TABLE OF CONTENTS

AUTHOR'S PREFACE

Thanks to the Tyndall Publications and Lilliput Press combination I am pleased to be able to make this memoir available in a second edition to an Irish readership, as well as to the many who were unable to get their copy of the 2003 US edition*; there were technical reasons for this. Since the appearance of the first edition I have responded to enquiries from aspirant readers, mostly students of history, by making available the hypertext version of the book, in which the footnotes are hotlinked into source material, or material closer to source. This has generated some feedback from historians researching the 1960s and interested in the attempt made then to take the gun out of Irish politics.

Typical is one comment which suggests that Chapters 7 and 8 should be seen as useful source material for a critical assessment of Seán Mac Stiofain's *Memoirs of a Revolutionary, Gordon Cremonesi, 1975*. I have also had feedback indicating disappointment that these chapters did not constitute a rounded history of the period. I felt unable to do this without unbalancing the memoir. But I think they do constitute a record of the aspirations and evolving world-views of various elements of the Republican Movement, primarily the left-oriented elements, and of the Marxist Left, in the context of a rapidly evolving and increasingly chaotic political situation in the wake of the Civil Rights movement in the North which we, as the 'Republican Left', had had a hand in initiating.

Those chapters should therefore be treated as source material for historians rather than as a rounded narrative for the general reader, though the latter may find aspects of it intriguing. The overall thrust of the book, however, is an attempt to show that some all-Ireland political thinking that was both innovative and non-violent was able to evolve from the liberal Protestant tradition that had fervently supported all-Ireland Home Rule, a tradition exemplified by my father Joe Johnston. His polemical book of 1913 *Civil War in Ulster*, re-published in 1999 by UCD Press, was an unsuccessful attempt to oppose the Tory-Orange conspiracy that shortly afterwards culminated in the April 1914 Larne gun-running, which event should be seen as initiating the twentieth-century cycle of political violence in Ireland.

Subsequently my father made his career in the Free State, and in the Seanad and elsewhere he consistently propagated an all-Ireland political perspective. In my own time I have tried to do the same in the various political environments available to me. This is a memoir of our successive attempts to develop an inclusive all-Ireland politics, one that would unite 'Protestant, Catholic and Dissenter under the common name of Irishman'.

Roy H W Johnston December 2005

* The December 2004 review of the memoir in *Studies* was based on a defective copy of this first edition.

ACKNOWLEDGMENTS

I have usually given acknowledgements along with notes and references, but it is appropriate to mention some people here to whom I am indebted for putting themselves out on my behalf. If there are some I have missed, I hope they will forgive me.

Norman Cardwell and William O'Kane in Dungannon were helpful when I was on the trail of JJ in his youth; also Winnie Acheson in tracking down the early Johnston residences. Kate Targett in the Plunkett Foundation, Oxford, unearthed many of his early co-operative studies. The librarians in the Lincoln archive and Bodleian Library in Oxford were helpful, also Gary Peatling and Roy Foster, the latter by encouraging me to think that my own memoir might be important. In Dublin the TCD Library MS room staff were helpful with the TCD Board minutes. The Central Office of Statistics in Rathmines, which holds the SSISI archive, was helpful with this. Plunkett House in Merrion Square (Dublin) was a helpful source of early co-operative movement publications to which JJ had contributed.

Ron Barrington (Greystones) was helpful with the Barrington Trust Archive, and RD Collison Black in Belfast gave useful insights, including the Salim Rachid contact in Illinois (Berkeley and the 'Irish School of Development Economics'). Tom Garvin in UCD deserves thanks for taking on the re-publication in 1999 of JJ's 1913 *Civil War in Ulster.*

John Killen in the Linen Hall Library, Belfast, deserves thanks for taking on board some of the archived source material. Maurice Laheen in Tuam was helpful with the RM Burke episode, and Prionnsias Ó Drisceoil in Kilkenny with the reports of the 1950s debates. Thanks are due to Ed Hagan for insights into Standish O'Grady.

Paul O'Higgins was helpful with insights into, and recollections of, the 1940s student Left. I am particularly indebted to Anthony Coughlan for enabling access to the Desmond Greaves Diaries, and the Wolfe Tone Society archive; these, I understand, he hopes to donate to the National Library of Ireland in due course.

I am indebted to Tomás Mac Giolla, Seán Garland and the Workers Party head office staff in Hill St, Dublin, for access to the 1960s Sinn Fein minutes. There is much archive material there relating to the 1960s politicisation process which remains to be accessed and analysed by historians. I had however to depend on the Ulster Quaker historian Roy Garland (no relation of Seán G) for a version of the (Sean) Garland Commission Report. Roy Garland has been studying loyalist-republican political interactions.

Mick Ryan (Dundalk) also deserves thanks in this context, as do Shay Courtney (Dublin) and Seán Swan (Belfast). The late Derry Kelleher should be thanked posthumously for making available his file of *Nuacht Naisiunta*, which ran from September 1969 up to the mid 1970s; this is now with the WP archive. Thanks also to Matt Treacy (TCD) for some National Archive material, including the 1965 'captured documents'.

I should thank Douglas Gageby for the opportunity to develop my 'science and technology' column in the *Irish Times* which ran from 1970 to 1976, providing me with the opportunity to ease myself constructively out of the political front-line when the latter became dominated by the pathology of violence. In this context I also owe gratitude to Gordon Foster for opening the possibility of constructive work at the university-industry interface.

I owe thanks to Brenda Swann for enabling my participation in the omnibus JD Bernal biography, published by Verso in 1999, which she edited. This ensured a significant Bernal input to subsequent books on Irish-rooted scientific achievements.

Finally, thanks to Brian Ennis (Irish Medical Systems), Derek Ennis (Coastline Solutions) and earlier Seán Breen (Interactive Multimedia Systems) for enabling me painlessly to develop the supportive hypertext knowledge-base.

Introduction: an Overview of the Century

This book is based mostly on publications by my father and myself, and on primary sources related to our respective lives and times. The unifying theme, if one can be said to exist, is based on a critical Enlightenment philosophical position, with strong radical Protestant and later scientific and Marxist flavours, mostly swimming against the tide of the Catholic nationalism which dominated the 20th century Irish environment.

I have, somewhat adventurously, adopted a method of making the notes and references more easily accessible to curious readers and to scholars than is the norm, taking advantage of the services provided by the Internet. The book exists in the printed version, with the notes and references in conventional format, except that some words will be seen to be underlined. The meaning of this is that in the hypertext version of the book, which exists on the Internet, a reader wishing to dig deeper into the background will find additional material, as they say, 'hot-linked'. To access the hypertext version, a dedicated reader will need to contact the author at rjtechne@iol.ie, who will be in a position to enable access either to the internet or via CD-ROM. Registered access initially will be a free service, in support of the development of the market for the book.

In these introductory notes I have given a few 'notes and references' which exemplify, and relate to, those given in the subsequent chapters. Where supportive material exists in the associated hypertext, occasionally where possible this is the complete document referenced. More usually it is an abstract or review of the referenced document, or focused essay based on primary sources(1). The underlining of the chapter references in the remainder of this introductory note implies that in the hypertext version one can jump directly to the chapter concerned, as one can from the table of contents.

I have tended, I hope consistently, to adopt the use of italics for retrospective comment, to distinguish it from the basic narrative. I use italics also for titles of books.

The critical overview of the century is developed in the following chapters, at the level of approximately one chapter per decade. The mid-century chapters divide into differing perspectives, as seen by my father Joe Johnston (JJ henceforth) and by the present writer Roy Johnston (RJ henceforth, though sometimes in the first person), but I try to conserve some degree of unity.

The experience can also be approached via 'threads', 'streams' or 'themes', dedicated to particular lines of activity, where it is useful to see the continuity of effort. The Appendices summarise these streams or themes.

JJ, Partition and the Free State

Chapter 1 deals with JJ's family background, his early political environment, schooling and early literary influences. His early politics were progressive, Liberal, Home-Rule supporting, with perhaps a tinge of romantic nationalism in the Thomas Davis tradition, supplemented by an overlay of Standish O'Grady(2).

Chapter 2 covers his 1910 JJ period in Oxford, where he did a further degree in the humanities, specialising in ancient history and archaeology, graduating in 1912. He moved in radical Liberal circles. He then returned to TCD where he did the Fellowship Examination in 1913, becoming among the last of the Fellows to become so 'by examination'. In 1913, after returning from Oxford and gaining his Fellowship, he wrote a polemical book(3) attacking Carson and the arming of the Orangemen. In 1914 JJ applied for and got an Albert Kahn (AK) (4) Travelling Fellowship (AKTF); with this he travelled round the world. The AKTF experience must have been the stimulus for his switch from classics to economics, which he proclaimed as his field from then on, without having studied it formally. As a consequence JJ found his academic career in TCD(5) becoming difficult and fraught with tension and controversy. JJ's Albert Kahn period, and subsequent contact with Charles Garnier(6) the AK Foundation Secretary (lasting right up to 1949), indicated a consistent role for him in support of Irish independence, with which the AK Foundation was in sympathy and to which it lent early support. This post-1914 career re-orientation helped JJ to relate to the developing political situation in Ireland, from a Protestant Home Ruler perspective. Post-1916 JJ seems to have been engaged actively in politics, but presumably with circumspection, as he has left few papers. He published in the Manchester Guardian and London Times, under a pseudonym, material which was supportive of the Canadian-type resolution of the political problem, in the context of the opportunity presented by the 1917 Irish Convention.

Chapter 3 shows how during the War of Independence he remained in touch with the AKF and kept Garnier briefed about Irish affairs, with a view to trying to influence French public opinion in the Irish interest. Subsequently in the later 1920s JJ was active in trying to support the declining co-operative movement (which had been split under Partition); he did extern lecturing, initially when the war of independence was on in Dublin in TCD to trade unionists, then later outside Dublin; these were mostly under the auspices of the Barrington Trust(7). The Barrington Lectures had been initiated a century earlier, in the aftermath of the Famine, and were in effect a sort of outreach campaign by the Statistical and Social Inquiry Society (SSISI)(8), with the aim of avoiding future famines through enlightenment.

In the late 1920s JJ sought election to the Seanad, initially however without success. He had published a book(9) in 1925 which attempted to popularise the basic concepts of economic thinking, and which contained some seminal ideas which now would now be recognised as relating the 'development economics' domain, emphasising the importance of getting a good deal for the agricultural primary producers. As regards political(10) activity, there is a suggestion that JJ had been involved in support of the Thomas Davis Society (TDS), which in the early 20s was a Sinn Fein 'front' in TCD. JJ participated in the first Agriculture Commission set up in 1922 by the Free State Government.

JJ and the Seanad, early RJ and the Emergency

Chapter 4 covers the 1930s when JJ began to farm for himself, to see how the system worked from below; he continued off and on in this mode right up to the 1960s, this being a cause of locational tension between his TCD job and his primary interest in agricultural economics. There were a succession of houses in the country, with land; he employed a farm labourer and kept the books. This was raw material for a succession of outreach(11) books and papers. The first impressions from the present writer RJ as a child begin to appear in this decade. In 1934 JJ published a polemical economics book(12) aimed at a lay readership, critical of the pure protectionist approach to economic development, and advocating that priority attention be paid to farm incomes, as a generator of demand for local industry. JJ served in the Seanad(13) on several occasions, being first elected in 1938; on this platform he stoutly defended the Protestant contribution to the Irish nation-building process.

Chapter 5 divides naturally into two parts, Part 1 covering the war and Part 2 the immediate post-war period. JJ became a member of the Royal Irish Academy in 1943, and the basis of his acceptance is a useful mid-career marker. He continued his critique of government policies in the Seanad. Post-war there were many articles, and more books. JJ served on the post-war Agricultural Commission, somewhat critically. He was also instrumental in building up the North-South Irish Association(14), this being the only intellectual think-tank having an all-Ireland dimension.

In the mid 1940s the present writer became associated with a school Marxist group, in which we tried to understand the war. This later evolved into the TCD student Left; this is covered in Part 2 of Chapter 5. We called it the Promethean Society, the objective of which was to re-introduce Marxist thinking into the Labour movement in Ireland(15). Our political impact as the post-war 'student Left' led to the reconstitution of the Students Representative Council, and the Irish Students Association, forerunner of Union of Students in Ireland. Our Marxism, which was based on Connolly, was rooted in bottom-up democracy: the role of the Promethean Society was as a sort of 'think-tank' to study the situation and come up with a solution to a perceived problem, which the membership of the democratic movement would be likely to accept when it was put to them(16). In my case, with my science background, it became necessary to make the link between the science and the politics creatively, and the catalyst was JD Bernal's writings(17). There was also the question of nuclear weapons, and the peace movement, with which Bernal was associated.

Parallel Universes

Chapter 6 for JJ covers the time in the 1950s when he was instrumental in getting TCD to develop an Honours Degree in Agriculture, for which purpose the College bought Townley Hall in Meath; this however was never brought to fruition, being frustrated by the inter-university politics which arose from the foundation of the Agricultural Institute with Marshall Plan money. During the 1950s my father increasingly got his fulfilment outside TCD; his long-standing membership of the Statistical and Social Inquiry Society had culminated in a period as President. He was also active as President of the Irish Association, continuing in that role up to 1954, and subsequently as a Council member, contributing papers and publications. In this context he was instrumental in organising a pioneering North-South debate(18) in Kilkenny between MacBride, Topping and others, on the national question. Despite his political isolation in

TCD, he managed to deliver a keynote paper at the Berkeley bicentenary conference(19) in TCD in 1953. In this he placed Berkeley firmly in the national political context. When de Valera returned to power in 1951, he brought JJ back into the Seanad(20) as a Taoiseach's nominee.

The present writer RJ spend the first two years of the decade in France absorbing the culture of the high-technology scientific laboratory. JJ and I remained, as it were, in parallel universes. I went in 1951 on a French Government *bourse*, and worked with Professor Louis Leprince-Ringuet, in the Ecole Polytechnique, on cosmic rays. This gave insights into theory-practice interaction, dialectics of experimental technology, competitive and co-operative team-work(21). I managed to get back to Ireland via the Dublin Institute of Advanced Studies, where cosmic ray work had been initiated under Janossy, a Hungarian anti-fascist refugee. This was an introduction to cutting-edge experimental technology, and indeed to systems engineering. There followed a creative period of 7 years in which I was able to do some scientific work of value, mostly on the experimental technology of high-energy particle physics. I was however aware of the problem of how work like this could be made relevant to the development of a relatively backward fringe economy; the 'science and society' problem, as identified by JD Bernal(22). The 1950s on the whole was a black period politically. The Sputnik however was a fortifier of the illusion that Soviet society had achieved a valid socialist model. I cultivated relations with various pioneering broad-left groups, and I was also in contact with Seán Cronin who had led the IRA 1950s border campaign. There were increasingly uneasy relations with the 'orthodox Left', and an increasingly perceived need for a 'broad Left'(23).

RJ and the Northern Crisis; JJ and the EEC

Chapter 7 deals with the 1960s, when JJ and the present writer tended to be active on parallel tracks, not being aware of each other as much as we should have been. This chapter divides naturally into 3 parts, Part 1 dealing with the period up to the foundation of the NICRA in 1966, Part 2 dealing with the development of the Northern situation up to when the arms were introduced by the B-Specials in the August 1969 pogroms, and then Part 3 dealing with how this disaster split the movement and how we tried to respond politically, though without success. During all this time RJ managed to keep alive his contacts and status in the scientific community, primarily at the interface between pure and applied science, and between both and the political economy of the national development process.

JJ wrote in the 1960s on the EEC accession, initially in favour of it, and then later critically(24). His main point was the negative effect of subsidised agriculture in developed countries on the world market accessible to developing countries. He attended international conferences in these issues. JJ's last book was an annotated edition of Berkeley's *Querist*, linked to a set of his own analyses(25). This was his 'magnum opus' and it sank without trace. It does however encapsulate his 'development economics' thinking, and he identified Berkeley as the Adam Smith of the development economics field. It was published in 1970 by Dundalgan Press, with some TCD sponsorship. Some copies were taken up by libraries; it got few reviews, and was remaindered(26). For his *Querist* book he was awarded in 1972, at the age of 82, the degree of D Litt; having done this he died, reasonably contented.

For the present writer RJ in the 1960s, after the DIAS epoch, which ended in the autumn of 1960, there was a period in London, in an industrial process innovation group in Guinness (Park Royal). Politically I identified with the Connolly Association, which had identified the problem as being to keep the Irish in London from being lost from Irish to British politics, and to try to mobilise them into an interest in Ireland(27). The chance to return to Ireland came in the summer of 1963, with Aer Lingus the national airline recruiting people to help them cope with the projected IBM 'real-time reservations system' deal(28).

In parallel with this came the opportunity to be associated with the politicising of the post-1950s Republican Movement, under the leadership of Cathal Goulding(29).

The history of this episode is quite complex. In summary, the movement was successfully politicised up to a point, in the context of active support for the non-violent Northern Ireland Civil Rights Association (NICRA) which had been a consequence of the Wolfe Tone Societies initiative, but the armed pogroms initiated by the B-Specials in the Falls Road in August 1969 was fatal to the politicisation process, and helped to promote the Provisionals, who had been lurking in the undergrowth in tacit opposition. The Provisionals were also encouraged by the Government party Fianna Fail, with a view to splitting the republican movement, which was actively engaged in exposing the shady land deals behind Fianna Fail financing, in the Dublin development environment. This was a preview of the situation currently being exposed in various Tribunals. As a consequence the Republican Left was marginalised and failed to develop, being also hampered by its own resurgent militarist illusions, in competition with the Provisionals. This latter process prompted the present writer's resignation in early 1972.

RJ, Science and Political Evolution

Chapter 8 covers the 1970s, which were for the present writer a constructive period scientifically, but depressing politically. I cultivated an Operations Research problem-solving consultancy on the fringe of TCD, with the support of Gordon Foster in the Statistics Department. Some of the work done in this period has been written up in a book by Julian Mac Airt. Some of the projects which we analysed using computer-based models were actually close to the type of pilot-project which my father had been promoting(30). I developed the *Irish Times* Science and Technology column, which ran weekly from 1970 to 1976(31). I initiated the TCD Applied Research Consultancy Group, which survived up to 1980, and employed up to 8 people. It turned out to be primarily a fringe enterprise generator, rather than primarily a problem-solver, though valid work was done. The College however stood it down, and went for a model where the spin-off enterprise was the main output.

Politically, an attempt to re-establish a working relationship with the 'orthodox left' proved totally barren, the pathology of the latter having gone beyond redemption following the Soviet invasion of Czechoslovakia. A subsequent period with the Labour Party proved to be equally barren, in that procedures for policy development, and analysis of problems in terms of feasible routes towards solutions, with membership participation, and a learning mode, were largely non-existent.

Chapter 9 covers the 1980s which were a nadir-period; I worked out my contract with TCD in various processes of attempted re-invention, with occasional bits of consultancy from State agencies(32). One such involved looking at the role of the Innovation Centre in Limerick and its relationship with the National Institute of Higher Education (NIHE), which had been somewhat abrasive. I proposed a model, based on the development of the NIHE postgraduate process as the prime innovation contact-point, which has since become the norm. Another project involved evaluating the Regional Colleges as sources of local innovative enterprise development(33). This work I understand has since proved useful.

Chapter 10 shows finally how by the early 1990s the Green Party had emerged into existence, and while it was initially somewhat 'crank fringe', it seemed to have enough going for it to enable a constructive interaction to take place. A constitutional reform procedure was initiated, in which I was able to participate, and a new model has emerged, which promises to be the makings of the necessary democratic vehicle for the development of radical conservationist policies, with full participation by a conscious principled membership(34). On the scientific front in the 1990s association with a young and vibrant software house has enabled me to contribute to the development of a philosophy of knowledge-base development, and this work is ongoing(35), representing a culmination of a lifetime of dedication to the inductive approach to problem-solving.

In the concluding 'reflections on the century' I make a modest attempt to produce a philosophical synthesis of the foregoing experience, relating development economics, science, the innovation process and politics, in such a way as perhaps to recapture the spirit of the 18th century Enlightenment in a manner adapted to the needs of the 21st century, primarily in battling with the new wave of religious fundamentalist obscurantism.

Notes and References

1. I have, at least partially, managed to index the source material, some of which it is hoped to archive; at the time of writing the archiving process is in course of negotiation, primarily with the Linen Hall Library in Belfast. There are separate source indexing documents for JJ and for RJ.

2. I attempt to construct some sort of feel for his intellectual environment from the analysis of books he had in his possession prior to 1910, and from analysis of the family background (Appendix 1), and the schooling in Dungannon. I have chronicled the details of JJ's participation in TCD student debates in the 1900s module of the 'political' thread. This is overviewed for the century in Appendix 10. The influence has become apparent in this context, thanks to EA Hagan's editing of his contribution to Larkin's *Irish Worker* (UCD Press, 2002).

3. *Civil War in Ulster* published in 1913 by Sealy, Bryers and Walker, Dublin; in its original edition it is on record in several libraries in Ireland, Britain and in the USA. It has been re-published in 1999 by UCD Press, with the present writer's introduction, and this is the version accessible in the hypertext.

4. For more about the Albert Kahn Foundation see the related AK background module in the hypertext; there is also an overview of, and entry-points to, this thread via Appendix 3. The dominant part played by India in his 1914-15 world tour was due to the opportunities presented by the presence there of his elder brothers in the Civil Service. The visits to Java, China, Japan and the USA are in less depth; they are treated in the hypertext summary of JJ's AK Report. The 'agricultural production' visit to France in 1916 he wrote up for the *Irish Times*; it was also published as a pamphlet by Maunsel, and is available in his papers. In these published accounts JJ emphasised the importance in the Irish context of good local government and a strong co-operative movement.

5. The Board minutes of the period have JJ on record in support of a better deal for the 'skips', or College menservants who looked after the students' rooms. JJ's interaction with academic life at this time was controversial; the Board minutes give something of the flavour.

6. I have abstracted for the hypertext the Garnier correspondence from the relevant file in JJ's papers (in the Linen Hall archive), where it is preserved in Folder 4.

7. The Barrington Lectures were initiated in 1849 by John Barrington, a Dublin merchant, with a view to providing for the instruction of the Irish people in Liberal economics. Before World War 1 they had been managed by the Statistical and Social Inquiry Society (SSISI). The Centenary Volume of the Proceedings of the Statistical and Social Inquiry Society of Ireland, published in 1947 edited by R D Collison Black, contains background information about the Barrington Lectures. There is given a complete series of Barrington Lecturers from 1852 to 1946 in the Centenary Volume. The most notable of the Barrington Lecturers pre-war was C H Oldham, who was a Home Rule supporter and a prolific contributor of papers to the Society between 1895 and 1925. He was an early influence on JJ.

8. For the background to the SSISI see Appendix 6, and for JJ's first paper, *Some Causes and Consequences of Distributive Waste*, see J SSISI vol XIV p353, 1926-7. For the Rockefeller Foundation background in context see Appendix 5 where I overview the 'academic research and publication' thread. The French component of his Rockefeller project are absent from his SSISI paper, but they surfaced strongly in JJ's work for the 1926 Prices Tribunal.

9. The earlier Barrington Lectures series by JJ seems eventually to have blossomed into his *Groundwork of Economics* , published by the Educational Co in 1925, or perhaps in 1926. (There is no date of publication given on the book itself.) It was certainly being reviewed in 1926, prior to the Seanad elections. JJ seems to have had in mind that his later Barrington series, outside Dublin, would have been promotional for his book. Subsequently in a Seanad speech, he referred to the difficulty in filling a hall during this period, in this context.

10. Evidence among JJ's papers is thin on the ground, but I have collected what I can find in the 1920s political module in the hypertext. He continued to receive communications from Erskine Childers. He wrote a letter of condolence on the death of Michael Collins, which was acknowledged. There was also contact with Dermot MacManus, an ex-service mature student, who had been the prime mover of the Thomas Davis Society from 1919, and who subsequently commanded the Free State Army in the West during the civil war. There are some intriguing hints, like copies of letters from Pierrepoint the hangman to the Governor of Mountjoy regarding clients in that institution: MacManus became Deputy Governor of Mountjoy Prison. JJ was also in the early 1920s involved in the work of the Boundary Commission, from the economic angle. There were papers to do with this, but they have vanished. I suspect them of being used by Kevin O'Sheil's biographer, and I remain in hopes of tracking then down. There is among his papers a copy of the 1923 *Handbook of the Ulster Question*, edited by Kevin O'Shiel, Director of the North-Eastern

Boundary Bureau, which is annotated in JJ's handwriting. The missing papers, if I can find them, and which I recollect from my earlier encounter with his papers in 1971, will indicate the extent of his role in the production of this Boundary Commission report. He remained in close touch with Kevin O'Shiel during the 30s and 40s, to the best of my recollection.

11. I count as 'outreach' JJ's work with the SSISI (Statistical and Social Inquiry Society), where he served on the Council during the decade, the related Barrington Lectures, which in 1932 he managed to bring in under the SSISI umbrella again, after their post-war period of alienation, and finally the Irish Association, of which he became a founder-member in 1938. In all three networks JJ consistently promoted all-Ireland thinking.

12. I abstract JJ's book *The Nemesis of Economic Nationalism,* published by PS King & Son, London, 1934, in a dedicated module in the background hypertext, and if re-publication in full turns out to be appropriate, as in the case of *'Civil War in Ulster'*, we will do this. This book also owes something to the co-operative movement; the Co-operative Conference Association had published a pamphlet written by JJ in 1933, of which a copy was among JJ's papers, entitled *The Importance of Economy in the Distribution of Goods.* Because it is rare I think it is worth reproducing in full, in the supportive hypertext, where it is accessed in the Plunkett stream. Also it contains embryonic versions of certain of JJ's key economic concepts, as developed in the *Nemesis of Economic Nationalism*, and his later attempt to establish consumer demand as the basis of credit. JJ sent a complimentary copy to Charles Garnier, at the Albert Kahn Foundation in Paris, with which he remained in touch during the 1930s.

13. JJ's Seanad election address I have given in full in Appendix 8, along with the names of his support committee. His maiden speech on May 11 1938 is on record in Column 99 of Vol 21 of the Seanad Reports; I also reproduce this in full in the hypertext support material; it is also hotlinked from the chronological summary of his speeches which I have collected in the 1930s Seanad module of the hypertext.

14. The Irish Association records, in the Northern Ireland Public Record Office, for the period of JJ's Presidency from 1946 to 1954 are extremely sparse, though quite detailed in other respects; it almost looks as if a conscious effort had been made to expunge them, by some hard-core Unionist agent who had never forgiven him for his *Civil War in Ulster*. I have however done what I could in the hypertext which is overviewed in Appendix 9. He did develop a good relationship with Irene Calvert the Stormont MP and the industrialist Sir Graham Larmour.

15. I have recorded my early political thoughts under the influence of the war when in school in the 1940s module of the political thread. Later when in Trinity College the Marxist influence developed, under the influence primarily of C Desmond Greaves, a London-based Marxist with an Irish family background, a member of the Communist Party of Great Britain, who specialised in the 'Irish Question', writing what has become a standard work *The Life and Times of James Connolly*, published by Lawrence and Wishart in 1960, followed by *Liam Mellows and the Irish Revolution*, also published by L&W in 1971; there were also numerous other polemical works.

16. The role of the aspirant democratic Marxist 'Promethean Society' is treated in the TCD section of the 1940s political module of the hypertext.

17. I have written some notes on our 'Science and Society' thinking under the influence of JD Bernal in the 1940s module of the this thread, which is overviewed in Appendix 11.

18. JJ had become President of the Irish Association, succeeding Lord Charlemont the founding President in 1946. His period as President is however very poorly documented. The Kilkenny Debates of 1954, in which Hubert Butler had a hand locally, was a high point of his Presidency, being the first time politicians from both parts of Ireland had appeared on the same platform. I have summarised the Irish Association thread in Appendix 9, and some details of the debates are given in the 1950s module of that thread.

19. This keynote paper was published with the title *Berkeley's Influence as an Economist* in Hermathena Vol LXXXII p76, 1953; I have reproduced it in full in the hypertext.

20. JJ made 31 speeches in the Seanad between April 1951 and July 1954. I have abstracted this record and it is available in the support documentation, along with his first and last speeches given in full.

21. RJ's published scientific papers are abstracted in the academic stream of the hypertext, together with an indication of their significance.

22. The science and society' problem had been addressed in the writings of the Marxist JD Bernal FRS, whose book *Science in History*, published by Watts (London) in 1954, was influential in the present writer's understanding of the role of science as a catalyst of social change.

23. The Greaves 1950s contacts however were influential in strengthening RJ's interest in the 'national question' and the ending of partition, while the Skeffington contact helped to encourage a critical view of the USSR, and to initiate the distancing of RJ from the Irish Workers' League. Greaves needless to say had no use for Skeffington.

24. JJ's attitude to EEC accession was initially in favour of it, publishing a book *Why Ireland Needs the Common Market* (Mercier Press, Cork, 1962) and then later, in his final years, he was critical with articles and letters to the newspapers.

25. *Bishop Berkeley's Querist in Historical Perspective,* Dun Dealgan Press, 1970.

26. This work has however since been referenced in the context of the 'development economics' domain by Salim Rachid in the University of Illinois, who has identified an 18th century 'Irish School of Economic Development' which included Swift, Berkeley, Molyneux, Dobbs and Prior, the latter two giving the group an important applied-scientific dimension.

27. The Connolly Association in the 1960s, led by Desmond Greaves, was the vehicle for this, and the key issue of the time was the release of the IRA prisoners, the 1950s IRA campaign being over, the people concerned having learned their lesson, and in process of deciding on the need to 'go political'. The idea of Civil Rights as being the key issue in Northern Ireland emerged on the agenda.

28. This enabled me to get into computer-based problem analysis, at quite a detailed hands-on level. I go into this in some depth, as it offers another handle on the inductive approach to organisational learning.

29. The Wolfe Tone Societies were the key influence behind the 1960s attempted politicising of the Republican Movement.

30. JJ's death occurred in the middle of the 1972 IFORS (International Federation of Operations Research Societies) conference, which took place in TCD. I was on the international programme committee. I contributed a response to one of the keynote speakers, on the topic of 'Simulation'. This paper was read on my behalf by Maurice Foley (who went on to be Chief Executive of Guinness Peat Avaition), as I was at the funeral.

31. I edited the material from the *Irish Times* Science and Technology column into a book *In Search of Techne* during the early 1980s, for publication by Tycooley, a firm specialising in servicing the UN development agency market. Unfortunately the firm closed down. I am taking this opportunity to publish the material in the present supportive hypertext.

32. This consultancy was mostly of a socio-technical character, resulting in reports which were not usually for the public domain; I have outlined some of them in the hypertext.

33. An 'executive summary' of the Regional Colleges report is available in the hypertext.

34. I have given an account of the development of the Green party during the 1990s in the 1990s political module.

35. Most of the work with the software firm Irish Medical Systems has been in the socio-technical domain, and I have outlined some of it in the hypertext, in particular that related to case-based reasoning, some of which is included in the book by Bergmann et al, *Industrial Applications of Case-based Reasoning*, published by Springer Verlag in 1999.

Chapter 1: The Period 1901-1910

Introduction

My father Joe Johnston (JJ henceforth) was born in the townland of Tomagh, near Castlecaulfield Co Tyrone, in 1890. His father John Johnston was a 30-acre farmer, the farm being leased from the Earl of Charlemont, and also a teacher in the Presbyterian stream of the national school system. Following in the footsteps of his five elder brothers, JJ went to Dungannon Royal School, and in his case he went on to Trinity College Dublin in 1906, where he took degrees in classics and ancient history, with two gold medals, in 1910. His early politics were progressive, Liberal, Home-Rule supporting, with perhaps a tinge of romantic nationalism in the Thomas Davis tradition, supplemented by an overlay of Standish O'Grady.

The political background, outlined below, in the Tyrone of the 1900s must have influenced the political thinking of the family. The family background focuses on my grandfather John Johnston (1834-1909) and my grandmother Mary Geddes, whom he married in 1873 he being 39 and she being 20.

The family moved house on 2 occasions, subsequent to my grandfather's retirement in 1897. During JJ's undergraduate years in Dublin University (Trinity College) he concentrated on his studies but found time to participate in the College Historical Society (Hist) debates. Early influences included the writings of Alice Stopford Green, CH Oldham, Rutherford Mayne, Standish O'Grady and others associated with the Home Rule movement.

Towards the end of the decade JJ encountered my mother, then in the Church of Ireland Teacher Training College

Political Background

The Tyrone MP TW Russell was a Liberal Unionist who succeeded Horace Plunkett in charge of the Department of Agriculture and Technical Instruction (DATI). According to Patrick Maume(1), whose book is a useful source for the political background in this period, Russell had led a Protestant farmers' agitation in favour of compulsory purchase. Russell held that if the land question was resolved the national movement would disintegrate.

Russell was close to Lindsay Crawford, editor of the Irish Protestant, then based in Dublin, and appealing to a working-class readership, with an evangelical and sometimes radical anti-establishment message. Crawford, originally from Lisburn, had been associated with a breakaway Independent Orange Order, which was critical of the landlord domination of the traditional lodges.

Another Liberal Unionist MP was WH Dodd, who became a judge in 1907. The seat remained Liberal, despite a Sinn Fein boycott. The nationalist vote at this time was mostly Redmondite, with supporters of William O'Brien and the All for Ireland League promoting an inclusivist Protestant-friendly policy, with Sinn Fein on the flanks promoting separatist policies, in some respects (eg on tariffs) taking a basically Tory line.

The All for Ireland League was supportive of an inclusive Home Rule political environment(2). It had attracted support from Lord Dunraven and significant numbers of Protestant improving landlords and business interests who saw Home Rule as an opportunity rather than a problem. Canon Sheehan of Doneraile was also associated with this movement.

In contrast, the pathologies of the Irish Ireland movement, and 'Catholic Nationalism' were beginning to emerge and to dominate the scene, with writers such as DP Moran, who edited the *Leader* (3). The separatist vision, insofar as it embodied exclusivist and restrictive principles, and rejected the inclusive mainstream of Enlightenment secular republicanism, was basically flawed. JJ was a critic of this flawed separatist vision, and I was also in my time, both of us in our own ways, during the whole of our working careers, perhaps on occasion with some modest success.

The current political perceptions within Trinity College, as picked up by JJ during his undergraduate career there, were basically Unionist and imperial, but there were critical voices, which JJ encountered in the College Historical Society debates.

Family Background

The Johnston family background(4) was Presbyterian, with somewhat of a scholarly, and probably radical, tradition. My grandfather John Johnston, by combining school-teaching with farming, had managed to rear a family of seven and put them all through college, with the aid of scholarships. In his earlier days he had given night literacy classes to farm labourers. My grandmother Mary Geddes also was an intellectual influence, helping her sons in succession to prepare for their exams.

As a consequence of this background, those of JJ's elder brothers who are accessibly on record, primarily James and John, show a spirited intellectual independence(5).

The Year 1901

When the century began, JJ was ten years old, living with his father John, his mother Mary, younger sister Ann and remaining elder brothers Harry and William in their farm-house on top of the hill at Tomagh, which is situated between Kilnaslee and Castlecaulfield, County Tyrone. The eldest brother James had by then become established in the Indian Civil Service, and was sending money home. The next brother, Sam, was in medical school, and young John was just about to enter Oxford. The farm was struggling on, with Harry, William and Joe helping the old man, who had retired from teaching in 1897.

I recollect JJ reminiscing about the sheer misery of work in the fields in winter, on tasks such as snagging turnips for cattle-feed, or picking potatoes, which occur in November. The context was my complaints about my own participation in such tasks, while helping to work the farm at St Columba's College, in the 1940s, during the war

.   This period however must have given him a hands-on feel for the role of the primary producer, which he never forgot, and focused his interest in his later career. His initial orientation would however have been to get out of it, as his elder brothers had done, via a classics degree and the Indian Civil Service. There is perhaps an echo here of the thinking attributed by Thomas Hardy to Jude the Obscure.

In his latter years he was crippled with arthritis, which he himself attributed to his early exposure to field-work in winter, though my sister from her medical experience questions this.

Dungannon Royal School

As well as details of the many prizes and bursaries won by the Johnston boys(6) the school archive contains newspaper cutting relating to the speeches of the Headmaster RF 'Boss' Dill on prize days, and to the winning of awards and prizes by DRS pupils. In this context JJ gets mentions in the Northern Whig on 14/09/06 and 2/12/07. The latter entry relates to his first-year results in TCD, where he got honours and first prize in classics, a term prize in French and a French composition prize, as well as term prizes for Latin and Greek composition.

The French prize indicates that he must have had an early mastery of the language, thanks to the employment in DRS pre-war of a native-speaking French teacher of some ability, and the practice of organising school visits to France, though my sister doubts whether JJ would have been able to participate in these. The quality of the teaching however made feasible his subsequent strong French connection, which began to assume some depth in 1916 when he reported on French agricultural organisation under wartime conditions, and was maintained in the 20s and 30s with his contact with the Albert Kahn Foundation.

There are no school records for James or Sam, the archive being incomplete. According to my sister, my grandmother Mary Geddes had coached James for entrance to Queens College Galway (according to my sister, at a very young age), whence he went on to Oxford. Sam she thinks went to College of Surgeons in Dublin. There are DRS records however for John, Harry and William (6). Harry went on to medical school in Edinburgh; John went to Oxford, as did William. There are no records for Ann, as the girls' school, then associated with DRS, was a separate entity; regrettably it no longer exists. According to my sister she went to Alexandra College in Dublin, and then on to Trinity, which she entered in or about 1915; she is on record as an active supporter of the Co-op, of which JJ was then Secretary.

Moving House

By the time JJ was in DRS, and William gone to college, it was evident that none of the boys was interested in taking over the farm, so old John began the process of getting out of farming. He had begun in 1900, the lease on part of the land (which was owned by the Earl of Charlemont) having been in that year transferred to William Hamilton, a neighbour. The remainder of the land was transferred in 1908 to one Ralph Hamilton(7).

The family then moved to a more comfortable house, at Dunamoney Wood, closer to Castlecaulfield, where the Presbyterian parish church was located. By this time John was on the way to joining James in the Indian Civil Service, and Sam had established himself in medical practice in Newcastle-on-Tyne. Harry was in medical school, on the way to joining with Sam, and William was in Oxford. The move took place some time after the end of 1906, when JJ would no longer have had to make the daily trip to Dungannon from Tomagh, with the aid of the Great Northern Railway, from Kilnaslee Halt.

Old John Johnston died while JJ was in college, towards the end of 1909. This left my grandmother and Ann, then aged 12, in the house in Dunamoney Wood, a relatively isolated spot, though in reach of Castlecaulfield. Ann by then was ready to go to secondary school, and to get from Dunamoney Wood into Dungannon would have been a problem. So they moved to Bessmount, in the townland of Ranaghan, near Dungannon, to the northwest, on the Cookstown road; this was in walking distance of the girls school associated with Dungannon Royal School, which Ann attended, probably from 1910, until she went to board at Alexandra College, probably in 1911. She is on record, perhaps as part of a school group from Alexandra, in the company of Douglas Hyde and others, in the group photograph of the 1912 Ard Fheis of Connradh na Ghaeilge, which is on display in the Hyde museum in Frenchpark.

The house at Bessmount, now a ruin, was substantial, with what looks like associated yard and mews. Local lore associates the house with family names Reid and Wiggins. My grandmother would probably have had a caretaking tenancy of a mews flat, with enough space to enable Ann and JJ to spend vacations there. She remained there until she moved to Dublin, first to JJ's place in Ranelagh, increasing the pressure for the move to Stillorgan, then eventually to Ann's place in Frescati Park Blackrock where she survived until 1939.

JJ's TCD Undergraduate Years

During JJ's time as an undergraduate in Trinity, he participated in College societies. The College Historical Society (the 'Hist'), founded in the 18th century, a platform for Wolfe Tone, Burke and others, contains several references to JJ during his undergraduate days, though he did not take a leading committee role, preferring to concentrate on getting good exam results.

He probably attended some of the meetings in his first year, picking up from its debate motions an impression of 'support for the Irish language', 'separation of church and state', and preference for 'small-nation independence' rather than 'embedding in a large empire'. On the strength of these early positive impressions he joined in November 1907(8).

One should hesitate to read too much into student debating attitudes, but it is tempting to use them as indicators of JJ's probable political position during his undergraduate years. The session 1907-1908 was dominated by a Tory backlash, and JJ was not moved to speak on any of the debates, which were mostly jingoistic. He stuck with it however, though he did not get around to making his first contribution to the debates until 1909-1910, his final year, the Tory jingoistic domination having continued during 1908-1909.

In JJ's final year he participated in at least one Hist debate; he led the opposition to the motion that 'the outcome of the Battle of the Boyne was beneficial to Ireland', the motion being defeated. Though JJ did not participate in subsequent debates, by analysing the attitudes of some of the active speakers who sided with JJ on the Boyne, it is possible to infer tentatively how JJ probably voted: he would probably have been 'critical of the current Irish fiscal position', 'sceptical about Irish literature', 'against labour exchanges', 'for municipal trading', 'against Westminster control of Irish finance', 'open-minded towards socialism', supportive of the 'soundness of modern society', and supportive of the 'reality of current Irish political issues'.

The foregoing would suggest a basically Liberal free-trade utilitarian type of outlook, with a positive attitude to the then-emerging politics of Home Rule for all-Ireland within the Empire. We will see later how this mixture evolves under the stress of the War, the national movement, the civil war and the Free State.

Books probably possessed by JJ in this period

Regrettably in JJ's many moves he never built up a consistent procedure for conserving a reference library. While he had access to the TCD Library for his varied scholarly interests, he did desire to possess certain books, and those he possessed and which survived his many moves he must have valued highly. Those which remained in his possession from this period(9) are therefore indicators of his then thinking. I note a selection of them in order of their date of publication.

In the box of JJ memorabilia relating to this period I have two issues, for 1892 and 1893, of a *Diary of an Irish Cabinet Minister*, which is a spoof Unionist anti-Home Rule polemic, outlining how the workings of the projected Home Rule cabinet were perceived in some Ulster quarters.

I have also a pamphlet dated 1898, published in Dublin, entitled *How Ireland is treated by her 'friends'* by one Wm Pentland, who claims to be a Westmeath tenant evicted in 1866, and who argues on behalf of the tenants evicted during the 'plan of campaign' and claims that the Land League is fraudulent.

This suggests an early critical questioning of the value of the 'peasant proprietorship' road taken by the Land League agitation.

There is a copy of *Lombard Street* by Walter Bagehot, first published in 1873, in a new edition dated 1904 (Kegan Paul, Trench, Trubner, London), edited by E Johnstone.

This analysis of the London money market seems to have been an early influence on JJ in the direction of economics.

He also possessed the Routledge 1905 edition of Adam Smith's *Wealth of Nations,* edited by Dugald Stuart. This and the Bagehot are underlined and have marginal notes by JJ.

The Facts and Principles of Irish Nationality, or The Fundamental Constitutions of this Realm, published in 1907 by Browne and Nolan, and authored by 'Éireannaigh Éigin', was also in JJ's possession. This is a well-written and scholarly analysis of the concepts of State and Nation, and of the course of Irish history, in 85 pages, price sixpence. It was '...not published by, or in the interests of, any league, association or society. It has been compiled mainly by one writer who however has received valuable suggestions from several quarters. To the assistance and exertions of some students of a well-known Dublin college its publication now is entirely due...'.

This book presents a critical view of Irish history which is a long way from the then current 'Irish Ireland' or Catholic Nationalist positions. The analysis of

1798 and the Union is very close to the contemporary detached 1998 bicentennial paradigm, and a long way from the Catholic-nationalist hijacking which took place in 1898.

Alice Stopford Green (ASG) was an important formative influence on JJ's approach to Irish history, though he fails to reference her in his 1913 *Civil War in Ulster*, preferring in this case to use impeccable Unionist sources on which to base his arguments for all-Ireland Home Rule and against Tory armed subversion of the UK democratic process. ASG's vision was of a united Ireland with its own Government, within the British Empire, conceived in terms later to be labelled 'Commonwealth'(10). According to Maire Comerford '...she was a nineteenth century Liberal who thought that British democracy would, given time, evolve to a perfect form of government by consent. Secondly her study of the decentralised old Gaelic State had led to a fanciful parallel between this and a decentalised British Commonwealth...'.

There was a drama dimension in JJ's formation(11); he was aware of the Belfast initiatives in the context of the national theatre movement, as embodied in the work of Rutherford Mayne and other Ulster playwrights such as St John Ervine and Lynn Doyle, who were associated culturally with the all-Ireland Home Rule politics of Bulmer Hobson, Alice Milligan and the Alice Stopford Greene network. This had Dungannon echoes, with local dramatists J and JM Muldoon writing romantic-nationalist plays with regional flavour, consciously attempting to portray '...the heroic virtues and lofty patriotism of Emmet, FitzGerald and Tone ...' (I quote from the preface of *For Ireland's Sake* published in 1910). Mayne tried to do for the Ulster Presbyterian peasantry what Synge had done for the Aran islands. JJ remained friendly with Mayne up to the 1940s, when the latter, like Bulmer Hobson, had become a Dublin civil servant, both being in effect refugee Protestant all-Irelanders.

There were also on our shelves at home during my youth three volumes of the Cuchulainn saga by Standish O'Grady. According to my sister, JJ gave them to her as a present. I used to read them for fun. They were also in the possession of Cyril and Cerise Parker, who ran Avoca School in Blackrock, where I boarded in the early war years. Cerise, who was a daughter of William Orpen the painter, used to read the Cuchulainn saga to us in bed in the junior dormitory. So the Standish O'Grady books were part of the cultural canon of the Irish Protestant community.

I did not recognise this as relevant to the present work, as an influence on JJ analogous to Alice Stopford Green, until I encountered Hubert Butler's(12) 1978 essay on Standish O'Grady, 'Anglo-Irish Twilight'. In this it is evident that O'Grady's vision was of a national-minded improving entrepreneurial landlord class, in the tradition of Charlemont and the 1782 Volunteers. He had tried to repeat this episode in Kilkenny during the Boer War, recruiting boy scouts to defend Ireland, and presenting an alternative to the Kilkenny Militia and the Irish Brigade who were then training to confront each other in the Transvaal.

As we have seen, the family farm at Tomagh was on the Charlemont Estate; JJ would have early been exposed to 1780s Volunteer lore. To my knowledge he always had respect for the type of landlord whom he regarded as 'improving', and who ran a productive estate generating employment. This all fits with the O'Grady model. The latter never came to anything, but JJ sought to transform it via his approach to co-operative estate ownership, as will emerge when we consider his work in the 40s as recounted in his 'Irish Agriculture in Transition'(13).

Other Possible Early Influences

There was in 1908 a meeting of the British Association for the Advancement of Science (BAAS). This was attended by one David Houston who later became scientific consultant to the Irish Agricultural Organisation Society, the co-operative movement co-ordinating body, on milk quality control procedures etc, and by one Edward(sic) de Valera, then a schoolteacher in Blackrock. JJ was at this time completing his second year. I have no indication that JJ took any interest in the 'British Ass' meeting, but then few did who were of subsequent national significance, apart from the two mentioned. Houston taught science at St Enda's, Patrick Pearse's school. JJ would however undoubtedly have come across Houston subsequently in the context of his work with the IAOS.

I mention the BAAS event to indicate the existence of a culture-gap between the science world, dominated then in Ireland by the 'gentleman-amateurism' of the 'big-house' culture, and the emerging national identity(14). The co-operative movement as it had begun to evolve was beginning to bridge this gap, and JJ was increasingly part of this process. This gap could also have been bridged by people like Houston, had the co-operative movement been allowed to develop as it did in Denmark, demonstrating a clear link between scientific competence and the development of a quality food export market, in a domain where science and practice were inseparable. Instead the co-operative movement was crippled by Partition, and the 'irregulars' in the civil war burned Sir Horace Plunkett's house into the bargain. I reference these events further in the 1920s decade.

The culture-link between science and the emerging national elite via de Valera was also flawed for different reasons; I go into this in the 30s and 40s, when de Valera set up the Dublin Institute of Advanced Studies, displaying a somewhat limited understanding of the nature of the process of transformation of scientific research into social utility. JJ however understood the need, and encouraged the present writer towards the scientific cultural direction, and perhaps also my sister, who started off doing Natural Science before switching to medicine.

The Protestant Liberal Home Rule movement during JJ's undergraduate period would have included people like CH Oldham(15) the economist who headed the Statistical and Social Inquiry Society.

The influence of Horace Plunkett, George Russell (AE) and the co-operative movement(16) must have been significant, because JJ early picked up on the discrepancy between farm gate prices and retail shop prices, deciding to act practically on the issue by forming the Dublin University Co-operative Society as a retail outlet to feed the students. This he did eventually, in 1913, but he must have picked up the motivation and the ideas through undergraduate interaction with the thinking of people like AE. Bulmer Hobson's paper *Irish Freedom* recorded an outcry from the Dublin retailers against it.

There is no doubt that in the lead-up to the expected Home Rule there was a sense of positive expectation in Irish industry. The annual Sinn Fein exhibitions of Irish manufactures were a focus for this. There was an innovative entrepreneurial spirit abroad, exemplified by the early flight pioneers, one such being Harry Ferguson, who subsequently became famous for the tractor with hydraulic lift. Sydney Gifford Czira, in her memoirs(17) describes the 1910 Sinn Fein Aonach na Nodlaig in the Rotunda which highlighted the Ferguson aircraft, with the promotion being done by The O'Rahilly. It is quite probable that JJ attended this, as it was a major public event, and from it he would have picked up a sense of vibrant national opportunity, with extensive participation by Northern industry, Ferguson being the star innovator.

I don't know to what extent JJ was aware of the Barrington Lectures(18) situation in his undergraduate period. They were then under the influence of the Liberal Home Rule elite (Oldham and co) who dominated the Statistical and Social Inquiry Society(19), and their focus tended to be on the UK as a whole, with emphasis on Liberal Free Trade. Arthur Griffith fulminated against them, from the German-inspired protectionist angle adopted by the early Sinn Fein.

JJ during this period was under the influence of his eldest brother James in India, who was a firm believer in Free Trade, and also in ensuring that the primary producers got their inputs as cheaply as possible, and added value to their outputs. After retiring from the Service he wrote polemical books criticising British policy in India, which he compared to the pre-Reform situation in Britain a century earlier(20).

The alternative to protection (which in British politics was a Tory demand, resulting from long-term British neglect of scientific technology as the basis for industry, relative to the Germans) was organisation of primary producers for maximum local added value, and maximum availability of technical competence, through technical education.

Industry developed on this basis would have strong local roots and would not need protection; the latter principle was at the root of all government corruption, with politicians bought by protected capitalists, as exemplified in the Indian Congress process, and repeated in Fianna Fail. This was James's view expressed in his book *Can the Hindus Rule India*. I suspect that it would by 1910 have begun to rub off on JJ in his undergraduate days, surfacing in his *Civil War in Ulster(2)* and emerging in its mature form in his critical analysis of de Valera's protectionism in the 1930s(21).

My Mother

Towards the end of JJ's undergraduate period in Trinity College he encountered my mother Clara Wilson. Her father was Robert Wilson, a schoolteacher in Ballymahon Co Longford, who had raised a second family. His first wife had died; there was a daughter Kathleen, who married the Rev George Harpur of Timahoe. This end of the family also had Empire connections, with India and Ceylon. The accepted role of the Irish Protestants was to be British Empire-builders.

My mother's father's second wife was Jenny Dunphy, from Windsor. My mother had two sisters, Florrie who married Jack Young, who came from a landed family in Queen's County (now Co Laois). The estate declined while Jack was serving in the 1914-18 war (he was at Gallipoli) and he ended up buying barley for the Perry brewery in Rathdowney. The other sister Isabel (Isa) married Bob Nesbitt, a Great Northern Railway clerk from Belfast. There were two brothers, one of whom died in the war.(22).

My mother trained in the Kildare Place Church of Ireland Training College as a national school teacher, and she taught for a time in Ballivor, Co Meath. She picked up some Irish via the Gaelic League, and made attempts to get the right to teach it in the school, but was blocked by the school manager, who was the Church of Ireland Minister.

When JJ went to Oxford in 1910 he was engaged to my mother, and he married her in 1914, before commencing the Albert Kahn Travelling Fellowship. Prior to the marriage he had, to please his prospective father-in-law, joined the Masonic Lodge in Longford, in which Robert Wilson was influential. He is on record in the Dublin headquarters as having resigned in good standing soon afterwards, rather than transferring to the TCD Lodge. I have scanned the names of the TCD Lodge members of the time, and they are mostly unmemorable.

JJ before he went to Oxford in 1910 I suspect must have had a vision which was perhaps analogous to, but somewhat less simplistic than, that of Thomas Hardy's *Jude the Obscure*. The Classics had taken three of the elder brothers into the imperial machine as administrators, but he must have been beginning to pick up their experiences, to the extent of making him question that channel, and look for alternatives.

Notes and References

1. Patrick Maume, *The Long Gestation: Irish Nationalist Life;* (Gill and Macmillan, 1999). I have been able to identify some of the notables associated with JJ's TCD undergraduate Hist debates thanks to this book. I have appended in the hypertext some notes and extracts as background to this period. Anyone wishing to research further the period, as well as reading Maume, should perhaps explore sources such as JJ used in his 1913 book *'Civil War in Ulster'*, primarily Louis-Paul Dubois, whose *'Contemporary Ireland'* gives an insightful view by an outsider of the then Irish scene. I have noted this author as a source for Chapter 9 of JJ's *Civil War in Ulster* (see Note 2 below). JJ seems to have picked up early a feeling for the French view of Ireland as an alternative to that of the English.

2. I have touched on Dunraven and the AFIL in my 1999 introduction to JJ's *Civil War in Ulster* (Sealy, Bryant and Walker, Dublin 1913, also UCD Press, 1999). In the additional support documentation, given in the context of this hypertext version of the 1999 UCD Press edition, there is an extract from the Asquith papers touching on AFIL.

3. Conor Cruise O'Brien, in his *Ancestral Voices* (Poolbeg, Dublin 1994), is an important source of insight into the pathologies of emergent Catholic nationalism.

4. Appendix 1 gives an overview of the family history during the century; where appropriate it references decade modules where detail is expanded.

5. I have found traces of the thinking of John in the Oxford records, as well as the school records of John, Harry and William, and have outlined these in the 1900s family module of the hypertext; this is referenced from Appendix 1.

6. Norman Cardwell, 16 Trewmount Road, Killymahon, Dungannon BT71_6RL, phone 01868-722-510, is currently working on a history of the School, target publication date

2002. I have included some details of bursaries won by the Johnston boys in the 1900s family module.

7. I am indebted to William O'Kane of Dungannon Heritage World (now moved to Donaghmore) for this information.

8. I have chronicled the details of JJ's Hist participation in the 1900s module of the 'political' theme. This is overviewed for the century in Appendix 10.

9. See also the JJ sources section where I have listed them in full. It is also worth recording that my sister Dr Maureen Carmody had many books from the library of her father-in-law, Rev WP Carmody, Dean of Down, who was of a somewhat similar political persuasion, ie a Liberal Protestant supporter of all-Ireland Home Rule. The Carmody books remain with her family; they represent an important collection relevant to this tradition in the pre-independence period.

10. I have added some notes on Alice Stopford Green based on RB McDowell's biography (Allen Figgis, Dublin, 1967) in the hypertext. I give also some notes on her *Making of Ireland and her Undoing* (Macmillan1909), and later her *Old Irish World* (Gill & Macmillan 1912). Her quasi-imperial 'Commonwealth' vision was made explicitly in a comment to her secretary during the war of independence; she was visibly upset by news of IRA ambushings of British troops. This was recorded by CD Greaves in his journal on March 12 1967 after an interview with Maire Comerford, who had been ASG's secretary at the time, and his notes are accessible in the hypertext.

11. I am indebted to my daughter Nessa Johnston for drawing to my attention *Sam Thompson and Modern Drama in Ulster* by Hagal Mengel (Peter Lang, Frankfurt am Main, 1986), in which the 1900s background in Belfast to the Dublin national theatre movement is analysed critically. This enabled me to pick up the significance of Rutherford Mayne, whose name had occurred among JJ's papers. I have expanded on this in the political stream of the hypertext. Mengel published a pre-view of his thesis in two articles in *Theatre Ireland* #1 (Sept-Dec 1982) and #2 (Jan-May 1983)

12. This Butler/O'Grady essay is reprinted in his book *Escape from the Anthill* (Lilliput 1985). For O'Grady's subsequent association with Jim Larkin and *The Irish Worker* see Edward A Hagan's edited version of his writings *To the Leaders of Our Working People*, UCD Press, 2002; my review of this for the December 2002 *Irish Democrat* is accessible in the hypertext.

13. *Irish Agriculture in Transition*, Blackwell (Oxford) and Hodges Figgis (Dublin), 1951. Some attempts were made by Munster co-operatives to resurrect this principle, and JJ describes one in the *Dovea* chapter, and also elsewhere in the book.

14. I have treated this question in a paper published in the *Crane Bag;* it is to be found in the 'Forum Issue', Vol 7, No 2, 1983. As published it is full of dreadful misprints; in the hypertext version given here however I have corrected it.

15. The Statistical and Social Inquiry Society was a focus of 19th century Liberal economic thinking; I go into its history in Appendix 6, which overviews JJ's long association with it. CH Oldham would have been an early influence on the development of JJ's economic thinking.

16. The Plunkett House theme is overviewed in Appendix 4.

17. *The Years Flew By*, Sydney Gifford Czira, Gifford and Craven, Dublin 1974. The Ferguson reference is on p60. The author was a sister of Grace Gifford, who married Joseph Mary Plunket in 1916 on the eve of his execution.

18. The Barrington Lectures at this time had a decidedly West-British flavour; I go into the background to these in Appendix 7. JJ did not begin to associate with them until after the war, when they had been abandoned by the Statistical and Social Inquiry Society; he resurrected them, and gave them a co-operative flavour.

19. JJ had a long-standing relationship with the Society, becoming President in the 1950s. He did not join until the mid 1920s. I overview this theme in Appendix 6.

20. James Johnston, *Can the Hindus Rule India?* (PS King, London 1935) (incidentally the same publisher who had taken Nemesis of Economic Nationalism for JJ).

21. Joseph Johnston, *The Nemesis of Economic Nationalism* (PS King, London 1934).

22. I go into the details of this via Appendix 1 which is dedicated to the family; this gives some insight into the impact on the Protestant community of the 2 world wars.

Chapter 2: The Period 1911-1920

Introductory Overview

In 1910 JJ went to Oxford, where he did a further degree in the humanities, specialising in ancient history and archaeology, graduating in 1912. He moved in radical Liberal circles, interacting with people like GDH Cole, who subsequently was the economic guru of the 1945 Labour Government, and Lionel Smith-Gordon who subsequently became a leading activist in Horace Plunkett's co-operative movement. He then returned to TCD where he did the Fellowship Examination in 1913, becoming among the last of the Fellows to become so 'by examination'. He was therefore in line for a distinguished academic career in the then fashionable classical studies domain, in which the civil servants of the British Empire were trained. His elder brothers James, John and William were by then established in the Indian Civil Service; James wrote books in the 1930s after he retired which were critical of the caste-based exclusivism of Hindu nationalism.

In 1913, after returning from Oxford and gaining his Fellowship, he wrote a polemical book attacking Carson and the arming of the Orangemen. He had encountered Carson in Oxford at the time Carson had addressed the Oxford Union, and had later thrown down the gauntlet of armed resistance to Home Rule with Tory support at Blenheim. This perhaps was JJ's greatest and most insightful political act, and he spent his subsequent career consistently attempting to undo the harm done by that disgraceful Tory conspiracy.

In 1914 JJ applied for and got an Albert Kahn Travelling Fellowship; with this he travelled round the world. The War initially prevented him from fulfilling the European sector of his world trip, but in lieu of this he was enabled to spend time in France in the autumn of 1916, doing an economic study of French agricultural production under wartime conditions. The AKTF experience must have been the stimulus for his switch from classics to economics, which he proclaimed as his field from then on, without having studied it formally. This gave rise to tension with the TCD authorities, which continued throughout his career.

Having decided to switch from the classics, and being determined to re-invent himself as a development political economist, with a primary interest in agriculture, JJ found his academic career in TCD becoming difficult and fraught with tension and controversy. He therefore sought to re-interpret elements of his classical background in terms of the development economics of the ancient world, and he was able to relate this, together with his AK experience, to the problems of the emergent Irish national state.

In the published account of his 1916 AK French agriculture project, JJ emphasised the importance in the Irish context of good local government and a strong co-operative movement, an exercise in analysis in the 'political economy' domain.

JJ's Albert Kahn period, and subsequent contact with Charles Garnier the AK Foundation Secretary (lasting right up to 1949), indicated a consistent role for him in support of Irish independence, with which the AK Foundation was in sympathy and to which it lent early support. He was responsible for a series of briefings to Garnier about the current Irish situation, which Garnier used in France as a means of mobilising French public opinion in the Irish interest during the war of independence.

This post-1914 career re-orientation helped JJ to relate to the developing political situation in Ireland, from a Protestant Home Ruler perspective. Much of his subsequent political and economic activity was directed at trying to undo the worst effects of Partition, by maintaining links with people in the North who retained all-Ireland vision.

Post-1916 JJ seems to have been engaged actively in politics, but presumably with circumspection, as he has left few papers. He published in the *Manchester Guardian* and London *Times*, under a pseudonym, material which was supportive of the Canadian-type resolution of the political problem, in the context of the opportunity presented by the 1917 Irish Convention. During the War of Independence he remained in touch with the AKF and kept Garnier briefed about Irish affairs, with a view to trying to influence French public opinion.

JJ in Oxford

JJ's Oxford period, 1910-12, had many diverse formative academic and political influences. These included his participation in the Lincoln College student debates, which are on record, and interaction with the historian HAL Fisher(1), whose book on *The Republican Tradition in Europe* would have been a topic of conversation. The English and American influences on the French Revolution were discussed in depth. Fisher was also interested in the Finnish question, and his essay on *Political Unions* covered Portugal and Spain 1580-1640, Belgium and Holland, Norway and Sweden etc.

Fisher probably was influential in pointing JJ in the direction of applying for the Albert Kahn Travelling Fellowship(2), though in later life JJ attributed this to Mahaffy in Trinity College Dublin. Fisher had himself applied for the Albert Kahn Fellowship in 1912 but failed to get it. Kahn was a philanthropist who had made a fortune in Africa and was concerned about the perceived European drift into inter-imperial war. He had set up his Foundation in 1910, the primary UK contact being HA Meiers the Principal of London University; there remain records in the UCL Library. The network extended pre-war to Germany, Japan and the USA, as well as the UK and France. Fellows became members of the 'Autour du Monde' Club, and Kahn hoped, by educating promising young opinion-leaders in the cultures of foreign countries, that the drift to war would be countered.

In Lincoln College JJ mixed with a Liberal set(3) who were supportive of Home Rule for Ireland, and whose leading members were active in defending the Liberal position in the Tory-dominated Oxford Union. This Oxford Liberal network extended into Balliol and included GDH Cole, who later became a key economic influence on the 1945 Labour Government, and into Trinity with Lionel Smith-Gordon. JJ remained in contact with both in later years, Smith-Gordon becoming a luminary of the Irish co-operative movement in Plunkett House.

JJ initially participated in the Fleming Society in Lincoln, which was philosophical rather than debate-oriented. Economics in ancient Greece was discussed in the spring of 1911. Perhaps this was among the factors which turned JJ from ancient history and classics to economics. He then switched to the Lincoln Debating Society, where he made his maiden speech on January 28 1912 in favour of votes for women, supported by Llewellyn Williams. The motion was defeated. Later that term, along with WJ Bland, he helped unsuccessfully to oppose a Tory motion '...that the party system is a fraud and a failure'.

JJ had been given the status of Senior Affiliated Student on account of his previous attendance at TCD and was thus able to complete his degree in two years. He was awarded first class honours in Literae Humaniores in Trinity Term 1912; the degree of BA was conferred on him on 10 October 1912. In his subsequent career, after waiting the decent interval and paying a fee, he was able to trade as MA (Oxon), on top of his Trinity College BA (Mod). He never got around to doing his doctorate in his early period, and he subsequently regretted this, achieving this distinction only in 1970, with a D Litt conferred on foot of his Berkeley book. The combination of the Albert Khan Fellowship and a period of intense political and journalistic activity between 1913 and 1923 undoubtedly came between him and the achievement of conventional academic distinction

JJ Returns to TCD

On his return to Trinity College Dublin from Oxford he sat the Fellowship examination in 1913, for the third time; he had tried without success in 1911 and 1912, during his Oxford period, perhaps even in competition with his Oxford agenda; he had clearly set his sights on the Fellowship goal, and pursued it with determination. When he achieved it in 1913, with some distinction, and at a relatively young age, he felt that his future was reasonably secure, and he could devote his attention to the current political issues of the day, the principal one at that time being the Ulster crisis.

In response to this crisis in 1913 he wrote his *Civil War in Ulster*(1), polemicising against Carson and in support of all-Ireland Home Rule, publishing it in October of that year, in time for the Protestant Liberal rally in Ballymoney in November. The basic approach of the book was Liberal Enlightenment rational argument; he suggested that the threat of Rome Rule, in the light of European historical experience, was illusory, and that Ulster Protestants had nothing to fear and everything to gain; it was certainly not worth fighting a civil war to resist. He underestimated seriously however the imperial mind-set of the Tory Party, and their ability to influence the subversion of the Army, with the 'Curragh mutiny' making the Larne gun-running possible, engendering a coup-d'etat against the Liberal Government and the Home Rule process.

The Trinity College Board(4) was at this time picking up the impression that the 'Fellowship by examination' procedure was allowing into permanent tenure a type of academic recruit whom they regarded as unsuitable. On Mahaffy's initiative they gave JJ leave of absence to take up the Albert Khan Fellowship with alacrity. I conjecture, given their hard-core Unionist political complexion, that they were glad to have him out of the way for a while, after he published *Civil War in Ulster*.

Trip Round the World

JJ had been courting my mother Clara Wilson during his Oxford period, and then when he returned and had won his Fellowship he married her in July 1914, before setting off on his world tour, in which she participated, somewhat adventurously. She went to her aunt in Australia while he did his economic analysis of India, facilitated by his brothers(5). They re-united in Shanghai in June 1915, and completed the trip round the world together, visiting China, Japan (where my sister was conceived) and the USA. This latter part of his trip JJ reported insightfully at the 'travellers tales' level, but the Indian part of the Report is in some depth, to the extent that the Travelling Fellowship experience must have been influential in turning his interests away from the classics and in the direction of development economics. He made many contacts through his brothers who were there in the Civil Service. He was much impressed by the positive economic developmental role of the co-operative movement, and critical of the way the legislation of the British hindered it.

JJ sought in vain evidence for the type of political community with which we are familiar in Europe. The concept of family and kinship had not begun to be transcended by those of the citizen and the nation-state. An important obstacle to this was the caste system, which existed not only among the Hindus but also among the Muslims. Among Europeans in India the caste system also de facto existed; they were far from giving a good example for the principle of egalitarian citizenship, to judge from the unwritten rules governing access to the 'station club'.

JJ remarked on the small proportion of people who understood and wrote English, all of whom had their training in an English environment. It was from this elite that Indian nationalism drew its support; JJ pointed out the anomaly that the Indian nationalist elite wanted to impose its own rule on the Indian masses using second-hand English principles, without any Indian character at all. He counterposed the need for a sense of Indian citizenship, capable of modernising and getting rid of child-marriage, suttee and other barbarisms.

He smelled corruption in the legal system, where barristers earned more per day than the judge did in a month. The temptation for the litigant to square the judge was considerable.

JJ went into the origins, dynamics and current statistics of the caste system. It was conjectured that it originated in the need of the Aryan invaders to differentiate themselves from their darker predecessors. The complexity of the religious concepts imposed the need for a numerous and skilled priesthood. Sometimes movements to eradicate the caste system emerged, but these simply tended to become new castes. It mattered little what one believed, as long as one obeyed the ceremonial procedures appropriate to one's caste.

JJ was highly critical of the over-dependence on use of text-books and rote-learning throughout the educational system, to the detriment of the ability to understand genuinely, and to reason. He was inclined to blame the Macaulay policy on education in the English language for this, and to call for a positive approach to education in the vernacular and in their own classical traditions, as embodied in the wealth of Sanscrit texts, while accepting a role for English as a national lingua franca. He argued that English should not be the medium of instruction until the basics had been taught in the vernacular, and a competent level of English had been learned.

In an extensive section on agricultural credit JJ then went into the details of how co-operative credit organisations were set up, the key motivation being the substitution of an interest regime of 12% on deposits and 18% on loans, this being a vast improvement on the 75% charged by the moneylenders. The purpose of the loan was discussed at lending-time. One got longer terms for sinking a well than for a wedding. The effect was to restrict extravagant expenditure on ceremonial feasts, and encourage productive investment.

The influence of the growing movement, and its role in training people for citizenship, was considerable. There was also evidence that it was helping to break down castes, in that low-cast people were taking responsible positions, and high-caste people did not have an automatic right to more favourable loan terms.

The *Calcutta Statesman* on December 31 1914 noted the fact that in the Punjab the joint stock banks had been in trouble while the co-operative banks weathered the storm and improved their position.

Later in his life JJ referred to writing his Albert Kahn Report(2) in 1915-16 while waiting for conscription to be imposed. This must have been a first draft, because it did not get finally published until 1920 after the war. He had a chance to put in addenda, in one of which he referenced a book by HW Wolff on *Co-operation in India* and highlighted the process of political citizenship training in the co-operative movement, leading to the possibility of enhanced local government. He contrasted the India situation with that in Ireland, where representative local democracy had fallen under the influence of gombeen-politicians, and co-operative initiatives tended to be attacked as conspiracies against trade.

The State in India JJ regarded as a relatively benevolent bureaucracy, in a position to act progressively without gombeen influence. I quote: '...Imagine a Parliament consisting of John Dillons, Lord Clanrickardes, and Sir Edward Carsons, and you will have a faint idea of what an elected Indian political assembly would be like. A proposal to establish co-operative societies for the benefit of rural India would the strangled at birth by a Parliament thus constituted...'.

Back to TCD: the Co-op

On his return to TCD from the Albert Kahn experience, JJ brought himself to notice by helping to found a consumer co-operative society in the College, to supply the living-in students with groceries, and incidentally incurring the wrath of the Dublin shopkeepers(6) .

The first meeting, with JJ present, took place on Tuesday November 11 1913; at this they planned the first general meeting which took place the following Friday, November 14, in the Graduates Memorial Building. Provost Traill had agreed to be the President, and there was an Honorary Council which included Sir Horace Plunkett, Father Finlay, Sir Henry Bellew, George Russell, Harold Barbour. The working committee included Professor Bastable, Joe Biggar, EW Deale, WJ Bryan and JJ, who was in a position to parade his recently-acquired status as FTCD.

The committee met subsequently on January 26 1914; there were 14 people present, including JJ; it was agreed that Sealy Bryan and Walker should print the annual accounts. (This firm of jobbing printers were, it seems, occasional publishers; their imprint is on JJ's *Civil War in Ulster*, which they had published the previous October. I suspect that JJ got them the co-op business, such as it was, as a friendly 'thank you' gesture.)

At the February 23 meeting, in JJ's absence, with 17 people present, Joe Biggar proposed JJ as Secretary and he was elected, and appointed to attend the general meeting of the Irish Agricultural Wholesale Society. Suppliers cheques for some £160 were passed.

The 46th Annual Co-operative Congress was held in Dublin, on the Whit weekend, 1914. The Handbook of this conference contains a review of the consumer co-op scene in Ireland, which was quite undeveloped; it would have been matched by one of the smaller English counties. The Congress was held in Dublin as a gesture in the direction of strengthening the Irish district, and mending fences with Sir Horace Plunkett's Irish Agricultural Organisation Society, with which they had been in dispute in the 1890s. The Co-operative Wholesale Society had attempted to establish creameries in Ireland, but these had mostly failed, being superseded by the IAOS creameries, which depended on local societies appointing their own managers. The emerging Irish movement had found the Co-operative Union structures too inflexible.

The embryonic Dublin consumer co-ops however remained with the Union; they existed in Rathmines, Inchicore, Thomas St, Dorset St and Fairview. The Inchicore one went back to 1859, and serviced the railway workshop workers; it was criticised in the Handbook for being exclusive. The Dublin meeting of the Union in 1914 however turned out to be a false dawn. It seemed however at the time to open for JJ a window into Irish co-operative politics, for which he then had hopes, but these proved illusory.

JJ would by then have applied for the Albert Kahn Fellowship, but I suspect that he regarded it as a 'long shot', and did not expect to get it, or he would not have taken on the responsibility of being the DU Co-operative Society Secretary. Meetings then become quarterly; there was one on May 4 1914; the minutes are in JJ's writing; there were 11 present; discount deals for students with firms were announced. As Secretary JJ was sent as delegate to the forthcoming co-operative conference., which took place before he left on his Travelling Fellowship.

Thus it would seem that the politics of the Irish co-operative movement was top of JJ's priority at this time, remaining so for more than a decade, despite the diversions of the national revolutionary period. He did however in the 1920s turn his attention to the Irish Agricultural Organisation Society (IAOS) and Plunkett House, once it became apparent that the Co-operative Union was not a viable prospect in the Irish context as it had developed.

The Dublin University Co-op lapsed somewhat during his absence, but when he returned he took it up again with enthusiasm, and it survived. At the November 22 1915 meeting, JJ took over doing the minutes. He wrote marginal notes on the earlier minutes, realising the extent to which things had fallen apart in his absence. At the December 3 meeting, with 10 present, JJ's detailed minutes include a decision to try to capture the trade of the College Kitchen for the Irish Agricultural Wholesale Society (IAWS), with some aggressive marketing. This came up at the Board, and the latter agreed to leave it to the Bursar's discretion, a rebuff. There followed a decision to cultivate relations with the IAWS, which was related to the IAOS rather than to the Co-operative Union; this was an indicator of a turn towards Plunkett House, and a response to the lack of College official support.

At meetings in the first months of 1916, with JJ as secretary, there was evidence of a major effort to get more business. There was an attempt made to do a deal with the Dublin Consumer Co-op secretary to encourage non-College Dubliners to shop in the College, making postal or phone arrangement; this looked somewhat like grasping at straws. Business was in decline because of the decimation of the College population due to the war.

Then came the Easter Rising, and the shop was occupied by the Officers Training Corps, which was defending the College against the insurgents. JJ as secretary was reduced to writing letters to the military HQ looking for compensation, which by the end of the year they received. JJ's last 1916 minutes were of the meeting on October 16. He continued to attend the meetings, with the status of Secretary.

The DU Co-op continued to be active in co-operative politics: at a meeting on May 7 1917 the question came up of whom to vote for as the Irish representatives on the Board of the Co-operative Union (the all-UK body). It was agreed to vote for Smith-Gordon, Tweedy, Palmer, Adams and Fleming. Smith-Gordon had been encountered by JJ in Oxford, where he had shone as a socialist debater in the Union. RN Tweedy was an engineer who subsequently became a founder member of the Irish Communist Party. The co-operative movement in this period was a focus for those who wanted to democratise the economic system from the bottom up, and who identified with the politics of the Left in this spirit. At a subsequent meeting on February 26 1918 RN Tweedy was nominated to the Board of the Irish Section of the Co-operative Union.

Thus on the eve of the 1916 Rising we have JJ at the beginning of an academic career, just having completed his Albert Kahn world tour, and living in a flat in Fitzwilliam Square, my mother being pregnant with my sister Maureen. He was engaged in lecturing students in ancient history who were being prepared for the Indian Civil Service examination(7). He was actively involved with Plunkett House, and in promoting consumer co-operatives in the context of the Co-operative Union, the College one being a sort of pilot-project. In this context he was friendly with people like George Russell ('AE') and had encountered James Douglas. He had many contacts on the Liberal Home Rule and co-operative networks.

Easter Rising Aftermath

Post-Rising, JJ was immediately enmeshed in the politics of the aftermath. There is among his papers a letter from the London *Times*, dated September 29 1916, covering payment for a 'special correspondent' role. He travelled round the country during the vacation and reported on the condition of things. His *Times* article had appeared on September 8 1916, headed *Ireland Today / Spread of Sinn Fein / Political Cross-Currents(8)*.

The article began with a scholarly reference to the fatalism expressed in the writings of Edmund Spenser: '...they say it is the fatal destiny of that land that no purposes whatsoever which are meant for her good will prosper and take good effect'. JJ went on to report on '...a journey...undertaken with the object of making an independent study of the condition of the country without the pilotage of leaders of political parties, though their opinions where sought received the great attention they deserve.' (The opening quote supports the hypothesis that this was JJ; also travel during the TCD long vacation would have been feasible.)

He noted that Sinn Fein had gained support from the Nationalists, the reasons given being (a) that the Nationalists participated in the Coalition, (b) that they agreed to the 'mutilation' of Ireland, and (c) that they omitted to procure for the Dublin rebels that measure of clemency with which rebellion in another part of the Empire was treated.

He went on to describe the wide variety of types of people who are in Sinn Fein: '...well-read, well-travelled and earnest...students of political history and political economy....the poor have been given ideals which they never before associated with politics.....Thus a great movement has developed...its strength and dimensions are visible everywhere.. ...portraits of the rebels exhibited in the shop windows.... It enlisted the support of a part of the labouring classes and then devoted itself to an object which could avail them nothing. That was probably a condition of its receipt of certain funds...'.

He went on further to contrast the violent denunciations of Redmond with the profession of admiration for Carson, regarded as strong, honest and just. '...who might well receive a cordial greeting in unexpected quarters ...'. *This complete misunderstanding of the role of Carson and the Larne guns was at the root of most subsequent disasters!* Further: '...it is thought likely that many who have given their sympathies to Sinn Feiners as a protest against recent events might support the Nationalists if a test were made with "exclusion" out of the way...'. *JJ was here clinging tenaciously to his vision of all-Ireland Home Rule.*

'The Nationalists...are confident of the unwavering support of such followers of substance as the shopkeepers and farmers. Among the latter however there is a growing disinclination to mingle ... in the tumult of politics. They are more prosperous than they ever have been. The co-operative movement has helped them towards that prosperity, and the Irish Agricultural Organisation Society has taught them to reap the great advantages which now come within their reach. Yet it is manifest that they are much less popular with the labourers than the "ould gintry" used to be... through settled ownership of land they are drifting from nationalism into a political category that has now no representation...'.

He also wrote from France journalistically for the *Times*, while travelling on his Albert Kahn project. There was an article on September 29 1916: 'War Agriculture in France / The Benefits of United Action / A Lesson to British Farmers', from a Correspondent in France; this was credibly JJ. He was also moved by his French experience to contribute a series to the *Irish Times* entitled 'If the French Ruled Ireland'. In this he also used material related to his Albert Kahn project, in which he had analysed how French agriculture was coping with production during the war, using co-operatively owned machinery, with positive local support for the co-operative organisation of agriculture from the State, administered by the Prefects(9). In his 'virtual history' *Irish Times* articles he basically transferred the French republican model to Ireland, with the British having in the 1880s got tired of Ireland, transferring her to France, for treatment as an offshore island like Corsica. He had the Meath ranchers going into tillage for winter-feed, with consequent increased productivity of finished cattle and livestock products.

He is also on record as having participated, by August 1916, in the committee of the Irish Constitutional Association(10) along with AE, Diarmuid Coffey, Maurice Moore, Edward McLysaght, Alec Wilson and James Douglas. The objective of this was 'full Dominion Status' for Ireland.

There is during this period a record of a controversy in the *Irish Times*, initiated by JJ in a latter dated November 20 1916, and published on the 21st, attracting editorial comment. He made the case that the anti-Redmond Nationalists are not necessarily 'seditionists', nor are they 'pro-German'; they are supporters of all-Ireland Home Rule, a constitutional policy which had been subverted by the Ulster covenanters and their political allies the Tories, with the introduction of the gun, to the extent that the Imperial Parliament was powerless to enforce a law of its own making.

JJ was thus pressing home the arguments of his *Civil War in Ulster(1)*. In it he developed an argument for all-Ireland conscription in return for all-Ireland Home Rule: '...the only policy worthy of a statesman is one which will be daring to the point of recklessness. Announce that the Act suspending Home Rule Act will be made inoperative from the 1st of February 1917. Invite a conference of all Irishmen representative of all sections of the country to meet together in the knowledge that, if they fail to agree about some better scheme of Irish government, the existing Act, with all its faults, will be in operation on February 1st... In any case, let the Government make it clear that it will enforce both conscription and Home Rule with equal impartiality in all parts of Ireland, and it will have no trouble in enforcing either ...'.

He went on: '...one of the facts I have endeavoured to face is that there is such a thing as a strongly nationalist point of view, and lately I have taken some trouble to estimate its force and understand its nature. Another ... is that at least three fourths of Nationalist Ireland do not read your able editorials on Ireland's duty in the war...'. This was an outcome of his journalistic travelling for the *Times* during the 1916 summer vacation. He felt that all-Ireland Home Rule could be pushed in the direction of Dominion-type status, and that all-Ireland conscription would pre-empt Orange armed resistance(11).

I am inclined to think that JJ's support for all-Ireland conscription was motivated by a combination of his feeling of the need for active support for France, and his understanding of the need to keep Ireland in one political unit, rather than primarily by support for Britain and the Empire. During all this time he was in correspondence with Garnier the Albert Kahn Foundation Secretary, whom he kept briefed with material for pro-Irish publication in France, in support of Irish participation in the post-war Peace Conference(12).

The Constitutional Convention

To return to the Irish Constitutional Association committee: this was influential in briefing Sir Horace Plunkett, and set the stage for the Irish Convention of 1917, over which Plunkett presided, and with which AE and James Douglas were associated, along with Alice Stopford Green and others. This group served as Sinn Fein link-points, direct participation being against Sinn Fein policy. There are indications that the Association continued to exist during the Convention, as a sort of informal caucus, meeting in Coffey's house, where Erskine Childers(13), the Convention secretary, was staying. The latter had been appointed by Lloyd George, on secondment from the British Navy, where he had been engaged in adventurous exploits based on his earlier experience of the Frisian coast, as documented in his *Riddle of the Sands*.

There is no direct reference to JJ in McDowell's book(14) on the Convention, although JJ was actively promoting Dominion Status wherever he could, in support of the Constitutional Association objectives. This is evident from the Garnier correspondence(15), and I understand that he wrote in support of this position in the *Manchester Guardian* and probably elsewhere, though perhaps pseudonymously. I have been able to track down some articles which could credibly have been JJ's in May 1917(16). The following key extract certainly reflects JJ's lifetime conviction:

'...the Irish people...have no use for the Government scheme of a truncated nationality....the existence or the pressure of .. Sinn Fein... does not affect the matter.... Partition is bad, partition without the vote of the counties affected is worse, but a partition scheme which, while refusing a referendum before dissection, insists on a referendum before the wound can be repaired, making reunion as difficult as possible, and subjecting it to the veto of the most inveterate of prejudices, is the worst of all forms of partition......The Ulster democracy has never voted for Partition... The interest and sentiment of commercial Ulster are against Partition, the interest of Protestant episcopalian Ulster are against it...'.

JJ and Agriculture in France

Between JJ's first contact with the Constitutional Association, and the impact of the latter on the Convention in 1917, JJ was able to complete his Albert Kahn Fellowship work, by carrying out a survey of agricultural production in France, and how it had organised to cope with the war(17). He used this report as a further argument for the development of co-operation in agricultural production. It was favourably reviewed by AE in the *Irish Homestead*.

During his absence in France my mother was left with my sister, a few months old, in the flat in Fitzwilliam Square. Her sister Florrie was then working in Dublin, as a 'typewriter', and living in Haddington Road nearby, so this probably contributed to the support system, which also would have included his sister Ann who was in college.

The reasons for JJ's switch from classics to economics are becoming increasingly clear. The Albert Kahn influence, his problems with the College (in part due to over-production of classics people), and his writings on the Co-operative Movement all point in this direction(18).

The Thomas Davis Society

In the final years of the decade, with the national independence struggle becoming increasingly intense, it is very difficult to find any documentary trace of JJ's activity, but I have heard, from a Queen's University historian, that he probably played a role in supporting, from the College staff angle, the Thomas Davis Society, which was in effect a Sinn Fein front among the TCD students. The leading element in this was one Dermot MacManus, with whom JJ remained friendly up to the 1960s(19).

JJ continued to take an interest in the Co-op in TCD; by 1919 business began to take up again, with students war-survivors trickling back. Roles of committee members were defined: there was a sub-committee to keep in touch with the needs of the junior years. Then at the end of 1919 they pulled off the deal that set them up viably for the long haul: they set up the Lunch Buffet, in the Dining Hall. This was an immediate success, and gave a good foundation to the wholesale purchasing operation, which they did via the IAWS. JJ then took over the Chair, which he occupied up to the end of 1922. He pulled out of active participation on co-op affairs once he saw it was on a sound business footing.

Notes and References

1. I have given some insights into the HAL Fisher influence in my supporting documentation for the introduction to JJ's 1913 polemical book *Civil War in Ulster* (originally Sealy, Bryant and Walker, Dublin 1913; it has been re-published by UCD Press in 1999 with introduction by the present writer, and preface by Tom Garvin).

2. For more about the Albert Kahn Foundation see the related background module in the hypertext; there is also an overview of, and entry-points to, this theme via Appendix 3. The dominant part played by India in his 1914-15 world tour was due to the opportunities presented by the presence there of his elder brothers in the Civil Service. The visits to Java, China, Japan and the USA are in less depth; they are also treated in the hypertext summary of the Report, the main body of which deals with India. The Mahaffy attribution he made in a 1952 Seanad speech.

3. Names associated with the Liberal set include H Llewellyn Williams, WJ Bland, FK Griffith, P Guedalla and others. During his Oxford period he on record as having been 'in digs' with one Mallampally Narasimham, an Indian student from a landed family with an interest in Christian doctrine, and Samuel Thomas, the son of a Welsh engineer, who had opted to go for the classics. The Oxford period constitutes an important aspect of his academic formation, though it did not give rise to published work. In the support documentation for *Civil War in Ulster* I have also gone in some detail into the student politics of the period, in the lead-up to the famous Union debate addressed by Carson, at which JJ and this group were present. JJ's political papers from this period are somewhat scanty, but I have outlined their scope for this decade in some supportive notes in the hypertext which relate to the 'political' theme.

4. In Appendix 2 I have given an overview of JJ's long-standing and uncomfortable relationship with the TCD Establishment. See also my notes in the hypertext on the TCD Board meetings, where the issue of 'Fellowship by examination' and the over-supply problem comes up.

5. For access to JJ's Albert Kahn records see note 2 above. I have overviewed the family background in Appendix 1 and given some more detail about my mother and her role in the Albert Kahn tour in the family module of the hypertext for this decade.

6. The hostility of the Dublin shopkeepers ti the TCD Co-op was reported by Bulmer Hobson in his paper *Irish Freedom* in June 1913. The 'co-op' episode occurred in the context of JJ's emerging interest in economics and alternative business models. He used the experience to write in Plunkett House publications subsequently. In an article in *Better Business*, the Plunkett House promotional publication, in April 1916 JJ contributed some of his experience of the movement in India. This must have gone to press on the eve of the Rising. The Board minutes of the period also have JJ on record not only in support of the College co-op in 1913, but also later on July 4 1917 in support of a better deal for the 'skips', or College menservants who looked after the students' rooms.

7. JJ's interaction with academic life at this time was problematic. He was attempting a personal re-definition from classics to economics, in an environment where, in the aftermath of the 1916 Rising, the Board was lionising Carson, the target of JJ's 1913 book.

8. JJ kept a scrap-book for this period, which he deposited in the 'rare printed books' section of the TCD Library. I have abstracted this for the 1910s module of the political stream of the hypertext.

9. I have collected more of JJ's journalistic comments, in summary or in full, in this decade's module of the 'political' thread in the hypertext. This is overviewed for the century in Appendix 10. His 1916 *Food Production in France* Report I have also summarised in the hypertext.

10. See p6 of the Introduction to J Anthony Gaughan's edition of the *Memoirs of Senator James G Douglas* (UCD Press 1998). JJ remained close to Douglas in later years; they co-operated in the Senate on issues relating to the North. Sources for the political interactions of JJ during this period are far from clear, those few I have are available with the JJ source material in the Linenhall Library, Belfast, by courtesy of John Killen.

11. I have given in the hypertext extract from the TCD Library scrapbook extensive extracts from JJ's arguments, which motivated his continuing support for the lobbying of the Convention.

12. I have abstracted for the hypertext the Garnier correspondence from the relevant file in JJ's papers, where it is preserved in Folder 4.

13. There is among JJ's papers some correspondence with Erskine Childers when the latter was Secretary of the Irish Convention; this relates to JJ's submissions to that body. The evolution of Childers' political philosophy is somewhat enigmatic and controversial: from a typical upper-class jingoistic position in the 1900s, to arming supporters of Home Rule in 1914; from Lloyd George's appointed Convention secretary in 1917 to anti-Treaty Republican publicist in 1922. Andrew Boyle's *Riddle of Erskine Childers* (Hutchinson, London, 1977) goes some way to explaining his trajectory, and his treatment was apparently welcomed by his son who became President. For the present writer however there remain questions unanswered, about the Asgard episode among other things.

14. RB McDowell, *The Irish Convention 1917-18,* Routledge and Kegan Paul, London, 1970. I can't resist remarking in this context that McDowell, like many others with a strong Unionist background, turns a blind eye to the Larne gun-running, despite its considerable scale, and its significance as the introduction of the gun into Irish politics in the 20th century. In his background introduction to the main theme of the book he mentions the miniscule Howth episode with the Asgard, but ignores Larne, though he goes in detail into the various political manoeverings for the exclusion of Ulster from Home Rule. There is a need perhaps for further analysis of the available background material. I append in the hypertext for example some notes extracted for this period from the Maume study of the politics: *The Long Gestation: Irish National Life 1891-1918,* Patrick Maume, Gill and MacMillan 1999.

15. Garnier was the executive secretary of the Albert Kahn Foundation; he and JJ corresponded right up the 1940s. The first Garnier letter I have on record is a response to documentation on the Convention sent to him by JJ. I have added some notes on the Convention in this Garnier module, to explain the background to the correspondence in the Albert Kahn context. This theme has political ramifications into the foreign affairs of the nascent Free State.

16. I have given extensive abstracts from these May 1917 *Manchester Guardian* articles in the section of the 1910s political stream of the hypertext which is based on the JJ scrap-book in the TCD Library.

17. When doing this he got accreditation from the *Irish Times*, and wrote up the experience in journalistic mode, as well as in his Report, which was published as a pamphlet by Maunsel.

18. I develop this aspect via the Plunkett House channel in Appendix 4, with the support of the Plunkett Foundation in Oxford. There are also strong indications that JJ was directly influenced by Standish O'Grady, who had been writing for Jim Larkin's *Irish Worker* prior to the war, promoting worker co-operative approaches to economic development; see his *To the Leaders of Our Working People*, ed EA Hagan, UCD Press 2002; I have reviewed this for the December 2002 *Irish Democrat*. For more on O'Grady's politics see Hubert Butler's 1978 essay, re-published in his book *'Escape from the Anthill'* (Lilliput 1985), which deals with his period in Kilkenny during the Boer War.

19. For the Thomas Davis Society reference, and Dermot MacManus's role in it, I am indebted to a lady QUB historian whom I encountered at a John Hewitt Summer School in or about 1996. It could have been Edna Longley, but perhaps not. To my eternal regret I have been unable to pin this down, having failed to note it at the time. Nor is there any record of the TDS in the TCD MS room. JJ had contact with McManus in the 1920s, when the latter smoothed the way for JJ's journalistic coverage of the post-civil war situation. Later in the 1930s their relationship became strained, with MacManus supporting the Blueshirts. There is subsequent correspondence in JJ's papers with McManus dated June 1965. McManus was then retired and living in Harrogate. He had contributed a paper to the Harrogate Literary Society entitled *The Irish Literary Revival 1890-1935*. I reference this also from Appendix 4, as the content relates to the cultural background of Plunkett and the co-operative movement, and also from the 1960s chapter, when JJ did some travelling in Mayo, trying again to pick up the co-operative trail on the fringe of what the present writer was doing. It is probable that he called at the McManus estate at Killeaden, having received some notes from McManus about its history.

Chapter 3: The Period 1921-1930

Introduction

In the 1920s JJ was active in trying to support the declining co-operative movement (which had been split under Partition); he did extern lecturing, initially when the war of independence was on in Dublin in TCD to trade unionists, often with Tom Johnson the Labour Party leader presiding, then later outside Dublin; these were mostly under the auspices of the Barrington Trust(1).

As regards political(2) activity, there is a suggestion that JJ had been involved in support of the Thomas Davis Society (TDS), which from about 1919 and in the early 20s was a Sinn Fein 'front' in TCD. He certainly was friendly with Dermot MacManus, who was a prime mover in the TDS, and who subsequently became a military leader in the Free State Army during the Civil War, acting mostly in the West. He wrote a series of articles for the Manchester Guardian in 1923, surveying the post civil war situation, and commenting on the motivations of the people concerned.

JJ participated in the first Agriculture Commission set up in 1922 by the Free State Government. This attempted to pick up the momentum of Sir Horace Plunkett's Department of Agriculture and Technical Instruction. Although most of its recommendations were sound, it was not adapted to the politics of the times, which were dominated by the demand for land-division. JJ wrote an addendum on the need for training of co-operative managers.

JJ began in the late 1920s to seek election to the Senate, although without success. He had published a book(3) in 1925 which attempted to popularise the basic concepts of economic thinking, and which contained some seminal ideas which now would now be recognised as relating the 'development economics' domain, emphasising the importance of getting a good deal for the agricultural primary producers. He also introduced the idea of the importance of know-how as a factor of production, along with land, labour and capital; this at the time was innovative.

During the 1920s and subsequently in the 1930s JJ campaigned for increased understanding of development economics in the Irish agricultural community, continuing to use as his vehicle the Barrington Lectures(4). These had been initiated a century earlier, in the aftermath of the Famine, and were in effect a sort of outreach campaign by the Statistical and Social Inquiry Society (SSISI)(5), with the aim of avoiding future famines through enlightenment. JJ joined the SSISI in 1924. In their original form the Barrington Lectures tended to dodge the key current political issues of land tenure etc. They survived in outreach form until rendered redundant by the advent of TV in the 1960s. They still nominally remain in the form of an annual SSISI Barrington Lecture on the home ground of the Society.

The Co-operative Movement

In the earlier years of the decade, when the war of independence and civil war was going on, JJ seems to have concentrated on working with Plunkett House, doing articles and reviews for *Better Business*; this later became *The Irish Economist* and then later blossomed into the *Irish Statesman*. He also kept up a low-key contact with the national movement(6), corresponding with Dermot MacManus, who had been the leading light in the TCD Thomas Davis Society, and by 1922 was commanding Free State forces in Limerick. MacManus later became Deputy Governor of Mountjoy Jail. In the latter context he seems to have leaked to JJ photocopies of handwritten letters from Pierrepoint the hangman, which JJ retained among his papers as curiosities. He probably found the McManus contact useful in the journalistic work he did for the *Manchester Guardian* in 1923.

JJ continued to publish promotionally for the co-operative movement(7) in various Plunkett House publications: an assessment of the experience of the TCD co-op, a review of the work of Sydney and Beatrice Webb, articles on 'Money and Credit', 'Free Trade and Protection for Irish Industries'; this was a forerunner of his book *The Nemesis of Economic Nationalism* published a decade later.

In 1925 JJ began to appear in the *Irish Statesman*, with UCD economist George O'Brien reviewing his *Groundwork of Economics*. JJ also had an article on municipal reform, and a letter on the Universities; at about this time he was standing for election to the Seanad. There appears the first of a series of Paris letters from Simone Tery, whom we have encountered with JJ in the Albert Kahn stream; it is reasonable to suggest that JJ might have contributed to encouraging her interest in Ireland, about which she wrote articles and a political book for the French market.

It can credibly be suggested that most of JJ's writings during this time were dedicated to the development of a public profile in the context of the 1926 Seanad election, in which however he was unsuccessful.

He had earlier had a supportive role in connection with the Boundary Commission, and he remained friendly with Kevin O'Shiel, the Secretary and author of the Report, during the 1930s and 1940s; I remember several social occasions, viewed from below, as a child. He kept among his papers some cuttings relating to the Boundary Commission, from 1924, and his copy of the Report is annotated. There is also a map of the Ulster and the six counties, with the distribution of electoral majorities by parish marked in. This appears to be a draft or earlier version of the map given on p83 of Kevin O'Shiel's *Handbook of the Ulster Question*, as the style is similar, though the representation is different.

The Barrington Lectures

JJ's main concern in the mid to late 1920s was to propagate in the outside world a critical view of the economic factors to be taken into account in the Free State situation. His main vehicle for this was the Barrington Lecture(1) series, which he managed single-handed between 1921 and 1932, when he managed to get them back under the control of the Statistical and Social Inquiry Society of Ireland (SSISI), from which they had lapsed after the First World War. During the War of Independence and the Civil War he delivered the earlier 1920s Barrington lectures on TCD ground, where they attracted support from the trade unions; Tom Johnson, leader of the Labour Party, on occasions presided.

Later in the decade he brought them round the country, making use of the Carnegie Library network, and later the Vocational Education Committees, when the library system was brought in under local government. In post-civil-war excursions to various remote places he seems to have had trouble in getting an audience; he mentions this retrospectively in a Seanad speech, in the 1940s. He attempted to prevent the withdrawal of the Carnegie Trust to Scotland, offering to take over the field-work after the resignation of Lennox Robinson who had been the Secretary of the Trust in Ireland, but was unsuccessful in this(4). He attempted in the correspondence to use the Barrington connection as leverage:

"The establishment of the Irish Free State has made more important than ever the task of creating a public opinion capable of appreciating the economic issues which are constantly being presented to us by our legislators. By means of its circulating libraries the Carnegie UK Trust has already done invaluable work in this, as in other, directions.

"For the last four years I have held the position of Barrington Lecturer in Economics. The Barrington Trust is a century-old Trust. The function of the Barrington Lecturer is to give lectures on Social Economics in 'the towns and villages of Ireland'. I have felt for some time that the value of these lectures was diminished because they were not preceded and followed by a course of appropriate reading on the part of those forming the audiences or classes.

"I have also felt that the efforts of the Carnegie Trust to create a reading public in rural Ireland would be assisted if the Library movement were more closely associated with an Institution like the Barrington Trust, which makes it possible for at least one Lecturer to give lectures or hold classes in out of the way places. Latterly, under the auspices of the Barrington Trust, I have been holding classes for non-university students in Dublin, but it is my intention to make a fresh start in the rural districts after the end of the present calendar year. It was also my intention to choose those districts where the Library movement had been most successful, with a view to the closer co-ordination of the work of the two Trusts."

In the course of further correspondence with Colonel JM Mitchell, the Carnegie Foundation executive in Scotland, JJ attempted to use the good offices of the Foundation to help him get access to the new County Library network, fearing perhaps that otherwise his TCD background might be a barrier. The Colonel replied positively for situations where Carnegie contacts had existed, namely in Antrim, Fermanagh, Galway, Londonderry(sic), Kilkenny, Sligo, Tipperary, Tirconaill, Wexford, Wicklow. JJ replied specifying his time-constraints, and offering 25 lectures per annum. The Colonel then back-tracked, referring the matter to the new County Committees. It seemed also that he regarded lectures in economic and social science as being subversive, especially in the then Irish context, and wanted to distance the Carnegie Trust from the process.

Later however there came a letter from the Colonel to the effect that he had heard from Miss Josephine M Walsh of Wexford, who expressed interest. He urged JJ to get in touch directly and gave the address. So the Wexford series was set up successfully; there is among JJ's papers a copy of a notice issued by the Wexford County Council, advertising a short course of Lectures in Economics, organised by the Library Service, in the Town Hall, the first one on 'Some Consequences of Economic Law' being fixed for Thursday March 8 1926 at 8pm. This was also in the lead-up to the 1926 Seanad elections.

There is also among JJ's papers a page setting out the topics for what look like a series of six lectures, along lines somewhat similar to the Table of Contents of the *Groundwork*, though differing in detail. It seems he hoped to give the series cohesively in the one location, and the purpose was didactic. Later, in the 30s, the lectures tended to be more critical and controversial on current affairs, and to be one-shot local events in various places.

The 1922-24 Agriculture Commission

JJ was recruited to serve on the Agriculture Commission(8) which sat from 1922 to 1924, along with George O'Brien, JP Drew and others. In order to have been so invited he must have been in good standing with the new Free State Government. His prior work(9) lobbying the Convention, and his work in support of the Thomas Davis Society in Trinity College would not have gone un-noticed, as well as his work with the Albert Kahn Foundation, which had both a national dimension, via his Garnier briefings for influencing French public opinion, and via his earlier work in 1916 on French agricultural production.

The Commission came out with a series of interim reports, on issues considered urgent. The series covered tobacco (in which there was some pioneering interest, though it never came to much), butter, eggs, credit and 'scrub bulls'.

The final report was basically a re-iteration of the classical Department policy from the Horace Plunkett era, derived from the Recess Committee, with emphasis on education and organisation, and as such was perhaps not in tune with the times, which were politically dominated by a populist demand for land re-distribution. JJ included a signed addendum in which he advocated resourcing the training of co-op managers, and also the imposition of an export tax on live cattle. He had early identified the need for combining tillage with livestock, enabling the finishing of cattle for beef by stall-feeding in winter, and supporting expanded winter dairying. This implied a co-operative approach to large-scale managed commercial farming, and was inconsistent with the division of land into small units. The Report was, unjustly, condemned in the political media as a 'rancher's charter'.

Political Journalism

There was a series of articles in the *Manchester Guardian* in 1923, which are JJ's from internal evidence, and which are referenced in the Garnier correspondence. These were headed 'An Inquiry Into Ireland' and I have summarised them more fully in the political stream(10).

In the first article JJ tried to explain why the Government had found it so hard to restore order, interviewing Republican supporters. It is difficult to organise the townspeople in self defence; they prefer to keep quiet and stay neutral. The Government depends totally on the Army, which is inexperienced and ill-disciplined. There are plenty of trained officers around, but the government is slow to take them on; too many British ex-officers would give the Republicans a propaganda point... Republican support is young unemployed, farmers sons etc.... professional men are withholding tax, agricultural labourers aspire to own land. Farmers withholding annuities worry about law enforcement regarding arrears.

Then on April 13 1923 JJ wrote of an interview with a group of six hard-core Republicans; regarding the election, they held that there was never a majority for the Free State vs the Republic, only a majority for the FS vs war. They would not feel bound by plebiscite unless the threat of war was removed. He quoted a source: '....the materialist majority are sheep who must be driven by the minority of energetic idealists ...'.

The April 14 1923 article contained a report from 'our special correspondent' on the Free State budget, which ran at an expenditure of £30M, at a deficit of £2.3M. Continuing the 'inquiry' series, JJ tried to find out what the 'republic' concept meant; most Free Staters saw the Free State as the 'stepping-stone' to the Republic. Some fear that a Republic now would mean civil war in the North. The majority would have voted for the Republic were it not for the threat of war. But now that civil war has begun, perhaps not; the 'republic' concept is now in disrepute.

The strong farmers had been the backbone of the war of independence, and it was the threat of conscription that had activated them. These however are now solidly Free Staters. 'The uncompromising republican idealists are drawn from the ranks of the intellectuals: professors, civil servants, teachers, young priests and women of leisure. These can't make successful war without the support of the farmers.'

April 17 1923: JJ described conditions in 'regular' country (there are 3 parts: regular, irregular and Ulster)..... Labourers quietly expand their half-acre to one acre by extending their fencing. Strong farmers do land deals with landlords, but can't agree on how to divide. The Land Bank refuses to help because they give priority to landless men. Law is beginning to exist, even for landlords. The unarmed Civic Guards are active.

April 18 1923: JJ spent time in Limerick, where the Free State troops were said to be 'the most effective in Ireland'; the average age of officers was 21, generals 30; there was said to be no looting or bullying. Experience of republicans was bad; there was much looting. However the Guards were becoming effective, and had established the ability to arrest without arms.

I suspect that JJ's contact with Dermot MacManus was relevant here. MacManus had written to JJ from Limerick earlier in the year, and even if demobilised would have been in a position to help with introductions and contacts.

He picked up some lore about de Valera in Tralee; a big crowd came to hear him; he asked them to vote for the Republic, and they all put their hands up. Dev went away thinking he had the people behind them and started the war. But the people had only come out of curiosity, and the felt that would get into trouble if they didn't put up their hands. 'That was the beginning of the irregularity'.

April 19 1923: In Tralee he picked up a picture of 'irregular' mountain country. The Free State was in Cork and in Tralee and in the coastal towns. .... It was impossible for the Free State to take over, due to lack of material and inexperience. The war here could drag on for the summer.

April 21 1923: JJ tried to analyse the thinking of the 'idealists'; their concept of culture was somewhat vague: '...one man cited the co-operative movement as an example of the way the Protestant aristocracy, even at its best, has never been anything but a fallacious guide endeavouring to persuade people to substitute material ends for the spiritual ideal of independence ...'. There was no clear idea how Europe should relate to tropical countries.. no idea of socialism... some talk of 'co-operative commonwealth'; '...the small-nation system will put an end to the sins of imperialism, capitalism and militarism ...'.

He evaluated them individually as being humble-minded, but '....as a class their conceit is astounding....the utmost concession...to democracy is to agree to be bound by the decisions of the nation in its best moments. But they themselves are to decide which are the nation's best moments....I am sure they can't be induced to drop their opposition to the Free State... they are as ruthless as any bureaucracy or autocracy... if only they could be persuaded to marry and to have children! ...'.

April 23 1923: JJ recounted some anecdotal travel episodes in Wexford, Waterford and Carlow. He stayed in a big house rented by a teacher and a Presbyterian Minister, near Kilkenny; Redmond supporters. He met a gardener who was out of work, and as a consequence somewhat blind to the patriotic virtues of burning country houses. He took a dim view of the type of pub-talk patriots who were being recruited to the Guards, and given land.

April 24 1923: there was a general desire to get back to work. It should be possible to establish a dead meat industry, and other industries subsidiary to agriculture, putting the money to work that was currently lying idle in the banks. No-one will venture money while there is danger of explosions etc. The Republican hope that the executions would bring people to their side was misplaced. Most 'irregularity' now is just criminal. A barracks was burned in Kilkenny because Guards interfered with salmon poaching.

The final article, on May 2, focused on the land question, which remained unresolved, with 25% of the land still under nominal landlord control, though with much rent arrears. He summarised the rest of the issues thus: '....the Ulster problem, the Labour problem, the demobilisation of 50,000 men, 2000 irregulars on the run, 15,000 republican prisoners, splitting the grass ranches and completing the land purchase ...'.

Steps Towards 'Political Economy'

JJ joined the Statistical and Social Inquiry Society in 1924, as an Oldham recruit, and was elected to the Council in 1925(5). He remained active on the Council for some decades. His first paper to the SSISI was on 'Some Causes and Consequences of Distributive Waste', delivered March 10 1927. This was the result of some work done with the support of the Rockefeller Foundation, which enabled him to travel to France to do some international comparisons. The results of his French studies are absent from his SSISI paper, but they surfaced strongly in the Prices Tribunal of 1926, to which he contributed an extended signed addendum, developing the argument for a National Economic Council to integrate the results of the various disparate enquiries and bodies which existed on economic matters. I have so far been unable to trace any actual integrated Rockefeller Foundation Report, though I have a copy of his application.

In March 14 1925 appointments were finally made in TCD to the School of Commerce: JJ at last got his lectureship in economics, CE Maxwell on economic history, John Cooke on commercial geography; there were lectures in French, German, Spanish etc, and TS Broderick lectured on statistical methods. The new School of Commerce seemed to be taking shape credibly. The Commerce School Committee had Bastable as the Professor, with Duncan and JJ as his Assistants. Bastable was also the Regius Professor of Laws.

The syllabus remained basically that of the pre-1920 Diploma; it showed no sign that JJ's efforts to promote the co-operative principle in commerce, via his Barrington Lectures and via his work with the Dublin University Co-operative Society, had any success. There remained however a nod in this direction, in the form of the retention of the Recess Committee Report, which had been on the syllabus since the beginning of the Diploma in 1906.

During the mid-20s we had the ESB and the Shannon Scheme, the Purser Griffith vs McLaughlin controversy regarding energy development policy; JJ does not appear to have been directly concerned with the 'development economic' aspects of this, though he retained in his possession TA McLaughlin's seminal pamphlet on the Shannon Scheme, in which the latter drew on the experience of the electrification of Pomerania. JJ also had the ensuing Borgquist et al Government Expert Report, which he got from EH Alton who then represented the College in the Dáil. Both these documents are among his papers. I remember him, in the early 30s, when living in Newtown Platin, near Drogheda, pointing out the new ESB high-tension poles with a sense of pride in achievement.

The Prices Commission: French Influence via Rockefeller

The TCD Board certainly was aware of JJ's economic work in the public service: on March 19 1926 there is a minute '...as the Government is desirous that Mr Joseph Johnston should be free to devote as much time as possible to the work of the Profiteering (sic) Tribunal and to the investigations incidental to it, and the Minister for Finance has agreed to pay deputies for him next term, he is allowed to take advantage of this arrangement next Trinity term.' Thus we have a further example of JJ's concern with, and availability for the solution of, problems of the outside world. There was a further reference on April 24 1926, in which leave of absence is confirmed for Trinity Term, with the School Committee to decide about a substitute. He was also granted a further fortnight in 1926, and one in January 1927, to take up a Rockefeller Fellowship for Economic Research in Europe.

In JJ's Addendum to the Prices Commission Report he described himself as Rockefeller Fellow for Economic Research 1926-27, and this embodied the results of his recent studies in France. He put emphasis on consumption as being the generator of demand for production, and on the importance of the distribution system working cost-effectively, so as to maximise the ease of access and affordability of the goods produced. He had in mind the potential for the development of the consumer co-op movement as a more cost-effective alternative to the large number of small retail outlets. He advocated a licencing system for retailing.

He produced evidence for this from his French studies, and went on to outline how the National Economic Council concept had been realised in France. The relevant sections I quote in full:

"43. By a decree of the 10th January, 1925, a National Economic Council was established in France. The object was to create a school for the dispassionate study of economic questions, from the point of view of the general economic interest, and to supply an organ of "inter-ministerial" co-ordination. In conformity with this idea it is attached to the office of the President of the Executive Council - not to any Ministerial Department. It is there to be consulted by the Government, but it has also the right to give its advice unasked on any matters in which it chooses to interest itself. Its membership includes expert officials from the Ministries of Finance, Agriculture, Labour and Commerce.

"It may also summon non-official experts –'techniciens', economists, and jurists to assist in its deliberations. The ordinary membership is based on a semi-representative principle, the governing idea being that the consumers' point of view should predominate. The Government decides what organisations shall be represented, and each such organisation freely appoints its delegate to the Council.

"There are 47 such delegates. Three are appointed by Consumers' Co-operative Societies, and six others represent directly various aspects of economic consumption. Eleven delegates represent managerial services in industry, agriculture etc, while fourteen represent wage-paid labour of various types.

"Industrial capital is represented by three delegates, land-ownership (urban and rural), by two, while the Capital associated with banking, insurance, and the Stock Exchange has a representation of three.

"44. Reports of the National Economic Council have been published in 'Annexes' to the 'Journal Officiel'. One such report deals with hydraulic production and distribution of electric power. Another deals with co-operation and agricultural credit as means of intensifying agricultural production, another with the electrification of the countryside, another with live stock, etc. It would appear from recent experience that the Saorstát has need of a rational and enlightened public opinion on questions like these, and in this connection a suitably constituted National Economic Council might play a useful part.

"45. It should contain in the first instance official experts from at least the economic Ministries -- Finance, Agriculture, Commerce and Fisheries. To these should be added experts from the Industrial Trust Company, the Tariff Commission, the Shannon Electricity Board, the Currency Commission, the Agricultural Credit Corporation, and the proposed Prices Board. The Chairman of the Currency Commission should be the Chairman of the Council, and the Secretariat of that Commission should act as the Secretariat of the Council. As in the case of France it should be attached directly to the office of the President of the Executive Council, and not to any Ministerial Department.

"46. Delegates from the more important professional economic organisations should belong to the Council, as in the case France, and be appointed by a similar method."

JJ went on to refer back to the 1922-24 Agriculture Commission, outlining some of the problems it had identified relating to the supply of milk. He drew again on the French experience:

"55. About forty miles north of Paris, at Lyons-la-Foret, there is a co-operative creamery which the present writer lately had the privilege of visiting. It was established in 1900, as a result of the intelligent initiative of some thirty farmers, who were tired of economic dependence on private milk collecting firms. It now numbers about 400 members who are bound by contract to dispose of all their milk through it. In 1918, when the membership was 284, the Society handled 3,442,186 litres of milk. The value of buildings, pasteurising and cooling plant, milk cans, butter and cheese manufacturing plant, motor lorries, horse-drawn vehicles, etc, now runs to some thousands of pounds sterling. It was originally established, mainly by borrowed money, but its debts have since been repaid, and the position is in the highest degree liquid.

"The premises of the Society are adjacent to a railway station from which there is a convenient train service to Paris. A depot is maintained in that city, the manager of which is in direct telephonic, communication with his colleague at Lyons-la Foret. It is also in close touch with the private retail milk vendors who are his customers in Paris. The latter are able to estimate very closely their requirements from day to day. They give their orders to the depot manager who, after a simple arithmetical operation, is able to telephone to the creamery manager forty miles away. telling him exactly the quantity of fresh milk which he should send in the next consignment. The milk cans, which are of ten, fifteen and twenty litres capacity, are sealed at the station of departure, and on arrival at Paris are distributed direct to the retailers without necessarily being brought to the depot.

"Nevertheless, a small cheese manufacturing plant is maintained there to deal with any surplus which the retailers might not be able to dispose of. All the milk is pasteurised at Lyons-la-Foret. Any milk not required for liquid consumption is retained there and turned into butter or cheese. Thus the substantial summer surplus is kept off the fresh milk market, and at all times of the year waste is reduced to a minimum. The suppliers are paid in proportion to their total milk deliveries -- a higher price of course in winter than in summer. In order to encourage winter milk production the refund, or dividend, payable at the end of the financial year, is paid only in respect of winter milk.

"56. The Society at Lyons-la-Foret is only one among some dozens of such societies, situated at an average distance of about fifty miles from Paris. Together they contribute one-third of the total fresh milk consumed in that city. The other two thirds are in the hands of two large private firms. Some of these societies go in for the manufacture of casein in the summer. I am informed by Senator Donon, President of the Federation of the Co-operative Creameries in the Parisian region, that certain societies find the manufacture of casein so profitable that they are able to pay the same uniformly high price for milk winter and summer.

"57. Twenty years ago, before the inauguration of this movement, milk was frequently sold in the country at nine centimes a litre to be re-sold at thirty in Paris. According to Senator Donon the position in the winter of 1926-1927 was as follows:-

"Collection, pasteurising, cooling, transport to Paris and distribution in Paris cost in all forty-five centimes per litre. The retailers, were allowed a margin of gross profit of fifteen centimes. The consumer paid one franc fifty centimes, and this left ninety centimes a litre as the farmer's remuneration."

The above figures are of course subject to wartime inflation, but the argument is clear: the ratio between farmer and consumer prices has been vastly improved by co-operative organisation of the distribution system.

The Protestant Role in Free-State Politics

There is among the few books JJ retained in his retirement the proceedings of a 'Conference on Applied Christianity' held in January 1926, on the theme 'Towards a Better Ireland' (11). This was an attempt on the part of the all-Ireland Protestant community to assert their role in civil society, and to address the uphill task of making democracy work under Partition. The Roman Catholic Church however did not participate.

This was addressed among others by Lionel Smith-Gordon, from the standpoint of the co-operative movement, and by the Ulster Liberal Professor RM Henry, who had participated in the group who went to Asquith after the Ballymoney Liberal rally of November 1913, in the hopes of stemming the tide of the Tory-Orange conspiracy which led to the April 1914 Larne gun-running.

The Albert Kahn Foundation and the French Connection

JJ still kept contact with the Albert Kahn Foundation in Paris, and was in ongoing correspondence with its Executive Secretary Charles Garnier(12). This was his 'international network' and it undoubtedly fuelled his progression into an Irish-based 'development economics' mode of thinking. He fed Garnier with material about Michael Collins, and promoted James Connolly; Garnier used the material to promote the Irish cause in France. Through this contact Simone Tery, whose *Irlande* had been published in 1923, was picked up as the Paris correspondent of the *Irish Statesman*.

There is reference in the Garnier correspondence to visits by Cosgrave to Paris, in 1923 and again in 1926, on which occasion Garnier was appalled to see him kneel before a bishop, and was thereby motivated to intensify his correspondence with JJ, with his projected book on Ireland in mind. The correspondence had been quite intense during the war of independence and civil war period. Garnier sent to JJ some unpublished research-source material, which he hoped JJ would be able to use as the nucleus of a Dublin 'Centre de Documentation' for the AK Foundation. JJ targeted the Plunkett House Library for this, but all trace of this seems to have been lost. He clearly regarded this as a more accessible location than the TCD Library, which Garnier would have preferred.

The documentation consisted of the proceedings of the meetings of a political and social studies group which had met weekly, in the Cour de Cassation, under Albert Kahn auspices. This material was not commercially available, being reserved for 'centres de documentation' in educational and research centres. Albert Kahn would have preferred such a centre to be established in Trinity College, in a small reading-room, accessible to qualified researchers.

At the time the material arrived the Civil War had not yet begun; the burning of Plunkett's house took place some time later, and JJ was optimistic about the future of Plunkett House in the Free State environment.

TCD Politics or Public Life?

JJ was active in TCD politics(13) in favour of the development of a significant school of commerce and political economy. In this he was supported by GA Duncan, who eventually got the Chair. Academic promotions, then as now, were hindered rather than helped by outreach work in 'civil society' such as JJ was doing. He engaged in a significant amount of work for the Government, on questions relating to consumer prices, and travelled abroad, on a Rockefeller Fellowship, for the purpose of carrying out international comparisons, particularly with France, where he had the prior connections, due to the Albert Kahn episode.

He published his book, *Groundwork in Economics(3)*, in which he popularised the basic ideas of economics, and attempted to relate these to the needs of the co-operative movement, which was struggling to survive in the hostile post-

Partition environment, the Munster producer co-ops having being severed from the Ulster consumer co-op movement. He had used the early 1920s Barrington Lectures as a laboratory for testing the *Groundwork* ideas against public perceptions, and for promoting the concept of local co-operative entrepreneurship.

During 1925 and 1926 JJ was active in public life, with an eye to the Seanad. There are preserved letters among his papers, dated September 24 and 28, 1925, from Louis Bennett, Secretary of the Women Workers' Union; this was an attempt, in the context of the coal dispute, with a view to mediation, '...to get three or four men such as yourself, outside the Labour Movement, but interested in the working classes of Dublin, to come together and consider if they could intervene in this dispute, and at least secure a truce between the two conflicting Unions ...'.

Also, dated September 26 1925, from John Busteed in Cork there is a letter seeking to enlist JJ as a judge in an essay competition organised by the Cork Chamber of Commerce, for the most constructive proposal for income tax; also one dated October 20 1925, from Michael P Linehan, Irish National Teachers Organisation, expressing doubt about the attendance of Trade Union officials at JJ's autumn course of lectures, given that the TUC was organising its own course.

Then on November 12 1925, from PJ Tuohy, General Secretary of the Irish Fishermen's Association, there was a letter seeking JJ's participation in a public meeting on Wednesday December 2 '...to focus public attention on the very unsatisfactory position of the Irish fishing industry... to review what has been done... to organise public opinion behind the just demands... particularly on behalf of a few important ports where the need is especially acute. The main speaker would be Col Maurice Moore, who was one of the vice-Presidents; the other was Thomas O'Donnell BL. The President was Rev CP White PP, and the treasurer was Prof EP Culverwell, TCD.

JJ went to this, and took out non-fisherman supportive membership for £1; there is a membership card, and a book of rules, which promote '...the benefits of combination in the sale of their produce, and the purchase of nets and gear...'. There was a standing committee named in the Rules for 1925-6, with groupings in the Dublin, Cork, Galway, Wicklow, Kerry, Louth and Donegal areas. They had an office at 5 North Earl St, Dublin. This was a serious organisation, and the fact that people like JJ and Culverwell were welcome supporters is an indication that the momentum of 'Protestant radical co-operativism' had persisted since the Home Rule period and had survived the burning of Plunkett's house by the 'irregulars'.

The 1926 Seanad Elections

JJ made his first attempt to get elected to the Seanad in 1926. If he had succeeded he would have been in for 12 years(14). There were 3 panels: 19 outgoing Senators for re-election, 19 nominees of the Seanad and 38 nominees of the Dáil. He got himself on the Dáil panel, as a Government nominee. The cumbersome electoral procedure militated against the election of specialist expertise, and he failed to get in, along with others, of the calibre of Douglas Hyde.

He produced a canvassing postcard with his picture, appealing '...for the support of all voters who desire the reconstruction of the Nation's economic life on sound economic principles.' He gave as his qualification his status as a Fellow of

Trinity College, Dublin, and Lecturer in the School of Commerce; also Barrington Lecturer in Economics, and Member of the 1922 Agricultural Commission.

The postcard continues, on the obverse side: 'In an effort to avert the serious consequences arising out of the Ulster situation, he published *Civil War in Ulster* in 1913. In *Groundwork of Economics*, recently published by the Educational Company of Ireland, Talbot St, Dublin (Price 2/6), he has sought to make the elements of this important science interesting and intelligible to all Irish men and women.'

JJ kept among his papers a newspaper cutting which gave the complete panel to go before the electorate for the 1926 Seanad; this was made up of 19 outgoing Senators, 19 chosen by the Seanad, and 38 chosen by the Dáil. JJ's name appeared among the latter 38; his name was followed by (G.) which suggests that he had got a Cumann na Gael nomination. There were a few (F.)s listed: John Ryan, James Dillon etc which suggests that the F stands for Farmers. Other Gs were Henry Harrison, TP McKenna, Marquis McSweeney; the G's were dominant. JJ had, it seems, joined with Cumann na Gael to get on the panel, which would be voted on as one ballot nationally.

Then finally we get the Seanad election results, analysed by constituency. JJ got a total of 1196 votes, and this compared with 1710 for Douglas Hyde, 601 for Dr McCartan, 1066 for Liam Ó Briain, 788 for the Marquis McSwiney, 509 for Darrell Figgis and 3722 for Sir Arthur Chance. The large numbers, leading to seats, went to people with high local profiles in certain constituencies, rather than to people with 'specialist niche' profiles such as the ones listed, none of whom got in. Thus the Seanad electoral procedure showed itself to be flawed, its aspirant role as 'panel of experts' being frustrated by the electoral procedure.

It is interesting to identify the constituencies where JJ picked up votes. Most were of course in Dublin, but after Dublin came in order of size of vote, Laois-Offaly, Donegal, Sligo, Wexford, Carlow-Kilkenny and Cavan. This would suggest that he had gone consciously for, or at least picked up, the Protestant vote. He had subscribed to a press-cutting agency and this had picked up items in the Church of Ireland Gazette advocating that readers should vote for JJ; there had also been a review of *Groundwork in Economics* in that same paper, linking its publication to his candidature in the Seanad election.

Internal TCD Political Barriers

Towards the end of the decade there occurred an episode in TCD internal politics which throws some light on JJ's subsequent development. The way in which the Board in 1929 attempted to set up the School of Economics and Political Science suggests a conscious move to block the aspirations of JJ, whose vision in this direction was becoming increasingly explicit, and whose public profile was expanding. On February 2 the Board asked Professor Bastable what requirements should be imposed on candidates for Fellowship in Economics and Political Science, for a competition by examination to be held in 1930. They were here reverting to the old examination procedure, and aspiring to impose a strong theoretical bias, in direct opposition to the type of experience that JJ had been acquiring, via his work on Government commissions, with Plunkett House, and with the Barrington Lectures, confirming, in the eyes of the Board, his 'enfant terrible' status.

On March 16 it was recommended that the principal subject of the examination should be Economic Theory, including History of Theories, this being testable by examination. Political Science should be regarded as a subordinate subject. The Fellow so elected should be fit for the Chair in Political Economy. In other words they wanted to recruit an external replacement for Bastable, then due for retirement, other than JJ or Duncan.

In 1930 on February 12 it was noted that three candidates for Fellowship in Economics had presented themselves: JW Nisbet from Glasgow, Alfred Plummer from London (earlier he had been an Albert Kahn candidate) and GJ Walker (Oxon). Two external examiners were selected, along with Bastable; one was Pigou, a world-figure. The externs however declined to act; two other were asked, Bowley and Clapham. The exam took place in May, there were 3 papers, Principles, Currency and Economic Organisation, Governmental Functions. The examiners reports were read on June 14, after which the episode sunk without trace. One can read into these events a sense of culture-shock. The world had moved on.

Family Pressures

During all this time however he was under considerable family pressures, with two grannies and three fostered nephews as well as my sister, and he had to move house several times. Of interest in the family context is a record of a visit by JJ's younger sister Ann to Budapest, at an international student Christian conference; she showed considerable insight into the post-Versailles politics of the Austro-Hungarian Empire, which she reported to JJ in correspondence.(15)

JJ had, as a result of his outreach and political activity, little output in the form of academic research papers. His main work was popularisation and polemic(16).

Notes and References

1. The Barrington Lectures were initiated in 1849 by John Barrington, a Dublin merchant, with a view to providing for the instruction of the Irish people in Liberal economics. Before World War 1 they had been managed by the Statistical and Social Inquiry Society (SSISI). The Centenary Volume of the Proceedings of the Statistical and Social Inquiry Society of Ireland, published in 1947 edited by RD Collison Black, contains background information about the Barrington Lectures. There is given a complete series of Barrington Lecturers from 1852 to 1946 in the Centenary Volume. The most notable of the Barrington Lecturers pre-war was CH Oldham, who was a Home Rule supporter and a prolific contributor of papers to the Society between 1895 and 1925. He was an early influence on JJ.

2. Evidence among JJ's papers is thin on the ground, but I have collected what I can find in the 1920s political module in the hypertext. He continued to receive communications from Erskine Childers. He wrote a letter of condolence on the death of Michael Collins, which was acknowledged. There was also contact with Dermot MacManus, an ex-service mature student, who had been the prime mover of the Thomas Davis Society from 1919, and who subsequently commanded the Free State Army in the West during the Civil war. There are some intriguing hints, like copies of letters from Pierrepoint the hangman to the Governor of Mountjoy regarding clients in that institution: MacManus became Deputy Governor of Mountjoy Prison. JJ was also in the early 1920s involved in the work of the Boundary Commission, from the economic angle. There were papers to do with this, but they have vanished. I suspect them of being used by Kevin O'Sheil's biographer, and I remain in hopes of tracking then down. There is among his papers a copy of the 1923 *Handbook of the Ulster Question*, edited by Kevin O'Shiel, Director of the North-Eastern Boundary Bureau, which is annotated in JJ's handwriting. The missing papers, if I can find them, and which I recollect from my earlier encounter with his papers in 1971, will indicate the extent of his role in the production of this Boundary Commission report. He remained in close touch with Kevin O'Shiel during the 30s and 40s, to the best of my recollection.

3. The earlier Barrington series seems eventually to have blossomed into JJ's <u>Groundwork of Economics</u> published by the Educational Co in 1925, or perhaps in 1926. (There is no date of publication given on the book itself.) It was certainly being reviewed in 1926, prior to the Seanad elections. JJ seems to have had in mind that his later Barrington series, outside Dublin, would have been promotional for his book. Subsequently in a Seanad speech, he referred to the difficulty in filling a hall during this period, in this context.

4. The Barrington Lectures had lapsed during the war, and post-war the Barrington Trust had fallen out with the SSISI. JJ did a deal with the Barrington Trust and managed post-war to <u>resurrect</u> them, but was restricted to Dublin by Civil War conditions. His attempt to integrate them with the Carnegie library system, and take the lectures round the country on Carnegie locations, was creditable but only partially successful. He must have had in mind the development of the market for his *Groundwork in Economics*, into which he integrated most of his Barrington lecture material.

5. For the background to the SSISI see <u>Appendix 6</u>, and for JJ's <u>first paper</u>, 'Some Causes and Consequences of Distributive Waste', see J SSISI vol XIV p353, 1926-7. For the <u>Rockefeller Foundation</u> background in context see <u>Appendix 5</u> where I overview the 'academic research and publication' thread. The French component of his Rockefeller project are absent from his SSISI paper, but they surfaced strongly in JJ's work for the 1926 <u>Prices Tribunal</u>.

6. Evidence among JJ's papers in third decade remains thin on the ground, but I have collected what I can find in the <u>1920s political</u> module in the hypertext. This touches on JJ's work with the Boundary Commission, with Ned Stevens and Kevin O'Shiel. He continued to receive communications from Erskine Childers. He wrote a letter of condolence on the death of Michael Collins, which was acknowledged.

7. In February 1921 in *Better Business* we have an assessment of the experience of the TCD co-op, and then in the February 1922 issue was a review of *The Consumers' Co-operative Movement* by Sydney and Beatrice Webb (London, Longmans, 1921). In August 1922 there was a review of *Money and Credit* by CJ Melrose (London, Collins, 1920), with an introduction by Prof Irving Fisher. *Better Business* blossomed briefly into *The Irish Economist*. Then, in what proved to be the final issue of *The Irish Economist* in January 1923, JJ had a paper 'Free Trade or Protection for Irish Industries?' which was a forerunner of his book *The Nemesis of Economic Nationalism* of a decade later. There is a gap in the Plunkett House series then until 1925 when JJ began to appear in the *Irish Statesman*. In Vol IV (14/03/25 - 15/09/25) we find the first appearance of JJ in this publication: George O'Brien reviewed his <u>Groundwork of Economics</u>. Vol V (12/09/25 - 6/03/26) contains a review by JJ of Foster and Catchings *Profits* and in this he referred to his earlier review of *Money*; this turns out to have been signed 'MS'; JJ was inclined to use pseudonyms when he wrote quasi-politically or polemically. Vol VI (13/03/26 - 4/09/26) contains a further article by JJ on Protection, presumably an update of his earlier one in the *Irish Economist* mentioned above. I have collected most of the texts of these papers from the Plunkett House Library, and they are available in the <u>1920s Plunkett House</u> module in the hypertext.

8. The 1922-24 <u>Agricultural Commission</u> was set up by Minister Hogan, and was an attempt to pick up the continuity of the Horace Plunkett Department of Agriculture, and support the development of an export-oriented commercial agricultural system.

9. JJ's work in the national interest in the period between 1916 and 1922 is ill-documented, but there is in his papers correspondence with Erskine Childers in the context of the Convention, and with Dermot MacManus, an ex-service mature student, who was the prime mover of the Thomas Davis Society, and who subsequently commanded the Free State Army in the West during the Civil war.

10. For this series the *Manchester Guardian* introduced an un-named 'special correspondent' who had done a similar analysis the previous year on India; this would have been spin-off from JJ's Albert Kahn Report, which was not published until after the war. I have outlined the series in the 1920s module of the 'political' thread, which is overviewed in Appendix 10. There is also evidence in this material that JJ was helpful during the Civil war period in getting journalists from Britain passes from the Free State Government.

11. I report on the 'Towards a Better Ireland' conference in the hypertext, and also summarise it in the 1920s political module, where I also give some insights into JJ's religious evolution away from Presbyterianism towards Unitarianism, under the influence of Saville Hicks. Also in this module is a record of correspondence with Kevin O'Higgins relating to the Commonwealth Conference in May 1927, shortly before his assassination, an a subsequent acknowledgement of a letter of condolence.

12. We have already met the Albert Kahn Foundation, a 'Liberal International' network, based in Paris. JJ remained in correspondence with its Executive Secretary Charles Garnier right up to the 1940s.

13. In College JJ was active attempting to pressure the Board via meetings of the Junior Fellows. He was bypassed in the first School of Commerce appointments, and did not get involved until the second round. When it came to the question of developing a School of Economics and Political Science, with a Chair, the Board attempted to backtrack and to re-institute the obsolete 'by examination' procedure, though in this they were unsuccessful, with extern examiners declining to act. The specification was strongly theoretical. I have treated these issues in some detail in the 1920s module of the TCD Politics hypertext stream, as overviewed in Appendix 2.

14. He kept a scrapbook and I have abstracted this in the 20s module of JJ's 'public service and Seanad' thread, which is overviewed in Appendix 8.

15. I have given some additional background to these pressures in the 20s module of the 'Family' thread, which I have overviewed in Appendix 1.

16. JJ did claim his *Groundwork* subsequently in his CV as presented at the time of his Royal Irish Academy election in 1943. There was substance in his claim, in that in Chapter 3 on the 'The Four Factors of Production' he adds 'Enterprise' as having equal importance with 'Land, Labour and Capital', the conventional three 'factors of production'; he also assigns a special additional role to Government. These two concepts I think were probably innovative in the context of the economic writings of the 1920s. His nearest approximation to a conventionally 'academic' output in the 20s was via the SSISI, where the papers were, and indeed still are, peer-reviewed. I review his 20s papers in the 20s module of the 'Academic Output' stream of the hypertext, which I overview in Appendix 5, where it will be seen that his output did expand substantially in the 30s and 40s, though it still remained primarily outward-oriented.

Chapter 4: The Period 1931-1940

Because the main core of this chapter is JJ's academic output, linked to College and national politics, I am including the titles (italics) and publication outlets (bold) in the narrative, the outlets often being tactical decisions in the context. This is despite the publishing convention that references should be relegated to footnotes, and italics reserved for book titles.

Introduction

In the 1930s JJ began to farm for himself, to see how the system worked from below. He continued off and on in this mode right up to the 1960s, this being a cause of locational tension between his TCD job and his primary interest in agricultural economics. There were a succession of houses in the country, with land; he employed a farm labourer and kept the books. This was raw material for a succession of outreach books and papers. The first impressions from the present writer RJ as a child begin to appear in this decade.

In 1934 JJ published a polemical economics book(1) aimed at a lay readership, critical of the pure protectionist approach to economic development, and advocating that priority attention be paid to farm incomes, as a generator of demand for local industry.

JJ served in the Senate(2) on several occasions, being first elected in 1938. On this platform he stoutly defended the Protestant contribution to the Irish nation-building process, though at the time he appeared mostly to be a lone voice. He did however team up with Senator James Douglas on occasion.

The 30s decade can perhaps be regarded as JJ at his best. In the 20s he had neglected his academic output, depending on his Fellowship for TCD status, and concentrated on outreach. When he failed to get a projected Chair in Political Economy, being leapfrogged by Duncan, he redoubled his academic publication efforts, and there emerged during the 30s a stream of well-researched papers, some of them of key significance.

He continued his political contacts with Cumann na nGael, and opened up contacts with Fianna Fail, while developing a devastating criticism of their 30s policies, which he was able to deliver in person to de Valera, both via the Seanad after 1938, and on at least one public occasion where they shared a platform.

In the background to this chapter the college-political(3), national-political(4), outreach(5) and academic publication(6) streams are closely interwoven, each one feeding the other on key occasions. The 'academic publications' in this decade provides a primary framework, with the other streams being folded in appropriately.

There were various family(7) episodes, involving moving house; education was a problem for a dispersed religious minority, and the need to take care of that of the present writer prompted JJ to give up his farm near Drogheda. The 'economic war' was also a factor.

College Politics

College politics for JJ centred round the Political Economy and Commerce question: on May 18 1932 the Chair of Political Economy was suspended for a year, on the resignation of Professor Bastable, and then on June 15 interim arrangements were set up for lectures in economics, with JJ appointed Lecturer in Applied Economics (money and credit, descriptive economics, commerce) at pass and honours levels. Duncan did economic theory, public finance, political and economic science, with the title Lecturer in Economic Theory. Constantia Maxwell did Economic History. This situation persisted for a while, and then on November 18 1933 they invited application for the Chair in Political Economy (at a supplementary salary of £150, so this was clearly an internal appointment).

In 1934 it was noted in the Board minutes (13/01/34) that the School of Commerce Committee included the Provost (EJ Gwynn), John Good, JCM Eason, Dr Bailey, the teaching staff and the Registrar. During the period Eason, the Dublin businessman, had been active with JJ on the Council of the Statistical and Social Inquiry Society. We can perhaps identify this as an indication of JJ's influence on School policy; the real world was important.

Moving House and Farming; Early RJ Memories

The move to Priorland near Dundalk in 1928 had whetted JJ's appetite for hands-on farming, but the commuting travel-time load must have been a strain, and my mother I gather had problems coming to terms with relative rural isolation. My sister went to Dundalk Grammar School as a day-pupil; it was within cycling distance. When I arrived in 1929 it must have increased the stress.

The Dundalk period gave JJ access to the neighbouring Barrow farm at Milestown, near Castlebellingham, and he analysed the economics of this successful labour-employing commercial farm in depth, using the results in published papers.

The decision to move nearer to Dublin, while still keeping in touch with hands-on farming, I suspect was made in 1931, before the Fianna Fail electoral victory in 1932. A move like that made in 1932 would have involved JJ ignoring strong warning signals. The farm near Drogheda was called Newtown Platin; there was a long low farmhouse, and a walled garden. There were monkey-puzzles in the front garden, conveniently placed for JJ to swing his hammock. (The lore was that when he moved house the existence of trees close enough to swing a hammock was a necessary condition!).

There was a farm-yard and stables behind, and a farm worker whose name was Brown lived there, with a young family; their names were Georgie and Vonnie, and I played with them. There was also an elder brother who had a job on the buses. JJ ran the farm by telling Brown what to do, and keeping the books. This was the beginning of the economic war, and of course the upshot of JJ's farming was disastrous, though it gave him practical insights for his writings.

My sister entered College in 1933, after finishing in Dundalk Grammar School as a boarder, and did medicine. She began doing Natural Science, at JJ's suggestion, and switched to the medical school subsequently.

We had a gramophone at Platin, and I recollect at this time a Maurice Chevalier record, 'up on top of the rainbow, sweeping the clouds away'. My sister had been in France in the 1920s during JJ's Rockefeller episode, when they stayed at the Albert Kahn Foundation.

I remember at Platin being lifted up one day, to look over the wall, to see the Blueshirts marching. Also I remember being driven into Drogheda in JJ's Model A Ford and JJ giving a lift into town to old Brown the grandfather of the family who lived in the stables. There was a further occasion when children living in cottages nearby threw mud at JJ's windscreen.

I remember JJ pointing out the electric transmission lines which crossed the field nearby, and relating them to the 'Shannon Scheme', of which he was aware and regarded as a good thing.

There was a visit by my uncles James and John to Platin; I suspect this involved a family conference on Geddes(8), whose role in Argentina seemed to have been open to question.

Academic Publications: the Global Crisis

Despite family constraints JJ in the 1930s had quite a substantial academic output, apart from his polemical work. This took the form of a series of papers, initially rooted in his classical and ancient history background, but concentrating on early financial and economic issues. Some of this aroused the interest of JM Keynes, and there was a correspondence. This led to his publishing in the **Economic Journal**, and to his making the transition to modern economics via the study of Berkeley, whose economic writings had hitherto been neglected.

The 'academic publications' theme(9) can be related to JJ's view of the developing Irish political economy, so that interspersing the political and outreach episodes makes sense.

In or about 1930-31 JJ must have begun to realise that if he was to get academic recognition and perhaps even a Chair, he would need to publish appropriately. His first step in this direction leaned on his classical background: he published *A Chronological Note on the Expedition of Leotychidas to Thessaly* in **Hermathena** the College-based learned journal (Vol XLVI p106, 1931). This is not among JJ's papers; it is accessible on the record, but is however not germane to JJ's mainstream thinking. It was his swan-song as a classicist in the pure sense.

At about the same time his 'winter milk' paper was published: *A Plea for Winter Dairying* in the **Journal of the Statistical and Social Inquiry Society of Ireland** Vol XV, no 33, 1930-31. This paper was read on March 19 1931, and JJ was introduced as 'Barrington Lecturer in Economics'. In this seminal paper, which remains relevant to this day, JJ questioned the traditional view that winter dairying was not practical economics for the Irish farmer. It was said that the winter feed required would cost more than the price of the milk would justify. The question of winter production had come on to the agenda as a result of the imposition of a tariff on imported butter, due to the winter market being flooded with imports from the southern hemisphere. This, being a peer-reviewed paper in applied economics, would have counted towards his academic recognition.

In *An International Managed Currency in the Fifth Century*, **Hermathena** XLVII p132, 1932, JJ managed to build on his classical erudition and make an insightful contribution to his standing as an economist. The paper deals with Croesus and refers to the 5th century BC. It is a highly technical analysis of the use of currencies in trading in the eastern Mediterranean, between Greeks, Persians and Phoenicians. JJ must have sent a copy to Keynes, because there is among his papers a letter from Keynes to JJ dated 11 April 1933:

"...I was much interested in your article on questions of ancient currency, a subject in which I have dabbled myself more or less seriously from time to time. I have the impression that the bi-metallic system of the Persian Empire worked efficiently for a long period of years, without either metal driving the other out of circulation, in spite of moderate disparities from the Persian ratio on the adjoining Greek territories, and have often pondered how this could have been achieved. I suspect that the Temple hoards operated to preserve the official ratio, much as a Central Bank with very large reserves might do today. We know what enormous figures the Temple hoards had reached by the time of Alexander, and if the Temples always rigorously observed the official ratio, this might well have produced the necessary stabilising effect. / Yours very truly JM Keynes"

At this time the global economy was in the depths of the great depression that had followed the 1929 Wall St crash. JJ was motivated to attempt to explain this, in academic-type publications which were read by decision-makers, such as the Proceedings of the **Institute of Bankers**, where he read his paper *The World Crisis: Its Non-Monetary Background* on November 17 1932. In this paper JJ focused on the dis-equilibrium between agriculture and industry, and on the various types of friction in the pipeline between the producer and consumer of agricultural goods.

There were echoes here of his 1926 Rockefeller project, and his work with the Prices Commission. As an example he considered how '...the butcher, the baker, the grocer and the milkman (were) left unpaid because the next instalment was due on the wireless set ...'. Price movement is the means of overcoming the various disequilibria, and in the pre-war world all prices were reasonably elastic. 'In the post-war world we meet a whole host of new price rigidities, for example the price of labour in sheltered industries, and the price of goods monopolistically produced...'.

Governments had tended to react to international trade dis-equilibria by imposing tariffs, rather than allowing supply to react to demand via the price mechanism. There was no longer a world price for wheat, due to European protectionism against cheaply-produced US wheat, the result being that there was a factor of 4 in the price of wheat (for example) between France and Argentina.

The drop in demand for producers goods was much greater, due to the high incidence of monopoly pricing. This deters new investment, and is the main obstacle to recovery. On the whole JJ used this Bankers platform as a means of launching his classic Free Trade onslaught on economic nationalism, later to be developed in his 1934 *Nemesis* book.

Dermot MacManus

It is appropriate here to mention JJ's friendship with Dermot MacManus, in whose house near Longford our family spent the Christmas of 1931. We were in the process of moving from Priorland in Dundalk to Newtown Platin near Drogheda, and spending Christmas away would have been a rest for my mother. Neither I nor my sister remember anything of the topics discussed, but they must have been quite intensive.

MacManus had been an ex-service student in TCD in the 1919-21 period, and JJ had supported his work with the Thomas Davis Society, which was effectively a Sinn Fein front in TCD. He had gone on to a position of military leadership in the Free State Army. Subsequently in 1932 he was actively involved with the Army Comrades Association and its transition to the Blueshirts. *This at the time would have been perceived by JJ as a reaction of the commercial farmers against the threat of Fianna Fail land-division, with de Valera perhaps perceived in a role analogous to that of Mugabe in Zimbabwe at the present time.* JJ and MacManus would have seen eye to eye on the matter of the economics of large farms employing labour. JJ however would have seen the potential for organising the labour as co-operative worker-owners, and had looked earlier to Tom Johnson and the Labour party. MacManus was more in the Standish O'Grady elitist tradition(10), and is on record as having attempted to bring in Yeats to the leading Blueshirt group which included O'Duffy.

The contact seems not to have persisted subsequent to this meeting; it is probable that JJ and MacManus agreed to differ, and their ways parted. MacManus however contacted JJ decades later, in the 1960s, at the level of seeking support from JJ for academic publication of literary critical work.

Shortly after this 1931 MacManus episode JJ was approached by Seán Lemass, and was appointed by the Fianna Fail government to a Commission to report on the workings of the Civil Service(11). JJ was prepared to give advice as an economist to whoever would listen.

Academic Publications: TCD Political Economy

Published in 1934, but I suspect produced earlier, before the *Nemesis* began to dominate his agenda, was JJ's paper *Solon's Reform of Weights and Measures* in the **Journal of Hellenic Studies**, Vol LIV, p180, 1934. This paper exudes classical erudition; quotations are given un-translated in the original Greek, making it difficult for a non-classicist to follow the argument. The essence would seem to be that Solon, when introducing economic reforms largely in favour of the common people, devalued the currency, and to make it look better, also reduced the values of the weights and measures by a corresponding amount, introducing some stresses and strains into inter-city trade, but preserving the local relationships between nominal prices and nominal quantities.

The **Economic Journal**, edited by JM Keynes and EAG Robinson, in its September 1934 issue (Vol XLIV no 175 p453) carried a paper by JJ on *The Purchasing Power of Irish Free State Farmers in 1933*. This was a quantification of the catastrophic collapse of agricultural purchasing power consequent on the 'economic war' arising from de Valera's policy on the land annuities(12). There are some ironical asides, like a reference to the fact that encouraging farmers to grow import-substituting tobacco, in accordance with the self-sufficiency policy, cost the exchequer £300,000 in lost duty on imports, excise on home produce being preferential. Farmers gained £187,500. JJ ordered reprints, with a view to using a paper in a prestigious journal abroad as a means of supporting his arguments at home.

In the 1930s JJ's efforts in academic politics bore fruit, in that there was at last set up a School of Economics and Political Science, with himself and Duncan in it as potential successors to Bastable, who retired. Duncan however ended up with the Chair; only later, in 1939, did JJ get a Chair ('for present holder only') in Applied Economics.

JJ had clearly hoped to get the chair, as he felt he needed the weight of the appointment to maximise the influence of his *Nemesis of Economic Nationalism* book. In the event he had to threaten the Board with the Visitors in order to get some financial support for its publication out of the Madden Fund. His continuing marginalisation in TCD(13) sharpened his interest in national politics.

He did however continue to be supportive of student societies which had a political flavour, remaining as a vice-president of the Gaelic Society, and supporting the new Commerce Society, bringing in outside names like Findlater, Jameson and Eason, representative of the Protestant business interest. He was also a supporter of the History Society, which was set up to encourage the serious study of history, as distinct from the Historical Society which was primarily for debating.

The Nemesis of Economic Nationalism

This book, published in by PS King, London, in 1934, was JJ's polemic against de Valera's policies which had led to the 'economic war'(1). I regard this as being a distillation of his experience in 'political economy outreach' focused via the Barrington lectures. Although popularising and polemical, it also deserves a place in JJ's academic stream because he mentioned it subsequently (in 1942) in his application for membership of the Royal Irish Academy.

I give primarily JJ's sub-heads; I give also some abstracts where he makes arguments of particular contemporary political relevance:

* Relative importance of world economy to different nations..
* The case of the USA shows that a nation may be nearly self-contained and yet collapse due to interdependence with the world economy...
  '..In particular the USA even before the Wall Street collapse failed to sustain the purchasing power of her agricultural population ...'.
* Agricultural producers for subsistence and for exchange react differently to falling prices...
  '..The peasant farmer's...reaction to falling prices is to buy less manufactured goods... raw materials... he will till more for subsistence ...'.
* The feasibility of economic nationalism depends on other nations not practicing it at the same time...
* Economic nationalism and monetary internationalism...
  '..A tariff war is an effort to separate (as for Siamese twins sharing a common circulation of the blood of commerce) two economically interdependent nations ...'.
* The correct reaction to the depressing effect of other nations' tariffs is a monetary one ...'...The way to expand consumption is to promote the production of capital goods. The workers engaged on the Shannon Scheme

were consuming food and clothing that were available there and then, and producing something that would not add its quota to the volume of consumers goods for some years...'.

- The State must now do deliberately what the gold standard formerly did automatically..."There are important departments of economic activity which by common consent have been abandoned to public or non-profit-making enterprise...(namely) educational services, transport facilities, the housing of the working classes, forestry and the Shannon Scheme (ie electricity generation)..."
- Creditor nations have it in their power to promote the production of capital goods...
- States should sometimes go to war with other things than foreign enemies... '...providing homes for living heroes instead of coffins for dead ones ...'.
- The bankruptcy of the world is more moral than economic. '..The nation which first turns the other cheek to the economic blows of its neighbours, and adopts ...a national economic policy whose chief recommendation is, not that it injures other nations, but that it benefits then as well as herself, will begin a new world era ...'.

Right and Wrong Methods of promoting National Economic Self-sufficiency.

He does not give sub-heads in this chapter. He begins with a critical comparison of Russia, Britain and the USA as regards policies of self-sufficiency. He then goes on to urge the transformation of Irish external assets (which then were considerable, as indeed they still are) into a massive infra-structural development program, importing the necessary capital goods and putting the people to work on public works projects. The concept is basically analogous to that adopted by Roosevelt, and shows the influence of his contact with Keynes, and indeed his reading of Berkeley, whom he is by then beginning to identify as the Adam Smith of what we would now call 'development economics'.

Lessons from Theory and Experience

In this chapter he reverts to the practice of sub-heads, which I therefore give, in lieu of abstracting; this I will perhaps do later.

- Correct relations of the economist and the politician...
- The economic value of our 'economic war'...
- Evidence that Great Britain too is the victim of economic warfare..
- Folly of economic war from Great Britain's point of view...
- The exact nature of the wound inflicted on us by the British taxes...
- The British taxes as part of a program for developing a closer balance between British agriculture and British industry...
- Evidence that agricultural production is diminishing in the Irish Free State.
- Competition for export markets...
- Tariff policy and the solvency of foreign debtors...
- Our bounty on the export of cattle favours the export of raw material and destroys the market for home-grown cereals...

- Even economic nationalists do not dispute that universal free trade would produce the maximum of wealth for all....
- Importance of maintaining the exchange economy and resisting the relapse to subsistence agriculture...

"..As an 'uneconomic' holder of 20 acres of County Meath land, I have lately altered my economy so as to produce a subsistence of potatoes and milk for about 20 inhabitants of the local village...paying no toll to transport or middleman agencies.....The new 30-acre farmers, whom it is proposed to plant on divided ranches, will, if they are wise in their own interests, practice a subsistence economy, and make little use of money, transport or shops. If they fail to produce a surplus for our townsfolk, will the latter take a leaf out of Lenin's book?..."

- Is it consistent to promote at one and the same time an industrial revival and a reversion to subsistence agriculture?

In this final section JJ has the following in italics:

"The main problem of the Irish economy now is, not the creation of new industries, but the expansion of the home market for the products of our agriculture and of existing industries."

He concluded with a critique of the retail trade, making the case for the development of a consumers co-operative movement. This represented a sort of afterthought, distilled from his earlier work with the Rockefeller Foundation in the 1920s, which was reported in his 1927 *Distributive Waste* paper to the Statistical and Social Inquiry Society (14).

The RJ Education Problem
After he published the *Nemesis* JJ was faced with the need to provide for the present writer's primary education, as well as with the adverse economic environment for agriculture presented by the 'economic war', so in 1934 he moved back to Dublin, renting a house in Waltham Terrace, Blackrock, not far from where he had owned one in the 1920s.

Church control of the education system, then as now, posed problems for Protestants living in rural areas. To assemble enough children to run a primary school required a substantial catchment area. The boarding school was the norm for second level, except for local concentrations in the main urban centres. This undoubtedly encouraged emigration, as teenagers would not have made local contacts. I have however encountered anecdotal evidence that where rural Protestant families made use of the Vocational Schools (which were not religious-dominated, and were under the local authorities), their children tended to stay on locally, and go into local businesses, or start things up. Secondary schools, as well as being denominational, tended to prepare people for the Civil Service or the professions; they were ill-adapted to the needs of a developing economy. The vocational education system was objectively better adapted, but was looked down on by the rural elite. JJ after 1938 got to be able to address these issues via the Seanad.

So, from Waltham Terrace in Blackrock Co Dublin I walked to Avoca School, then in Carysfort Avenue. Shortly afterwards it moved to Newtown Park Avenue, to the present site of Newpark Comprehensive School. (This prompted JJ to move to another rented house, Charleville, close by.) I have mostly fond memories of Avoca; the head was Cyril Parker, and he was very anti-war, based on 1914-18 experiences. He was hostile to the Boy Scout movement, which he considered militarist, though there was a troop associated with the school, which he tolerated grudgingly. He was married to Cerise Orpen, a daughter of Orpen the painter. The school was patronised by the Protestant intelligentsia, with business connections, who were in process of defending their inherited leading role in the 'civil society' of the emerging nation.

Irish was taught initially by one Boland, later by Cecil Hyde, who was I think a nephew of Douglas Hyde. We learned Irish quite successfully; I don't recollect any sense of imposition. We absorbed Irish history from the Carty texts, which are now disparaged, but we relished the drama of the narrative, and we cheered on the few occasions when the Irish won the battles.

Erskine B Childers I counted among my friends; we stayed in each other houses; his father, who subsequently became President, was then a Minister in the Government. I recollect being in the Childers house one weekend some time around 1937 or 38, when we all went to the Guinness house at Chapelizod, and played with the Kinderslys, who were about the same age; we ran around the house and across the covered bridge which crosses the road between the two parts of the house.

I have often wondered what Childers, the Fianna Fail Minister, was doing socialising with the Guinness family at that time. Could it have been part of the process that led to the ending of the economic war, with the 1938 trade agreement? The brewery in Park Royal had been built as the Guinness response to the 1932 Fianna Fail government; there was a 'flight of capital' process going on; Jacobs had expanded to Liverpool. The effects of doctrinaire protectionism, as predicted by JJ in his 1934 *Nemesis of Economic Nationalism*, were biting hard, with the shrinking home market.

Erskine B Childers and I were in the Boy Scouts, and we united politically to get them to drop God Save the King and substitute the Soldiers' Song.

JJ as Political Consultant

Politically JJ was close to Fine Gael, and on December 3 1934 there is on record a meeting(15) he had with their top leadership, from which it is possible to confirm that he saw the way forward via an alliance between the larger commercial farmers who employed labour, and the urban labour movement, whose ranks he hoped to see swelled by an expanded agricultural and food-industry labour force supporting an expanding export-oriented commercial agriculture. He also tried to win them over to a Roosevelt economic policy:

"...The State can do much to maintain private property if it takes the part of intervening when things are bad and retiring as much as possible when prosperity returns. but the simple transfer of a certain volume of purchasing power from one set of individuals to another in the community will not involve any net increase in purchasing power.

"Purchasing power is, to a considerable extent, bound up with the production of capital goods and when the production of capital goods slows down, purchasing power contracts. This is the trouble in the USA at present. The capital goods industries in America through decline in production have left about six million people unemployed. Roosevelt's NRA policy can only find employment for approximately two million out of a total of 12 million unemployed. The great problem in America, therefore, is to increase production and marketing of capital goods. This great difficulty, however, is not present to any great extent in Ireland. The NRA plan would stand a better chance of working here...."

The Fianna Fail land-division policy was anathema to him; he had shown definitively that 300 acres employing 10 men with a properly managed productive system was over twice as productive as 10 30-acre subsistence farms. Likewise the protectionist industrial policy was anathema; he saw it as simply reducing the effective size of the home market and increasing farm input costs. Industry should build on productive agriculture, on the Danish model(16).

Academic Publications as Critical Polemics

Then in June 1935 JJ published *Agriculture and the Sickness of the Free Economy* in **Studies**, XXIV no 94, p295. I count this among the academic stream, given that the Jesuit quarterly **Studies** is refereed and has a scholarly reputation. It is however polemical, and also belongs in the outreach category treated in the Barrington and Statistical and Social Inquiry Society streams; again he got reprints for distribution.

The de Valera 'self-sufficiency' policy was it its height, and agricultural exports were crippled by the 'economic war'. Drawing on sources as diverse as the Roman Empire, the USSR, the USA, Adam Smith, the Physiocrats and the Merchantilists, JJ diagnosed the sickness of the economy in terms of the inadequacy of agricultural incomes, and homed in on the need for enhanced agricultural productivity via 'large mixed farms where machinery is used'.

The experience of the Roman Empire and the USSR he identified as '...systematic exploitation of masses of agricultural producers in the interests of an urban bourgeoisie and proletariat, and later of a bureaucratic imperialism...producing an economic situation in which the peasants no longer found it worth while to produce on any serious scale for exchange ...'.

During the lead-up to the de Valera Constitution JJ felt he needed to take public stands where he could, on the issue of the role of the Protestants in the Free State. Thus on December 21, 1935, he was reported in the *Irish Times* as speaking at Wesley College, covering teaching through Irish, Protestant interests in Ireland, and the Free State industrial revival. He supported learning Irish as one might learn French at school, but opposed teaching other subjects through it where English was the mother tongue. He supported stoutly the Protestant identity as part of the national mainstream: '...we do not regard ourselves as in any sense outlanders in this island, which is our native land ...'. He foresaw negative outcomes of current economic policies: '...is there not some danger that the nation will be exploited by industrial monopoly, or a series of industrial monopolies, in the interests of an ascendancy class which is not entirely native Irish, Protestant or Catholic?'.

The *Independent* also took it up, with the header 'Protestants Get Square Deal'; they picked up JJ's reference to Partition, which '...was in the highest possible degree an injury to the Protestant interest, north and south...'.

Addressing British Public Opinion

JJ felt motivated to keep trying to explain Ireland to those he regarded as opinion-leaders in Britain, and with this in mind he published on *The Anglo-Irish Economic Conflict* in **Nineteenth Century and After**, DCCVIII, February 1936. This periodical, which was published by Constable, had had a long run; it was originally 'The Nineteenth Century'. It seems to have been a sort of 'think tank' or theoretical journal of the Liberal Party. The copy which survives among JJ's papers is a reprint, and from internal evidence it was a public lecture read on some occasion, perhaps at his Alma Mater in Lincoln College Oxford, but this is a guess.

JJ used the occasion, whatever it was, to give an English audience an overview of the current Irish political environment. He led in with a reference to his 1920s Barrington Lecture experience, during which '...in the first year or two (he) had to compete with the rival entertainments provided by bank robbers and civil warriors ...'. He was '...vaguely conscious that the academic outlook was somehow divorced from the point of view of the man who was in daily contact with economic realities ...'. He had '...sat on more than one Government Commission, and had numerous opportunities of hearing practical men give their views, and yet we seemed to speak a different language ...'.

He recounted how in 1928 he had taken up residence in the country, and had begun to keep a few cows and hens as a hobby, '...seeking to acquire the art of expressing elementary economic truths in language which our agricultural population can understand and appreciate ...'.

This suggests that his attempts in the 20s to bring Enlightenment Liberal political economy to the Irish rural masses had been in vain, and he had learned a lesson from the experience.

After 1932 he found himself '...diametrically opposed to the policies which are now the official policies of our Government ...'. He was however '...glad to be able to state that (he had) enjoyed complete freedom of speech in both town and country; on two occasions Ministers (had) occupied the same platform...argued their view in opposition... thus helping.... in giving wider publicity to the policies (he) recommended.... De Valera and his colleagues have always been most friendly...'.

Arguments about 'breaking up the ranches' were supported by the production per acre being greater on small farms. Production per farm worker on large farms well managed, as integrated multi-product enterprises rather than ranches, however was substantially greater still(17). Larger total production must be taken up by exports, given that agricultural production already is twice domestic consumption. The current British tariff and quota system generated by the 'economic war' was bankrupting the productive large farmers.

In 1933 he had set himself the problem of how to 'win' the economic war, and to keep the land annuity payments in fact as well as in form (they had de facto been paid via the export bounty process). In his *Nemesis of Economic Nationalism* he had advocated the use of our substantial realisable foreign assets for an investment programme, employing '...our dislocated workers in tidying up our national household without any danger to currency stability ...'. Imports, as a 'war' measure, could be from non-British sources, thus perhaps depressing the foreign exchange value of sterling.

The loss in capital value of Irish agricultural assets JJ estimated at £100M, and this was simply destruction, not just robbery, as it had been in the time of the landlords who confiscated tenants' improvements.

Unfortunately there was no clear message regarding what he wanted his audience, presumably of English Liberal intellectuals, to do next. This was perhaps a basic weakness in JJ's critical position. The natural target for his arguments at this time was the political Labour movement, but he was some way from identifying this, although Plunkett had tentatively done so in his 1920 speech(18).

Continuing his efforts to keep public opinion in Britain informed about the Irish situation, JJ published his *Irish Agriculture, Then and Now* paper with the **Manchester School of Economic and Social Studies** journal in October 1940, pp105-122. This paper reviewed critically the 'economic war' period and analysed the relationships between cattle, pigs, poultry, milk, grass and cereals. JJ introduced it with an outline of his experience of farming and market gardening between 1928 and 1934, when he '...abandoned the unequal struggle and devoted his spare time to poltico-economic agitation ...' becoming a Senator in 1938 and then '...graduating back again into agriculture with the ownership of a 25 acre grass farm some 30 miles from Dublin ...'.

It constituted a useful review of academic and practical insights into the main inputs and outputs of Irish agriculture during the 1930s, summarising much of his work during this period.

Self-Sufficiency in Wheat

Back on the home ground JJ attempted to analyse the effect of the then current 'self-sufficiency in wheat' policy, with his paper *The Place of Wheat in Irish Agriculture*. This paper exists in typescript form among JJ's papers, with the note 'written in 1937' appended to the title. He seems to have attempted to get it published at the height of the 'economic war' but was unable to do so. Some of the elements in it, particularly the economics of stall-feeding, relate to the following **Economic Journal** paper; it seems he put it aside and reworked it as an 'export publication'. He subsequently came across it and contemplated using it in the context of his Berkeley project, as it has deep roots in the economic history of the 18th century. This I think is when he prepared the typescript. In the end for the Berkeley project he confined himself to published material.

Because of the importance of the Fianna Fail wheat policy in the 30s this unpublished work deserves some attention. He used the material in his Seanad speeches subsequently, when he needed to develop a critical approach to current wheat policies. In the paper he had also developed the argument that the wheat policies of the 1780s and 90s, which were currently viewed as supportive of the de Valera 'self-sufficiency' policy, were in fact long-term disastrous, and contributed to laying the basis for the Famine(19).

JJ then tried another angle on his wheat argument, using the prestige of publication by Keynes: *Price Ratios in Recent Irish Agricultural Experience*, **Economic Journal** (ed Keynes & Robinson) December 1937; Vol XLVII no 188 p680.

In this paper JJ developed a classical Adam Smith argument from the Wealth of Nations, regarding the need for a certain ratio between the price of cattle and corn to exist, if continuous improvement of arable and pastoral land is to take place. It take 7 pounds of cereal under stall-feeding conditions to produce 1 pound of beef. The price of oats relative to cattle between 1891 and 1929 was stable, even during the war. Then came 1933 and the economic war. There was a huge jump in the ratio, to the extent that it would require 3.3 pence worth of oats to produce 2 pence worth of beef. The cattle population therefore dropped in 1936 to below the 1881 level. He produced a similar argument for poultry and pigs. He concluded that nothing could take the place of cattle as the central product of Irish agriculture, and cereal production could only thrive if cattle were profitable enough to require stall-feeding.

Berkeley as Economist

On the TCD home ground JJ then published his *Irish Currency in the Eighteenth Century* in **Hermathena** LII p3, 1938. This paper appears subsequently as Chapter VI of his 1970 *Berkeley's Querist in Historical Perspective*, with some revisions. It is a highly technical paper, in which he adduces arguments made by George O'Brien subsequently, and at the time by Thomas Prior and Dean Swift, as well as those of Berkeley. There are echoes in the argument of the earlier experience of Solon and Croesus.

Continuing in this vein in the international literature, we have his *The Monetary Theories of Berkeley* published in **Economic History** (a supplement to the **Economic Journal**, edited by JM Keynes and EAG Robinson), February 1938.

In this JJ identified in Berkeley forerunners of ideas expressed in Keynes General Theory: "Berkeley anticipated Mr Keynes' view...that an increase in the quantity of money, if used for productive purposes, would increase the volume of employment."

He went on to relate some of Berkeley's queries to "...the most important of all the important facts formulated in Mr Keynes' General Theory is that capital is brought into existence not by the propensity to save, but in response to the demand from actual and potential consumption...".

He concluded: "..in his emphasis on the importance of consumption as a factor in the production of wealth, in his realisation of the vital part played by the quantity of money in the promotion of commerce and enterprise, Berkeley must be regarded as a precursor of Keynes. In his analysis of the nature of money itself, and of the function of gold in relation to it, Berkeley showed a complete emancipation from the merchantilist opinions of his time, and he takes high rank as one of the most modern and 'advanced' of monetary thinkers."

In pre-publication correspondence with Keynes JJ received the following letter dated April 5 1937:

"I much prefer the new version of your comments on Berkeley. But your note is now open to a new objection:- by relating it more closely to my views, you are in danger of bringing it within the objection that I am now having to attend to, that far too many articles sent to the Journal are on this and on analogous topics.

I have, however, in the enclosed suggested some small modifications which would do something to meet this. If you could accept these and are ready to let me publish it in **Economic History**, where there is much less pressure on my space, I should be glad to accept it.

I read Berkeley's *Querist* a few years ago, but I admit that his theories were not vividly in my mind when I was writing my General Theory.

Yours very truly, JM Keynes."

This issue of **Economic History** contains also a paper by J M Keynes on Adam Smith as Student and Professor, giving interesting biographical insights, like falling into a tan-pit while demonstrating division of labour.

JJ also was actively cultivating transatlantic contacts in support of his economic war polemics: he had among his papers a copy of an article in the **New York Times Magazine** of April 3 1938 by Harold Callendar, and a covering letter from the author dated July 8; he had been in Spain when it appeared and had only then got back. The article was headed *Riddle of the Two Irelands and an Empire* and was an analysis, with some historical depth, of the then current Anglo-Irish scene, in which Callendar had used JJ's work on the evaluation of the economic war and its effect on agricultural production.

College Politics and the Seanad

In College politics JJ was active in the democratic reform movement among the Junior Fellows which was aimed at displacing the then ruling gerontocracy. He was however by this time on the verge of becoming a gerontocrat himself, and he had become one by the time the movement succeeded, so that he missed the boat, by, so to speak, being too early for it[20]. It could be argued that by concentrating on national politics in the Seanad, he had isolated himself from the internal reform movement in TCD which finally surfaced with AJ McConnell's Provostship in the 1950s.

The first elections to the Seanad after the new Constitution was enacted took place in 1938, on the basis of nominally vocational panels, though this was rapidly subverted into political channels for most panels, the electorate being dominated by local councillors. The University seats however managed to avoid this process, and JJ sought election by the TCD graduates[2].

In his election address he listed the following of his published works as being relevant to political image he wished to project:

Groundwork of Economics (The Talbot Press, Dublin), *The Nemesis of Economic Nationalism* (PS King & Son, Ltd, and The Talbot Press, Dublin), Articles in **The Economist, The Economic Journal, The Nineteenth Century**, and in the current (February, 1938) number of **The Fortnightly**.

This attention to detail paid off, and he was elected. His maiden speech on May 11 1938 is on record in the Seanad Reports; he commented on the Agreement with the UK (Capital Sum) Bill 1938, second stage, introduced by de Valera as

Taoiseach; he gave his initial assessment of the outcome of the Economic War, and placed the arguments firmly in an all-Ireland context.

I quote the following extracts:

"...I felt that the Predominant Party in the country, and the leader of that Party, had their hearts set on that new Constitution, and that it was good citizenship for me to put no obstacle in the way of their achieving that constitutional change, hoping and believing, as I did, that when that Constitution had been enacted, that then the statesmanship that we even then hoped was latent in the character of our Prime Minister might somehow manage to emerge, and we have not been disappointed in that hope.

"After six years in the wilderness, and six years of economically riotous living, I rejoice to welcome the prodigal home, but I regret it is not possible to sacrifice any fatted calf in celebration of that event, because the animal that I had in mind to sacrifice was sacrificed in a different cause some three or four years ago...."

"...One of the problems of the future is the problem of relating the present and the past of Ulster to historical traditions, some of which bind them to us and to the Irish nation as a whole. On this question of Partition, the minority here have every reason to desire the reunion of all Ireland, if it can be obtained on the basis of consent. I think we have even more intimate and personal reasons for so desiring that than even the majority have here. After all, we are but a small minority. The bulk of our co-religionists are outside our political fellowship and it is a sad business for those of us born in Northern Ireland to realise when we visit that country the extent to which its particular conditions and local circumstances, and the absence of that fellowship and political unity -- the extent to which these have altered their outlook in life. We are still good friends, but the point is that, owing to the difference of political conditions, we have not so many interests in common as we would like to have and retain.

"The fact is that one does not feel quite so much at home in the Six Counties as one does in the Twenty-six Counties, and I am sure that most members of the minority here would like to feel at home in the Thirty-two Counties. There are obstacles to reunion, and perhaps the best contribution one can make to the removal of these obstacles is to try and explain as clearly as may be what the objective nature of those obstacles is. At the same time we should remember that times change and time also changes things which at first sight may appear unchangeable...."

In the ensuing debate, Senator James Douglas, with whom JJ subsequently regularly collaborated, wanted to help industry to get into the British market (anticipating the thinking of 2 decades later), and wanted an open declaration of attitude to the Commonwealth. He also wanted an end to tariffs on goods from the North.

Shortly afterwards JJ had the chance to interact in public with de Valera(21) on the basis of the arguments of a subsequent speech on agricultural issues. I again give some extracts:

"...The question, as I see it, before the House is how best we may perfect the machinery of co-operation between the Seanad and the Government. One idea which is supposed to he embodied in this House is vocational representation, and one idea associated with that representation is that expert minds, free from political or partisan bias, should give of their best in service by way of advice to the Government for the time being in power. Therefore, if we can in any way develop the vocational agricultural element that exists in this House, strengthen and develop it, it may form the nucleus of a permanent consultative council to give advice to the Minister for Agriculture. Along such lines we may he able to arrive at some commonly agreed solution.....

"....Agriculture at the present time is engaged in licking its wounds after the battle, and it is, I think, in order that I should attempt to analyse the extent and the seriousness of those wounds. The evidence from official statistics and other sources of agricultural decay in the last few years are, I think, quite incontrovertible. Whether we take it from the point of view of diminution in gross output or diminution in net output, there is no doubt whatever that our agricultural industry has passed through a most serious and difficult time. We know from official sources that gross output is down by more than £20,000,000 per year from the very inadequate total it had reached some ten or 12 years ago....

"...the average remuneration of the 625,000 persons occupied in agriculture amounted to £88 per annum 12 years ago. Between 1932 and 1936, that average remuneration amounted, if my calculations are right, to not more than £60 per annum, the equivalent of an income tax -- although most of that money went to waste and did not enrich the national revenue -- of more than 25% on persons occupied in agricultural production. That is a serious economic loss to the interests concerned....

"...Another important aspect of livestock agriculture in the feeding of an adequate protein ration to animals, especially in the winter time, when grass is inadequate for their complete nourishment. Protein in the form of one other of the oil seed cakes is one of the agricultural raw materials we simply must import. Therefore, the annual import of oilseed cake raw material is an admirable index of the extent to which we are using this necessary protein ingredient in out ration...

"...In 1927 we imported 1,000,000 cwt of oilseed cake and meal, and, in 1931, we imported 1,136,000 cwts. of oil seed cake and meal. In 1936, we imported 429,000 cwts. of that most necessary raw material. The importance of that is not only with reference to the weight and quality added to the animals which are fed that ration but also with reference to the fertility of the soil, which is preserved by properly feeding the live stock which graze on that soil. I should not he the least surprised to find that, owing to the inadequate feeding of our live stock for the last few years, the fertility of the soil, so far from being enriched, has steadily deteriorated. That is evidence of a serious development in our agricultural situation requiring the attention of some body specially qualified to investigate it....

"...Grass is our greatest natural resource, and basic slag is one of the most important of grass manures. In 1927, we imported 28,000 tons of basic slag. In 1934, we imported none at all, and, in 1936, we imported 15,000 tons. I submit that that is evidence of neglect of one of our most important assets....

"...The most striking thing we see when we look into the matter in this way is that by far the most remunerative source of taxation to the British tax-collector was the tax on our cattle. In 1935 the British collected £2,500,000 on cattle which we sent out, and the amount of bounty paid on this side in respect of these cattle exports was only £297,000, so that we may truthfully say that the cattle industry was allowed to bear its full share, and more than its share, of the brunt of that economic east wind...

"...In 1934-35 the British collected £444,000 from our dairy exports, and, in the corresponding year, we paid in bounty and subsidy something like £2,000,000, so that the dairy industry during this last six-year period was able to command a higher price for its products than it would have commanded if there had been no economic war and no bounty or subsidy. The important fact that emerges from that is that the economic war and the hand-to-mouth policy adopted from time to time in dealing with that war must have had a certain effect in distorting our agricultural economy from the form it would otherwise have occupied. Whether that distortion was intentional or not I do not know. At all events, it did distort it, and the fact of that distortion and the general tendency resulting from that distortion is one of the things which I should like some such expert body as this council to consider very carefully in the most impartial manner possible....

"...The shock of the settlement of the economic war has, therefore, in a way, been nearly as disastrous to certain sections of the agricultural industry as the original shock of the outbreak of the war was, because those people who, if they are able to maximise production -- it is our interest and the national interest that they should do so -- will have to be in a position to increase to full capacity the stock they carry on their land, now find that that stock is going to cost them far more money than it would have cost them if the economic war had continued. That is the principal reason why liberal credit facilities should be made available for such farmers as find it impossible to stock their land, because the value of cattle has increased in consequence of the settlement....".

Here JJ was making the case for something like the Agricultural Institute; this did not however get set up until the late 1950s. Until then, with his 'hobby farming', employing a man and keeping the books, trying various things, he was in effect a small-scale amateur Agricultural Institute.

Berkeley and Money

Continuing his economic history project, JJ published his *Commercial Restriction and Monetary Deflation in 18th Century Ireland* in **Hermathena** LIII, p79, 1939. This paper appears subsequently as Chapter IV of his *Querist*. According to JJ '...Berkeley was profoundly right in thinking that Ireland was to a much greater extent the victim of merchantilist monetary thought (or prejudice) at home than of merchantilist commercial policy abroad ...' The solution to the problem was '...well within the power of the Irish Government, in spite of the limitations of its constitutional authority ...'. JJ accessed the TCD estate records and analysed the values of the leases, in the context of the disastrous currency change of 1701, which he identified as being much more significant that the woolen restrictions.

There had been, earlier, a review by JJ of two books relating to this period: Irish Life in the 17th Century *by E McLysaght (Longmans, London 1938) and* The Economic History of Cork City *by W O'Sullivan (Longmans, 1937). In these reviews JJ identified tentatively the 1701 deflation as being the key factor underlying the poverty of the early 18th century, and related it to a similar episode under Elisabeth I. I conjecture that these review might have been the trigger for his 1939 paper.*

Continuing in this productive vein JJ then published *Berkeley and the Abortive Bank Project of 1720-21* in **Hermathena** LIV p110, 1939. Banking in the early 18th century was private and prone to failure, yet banknotes of all sorts circulated, and in fact constituted a currency, even though the credit on which they were based was often flimsy. "Whether current banknotes may not be deemed money? And whether they are not actually the greater part of the money of this kingdom?" (Berkeley's *Querist*). I quote JJ: "...one would have thought that the proposal to establish a solid and substantial corporate bank, which appeared in 1720, would have received a warm welcome... (there was) a petition from the Earl of Abercorn...to raise a fund of £500,000....The King approved...".

There was however considerable hostility aroused, from Swift and others; JJ analysed this, and identified as one factor the perception among the colonial elite that "...the Papists cannot purchase lands and are at a loss how to lay out their money. They will buy Bank stock and get control of the Bank to the weakening of the Protestant interest..". JJ's hero Berkeley alas at this time was away on his travels, and so was unable to intervene in the dispute. JJ argued that Berkeley would have held out, in accordance with his writings, that the bank should have been nationally owned rather than privately.

Returning more to polemical outreach mode, while remaining scholarly, JJ published his *An Outlook on Irish Agriculture* in **Studies** XXVIII no 111, September 1939. This continued the arguments of his 1935 paper, in the light of subsequent experience. Aggregate money income in agriculture declined from £52M in 1929 to £29M in 1933 and by 1938 had increased again only to £38M. The increase in industrial production under protection had increased the wealth of the towns but had increased the prices of industrial goods bought by declining agricultural incomes. A section of the paper is headed *Fallacy of 'Increasing Home Market' by mere Distribution of a Declining Population.* The policy of division of large farms is again looked at critically, in the light of the potential for increased productivity, per man and per acre, presented by mechanisation in a well-managed large-scale mixed farming environment consisting of specialising large and small farms. Again, he got reprints for distribution.

A Synopsis of Berkeley's Monetary Philosophy, published in **Hermathena** Vol LV p73, 1940, appears as Chapter VII of JJ's 1970 *Querist* edition commentaries. He makes a case for the inseparability of Berkeley's social and monetary philosophies: '...whether money be not only so far useful, as it stirreth up industry, enabling men mutually to participate in the fruits of each other's labour? ...'.

"For, in its essence, money is only a means of conveying and recording power to command the industry of others, and others will not give their services in exchange for it unless they have confidence that they in turn can get what they want in exchange for money". This far JJ; he then quotes Berkeley: "Whether all circulation be not be not like a circulation of credit, whatever medium (metal or paper) is employed, and whether gold be any more than credit for so much power?".

JJ stressed the identity of money and credit as seen by Berkeley, and related this to his promotion of the need for a national publicly-owned banking system.

Private ownership of the banking system, as is has evolved, regards the distinction between money and credit as being of great importance. For a modern financier, a debt is liquidated when money is repaid. For Berkeley, monetary obligations are only liquidated when transformed into solid goods and services. The latter was JJ's position.

JJ concludes by remarking that '... the idealist philosopher who disbelieved in the independent reality of matter was before all else a realist in his economic thinking.'

The foregoing, to my mind, puts the economic thinking of both JJ and Berkeley firmly on what in modern terms has come to be known as the 'political Left'.

Sticking with **Hermathena** for his Berkeley work JJ then published *Locke, Berkeley and Hume as Monetary Theorists* in Vol LVI p77, 1940. I feel I should give two quotations from this paper, which appears as Chapter VIII of his 1970 *Querist* commentaries:

"Berkeley must have read Locke's monetary pamphlets, and Hume may be supposed to have read the *Querist*. Hume's ideas were absorbed by his bosom friend Adam Smith, and passed by this channel into the main British stream of accepted monetary doctrine. And yet, as we shall see, essential elements in Berkeley's monetary philosophy failed to penetrate the mind of Hume, and accepted monetary doctrine has been impoverished as a consequence. The theory of money that appears in Adam Smith's *Wealth of Nations* stands decidedly apart from his main line of reasoning."

After some five pages or so of close argument he concludes: "...Thus Hume deliberately opposes not only the main theme of Berkeley's book (national banking), but what the event has proved to be the inevitable and necessary form of commercial and monetary development - the growth of paper credit...".

The Irish Association

Towards the end of the 30s there was a move on foot in Northern Ireland among some academics and business people, who were unhappy with the environment, to initiate an organisation which would cultivate an all-Ireland view without stressing unduly the political dimension. There emerged the Irish Association(22), and my father was a founder member, subsequently in the 40s becoming President. The first President was Lord Charlemont, who was an 'improving landlord' in the liberal tradition. (My grandfather's farm at Tomagh near Castlecaulfield was leased from the Charlemont estate, but I think this is coincidental).

The origins of the Irish Association were rooted in the perceptions of the de Valera Constitution of 1937, as seen from the angle of the Northern Protestants. It was a conscious attempt to stem the increasing divergence of outlook, and to preserve the opportunities for all-Ireland interaction presented by the status of the Free State within the Commonwealth. Names associated with its foundation were Frank McDermot and General Hugh Montgomery.

Academic Recognition

On June 14 1939 the TCD Board agreed to create Chairs, for the lives of the present holders only, in Applied Economics for JJ and in Economic History for Constantia Maxwell. So in the end JJ, at the age of 49, achieved some degree of academic recognition for his not inconsiderable outreach work on government commissions and extern lecturing in popularising mode, under the Barrington banner, and perhaps for his new role in the Seanad. JJ during the 30s decade JJ still remained in touch with the Albert Kahn Foundation(23), though more marginally than he had done in the hectic 20s. There was a visit by the Executive Secretary Garnier in 1939, in the context of the latter's chronic book on Ireland, which was later reviewed by TW Moody. When JJ was elected to the Seanad, Garnier had written to him inviting him to become officially a foreign member of the 'Cercle Autour du Monde', and JJ accepted.

Family Events
In 1939 my sister Maureen married Dermot Carmody, the second son of Dean Carmody, of Down, who had been a friend of Alice Stopford Green, and had a library containing most of the significant books relating to the national revival and Home Rule. Dermot had studied divinity in TCD and had been ordained; for a while he served in Enniskillen Cathedral, and then served in Christ Church, Dublin, and from that situation he married my sister. They lived initially in Sandymount.

The move to 'The Glen', near Drogheda, which took place in 1940, as a war expedient, I treat in the 1940s module (I have tended to include the year ending in 0 with the previous decade, but here I make an exception).

Notes and References
1. I abstract the *Nemesis of Economic Nationalism* (PS King & Son, London, 1934) in a dedicated module in the background hypertext, and if publication in full turns out to be appropriate, as in the case of *Civil War in Ulster*, we will do this. This book also owes something to the co-operative movement; the Co-operative Conference Association had published a pamphlet written by JJ in 1933, of which a copy was among JJ's papers, entitled *The Importance of Economy in the Distribution of Goods*. Because it is rare I think it is worth reproducing in full, in the supportive hypertext, where it is accessed in the Plunkett stream. Also it contains embryonic versions of certain of JJ's key economic concepts, as developed in his *Nemesis*, and his later attempt to establish consumer demand as the basis of credit. JJ sent a complimentary copy to Charles Garnier, at the Albert Kahn Foundation in Paris, with which he remained in touch during the 1930s.
2. JJ's election address I have given in full in Appendix 8, along with the names of his support committee. His maiden speech on May 11 1938 is on record in Column 99 of Vol 21 of the Seanad Reports; I also reproduce this in full in the hypertext support material; it is also hot-linked from the chronological summary of his speeches which I have collected in the 1930s Seanad module of the hypertext.
3. The highlight of JJ's interaction with the TCD Board in the 1930s was when in 1934 he had to 'threaten them with the Visitors' to get a small subvention for publishing his *Nemesis of Economic Nationalism*.
4. The 1930s political thread was undoubtedly fed by some of his quasi-academic publications, most of which gave him ammunition for his Seanad participation from 1938. He also had media exposure, often arising from the Protestant school speech-day circuit.
5. I count as 'outreach' JJ's work with the SSISI (Statistical and Social Inquiry Society), where he served on the Council during the decade, the related Barrington Lectures, which in

1932 he managed to bring in under the SSISI umbrella again, after their post-war period of alienation, and finally the Irish Association, of which he became a founder-member in 1938. In all three networks JJ consistently promoted all-Ireland thinking.

6. The criterion I have adopted here is that of 'peer-review', but even with this constraint it is evident that a high proportion of JJ's 1930s academic output was motivated by the developing Irish 'political economy' environment. He published not only in the TCD *Hermathena* but also in the SSISI Proceedings, in the Jesuit quarterly *Studies* and in JM Keynes's *Economic Journal*.

7. JJ moved from Dundalk to near Drogheda in 1932, here he again farmed with rather more dedication, but less success, due to the economic war. He moved back to a rented house in Dublin in 1935, and to another in 1937, and then in 1940 he bought a farm, again near Drogheda, where we survived the Emergency in relative comfort. This trail is followed in the family thread of the hypertext.

8. JJ's orphaned nephew Geddes had aspired to a life in the open air, abroad, and JJ in the end managed to fix him up on a ranch in the Argentine, through Mahaffey in TCD; there was a Traill property there. There is extensive and rather acrimonious inter-family correspondence about Geddes around this time, on record among JJ's papers. It seems one option being promoted by JJ was to bring him back and get him into a management role in some agricultural enterprise, but he did not buy this, preferring to continue his somewhat adventurous gaucho-like role. The correspondence peaked in 1932, and then ceased, so the issue whatever it was must have got sorted out, and we lose sight of Geddes until he came back in 1940 on his way to join the RAF. He was shot down over North Africa. It would be somewhat of a red herring to develop the Geddes saga in full here, but there are indications that it may surface in another context.

9. I have overviewed JJ's academic publication stream in Appendix 5, and expanded on the details in the 1930s module of the hypertext. In this decade narrative I have selected the key papers and given their references in the text.

10. However in later life Standish O'Grady was promoting co-operative communes in Jim Larkin's *Irish Worker*, in 1912-13. See his *To the Leaders of Our Working People*, ed EA Hagan, UCD Press 2002. There are references to Dermot MacManus in Maurice Manning's *The Blueshirts*, Gill & Macmillan (1971, 1987), and in Mike Cronin's *Blueshirts and Irish Politics*, Four Courts Press (1997); this documents the Yeats episode. I have expanded on this in the 1930s political module of the background hypertext. According to Micheál O'Riordan, the retired Irish Communist Party leader, (*Irish Times* letter, 22/01/2001) the 'ordinary Blueshirts' were not fascists, but their leadership did consciously support the German and Italian models, as evidenced by JA Costello's Dáil speech on February 28 1934, which he quoted. O'Riordan went on to concede that by 1948 Costello had retreated from that position.

11. On November 28 1932 Seán Lemass, then Minister for Finance in the new and dreaded Fianna Fail Government, wrote to JJ inviting him to participate in a commission of enquiry into the Civil Service. JJ accepted, and contributed to the work of the commission, though not so significantly as he had done on his earlier Agriculture and Prices commissions in the 1920s. I have also referenced this episode in the 1930s political module of the background hypertext.

12. *The 1935 Yearbook of Agricultural Co-operation*, an annual publication of the co-operative movement in Britain, has on p67 an article by HF Norman headed *The Irish Free State* in which JJ's analysis of the situation is quoted, based on this paper in the Economic Journal. I have made this available in the 1930s Plunkett module of the hypertext.

13. As an example of the flavour of the Board at this time, I feel I should mention the censure by the Board of JM Henry, a Mathematics lecturer and Junior Fellow, for his book *The New Fundamentalism*, as being inconsistent with his role as a tutor Fellow. Presumably he was considered in danger of corrupting the youth. A motion to deprive him of his pupils was narrowly defeated. According to McDowell, Henry '...took such a wide view of culture that he tried to combine all elements of it together. Mathematics, psychology, philosophy, comparative religion, education, dietetics, fringe medicine, all were grist to his mill....a credo of an eccentricity which places it in the outer fringes of the curiosities of academic literature....his genuine surprise at the indignation caused by an implication, tossed off incidentally in his book, that the Virgin Mary was a respectable Temple prostitute...'. The foregoing throws light on the nature of the incubus under which JJ laboured, as a result of his having been, like Max Henry, a pre-1919 Fellow. He had to work all that much harder to avoid being labelled as a polymath, dilettante or guru. I expand on this in the 1930s TCD college politics module in the hypertext.

14. 'Some Causes and Consequences of Distributive Waste' (JSSISI vol XIV, p353, 1926-27).

15. There is a draft minute of this meeting among his 1930s papers, and I have embodied this in the 1930s module of the political thread of the hypertext, which is overviewed in Appendix 10. In the minute JJ's contribution is treated anonymously, as an 'economist'. This could perhaps have been at his own request. While recognising that Fine Gael was trying to look after the interests of the labour-employing commercial farmers, JJ would probably have been uneasy about the extent to which the then Fine Gael was becoming identified with the Blueshirts, and consciously supporting the German and Italian models. (see note 10.)

16. JJ's ideal vision was commercial farming in large units, whether Milestown-type capitalist, as described to the SSISI, or Ralahine-type co-operative, as described by James Connolly in *Labour in Irish History,* and envisioned later by JJ in his *Irish Agriculture in Transition.* This implied a large farm labour workforce, potential Labour supporters. We have here perhaps a foreshadowing of the Labour-Fine Gael coalition which was later to emerge, though without the type of co-operative-oriented policies to which JJ aspired. The Fianna Fail land division into 30-acre subsistence lots was anathema, as was protectionism, which he saw as the road to cronyism, based on his brother's Indian experience. Despite this Fianna Fail valued his services and aspired to use them, as evidenced by the 1932 Lemass letter.

17. JJ had recently published a Statistical Society paper to this effect, 'Aspects of the Agricultural Crisis at Home and Abroad', (JSSISI XV, 79, 1934-5). He expanded on it subsequently, in his 'Capitalisation of Irish Agriculture' (JSSISI XVI, 44, 1941-2), instancing three farmers who between them farmed 700 acres and employed 50 workers.

18. The occasion was a dinner in honour of Sir Horace Plunkett on March 4 1920, at which Plunkett commended the British Labour Party for their support of the Irish Dominion League, which was holding out for a united Ireland within the Commonwealth.

19. This paper is reproduced in full in the background hypertext. The '1790s utopia' arguments used by economic nationalists he demolished using eyewitness evidence from Arthur Young's travels. On May 30 1936 the *Irish Times* had a report headed 'Drawbacks of Wheat / Present Systems Dangers / Warning by an Economist'. This was JJ's Athy Barrington Lecture. The contents of the report is basically that of the unpublished 'wheat' typescript which I have reproduced. This report therefore identifies it with the Barrington Lecture stream, which was an important political outlet for JJ's ideas. I have collected some press cuttings reflecting JJ's public campaigning in the period 1935-38 and they are accessible in the 1930s political module of the hypertext.

20. I treat the emergence of the democratic reform movement, later associated with the emergence of AJ McConnell as Provost, in the latter part of the 1930s TCD college politics module of the hypertext. The process was helped by progressives like RM Gwynn joining the Board, on the decease of McCran; the flavour of Board decisions improved significantly towards the end of the decade, with support for projects such as the Irish Students Association as an all-Ireland body, inviting Robin Flower, of Blaskets fame, to give the Donnellan Lecture, and sanctioning the Dublin University Fabian Society, founded on the initiative of Owen Sheehy-Skeffington.

21. On July 10 1938 in the Sunday Times there was a report by their Dublin correspondent of the Centenary Reunion of the past graduates of the Albert Agricultural College, which was addressed by de Valera, and by JJ. This was in a sense a public celebration of the ending of the 'economic war', with de Valera admitting the need to develop agricultural exports. JJ used the occasion to go over the ground of his July 6 Seanad speech, in the presence of de Valera; this is accessible in full via the Public Services and Seanad stream of the hypertext. The speech was also reported positively in the *Sunday Independent* on July 10, 1938, and there had been a preview of the speech when JJ had presided at the end of term celebrations in the Royal School Cavan, as reported in the *Irish Times* on July 2 1938. Charles Garnier had been in Ireland during JJ's Seanad campaign, and on hearing of his success invited him to become officially a Membre Etranger of the Cercle Autour du Monde, which JJ accepted in October 1939.

22. The background to the Irish Association is given in some detail in the associated hypertext 1930s Irish Association module, and in Mary McNeill's 1976 paper, as published by the Association in 1982.

23. See Appendix 3 for an overview of the Albert Kahn Foundation; I have expanded on his contacts in this decade in the 1930s module of this thread of the hypertext; the Moody review of Garnier's book in *Irish Historical Studies* (Vol 2 no 5, March 1940) is included with the Garnier letters.

Chapter 5 Part 1: The Period 1941-1945

This chapter falls naturally into two parts: the war years, and the immediate post-war years with the present writer active in the TCD student left. The introductory section below overviews both parts.

Introduction

When the war came, JJ moved back to Drogheda, to a 30-acre farm, with a substantial ex-Ascendancy house. I boarded initially at Avoca School, then from 1942 at St Columba's College near Rathfarnham. We endured the privations of the emergency from the relative comfort of JJ's professorial salary. At school in St Columba's we had access to newspapers and radio, and we followed the war avidly, trying to understand the politics. A group of us took up Marxism, under the influence of the war, with fellow-pupil Paul O'Higgins as focus. We had support from a teacher EL Mallalieu, who subsequently became a Labour MP in England; we stored our Marxist library in his rooms.

What follows here, where it relates to JJ, is an overview of the domains where he was active during the decade, and in most of these I have collected a significant amount of background material, referenced in footnotes and their associated hypertext hotlinks. By far the most significant part of JJ's 1940s contribution was made via his membership of the Seanad, until his defeat in the 1948 election. JJ also served on the Post-war Agriculture Commission, somewhat critically.

JJ continued to be active in the Statistical and Social Inquiry Society (SSISI)(1) and in this context the Barrington Lectures(2) continued to be of significance. His Barrington and SSISI material, supplemented by field work in the late 40s when travel became again feasible, took shape as a book *Irish Agriculture in Transition*(3). In this book JJ elaborated his vision of a highly productive, mechanised and labour-intensive agricultural system, based on managed large-farm units, co-operatively owned, making use of practical examples from real-world sites demonstrating the principles he was advocating. The failure of Irish agriculture to develop systematically along these lines post-war is one of the great lost opportunities. He continued to make the case for productive agriculture via the Seanad(4), where he held on to his seat for most of the decade.

The foregoing I count as one of the missed opportunities for constructive father-son interaction, in the field of politics and economic organisation. JJ's vision had been, since the 30s, at least partially realised by RM Burke, whose estate near Tuam Co Galway he had transformed into a working co-operative or collective farm, avoiding division by the Land Commission into uneconomic 30-acre units. I visited it in or about 1947, in the context of the development of our TCD 'student left' group, the Promethean Society, seeking role-models on the home ground, rather than in Eastern Europe, and I go into this further in Part 2. At this time however I was not aware of JJ's vision of productive estates converted to co-operative organisation, and I failed to make the connection, though JJ himself had been invited as a Barrington Lecturer to Tuam in October 1947, largely on the initiative of Burke(5) .

During the 40s JJ tried as best he could to keep in touch with TCD Board politics(6). In this arena he was however sidelined in the McConnell 'revolution'; the 'new wave' with which he had been associated as a Junior Fellow matured after he became a Senior Fellow in December 1943, and thus became identified with the 'gerontocrats'. He did however participate in the politics which developed between Government and the Universities over the question of the investment of the Marshall Plan money into agricultural research. In this area he played a leading role, along with Frank Mitchell, positioning the College to participate in the project, with the Kells Ingram Farm.

He had significant published academic output, and became a member of the Royal Irish Academy in 1943 at the invitation of Eoin MacNeill(7). His Academy citation, on the basis of which he was elected, looks as if it was prepared in a hurry, and does not reference much of his real academic work. This was the time when de Valera was in process of setting up the Dublin Institute of Advanced Studies, and he had had little support in this from the Academy 'old guard'. Eoin MacNeill becoming President however constituted an indication that the Irish State was becoming recognised as being 'here to stay'. Eoin MacNeill had earlier been associated with a move to set up an alternative National Academy; this process had been initiated but abandoned under the pressures of the Civil War period. So it seems appropriate to suggest that JJ's election to the Academy might have been part of an Eoin MacNeill recruitment of scholars known to be favourable to Irish independent statehood, and in this context JJ had indeed proved himself, in service on a series of Free State government commissions, and latterly in the Seanad.

The Albert Kahn contact(8) remained tenuously in existence, despite the war. JJ remained active in the organisation of resistance to the worst effects of Partition, via the Irish Association(9), of which he became President in 1946. In this context to tried, usually without much success, to ensure that Northern organisations participated on an all-Ireland basis, in the post-emergency / post-war reconstruction process.

This ends an introductory overview section. I build the structure of this two-part chapter for JJ initially around his Seanad speeches, with his College role in the Board, and his role as President of the Irish Association, taking over after 1948. For my own part, the focus is on the development of Marxist political thinking under the influence of the war, and its transition from school to college environment.

RJ at School

The decade began just about when the war became 'real'. There was a rallying of the remote Johnston cousinhood, from the ends of the earth, in support of the defence of Britain. This is recorded in the 'family' thread(10). JJ moved to a farm near Drogheda for the duration, requiring the present writer to attend boarding-school, initially at Avoca School in Blackrock, where I had been since 1935.

In school we set up a war map on the classroom wall. People discovered books about the first world war, and brought them in. The general feeling in the school, being Protestant, was pro-British. There was a boy scout troop, somewhat on sufferance; the head master Cyril Parker disliked the scouts, as he felt they were too militaristic. He had also served in the previous war, and had become a total pacifist. But to return to the scouts: Erskine Barton Childers and I were in the same class, and were good friends; we week-ended in each others houses occasionally. His father, who subsequently became President, was a Minister in de Valera's Government at the time. Erskine and I were in the scouts. The scout routine involved learning the National Anthem, and the norm at this time, in the Protestant school scout-troop environment, was God Save the King. Erskine objected to this, and I backed him up. We got our way. This was my first political act.

The war dominated my dawning political consciousness however from then on, and I identified with the British. I was conscious of Irish neutrality but aware of a general sympathy with the British, and a genuine fear of German invasion, grounded on the realities of the worst period in 1940-41. In the spring of 1941 I was still at Avoca, though as a border, JJ having moved to a farm near Drogheda; he felt safer in a rural environment in the threatening situation. I remember the physical training instructor, one Sergeant O'Neill of the Free State Army, regaling us with what the military view of the situation was at that time, to the effect that a German landing in the south was imminent.

JJ evidently was of the same view, because for the summer term of 1941 he took me out of Avoca, and sent me as a day-boy to Drogheda Grammar School, along with my cousin Ian Nesbitt, who had been sent down from Belfast. If the Germans had landed, at least the family would have been in the one place, with access to food.

We went camping with the Drogheda scouts in June 1941, and when in camp we got the news of the German invasion of the USSR. This immediately changed the scene as regards danger of invasion, and I was sent back in September 1941 to board at Avoca, where we followed the war on the classroom map.

St Columba's College

I did the entrance scholarship exam for St Columba's College, and went there in September 1942. The school was, and still is, situated in the foothills of the Dublin Mountains. It had been founded in 1841 by a group of progressive landlords, Adare and others, to enable the landed and church elite to communicate with their Irish tenantry in their own language, and thereby to develop some social and religious cohesion, along with a supportive educated artisan class, thus undermining the alien influence of Rome(11). The core idea here was the attempt to transform parasitic landlordism into a bourgeois-national elite capable of leadership in the positive sense; the language was to be the bond, with the Roman Church marginalised.

The teaching of Irish was competent; one Brooks was the teacher. Vestiges of the founder's vision remained in the form of a service in Irish in the Chapel on St Patrick's Day. The most positive remaining aspect however of the founders' vision however was the emphasis on access to technical education, and to the farm. There was woodwork, metalwork, including a blacksmiths forge, a printing works, and in my time, an electrical and electronic workshop. There were good science laboratories, the science teacher being one George Lodge, a veteran republican, who had driven the car during a famous episode involving a rescue of de Valera from prison in England during the war of independence. He had graduated from the

College of Science, and served his time as an industrial chemist during the first world war.

I recollect following day by day the battle of Stalingrad on the copy of the *Irish Times* which was accessible in the junior common-room. We cheered on the Russians. The 'radio club' (as the electronic workshop was known) was a bit exclusive; juniors like me were not allowed in. I managed however to get into building radios at home during the vacations. My sister when in college had been friendly with one Cyril Dugdale, in the medical school; he became an excellent dentist. Like most dentists, he liked working intelligently with his hands, and he had been a hard-core radio buff in the 30s; he has made radios for us. These had fallen into disuse, but I stripped them, and used the bits and pieces to build my own; I learned how to solder. In or about 1943 I made my first successful radio set, and I got it to work on the short wavebands, so I could listen to the news of the war from all over the world, by-passing the Irish censorship. This fed into our understanding of global politics at school.

I remember coming back to school in September 1944 and getting to talk to Paul O'Higgins, Dick Stringer and Paddy Bond, who it seems had already become the makings of a sort of Marxist underground group. The topic was the civil war then going on in Greece, which I had initially found incomprehensible from the news reports. They filled me in on what was going on: it was Churchill using the British Army to prevent the Greeks having a social revolution and installing a post-war government friendly to the USSR. From then on, the jig-saw puzzle of world events began to fit together into the Marxist world-picture.

Paul O'Higgins was unusual in St Columba's College, in that his parents had rejected the Catholic Church, and Paul was consciously an unbeliever. He went to the College Chapel, and fulfilled the necessary rituals, with the exception of bowing his head at the name of Jesus during the creed, which was then the norm; perhaps it still is, I don't know. This engendered a degree of respect in many, and I seem to remember one or two others following suit.

Apart from myself our Marxist group consisted of Paul O'Higgins (background as above); Paddy Bond (landed gentry from Farragh, between Longford and Edgeworthstown; Oliver Bond of 1798 fame was ancestrally related; he went to Cambridge University and remained active in Britain with the Communist Party and the Connolly Association until his death in ~1990), Dick Stringer (he went to Liverpool University and eventually became Dublin County Architect), George Fairbrother (studied law in TCD, supported the Promethean group in TCD, then became a solicitor in Cavan). George joined the group as a result of the performance of Stringer and myself in a school debate in which we promoted Marxist ideas.

There was a friendly teacher, one EL Mallalieu, subsequently a Labour MP for Colne Valley in England, winning a seat in the 1945 election. We kept our library of Marxist books in his room, with his blessing. We bought them in surreptitious visits down to Dublin, to New Books, 'Johnny Nolan's Bookshop', which was the residual contact point for the Irish Communist Party, then disbanded due to the war and the politics of neutrality.

We recruited a few more; Adrian Somerfield (who ended up teaching science as George Lodge's successor), Fred Marshall (who made a career in music in

London), one Mercier who went to college in Scotland; we lost track of him. Adrian edited trenchantly a 'wall-newspaper' called the 'Beresford Free Press' which developed a sort of muck-raking left-wing journalism. Fred played the organ in the Chapel and on VE day improvised around the anthem of the USSR.

Somerfield and I moved in on the Radio Club, its earlier denizens having lost interest. We attempted to develop a transmitter, with a view to conveying the liberating message of the Left to the Dublin masses. We managed to transmit from the radio club workshop to the senior common-room. We developed a portable test rig, which we brought up the mountain, to try to get a feel for range measurement, but this turned out to be out of range; we only had a few watts.

One of the earlier radio buffs, I should say, was the younger brother of a subsequent Stormont potentate. We learned from him the essential principles of Orange patronage: there was a weekly issue of toilet paper ('bumf') in the school latrine, it was somewhat scarce under war conditions. He used to get there early, stock up with it in his pocket, and issue it to his friends, thus illustrating the essentials of bourgeois politics!

At this point it is appropriate to use George Lodge, the science teacher, as a hook on which to hang a comment on the science tradition in Ireland. He got his training in the College of Science, which was outside the Irish university system. It had been founded by the British when they discovered that the Germans had been investing in education in science and technology for industry, and this constituted a competitive threat. It was a producer of the industrial chemists who had fuelled the British war machine during the World War 1, George Lodge among them. Prior to 1906, with the foundation of the National University of Ireland, this was the main channel for Catholics to get a scientific education, access to Trinity College and the 'godless colleges' in Cork, Galway and Belfast being banned or discouraged by the Catholic Hierarchy. Cardinal Cullen's ban on the 'godless colleges' had discouraged generations of the rising Catholic bourgeoisie from accessing scientific technology; some like Robert Kane went abroad. The result was that the culture of science tended to be a Protestant preserve.

This was reflected in the curricula of second-level schools. When JD Bernal's mother visited Clongowes, seeking to evaluate science opportunities for young Desmond, she decided in favour of boarding him in England. There was good science in St Columba's, set up by Joly, but the religious barrier would have intruded, the Bernals being Catholic. Thus Bernal(12) was lost to Ireland.

We celebrated the ending of the war in Europe in May of 1945. We got to see films which had been banned under the neutrality censorship. I happened to be down in town on the day of the TCD flag-burning, and I observed it from a distance, not fully understanding its political implications. I was with the Carmodys(10) (my sister and brother-in-law) in Ballinaclough near Nenagh when the Hiroshima bomb was dropped; having a feel for physics I immediately grasped its implications. Later in September, back in school, it was a topic of conversation, and we tried to come to grips with the politics of the new post-war situation.

JJ in the Seanad

Continuing his campaign in the Seanad for agricultural organisation based on well-managed and capitalised large-scale units, JJ along with Senator Counihan introduced on January 29 1941 a motion in support of special arrangements for agricultural credit, with a Debt Adjustment Commission, on the New Zealand model. The situation was that there were many small farmers without capital and the only source of capital was bank credit. Having raised the issues, he withdrew the motion, after mentioning in passing that those who had resisted the wheat policies of the 30s now had pasture in good enough heart to enable wheat to be grown, while the 30s wheat growers had in effect mined their land, leaving it now exhausted, without adequate manuring.

In March 1941 JJ made repeated efforts, on various issues, to get the Government to do a beef export deal with Britain, based on upgraded agricultural productivity, in return for access to key imports. For a while in 1941 it looked as if things were going JJ's way, with the foot and mouth disease, and a British ban on import of live cattle, introducing an additional supporting factor. What JJ wanted was (a) local abattoirs, dealing with local farmers, to have the right to get into the export market, thus keeping up the prices, (b) buyers from the 'Emergency Purchasing Committee' to be discouraged from spreading foot and mouth disease with their muddy boots on direct farm visits, and (c) Dublin buyers, similarly, to deal wholesale with the local abattoirs, rather than dealing directly with farmers.

In May 1941 the Fianna Fail government made its first attempt to get rid of Proportional Representation, and a Government Senator adduced arguments suggesting that PR was at the root of the current state of European politics. JJ took strong exception to this, defending PR as a 'valuable feature of the Constitution...which in particular appeals to the minority...PR modified by the existence of a two-party tradition works reasonably well...has not prevented...a single-party government...'

Referring to Northern Ireland JJ reminded the Seanad that PR '...was part of the original Constitution and that it was generally regarded as a retrograde step when it was abolished...at the time (its abolition) was denounced as a flagrant violation of the rights of the minority.' He harked back to the First Home Rule Bill, which was defeated in the Commons, and in the ensuing election more voters voted for Home Rule candidates but owing to the English system a Unionist majority was returned. So if there had been PR in Britain in 1886 '...the whole history of Anglo-Irish relations would probably have been altered, and altered for the better.'

Later on the milk supply question JJ drew attention to the factor of about 5 between what the farmer got and what the consumer paid for a pint of milk, and to the under-consumption of milk in Dublin, which had public health implications. He called for a rationalised municipal distribution system, and for a deal to be done with producer co-ops remote from Dublin for milk pasteurised at source. He wanted the quality farm-based producer-distributors near Dublin to get some recognition, and for the sub-standard back-yard urban cow-keepers to be phased out, being a source of disease, both in cattle and humans.

The debate went on to the economics of winter milk supply. JJ wanted there to be free trade in milk; anyone who undertook 12-month continuity of supply to be able to contract in to the Dublin system, not just an existing vested interest of suppliers in a designated Dublin production area. JJ's amendment was withdrawn on the assurance from Minister Ryan that he was considering the municipalisation of Dublin milk distribution.

In the following July on the Finance Bill JJ accused the Minister of erring unduly on the side of rigid financial virtue, given the needs of the emergency situation; government borrowing from the banks in the UK was much greater. He reminded the Minister that the Banking Commission had advocated setting up a Research Department in support of public policy development. JJ warned the Minister about trying to increase taxation in a situation of declining real incomes, and drew his attention to the abnormal profit-making which had gone on in some favoured sectors, particularly the millers. He re-iterated his call for improved credit facilities for farmers, and warned the Minister against attempting to increase taxation on agricultural business. The credit of the State depends '...on the productive capacity of the citizens ...'.

JJ then read what amounted to a Keynsian lecture on the role of the State in a deficit financing situation, based on current British experience, where State borrowing had increased but inflation had been contained.

In January 1942 there was a debate on the Minimum Price for Wheat in which JJ again attacked the policy of the Government over the previous 10 years, and indicated how it had now left us on the verge of actual starvation, quite unnecessarily. The crisis was due to a combination of land exhaustion due to unnecessary growing of wheat in the 30s, and land subdivision in favour of 'landless men' who lacked the capital to develop the production of their smallholdings, and for whom the growing of wheat was quite unsuitable(13).

In February 1942 in a debate on Wages of Agricultural Workers JJ gave a preview of a paper which was to be delivered a couple of days later, to the Statistical and Social Inquiry Society, on the *Capitalisation of Irish Agriculture(14)*. The gross output of Irish agriculture was about £60M and the net output some £53M. The capital invested in Irish agriculture he estimated at £466M and he proposed to remunerate this with a return of £23M (ie a modest 5%) leaving £30M to remunerate labour, to be divided among the 600K people then said to be engaged in agriculture. This figure was of course inflated by the Land Commission subdivision into 30-acre lots. This gave an average income per head of £50, which was substantially less than the weekly minimum wage of £1.50 which was on the table.

Analysing this somewhat absurd conclusion JJ concluded that '...the great bulk of the persons occupied in Irish agriculture are sitting around on the small farms of 30 acres or less are really superfluous to the work to be done on them... (earning) less than £50 per person per year... (while) in the few cases which I have personally investigated...large well-equipped and adequately capitalised farms, I arrived at the conclusion that the net output per person occupied in such farms reached as high as £215 per person per year, and in other cases well over £100 per person per year.'

He went on: '...whereas we have nearly 400,000 ... holdings there are only some 50,000 farmers who employ any wage-paid agricultural labour at all... the output per person is, on average, much higher on the larger farms...'.

On March 19 1942 on the Central Fund Bill (this was an opportunity for airing general economic ideas for taking care of the emergency, which by this time had become quite acute) JJ argued that a controlled degree of inflationary finance should be allowed. Britain had acquired 5% of the real income of the nation by simply issuing new money (i.e. borrowing from the banking system) with quite easily manageable inflationary effects.

He then came around to how compulsory tillage was working, in the non-tillage areas where it was imposed. Land was being let on conacre to contractors who mined it. He drew attention to this as a disastrous procedure, and counterposed the current English procedure, which was based on a plough-up subsidy. He predicted a declining yield per acre, and a need to increase the acreage.

He then went into agricultural productivity per person. One person in Ireland on the land was producing food enough for 10 persons. The comparable figure in Britain was 15. He reiterated his call for increasing the employment of labour on the larger and better-equipped farms.

On fuel he urged that the State should deal with voluntary co-operative organisations of local labour, as well as importing mobile labour from a distance. On food he urged increase uptake of potatoes to offset the shortage of bread, and relocation of people from the towns back to the country, to be nearer to the sources of food. Communal feeding in the towns would enable potatoes and vegetables to be cooked with fuel economy.

In April 1942 on Family Allowances for Agricultural Workers JJ analysed the relationship between wages and family income requirements, and made the case that just as in a business they make systematic provision for depreciation and maintenance of plant and equipment, so society should make social provision for the replacement of its members. He leaned heavily on a book by Dr Eleanor Rathbone, which made the family allowances case in Britain.

As regards financing the scheme, he offered various options, one being a fund to which employers and workers would contribute out of a projected wage increase *(a foreshadowing of contemporary PRSI)*, another being for the State to take over and legalise the existing black market in white flour and tea, thus turning the racketeers' super-profits to the social advantage. The amendment providing family allowances for farm workers was carried on May 6.

Returning on June 2 1942 to the vexed question of the Minimum Price for Wheat, JJ attempted to link it to a post-emergency policy for a relationship between grass and tillage, pointing out the best grass farmers were often the best tillage farmers. The policy should also relate to agricultural credit, and to dairy farming, and calf rearing, and fat cattle production. It should allow for collaboration with our British neighbours.

He pointed out that there would be absolutely no reason to continue the wheat growing policy after the war, as the granaries of the US and Canada were overflowing, with ample stocks for the whole of Europe during post-war recovery. There was no reason why we could not get this at world prices.

He urged that if there was to be a fixed price for wheat there should be a related fixed price for oats. He blamed the bad relationship between cereal and livestock prices on British policy which had penalised Irish production of fat cattle for export, and blamed the Government for not making a public issue of this, as a serious national grievance. As a consequence of this policy, stall feeding had been abandoned and as a result there was a shortage of manure. What we want is a price for fat cattle that is at least 5 times the price of oats; this is the Northern Ireland situation under UK market conditions.

He went on to criticise the 100% extraction of wheat flour, which had introduced into the human diet indigestible material better suited to feeding to pigs and poultry.

In the debate on the Finance Bill in June JJ reiterated his arguments for coming to an agreement with Britain over the enhanced supply of food, and expanded on his earlier suggestion that the Government take over the black market in white flour; people in Donegal were prepared to pay a guinea a stone for flour bought for 3 shillings in Derry. Why not mill 10% of the wheat into white flour, put an excise of £100 per ton, and make it available at a guinea a stone to those with the money to pay for it? Why should the State allow the black marketers to levy a private taxation?

On June 18 1942 the Price of Bacon Pigs was debated; JJ was able to encapsulate the essentials of emergency agricultural policy across a broad spectrum. The British would rather lose the war than accept food from Eire. The Government should do a deal with the British to get parity with Northern Ireland prices.

He then went into pig production models: there was the 'pig as by-product' model and the 'pig specialist' model. The second was dominated by the 'hog-corn ratio' and could currently be done in the US profitably, with cereals in glut, and shipping space to Britain at a premium. No way could we compete with the US for the supply of bacon in this mode. We could however post-war, and it would be necessary to maintain a pig population to enable this. The 'pig as by-product' fulfils this role, and the natural feed is skim milk and potatoes.

The trouble was that skim occurs in the summer and the potatoes occur in the winter. It is however feasible to bring them together by the expedient of (a) encouraging winter milk production, with autumn calving, and stall-feeding with silage and roots and (b) making storable 'potato silage' in the spring with the residuum of the crop, before it begins to sprout, cooking it and storing it under sterile conditions.

He concluded by again attacking the 100% extraction wheaten flour, of which the 15% bran was in fact best for pigs, and quite indigestible by humans. In the best polemical tradition he concluded: '...the Minister in his career as a successful politician had doubtless had occasion to hand out chicken feed to his followers, and I might say to him in this particular matter that he is handing out not only chicken-feed but pig-feed and expecting humans to digest it...'.

On September 23 1942 on the Central Bank Bill JJ contributed a highly technical speech(15), which probably went over the heads of the Senators, but perhaps contributed to the bank of expertise available to the Department of Finance. JJ began by reminding the Government that he had advocated the setting up of a Central Bank nearly a decade ago, and he quoted from Page 100 of his 'Nemesis of Economic Nationalism: '...it is amazing to me that the State has not yet done anything to create a national short-term money market. The first step in that direction is to turn the Currency Commission into a Central Bank.... to give leadership to the ordinary banks in the practice of a national credit policy...'.

He went on to regret the 30s as a lost opportunity for adopting a liberal monetary policy and borrowing millions for the purpose of national reconstruction and readjustment '...from the general public ...though a mechanism which in those times would have been anti-inflationary'. The criticisms of the Banking Commission which had sat from 1934 to 38 had largely been ignored. The Central Bank Bill '...positively oozed monetary orthodoxy of a late Victorian kind ...' as if the Government was trying to atone for its 30s economic heresies with 'a swan-song of monetary orthodoxy'.

JJ then homed in on the all-Ireland nature of the banking system, and the constraints this put on the relationship with sterling. The sterling reserves held by the banking system were so big that we could have considerable economic departure from parity without noticing it in financial terms. He went in some depth into the question of the jurisdiction of a 26-county central bank on a 32-county banking system. He concluded that '...the real cash basis of the Irish commercial banks is the plaything of the trade balance between our country and Britain, and is consequently completely outside the control of the central bank'.

He concluded with some remarks on the legal debarring of the right of the central bank to lend to the Government, which he criticised as a very negative means of preventing inflation. The bank would do little for the emergency situation, and was perhaps relevant to the post-war situation, in a way which it was difficult to foresee. He called for the Board of the bank to be constituted in such a way as to command the respect of the whole community 'even from the Labour Party'.

The foregoing long speech by JJ came immediately after the Minister Seán T Ó Ceallaigh had introduced the Bill for the Second Reading. The key issue was the central management of the sterling reserves as backing for the currency.

In the Committee Stage of this Bill in October 1942 JJ tried to raise again the question of agricultural credit, in the context of who should be on the Board of the Central Bank. Later in the final stages JJ came in briefly to remind the Minister of the need to build industry on the fruits of agricultural exports, as the USA and Denmark had done, and to be selective in what industries were built. Industry should be dibbled in rather than sown broadcast, and where the latter had been done, the weaker seedlings should be thinned. Post-war the same problem would exist all over Eastern Europe: how to make the transition from a primarily subsistence agricultural country to a system of commercial agriculture feeding healthy industry.

In November 1942 in the Censorship of Publications debate JJ intervened to suggest that much of the Bible, Shakespeare and Greek, Latin and Gaelic classics should be censored if the practice of the censors were to be applied consistently.

In January 1943 in the School Attendance Bill debate JJ moved an amendment, seconded by James Douglas, to defend the rights of Protestant parents for access to all relevant schools in Ireland, including the North. He further defended the rights of parents to sent children to school in England, on the grounds that '...some people only find their Gaelic soul when they are thoroughly immersed in the atmosphere of the English public-school system. Some of the most enthusiastic Gaels I know received their education in their formative years in English public schools...'. After placing on record the foregoing arguments he withdrew the amendment.

In the above argument I suspect that JJ had in mind Claude Chevasse, whom he had met in Oxford, and who had inaugurated a branch of the Gaelic League there, which JJ had joined.

This debate was taken up again some days later, and JJ instanced his own family experience, with access to Oxford and Edinburgh seen as a positive educational experience; he also urged the utility of having people from abroad educated here, on an exchange basis.

In the ensuing debate Professor Magennis (UCD) opposed the amendment strongly, identifying it as a demand of an ascendancy group for privilege. The debate had been opened up in the direction of this type of opposition by the intervention of Sir John Keane, from whose support JJ attempted unsuccessfully to decouple himself.

In his concluding speech JJ ended by deploring '...the fact that he had succeeded so little.' He had not been suggesting that there should be any escape from compulsory education; he had been urging a different machinery of enforcement. Nor was he advocating that a privileged section of the community be exempted. He withdrew the amendment.

The February 17 1943 debate on Artificial Fertilisers and Exports was another occasion in which JJ was able to rub the noses of the Government in the disastrous effects of the Economic War on national survival potential in the Emergency. The Minister was not present, reflecting perhaps his being somewhat tired of JJ's criticism. He reminded the House that the current shortage of artificial manures was not new; it had been originated as a self-inflicted wound in the 30s, under the doctrinaire self-sufficiency policy. He then re-iterated his argument about the role of stall-feeding of cattle as a source of farm-yard manure, and came up with figures from Rothamstead showing that the nitrogen content of FYM from cattle stall-fed for beef was higher than that from dairy cows.

The results of applications of basic slag only became realised over a 5-6 year period, and imports of this had dropped to zero during the economic war; we were reaping the fruits of this in the Emergency. He went on to argue that it would be in the British interest that they arrange to let us have some artificial manures now, in order for us not to have to increase further tillage and reduce grass, reducing their access to beef.

He urged also that the sugar produced from our sugar-beet harvest, of which he had in the end came round to showing some grudging approval, having grown some himself, should be officially shared with consumers in the North (a process which was going on unofficially via the smuggling process), and that flax should be grown to supply Northern industry, with these being used as arguments in discussions with the British Government.

Then on March 18 1943, on the Central Fund Bill, JJ used the opportunity constructively; *I would like to be able to scan in the whole of this speech, but the yellowing emergency-quality paper makes it difficult.*

He began with an account of his conversion to the cult of sugar-beet: the key factor had been the award of a stone of sugar for every ton of beet produced. He had fallen for this, and persuaded his neighbours in Drogheda to do likewise, on the grounds that it opened up the possibility of conserving the fruit harvest from their gardens in the form of jam.

I have fond memories of being a part of this production process, during the school vacation.

He had put down a half an acre of beet and got the sugar, and indeed the pulp for animal-feed. He went on to do the sums: half an acre on 400,000 farms would give us an export surplus which could be traded with the British for fertiliser.

He then went on to re-iterate his arguments in favour of the productive efficiency of larger farms employing labour, quoting extensively from an article which he had written recently in the *Irish Press*, in which he argued for investment in agriculture of £100M over the coming decade, leading the employment of one extra farm worker on each of the 50,000 farms currently employing paid labour.

He concluded by deploring the fact that the graduates of the agricultural colleges rarely actually went into farming, and urged that the then projected Agricultural Credit Corporation should take over the land of defaulting debtors, and make it available to a Development Corporation, which should let out the land '...on lease, with covenants ensuring the use of proper methods of husbandry, to persons of adequate agricultural knowledge and possessed of enough working capital, preferably persons who had graduated from one or other agricultural colleges...'. The latter is a quotation from his *Irish Press* article.

On May 13 1943 JJ supported a motion on increase of agricultural production, with a view to making available food in post-war Europe. He stressed the need to keep in existence an exportable in-calf heifer population to help build up the European breeding stock. As a lead-in to the discussion he harked back to the Ottawa agreement of 1932, which combined with the Harvey-Smoot Bill in the US, set the stage for the rise of Fascism in Europe, by their general disruption of international trade.

As a consequence of both the war and the epoch of pre-war protectionism, agricultural surpluses in Ireland in most areas had disappeared, except for cattle. To illustrate the European scene he read extracts from the *Central European Observer* (April 30 1943) '...the French people have already eaten all their turnips, they have finished off their crows and sparrows. In the north they eat acorns and tree bark. In Greece they chew at bushes. Shadows roam the streets of Athens. They used to be scientists and workers, artists and students. They are not conscripted for work because they have not enough strength to lift a spade. The dogs have disappeared -- they have all been devoured ...'.

He then addressed problem of agricultural prices in Britain, and how under present conditions these would actually discourage the build-up of the Irish livestock population, by encouraging the export of milch cows to the UK. He came around to the need to subsidise the production of butter for the home market, in order to compete with the demand for the export of milch cows to Britain, and keep open the option of exporting heifers to post-war Europe as breeding stock, rather than to Britain for beef.

On May 19 1943 on the Finance Bill JJ referred to the coming election, and empathised with the Minister, on the principle that politicians usually get punished by the electorate for their virtues. He supported Senator Douglas's call for greater dependence on individual and group efforts and less on the State, with a view to '...averting State omni-competence and an ever-increasing and ever more costly Civil Service.'

He went on to remark on the fact that despite the increase in tillage, there had been no overall increase in agricultural production, due to the restrictions on importing feedstuffs. He urged a consistent set of floor prices: we had the previous year had the collapse of the price of oats, and now that of potatoes. He contrasted Northern Ireland where there was a subsidy of £10 for every acre of potatoes, and £3 per acre for wheat or oats planted. With a well-structured set of consumer subsidies the cost of living in Britain had been kept down to 20% of the 1939 level, whereas ours was up 60%. He expressed concern about the additional inflationary effect of the increasing external assets, a consequence of the fact that we were exporting more than we imported. On balance however he felt himself able to congratulate the Minister on a sincere and honest Budget.

On July 14 1943 in the Central Fund debate JJ made his last speech before the election, impromptu, in response some Fianna Fail backbench rumblings, which stimulated him to re-iterate his arguments about the need to re-negotiate the 1938 agreement in favour of getting the right price for fat cattle. The consequences of the British differential price policy had influenced all aspects of agriculture, including tillage. The result was that we were exporting agricultural labour to Britain rather than produce, and exporting female cattle stock for breeding in Britain. The case should be made that it is in Britain's interest to do a deal.

Thus ended JJ's first term in the Seanad. He had, perhaps, made a name for himself as a persistent critic, and as an advocate of a point of view which was running against the tide. He had not acted primarily for TCD but for what he saw as the interests of the nation, with agriculture as its primary source of wealth, and intensive farming of large units, whether capitalist or co-operative, as the road to productivity per worker and per acre.

When de Valera called his mid-war election in 1943 my father was living in 'The Glen', a house near Drogheda which he had bought at the start of the war; there was a 20-acre farm attached, which he farmed, employing a man and keeping the books, as he had done over a decade earlier. This decoupled him somewhat from College politics, and he was not in such a good position to canvass and organise his support-group as he had been in 1938, though he had managed to add about 20 people to it. As a result he lost the seat, to TC Kingsmill Moore(16).

Although he had in his nominating group more people than he had had in 1938, mostly clergy, whose support he had perhaps picked up through his son-in-law Rev Dermot Carmody, and there were no notable defections from his 1938 panel, he still lost his seat. I suspect his acceptance of 'front-bench status' might have told against him. While De Valera, in offering him front-bench status, apparently appreciated his critical feedback, the apparent approval of de Valera would perhaps have counted against him with the TCD graduate electorate.

Post-Emergency Agricultural Policy

JJ's input to the Seanad during his second spell, from 1944, was somewhat marginalised by the fact that during the latter part of 1943, and most of 1944 and 1945, his main attention was on the Post-Emergency Agricultural Policy Committee, which produced a series of Reports(17). After losing his seat in the 1943 General Election he was recruited to participate in this Committee, along with TA Smiddy (who chaired), RC Barton, C Boyle, Professor JP Drew, Henry Kennedy (Chief Executive of the IAOS), J Mahony and EJ Sheehy. Both Professor Drew and JJ had served on the earlier Committee from 1922 to 1924.

The key input by JJ to this work is touched upon in the third section on Production of Store and Fat Cattle; it is quite short, and states the problem of British policy on fat-cattle subsidy, with its 3-month residence requirement, generating an artificially high demand for 'forward stores', but takes it as a necessary constraint. JJ's arguments about the need to negotiate this politically, to get parity with Northern Ireland, and build up stall-feeding with consequential tillage-enhancement, was not however taken on board. It was simply recommended that stores be de-horned for ease of transport. The idea of developing a trade in veal, on the continental pattern, was entertained.

The fourth and final section on Feeding of Cattle however homes in sharply on the key issue: winter feed supplies. No breeding programme will be any use unless the animals are fed adequately; and estimated extra 150 gallons of milk annually per cow was feasible with proper feeding alone. A radical change in grassland management was called for, with production of silage, supplemented by hay, roots, straw and green forage crops. This section contained what JJ had been campaigning for during the previous decade.

JJ Returns to the Seanad in 1944

When JJ returned to the Seanad in the 1944 election, he replaced Dr Rowlette, and served with TC Kingsmill Moore and Professor Fearon. At the same time for UCD Tierney was replaced by MJ Ryan.

In October and November 1944 JJ spoke on the Transport (no 2) Bill which involved the take-over of the Great Southern Railway (GSR) and the Dublin trams and buses to form Coras Iopair Eireann (CIE). JJ supported it, but not without critical comment on the way in which leakages had occurred in the spring of 1943 such as to enable speculators in the know to acquire GSR shares at rock-bottom price and make a killing. He introduced amendments which attempted to provide some compensation for GSR shareholders who had sold out at rock-bottom prices in 1943 to speculative buyers who had access to inside information regarding Government intentions.

He had no success, and in his concluding speech, which he made after the Bill was passed, he warned against a tendency under capitalism for a sort of economic cannibalism to emerge, in which new capital indulges at the expense of old: '...interests connected with the development of road transport have battened on the vitals of the capitalist interests connected with the railway company....now that the vitals of the of the old railway company have been attenuated almost into non-existence and we have.... nationalisation of transport.... I foresee the danger that the cannibal instincts of certain interests, instead of being directed against the helpless shareholders, will be directed against the helpless taxpayer. There will be a tendency to try to further the interests of certain highly organised concerns at the expense of the State and the community in general...'. In the course of the debate a called for some control over road hauliers by means of a licensing system.

Then on November 23 1944 we had the Land Bill which related to the work of the Land Commission in the redistribution of land, in the form of large farms or estates compulsorily purchased from owners who were usually identified with the ex-Ascendancy class. JJ had consistently made the case that large farms of this nature should be kept integral and worked productively, thereby employing more labour than could be supported on sub-divided subsistence units. In this debate he approached the question from the angle of elementary justice: "...is there any justice in confiscating the property of people in this generation because the property of certain other people ...300 years ago was confiscated...? It surely is not going to be seriously argued that the people whose social position it is sought to raise by such a policy are in that low social position because...their ancestors backed the wrong king in the 17th century.."

He went on to claim equal citizenship rights under the Treaty for all, whether "...people who were disparagingly called the old ascendancy class..." or not, and quoted Thomas Davis's verse "what matter that at different shrines we pray unto one God, what matter that at different time our fathers won this sod..". He then brought in the question of agricultural credit, and how it would be undermined by the threat of confiscatory pricing of land, and likened the process to the selective taxation imposed by Henry VII, under the name of 'benevolences'. The worst victims of the process were hitherto successful commercial intensive farmers, employing labour, who found their credit with the bank undermined by the perception that they had a Sword of Damocles hanging over them, in the form of the Land Commission.

He concluded by estimating that the capital required to make Irish agriculture productive was in the region of £100M over the next 10 years, but this would not get invested if the foundations of agricultural credit was undermined by rendering insecure the title to land of successful commercial farmers.

On December 6 1944 it seems that there was a debate which the Minister prevented from being reported in the press. JJ kept among his papers an *Irish Times* poster for Tuesday December 6 which I think must have been 1944, judging by the relationship between day and date. The poster, of the type used by news-stands, reads 'Senator Johnston on Irish Re-union'. It seems from the subsequent Seanad record that there was an altercation between JJ, Sir John Keane and Frank Aiken (see below). *There is unfinished business here.*

On February 22 1945 we had the Tuberculosis (Establishment of Sanitoria) Bill, which was a precursor of the later efforts of Dr Noel Browne. While being supportive of this Bill JJ held out for better housing, clothing and nutrition as being important preventive measures against the spread of tuberculosis.

From his then current work on the Post-Emergency Agriculture Committee JJ was well aware of the potential for the expansion of the national income by proper use of national resources.

Later on the same day, on the resumption of the Censorship of Parliamentary Debates motion debate JJ registered a protest about the December 6 suppression of press reporting. He distinguished himself from Sir John Keane, who had it seems declared himself a supporter of Cromwell, by declaring that he regarded Cromwell as 'the most successful leader of a Fascist Revolution in his own or any other European country'. He then went on to identify the Minister with the Cromwellian Orangemen of South Armagh, whose attitude a friend of his had encountered when canvassing in the 1918 election for Sinn Fein.

JJ here identified the historical process which has perverted progressive republican democratic reform movements into throwing up autocratic leaderships such as Cromwell, Napoleon, Hitler and Stalin. He was perhaps hinting implicitly at a similar process behind the rise of de Valera.

Coming now into 1945, on March 7 JJ welcomed the Electricity Supply Bill, with some degree of caution. It provided for the extension of the services of the Electricity Supply Board to rural areas, at some cost to the taxpayer. The Bill had been introduced by Seán Lemass, hitherto regarded by JJ as unsympathetic to agriculture, and JJ took the opportunity of reminding him of his past record, building the industrial house from the roof downwards, without taking care first of the agricultural foundations. He was therefore initially inclined to view Lemass's incursion into investing in agriculture with some suspicion.

He regarded the Bill as an isolated contribution to the problem of agricultural development; this however had many and complex aspects. The priorities for investment, as seen by the Committee of which he was a member, were the restoration of the deficiencies of lime and phosphates, technical education, and the provision of buildings. The provision of electrical supply would then follow as a development requirement.

The relatively high cost of rural electrification arose as a consequence of the culture of the isolated farmhouse. He urged however that where new housing was provided, for example farm labourers' cottages, that they be clustered, and near to existing villages. This would reduce the cost of supplying electricity(18). He concluded by remarking that the need to import copper and equipment would stimulate the need to expand agricultural exports.

From April 19 up to May 9 1945 the Mental Treatment Bill was debated. JJ began by drawing attention to the need for statistical analysis of the occurrence of mental illness in the population, before deciding whether it should be a local or central funding matter. He mentioned the possible impact of the low marriage rate in rural areas, and the possible correlation with high intelligence. He came up with the idea that there was a spiritual dimension, and urged that theological students receive training in psychology, with a view to their role as chaplains in mental hospitals. This led him to what he identified as a flaw in the Bill, the exclusion of hospital chaplains from superannuation rights.

The Minister came out with figures to suggest that the numbers of Protestant inmates was trivial, with the result the Protestant chaplaincies were somewhat nominal, and not deserving of pension rights. To which JJ replied '...I would like to assure the House that in proportion to our numbers we Protestants are just as mad as you are ...'. The Minister had produced figures '...carefully chosen to suggest that there was hardly any insanity at all among certain sects of Protestants ...'. and he went on to claim that he knew of at least one place where there were 40 Church of Ireland inmates. He conceded that the amount of salary and pension should have some relation to the workload. In the end his amendment was lost.

In the final stage of the Bill JJ made some comments on the Church and State question, and registered a protest about the question of Catholic access to Trinity College. This issue had arisen because in the third reading of the Bill JJ had picked up a perception that the question of Church and State, insofar as it concerned chaplaincies in mental hospitals, was regarded as not appropriate for the likes of him to be discussing. So in the final reading he 'trailed the coat' by mentioning the 'Catholics in TCD' issue. The Minister tried to block him, but the Chair allowed him to continue.

He then went on the put on record how when an undergraduate he had come across the writings of Thomas Davis, and urged that '...the conception of citizenship and nationality which Thomas Davis advocated in his day is one which we would do well to remember now...' and he managed to close, after being ruled out of order finally, with Davis's verse 'And oh! it were a gallant deed / To show before mankind / How every race and every creed / Might be by love combined ...'.

On July 19 1945 the Agricultural College Bill dealt with the gift to the State of Johnstown Castle, and JJ attempted to open up a general debate on agricultural education, but was ruled out of order. He managed to put on record the extraordinarily low level of participation in agricultural colleges by farmers' sons.

I suspect that JJ would have homed in on the question of control of such colleges by religious orders, if he had got the chance. Incidentally Johnstown Castle, near Wexford, subsequently became the Soil Science focus of the Department of Agriculture and then later of the Agricultural Institute; this process was the launch-pad for the career of Dr Tom Walsh who headed the Institute.

The July 25 1945 debate on the Appropriation Bill was memorable: the war was over, and JJ was having fun; his main work had been in the Post-Emergency Agriculture Committee and during this period he was inclined to treat the Seanad with levity. He began with some basic Irish which he had picked up from the radio lessons of Aindrias Ó Muineacháin, and then when pulled up by the Chair, got down to the guts of the matter: the recent war and Partition. He hung his argument, somewhat tenuously, on the new Minister for Finance's earlier role as Minister for Foreign Affairs, in which he had managed successfully to steer a course which amounted to moral neutrality in a conflict which the Pope had since declared to have been with Satan. He had high hopes of someone as skilled being in charge of Finance.

He then expounded the 'blessings' of Partition, which not only had kept us out of the war, but had kept the Seanad free from '...at least a dozen or a score unpleasant Ulstermen like myself in this House... the atmosphere ...instead of being the pleasant little family party that it is would approximate more ...to that of a frontier district in Belfast...'. He went on to remind the House that Partition derived from '...the successful appeal to force made by the Ulster Protestants in the years from 1912 to 1914... (which)... produced the Sinn Fein movement...' and indeed the Minister and many others who came into public life.

Despite heckling from Senators who accused him of 'reading his speech', he went on to put on record that the British seaplane base on Lough Erne, flying out over Donegal, had helped win the war, and that no anti-aircraft guns had defended our neutrality in that situation.

Having made his point about the collusive nature of our neutrality in the war, he then switched to the question of the sterling balances, which had accumulated over the previous 5 years, due to our inability to import enough to match our exports. He expressed support for this, as representing Government policy of supporting the British war effort in effect with a long-term loan. He urged that we should now say to Britain 'we were glad to do that much for you in your time of need ...'.

This triggered another round of heckling; Quirke again accused him again of reading his speech; the Chair however insisted he was consulting his notes, and

Kingsmill Moore confirmed this. JJ went on to the effect that we had nothing to be ashamed of in our war record; we had in fact helped Britain to win it. We were now well placed to engage in post-emergency reconstruction; the farmers had money in their pockets, and would be better placed to be a market for any industrial development, which would be on a sounder foundation than in the 30s. He urged that the relatively high level of agricultural wages should continue, giving a better balance between rural and urban incomes.

Later in the debate, the Minister accused JJ of being the 'spiritual father' of the students who had burned the national flag on the roof of Trinity College on VE day. In the 5th stage of the debate, against further heckling, JJ managed to put on record his absolute dissociation from the flag-burning incident, which he said '...was an act of either very disloyal citizenship or of a person or persons who were enemies of this State.'

He went on to state that the Provost had apologised and that the Taoiseach had accepted the apology, and this was then confirmed to the Seanad by the Minister present, Frank Aiken. JJ's final remark was to the effect that de Valera had been a student in TCD and he could then claim to be the spiritual father of de Valera.

In the course of this wide-ranging debate the Minister, Frank Aiken, attacked James Douglas for being 'pro-Blueshirt'. On the whole, the debate was somewhat heated, even rancorous.

James Douglas, the Quaker businessman, had been close to JJ ever since together they had lobbied the Convention in 1917. The 'Blueshirt' jibe from the Fianna Fail benches confirms the need for a revaluation of that movement. JJ had also been close to Dermot MacManus, identified by Maurice Manning as part of the Blueshirt intellectual support system. JJ had consistently supported commercial farming against land-division into subsistence units. Contemporary historical analysis tends to treat the Blueshirt movement as primarily grassroots support for this principle by existing commercial farmers(19), and to decouple it from the European 'shirt' movements.

The ending of the 'emergency' is a natural break-point for this 1940s chapter. In the second part I deal with my own transition from school to College, with the development of the student Left; I then continue with JJ in the Seanad, in College politics and in outreach, and return finally to our somewhat sterile attempts to develop a Marxist left nationally.

Notes and References

1. JJ continued on the Council of the SSISI and in 1950 became its President. For an overview of JJ's contribution to the Society see Appendix 6.

2. I have found reports of JJ's 1946 Tuam lecture from the local papers, and his 1947 Athlone lecture from the *Irish Times* via the Seanad record, where he referenced it. See the 1940s Barrington module of the hypertext. It has subsequently emerged that the then US Ambassador had even then got both my father and myself labelled as Marxist. At this time I had no idea of my father's earlier interests, or their significance, and I had him mentally labelled as a bourgeois economist of the Establishment. It is only many years later that I realised how much non-Establishment he was, and how close his thinking was to the creative strand of Irish Marxism, as embodied in Connolly; in fact he had commended Connolly's writings to Garnier, the Albert Kahn Foundation secretary, in the early 1920s.

3. *Irish Agriculture in Transition*, Hodges Figgis (Dublin) and Basil Blackwell (Oxford), 1951; I have made available significant extracts from this in the hypertext.

4. I abstract, as the backbone of this chapter, the highlights of JJ's 1940s Seanad performance. For the overview of JJ's public service and Seanad work see Appendix 8.

5. I am indebted to Maurice Laheen the Tuam local historian, and to John Cunningham, who wrote a chapter on RM Burke's life and times for John A Claffey's *Glimpses of Tuam since the Famine* (Tuam 1997; ISBN_0_9530250_0_4), for additional background to my brief encounter.

6. JJ's interaction with the 1940s TCD Board is treated in the hypertext module, and an overview of his role in College politics is given in Appendix 2.

7. JJ's 1940s academic output is reviewed in the hypertext, his main interest increasingly being the economic writings of Berkeley. He became a member of the Royal Irish Academy in 1943. His overall academic output is reviewed in Appendix 5.

8. The Albert Kahn contact remained at the personal level through Charles Garnier, but by this time its significance had declined.

9. The Irish Association records, in the Northern Ireland Public Record Office, for the period of JJ's Presidency from 1946 to 1954 are extremely sparse, though quite detailed in other respects; it almost looks as if a conscious effort had been made to expunge them, by some hard-core Unionist agent who had never forgiven him for his *Civil War in Ulster*. I have however done what I could in the hypertext which is overviewed see Appendix 9. He did develop a good relationship with Irene Calvert and Sir Graham Larmour.

10. I have recorded this in the 1940s family thread of the hypertext, the overview being in Appendix 1.

11. An abstract of a document, written by Adare in 1841, outlining this founders' vision for St Columba's College, turned up in a file of JJ's papers relating to the present writer. It is accessible also via the 1940s family stream in the hypertext. Standish O'Grady later took up this vision, belatedly. Aspects of it are echoed faintly in the thinking of AE, Horace Plunkett, Constance Markiewicz, Claude Chevasse, and, later in an attenuated and reoriented form in my own generation, of Paddy Bond and Neill Goold. For more detail about the Promethean Society and its origins in St Columba's College, see the 1940s political module of the hypertext.

12. I have expanded on this in my contribution to *JD Bernal: a Life in Science and Politics*, edited by Brenda Swann and Francis Aprahamian (Verso, London, 1999), and also treated it in the hypertext in the 'science and society' thread, overviewed in Appendix 11.

13. I have reproduced this January 15 1942 speech by JJ in full in the hypertext, as it summarises well JJ's views on the handling of the emergency by Fianna Fail.

14. I have abstracted this paper in the 1940s SSISI module; the reference is JSSISI xvi, 44, 1941-2.

15. JJ had recently published his 'Bishop Berkeley and Kindred Monetary Thinkers' *Hermathena* LIX p30, 1942. In this paper JJ '...detect(ed) in Berkeley's monetary philosophy certain elements which occur(red) also in Aristotle, and in the writings of the French economist Boisguilbert ...' and went on to link these with the economic ideas of Aristotle and Adam Smith, relating them to the then current ideas as expressed by Keynes in the General Theory. This paper is full of quotable bits, like '...the practical navigator would pay little attention to a science of navigation based on the long-run tendency of the sea to present a flat surface...'. I have abstracted the paper in the supporting hypertext.

16. JJ's election address is available, and I reproduce extracts from it in Appendix 8, as it summarises his then political position.

17. There were three Reports, bound as a single volume, I think subsequently, perhaps by JJ himself. The Stationary Office reference numbers are 6624, 6895 and 7175. I have abstracted these in the hypertext.

18. This argument relates to JJ's support for the <u>Orpen model</u> of rural development, as outlined in *Irish Agriculture in Transition*, and in his *rural civilisation* <u>SSISI paper</u> (JSSISI xviii, 1, 1947-8).

19. There are references to Dermot MacManus in Maurice Manning's *The Blueshirts*, Gill & Macmillan (1971, 1987), and in Mike Cronin's *Blueshirts and Irish Politics*, Four Courts Press (1997). I have expanded on this in the <u>1930s political module</u> of the background hypertext.

Chapter 5 Part 2: The Period 1946-1950

Introduction

In this second part of the 1940s chapter I begin with an outline of the aspirations and experience of the student Left, and then go on to treat JJ's TCD, Seanad and outreach worlds, with us, as the student Left, lurking in the undergrowth of the first and groping our way into the third of JJ's domains; we were largely unaware of the second. I identify a few contact-points. I then return to an assessment of the role of the embryonic Left which emerged nationally, to which we as student Left contributed. There was a serious gap between the European Marxist vision which we espoused and the intellectual requirements of Irish radical political practice as it then was. Into this vacuum flowed the resurgent IRA of the subsequent decade.

In 1950 the Korean War broke out, and the cold war situation became impossible. The student Left became increasingly isolated, and the student Representative Council was taken over by destructive elements who abandoned it, so that student democracy in effect ceased to exist for the following decade. JJ retained a critical view of the US version of events; I recollect his publishing a letter, perhaps to the *Irish Times*, in which, with a quote from a credible US-based source, he suggested an alternative analysis of the situation. *This helped no doubt to confirm the CIA's impressions about the Johnston family. I have alas been unable to track this down.*

RJ and the school-college transition

In the late 1940s our school group evolved into the TCD student Left, via the Promethean Society (PS). The objective was to re-introduce Marxist thinking into the Labour movement in Ireland. Of the people who were associated with the PS, few remained on in Ireland; the only ones to make it to any degree of public prominence were Justin Keating, who became a Minister in the 1970s coalition government led by Liam Cosgrave, and myself. Paul O'Higgins made his career in Cambridge as an academic lawyer.

In my final year in St Columba's College, the Promethean group had been missing Paul O'Higgins, who had been expelled the previous summer, under circumstances which seemed to us to be discriminatory. (It was a matter of going down town at night; there were others involved, but Paul was singled out.) We kept in touch with him, calling to his parents' flat in 104 Lr Baggot St if ever we were in town. When he entered TCD to do medicine in October 1945 my father, at my suggestion, allowed him to lodge in his rooms in #36. We took up a collection for him among his friends in school, and he bought books with the money, each of which he labelled 'munus columbanensis'. Various meetings were organised, addressed by John de Courcy Ireland, RN Tweedy, Owen Sheehy-Skeffington, Arnold Marsh and others. We used Deirdre MacDonagh's bookshop in Baggot St for Promethean meetings pre-TCD. We encountered Paul Keating and the TCD Fabians. We picked up contact with a floating population of disaffected critical intellectuals, such as John Jordan, Anthony Cronin, Arthur Reynolds, Rex Cathcart and others whom we identified as the raw material of an emergent Left.

Our early attempts to contact the remains of the old Left via New Books, the Pearse St bookshop run by Seán (Johnny) Nolan, and via Bill McCullough in the CPNI in Belfast, were not fruitful; they preferred to keep a low profile, and were somewhat suspicious of intellectuals. We did however support the Irish Review, the monthly paper edited by Seán Nolan and sold around the pubs by the handful of residual ex-Communist Party stalwarts. We contributed our first political writings to it, such as they were. I remember being told by Johnny Nolan, having submitted a manuscript, that 'the material had been treated editorially', which I suppose was a relatively civil put-down.

When I entered TCD in October 1946, and took up lodgings in JJ's rooms along with Paul O'Higgins, an ongoing role for the Promethean Society(1) took shape. It was defined as a Marxist 'think-tank', for sharpening up the ideas necessary for transforming the political situation. These we would promote in wider circles, and try to get people to agree with them, towards the achievement of various realisable democratic objectives, thus helping people to understand the essentials of the political process. Viewed in retrospect, our aspiration was similar to that of the young Marx, and a long way from the centralising Stalinist pathology which had gripped the international movement under the influence of the USSR. Our first step into the circle of wider politics was the Dublin University Fabian Society, but we also set our sights higher; we wanted to get broad-based student representative politics set up officially, by reforming the Student Representative Council.

We recruited to the Promethean Society mostly mature students with a British CP background; we attempted to develop a broad-based student politics based on principle. In this context we encountered C Desmond Greaves (CDG) who had earlier been in touch with de Courcy Ireland and the TCD Fabian Society; he was researching Irish left-wing politics on behalf of the international affairs committee of the Communist Party of Great Britain (CPGB), where he was emerging as the expert on the Irish situation. Greaves' role(2) in our political education was significant, though he did I think place too much reliance on a process of inducting us into the Marxist experience of the CPGB. We tended to accept this uncritically, although in retrospect it was mostly a valid transfer of relevant experience, not unduly dominated by the USSR; I am thinking of the historical analyses done by people like Eric Hobsbawm, Christopher Hill and TA Jackson to which we were exposed.

In some respects this CPGB contact, and implied USSR orientation, was however a negative factor, in that it soured our relationship with Owen Sheehy-Skeffington(3), and focused too much attention on what was going on in Eastern Europe. Justin Keating, who had joined us from UCD, and the present writer, however bucked this trend, and we tended to seek our contacts in Ireland, among the politicising ex-republicans who had been interned in the Curragh during the war.

Our political impact as the post-war 'student Left' led to the reconstitution of the Students Representative Council (SRC), and an attempt to revive the Irish Students Association(4), forerunner of Union of Students in Ireland. Our Marxism, which was based on Connolly, was rooted in bottom-up democracy. The role of the Promethean Society was as a sort of think-tank to study the situation and come up with a solution to a perceived problem, which the membership of the democratic movement would be likely to accept when it was put to them. This in retrospect was

Marx's own approach to the 'leading role of the Party' rather than that which evolved in the USSR under Lenin and Stalin, though at the time we did not identify the extent to which the USSR Party had been degraded by Stalin's influence. This was the primary bone of contention between ourselves and OS-S.

The relationship between the Promethean Society, Fabian Society and Student Representative Council during the late 1940s is an example of how the development of the Marxist left, the broad left and the democratic movement was constrained and soured by the Stalinist influence on the Marxist left. We as the aspirant Marxist left understood the potentially positive role of broad-based student democracy, and we campaigned for a new constitution for the Student Representative Council. The old one had been dominated by the major College societies; we managed however to get direct elections in which all students could participate. In this context there emerged a leading group based on a loose alliance between the socialist elements and the Student Christian Movement. We set up useful services, like a book mart and a mass radiography against TB (then endemic).

In this forum however issues arose regarding international affiliations. A conservative group wanted to affiliate to the NUS in Britain, while we of the Left had set our sights on the International Union of Students (IUS) which had been set up post-war, had UN recognition, and could have been a source of travel opportunities. But the 'cold war' had begun, and the IUS was a battleground; the attitude to it split the Left. Then came the Korean War, in the summer of 1950, and in the subsequent SRC elections there was a right-wing landslide, electing a no-good do-nothing committee which in effect killed the SRC; it subsequently sank without trace, only re-emerging in the 1960s.

These cold-war issues also divided the Fabian Society(5); we attempted to get support for various peace initiatives in Western Europe which were attacked as 'Stalinist propaganda', and fell foul of OS-S, who had been Chairman of the Fabian Society; we voted him out. Had it not been for the heavy-handed role of the USSR and the 'international movement', in continually being seen to 'bring the Western European Marxist into line', a constructive relationship could have developed between independent-minded liberal socialists like OS-S and the rising generation of Irish Marxists who looked to build on Connolly. Such a relationship developed earlier between JJ and the Thomas Davis Society in the 1919-21 period, via Dermot MacManus(6). It also existed between RM Gwynn (in whose rooms in 1913 the Citizen Army was founded) and the Fabian Society founders in the 1930s, who included OS-S; they had the clout and understanding to be able to pull in people like Robert Lynd to be the honorary President. In our generation however the influence of the 'international movement' must in retrospect be assessed as having been largely destructive.

We made contact with the emerging Dublin-based working-class Left, which at that time was being reinforced with people who had been interned in the Curragh, and had become, after a fashion, politicised towards the left there. There was a sort of division of perspective within the PS, with Paul O'Higgins and others looking towards Eastern Europe, where the illusion was being rather effectively presented that the vision of the Left was in process of becoming reality, and on the other hand myself and Justin Keating (who was the only PS contact in UCD) looking towards Dublin and Ireland.

I remember increasingly finding it necessary to consider the science aspect as well as the political aspect; in JJ's case his politics and his career were intertwined in the natural course of things; in my case it became necessary to make the link between the science and the politics creatively, and the catalyst was JD Bernal's writings(7). There was also the question of nuclear weapons, and the peace movement, with which Bernal was associated. The relationship between the Western Left and the USSR was dominated by the need for the latter to use the former to slow down the arms race while they caught up with nuclear arms. In the atmosphere of cold-war politics the Stockholm Appeal caught the imagination of the visionaries of the Western Left. We supported it as best we could, in a hostile atmosphere.

JJ in the Seanad

Although elected by the Dublin University constituency, JJ seldom actually 'represented' it; he used it as a platform for comment as a development economist on national affairs. I have therefore treated this as a single section covering the period 1946 to 1948, and have refrained from interspersing his 'college politics' episodes, which I have collected in a subsequent section. His outreach work with the Irish Association, and the research for his 'Irish Agriculture in Transition' was subsequent to his Seanad period. I have occasionally interspersed retrospective comment in italics.

On February 28 1946, debating the Rent Restrictions Bill 1944 (final stages) JJ likened the workings of the Act of 30 years previous to the workings of the Land Acts, in that the tenant was in effect awarded a share of the value of the house as the market appreciated. It became no longer advantageous for a landlord to let a house; it was better to sell it. He illustrated from his own experience of a tenancy in a house in Ranelagh between 1918 and 1921.

He went on to urge the development of housing associations, along the lines of Associated Properties ltd, which currently had some 1000 or so houses for rent in Dublin, at rents which were reasonable, and were not under threat from the Act. Such an enterprise could raise capital by mortgaging its property at rate of interest more favourable than an individual could obtain, and then use the capital so raised to build more houses for rent.

In March 1946 the Harbours Bill was debated; the question arose of what interests were to be represented on the Board. JJ urged that the livestock exporters be represented; he made the case that if the Federation of Irish Manufacturers had a place, despite their then minimal interest in exports, the livestock trade should a fortiori have one.

On March 21 1946 on the Central Fund Bill JJ attempted an analysis of post-war inflation. It was not due to increased wages or salaries, or to expanded bank credit. It was due to our exporting more than we imported. The people who got paid for their exports regarded the revenue as income. The existence of the quota system of import control limited what this income could be spent on. Prices in Britain were some 35% above the 1939 level, while in Ireland they were 70%.

He went on to urge the development of procedures for converting the banks' deposits held abroad into capital goods for the development of both industry and agriculture (reiterating his 1934 arguments). He welcomed the Beveridge Report *Full Employment in a Free Society*, though warned against its uncritical application in the Irish context. He mentioned Arnold Marsh's *Full Employment in Ireland(8).*, which however he regarded as containing serious defects in analysis. He urged putting full employment on the agenda, but declared himself unable to come up with any comprehensive policy, though he was aware of many ways in which public expenditure could be used in the promotion of enterprise. He urged the Minister to call a conference of those in a position to make a useful contribution.

In April 3 1946 there was a Proposed New Ministries motion proposed by Sir John Keane, to enable the Seanad to have a critical look at the Departments of Health and Local Government. It was formally seconded by James Douglas, and then JJ came in immediately, developing arguments about the relationship between central and local government, and calling for a White Paper for discussion in depth, cross-party, before the Government legislated.

JJ argued against over-centralised control of local government, as being inimical to local public spirit and initiative. He questioned the county system, as set up 300 years earlier; the units were both too large and too small, nor do they coincide with any natural social or economic regions. He called for groupings of counties to match the scale of the older divisions such as Ossory or Oriel. The authorities of such regions should be able to relate to the government as a whole, rather than with one department dedicated to Local Government.

The present writer has since developed these arguments; they have made a contribution to the policies of the Green Party(9).

Then on April 10 1946 on the Forestry Bill 1945 JJ objected to putting an artificial limit on the price of land to be purchased for forestry, mentioning the impossibility of accurately foretelling the value of timber in 30 or 40 years time, but expressing the view that given world trends the value of forest products was likely to be upwards. He was critical of the low target of 10,000 acres annually set by the Minister, and the low overall target of 6-700,000 acres. He urged increasing the planting rate by a factor of 10, and making use of the available winter labour surplus.

He went on to urge the development of deals with individual farmers for planting on private land, with the option of either the farmer or the State to own the resulting timber harvest when the time came. (Later, on May 8 in the Committee stage, the Minister Moylan 'did not think well of it' but did not elaborate.) JJ finished by urging the planting of a proportion of broadleaf rather than total concentration on conifers, and remarked that we would have got through the Emergency more easily if we had had this policy 20 years earlier.

This has in the end become the policy of Coillte, the State agency concerned.

On April 11 1946 in the debate on the Turf Development Bill it emerged that the target production figure was 1M tons annually, and the amount of coal imports when imports were unconstrained was 2.5M tons of coal. JJ questioned the suggested equivalence between a ton of coal and 2 tons of turf, suggesting that for the type of turf they had been getting in Dublin it was more like 4 tons. The quality of turf delivered to the towns in the emergency filled him with loathing, as compared to 'country turf', for which he had nothing but admiration.

The cause of this was the imposition of regulations insisting on sale in towns by weight, which motivated merchants to cut the necessary drying stage short. Turf in the country was sold by the 'load', the volume that could be taken in a standard horse-drawn cart. I am surprised JJ was not on to this.

He went on to adduce continental experience, from Germany, Russia and Sweden, listing the various organic polymer products which could be extracted from turf as by-products of the carbonisation process, and urged that this should be the objective of scientific research based on the turf industry.

On May 1 1946 Land Bill 1945 was discussed; the purpose of this Bill was to set up procedures for getting rid of people who had been allotted land but were not working it. It was proposed to insist that someone allotted land should live in the house provided. JJ proposed an amendment which would re-direct the pressure along economic lines, adjusting the annuity. The value in capital terms to the allottee of the land, in adjusted annuity subsidised by the State, was of the order of £1000.

It is worth remarking that this allocation of land individually to landless people in rural areas was the way in which Fianna Fail in the 1930s purchased votes using public money, generating the pathological political culture in which subsequently corruption has flourished.

The effect of JJ's amendment would be that non-farming allottees of land who had decided to sell up should not be able to cash in on the State bounty in giving them land. He went on '...another objectionable feature is that some of these tenants get this land, pay the nominal annuity and let the land on the 11 month system, becoming in fact a kind of 18th century landlord on a small scale and profiting on the land to the amount of the difference between the annuity they pay and what they get from the lettings on the 11-month system. The margin ... is very wide indeed...£5 or £6 an acre ...'.

On July 9 1946 on the Appropriations Bill JJ argued for special salary arrangements for high-grade specialist Civil Servants, using the arguments of a Report which had been prepared by Professor Duncan of TCD, assisted by Louden Ryan. 'If we want the best brains in the Civil Service or elsewhere we shall have to pay for them'. He then went on to propose a model for a public-private hybrid enterprise, based on the experience of the War Agricultural Executive Committees in England, which owned and managed machinery pools in support of farmers' needs. Such co-operative machinery contactors here could usefully supply the needs of drainage and land reclamation, using heavy machinery.

On July 24 1946 on the Industrial Research and Standards Bill JJ warned against a blinkered sub-division of research into industrial and agricultural categories, and urged that if and when agricultural research were to come on the agenda, the interface between whatever agency were to emerge and the IIRS should be dynamic.

This warning was unheeded; the Agricultural Research Institute did not come into existence until over a decade later, and when it did, the gulf between it and the IIRS was considerable. I had occasion to comment on this in my Irish Times column in the 1970s.

On November 13 1946 in the Seanad the Economic Price for Fat Cattle Bill gave JJ an opportunity to develop definitively his arguments around what he regarded as the central issue in Anglo-Irish relations, taking up 6 pages of the Seanad report doing it, from his standpoint of having serviced the Committee on Post-Emergency Agricultural Policy. He began by suggesting that in their negotiations with the British they had not been aggressive enough in seeking a consistent price on the British market whatever the origin of the animal.

Stall-feeding of cattle in winter for beef had been killed for the previous 14 years by the British differential price, which favoured the export from Ireland of 'forward store' cattle for finishing in Britain. This had restricted the supply of manure, and this had reflected itself into the declining yields of wheat, oats and barley. Total cattle had remained constant, but output had declined, because cattle inadequately fed in winter take longer to mature.

He then went on at length to the effects of the British taxpayer subsidising British food producers on the prices available to Irish producers. He read into the Seanad record an extensive paper which he had tried and failed to get accepted in the Report. The conclusion of his analysis was '...We are strongly of the opinion that equal prices for equal qualities of produce, sold in the UK, is the policy which would best facilitate agricultural production in, and export from, our country. We recommend that a joint conference be held to see if the problem can be solved in a manner that will be compatible with the national interests of both countries.'

Turning then to the dead meat trade, he made use of correspondence with a British meat trade expert, Thomas Shaw, who had recently contributed an article to *Studies*(10) on the importance of the dead meat trade to Ireland. He hoped, by promoting a public understanding of the situation, using the expertise of Mr Shaw and his interactions with the Minister in a public meeting scheduled for the TCD Commerce Society on December 3, to develop political pressure for a top-level approach by the Government to John Strachey, the then British Minister for Food.

The 'win-win' situation JJ had in mind was that if the Irish were allowed to upgrade their beef production by finishing cattle in Ireland and exporting as meat, the British would get more of what was still a rationed commodity, and the Irish agricultural production system would be transformed by improved winter feeding practice. He had been making this case again and again during the 'emergency', with first-hand comparative knowledge of agricultural practice North and South. He wanted the UK agricultural environment extended to include the whole of Ireland, to the benefit of both Ireland and Britain.

On December 12 1946 the Industrial Alcohol (Amendment) Bill 1946, second stage was debated; JJ supported industrial scientific research, and approved of the idea of having a pilot plant to explore the feasibility of chemical production processes, this being provided for in the Bill. He then went on to compare Denmark industrially, remarking that Danish industrial strength was a result of having put their agricultural development first. In contrast the Irish industrial experience had been parasitic on agriculture, with the value of the latter being reduced. He then went on to measure things by the consumption of phosphates, with seven lean years 1932-39, followed by seven absolute starvation years of the war, leading to an overall phosphate deficiency of 2M tons. He was critical of dependence on nitrogen in the form of ammonium sulphate, and urged greater dependence on clover, and on proper management of the farmyard manure-heap.

The contemporary Green movement could credibly claim JJ among its progenitors, if we add this clover preference to his support for clustered interdependent rural housing, and reconstructed local and regional government.

Continuing the above debate on January 15 1947 JJ introduced an amendment urging that the Minister should '...issue a licence for the import free of duty of any chemical product which is used as an agricultural raw material in all cases where the corresponding product of domestic manufacture is available only at a higher price.'

The key issue here is that '...all our industrial development is directly or indirectly based on agricultural productive and export capacity'. JJ then went back into the history of the economic war, rubbing the Minister's nose in it along the lines '...that it was necessary to throw Kathleen Ni Houlihan into the water in order that the Minister should effect a heroic rescue', along the lines of a PG Wodehouse story.

Industrial development in the 30s had been done at the expense of the profits made by Irish farmers during the first world war. He urged prioritising such industrial development as was agriculture-based, or serviced agricultural needs (as indeed did cement, which was based largely on native raw materials). The cement industry was kept going during the war with prioritised supplies of coal, and much of the produce went to Northern Ireland, an act of benevolent neutrality. The electrical industry was well-founded, but there were some industries which were not well founded, in that they simply added to the costs of other industries. Any increase in agriculture costs decreases productive and export capacity. JJ did not want this Bill to provide a cover for building a fertiliser factory of which the products would be more expensive than imported products, and this was the thrust of his amendment.

The above amendment being defeated, JJ tried again on January 22, along the lines that the Minister '...shall have regard to the desirability of making available at all times the chemical raw materials of agricultural and industrial production at prices which compare favourably with the prices at which similar chemical material could be imported.'

JJ had taken on board criticism of his earlier amendment. In support of his revised amendment he adduced comparisons with Britain during the war, where agricultural production had increased by 50%, while ours had declined. He was aware of the availability of native gypsum but wondered where the nitrogenous component would come from. Would it be techno-economically possible to produce ammonium sulphate at a price to compete with imports?

On January 22 1947 JJ had another bite at the Land Bill 1946, second stage. The problem as then perceived was the inflated price of land consequent on the influx of foreign buyers, mostly wealthy refugees from British Labour Government policies. JJ used the debate to reiterate his arguments for expanded commercial agriculture. The State should intervene to buy land when the price was low, and should lease land to 'persons having agricultural knowledge who would farm them as tenants of the State'. He urged an increase in the number of farms employing labour, and an increase in the number of farm workers, and an increase in their wages, in an expanded commercial agricultural sector, with expanded facilities for agricultural credit.

JJ must by now have been tired of the need to reiterate these arguments, and of being not listened to; Fianna Fail backbenchers, dependent on masses of bought 30-acre votes, must have found this reiteration uncomfortable and boring.

On February 26 1947 the Dublin Institute of Advanced Studies (DIAS) was debated. There was a lot of criticism of the Institute, on the basis that it should have been attached to the Universities. JJ came to its defence, on the basis that there existed some areas of research which did not easily combine with a teaching load, and that TCD experience of co-operation with DIAS was positive, especially as it provided a common meeting-ground for people from the two Universities.

JJ then went in some detail into the history of Dunsink Observatory, and the contributions to science of Brinkley, Hamilton and their successors, up to the time of Plummer, who had left TCD in 1921, after which they had the observatory but no Astronomer Royal, and TCD had been somewhat embarrassed by Dunsink, as increasingly a white elephant. They could have sold it at a high price, for greyhound racing or whatever, but the College had hung on to it, in the hopes that something would turn up. In the end it did, and TCD were happy to do a deal with the DIAS in the confidence that the asset would remain of scientific value in the new context.

On March 12 1947 the Agricultural Credit Bill 1946 (second stage)was debated; putting into effect one of the minor recommendations of the Committee on Post-Emergency Agriculture, in which JJ had participated. The Agricultural Credit Corporation was to be set up, thus distinguishing the special needs of farmers from the market normally served by the banks.

JJ began by referencing Doreen Warriner's *Economics of Peasant Farming* in which the number of families fed by a family farm is estimated for various countries, being 1.5 in Poland and India, three in Germany, five in the USA and eight in Britain. In Ireland we come between India and Germany, at about 2 to 2.5, with half of the 1.5 non-farm families fed by the farm being in Ireland and the other half in Britain.

Alternatively, for every 125 units of food we produce, we consume 100; our exports are only 25% of our total output. Thus a 20% increase in production would enable exports to be doubled. The real comparison to be made is between the best farmers and the worst, with a view to bringing all up to the level of the best. In this context he leaned on his recent SSISI paper on capitalisation of Irish agriculture(11). The essence of the argument was that the output per worker on a well-managed large farm was substantially greater than that on an equivalent area of 30-acre farms run by the same number of people.

He went on to call for a farm survey, and to draw on the experience of the British War Agricultural Executive Committees, which had led to the development of co-operative ownership of machinery centres(12). The credit-worthiness of an application for a loan should be a matter for such a committee, rather than the opinion of a Civic Guard. In general the ACC should deal primarily with large farms or with co-operative societies, relying on mortgage or collective security(13).

On March 13 1947 JJ spoke on the Butter Production and Milk Prices motion, developing further his arguments in the post-Emergency Agriculture Committee, going on to urge the 800-gallon cow and the scientific use of grass in all its forms.

The argument continued over the need to re-establish a free market in butter, and to bring this under some sort of organised control by the dairy industry as a whole. JJ referred to the existence of a civil servant Butter Marketing Committee, and urges that this function be taken over by the industry, thus foreshadowing what later became Bord Bainne.

Then on April 16 1947, debating State Intervention in Public Enterprise: JJ referenced an article of his which had appeared in the day's *Irish Times*, on the same question(14).

This was based on a report of an Athlone Barrington lecture, under the auspices of the Vocational Education Committee. In this wide-ranging and radical paper JJ laid down criteria for recognising situations in which the public good would best be served by public enterprise, instancing utilities, education and scientific research. He drew on the experience of the Tennessee Valley Authority regarding demonstration farms, run on a scientific basis, with good record-keeping accessible to their neighbours.

He welcomed the rural electrification programme of the ESB as a factor in the future development of farm productivity, but again urged the need for co-operative pooling of investment in machinery, along the lines seen in Britain under the influence of the War Agricultural Executive Committees.

His most radical proposal was the taking over of derelict farms by the local authority, and their leasing to worker co-operatives, or to existing farmer co-operatives, to be run under the direction of people properly trained in agricultural best practice. He pointed out that the local authorities had the power to do this, under Section 99 of the Local Government Act 1946, conventionally considered as being related to housing needs, but extensible by implication towards a process of agri-village development.

This is relevant to the needs of the contemporary 'eco-village' movement, which is seeking to develop a positive approach to rural resettlement economics. It was a good practical proposal which could credibly have been taken up by the nascent Left, had we been aware of it.

JJ went on to commend the ESB as being a model State enterprise, and urged the need for development of State enterprise where there was a natural monopoly situation, like public transport. He expressed concern however about a variety of hybrid organisations where State and private interests were '...mixed up in the most extraordinary way...' He instanced the Sea Fisheries Association and the Roscrea meat factory. He warned of the danger of State investments ending up in private hands, in a way '...which escapes the knowledge of the public and completely escapes parliamentary control ...'.

He urged that enabling Acts should set up constitutions for such hybrid activities, with rules of the game, distinguishing subsidies from 'loans', capital from income. In this context he instanced the Dairy Disposal Company, as a long-term embodiment of what was originally defined as a transitional situation.

We have here an early warning of the situation which has led in recent times to the series of Tribunals exposing corruption in high places.

On May 21 1947 the Slaughter of Calves (motion) was debated; this related to what was the beginnings of the switch in the dairy areas from the Shorthorn dual-purpose animal, whose male calves were bought by the dry-stock farmers for beef, to Frisian, whose male calves were not worth feeding. JJ urged that detailed attention be given to the implications of this 'completely new factor in our whole agricultural economy'. It would be necessary to encourage the dry-stock farmers to go into rearing their own calves, and thereby produce better beef in a shorter time than under the traditional procedures.

Then on June 17 1947 the Finance Bill (second stage) presented an opportunity for JJ to thank the Government for taking into account the needs of Trinity College in the Estimates, to put on record the positive attitudes that TCD had in 1912 and in 1922, and to comment appreciatively on the role of the State in the appointments of Provosts *(The College electoral procedure comes up with three ordered preferences which it submits to the Taoiseach, who up to now has always accepted the first)*. He went on to comment on the world economic situation, warning of the need for the US to find markets for its expanded production, if another 1929 was to be avoided.

He urged the maximum development of intra-European trade, and the avoidance of imports from the dollar area of raw materials which could be obtained in Europe, using current economic data from the *Central European Observer*. He expressed concern over the early exhaustion of the US dollar loan to Britain.

JJ was foreshadowing the situation that led to the Marshall Plan in 1948, and by implication urging that scarce dollars be used with priority for capital re-equipment purposes.

After supporting a revised schedule for expenses of members (the 'free service' idea reserved Parliament for the rich) on July 16, on the Appropriation Bill, JJ responded constructively to some of the points made earlier in the debate. He supported the idea of 'dower-houses' for aging farmers to retire to, and hand over the farmhouse to the coming generation. He approved of the attendance of the Government at the recent European conferences, predicting that we could have an influence disproportionate to our small size.

He then spent some time on Partition, urging the routine exchange of reports, blue books and white papers on related topics. He noted that the Veterinary College was all-Ireland, and that problems of disease elimination had to be approached on an all-Ireland basis. He noted with approval the Erne hydro-electric scheme. He urged discreet co-operation at the working level, such as to help undermine the prejudices of the Protestant working people, who currently regarded '... their Roman Catholic countrymen in all parts of the country as one of the most regrettable mistakes of the Almighty ...'. He warned against regarding either Senator Douglas of himself as '...in any sense typical Protestants ...' and pointed out that it would be '...a slow business to get the majority of the Northern Protestants to take a more Irish outlook on things ...'. He then commented on the proposal to encourage the raising of tomatoes in greenhouses in the Gaeltacht, supporting it with some enthusiasm, and urging that the greenhouses be heated with stoves burning locally produced turf fuel. He had himself constructed one in his own greenhouse.

I remember this episode; he used a Russian stove design, from Nick Couris of the emigre Russian colony in Collon, and built it himself. It worked quite effectively, storing heat in the brickwork for slow release, and did not require much attention, though in the long run there would have been build-up of tar in the flues, had he persisted. I remember him discussing the combustion technology with Dusty Miller, then head of R&D in Bord na Mona. Dusty understood the problems of combustion of high-moisture fuels, and tried to convey them to JJ, who persisted in underestimating them. Basically, however, JJ was 'right in principle', though perhaps underestimating the practical obstacles.

Regarding the Gaeltacht greenhouses: these were built, without heating; few of them survived the Atlantic winter storms. To implement the plan, and to bring in effectively the heating dimension, would have required some collaborative design between engineers and greenhouse experts. The concept however has re-emerged, with the energy for heating provided by a wind-generator, and this system was piloted in the 1980s in Baile an Fheirterigh at the tip of the Dingle peninsula, though apparently without long-term success on this scale. Wind-farms on the scale of megawatts are however currently a good commercial proposition.

Continuing this omnibus contribution JJ got on to strawberries, which grow in Mayo virus-free, and could form the basis of an export enterprise. He wondered if documentation was available in Irish to enable the Gaeltacht people to pick up this type of know-how.

He then digressed into the utility of Irish as an all-Ireland cultural unifying factor, via the interest in the North in understanding the place names, and concluded on a positive note on the need to keep alive this unique link with pre-Roman (European) culture, which was attracting the interest of 'scholars of European fame'.

While supporting the idea of a National Health Council in July 1947 JJ was critical of the procedure of Ministerial nomination; there should be a defined nomination procedure by expert groups. He similarly opposed direct Ministerial control of food premises licensing procedures.

Then on November 19 1947 on the Finance (no 2) Bill JJ spoke at some length, praising the Minister for doing many of the right things, at the risk of becoming unpopular *(as indeed they did, losing the election in the following year!)*. He began however by querying the increase in car tax for all users: might there not be a case for favouring some for whom the use of the car was essential, like for example rural Protestant Ministers with scattered parishes?(15)

Coming to the main features of the Budget: it was balanced, not inflationary. Under the Budget the lower income groups would gain more from subsidy than they would lose by taxation. He however discounted the claim in 'irresponsible quarters' that the cost of living could be reduced by 30% by taxing incomes of £1000 or more, exhibiting the necessary numbers, to Minister Aiken's approval.

He welcomed the agreement with Britain making available phosphates, of which the land had been starved. While the agreed price for beef cattle was not up to Northern Ireland standard, it would again begin to make stall-feeding feasible. He urged some strategic planning between ourselves and the British regarding the long-term management of agricultural prices, and warned against the British extremes of subsidising of food. A budget like Aiken's then current one would be much better for the British, and it was a pity Aiken was not advising them; '...unfortunately, we gave the British Home Rule some years ago....'

Currently the British wages and prices policy was highly re-distributive, but unfortunately this had the effect of surplus money spilling over into all sorts of undesirable economic activities.

He then ranged over France, where they had pegged the price of wheat and left all other prices to drift, the effect being danger of actual starvation, and the US, where the price of wheat was comparable to the Irish price, reflecting an overall global scarcity.

He complemented the Government on taking part in world conferences and generally acting the good neighbour in regard to European recovery. His concluding remarks, based on the Prodigal Son story in the Bible, are worth quoting in full:

"...During the past 15 years the Minister's Party has by no means been in the political wilderness - on the contrary it has enjoyed the fruits of office - but perhaps during much of that time it was in a sort of moral wilderness, living on the husks of exploded political, economic and ideological fantasies. But lately, and altogether to its credit, it has decided to come out of that moral wilderness, and to return, so to speak, to its father. The Irish people, the father in question, so unlike the father in the parable, has slaughtered the fatted calf and fed it to the greyhounds and is entirely disposed to send the Minister's party back again into the political wilderness. That is just not fair and the Minister's Party has my utmost sympathy..."

On December 11 1947 on the Poultry Hatcheries Bill, the purpose of which was to licence hatcheries, with a view to the control of disease, JJ was able to complement the Minister for implementing one of the proposals of the Committee on Post-Emergency Agriculture, but he was critical of the heavy-handed and arbitrary nature of the licensing procedure, which appeared to require a licence for all incubators, whether for commercial production of chicks for sale off farm, or not.

This was another example of undue dependence on Ministerial regulation and arbitrary rule of inspectors. '...I would remind the Minister that, on a famous occasion, James II claimed to exercise that power, and that, in consequence of that claim, he went on his travels and lost his job. I would ask the Minister, is he not afraid of something similar happening to himself? I think it ought to be possible, on the Report Stage, to draft and amendment which would give effect to the licensing provision in the more restricted manner which I recommend, and to deprive the Minister of that wide degree of autocratic power which he is claiming for himself under the terms of this and other sections.'

Later in the debate, JJ pointed out that the clause '...The Minister may, in his absolute discretion, revoke a poultry hatchery licence...' would be a total disincentive to any agricultural entrepreneur investing money into a hatchery.

On January 8 1948, on the Garda Siochana Bill, JJ attacked this same process of including excessive Ministerial arbitrary powers in the legislation: '...in that procedure the legal rights safeguarded by the Oireachtas have been shot away and there is substituted the discretional power of the Minister ...'.

We see here an attempt to nip in the bud what has become standard political patronage practice over the decades since, the consequences of which are currently being uncovered in the Tribunals.

After the election, on March 11 1948 a Milk Yield of Dairy Stock motion was debated.

This was JJ's last intervention before he lost his seat; the election had taken place for the Dáil, and the new Government was in, with Dillon as Minister for Agriculture. The Seanad election had not yet taken place.

JJ began by asserting his Independent status, and expressing agreement with most of Minister Dillon's speech, to which he had some points to add, arising out of the Report of the Post-Emergency Agriculture Committee. Better Dairy Shorthorn bulls were needed in the dairy areas. It would be necessary to again abolish the Beef Shorthorn bull premium, as the former Minister had done, following the good advice of the Barrington Committee to the Northern Ireland Government. *Dillon had reinstated it.* He urged the Department to produce Monthly Reports along the lines done in Northern Ireland, or if not, to circulate the NI Reports. Beef Shorthorn bulls with Dairy Shorthorn cows produce heifers which are indistinguishable from those with Dairy Shorthorn sires, with the '...danger that they will filter into the dairy herds and prove to be ...unprofitable ...'.

He then went into cow-testing procedures, and attacked the procedure of making the supervisor dependent on the number tested, proposing instead a levy on creamery milk volume, with State subvention, and the building up of the link with the Cow-Testing Associations, developing them into Dairy Cattle Improvement Associations working closely with the existing creameries.

JJ was acting as a sort of precursor of the Agricultural Institute, and was a fount of technical knowledge, which he got from reading the international literature, and with hands-on experience with his own small-scale farm experimentation. It is probable that this role was beginning to be recognised (though not alas in TCD) so that when he lost his seat in the Seanad in 1948, he was, in fact, missed. This may have been a factor in his next spell in the Seanad, as a de Valera nominee, in 1952.

My father had been re-elected in 1944, and so in 1948 he was in the position of defending his seat, in which however on this occasion he was unsuccessful, losing out to the classical scholar WB Stanford.(16)

JJ and TCD Politics

Consider now the 'TCD internal politics' theme. On May 15 1946 JJ participated in a committee to consider future relations with Magee College, Derry. Apart from JJ it consisted of the Provost, the Senior Lecturer, the Registrar, Godfrey and two representatives from Magee. On June 15 this committee reported, along the lines that Magee students should spend one or more years in TCD, with access to rooms, and Magee staff were to be involved in course planning and exams. This arrangement was close to JJ's heart, as he was always a defender of the role of TCD in supporting all-Ireland culture in the Presbyterian context, and the Magee contact was essential for this purpose.

Then on November 6 it was noted that the Provost and the Registrar were to discuss the needs of the College with de Valera. An Honorary Degree for Seán Lester was projected for July 1947, in appreciation of his role as the Irish representative in the League of Nations, which role he had fulfilled throughout the war. It is difficult not to associate this with the politics of the developing attitude of TCD to de Valera, pre-dating the 1952 McConnell Provost-ship. JJ was influential on the Board, being still an 'enfant terrible' among the gerontocrats.

On December 11 the Board approved a memo to the Government, in which they welcomed the formation of an Irish Universities Council, to include Northern Ireland, as an opportunity for consultation on an all-Ireland basis.

At the TCD Board on February 26 1947 the Provost and Registrar reported on the meeting with the Government, but no details were given. Then on March 12 the existence of a State grant of £35K was mentioned in the estimates, so this must have been the fruit of the encounter.

Then on May 17, a committee was set up to consider suggestions for departmental·grants from the Government money. This included JJ, the Bursar, the Registrar and Professor Purser (Engineering School). Two other committees were to consider appointments and building maintenance.

The period 1944 to 1950 can perhaps be identified as one in which JJ is at the peak of his College political influence. Episodes noted in the Board minutes, where I suspect he must have been a supporter or a prime mover, included a reply in Irish verse to an Address from the Oireachtas of the Gaelic League (Jan 14 1948), refusal of access by the Colonial Office for purposes of graduate recruitment (Jan 21), permission for the reproduction of the Book of Kells by Titus Burckhardt of Berne (Feb 25), support for the 1798 150-year commemoration by loan of exhibits (October 20), and the rejection of a request to form an Orange Lodge (December 1 1948).

The foregoing juxtapositions suggest a conscious policy on the part of the College to raise its political profile, and a key role for JJ in the process.

Other indications of his role in this period included his joining the Agriculture School Committee (February 4 1948), and the assertion by this committee of its own right to appoint a committee to supervise entry, a devolutionary move from centralist Board control (February 25). Then on June 2 JJ, Duncan (economics) and Broderick (mathematics) considered applications for a Lecturer in Statistics, appointing EH Thornton on October 1.

JJ's role on the Agriculture School Committee laid the basis for his survival into the 1950s as an influence in College politics, despite marginalisation by the incoming McConnell Provostship. Later JJ was nominated by the Board to serve on a Committee to watch developments in relation to the Agricultural Institute, along with the Provost (Alton) and Professor Purser. This set the scene for the next decade, and the saga of the Kells Ingram Farm, at Townley Hall, Co Meath. This episode, conceived initially as part of the projected Agricultural Institute, was to be JJ's last attempt to introduce estate-based integrated commercial farming into the Irish agricultural scene. We treat this in the next chapter.

On October 23 1950, the College welcomed the idea of the projected 1953 Berkeley Bicentenary Conference, organised by the Mind Association and the Aristotelian Society. This, as we shall see, turned out to be JJ's opportunity to contribute a keynote paper(17) identifying Berkeley's status as an economist.

JJ's post-Seanad political outreach

Towards the end of 1949, after his defeat in the Seanad elections, there are some indications that JJ reacted politically to the phony declaration of the 'republic' by the coalition government. He was at the time President of the Irish Association and must have sensed the alienation of the Northern members. He seems to have made an attempt to get Ireland's part in the European Recovery Program debated in

Queens, with the relevant Ministers present from North and South, but failed. The declaration of the 'republic' would appear to have triggered Lord Charlemont's resignation(18).

He was however active at the level of being an invited speaker on the Protestant secondary school circuit, from which platform he received some publicity, and he almost certainly did this in support of his Irish Association Presidential role. He kept some records of these episodes among his papers.

There is a front-page photo on the *Irish Times* of October 7 1949 of JJ at the distribution of the prizes in Drogheda Grammar School; he was at that time Chairman of the Board of Governors, and had helped to turn around the fortunes of the school, enlisting financial support from Mrs Balfour, of Townley Hall, who was a daughter of John Kells Ingram(19), author of 'Who Fears to Speak of 98'. Ingram had died in 1907, and had become a Fellow of TCD in 1846, at a time when the Thomas Davis republican vision was making an impact in TCD. This episode got the full treatment from Editor Smyllie on October 15 1949, in his 'Nichevo' column; he had been invited by JJ to the event, and went at length into JJ's CV, and about the school, its background and current resurrection with local support. There had been also a feature on the school on October 7, headed 'Children who Should be Proud'.

Then on October 28 1949 JJ was the distinguished guest at the Dungannon Royal School speech day; he tried to counter the then current anti-partitionist rhetoric being promulgated by Fianna Fail out of office, via the Anti-Partition League and otherwise, calling for co-operation between north and south, and promoting, in somewhat veiled form, his long-held belief in all-Ireland government within the Commonwealth. He suggested that 'republicanism was only skin deep', given the attention paid by many in the South to the doings of the royal family.

He kept the letter of thanks, dated October 31, from the headmaster AdeG Gaudin, who mentioned that a number of people had expressed to him in the previous few days their interest in JJ's remarks, referring to the pride with which the old school must consider his career. JJ was clearly holding out a hand to his home ground, in an attempt to preserve his all-Ireland vision, within which the Protestant community had a positive role to play.

There is among JJ's papers a copy of a letter to the *Irish Times* dated 01/06/50 in which he reacted to a letter from David Gray, the US Ambassador, on the previous day. It is worth reproducing in full:

"A propos Mr David Gray's letter in your issue of May 31 an episode took place in the early summer of 1940 which, if my interpretation is correct, places Mr de Valera's attitude in a very different light.

"At a time when German military power was sweeping over Western Europe I, in my capacity as a Senator, sought a private interview with Mr de Valera. I suggested to him that in spite of our neutrality our national safety was very precarious, and that it might be a good idea to suggest to neutral America the advisability of guaranteeing the integrity of our shores, and making good that guarantee by acquiring naval and air bases here by agreement with our Government.

"Mr De Valera discussed the suggestion in a most friendly manner and said he would make inquiries about the possibility of it.

"A few days later, when we were both going into the debating hall of the Senate, he told me that he had made inquiries and ascertained that it was utterly impossible. It was impossible to pursue the subject then, but I understood that American public opinion was at that time too neutral and too isolationist for President Roosevelt's Government, however sympathetic, to be able to entertain this suggestion.

"Am I right in this interpretation, and if I am who is to blame if America did not have bases in Eire when their country finally entered the war? "

JJ and *Irish Agriculture in Transition*

I can preface this section with some of my own experience. In the summer of 1947, in the context of the political educational program of the Promethean Society, Malcolm Craig and I went on a sort of political tour of Ireland, using a tandem bicycle which we bought second-hand. We visited Cork and encountered some of the Cork Republican Left ex-internees (Jim Savage and others) and some Labour left trade unionists. We stayed in youth hostels and in friends' houses where we had contacts. We went north to Belfast via Tuam, Kiltimagh and Cavan.

Our reason to go to Tuam was that we had picked up about RM Burke's 'collective farm'(20) from Paddy Bond in Longford, who somehow had discovered it, and had written to us about it from Cambridge, where he was in college (rather than Trinity; the Bonds of Farragh, though descended from, or at least related to, Oliver Bond of 1798 fame, were decidedly 'landed gentry', for whom the educational system in Ireland was judged to be inadequate; I suspect that the only reason he went to school in St Columba's was the war).

In Tuam we spent a couple of nights in RM Burke's house; he had built a small bungalow for himself, having plans for using the big-house in some socially useful mode after his mother's death, apart from its role as the management centre for the estate. He showed us round what was clearly a well-managed commercial agricultural enterprise, encountering some of the workers, who however appeared to treat him with the type of respect one would expect from their relative class positions.

I regaled Desmond Greaves some time later with our impressions of the Burke scene; he was aware of it, having seen it on his own political travels, and was sceptical: 'why then do they call him Sir?'. In retrospect I am inclined to discount this type of critical view. There clearly was a culture-gap; the estate workers had little schooling, and little chance to accumulate experience of co-operative organisation. This situation however was remediable, with the aid of an educational programme. RM Burke himself was working in effect as the co-op manager; subsequently, when he got into the Seanad via the Labour Party, he employed a professional manager.

Burke's time in the Seanad, 1948-50, did not coincide with JJ's, and as far as I can find out they never worked closely together, although they had met, and were known to each other, at least by repute. Bobby Burke was almost certainly responsible for organising JJ's October 1947 Barrington Lecture in Tuam.(21).

If JJ and RM Burke had been in a position to collaborate, it is possible that their combined forces might have helped the Tuam co-operative to succeed, because JJ would have been supportive in the need for education in co-operative principles, and in particular for training of co-operative managers.(22). The Burke motion urging support for a co-operative approach to commercial-scale managed-estate agriculture was withdrawn for lack of support; had JJ been there he undoubtedly would have supported it. By 1952 when JJ got back to the Seanad, RM Burke had given up and gone to Africa.

It is quite possible that the professional manager employed by Bobby Burke, during his time in Dublin-based politics, would have acted as a traditional estate manager for an absentee landlord, and this would have soured the work-force, to the extent that in the end they opted for the division of the estate, whereupon Bobby Burke, in some disillusionment, went off to do development work in Africa. He returned from Africa in 1978 and ended his days in retirement in Belfast, close to his wife's family. He was honoured by Tuam Urban Council in 1988, for his generosity and services to the community, with a civic reception and a plaque on the wall of the Town Hall. He died in Belfast in 1998, at the age of 91, having spent his retirement working for peace and reconciliation in Northern Ireland.

While the present writer was engaged as above, trying to build the student Left in TCD, and developing links with the shreds of the Connolly tradition which survived among the Dublin working-class, and the scattered remnants of the 1940s Republican Movement all over Ireland, JJ was pursuing what remained of his vision rooted in Horace Plunkett and Standish O'Grady. In 1947, in his last year as an elected Senator, he engaged in what he called an 'Arthur Young's Tour of Ireland' and gathered material for his book *Irish Agriculture in Transition*(23).

The starting-point for JJ's analysis was the same book which he had used in 1913 as background to his *Civil War in Ulster*, namely Dr Moritz J Bonn's *Modern Ireland and her Agrarian Problem*, published in English translation in 1906. The process of State-subsidised tenant purchase left in existence many isolated holdings without any social organisation such as had been provided, in a rudimentary and exploitative form, by the landlords, bailiffs and agents. There was no organised link via village communities, as was the case in most other European countries. The co-operative movement could have provided such an organisation, but failed to do so, except insofar as it organised the processing of milk. According to Bonn "...it cannot be said to have established in the country as a whole any system of 'communal agricultural organisation'...".

In his introductory chapter JJ contrasted the unorganised mass of desocialised 30-acre farmsteads with '...a well-known 2000 acre mixed tillage farm in the midlands (where) 100 workers are permanently employed, a ratio of 5 persons to 100 acres....Can we reproduce under a co-operative system the technical and other conditions which enable our best-managed, privately-owned large holdings to show a high density of employment and a high output per man and per acre?...'.

There is among JJ's papers a letter from George O'Brien, dated 20/04/1948: '...I have read your manuscript with the greatest of interest and I am passing it on to Duncan. I think your idea of "Young's Tour of Ireland in 1947" an excellent one... There is no gainsaying your thesis that larger-scale farming should be attained, if at all possible. The scope for large farms is limited by the passion for land division, but the possibilities for co-operation are very great. Your insistence on the advantage of large scale production is very timely and I hope to see it published... The second part of the manuscript is one of the most acute analyses I have read of the underlying foundations of Irish agriculture...'.

In the course of the field work for this book he visited several co-operatives in Munster which had developed large-scale labour-employing agricultural enterprises, and he also visited Bobby Burke in Tuam on the Barrington circuit. He devoted several chapters to the Munster farms, but there is no mention in the book of Burke; he must have concluded that the Burke model as it stood was unworkable. Nowhere however did he find anything approximating to his 'rural civilisation' vision(24). The Munster farms were commercial capitalist farms owned by absentee shareholders who happened to be dairy-farming owners of a co-operative creamery.

The book was, perhaps, a modest success; I have met people who remember it, and thought highly of it, but it had no impact. The damage was done, the Plunkett/AE vision had been killed by the land policies of successive Free State governments. Isolated 30-acre farmsteads without social cohesion, owing their land to Fianna Fail patronage, dominated the landscape. Those with a little more capital leased land from their neighbours, who got jobs on the roads, another vehicle of Fianna Fail patronage. Those who succeeded by getting more land supported commodity-processing co-ops, with production cycles following the growth of the grass. The concept of a managed estate, with many food products, absorbing its own by-products, generating added-value local industries, and catering for year-round quality market demand, never managed to emerge as the norm.

Building the Marxist Left

To return to the role of the student Left, as introduced earlier: some of us were influential in trying to pull together the makings initially of a Dublin Left, and later of a national movement of sorts, though we can not claim much success. Our reasons for failure are worth analysis, because it left a vacuum into which the 1950s IRA expanded(25).

The present writer was also beginning to be concerned with 'science and society' issues, and with the interactions between science and government. I had been observing the high emigration rate among science graduates, and had personally set an agenda to explore how the Irish environment could be adapted to take up the amount of science know-how which it was exporting. An influential factor at the time were the writings of JD Bernal FRS, who had visibly made the bridge between Marxism and contemporary science; Desmond Greaves, who had an applied-scientific background in industry, also contributed, though not always from a consistent scientific position(26).

Desmond Greaves and the Irish Workers' League

There is regrettably no record in the Greaves journals(2) of the interactions with the TCD students during the early days of the Promethean Society and the Fabian Society, from October 1946 when the present writer went to college. I recollect however that he made contact with us in 1947, and was actively promoting the idea that some sort of Marxist political group, or perhaps Party, needed to be started, and that we as students could be helpful in making it happen. In retrospect, it is clear that the key flaw in this procedure was the lack of understanding on the part of the mainstream British Marxists of the complexities of the Irish national question. Greaves early came round to identifying this as the key obstacle to constructive interaction between the British Communists and the nascent Left in Ireland.

We as the Promethean Society were in touch with Seán Nolan, Geoff Palmer and the group around the Pearse St bookshop 'New Books', and also with John de Courcy Ireland. We were also in touch with the Connolly Group, mostly of ex-1940s internees, which included Denis Walsh, Seán Mulready, Ned Stapleton, and some others who joined subsequently, like Seán Furlong, Brian Behan (Brendan Behan's half-brother and brother respectively), Alfie Venencia and others. It was agreed to attempt to inaugurate an open Marxist political group, to be called the Irish Workers' League; the inaugural meeting was planned for some time early in 1948, and it took place in Deirdre MacDonagh's bookshop in Lower Baggot St.

There was a good attendance, mostly of people with a 1940s republican background, who had their period of education and reflection behind the wire, and were keen to go political. Seán Nolan for the bookshop group and Denis Walsh for the Connolly Group were presiding at the table; also I think Paul O'Higgins for the students group. There was a draft document on the agenda, and we discussed it. *It may turn up in the CPI archive, and if so I will reference it here.* It was quite tentative and was a long way from being a founding document for a Communist Party of Ireland.

I was present, and I remember during the discussion Greaves standing up and introducing himself as acting on behalf of the International Affairs Committee of the CPGB. He supported the proposal. A probable consequence of this (though there could have been other factors) was that the next meeting, when it occurred, was very poorly attended, and the IWL got off to a bad start. The negative image of Communism as imposed in Russia under Stalin dominated the scene. Greaves picked this up later when on his travels; the perception was dominated by Stalin's purges and the forced collectivisations. I think he later regretted his premature intervention on that occasion. He was then in his 30s and his thinking was dominated by the post-war euphoria; his knowledge of Ireland was superficial; he was only beginning to realise how much he didn't know.

Later, during the summer of 1948, Denis Walsh, Seán Mulready, Ned Stapleton (all Connolly Group people, ex-internees) and I went travelling around Ireland. I had the use of JJ's old Ford Anglia (he had upgraded to a Morris 12), and we had tents. We called on 1940s IRA and other contacts, hoping to set up the IWL network in some sort of effective structured manner. I remember meeting Peter O'Connor, an International Brigade veteran from the Spanish civil war, in Waterford, Tommy Molyneux in Killarney, Bernard Kennedy in Cork, Jack Gavaghan in Loughrea, John Joe Hoey and Packy Gralton in Leitrim, Walter Dwyer in Swinford, Tommy Kilroy in Kiltimagh, and perhaps others. In the case of Hoey we had a living link with the 1934 Republican Congress, but he was living in poverty on a smallholding, with one cow, which he milked outside into a pail, for our breakfast porridge and tea. Later I heard he emigrated to the USA. I remember also hearing the Jim Gralton saga from Packy Gralton, by the light of an oil lamp in the latter's cottage, where we shared lumpy beds.

This was not a productive exercise. At the same time Gearoid Mac Carthaigh was reconstructing what became the 1950s IRA from a similar but unrelated contact network, and he succeeded. The vision which the IWL at that time projected was not a marketable package. It was basically flawed and not related to the needs of the time. The gap between the post-war European Left experience, and that of Irish insularity and war-time neutrality, was far too wide.

The 'student Left', apart from the present writer, was mostly decoupled from this process, and tended to concentrate on student politics, with some success as regards broad student democracy, but this effort was counterbalanced by their tendency to look East for international affiliations which were perceived by most students as being irrelevant. On the whole we did not succeed with our analysis of the situation; we failed to lay the foundation for next-generation politics, and condemned the aspirant Connolly-Marxist movement to be by-passed by the 1950s republican revival and the IRA armed campaign. In retrospect, our student Marxist group could perhaps have been compared to that described by Doris Lessing during the second world war in Rhodesia: well-meaning left-wing people with British connections reacting to European politics, oriented towards the USSR and totally unaware of what was going in the undergrowth of the emergent Zimbabwe.

The Irish Workers' League's Internal Development

There was an IWL conference in November 1949; this could be regarded perhaps as the fruit of our organising trips the previous year; there had been subsequent ones in the autumn. Typically, the conference material is all analysis and little of immediate practical utility(27).

A Constitution was adopted; among the objectives was the establishment of diplomatic relations with the USSR; the primary objective was 'to achieve socialism in Ireland, ie, a social system in which the means of production and exchange shall be publicly owned'. 'The establishment of a united, independent and democratic republic for all Ireland' was seen as an intermediate objective. A branch structure was envisaged, and an annual conference. The Executive Committee was to have Political and Organisational sub-committees. Membership was defined.

Clearly there was the makings of a genuine radical socialist movement here, which might have collected support had it not been for the negative impact of the international scene, the emerging 'cold war' tensions, and then in the summer of 1950 the Korean war, which drove the IWL practically underground.

Subsequent to the conference, the IWL embarked on an internal educational programme, which was very much slanted towards current European Marxist ideology, and was decoupled from the current Irish needs. For example, the first issue of the IWL Education Bulletin consisted basically of a listing of the various Marxist publications available in New Books, 16a Pearse St; the orientation is towards Britain, France and Russia, and there is practically nothing with an Irish flavour. Understanding and defending the USSR was always high on the agenda.

In a subsequent issue I was concerned that people talking about 'developing the forces of production' should have been given some idea what it meant in real terms, and suggested Hogben's 'Science for the Citizen' as useful reading.

Viewed in retrospect, this was a formula for producing boring autodidacts, decoupled from the real situation in Ireland.

Subsequently there were calls for development of a sound theoretical basis by the analysis of the class forces in Ireland, and their relationships with external imperialism, and for a 'theory of allies'. A subsequent item however illustrates the gulf between the vision and the practice: it is a review by the present writer of Lenin's 'Materialism and Empirio-Criticism', a book of some interest to specialists in philosophy, but about as remote from the immediate needs of a struggling radical working-class party as one could get. There follow some letters from readers, one critical of the bookish orientation of the aspirant educators, including the present writer.

The September 1950 issue has a note by Sam Nolan on the circulation of the paper *Irish Workers' Voice*; they had targeted 6000 and were attaining about 1000, of which about 400 were personal sales by members, a derisory amount.

I recollect trying to sell the paper in public places and encountering personal hostility, a consequence of the apparent promotion of support for the USSR and the post-war Eastern European scene. Anti-communism was ingrained in Irish culture, a consequence of the perceived attitude of Communist governments to religion. The atmosphere had been made much worse by the Korean war. Our earlier attempts to make contact with the CPNI, and to begin developing some analysis of the national question, under Greaves' influence, had foundered; the Northern comrades, mostly crypto-Unionists, were glad of any excuse, such as that presented by the priority of the 'peace issue' seen globally, for not discussing all-Ireland issues. Our failure to do this undoubtedly fuelled the 1950s IRA.

The December 1950 issue is dominated by feedback from the Warsaw Peace Congress and the November Cominform meeting. There is a 'Salute to Stalin'. There is a call by Máirín Mooney (whom I subsequently married in January 1952) for the leadership to run special classes for women members on women's issues, and a review by Paddy Carmody of TA Jackson's 'Old Friends to Keep'. This book in its time was seen as serious contribution to Marxist literary criticism.

Thus ends the 1940s decade. The 'Left' in Ireland had on the whole got off to a bad start; dominated by bookishness, by respect for Stalin and the Cominform, turned in on itself, doctrinaire, it provided meagre raw material for intelligent Marxist analysis of the Irish situation. There was, however, nowhere else for the aspirant radical critical intellectual to go. The present writer stuck with it, and fought for a genuine critical view where and when he could.

Notes and References
1. For more detail about the Promethean Society and its origins in St Columba's College, see the 1940s political module of the hypertext.
2. C Desmond Greaves, author of the *Life and Times of James Connolly* and *Liam Mellows and the Irish Revolution* (Lawrence and Wishart, 1960 and 1971 respectively). He had set himself the task of encouraging the development of independent Marxist thought within Ireland, and ensuring that the Irish when they emigrated to Britain learned to act politically in the Irish interest, the vehicle for this being the Connolly Association, with its paper the Irish Democrat. I have partially abstracted his journal, which he kept from the 1930s to his death in 1988, where it bears on this narrative, in the hypertext. An overview is accessible from Appendix 10 and there is a 1940s module which expands on the background to these TCD and other Irish contacts in the 1940s. I am indebted to Anthony Coughlan, who is CDG's literary executor, for access to the Greaves journals.

3. Owen Sheehy-Skeffington (OS-S) was a leading liberal socialist, on the staff of the TCD French Department, a founder member of the Dublin University Fabian Society, which was an accessible forum for socialist thought. We as a student group had a somewhat difficult relationship with OS-S; he had us identified in his mind as a pernicious Stalinist cult, and in retrospect he can, to some extent, be forgiven. It could be argued that the Trotskyist position, with which he identified, was equally pathological, though in different ways. An account of the relationship between OS-S and the student left has been given by his widow Andrée Sheehy-Skeffington in *Skeff*, a biography published in 1991 by Lilliput, Dublin. I contributed some notes to the author, and have included some subsequent comments by myself and by Paul O'Higgins in the 1940s political module.

4. The Irish Students Association had been founded originally in 1931, and was one of the all-Ireland bodies which the Irish Association had attempted to foster after its foundation in 1938. The NUI authorities had opposed the ISA, while TCD encouraged it; there is correspondence with de Valera on the topic in the Irish Association archive which is in the NI Public Record Office; see the 1930s module of the Irish Association theme.

5. The personnel who were in the lead in the Fabian Society and the Student Representative Council are partially on record in the TCD Calendar editions of the period, though there are gaps and lapses. I have tried to set the record straight in the 1940s political module, in the section headed 'Fabian Society'. I have also expanded on the Promethean Society role.

6. See Chapter 2 for some background to MacManus and the Thomas Davis Society.

7. I have overviewed the role of JD Bernal FRS (1901-1971) in the 'science and society' context in Appendix 11 and supportive hypertext.

8. Arnold Marsh was a Quaker schoolteacher (Newtown in Waterford, Drogheda Grammar School) with a background in economics who was a leading Labour Party member. His book *Full Employment in Ireland* published in 1946 was regarded in left-wing circles as an Irish approach to the problems identified in the Beveridge Report, and widely welcomed.

9. 'Local and Regional Government in Ireland', Roy H W Johnston, Regional Studies Association, 15/09/1990. This paper is part of the raw material for the 1990s chapter and is accessible in the hypertext.

10. 'The Irish Meat and Livestock Industry', Thomas Shaw; reprint from *Studies* September 1946. There are comments by JJ, TA Smiddy, J Hughes and EJ Sheehy in the same issue.

11. This argument relates to JJ's support for the Orpen model of rural development, as subsequently outlined in *Irish Agriculture in Transition*, and currently in his 'rural civilisation' SSISI paper (JSSISI xviii, 1, 1947-8). These were all developments of his earlier 1941 SSISI paper on 'Capitalisation of Irish Agriculture' (JSSISI xvi, 44, 1941-2).

12. The present writer had encountered in England in 1947 the workings of the 'War Ags', having worked as a farm worker during the College vacation, after attending a CPGB 'summer school'. They were regarded as a progressive consequence of the war emergency situation, on which it was hoped to build politically, and Party personnel were involved.

13. There is the embryo here of JJ's 'Berkeleyan theory of credit' as subsequently developed in the 1960s, in an unpublished monograph.

14. This article was a report of his Athlone Barrington Lecture, and I have summarised it in the Barrington module.

15. JJ was acutely aware of the economic problems of his son-in-law, then Rector of the parishes of Ballinaclough and Templederry, south of Nenagh; I expand on this in the 1940s family module of the hypertext.

16. I have reproduced JJ's 1948 election address in Appendix 8. I have also added some notes on his attitude to the 1949 elections, which in the end he decided not to context.

17. This keynote paper was subsequently published: 'Berkeley's Influence as an Economist', *Hermathena* Vol LXXXII p76, 1953.

18. I go into the details of JJ's Presidency of the Irish Association in the 1940s hypertext module of this theme; it had been founded in 1938 by a group of liberal Unionists with an all-Ireland vision, headed by Lord Charlemont (who incidentally had been old John Johnston's landlord). JJ succeeded the latter in its Presidency in 1948. In the NI Public Record Office the Irish Association archive of JJ's Presidency however is somewhat deficient. I overview the history of the Association in Appendix 9.

19. This contact undoubtedly led later to the Kells Ingram Farm episode in the TCD School of Agriculture saga, treated in the TCD Board thread of the hypertext.

20. Bobby Burke was a progressive landlord near Tuam who had attempted to convert his estate to an integrated worker-owned co-operative farm. He became a leading member of the Labour Party and was elected to the Seanad in 1948.

21. I am also indebted to Maurice Laheen, the Tuam local historian, for picking up this event, which is described in the 1940s Barrington module of the hypertext.

22. JJ in his contribution to the report of the 1922-24 Agriculture Commission had written an Appendix calling for training in co-operative management. I have referenced this, and other related work for the 1926 Prices Commission in which he recorded French agricultural co-operative experience, from Chapter 3.

23. *Irish Agriculture in Transition*, Hodges Figgis, Dublin and Blackwell, London, 1951; I have abstracted this substantially in the hypertext.

24. JJ did succeed in tracking down an estate which might, under more favourable political circumstances, have evolved in the direction of this model at Dovea, an estate owned by the Ballyduff Co-op Creamery, near Thurles.

25. I have given more background detail in the 1940s political module of the hypertext.

26. I had begun to analyse the science and society problem under Bernal influence in this 1940s decade, and have overviewed this theme in Appendix 11. In our student political experience we had an encounter with the Lysenko episode, and in this context the Greaves connection was decidedly negative, influencing Justin Keating in the direction of accepting Lysenko as genuine; he was subsequently very civilly put down by Professor Gatenby (Zoology) in a Fabian Society meeting.

27. I have again given more background detail in the 1940s political module of the hypertext.

Chapter 6: The Period 1951-1960

Introduction

During the 1950s JJ was instrumental in getting TCD to develop an Honours Degree in Agriculture, for which purpose the College bought Townley Hall in Meath. This however was never brought to fruition, being frustrated by the inter-university politics which arose around the foundation of the Agricultural Institute with Marshall Plan money.

In the 1950s also we follow the evolution of the present writer (RJ), his politics and his science, in the hostile atmosphere of 1950s Ireland, after an initial creative scientific incubation period in France.

During this period my father increasingly got personal fulfilment outside TCD as President of the Irish Association, and as President of the Statistical and Social Inquiry Society. Despite his political isolation in TCD, he managed to get to deliver a keynote paper at the 1953 Berkeley bicentenary conference. When de Valera returned to power in 1951, he brought JJ back into the Seanad as a Taoiseach's nominee.

The present writer RJ spent the first two years of the decade in France absorbing the culture of the high-technology scientific laboratory. JJ and I remained, as it were, in parallel universes. I went in 1951 on a French Government *bourse*, and worked with Professor Louis Leprince-Ringuet, in the Ecole Polytechnique in Paris.

I had in mind to get back to Ireland via the Dublin Institute of Advanced Studies, where cosmic ray work had been initiated under Janossy, a Hungarian anti-fascist refugee, and I succeeded in this objective, thanks to an encounter with Cormac Ó Ceallaigh at a conference. There followed a creative period of 7 years in which I was able to do some scientific work of value, mostly on the experimental technology of high-energy particle physics.

The 1950s on the whole was a black period politically. I attempted to make my peace with Owen Sheehy-Skeffington, visiting him in hospital in 1956, after he had his heart attack. The Greaves contacts also continued, and we had the first rumblings of the crisis of Utopia: Hungary. I cultivated relations with the *Plough*, a 'Labour-Left' publication, and I was also in contact with Seán Cronin who had led the IRA 1950s border campaign. There were increasingly uneasy relations with the IWL, and a perceived need for a 'broad Left'.

JJ meantime was farming and market gardening in Laois, on a small scale, with the TCD kitchen as his (slightly captive) market. He was developing his long-term thesis that small-scale farming could combine with market gardening to generate an adequate income, provided that the marketing was organised, and the key to this process was co-operation, though at this time and location he had no opportunity to develop this aspect of the process.

The concept of a pilot project, with decisions being made about a trial system in a defined environment, was then, and still remains, foreign to the economics fraternity; it is more comprehensible in Operations Research terms. JJ felt that the inductive approach, of learning from actual experience at the micro level, was no longer being listened to or appreciated, and that economics was going increasingly towards abstractions, which he mostly found incomprehensible.

RJ's Final Year in TCD and the Nascent Left

The Irish Workers' League was still struggling for its right to exist, experiencing difficulty in finding a place to meet. I contributed to their new internal education bulletin, with reviews of books and suchlike. This was edited initially by George and Marion Jeffares; George had a TCD modern languages background, and Marion was a talented artist with a CPGB political background. They had married when George was teaching in England, and returned to Ireland, where George developed a business as a motor-car salesman.

The January 1951 issue of the *IWL Education Bulletin(1)* had an article by George Jeffares (GJ) on 'Unity with the Republican Forces', and a review by the present writer of Vassili Robertovitch Williams' 'Principles of Agriculture', in which I noted the existence of a market for the English translation of the book from the Russian, and hailed it as a seminal work on the understanding of soil science(2). I managed to link some of the ideas with critical observations of agricultural practice in Kildare and Tipperary. GJ promoted the idea that the IRA was the strongest anti-imperialist force, and noted that the *United Irishman* had ceased publishing anti-Soviet articles, and that at Bodenstown they had vowed never to support an imperialist war, even in return for the ending of partition. Micheál Ó Riordáin commented on the Congress of the Scottish division of the CPGB, which he had attended. It was clear that the Korean war situation had prevented serious attention being given to the question of Scottish independence, though this issue was given a somewhat grudging recognition. There was much padding with 'international movement' stuff, and the usual deference to Stalin.

The February 1951 issue, edited by Marion Jeffares, led off with a statement of the agenda for the development of a Marxist theory of the Irish revolution, to fill the post-Connolly vacuum, occupied sparsely by books like Brian O'Neill's *War for the Land in Ireland* and TA Jackson's *Ireland Her Own*. The agenda she set was broad-based and in some respects insightful, but was ill-adapted to the available IWL intellectual resources, and as usual dominated by the Korean war and US imperialism seen as the 'main enemy'. There was not even a nod in the direction of the Irish national question and Partition, despite an earlier effort by George on this topic. There was wide-ranging negative response to the latter, mainly from ex-IRA people who had evolved to the Left. There was visibly some confusion as to what the 'republican movement' was: did it include Fianna Fail and the IWL, both these bodies aspiring to the all-Ireland Republic? There was a message of solidarity from Gus Hall on behalf of the CPUSA. The 'international movement' was treated with respect, and usually given some priority.

The foregoing is a snapshot of the position of the embryonic aspirant-Marxist Left in Ireland before I went to France. At about this time the scene was sampled by C Desmond Greaves (CDG), who had recently given up his job as an industrial chemist, to dedicate full time to editing the Irish Democrat. I remember at the time picking up that it was his intention to isolate himself with the notes, with a view to drafting a book on the history of the Irish working-class, which eventually evolved into *The Life and Times of James Connolly*. The Workers League had relatively recently been set up; I distinctly recollect it being said in IWL circles that he wanted to have residential status in Ireland so as to be able to participate in IWL events should the need arise. This could have been rumour based on wishful thinking in IWL circles; there was a perceived leadership vacuum. CDG's main priority however undoubtedly was his book.

In his Diaries(3) however he indicated that he regarded the stay in Curraun as an extended vacation, time for reflection, and getting the measure of the size of the Connolly project, which did not mature until almost a decade later. There is little explicit politics, but many acute observations of life in the West of Ireland; this, I surmise, must have reinforced his growing belief that the simplistic 'class struggle' formulations of the CP in Britain were quite remote from the Irish reality.

It was in the spring of 1951, my final year in TCD, that I visited him for a few days during the Easter vacation. We must have had much political discussion, but there is nothing on record in the Diary, apart from the fact that we climbed the Curraun mountain, which gave a great view over Achill, Clew Bay and Croagh Patrick. There is a reference to the election, and to the Dr Browne issue. He picked up odds and ends of local politics and gossip. There was also a visit from some IWL activists, including Justin Keating, the objective of which undoubtedly would have been to discuss issues arising within the infant IWL, but no hint is given as to what these issues were. There is much detail on how turf was won, and about some innovative small-scale machinery for use in that context; he provides photographs.

He went up to Dublin for the elections, observing the final rallies with Paul O'Higgins. He remarked on how old and tired de Valera was, losing his magic. The Clann rally was much diminished. He spoke to the TCD Fabians, sharing a platform with Dorothy MacArdle, Desmond Ryan and Eoin (the Pope) O'Mahony. Afterwards they discussed Connolly's background, including his birthplace, then thought to be Monaghan. My parents must have invited him for a meal at our then house in Raheny; I remember the event; I would have had a hand in organising the Fabian meeting. The only reference to this is: '...As I left Dublin Joe Johnston remarked "this is the fateful day, the day of decision between Tweedledum and Tweedledee" ...'.

From March 1951 onwards the Bulletin ceased to have a named editor, and showed signs of having been 'taken in hand' by the leadership; the format was improved, but it remained dominated by the 'international movement' and touched on Irish issues only rarely. The March issue concluded with a definitive put-down of the earlier Jeffares article on 'Republican Forces', in the form of a Political Committee statement; the 'so-called IRA-Sinn Fein group' in the July 1950 issue having basically given an endorsement of Mulcahy's and MacBride's line. Also 'Ireland's economic subservience to Britain fits in to the aims of American monopoly capitalism... the role allotted to Ireland in the Marshall Plan... favouring more up-to-date methods... of supplying Britain with more cattle ...'.

The July-August issue led with an analysis of the elections, which had taken place in May. It was said that "..Con Lehane for Clann na Poblachta claimed the 'workers' while Fianna Fail claimed to be the 'real' Labour Party...". The problems posed by the IWL's electoral experience were listed: the role of the Church, the IWL attitude to religion, civil liberties issues, the need to clarify the attitude to the national question, the method of approach to the people; the call was 'back to Connolly'. Pseudonyms were increasingly in vogue due to pressures on people in their work-places, a measure of the level of repression.

September-October 1951 issue showed concern with the problem of how to adapt the requirements of the 'international movement' (eg collecting mass signatures for the Stockholm and Berlin peace appeals) to the Irish environment, dominated by extreme hostility to anything to do with the USSR. There was an article by Paul Robeson, reprinted from *Masses and Mainstream* the US Marxist periodical, arising from a conference held in Chicago which called for a cease-fire in Korea.

By this time the present writer was in France, and out of touch with the IWL, though marginally in touch with French politics, and with the Irish Democrat in London, to which he contributed occasional Paris letters. I continue however to abstract the IWL Education Bulletin series, as it helps set the stage for the political scene which I confronted on my return to Ireland in September 1953.

While I was in France the **Ballyfermot Co-op** episode took place. This is important because it illustrates the vicious nature of the opposition at the time to any sort of democratic, bottom-up, economic organisation of working people. In a new working-class housing estate, remote from shops, there is a clear motivation to set up a retail distribution system on the consumer co-op principle, and such a system was set up, initially in 1946, in Inchicore, where there was a co-op tradition among the railway workers, as earlier noted in the context of the 1914 Co-operative Union conference in Dublin, which my father attended (see Chapter 2). In 1951 it relocated to Ballyfermot, by which time it had some 700 members. Joe Deasy, who had become a Labour Councillor in the 1945 election, was the Chairman. Around this time he resigned from the Labour Party and joined the Irish Workers League.

The co-op for a while was a success, but the local retail traders used Church influence to raise a McCarthyite anti-communist witch-hunt. The co-op was put out of business and its membership disbanded(4).

JJ and College Politics

The decade began for my father with his being aware of his increasing marginalisation in TCD politics. He had been a radical too early, and was now classed by the new wave of 'young turks' in the College with the 'old guard'. As a result he came off badly as a result of the McConnell reforms.

According to McDowell(5): '...a dangerous atmosphere of frustration and...personal hostility such as the College had not known for the past 40 years...a general meeting of academic staff to discuss constitutional reform...on March 1 1951...'. There was a problem however in that the non-Fellow Professors would not agree simply to increase Junior Fellow representation. The Board then voted themselves a 10% increase in salary, and this increased the tension. It was noted that not one of the current Senior Fellow Board members, apart from Alton the Provost, had ever been elected as a Junior Fellows representative.

My father increasingly got his fulfilment outside TCD; his long-standing membership of the Statistical and Social Inquiry Society had culminated in a period as its President(6). He was also active as President of the Irish Association(7), continuing in that role up to 1954, and subsequently as a Council member, contributing papers and publications. In this context he was instrumental in organising a pioneering debate in Kilkenny between Seán MacBride, Colonel Topping (a leading Stormont politician) and others, on the national question.

Despite his political isolation in TCD, he managed to deliver a keynote paper at the Berkeley bicentenary conference(8) in TCD in 1953. In this he placed Berkeley firmly in the national political context, with his concluding paragraph: 'John Mitchel, Thomas Davis, Isaac Butt, and in our own day Arthur Griffith, George Russell and Éamonn de Valera, have frankly recognised the debt the nation owes to the heart as well as the head of this great Irishman.' This paper was a sort of dry run, or 'executive summary' of his Berkeley material which he was later to pull together for his annotated edition of Berkeley's *Querist* (Dun Dealgan Press, 1970).

He had considered standing again for the Seanad on behalf of the College, but had concluded that his political base was untenable. He had made enquiries, primarily via Senator James Douglas, about the possibility of his getting in via one of the 'vocational panels', but had been discouraged by the response (I have treated this towards the end of the previous chapter). This encounter however bore fruit, and when de Valera returned to power in 1951, he brought JJ back into the Seanad(9) as a Taoiseach's nominee.

Background to JJ's final term in the Seanad

During this his last spell in the Seanad, he pulled no punches, 'going for broke' on what he regarded as the key issues facing Irish agriculture. For example, he contributed an article in commemoration of the Plunkett(10) centenary to a publication of the National Co-operative Council, a gadfly-body on the fringe of the mainstream commercial co-operative movement. There was a centenary event organised, on a modest scale, in Pearse St Public Library, presumably by the NCC, on October 18 1954, of which the proceedings were published. I treat this below.

JJ continued his economic polemical and critical work, in the Barrington Lecture tradition, though increasingly through more marginal publication channels(11).

He moved house again, to a farm(12) near Stradbally in Laois, and began to re-develop his model for linking small-farm economics with market gardening. He contributed this experience to the Statistical and Social Inquiry Society(13) during this period, though the new wave of econometric specialists were increasingly inclined to dismiss this type of analysis as 'anecdotal'. What he was describing was however in fact a quantified productive system in an economic environment, and JJ was therefore close to what would now be recognised as an 'Operational Research' or 'techno-economic' approach.

JJ as a Dev Nominee

When JJ returned to the Seanad in 1951 as a de Valera nominee(9), his first intervention was in connection with the Supplies and Services Bill on December 13 1951. This was a substantial review of his then current thinking on a range of issues, and I summarise it here. He covered the following topics:

- The role of sterling assets and how their repatriation for capital investment purposes necessarily involves imports of consumer goods for the people involved in realising the investment process;
- Any attempt to restrict imports, out of concern for the balance of payments in such a period of investment, would be inflationary;
- Subsidising consumer goods for the poor is bad economics; better to sell at market price and increase the incomes of the poor;
- The future of sterling itself was seriously in doubt, given the impact of the rearmament program on the British economy;
- No-one in the USSR was personally making money out of rearmament, but some people in the capitalist world were, and these were influencing governments;
- In some quarters in the West, preparing for war was seen as better than a return to the 1929 depression;
- Invoking his old Oxford friend GDH Cole, he quoted at length from the latter's pamphlet *Weakness through Strength*;
- The triangular trade between Britain, the sterling area and the dollar area had reasserted itself post-war, but was now being disrupted by the arrival of Germany and Japan, and the rearmament process;
- There had been ideological conflicts before, like Protestantism vs Catholicism, which had led to wars, but people had since learned to live with them peacefully;
- The Ulster Volunteer movement in the period 1912-14 had brought back the principle of violence in Ireland, in which context he had made his first political act, in the form of his 1913 book *Civil War in Ulster(14)*;
- Communists should be regarded as erring children who would not be converted by atomic bombs; Attlee's recent visit to Washington had helped to prevent the US using the atomic bomb on China, which would have unleashed the third world war;
- We should have nothing to do with the madness of rearmament and should recognise the immediate danger of the rearming of Nazi Germany.

With the foregoing uncompromising speech he re-asserted his political position as an independent Protestant democratic critic, despite his then novel status in the Seanad as a de Valera nominee. He was, of course, fully aware of the present writer's dedication to Marxism, and he was visibly trying to make some political space where his son's ideas might get a hearing.

Then on the Undeveloped Areas Bill on December 19-20 JJ begged to differ with Professor George O'Brien, who had taken a somewhat pessimistic 'dismal science' view; JJ welcomed the Bill as a step forward, but was critical because it had not gone far enough. The main thrust of the Bill was directed at the 'congested districts' of the West, which were dependent on remittances from migrant labour, usually from the US and from Britain. As an interim arrangement he urged that arrangements be made to make available migrant labour to commercial agriculture in the East, where the production was limited by the availability of labour at harvest-time.

Chapter 6: The Period 1951-1960

Regarding subsidy to Gaeltacht industry, he differed with George O'Brien in his assessment of the risk of this subsidy being continuous. Once the initial friction was overcome, the presence of industry would attract more industry, and the need for subsidy would evaporate. He instanced the Canadian model provided by Quebec.

He went on to be critical of individualist capitalist models for development, quoting from his then recently published book *Irish Agriculture in Transition*, where he had drawn on the writings of James Connolly and Estyn Evans in support of the 'clachan' or cluster of houses as opposed to the individual isolated farm, and the implied deep-rootedness of the co-operative principle in the culture. He warned of the danger of fortifying the local power of the 'gombeen man' by undue reliance on capitalist individualism.

He went on to instance at some length the experience of the Templecrone Co-operative, initiated in 1906 by Paddy Gallagher in Co Donegal, which had extended itself towards industrial development and electricity generation. He regaled the Seanad with anecdotes about how the Donegal men had learned to pack eggs from a poultry society in Derry, run by one Mr Barr, an Orangeman. The Cathaoirleach became impatient at the level of detail JJ was giving, and as a result JJ wound up with a call that the Templecrone co-operative experience be used as the basis for Gaeltacht industrial development.

Continuing the debate in the next session on January 9 1952 JJ proposed amendment no 4: 'before Section 5 to insert a new section as follows:

( ) In the course of its operations the (Gaeltacht Development) Board shall have regard to the following major considerations:-

(a) the desirability of developing on an appropriate economic foundation a social and economic organisation in which Gaelic culture and civilisation may survive, flourish and expand;

(b) the desirability of integrating industrial development with a general economic structure in which agriculture, industry, afforestation, fishing, tourism, turf production and the arts and crafts play their respective parts;

(c) the desirability of co-ordinating the activities of the Board with those of Bord na Mona, the Irish Sugar Company, the Forestry Department, the Electricity Supply Board, the Arterial Drainage Board and all central and local government agencies which are in any way concerned with ameliorating conditions in the undeveloped areas.

When introducing this amendment JJ harked back to Horace Plunkett and George Russell, and attempted to analyse the nature of the vicious circle of unproductivity that dominated Connemara at that time, urging the development of industry based on local products, such as a bacon factory in Clifden supplied by pigs from Connemara fed with locally produced potatoes and oats; likewise jam and chutney factories supplied by locally produced strawberries and tomatoes etc.

He insisted that the 'three wise men' who were designated to lead the development process should be locally based, and urged that the Department of Agriculture instructors should be brought in on a training programme oriented towards industrial production based on local agricultural resources. He argued for a co-operative marketing organisation, instancing the price differential between Clifden and Dublin for fowl and eggs, which was of the order of a factor of two.

Lemass in his reply was inclined to be dismissive of the need for the 'three wise men' to be local, their role being perceived as being to persuade outsiders to invest. JJ responded robustly to this, accusing the civil servants of only going to Connemara for the summer holidays, and being quite unaware of the problems as seen in the winter. Connemara shopkeepers preferred to deal with Galway wholesalers rather than accept local produce, and this problem needed to be addressed by co-operative organisation.

JJ was here attempting to generalise the type of integrated bottom-up development based on a combination of small-scale farming and market gardening which he was planning to pilot by his move to Grattan Lodge, Co Laois.

Local Economic Policies in a Global Context

After intervening on February 13 1952 on the Milk (Amendment) Bill 1952 in favour of opening up the Dublin milk market to unregulated supply from the whole country, with the surplus being used for production of cheese, on March 27 1952 he again expanded at length on the Central Fund Bill. This was the second day of the debate, and JJ chose to come in with his professional economist's hat on, George O'Brien having contributed on the previous day; the infliction of economics was therefore spread over the two days, avoiding overload.

He adverted to his peculiar status as an economist; when he had become a Fellow of Trinity College in 1913 he had been a classics and ancient history scholar. Mahaffy who was then Provost, alive to the danger of unleashing someone so young and inexperienced on the academic community, pointed him in the direction of the Albert Kahn Travelling Fellowship, in which context he saw the world, including India, China and the USA. This aroused his interest in economic affairs, as a result of which he '...abandoned culture... and developed a keen interest in social philosophy, and especially agricultural co-operation ...'.

As a result of this background JJ always tended to look at Irish problems in a world setting, and most of the current problems were a consequence of the arms race. It was regarded therefore as most important to get into UNO, and to recognise that the blocking of our entry currently came from the US, having previously been from the USSR. The one UN body of which we were a member was the Food and Agriculture Organisation (FAO), and JJ commended to the House the book *The Geography of Hunger* by the Chairman of the FAO. It was important to retain our neutrality and to realise that we were in good company with Sweden and Switzerland.

He mentioned his opposition to the self-sufficiency policy in the 30s but stressed that in the current world situation the maximum of self-sufficiency was desirable. In this context he referenced his recent *Irish Press* articles, in which he had made several currently relevant economic arguments:

- The need to get rid of food subsidies, especially butter, which was depressing the price of farmers' butter, and therefore reducing the population of cows in the non-creamery areas.

- Ranging over the world market for butter, he indicated that there would emerge an export potential for the butter surplus if the price was right.
- He reiterated the point he had made earlier about capital investment at home converting itself into an increased demand for consumer goods.
- Capital invested in fertilisers for agriculture would give a remarkably quick return, especially when associated with the upgrading of pasture.
- The previous Minister for Agriculture, Mr Dillon, while having been popular with the farmers, would happily have led us into '...an Anglo-American Alliance which, if certain wild men had their way, might bring us into a third world war ...'.
- The devaluation of our external assets had been proceeding at a rate of 23% over the past 3-4 years, so we needed to dedicate their investment for maximum rapidity of return.
- He advocated development of production of Ymer barley, at a guaranteed price per ton, for use as feed at a subsidised rate, with the subsidy being paid for by a tax of £5 per head on cattle exported on the hoof. The current excessive price for beef cattle was undermining the breeding capacity of the national herd, by biasing the market against in-calf heifers.
- On problems of the national rail network, he advocated a preferential vehicle tax for short-haul road transport, to encourage servicing the railheads for local distribution.

Internal College Politics in TCD

Meanwhile in the College on February 19 1952 Provost Alton died, and on March 18 AJ McConnell became Provost. McConnell not being Church of Ireland, the Chair of the Divinity School fell to the Vice-Provost. Duncan was appointed Registrar. On May 24 McConnell made an attempt to get the College Constitution revised; a motion to force retirement at 72 was lost, and a motion to increase the Junior Fellows representation was lost. A motion to abolish the fine for non-attendance at Board meetings however was carried. This had the effect of undermining the influence of the gerontocracy. JJ is on record as having voted against all three motions, believing that he and the other old-timers had a positive role. The new McConnell regime took a realistic positive view of the Dublin Government, abandoning the residual unionism of its predecessors. Despite this adoption by the new Board of his own long-held views, JJ did not get any of the key influential administrative posts, and remained politically out in the cold. He did however become the keeper of the Board minutes, which role continued for the best part of the 50s decade.

On June 6 it was decided that the informal Appointments Association, whose job it was to help graduates get jobs, became the Appointments Office, part of the Establishment, a significant modernising step.

On June 28 there was an echo from the student Left: it was laid down that in the Fabian Society non-College members of the Society must not have voting rights. This was a consequence of the existence of the Fabian Society, which had attracted people from outside College who needed a forum for the exchange of radical ideas.

The influential rule of Archbishop McQuaid in Dublin at the time was such that it was impossible to get a hotel room for a left-wing meeting.

Also on the same date it was noted that five professors in the Veterinary College were to be recognised as College teaching staff. This was an echo of the ongoing struggle between TCD and UCD for control of the Veterinary College, in the context of the emerging new State-supported agricultural research regime.

On July 4 the present writer's French Government Bourse was renewed. *This apparently was not simply between the present writer and the French, it required the blessing of the College. It is far from obvious by what channel they knew I was not wasting my time. In such a discussion it would have been customary for JJ to withdraw.*

Then on October 8 1952 it was agreed that the Provost and Dr AA Luce were to handle the Berkeley Bicentenary invitations; there was no mention of JJ in this context. Luce, although a gerontocrat, was of course a front-runner in the field, from the philosophy angle. JJ's role was perceived as being more marginal.

The question of JJ's lecture load continued on the agenda; he was to still have six per week, to be reviewed soon. The following week, October 15, they increased JJ's salary to £1600, and Brian Inglis was renewed as his deputy, with his pay however to be deducted from JJ's salary (this was decided the following week).

These events, which he took as a rebuff, probably were the trigger for his decision again to leave Dublin (he was then living in Mount Merrion) and seek a farm where he could try things out, and do his TCD work by looking in occasionally. He went to Grattan Lodge, in Laois, where he again attempted to get his model for combining small-scale farming with market-gardening to work(12)

The Seanad: TCD, Berkeley and Tariffs

Let us return to the Seanad: JJ intervened briefly on June 26 1952 on the Tourist Traffic Bill, in defence of buildings of possibly historic status in danger of losing their roofs in order to avoid the payment of rates. Then on July 30 1952 JJ spoke at length on the Appropriation Bill. The Government had made a substantial contribution to the revenues of TCD, and JJ felt moved to thank them, though no longer in a TCD-representing capacity. He chose to take his status as a Taoiseach nominee as evidence that service to the University was regarded as service to the nation, on both sides of the Border.

He went on to regale the House with the way in which the late Lord Glenavy, then Sir James Campbell, MP for TCD in 1912, had attempted to get TCD excluded from the Home Rule Bill in 1912. A meeting of the Fellows and Professors took place which repudiated this move, and he had to drop the amendment. The College elected to remain part of the nation. Similarly, when Carson abandoned representing Trinity in 1918, '...after he had tarnished his name with the abominable policy of Partition ...', Provost Mahaffy had remarked to JJ at the time, in effect, 'good riddance'.

JJ went on the promote the thoughts of Bishop Berkeley, being then involved in organising for the 1953 commemoration of the bicentenary of his death. He quoted at length from Joe Hone's edition of the *Querist*, in the introduction to which we are reminded of his status as the founder of a truly Irish political economy, as seen by John Mitchel and Arthur Griffith.

He light-heartedly introduced the topic with 'Whether if drunkenness be a necessary evil, men may not as well get drunk with the growth of their own country?' In other words, drink Guinness or Jameson if you must drink. He then went on to dig out a query for practically every Department involved in the Appropriations:

"Whether, if our exports be lessened, we ought not to lessen our imports?"

"Whether there be any other nation possessed of so much good land, and so many able hands to work it, which yet is beholden for bread to foreign countries?"

"Whether a wise State hath any interest nearer heart than the education of youth?"

"Whether, by a national bank, be not properly understood a bank, not only established by public authority as the Bank of England, but a bank in the hands of the public, wherein there are no shares, whereof the public alone is proprietor, and reaps all the benefit?" *JJ was particularly emphatic about this advanced concept.*

"Whether interest be not apt to bias judgment? and whether traders only are to be consulted about trade, or bankers about money?"

"Whether one, whose end is to make his countrymen think, may not gain his end, even though they should not think as he doth?" *JJ identified with this role, in his public life.*

"Whether there can be a worse sign than that people should quit their country for a livelihood? Though men often leave their country for health, or pleasure, or riches, yet to leave it merely for a livelihood, whether this be not exceeding bad and sheweth some peculiar mismanagement?"

"Whether the industry of our people employed in foreign lands, while our own are left uncultivated, be not a grave loss to the country?"

"Whether it would not be much better for us, if instead of sending our men abroad we could draw men from the neighbouring countries to cultivate our own?"

"Whether we had not, some years since, a manufacture of hats at Athlone, and of earthenware at Arklow, and what became of those manufactures?" *JJ used this particular Query in positive recognition of some of the results of the 1930s Fianna Fail industrialisation policy.*

And then finally "Whether it be not wonderful that with such pastures, and so many black cattle, we do not find ourselves in cheese?"

On this latter matter JJ applauded the recent modest development, but called for more, and pointed out the relatively low consumption per head.

In the latter part of his speech JJ dealt with the question of how to measure the reproductive capacity of the national herd. In-calf heifer statistics were only taken on June 1 and showed what must be a serious underestimate, knowing the herd size and the mean cow lifetime. They should be taken biennially.

Then on December 3 1952, on the Imposition of Duties (no 2) Bill, JJ picked up again the arguments used in his *Nemesis of Economic Nationalism*, pointing out that protecting an industry employing a measurable number of people sounded good at first sight, but the resulting rise in prices eroded jobs elsewhere, to an extent that was not easily visible, being spread thinly. While he approved of protecting

Waterford Glass, a traditional industry worthy of revival, to involve other firms in the protection process could increase the price of equipment necessary on the farm and in the farmyard, where the bulk of the wealth was produced.

Later in the same debate Senator James Douglas supported JJ's arguments for tariffs in favour of industries having a historical background, and thus a probability of survival. He adduced evidence from his own experience, relating to the Liberties weavers.

On December 4 1952, George O'Brien introduced a motion on the Income-tax Code seeking to set up a Commission to look into it. JJ supported this, with reference to the need to make medical expenses deductible, a device which would give for the first time a measure of incomes in the medical profession, as was the case in the USA. JJ then went on to the question of farm incomes, and how they were taxed currently based on the Griffith valuation. He regarded the latter as positive, as it gave an incentive to increase production, though it became a disincentive if they were so successful that they came into the tax net on the evidence of accounts kept. He wanted to design a system which would penalise sloth and reward enterprise. He then tried to get into discussion of the effects of the conacre system (11-month lettings), this being a source of income for many non-active owners of land, but was ruled out of order.

On December 10 1952, in the debate on the Finance (Excise Duties - Vehicles) Bill, JJ made an attempt to get an incentive built in, such as to encourage owners of small and medium lorries to work within a restricted radius, thus encouraging the use of the railways for goods transport, and to restrict the access of heavy lorries to roads fit to carry them.

He continued this effort on the next day, introducing, in two successive versions, an amendment entitling the Minister by regulation to enable locally-owned vehicles to service deliveries via the nearest public transport node, offering a favourable rate of taxation for this purpose. This however was dismissed by the Minister as impracticable. The debate tailed off into issues arising for the use of tractors for tasks other than agricultural.

Continuing what must by now have become a routine, on December 11 1952, on the Supplies and Services (Continuance) Bill, JJ again drew attention to the failure of agricultural production to increase in volume, despite the under-utilisation of land resources. He pointed out the contrast between the few effective farmers and the many who did as little as possible and allowed weeds to grow on their land. He urged consideration of passing a law to enable efficient farmers by compulsory purchase to expand their holdings at the expense of neighbours who neglected their land. He offered to give to the Minister privately examples of where so-called farmers preferred to leave land derelict than to sell it to a neighbour who could use it productively.

JJ as President of the Statistical and Social Inquiry Society

JJ's paper to the Statistical and Social Inquiry Society 'Economic Leviathans'(15) was the second of his Presidency; it was delivered on February 5 1953. It was a monumental attempt to summarise the history of the interactions between the 'leviathans', Britain and the US, in the interstices of whose turbulent movements we in our small boat, and other European nations, have to survive.

Chapter 6: The Period 1951-1960

JJ reminded his audience that the protectionism of the US in the 1920s had crippled the re-development of Europe's export trade, and led directly to the 1929 debacle. He went on to relate this to the dollar crises which followed the second world war, and predicted the demise effectively of the 'sterling area'. He analysed the effects of the Marshall Plan, including the negative effects of its coming to an end, and then the effects of the price perturbations introduced by the Korean war.

Commenting on the 'Colombo plan' he remarked that the indigent citizens of the colonial empire were being expected to subsidise both Britain's welfare State and her rearmament drive.

He went on to note the re-emergence of Germany and Japan as significant actors in the export markets of the world, and commented on the probable effects of the industrialisation programme in Eastern Europe, which he predicted would be crippled by the restriction of east-west trade.

This paper constituted a critical assessment of the way world trade had been developing under the influence of the Cold War and rearmament. He remarked that the US would rather spend $1B on rearmament than $100M on investing, perhaps with some risk, in the development of an impoverished country regarded as untrustworthy. He concluded that '...any sudden outbreak of real peace would inflict a most serious shock on capitalist economies...'.

The ensuing discussion included TK Whitaker, Prof GA Duncan, Mr Bourke and Dr Geary.

Science, TCD, UCD and Agricultural Research
On February 18 1953 at the TCD Board the Provost agreed to invite the British Association for the Advancement of Science to hold its 1957 meeting in Dublin. It is not clear whether this was a TCD initiative or a joint Dublin Universities action. I suspect the former, as I have not found any reference to the episode in Donal McCartney's *UCD a National Idea* (Gill & MacMillan 1999). But I do recollect the UCD science faculty people participating with enthusiasm, and we also contributed from the Dublin Institute of Advanced Studies, where I was working as a research scholar from 1953 to 1957, and then as Assistant Professor up to 1960.

Then on February 24 1953, after receiving a letter from the Department of Agriculture, the Board agreed in principle to support an Agricultural Institute. JJ, despite his marginalisation, still had some clout in this domain, and on April 29 the Board appointed him to attend as an observer an meeting of the International Seed Testing Association, to be held in Dublin on May 26-30. JJ continued to attend the Board, and write the minutes, despite being excluded from positions of influence. On November 25 the question of the Agriculture and Forestry course came up: there was a fees deal done with UCD, with TCD recognising UCD fees paid. This was a further step in the evolving agricultural role of TCD, in which JJ had a continuing interest.

The role of the TCD Board in supporting science-based initiatives during a 'dark age' of governmental neglect of things scientific perhaps needs to be analysed, and JJ on such matters was well-informed and supportive.

The Seanad: Gombeen Capitalism and other issues

Returning to the Seanad, on March 12 1953 the Restrictive Trade Practices Bill provided JJ with an opportunity to recycle some of his earlier work, published in Hermathena and elsewhere, on the classical origins of trade and the invention of money. He regaled the House learnedly with Plato, Aristotle, Berkeley and Boisguilbert, the main message being the positive effect of mass consumption on the overall health of the economy, quoting from the latter '...If the rich understood their interests they would wholly relieve the poor of their taxes, which would immediately create more well-to-do persons ...'.

Responding to a reprimand from the Chair, he then came down to earth with discussion of retail price maintenance, and re-iterated his criticisms of the retail trade that he had originally produced in the 20s and 30s; basically that there were far too many people engaged in it, and the whole could be handled by the top 7% of the shops doubling their capacity. He instanced his own experience with trying to sell *Irish Agriculture in Transition* outside the retail bookshops, with special deals for farmers clubs and so on. He had been told that he was welcome to do this if he liked, but that if he did, the retail trade would then refuse to handle it.

He concluded with some remarks on the nature of the capitalist system, which he regarded as basically trying to be co-operative, but being frustrated by the psychological emphasis on competition and conflict of interest. Increasing personal wealth at the expense of others was preferred by many to increasing wealth by supplying the genuine needs of others. The Bill emphasised the social obligations of economic decision-makers, and he therefore welcomed it, as far as it went, but he would have preferred a Bill pointing in a more consciously co-operative direction.

JJ has here put his finger on the essentially 'gombeen' nature of modern Irish capitalist culture, originating as it did with people who enriched themselves at the expense of their emigrating neighbours in the aftermath of the Famine.

Then on June 3 1953 we had the Great Northern Railway Bill. While congratulating the Minister (Lemass) on this Bill, JJ re-iterated the sense of injustice felt by the shareholders in the Irish railway system at the raw deals they got from the two Governments. Taking the GNR as an example, it would cost £30M to rebuild it at current prices, the sale of the assets would realise perhaps £10M, but the shareholders only got £4.5M for it. Leaving this aside, he went on to address the question of the overall cost of transport in Ireland, which was 5% of GNP, while in Britain it was 3.5% and in the US 2.2%. The problem was that production was insufficient to make full use of the transport infrastructure provided.

In the specific case of the GNR, the transport system was additionally damaged by Partition, which had restricted trade across the Border, despite, as JJ used to say, the '...three powerful links binding North and South... God, Mammon and the GNR...' (the Churches and the Banks being effectively all-Ireland bodies). He went on to stress the need to undermine Partition by not attacking it directly, in the aggressive mode current in the Anti-Partition League, but by concentrating on developing functional co-operation in economic and social life, of which the new GNR joint venture was an example, which was a 'link of steel' echoing the Thomas Davis quatrain.

On June 17 1953 they debated the Turf Development Bill. After congratulating the Minister on an excellent Bill, JJ went on to point out some of the problems that had arisen as a result of Bord na Mona activities in the midlands, in particular, the denuding of midland farms of access to farm labour. On the other hand, the settlements with housing, built by Bord na Mona, would remain after the bogs had been exhausted, and the people living there would have the opportunity to develop the cutaway bog as new farmland.

One farmer he knew(16) had stopped growing crops through lack of labour, and had concentrated on intensive feeding of cattle, using silage, and stall-feeding in winter. For this purpose however he was now unable to get straw for bedding, and JJ wondered if it would be possible to get peat mould from Bord na Mona at a price consistent with using it for bedding, so that the manure generated could be put back to the land.

JJ concluded by noting the existence of the Bord na Mona research unit at Newbridge, and wondered if the technology would become available for gasification of peat by distillation or pyrolysis, leading to other industrial raw materials as by-products.

JJ had almost certainly picked this latter idea up from the present writer and/or Desmond Greaves, who had, up to 1951, been a carbon technologist working for Powell Duffryn. At the same time Greaves fulfilled the role of a Marxist guru, interacting with the nascent Irish Left, in which capacity he had on many occasions shared a family meal in the Johnston house. I treat this as part of my own memoirs elsewhere in this chapter, and in more depth in the left-political stream.

After a brief incursion into interest rates on July 1 1953 on the Land (no 2) Bill, on July 15 1953 in the debate on the Imposition of Duties Bill JJ was provoked into his *Nemesis of Economic Nationalism* mode of thinking, and accusing the Minister of operating a shotgun policy of protective duties on all sorts of disconnected items, from plastic hair slides to art paper, when he should be developing agricultural production and industries based on agricultural raw materials. He was backed up in this by Senator WB Stanford, who had taken JJ's TCD Seanad seat. These policies were not reconcilable with the IBEC Report.

This drew a predictably robust response from Senator Summerfield, the leader of the protected industry lobby, who however was somewhat coy about naming protected industries fit to compete in the export market, when challenged to do so by Senator Stanford.

On July 16 1953 in the Finance Bill debate JJ was able again to ride a few hobby-horses, attacking subsidies on principle, being particularly scathing about subsidised housing, the need for which he attributed to the distortion of the market caused by the Rent Restrictions Acts of the first world war, which had made it impossible for capital to invest in housing for rental.

He commented on the recent interest-rate rise, and supported George O'Brien in calling for a more intelligent procedure than interest-rate adjustment to govern capital investment priorities. He warned against the State soaking up too much capital. He questioned the concept of the 'right to work', warning of the danger of its becoming an obligation to work at whatever the State dictated, which he identified with 'communism'.

State spending on amenities should be tax-funded, while state investment in productive enterprise (e.g. electricity generation) could be funded by borrowing. State funding in support of industrial development should be rifle rather then shotgun or blunderbuss. He supported the IBEC Report. Most industry depended on imported raw materials, and the value of industrial exports was only 8% of the total; the value of imported raw material was four times as much. The balance was made up by agricultural exports.

He attacked income tax as counter-productive and called for local government tax relief in agriculture to favour new farm buildings.

Then on July 29 1953, on the Central Fund (no 2) Bill 1953, 2nd stage, JJ again brought up the question of housing for rental, and the extent of subsidy of local government housing, which he asked the Minister to reassure him was being paid for out of taxation and not by borrowing. He then went on to the question of unemployment in the building trades, which was not dependent on the extent of the housing subsidy, and un-stabilised by any ongoing demand for maintenance of the older housing stock, which was going to rack and ruin as fast as new houses were being built, thanks to the Rent Restrictions Acts introduced by the British during the first world war. He produced a letter from a 71-year old widow dependent for her income on rent from a dilapidating controlled-rent house.

He then went on to relate the housing shortage in Dublin to the depopulation of rural Ireland consequent on the failure to increase agricultural production, and to develop local industries based on agricultural raw materials. He adduced international comparisons, with countries in Europe recovered from the war, among which Ireland was at the bottom of the output per hectare list, and near the bottom for output per head.

The opportunity to get fresh capital and know-how into Irish agriculture had been squandered by the 25% tax put on buyers of Irish farms from abroad. Had they been allowed to settle they would rapidly have been culturally absorbed, according to tradition, becoming 'more Irish than the Irish themselves'.

He castigated the dairy industry for its hanging on to the 'dual-purpose cow' and crippling itself and the beef industry by expecting the one to be the by-product of the other. He called for a farm survey, with some grading system for farms, with Grades A and B getting absolute security of tenure, and Grade C taken over by the Land Commission and leased to farmers' sons who had been through agricultural college. In support of this he quoted Michael Davitt: '...multiplication of land-owners through State-aided land purchase would not remove the evils inherent in the private ownership of land...'(17).

He concluded by advocating the Danish system of farmers' sons working as labourers on neighbours' farms for a real wage, rather than for a pittance on their fathers' farms.

On August 6 1953 the Health Bill 1952 was debated. This was Fianna Fail's version of the ill-fated 'Mother and Child Scheme' of Dr Noel Browne. JJ had not been in the Seanad at the time of the controversy, but I remember him being acutely aware of the issues.

He began with a *Querist* quotation:

'Whether interest be not apt to bias judgment and whether traders only should be consulted about trade or bankers about money',

and extended it to include 'doctors about health'. Doctors had a vested interest in the ill-health of the wealthier classes. The Chinese however pay their doctors when they are well, and stop paying when they are sick. JJ hoped this Bill was going in that direction. On the whole however the medical profession had been re-distributive in its services over the years, subsidising the treatment of the poor by their fees from the rich. He himself had had free service from Sir Robert Woods when a student, with nasal surgery, to his lasting benefit. Better to put resources into good health for the young than adding a year or two to the age of old crocks.

He went on to warn against opening the health service to abuse, as had happened in the UK; he gave anecdotal evidence from Belfast, where the waiting rooms had become social centres: '...I didn't see you at the doctor's, was there something wrong with you?'.

On November 18 1953 JJ used the Supplies and Services Bill as an opportunity to comment on the international situation, attacking the implication that we would be pleased to join NATO if only Partition were ended. NATO he castigated as being inconsistent with the principles of UNO. He was pulled up by the Chair for taking this issue up; JJ defended himself on the basis that the international situation determined the economic environment, but in the end gave in. As a parting shot he tried to discuss transport policy, with the closure of the railway station at Naas, and the neglect of the by-roads.

In the end he agreed to postpone these issues until the Appropriations Bill, which came up on November 26 1953. JJ welcomed the fact that the Minister for External Affairs was responding to the debate, and used the occasion to stress the common economic problems in all European countries, with inflation being fuelled by rearmament. Membership of NATO should be avoided even if Partition were to be ended. The practical response to the Communist challenge was to make capitalism work, pointing it in a co-operative direction along lines pioneered by Sir Horace Plunkett and George Russell. Rearmament was '...like the person who decides to commit suicide for fear he might get killed ...'. He did not think the Russians were thinking of aggression, having lost 10M dead in the recent war.

The Chair asked him to come back to home affairs, so he homed in on the proposal to build a fixed bridge at Athlone, urging the development of the Shannon and the waterways not only as a leisure activity, instancing the Dromineer regatta, but also for economic activity, instancing the transport of the coal supply from the Arigna mines, near Lough Allen. The canal connecting the Shannon Navigation with Lough Allen had been abandoned as a result of the ESB control of the lake level.

We come back to *Nemesis* country on December 2 1953 with the Imposition of Duties (no 2) Bill: JJ complained about there were duties on standard farm inputs like wire mesh, and blades for a Bushman saw.

In the next session on February 24 1954 on the National Development Fund Bill JJ showed signs of weariness, having been over this ground before so many times. He attempted, unsuccessfully, to steer the debate in the direction of agricultural added value, instancing the Dingle Peninsula onion-growers, and the need for capitalising the under 50-acre farms via dairying, rather than paying their occupants the dole for doing nothing.

Later in the debate on the same Bill, on March 4, he supported an amendment oriented towards supporting some sort of voluntary agency, or alliance of relevant organisations, in support of the economic development of the Gaeltacht, along lines pioneered by the French-speakers of Quebec. There were again signs of weariness; he had been over this ground before.

Then on March 16 1954, on the Central Fund Bill, with the Dáil in process of dissolution, JJ spoke at length, with a view to getting as much of his views on the record as possible, knowing that he was unlikely to get in again(18). He declared the intention of addressing the problem of the inelasticity of agricultural output over the previous 20 years, but first made some points on the current Estimates.

He expressed appreciation of the increase in capitation fees paid by the State in respect of secondary education, as being of particular value to the smaller schools attended by the religious minority. He compared the situation with that in Northern Ireland, where the expansion of second-level schooling had been considerable: in Dungannon Royal School in his time there were some 60 pupils; now there were 250. The Republic was lagging behind this rate of increase.

He expressed concern at the rate at which historic buildings were being demolished, particularly via a process of de-roofing to avoid paying rates. Some 'big houses' would be marketable to foreign buyers who desired to live here or to retire here, and such people should be encouraged to play a care-taking role with our heritage of historic buildings. The 25% tax burden on such purchases should be scrapped.

Turning to agricultural stagnation, in contrast to the industrial increase, JJ took up some European comparisons, using UNFAO statistics. The output per hectare was the lowest of the 14 European countries considered. Output per person was in the third quartile, ahead of Greece and Italy. 'We would have to double... before we would achieve the standards achieved in Denmark and Belgium and treble... (to) achieve the results achieved in the UK'.

He then went into the history of production over the decades, and concluded that '...for one reason or another we failed to integrate our cash-crop cultivation with our livestock production ...'. He then went on to compare the declining pig and poultry populations in the Republic with the thriving situation in the North.

He identified the key issue as being the relationship between the price of store cattle in the autumn and fat cattle in the spring, this being what determined the decision to stall-feed in the winter, generating the manure required by tillage. This price-ratio was unfavourable due to British policy. Similarly the price of feed relative to the price of produce dominated the activity of the small farmer attempting to produce pigs and poultry.

He went on to be critical of the 'dual-purpose cow', again using European comparisons: small-farm prosperity in Western Europe was based on '...a plentiful milk supply produced on the farms and on the production of by-products that depend for their existence on a plentiful supply of milk ...'. A consequence of the abandonment of the dual-purpose cow and the switch to high-yielding milk breeds would be that the beef people would have to breed their own supplies of beef animals. The link between the two sectors would then no longer be via calves, but would need to be developed via fodder crops, particularly feeding barley.

The 1953 decision regarding a support price for wheat had resulted in far too high an acreage, and had pulled up the price of feeding barley to uneconomic levels. There was a case for keeping some wheat production going for strategic reasons. High wheat prices were subsidised by the taxpayer via the bread subsidy. They led to 'wheat ranching', which impairs the stored fertility of the land, straw being left in the field to rot rather than ending up as manure via livestock stall-feeding.

He concluded by again urging that the agricultural horse be put before the industrial cart, as had been done in Denmark, with expansion of the former fuelling the latter.

Back to *Nemesis* on April 7 1954 with the Imposition of Duties Bill: JJ castigated Minister Lemass for imposing a duty on milk cans, thus increasing the costs of the dairying industry which was far from prospering, indeed requiring consumer subsidy.

The 1954 Kilkenny Debates

On April 22 1954 there was a debate on Partition in Kilkenny; this was the first occasion when politicians north and south shared a platform. JJ and the Irish Association had a hand in organising it, and JJ participated. The local organisation of the event was in the hands of the Kilkenny Debating Society, which was a subsidiary body of the Kilkenny Arts Council. One can here also see the local influence of Hubert Butler(19).

The motion "that the best interests of 'Ulster' lie with the United Kingdom" was proposed by Col WWB Topping, then Chief Whip of the Stormont Unionist Party, supported by William Douglas OBE, the Party secretary. Seán MacBride led the opposition, supported by Eoin (the Pope) O'Mahony. Professor Myles Dillon from the Dublin Institute of Advanced Studies was in the chair.

Col Topping, speaking as an Ulsterman, an Irishman and an Orangeman, listed some reasons why the price of losing the UK connection was seen as too high. He homed in on the hypocrisy of the official Irish language policy: the Dáil Debates were printed in both languages but only indexed in English. Free trade with the UK for manufactured goods was important to them as an industrial economy. Farmers had guaranteed prices within the UK. Government orders for ships and aircraft were supplied. The 'Eire' government was dominated by the Roman Catholic Hierarchy, as evidenced by the 1951 'mother and child scheme' of Dr Noel Browne, and the oppressive censorship of books and films. All this did not prevent the two parts of Ireland from being good neighbours.

Seán MacBride mentioned the higher level of tax in the North, and insisted that there was a mutually exclusive choice between being British and being Irish. He stressed the linguistic diversity of many European states. He mentioned the common problem of Irish-owned assets abroad, with lack of investment in Ireland; this was substantial and common to both parts of the country. He suggested that the Government in Britain would be unlikely to enact legislation unapproved of by the Church of England, and that the C of E had been responsible for deposing their

King. He questioned the level of tolerance in a society which allowed slogans like 'to hell with the Pope' to be written on walls.

William Douglas praised the economic record of the North, mentioning newly set-up firms like Courtaulds and Dunlop. The only place in the English-speaking world where the State aided Roman Catholic schools was Northern Ireland. He quoted Cahir Healy, the Nationalist MP, in support of the non-existence of discrimination in housing.

The 'Pope' O'Mahony(20) argued for north-south agriculture-industry interaction as the route to prosperity, and pointed out that a new 'Ulster Plantation' was going on, with all people in key leading positions increasingly being English, especially in the university system, with Ulster intellectuals leaving to take up posts in Britain.

In the context of the motion 'that the Society was worthy of support' JJ referred to Kilkenny as the Athens of Ireland; he mentioned Lord Charlemont his predecessor as President, and his own Presidency, of the Irish Association, and the role of that body in encouraging mutual understanding and goodwill.

Mary O'Malley, a Nationalist member of Belfast Corporation and a member of the Irish Association, gave clear evidence of discrimination in housing against Catholics, and referred to censorship on the part of the BBC regarding the Special Powers Act.

Arnold Marsh(21) pointed out that 75% of Ulster industry was foreign-owned and that they had thrown away their independence.

While JJ was still in the Seanad, and President of the Irish Association, he actively promoted the role of public enterprise and the industrial infrastructure, and its significance in an all-Ireland context, via a delegation of Irish Association members from the North, who visited Bord na Mona installations in 1954. This episode was almost certainly a spin-off from the Kilkenny debate itself, or the contacts made while organising it(22).

TCD and Agricultural Research

On April 21 at the TCD Board JJ for once did not do the minutes; the Board had extended to the Saturday, and JJ was by now living in Laois. He was also actively involved on this occasion with the Kilkenny Debates, as summarised above, on behalf of the Irish Association. On May 5 however he was back doing the minutes, and was still apparently regarded as relevant when it came to matters agricultural: JJ and Frank Mitchell (Registrar and counting as a new-wave heavyweight) being delegated on May 26 to meet with the Minister for Agriculture to discuss the future of the Veterinary College. There were 8 TCD veterinary students annually, but there were fee anomalies; to equalise required a departmental grant. The Veterinary College had become a shared TCD/UCD facility, a situation giving rise to all sorts of problems.

I remember discussing the question at the time with Justin Keating, who was on the staff, and was convinced there were behind-the-scenes conspiracies, involving 'Knights and Masons'.

At this point it is relevant to remark that there is need for research and publication of the background story of how the Government and the Universities interacted around the problem of funding agricultural research, a process which led in the end to the foundation of An Foras Taluntais (the Agricultural Institute) as a State applied-research institute without initially any University linkages.

Was this the State's way of saying 'a plague on both your houses' to the Dublin Colleges, which were effectively partitioned on the basis of religion? There undoubtedly is a story here to be unearthed by someone with the energy to dig. Justin Keating would be a good source of first-hand worms-eye experience. I understand that Pat Fox in NUI Cork has been researching this background, and look forward to seeing the results..

In June the annual appointments come up. After some political manoeuvres, with JJ initially nominating himself for Senior Dean, against the Provost's nomination of Godfrey, in the end JJ backed off from Senior Dean and got to be Senior Proctor, a post which had to do with the formal awarding of degrees to those entitled to them, a somewhat nominal role. *The fact that the award of the present writer's PhD was coming up soon may have figured in JJ's motivation.*

On October 27 a motion from the Junior Fellows viewing with abhorrence the invitation of Sir Oswald Mosley to a College society was considered and supported. At the same meeting it was decided to set up a School of Veterinary Science; this must have been a further step in the Agricultural Institute background saga. Then on November 10 the Veterinary College staff were recognised, and a School Committee was set up, with JJ involved.

Also at this meeting there was recorded, for the first time, the 'approval of the Proctor's Lists'; this must have been a consequence of JJ being Senior Proctor (a job hitherto regarded as nominal) and also keeping the Board minutes: he wanted to assert the legal standing of the role, as something other than nominal. In fact later on there appear recorded amendments to the lists, suggesting that JJ had successfully re-asserted a positive role for the Board in the awarding of degrees. Then on December 1 there was recorded the award of the degree of PhD to Conor Cruise O'Brien.

Seanad Swan-song

My father's final speech in the Seanad was on July 7 1954 with the Finance Bill. This took place after the election, with a new Government; the Seanad elections take place after a short delay. JJ used the occasion to put on record as much as he was let of the distillation of his experience(18).

He began by criticising the continuation of the butter subsidy, pointing out the adverse effect it had on the production of farmers' butter outside the creamery areas.

He then went into the basics of the principles of levies and subsidies, and used it as a means of developing a spirited defence of an article he had written two years previously, advocating a levy on the export of store cattle, to be used as subsidy for home-produced animal feeding-stuffs. He read into the Seanad record the text of this article, and subsequent press correspondence, after an altercation with the Chair; he made the case that his position had been attacked and misrepresented in the Dáil, and the chair allowed it.

In this final distilled argument, the culmination of long political battles going back to the 1920s, he managed to encapsulate many of his critiques of a pathological production system which had been crippled by the imposition by Britain of conditions leading to the dominance of the store cattle trade.

Plunkett Centenary

In 1954 the National Co-operative Council published the *Sir Horace Plunkett Centenary Handbook* and JJ was invited to contribute. This was the Proceedings of a centenary event organised, on a modest scale, in Pearse St Public Library on October 18 1954. It was opened by JJ, who was reported in the Press as having attributed to Plunkett's influence the opposition to Communism in rural Ireland.

The National Co-operative Council, as we have seen, was a gadfly body, on the fringe of the mainstream movement, attempting to activate the latter via the re-discovery of co-operative principles and the education process. It never achieved much success, though there were I think one or two worker co-ops initiated as a result of its activities.

I quote the following key paragraphs from JJ's paper as published in the *Handbook(23)*:

"...Plunkett issued a clarion call to self help through mutual help. Irish farmers were, and still are the principal wealth producers in Ireland. Their low standard of production and living was the central economic and social problem of the nation. Centuries of alien misrule had confirmed an instinctive belief that "the Government" was the principal cause of economic distress. The recent change in the attitude of Government from policies of mere repression to policies of conscious and conscience-stricken amelioration was creating the even more demoralising belief that Government was the only possible source of economic improvement....

"...Sir Horace Plunkett was deeply concerned to bring the commercial and industrial interests of Belfast more fully into the current of the national life. Some of his closest associates in the Recess Committee and in the IAOS were prominent Ulster industrialists. Partition, of which the IAOS was also a victim, has effectively restricted this helpful co-operation between Northern industrialism and Southern agriculture. The fact of Partition even to-day operates in much the same way as the fact of alien Government in the past to promote a spirit of personal apathy, or at least to divert to political agitation energies that would be better employed in more constructive work....

"...The Marxians hold that individual character is formed and dominated by economic environment. Sir Horace regarded individual character as of paramount importance. By free voluntary co-operation with his fellows the individual would learn to seek his own economic welfare only by methods which at the same time promoted the economic welfare of his fellows. A social organisation based on such an economic system could not fail to make its members better men and better citizens.

"The essence of the matter is that the individual should freely choose to seek his own good through such association. An outwardly similar organisation imposed by authority, however benevolent, could not have the same moral influence and psychological value.....

"...When Plunkett began his propaganda the tenants had already been liberated. But no social organisation had been imposed, or even conceived, which could bind the isolated units of the mass of peasantry into a coherent and self-conscious rural community. '...In Ireland the transition from landlordism to a peasant proprietary not only does not create any corporate existence among the occupying peasantry but rather deprives them of the slight social coherence which they formerly possessed as tenants of the same landlord ...' (*Ireland in the New Century* p49).

"Both Communism and Capitalism in its cruder forms sacrifice the individual to the material power of the State in the one case and the material gain of the capitalist in the other. By organising the economic activities of farmers on a co-operative system Plunkett sought to give the national economy as a whole a co-operative outlook, and permeate the national being with a social philosophy in which the individual would be exalted because he was part of a social structure wherein economic efficiency was promoted in an atmosphere of friendly co-operative association.

"Co-operation, as envisaged by him, is simply the application of elementary Christian principles to economic relationships and social organisation. If two hostile worlds now confront each other in threatening hostility, surely the Plunkett philosophy -- in action -- is infinitely preferable to a 'cold war', or to a third 'hot war' which must destroy us all. We in Ireland cannot claim to have made that philosophy fully articulate either in thought or action, but at least we owe it to his memory to make ourselves familiar with the full scope of his far-seeing wisdom, and to approach our everyday problems in the spirit of his inspiring message...."

It is evident from the above that the Press totally misunderstood JJ's message, which was directed against top-down central-state autocracy, and in favour of bottom-up democratisation of economic organisation, which is Marxism in the sense understood by Connolly and the present writer, and constituted basically the Communist vision before the latter was perverted by Stalin.

TCD and the Kells Ingram Farm

It is appropriate at this point to abstract JJ's role on the Board regarding the Agricultural Institute and the Kells Ingram Farm.

Towards the end of 1955 came a serious attempt by TCD to get its foot in the door of the process whereby the Government was setting up the Agricultural Institute. On November 2 they issued a press statement on Agricultural Education, which they were currently discussing with the Minister, the TCD spokesmen being JJ and Frank Mitchell. The statement pointed out the TCD track-record: they had been active since 1906; it was part of the science faculty; they did their practicals at a farm near Kells up to 1912 and then at the Albert College in Glasnevin, which was then under the Department of Agriculture and Technical Instruction (DATI), and also serviced UCD.

Then in 1924 the Dáil handed over the Albert College to UCD, along with the College of Science, without consultation with TCD. The TCD Board at the time then made ad hoc arrangements with Coffey, the UCD President. In 1953 the

Minister for Agriculture had invited TCD to take part in the proposed arrangements for the projected Agricultural Institute; the idea was to bring together the two Universities and the professional organisations. There was in prospect either a central agricultural faculty, or else upgraded faculties in both Universities. The statement was signed by GF Mitchell, Registrar.

At a TCD Board meeting on January 11 1956, minuted by JJ, John Garmany of Magee was invited to join the School Committee of Economics and Political Science, emphasising the fact that the Magee connection was not only about Presbyterian theology. We will have occasion to encounter JG in the context of JJ's SSISI network (and the extension of the Barrington Lectures northwards), and also on JJ's Irish Association network, where he participated in the seminal Derry Whit weekend meeting in 1965, at which the seed-bed for the Civil Rights movement in the North was prepared.

JJ was prepared to use every possible lever he could lay hands on to keep alive the all-Ireland cultural and educational links within the Protestant community, and to keep TCD in the picture as a national institution, despite the 'intellectual partition of Dublin'.

On January 18 1956 Máirtín Ó Cadhain was recruited as a Grade 2 lecturer in Modern Irish, just about a decade after his release from the Curragh. He subsequently occupied the Chair. This was an enlightened move on the part of Trinity, emphasising the continuing aspiration to become part of the cultural mainstream without yielding to Catholic cultural hegemonism.

On March 14 it was proposed to develop a School of Agriculture in association with the projected Agricultural Institute, and a printed memorandum was projected, critical of the Government proposals, which were described as vague. If the entity was centralised, TCD wanted unrestricted access. If decentralised, TCD wanted full faculty status. The memo suggested four university-based faculties, each tackling different research problems. TCD was making a bid for soil science, with emphasis on upland soils. A location for a farm in south Co Dublin was sought, with access to upland. The farm was to be run on commercial lines. The other locations were to be related to UCD, UCC and UCG. The memo was presented to the Minister at the end of May by the Provost and Registrar.

According to the 1956-57 Calendar, JJ was on the Agriculture School Committee; he had by now dropped off the Commerce School Committee.

Early in 1957 the agriculture issue reasserted itself: on February 20 the DU Agricultural Society was sanctioned; this provided a forum for the agricultural students, a source of political support. The next week, on the 27th, the Board agreed the purchase of Townley Hall, an estate on the Boyne, near Drogheda, not far from the site of the famous Battle.

The farm was to be called after John Kells Ingram, who in his youth, in the Young Ireland epoch, had written the words of the song "Who Fears to Speak of '98", and who later had been active with Fitzgerald in the politics of the Royal University and the background to the foundation of the NUI. This naming was also a political assertion of TCD as a force in national mainstream politics, and a refusal to be marginalised by the 'Catholic nationalist' politicking of UCD under the leadership of Michael Tierney, which had the downgrading of TCD as its objective(24).

The issue was contentious, and the Board divided, the names being registered. The Provost, Parke, Gwynn, Luce, Stanford, Wormell, Mitchell, Chubb and JJ were for; against were Thrift, Godfrey, Fearon, Duncan, Poole and Torrens. *There is digging to be done if we are to understand the political rationale for this division. Both old-timers and 'new wave' are on each side. Opposition seems to focus on the science and medical faculties.* Duncan, who held the Chair of Economics, was opposed. But Provost McConnell and Registrar Mitchell were supportive, and JJ for a time got to ride with 'new wave' college politics, until later when the project went sour under the stress of what perhaps can be identified as Government centralist institutional politics.

I can perhaps put forward as a working hypothesis that those against represented the old Protestant defeated-ascendancy view (keep your heads down, don't rock the boat, accept Catholic nationalist hegemony, and hope to survive unnoticed in the undergrowth) while those for represented a positive assertion of Protestant participation in mainstream national development. The Provost, Gwynn, Stanford, Mitchell and my father were certainly all of the latter view.

A farm management committee was set up consisting of JJ, Mitchell, Byrne and one Lett, who would appear to have been the farm manager. It was agreed that the committee should open a bank account in Drogheda. The Veterinary College question was still smouldering: the Provost, the Bursar and Jessop were to meet with the Veterinary Council. These issues were all connected with the question of the relative roles of TCD, UCD and the Government in organising for the allocation of resources to agricultural research.

According to the 1957-58 Calendar, where a mention of Townley Hall first appears, the house was built by Francis Johnston in or about 1800. Mrs Townley Balfour, who had owned it, had died in 1955; she was a daughter of JK Ingram. The College was the beneficiary of a legacy left by her brother, Captain J Kells Ingram, who died in 1956.

When the Annual Offices came around on June 19 JJ managed, with the momentum of the Kells Ingram Farm victory, to get his way with regard to appointments. The Provost wanted Mitchell for Bursar and Chubb for Registrar, while JJ wanted these reversed; Mitchell had done a good job as Registrar along with JJ, representing the College with the Department of Agriculture, and JJ wanted continuity of experience with this role in the context of the Kells Ingram farm committee. JJ got his way. It was then agreed that Mitchell as Registrar should, as a routine role, represent the College in negotiations with external bodies.

On November 13 1957 it was agreed that the Kells Ingram Farm was to be accessible to second-year agricultural students from the following Hilary term, and the Department of Agriculture was to be asked to support a research programme in farm economics. This represented the culmination of JJ's attempts to get a scientific understanding of scale effects in farm organisation(25). We have here a 300 acre unit, with timber, crops, livestock and a walled garden, an integrated traditional manor farm unit, supporting over 10 families and generating substantially more added value than 10 30 acre units would produce, if the farm were to be divided according to the political objectives of Fianna Fail.

From now on JJ's main interest was the Kells Ingram farm. On March 19 1958 the management committee was strengthened by adding the Bursar and Webb (the botanist) to Registrar Mitchell, JJ and manager Lett. They were authorised to sell some timber. The bank account was moved from Drogheda to Dublin. One can here read between the lines; economic life in Ireland was at its nadir; there were mass demonstrations of unemployed in the streets of Dublin. Emigration was at its peak. The College was concerned: has it over-extended itself? On April 30 however they declared confidence in the future and invested £3500 in building a bungalow for the manager. The manor house itself was more suited as a conference centre, which role they later tried to develop.

On May 5 they agreed that GF Mitchell, the Registrar, was to represent them on the Board of the Agricultural Institute, and Jessop was to represent them on the Veterinary Council. On June 25 the farm accounts were noted, without comment.

By October of 1958 there were indications of unease in the Agriculture School: students were on the agenda, requiring permission to do supplementary examinations.

In November Duncan emerged in the lead of the opposition to the Kells Ingram Farm: on December 10 the matter came up, and Duncan wanted the discussion postponed until he could be there. He did not get his way; the matter was discussed, and it was agreed that the farm should seek credit subject to the College Finance Committee. Then on January 28 the Kells Ingram Farm again came up; Duncan proposed and Fearon seconded that the College should get rid of it. On the recommendation of the Finance Committee, a development budget of £20K was agreed, over the period 1958-63, to be regarded as a loan. The pro-farm group was still getting its way, and fighting a rearguard action.

The handing over of the farm budget to the College Finance Committee was a stimulus for JJ to take a look at College investment policy, which he did in a memo on February 11. He compared it unfavourably with the Church of Ireland Representative Body, which had gone for an equity portfolio a decade earlier.

On April 22 1959 there was a reference to the installation of a cobalt 60 radiation source at the Kells Ingram Farm, with a view to experiments in genetics involving irradiation of seeds etc. The Farm, and its possible role in the still nascent Agricultural Institute was still high on the agenda of the academic leadership: Mitchell and Pakenham-Walsh were sent to attend a conference of Schools of Agriculture in Paris on July 27-31, under the OEEC (Organisation of European Economic Co-operation), the 'Marshall Plan' body which was funding the Irish investment in the Agricultural Institute.

By April 29 JJ was no longer doing minutes. On May 6 they approved the initiation of an Honours course in Agriculture. JJ was absent on May 20 ad May 27; about this time he moved from Grattan Lodge near Stradbally to Bayly Farm near Nenagh. He got back to attend Board meetings on June 3; after this there are no more minutes in his writing. His increasingly poor hearing was by this time becoming a serious barrier.

On July 1 the Kells Ingram Farm came up again. Pakenham-Walsh and P McHugh the manager (he has apparently succeeded Lett) signed the cheques. The accounts were accepted on October 1, in JJ's absence, and the report was noted. There was set up a School Committee for Agriculture and Forestry; Pakenham-Walsh was Registrar and the committee included McHugh the Manager, the Bursar, JJ, Mitchell and LG Carr-Lett, who apparently now had an external advisory role. Much of the work within the TCD School of Agriculture was actually done in UCD; I interpret this as evidence of an attempt on the TCD side to develop inter-university co-operation, in the context of the opportunity presented by the OEEC funding, despite Tierney's ongoing hostility, as documented by Donal McCartney in his *UCD a National Idea*.

During this time my father remained as Senior Proctor; he held this post until 1962, after which he ceased to hold any annual office.

He remained active in defence of the TCD role in agriculture, insofar as he could, from his distant base in Bayly Farm near Nenagh. He tended to come up for the mid-week, live in his rooms, and take in the Board meetings on a Wednesday. Sometimes however they overflowed to a Saturday, and these he missed.

He was absent on February 10, 17 and 24 1960. On the latter date the Board agreed to drop the Arts requirements for the School of Agriculture; this meant dropping the French and German options. JJ had almost certainly put these requirements in, on foot of his earlier experience of trying to get the Irish agricultural community to look to the Continent rather than to Britain for external experience.

On March 16 they decided to empower the Vacation Committee to conclude an agreement with the new Agricultural Institute for setting up an Applied Genetics Unit. Then on April 20 they employed a Research Assistant, Saeve(sic) Coffey, at the Kells Ingram Farm, and the following week they agreed to give Mitchell residential status there, while he remained Chairman of the Farm Committee.

On May 11 it was agreed that George Dawson in Genetics should undertake work for the Agricultural Institute, and on June 1 they decided to expand the Veterinary College building into the College Botanical Gardens. They were still clearly aspiring to have an ongoing role in both agricultural and veterinary science. Dawson's Genetics Unit was set up on June 29 at the Kells Ingram Farm, the agreement with the Agricultural Institute having been made successfully.

By November 1960 it was apparent that they needed to spend money on Kells Ingram farm again; they agreed on 2nd to seek tenders for alterations. On November 5, which was a Saturday, JJ was absent; the Board shows its liberal colours by agreeing to use the College Chapel for any denomination, provided there is a Chaplain nominated by a Church.

On November 9, JJ being present, 5 students were excluded from the School of Agriculture, suggesting that the system was under some strain. However JJ got to represent the College at the National Horticultural Research Conference to be held in Dublin in December. He was however absent on Saturday November 19, when the question of evidence for the Higher Education Commission was discussed.

To conclude the decade for JJ: one gets the impression that his pet projects, the Kells Ingram Farm, and the Honours School of Agriculture, were under some strain, and he was losing interest, turning to the completion of his Berkeley book.

***

I have touched on my initial political role in the 1950s above, before leaving for France, and I expand on it below during the time after my return. In retrospect, my scientific work was central, and I gave it priority. Insofar as political work in the undergrowth of the nascent Left was feasible, I did also try to give it some marginal-time attention.

RJ and High-Energy Particle Physics in France

The Ecole Polytechnique physics laboratory, which I joined in October 1951, had three 'cloud-chamber' groups and an 'ionographic emulsion' group. A 'cloud-chamber' is a device for making tracks of charged particles visible, in the form of a trail of droplets of liquid in a super-saturated gas. The group of which I became a member ran a cloud-chamber installation at the Pic du Midi in the Pyrenees, which consisted of two large chambers, the upper one being in a 250KW solenoid, producing a magnetic field for measuring particle momentum, and the lower one containing lead plates, for measuring the range of stopping particles.

I found myself contributing to the maintenance and development of the electronics. I had picked up in my final year in TCD some experience of pulse electronics, thanks to a course laid on in the Dublin Institute of Advanced Studies by one McCusker, who had a cloud-chamber experiment running in the School of Cosmic Physics, Merrion Square. The key text was Elmore and Sands, which enshrined the pulse electronics experience from the Los Alamos 'Manhattan Project' (ie the atom-bomb). Surprisingly this had not reached France yet, and I found myself regarded as an expert. The electronics had been developed at the then existing level of technicianship, with the gain of amplifiers dependent on various random and time-dependent factors. I introduced the principle of the negative-feedback amplifier, where the gain depended on the ratio of two resistors, and was more or less independent of the state of the vacuum tubes (transistors were then unheard of). Getting a good square pulse, with fast rise-time, for use in coincidence and anti-coincidence logic circuits, was embedded in the Elmore and Sands text, and we absorbed it avidly.

There was also a problem with the photo-flash tubes, which were driven at high voltage from a bank of heavy-duty capacitors ('ici, c'est la chaise electrique'). Sometimes one of the 3 flash tubes did not work, and in this case the chamber illumination would be uneven, and the picture useless. I rigged up a handy little indicator, with neon lights, which showed whether all 3 flashes had worked, and if not, which one was at fault. This was regarded as pure magic, and from then on my reputation was assured.

While none of this work was 'world-shaking' in scientific terms, the experience was part of a global scientific culture which has thrived and continued to give increasing insight into the laws of nature. It was my privilege to have been part of this culture, and to have benefited from it in human terms. One of the lasting memories is of the relationship between the members of the physics community and the technicians who worked with them making their equipment, and getting it to work; this was based on mutual respect between people having complementary skills, unsullied by exploitation. I shared with JD Bernal(26) the vision that this might be a glimpse of the human side of the productive process in some post-capitalist future, owned by those directly concerned and not by some remote alien capitalist consortium.

I should perhaps record an exception; one Mayer, who came from Brazil, from an upper-crust Hispanic background, refused to help with the cleaning of the windows of the cloud-chamber, insisting that this was not physicists' work. It is actually quite a crucial part of the preparation of the chamber when stripped down for maintenance, and everyone concerned had to know how to do it correctly; it is part of the 'black art'. This perhaps says something about Latin-American society. In fact, most of the physics world, being usually at the frontiers of knowledge, has to live with the need for hands-on mastery of its technical practice by its scientists, who then, when they can, pass the knowledge on to the technician community by apprenticeship or osmosis. There is no room for disdain of dirty-handed processes.

In July 1953, towards the end of my spell in scientific work in France, there was a Cosmic Ray Conference(27) at Bagneres de Bigorre, which was the base-location for the Pic du Midi operations. This was held there in honour of our cloud-chamber installation, which was ground-breaking, and at the time the largest in the world. The conference explored competitively the utilities of the cloud-chamber and ionographic emulsion as tools; the bubble-chamber was an additional competitive threat on the horizon, as indeed was the next generation of particle accelerators. Cosmic rays were still the main source of particles having energy enough to produce heavy mesons and hyperons from protons and neutrons. We did what we could with the tools to hand. When the new tools arrived in the mid to late 50s, the then 'cosmic ray community' split into those looking at cosmic rays cosmologically, seeking their origins, energy spectra etc, and those interested in cosmic rays primarily as sources for generating high-energy nuclear interaction; the latter gravitated towards the accelerators as sources, continually refining their experimental technologies. I followed the latter path.

Return to Dublin

Cormac Ó Ceallaigh attended the Bagneres conference, and we met there for the first time. He was a pioneering luminary of elementary-particle physics, being the recognised discoverer of the K-meson, and in that capacity had just then secured appointment to the Chair in the School of Cosmic Physics in the Dublin Institute of Advanced Studies. He regarded encountering the present writer at Bagneres as a piece of luck, and he recruited me on the spot to join his team.

During our spell in Paris my wife Máirín had joined the team at the Ecole Polytechnique and trained as a 'scanner'; she learned how to scan with a microscope through the volume of the ionographic emulsion, recognising 'interesting events' and recording their exact position, to within a few microns, enabling them to be studied in more depth using various analytical techniques. She had become very good at this, and Ó Ceallaigh recruited her also to the team.

Máirín and I, during our first few months of work in the DIAS, were lucky: she picked up the track of a relatively heavy particle which emerged out of a 'star' (i.e. where a high-energy particle had encountered a nucleus and shattered it into many visible components) and which came to rest in the emulsion, causing another small 'star'. One can tell a particle is coming to rest by the way its 'scattering' (ie tortuosity of its path) and 'ionisation' (blackness of its track) increases. She recognised an unusual example of this process, and drew our attention to it; we immediately knew we were on to something, and began intensive work to characterise it.

The mass was some 2300 electron masses, and the amount of energy involved in the small terminal 'star' was such that it implied that much of the decay energy had gone into a neutral particle, perhaps a pi-zero, or a lamda-zero, either of which would be invisible. The fact that it had ended up disrupting a nucleus implied it was negatively charged. There were at this time only two other such events in the world, both subject to uncertainties. This one was the clincher; it was later labelled the Sigma-minus, and entered the extended family of 'hyperons', which can be visualised as nucleons with a meson stuck on. This enabled us to produce our first DIAS paper(28).

This work continued productively until the end of the 1950s, when its significance began to decline; our experimental technology was rapidly overtaken by that of the major particle accelerator laboratories abroad, with their liquid hydrogen bubble-chamber detectors, and increasingly computer-based analysis of the pictures obtained. For a time however the procedures we developed became the standard in the European laboratories with which we were associated: Bristol, University College London, Brussels, Milan, Genova..

Our work-team foreshadowed the multi-centred work-teams which have since become commonplace in European Union collaborations.

There was one Gideon Alexander, an Israeli student who joined us for a time in the team; he subsequently, I believe, became influential in the nuclear physics establishment in Israel, perhaps with nuclear weapons, I hope not, if so, it would be on my conscience that I had helped him establish himself in that mode!

Jack Lynch, later to be Taoiseach, was in the mid-1950s Minister for Education. Round about this time he would have been presiding over events such as the sacking of writer John McGahern from his job as a primary teacher by the clerical manager of the school. Ó Ceallaigh had to spend a lot of his time defending the very existence of the DIAS, and on one occasion the Minister Jack Lynch visited the place. He encountered Gideon and the present writer working on our particle 'scattering' and 'ionisation' measurements, and we explained to him as best we could what was going on. It became clear from his contribution to the conversation that he regarded Gideon as a 'foreign expert' we had brought in, this then being the dominant Establishment attitude to science. Slave-minded deference to Church and foreign expert went hand in hand. It never occurred to them that the DIAS was a place to which foreigners came to learn, from people like Ó Ceallaigh, Pollak, Synge and Lanczos who were, in their own scientific fields, world figures.

There was a paper produced for the second UN Geneva Conference in the 'Atoms for Peace' series, which took place in 1959. It was edited review of the combined DIAS and UCD work done in the previous 2 or 3 years(29). This I suspect was a political nod in the direction of the United Nations, Ireland having recently joined. Ó Ceallaigh delivered the paper; I don't think any of the others got to go.

It could also have been a device by Ó Ceallaigh to try to draw to the attention of the Government that there was world-class scientific work going on in Ireland, on a shoestring. He had recently reported to the Government on the question of what to do about the offer by the US of a 'research reactor', as part of the promotional process for nuclear energy. Ó Ceallaigh pointed out in his Report that the cost of this 'gift' to the Government would be, in ongoing running costs, more than the total then current funding for science in Ireland, and it therefore should be rejected, until such time as they set up a science budget fit to accommodate it. This episode I suspect must have influenced the Government to commission the subsequent 1964 OECD Report *Science and Irish Economic Development*, by Patrick Lynch and HMS 'Dusty' Miller, which in turn influenced the setting up of the National Science Council in 1970.

In major States, Government support for 'big physics' was in the 1950s analogous to Machiavelli's successful alchemist kept by the Prince, where success had been measured by earlier production of innovative weaponry. Ireland however was not in this league, although it had been in the late 1700s, when Dunsink Observatory was set up, that being the 'big science' of the time. Such traces of the 'belle epoque' of Irish science as remained were ignored by the Government, although they did constitute building blocks for an innovative science culture, should we ever get around to recognising them. The DIAS, with which Dunsink had become associated, was such a building block(30).

Scientific research at the frontier has an important role in training for other things. There was however a wide gap between the frontier and what was then currently realisable as it affected the people, especially in the Irish post-colonial situation. The full creative role of the DIAS was not understood by de Valera when he founded it; he simply regarded it as 'scholarship'(31) in the abstract.

Towards the end of the 1950s, shortly after the Industrial Development Authority (IDA) was set up, I sought it out, with the concept in mind that if the flight of capital and the flight of know-how could be brought together, both might be creatively employed in Ireland. I remember finding a small office, with some civil servants in it, to whom I attempted to make the case for reversing the brain drain, and linking it with an alternative route for expansion for those firms which had saturated the Irish market and were poised for expansion. I had, of course, no business training or experience, and I doubt if I presented the case well. In addition however I ran into a complete culture-gap; this was my first experience of attempting to deal with a bureaucracy which had been trained totally from Leaving Cert level in bureaucratic procedures and little else. I got from this encounter a measure of the extent of the failure of the scientific and national cultures to interface.

In the Political Undergrowth: post-France

On my return from France the IWL was still attempting to pull itself together, in the hostile cold-war atmosphere. The membership record shows horrendous decline: June 1952: 102; June 1953: 79; October 1954: 59; the breakdown is as follows: industrial workers 27, other waged and salaried workers 15, students 6, housewives 6, self-employed 4, unemployed 1.

Losses were due mostly to 46 lapses and 17 emigrations. There was a Conference in 1954, which I probably attended, though I have no recollection of it. I would have been concerned to consolidate my working situation on return from France. We were under pressure from the then developing anti-Communist witch-hunting campaign orchestrated by the extreme-right weekly paper, the *Catholic Standard*, which was clearly having the effect of driving the IWL practically underground.

The Issue #1 (New Series) of the *Educational Bulletin* (undated, but circa December 1954 from internal evidence) blamed the lack of lead by the Labour party for not enthusing the youth and leaving them open to attraction by the IRA. It went on to compare the IRA to the Narodniki in the history of the Russian Revolution, and to call for working-class unity rather than sectarian wars: '...in the south there are those who would replace the word 'Irishman' with 'Catholic' and who would attempt to smother the great liberal tradition of the past leaders.... the IRA could be responsible for the unleashing in Northern Ireland of a flood of sectarianism ...'.

The aspiration was to achieve a united all-Ireland working class including the Protestant workers of Belfast, and this aspiration was clearly threatened by the IRA campaign. However the key text for the education of Party members was the 'History of the CPSU(B)' which was subsequently attributed to Stalin. This new series was launched in response to the beginning of the IRA campaign with the arms raids at Armagh and Omagh.

I have a copy of the Rules as adopted by the IWL Conference in October 1954(32). It would be hard to fault the actual Rules. The Stalinist culture in practice however asserted itself via unwritten procedures, such as the practice of the EC nominating its successor at the annual conference, with rubber-stamp voting. The aims were (a) to establish in Ireland a Socialist society... based on the public ownership of the means of production and exchange (b) to ensure that a united Irish working-class led the movement for unity and independence and (c) to develop a militant Labour movement based on the Socialist principles of Connolly and Larkin. It goes on to define membership, its rights and duties, and to define a structure, with a conference at least once every 3 years, electing an executive committee.

It is worth remarking that 'public ownership' is left undefined, and the implication, from Soviet practice, is that the central State is involved. This was of course the fatal flaw in the case of the USSR, where the Party in fact became a sort of collective monopoly capitalist owner of the State.

One can get the flavour of the degree of isolation of the Left in the 1950s from these newsletters and conference reports. The present writer had more or less given up on the IWL as providing a creative political forum, and was searching around, encountering things like the 1913 Club (with Owen Dudley Edwards and others), and later the *Plough,* which was an attempt to develop a broad-left paper, edited by Maisie McConnell, and supported by a group of ex-supporters of Noel Browne, whom he had alienated. (Dr Browne had a reputation of being somewhat of a 'prima donna', doing things on his own initiative, and keeping his successive support committees in the dark.) A key supporter was May Keating, Justin's mother; Justin at this time was lying low in the hopes of getting a job in the Veterinary College.

The Hungarian Episode

Desmond Greaves (CDG) on November 13 1956 recorded in his diary(33) attending a Central London meeting of the British Communist Party on Hungary. This attempted to understand the overthrow of the post-war Communist Government, led by Rakosi, by what was regarded as a right-wing nationalist insurrection, followed by an invasion of that country by Soviet troops. The extent of the disaster was rapidly becoming apparent. The next day he discussed it with Pat Clancy, a leading Connolly Association member, who was in despair: '...set us back generations.. war inevitable... little hope remains ...'. The occasion was one of mass walk-out by Party intellectuals. Subsequent entries recorded build-up of anti-communist hysteria in Hyde Park. On the 20th CDG noted that Flann Campbell has resigned from the Party.

Then on November 21 1956 CDG recorded that he had heard from Cathal Mac Liam, who had recently returned to Dublin from London to avoid conscription, that I had managed to get him a job in the Advanced Studies, presumably as a technician. *Either this was a false trail, or he did not take it up, because I don't remember it. Perhaps I tried. In the end he got an electronics job with Unidare.* The IWL was still cold-shouldering Mac Liam. He was worried about Hungary: '...can any ends ever justify such means?' Justin Keating added a footnote to the effect that the Dublin Labour movement has collapsed, including the Left. CDG: '...Roy is closer to the IWL, never having lived in England. He can get nothing out of Nolan but "we're in for hard times". The hoodlums who smashed the shop have been fined and made pay damages. As for the North, Roy's acid Protestant wit came into full play. When some Party activist held an open air meeting Falls Road and Shankill Road hooligans combined to attack him. "Working-class unity at last" says Roy ...'.

On November 29 CDG arrived in Belfast, on what amounted to a damage-limitation tour of the Irish left, triggered by the Hungarian events. He was met by Jack Bennett, and spoke to the CPNI people. There were mentions of Peadar O'Donnell and Anthony Cronin; the latter had gone to Russia with an Irish group at Peadar's instigation, and written it up for the *Irish Times*. Then on December 2 Greaves went to Dublin, where he encountered the IWL stalwarts: Cathal Mac Liam, Justin Keating, the present writer, Seán Nolan, Micheál O'Riordain, George Jeffares, Seán Mulready. There was much talk of the Eastern European scene. Then he went round the country, meeting with groups of IWL supporters in Waterford: Peter and Biddy O'Connor, Jim Duggan, Gabriel and Mrs Lalor; also in Cork: Jim O'Regan, Cal O'Herlihy, Mrs O'Shea, Con O'Lyhan (sic, perhaps Ó Liatháin), Norman Letchford, Donal and Maire Sheehan.

He attempted to encourage some sort of critical Marxist analysis of the current Irish situation, despite what went on in Hungary. There was no precise record about what this analysis was, but I remember him pacing up and down in our house in Sandymount, delivering what must have been a dry run for his position statement, which depended on a virtual historical analogy, and it ran something like this:

"Imagine that a socialist Britain had been in a war with the capitalist US, and had driven the US out of Ireland, installing a government in Ireland composed of the current Irish Workers League leadership. Imagine that the Irish people had risen against this imposed government, with US aid, and that the British had again intervened to suppress the rising, and installed another imposed government, this time selecting their people a bit better. Which side would we be on?" *One can indeed see the difficulty of the position of the Left!*

The Unemployed Movement

On February 15 1957 I looked in on Desmond Greaves in London, having been to Bristol and Harwell on DIAS business, and decided to make an opportunistic visit to the metropolis. I filled him in on the Dublin unemployed movement; Sam Nolan, then an Irish Workers League activist and subsequently a leading trade unionist and Chairman of the Dublin Trades Council, was the leading figure. Greaves recorded what I told him, adding comments: '...That two-faced scoundrel Peadar O'Donnell is intriguing with them.... he received a deputation from them in the Shelbourne, and advised them to confine their demands to that for "work", and put up a candidate in Dublin South Central, where Sinn Fein might rob FF of votes.... The lads demurred. Where was the money to come from? Peadar assured them that the money would be available...'. CDG immediately pounced on this: it must have come from Fianna Fail.

It is noteworthy that it was even then Fianna Fail practice to put up money for movements which were alternatives to the development of a political left, a foreshadowing of the way in the 1960s that they encouraged the diversion of the republican politicisation process in the 'provisional' direction.

On March 4 1957 CDG stayed with us in Sandymount. He came over to primarily on his Connolly research, but also took advantage of the visit to observe the election, and attend some of the rallies, including that of the unemployed, in his capacity as Irish Democrat editor. Meeting Jim Collins at the Dublin Trades Council he found him gloomy; Labour was in for a trouncing. The unemployed meeting was addressed by Sam Nolan, Steve Mooney (Máirín's brother), Packy Early (a former Connolly Association supporter who had returned to Ireland) and one Liam O'Meara, whom CDG compared to Jim Larkin. He stayed over a few days, meeting Paul O'Higgins, Justin Keating, Desmond Ryan, Cathal and Helga MacLiam.

According to PO'H they (ie Seán Nolan and the leading IWL people) were talking of closing down the IWL and opening a non-political bookshop, under the guise of 'reorganising'. Their failure to make any statement on Hungary or on the IRA was due to their being afraid of injuring O'Riordan's prospects for a trade union position. Later the unemployed movement evolved into a small circle advising Jack Murphy, the unemployed TD. There was talk of a march on the Dáil; there was interest from the Trades Council, but Murphy was talking to John Charles McQuaid the Archbishop. The in-group advising Murphy felt that they were losing control. In the end Murphy resigned his Dáil seat and emigrated to Canada.

The Embryonic Dublin Left and the Republicans

On May 25 1957 CDG encountered Cyril Murray who turned out to be an IWL member with a Belfast republican background. He has heard of CDG though his being continually attacked by the IWL leadership and wanted to meet him. The perception in IWL circles was that CDG only talked to ex-CA people when in Dublin and never went near the bookshop. The present writer and his then wife Máirín were involved in the episode, which took place in Cathal Mac Liam's house in Finglas, where CDG was staying. *He preferred to go there so as not to impose on Máirín who was pre-occupied with our first-born Una.* CDG outlined his thinking on the relative priorities of socialism relative to the achievement of national unity. He picked up a whiff of Murray's 'republican' sentiment, and was critical of the IWL for allowing the 'republican' (CDG's quotes) movement to claim a monopoly of the national question(34).

During the tail-end of this extended Dublin visit, during which CDG's main concern was gathering material for his Connolly book, there was an account of an attempt made by Cyril Murray to open up the debate on 'The Left and the National Question'. On May 27 there was an abortive lunch arrangement with the present writer, Cyril Murray and CDG, to which O'Riordain and Nolan were also invited. O'Riordain declined, but Nolan accepted and then declined. CDG was amused at CM's attempts to broker an encounter. On 29th he called to the bookshop, so he was able to tell CM the next day that he had seen Nolan, much to CM's surprise. Then on June 2 it turned out that Cyril Murray was driving Jack Murphy and Sam Nolan to Cork for an unemployed meeting. Jack had not yet succumbed to the Archbishop's pressure.

Later on June 3 1957 there was an attempted meeting of the IWL which CDG attended; Carmody, Jeffares, Murray, Cathal MacLiam, Mulready and others are there, but no Nolan or O'Riordain, the IWL Chairman and Secretary; the latter couldn't come, and Nolan was said to be sick. Carmody took the chair and proposed an adjournment, since the importance of the topic requires the presence of the leading people. After some heated discussion they adjourned the meeting, but invited CDG to say a few words, which he did, along the lines of calling for unity among all Irish socialists based on agreement reached by free and open discussion. One can understand Murray's frustration; he had clearly worked to set this up, and was upset when the leading people were absent. We clearly have a pathological situation, with apparently CDG *persona non grata* when in Dublin among the leading elements of the struggling embryonic Left.

Subsequently CDG lunched with Murray, who said that they had 3000 at the Cork unemployed meeting, but no resolution or declaration of policy was passed, 'a regrettable omission'. The next day he called to the bookshop and found Nolan '...extremely affable.. I never knew him like it ...'. He went to remark on how the movement was depleted, many key people having emigrated to England.

The Interface between the Left and Civil Society

After the foregoing episode I more or less gave up on trying to work with the Irish Workers' League in the direction of developing a sensible practical 'civil society' approach to the unification of Ireland and establishing social control over the means of production. The orientation of the IWL was totally towards the perceived Eastern utopia. Insofar as they interfaced with broader organisations, they only understood the trade unions; anything else was regarded with suspicion. Their members had absorbed the worst practices of the 'international movement'; for example some of their emigrant members had been engaged in dubious trade union practices in the Electrical Trades Union, which later developed into the election-rigging scandal(35).

Also earlier, in 1956, I had visited Owen Sheehy-Skeffington(36) in hospital, and we had corresponded; the effect of this must have strengthened my resolve to try to find some alternative model than that presented by the USSR, to which the IWL gave unconditional obedience.

I searched around and found things like Tuairim, the 1913 Club and the *Plough*. The first of these included people like Frank Winder, Donal Barrington, Miriam Hederman and a few others, a handful of intellectual critics of the then current Irish scene. They held occasional meetings in Jury's Hotel, then in Dame St. I remember Frank Winder (later Professor of Biochemistry in TCD, and earlier one of our few UCD contacts, along with Justin Keating, in our 1940s Promethean Society epoch) talking about the role of scientific research in Ireland, and pointing out that it was not necessary to be making great discoveries, but to be enough 'in on' the global network of science to be able to know when a discovery was significant, and to be able to organise locally to profit by it, both scientifically and as regards related technology.

Tuairim organised some meetings around the question of the UCD move to Belfield; they had an alternative vision of allowing UCD and TCD to expand into the Government-occupied ground between their locations, eventually merging, with the Government moving out elsewhere. I don't think they went so far as to urge a Canberra model in Athlone, but that idea was floating around, in the context of a regionalised reconstruction. I remember Frank Mitchell remarking that if they do move to Belfield, then there will be no doubt as to which is Dublin University.

So much for Tuairim; as regards the 1913 Club I never got to go to it; Owen Dudley Edwards was one of the prime movers, as was David Thornley; it attempted to be a radical Labour party think-tank. I applied to join, but was blackballed; it seems they did not approve of my Marxist aura.

The *Plough* was a monthly paper published by a group of Dr Noel Browne supporters, mostly Labour Party members; the Editor was Maisie McConnell, and May Keating, Justin's mother, was associated. Dr Browne had distanced himself from them, but the group continued and the paper survived from the late 50s up to the early 60s. I contributed some articles on the analysis of capitalism in Ireland, adapted versions of ones I had earlier done for the Irish Democrat. I indicated that the three main groupings in Irish industry were (a) the older firms like Guinness and Jacob which had expanded into Britain, (b) the British firms which had set up in Ireland under Protection, and (c) the State sector, which had taken up socially important areas deemed to be unprofitable. We were feeling our way towards a politics of how to expand the State sector to include areas which the national and imperial bourgeoisies found profitable.

I also got into correspondence with Seán Cronin, who had led initially the 1950s IRA border campaign, and was then interned. I met him later when he came out. The idea emerged that the politics of a united Ireland needed to be seen as being to the positive advantage of the working people. It was not a military issue, it was a political issue, and those who had been interned as a consequence of the 1950s campaign needed to learn how to treat it politically.

This encounter was followed by further articles in the *Plough:* I recollect one, 'The Pound and Partition', in which I argued that the all-Ireland nature of the banking system had been an important factor keeping us at parity with sterling, and an all-Ireland economy under a united government could allow the value of its currency to float, giving us a price advantage as an exporter, and an incentive to satisfy as much as possible of the home market with home-produced goods, imports being dearer. In the *Plough* generally I argued that the Labour movement needed to take the initiative on the national question, and not leave it to the IRA, the sterility of whose campaign was becoming increasingly apparent. In this I was trying to develop the seeds of ideas planted by Greaves earlier, and rejected by the IWL in the Greaves-Murray episode.

DIAS End-game and the Move to London

Unfortunately in September 1960 the DIAS contract came to an end, and Ó Ceallaigh did not renew it. I have yet to discover why this happened; it could have been political pressure, but I have no direct evidence of this; circumstantially it is worth remarking that Japanese physicists like Kuni Imaeda, whose scientific work was marginal and obscure, stayed on indefinitely, while I got marching orders, although we had been pushing at the frontiers quite successfully. By this time however I was in somewhat of a cul-de-sac experimentally. My preferred hypothesis is that Ó Ceallaigh gave me the push for my own good, realising that I was primarily a technologist rather than a scientist, having served my time in the underlying technology of scientific experimentation.

During my last year at DIAS we had been producing masses of multiple scattering measurements, requiring large volumes of trivial calculations. I decided this was worth trying to automate, and to do this I developed what amounted to a small special-purpose computer, after exploring the feasibility of using the HEC in the Sugar Company, which we had used earlier for curve-fitting. The data-preparation load would however have been impracticable. We needed something like an adding machine, into which we could quickly type in a sequence of numbers, and the computer would need to come up with the total of the moduli of the second differences. The average value of these could be used to calculate the momentum of the particle. We did this successfully, using electronic components which were to hand, and the project formed the basis for a paper subsequently published(37).

However, having been given marching orders, I made a few enquiries; I contacted Leo the pioneering computer firm, and one or two scientific instrumentation firms in England; I looked at medical physics, but none was suitably located. If we were going to England I wanted to be in reach of where the Irish situation was focusing political effort: the Connolly Association in London, where Desmond Greaves was beginning to come up with the 'civil rights' approach to the Northern question. Just like my father, I was obsessed with the negative effects of Partition, which had produced the Catholic-hegemonist environment in the 'republic' within which critical thought was decidedly unwelcome, and the obverse Protestant-hegemonist northern scene. It had to be London.

Then by chance the managing director of Guinness Dublin made some public statement about science in industry, and I wrote to him, looking for a job. He invited me to lunch with himself and the Head Brewer. I was offered a job with a new Production Research Department then being set up, in Park Royal in West London. In Guinness the science was in Dublin, and was dominated by brewing chemistry and yeast biology, but technological development was in Park Royal, presumably so as to be accessible by suppliers; this made sense given the backward technological infrastructure in Ireland. So in the autumn of 1960 I set off to London, initially on my own, to find a place where we could live; we decided we would hang on to the house in Belgrave Road, and find a tenant for it.

Initially I stayed in a Quaker vegetarian guest-house in London where Anthony Coughlan lived at the time; he fixed me up with the contact. Brian Farrington was returning to France in his 2CV, and we chugged down the A5 from Holyhead at a leisurely pace, heavily burdened with my stuff; he dropped me off in Anthony's place in Ladbroke Grove. From this I went to work in Park Royal by a rather complicated bus-route. I borrowed Desmond Greaves's bike and went flat-hunting; I put out enquiries also on the Connolly Association network, and on the Communist Party network. The latter came up trumps with Bardy Tyrrell's place in Hammersmith; she was an upper-crust curmudgeon who was a Party supporter. So Máirín, Una and Fergus were able to come over in or about November 1960, and our period in London began.

Notes and References
1. I have given more detail in my abstracts of political experience in this period in the 1950s module of the political thread.
2. This review occurred in the context of the impact of the Lysenko episode. Russian pioneering work in the field of soil science, which is internationally recognised (Russian technical terms like 'podzol' relating to soil typology having been accepted in the vocabulary), helped to provide a background which enabled Lysenko to gain some degree of credibility.
3. I have made some abstracts from the Desmond Greaves Diaries for the 1950s where they relate to developments in Ireland, by courtesy of Anthony Coughlan in TCD, who is prepared to waive his copyright subject to check for accuracy.
4. I have embedded some documentation which tells the full story of this episode in the 1950s political module of the hypertext.
5. RB McDowell, in his *Trinity College 1592-1952*, claimed that the average age of the Board members was 73 and the youngest was 67; this latter figure however is incorrect, as JJ at that time was 61, still the 'enfant terrible' who gave so much attention to extra-curricular activity; he was a reluctant gerontocrat, and had been in the reform camp for decades, though perhaps too early there. I give a blow by blow account of JJ's interaction with the TCD Board in the 1950s module of this thread of the hypertext, which is overviewed in Appendix 2.
6. JJ was President of the Statistical and Social Inquiry Society from December 1950 and he contributed two papers during his presidency, the second on February 5 1953 being a survey of the global macro-economic scene, entitled 'Economic Leviathans'. Later in the decade he fell out with the new wave of econometric specialists, who were inclined to dismiss his work as philosophical and anecdotal.

Chapter 6: The Period 1951-1960

7. JJ had become President of the Irish Association ('for social, economic and cultural relations'), succeeding Lord Charlemont the founding President in 1946. His period as President is however very poorly documented. The Kilkenny Debates of 1954, in which Hubert Butler had a hand locally, was a high point of his Presidency, being the first time politicians from both parts of Ireland had appeared on the same platform. I have summarised the Irish Association thread in Appendix 9, and some details of the debates are given in the 1950s module of that thread.

8. This keynote paper was published with the title 'Berkeley's Influence as an Economist' in *Hermathena* Vol LXXXII p76, 1953; I have reproduced it in full in the hypertext.

9. I give some background to the James Douglas encounter in the context of possible re-election on one of the non-university panels in the late 1940s module of the hypertext Seanad notes. My father made 31 speeches in the Seanad between April 1951 and July 1954. I have abstracted this record and it is available in the support documentation, along with his first and last speeches given in full.

10. I have reproduced this article from the *Horace Plunkett Centenary Handbook* (National Co-operative Council, 1954) in the 1950s module of the Plunkett thread of the hypertext. Other contributors to the Handbook included Louie Bennett, the pioneer feminist trade unionist, and 'Rex McGall' or Deasun Breathnach, subsequently a contributor to, and perhaps for a time editor of, *an Phoblacht* the Provisional paper during the 1970s. *For most of this period I was in France, and I had no idea how JJ's politics was developing; it is to my eternal regret that my father and I did not interact more intensively during that epoch.* The reportage of the Plunkett commemoration event was picked up by Brian Farrell in his TV series which ran during the year 2000, and was each day dedicated to identifying what happened of significance on that day during the previous century.

11. His *Sickness of the Irish Economy* was published by the Irish Association, with some modest industrial sponsorship, and a preface by Sir Graham Larmour, his successor as President of that body. I have reproduced it in full in the hypertext.

12. This move also decoupled him somewhat from contact with the family, and left my mother isolated; I treat this in the 1950s module of the family thread in the hypertext.

13. He reported this experiment at a 'Symposium on Economic Development' organised by the SSISI in response to the 1957 Whitaker White Paper, which included contributions from Donal Nevin of the Irish TUC, and Labhras Ó Nuallain, the Galway economist, who had written on the finances of Partition.

14. JJ's 1913 book *Civil War in Ulster* appealing for non-violence in Irish politics was re-published in 1999 by UCD Press, and is available in full in the hypertext with their permission.

15. This paper is to be found in JSSISI xix pt 1, 42, 1952-3; I have summarised it in the 1950s SSISI hypertext module.

16. This would have been my cousin Alan Johnston, who at that time ran a farm near Kildangan. I suspect that JJ's move to Grattan Lodge in the 1950s was influenced by a desire to be a neighbour of Alan, and to access his experience of practical farming matters. See the 1950s Family module of the hypertext.

17. His source was *Michael Davitt and the British Labour Movement* by Professor TW Moody of Trinity College.

18. In the event he managed to get a second 'swan song' on July 7, which I reproduce in full in the hypertext, as well as summarising here.

19. Hubert Butler (1900-1990) was a Kilkenny Protestant landowner, with an estate near Bennettsbridge; he travelled widely in central and eastern Europe and spoke many languages, writing up his experiences in essays published somewhat obscurely at the time. He fulfilled a gadfly political role. In his 80s he was 'discovered' by Antony Farrell and his collected works have been published to some acclaim by Lilliput Press. I am indebted to Prionnsias Ó Drisceoil, the Arts Education Organiser for the South-East, based in Kilkenny, for unearthing the *Kilkenny People* report, dated 22/04/54, of this Partition debate in which JJ and the Irish Association had a hand in organising, and at which JJ spoke.

20. Eoin ('the Pope') O'Mahony was an itinerant Cork barrister, who knew, or appeared to know, the seed, breed and generation of everyone in Ireland. He was good company, a great conversationalist, and in demand for public occasions. He had played a role in the campaign for the release of the IRA prisoners in the late 1940s.

21. Arnold Marsh, a Quaker schoolteacher, wrote a book entitled *Full Employment in Ireland* in or about 1946; he was influential in the Labour Party at the time.

22. I picked this up from a reference in JJ's subsequent book *Why Ireland Needs the Common Market* (Mercier Press, Cork, 1962); in Ch8, p97 he recorded the 'envious admiration' of the visiting group of Northern businessmen and politicians. There is, alas, no record of this episode in the Irish Association archive in the NI Public Record Office, nor of the Kilkenny debate, nor indeed of any events connected with JJ's Presidency.

23. The article in full, and the table of contents of the *Handbook*, are reproduced in the 1950s Plunkett module of the hypertext.

24. This is explicitly treated in Donal McCartney's *UCD, a National Idea*, published by Gill & MacMillan in 1999.

25. JJ had made this argument repeatedly in lectures and papers, in the SSISI and elsewhere, over the years from the 1920s.

26. The science and society problem had been addressed in the writings of the Irish-born Marxist JD Bernal FRS, whose book *Science in History*, published by Watts (London) in 1954, was influential in the present writer's understanding of the role of science as a catalyst of social change.

27. The Proceedings of the Cosmic Ray Conference in Bagneres de Bigorre, July 1953, was published by the Ecole Polytechnique, Paris. It contains my first scientific publications. I have expanded further on this theme in the 1950s academic module of the hypertext.

28. 'Evidence for the Nuclear Interaction of a Charged Hyperon Arrested in Photographic Emulsion'; RHW Johnston and C Ó Ceallaigh; *Phil Mag*, ser 7, vol 45, p424, April 1954. There followed a series of some 12 or 13 papers based on the DIAS work; I have outlined this work in greater detail in the 1950s academic module of the hypertext.

29. 'Investigation of the Strong and Weak Interactions of Positive Heavy Mesons'; G Alexander, F Anderson, RHW Johnston, D Keefe, A Kernan, J Losty, A Montwill, C Ó Ceallaigh and M O'Connell; in *Proc UN 'Atoms for Peace' Conference* (Pergamon Press, 1959).

30. This is a contact point with JJ, who had in a 1947 Seanad speech gone into the history of Dunsink Observatory, on the occasion of its being sold by TCD to DIAS.

31. I had at this time begun to be aware of the 'science and society' cultural gap problem, as instanced in the related 1950s module of the hypertext, where I also begin to treat some socio-technical issues.

32. Some of the conference documentation, including the members of the Executive Committee, is embedded in the 1950s political module, following on the Ballyfermot material.

33. This and the following sections are condensed from my notes on the Desmond Greaves Diaries for the 1950s; these may remain for a period under embargo but will eventually be accessible in the National Library.

34. This encounter, also recorded in the Desmond Greaves Diaries, was influential in turning my attention towards exploring the political potential of the republican movement as it then was.

35. In Dublin on December 14 1968 CDG recorded in his Diary (Volume 20) encountering the remains of the IWL group who had been so destructive of the CA a decade previously. Carmody (an IWL stalwart) wanted to talk with them, expressing sympathy with Pat O'Neill who had been 'crucified' while in the Electrical Trades Union. According the Greaves '...the "crucifixion" consisted of touring England in a motor-car posting bogus election papers for Haxell. It would be impossible to have the slightest sympathy for anybody involved in that discreditable operation ...'. This could perhaps be taken as evidence that the deep-rooted corruption of the USSR-dominated 'international movement' extended in some cases right down to the membership and practice of its component member-parties. Most members of the CPGB and the IWL, in the present writer's experience, were however motivated by an honest desire to achieve a Socialist vision.

36. I contributed some notes to Andrée Sheehy-Skeffington at her request, towards her biography *Skeff*, published by Lilliput (Dublin, 1991). I have expanded on these in the hypertext, and commented on the *Skeff* references to our student left in the 1940s. I have also included some of the April 1956 correspondence. The Greaves contacts however were influential in strengthening my interest in the 'national question' and the ending of partition, while the Skeffington contact helped to encourage a critical view of the USSR, and to initiate my distancing from the Irish Workers' League. Greaves, needless to say, had no use for Skeffington.

37. I have expanded on this in the 1960s techno-economic module of the hypertext; the paper was published in the June 1963 issue of *Electronic Engineering*.

Chapter 7 Part 1: The Period 1961-1966

In view of the large amount of RJ 1960s material, it has been necessary to split this chapter into three parts; I have kept the RJ and JJ stuff interspersed.

JJ in the 1960s: Overview

This overview of JJ's work in the 1960s touches on all three parts of this Chapter.

In TCD JJ's primary interest was the Kells Ingram Farm, and the unsuccessful attempt to position TCD to get a share of the agricultural research action, this then becoming a source of government funding. In TCD politics(1) he had been manoeuvred into a backwater, although he retained the somewhat nominal role of Senior Proctor up to 1962.

After JJ's Presidential term with the Statistical and Social Inquiry Society (SSISI)(2) he became disillusioned with the current economic orthodoxy and its gurus. Isolated in TCD he again turned to newspaper articles and pamphleteering, reverting to his earlier Barrington-like(3) outreach mode, though without the actual label this time. The 'Barrington lectures' as such had by now subsided towards an annual SSISI event. After the demise of the Kells Ingram Farm JJ reverted to his scholarly (4) role, drawing together his Hermathena papers into his Berkeley book, and into a monograph developing the Berkeley theory of credit, which I treat elsewhere(5).

JJ continued his association with the Irish Association(6), as a 'Past President', and attended some of the functions. He had registered to attend the Derry Irish Association Whit-weekend conference in 1965, but was apparently unable to come; if he had, he would have attended an interesting seminal event which laid the basis for the subsequent development of the Civil Rights movement; it was attended by many of the people concerned, including myself and John Hume.

There was also a revival of correspondence contact with Dermot MacManus(7). The context was an attempt by the latter to get a paper published on the history of the literary revival.

After JJ published his *Bishop Berkeley's Querist in Historical Perspective* in 1970 he submitted it for the degree of Litt D. The degree was conferred in May 1972, shortly before he died.

This completes the introductory overview of my father's contribution to this chapter. In what follows, most of the material relates to my own work on developing a theory-practice dialectic, in left-wing politics and in applied science. Where highlights occurs in my father's work I intersperse them.

RJ and Industrial Applied Science

In introducing this section I should say that I found, with the Guinness (Park Royal) production research experience described below, a very positive sense of team cohesion (between scientists, engineers, technicians and process workers). I was reminded of the earlier period at the Pic du Midi. One got a pre-view of the cohesion which might become the norm in a future society where the various elements of the economic system would be socially owned.

This experience also gave some insight into the workings of the applied-scientific community in Britain, and into socio-technical and techno-economic issues. The 'science and society' domain (8), as defined earlier by JD Bernal, remained dormant, except insofar as I was motivated to join the Association of Scientific Workers, which was a trade union that had been set up in the 1940s by Bernal and others. This was in process of evolving into a typical run-of-the-mill British trade union, catering for technicians' working conditions, though it was supported by a handful of scientists who possessed the Bernal vision, and believed that their technicians were important and should be looked after.

I was a member of the West London Branch of the AScW, and in this capacity I got to represent them on the Acton Trades Council. I developed some insights from this experience which were relevant to Irish politics; it would have been quite easy for me, had I been motivated to get into London politics, to get nominated from the Acton Trades Council to the local Hospital Board. The accessibility of local government structures to democratic nomination from below is an extremely important feature, in which Irish local government is deficient. Here was an item for the home political agenda. (9).

***

The Production Research Department in Guinness (Park Royal, London), in the period 1960 to 1963 headed by Michael Ashe, was on the scale of a 100-barrel per day pilot plant (10). Beer we produced was rarely up to standard, so it was blended off with the 'added beers' into the general production. We ran the system only occasionally, most of the time being taken up with modifications prior to the next run.

The relationship between the Production Research Department of Guinness in Park Royal and Statistics Department, run by Stella Cunliffe, was somewhat problematic. The key question was getting recognition, in the dynamic context of process control, for the 'Philosophy of the Unplanned Experiment' in a context dominated by the classical statistical philosophy of 'experimental design' as it had emerged in a static agricultural 'experimental design' situation.

There was a rotary filter with which the 'wort' (i.e. unfermented soluble malt extract) was drawn off from the 'mash' (milled malted barley to which water had been added for extracting the solubles). The mash was then 'sparged' with hot water, to rinse out the last of the wort. If you sparge too much, the resulting wort ends up too dilute.

The wort was then boiled with hops; this was done in small batches in a sequence of vessels in rotation. An attempt was made to compensate for the variability of the hops by measuring a key component of the extract, a biochemical known as 'iso-humulone', and a member of the team, George Philpotts, had attempted to develop some instrumentation for this purpose, using auto-analyser technology.

The wort, after boiling with hops, had to end up at a specific gravity of 1.0459, so that measurement of 'gravity' was crucial. In the traditional process one does this with a hydrometer, a relatively simple task, but the object of the development was to make the process continuous, so this meant on-line instrumentation and a control system. My task was to try to get on top of this instrumentation problem.

The hopped wort, at the desired gravity, was then declared to the Excise in a batch vessel, from which the continuous fermenter vessels drew. I spent most of my time at this end of the process, though some of the instrumentation was relevant upstream, and we ran a sort of test-bed for gravity-related intrumentation of all sorts in the neighbourhood of the rotary filter.

The output of this work is perhaps best measured by three patents (11) registered during my time with Guinness. The first, 976,663, is headed 'Examining Solutions Photoelectronically', and covered our 'Yeast Concentration Meter'. The novelty was in the use of a photo-multiplier tube to pick up back-scattered light from a liquid containing suspended solids. This could not have been done with the usual type of photo-cell, the intensity being too low. It was, I think, the first example of the use of the photo-multiplier in industrial instrumentation.

The photo-multiplier output signal was a linear measure of the concentration of yeast in beer, and it did not matter if the beer was dark. The then current 'nephelometry' instruments (which measured reduction of intensity of a beam of light passed through a liquid) were quite useless in Guinness, the liquid being dark, and anyway they had a non-linear output. It was a good instrument, with many possible applications, and was subsequently made commercially under licence by Evans Electroselenium. If it had been used outside brewing (eg in paper pulp) I understand I should have been entitled to a royalty, but I never pursued this.

I wrote this up in *Research and Development for Industry*, no 31, March 1964, giving examples of how it had been applied in the control of the Guinness pilot-scale continuous fermenters.

The second patent, 986,343, was headed 'Controlling Yeast Fermentation' and was in effect an attempt by Guinness to evade infringing the then current patents of, if I remember correctly, Coutts in Australia and Lebatt in Canada. The novelty was in splitting the feedstock between a yeast growth vessel and one or more main fermenter vessels. The yeast concentration in the main fermenters was maintained high by a system for restricting the amount washed out, the yeast being flocculent, and wanting to settle, but being prevented from doing so by a stirrer. The outlet however was via a settling-tube of which the setting could be varied; this shielded the outgoing liquid from the action of the stirrer, thus holding back the flocculent yeast.

The main fermenter got a portion of the feedstock directly, the other portion feeding the vessel where yeast was grown, under aerobic conditions. The output of this growth vessel was fed into the main fermenter, replenishing the yeast supply therein, at a controlled rate.

We developed instrumentation to measure the oxygen level in the growth vessel, and to measure the gravity in the fermenters, and to keep track of the amount of yeast that came out. The rule was, everything must go downstream; no recycling of yeast. This latter feature dominated the Coutts and Lebatt patents, but Guinness wanted to maintain their own system distinct from this, the key idea being to start with pure yeast culture under laboratory control, and not allow a population of wild or mutant yeasts to build up, as would happen under a recycling regime.

We did the best we could, but the system was wildly unstable, and would have required a sophisticated feed-forward control system, based on totally reliable instrumentation. There is a non-linear relationship between the gravity of the fermenting beer and the extent to which the yeast flocculates. The attempt to control yeast concentration in such a way as to achieve the target beer gravity at the outlet, while staying within the 'no recycling' constraint, was doomed to failure.

In this situation, Stella Cunliffe in the Statistics Department was trying to impose on us a pattern of meticulously planned experiments, derived from the procedures used in agriculture for evaluating barley and hop production. This however was wildly out of phase with the requirements. It was all we could do to keep the process going, with the resulting beer fit to add to the 'added beers' (after all, excise had been paid, and to dump it would have been a mortal sin!). So what we did was treat the plant as an ongoing 'unplanned experiment', keeping records of the parameters at the various stages of the process, and working over the data afterwards to try to draw some conclusions. We were able to do this, and we wrote reports, the results being meaningful experience, and the general message being that continuous fermentation without yeast recycling is intrinsically unstable and Guinness should not pursue this road, a useful negative result. This experience of an 'unplanned experiment' in a continuous process however was an early example of the 'operations research' approach to industrial process control statistics.

We were able to model the performance of the 3-vessel continuous fermentation system using a set of differential equations, and at one stage we had this working on an analogue computer. I drafted a paper on this, and showed it to Sir Cyril Hinshelwood FRS, who was then consulting with Guinness, and he thought it should be published, but I never got round to it. The key concept was in the separation of the aerobic growth from the anaerobic fermentation phases; these processes obeyed different dynamic laws. It was, I think, an innovative example of a mathematical application in biodynamics.

In the end Guinness went back to the classical batch process, which is self-stabilising and easily manageable. Again, the experience was interesting and useful; one can learn from failures perhaps more than if one has one's head swelled by successes. Above all, we had fun doing the work, and there was a great sense of team cohesion.

I should add that we attempted to develop an on-line gravity-meter, in association with Solartron-Schlumberger (currently a world-leading oil-well instrumentation specialist), which depended on the vibration frequency of a metal tube being modified by the specific gravity of the liquid in it. I don't think this led to a working prototype, but we had observed and measured the gravity effect in another Solartron instrument which depended on vibrations, designed to measure viscosity.

The third patent, 1,004,693, headed 'Continuous Production of Alcoholic Beverages', was a product of some laboratory prototyping; it never scaled up. (The work mentioned above I should say was on a large pilot scale, of the order of 100 barrels per day). The novelty was to ferment wort to beer by trickling it down a column containing concentrated yeast, in the form of a carbon dioxide foam, the yeast being in the walls of the bubbles. The foam was generated by compressing the liquid and releasing the pressure through an orifice, much as the foam on the pint is generated to this day.

We got this to work, after a fashion, on the bench, but scale-up problems would have been horrendous, and it remains a curiosity. The patent agent however was very taken by it, and had great hopes, and Michael Ashe was persuaded to go through with the patenting.

RJ and Emigrant Political Organisation

The relevant emigrant organisations in London were primarily the Connolly Association(12), but also Clann na hEireann which was associated with Sinn Fein. There were also the County Associations, and Tuairim which catered for expatriate intellectuals who mostly had been associated with Tuairim in Dublin in the 1950s, where the present writer had encountered it.

There was a somewhat edgy relationship between the Connolly Association (CA) and the British Communist Party (CPGB); the CA competed with the CPGB for the attention of political-minded Irish emigrants, and also with Clann na hEireann, the republican emigrants grouping, for the attention of emigrants whose formation was primarily in the republican tradition. In summary, it could be said that the CPGB thought in terms of the 'British working-class' and was hostile to what it regarded as nationalist diversions; Clann na hEireann thought in terms of money and support for the movement in Ireland; the Connolly Association tried to mobilise Irish workers in support of Irish interests via a process of lobbying Parliament and influencing opinion-leaders in the Labour Party and trade unions. The present writer devoted all of his marginal time to Connolly Association politics.

After the initial few months in Ladbroke Grove I lived (along with my wife Máirín and the two children Una and Fergus) in Hammersmith and then in West Acton, so the basic unit for political activity was the West London Branch of the Connolly Association, which met weekly in a pub in Shepherd's Bush. We did our best to have a talk at each meeting by someone who was knowledgeable on a current topic, or on some aspect of Irish history or culture. We sold the Irish Democrat, the Connolly Association monthly paper, in the Irish pubs on the weekends. This task, while apparently menial, in fact was a fruitful source of insights into the way the emigrant Irish were thinking, from the numerous friendly conversations which ensued.

There was also a local branch of the Communist Party, of which I became nominally a member, attending an occasional meeting. It was rare however to find any useful ideas in that environment; I recollect one meeting at which some development in the Soviet legal system, the nature of which I forget, was 'explained' at length by a leading member. One could not help thinking in terms of a millenarian religious cult with a remote utopian vision. It is worth mentioning in passing however that local CP activists helped, in a valiant rearguard action, to keep going the democratic system on which the London consumer co-operative movement depended. One could however sense the tension between the ideology of the visionaries and the management practice of the London co-operative retail outlets.

Analysis of this is necessary to explain the decline of consumer co-operation in the advanced capitalist environment. It is perhaps possible to relate this to JJ's experience half a century earlier.

In the Acton Trades Council, where I represented the West London AScW, it was also possible to observe the ideological divisions. After the meetings of this body, people went for a drink to two different pubs. The significance of this I soon learned was that the Communists drank in one and the Labour people in the other. It was an 'us and them' scene of the worst description. My priority being the Irish movement, I used to drink alternately with both, and kept my distance from the in-fighting of the London Left.

Keeping the Connolly Association branch going required a significant amount of marginal-time effort. Activities included identifying and getting hold of appropriate speakers, lobbying the local MP, outreach work with local trade union branch meetings explaining the nature of the Irish situation to them, all this as well as keeping up the circulation of the Irish Democrat. The key issue at the time was the Special Powers in Northern Ireland, and the internment without trial of the people who had been involved in the 1950s IRA campaign. Supportive of this was the campaign for an enquiry into the working of the Government of Ireland Act, ie the Northern Ireland 'Constitution' as set up by the British.

During this period the embryo of the 'Civil Rights Movement in Northern Ireland' concept emerged, the prime mover being C Desmond Greaves (CDG), who during this period spent much time in Ireland researching for his book on Liam Mellows. According to his Diary, CDG spent from November 1 to 9 1962 in Belfast (13). The context was his perceived need for an analysis of, and response to, the Barritt and Carter book *The NI Problem: a Study in Group Relations*. He discussed this with the CPNI people, in the Belfast Trades Council office. Was NI subsidised? The nationalists said yes, the Unionists said no. He leaned heavily on the evidence picked up earlier from my father Joe Johnston, to the effect that the agricultural subsidies were worth £30M. The earlier *Isles and Cuthbert Report* had cast no light on the issue. He also talked to Seán Caughey, the Sinn Fein political spokesman in Belfast, who wanted a 'National Liberation Council' composed of various organisations, but CDG countered with an National Council for Civil Liberty (NCCL) proposal for a conference on the franchise; Caughey however was not convinced.

Then on December 11 1962 CDG noted the prospect of a debate on the thesis of the Barritt-Carter book; Carter however refused to debate in person, and put up Norman Gibson instead. CDG however had no desire to debate with Gibson, of whom apparently he had never heard. In fact Gibson was then a rising young economist who was putting feelers out in the direction of the Republic; I had encountered him at a Tuairim conference in Greystones, in or about 1959 or 1960, considering the implications of the Whittaker Programme and the then innovatory orientation of industry in the Republic towards exports. CDG was, in my opinion, wrong to dismiss him as a nobody; I had certainly heard of him. It is a pity this opportunity was missed. Any interest shown by economists in the North in the economics of Ireland as a whole should have been welcomed. The Greaves response to the Barritt-Carter book later took the form of his book *The Irish Crisis*.

The August 1 1963 Greaves diary has a revealing entry relating to the present writer: '...Roy goes back to Ireland on Tuesday to take up his post with Aer Lingus. He wants to talk to everybody about his "role" there. But he is incapable of pursuing single-mindedly a political course of action, let alone originating one. So I made no suggestions. And in any conflict between his duty and his interests or convenience, his interests or convenience are bound to win. Still he is not the worst...'. On the previous day he had recorded something of the problem we had getting back into our own house, currently occupied by Jim Fitzgerald(14) and family upstairs and Anthony Coughlan down below. Certain rearrangements would obviously be necessary, and money was involved. In this context he interpreted my concern with the financial side of things as being 'miserly'.

The foregoing says something about CDG's judgment of people, and his confidence in their ability to grasp his strategies. The Civil Rights approach within the NI situation was in gestation, and he had already set up some contacts. Yet he chose not to tell me anything about it, in a farewell briefing, which I had asked for. If he had briefed me, it is quite possible that the Wolfe Tone Society in Dublin would earlier have been able to help this process along, with its Belfast contacts, which included Jack Bennett, and, later, people like Alec Foster (Principal of 'Inst' and Conor Cruise O'Brien's father-in-law), Michael Dolley (the Queens historian), John D Stewart (a leading critical journalist), and Kader Asmal in Dublin (in the TCD Legal Science Department). But he seemed to be dismissive of the potential of all-Ireland democratic intellectual networking, preferring when in Ireland to cultivate the 'intellectual undergrowth' of the CPNI and the IWL. He expected all intellectuals to go the road taken by Cal O'Herlihy, who was lecturing in bourgeois economics in Queens, and Justin Keating who was in the Veterinary College and aspiring to a Labour Party Dáil seat, and he automatically wrote them off politically.

I recollect how on this occasion Greaves turned our conversation towards the potential for exotic vacations which presented themselves for airline employees with concession travel, suggesting the flora and fauna of the Amazon as being accessible should I so desire. This was, of course, a leg-pull, but it indicated that CDG was far from 'sending me back to Ireland on a mission', as Mac Stiofain has alleged; he was clearly indicating to me that I was on my own, and as far as he was concerned, I had established myself in his mind as being somewhat of a political dilettante. It also suggested that he had absorbed the lessons of his premature intervention on the occasion of the founding meeting of the Irish Workers League, and wanted any political developments in Ireland to be genuinely indigenous, from the bottom up.

Anthony Coughlan had returned to Ireland in August 1961, to take up a job as a lecturer in the Social Studies Department in TCD, for which his London postgraduate work in social administration policy was relevant. This was his own decision. My job in Aer Lingus came up as a result of having had earlier contact with Finbar Donovan the Sales Manager, when the latter was in touch with the DIAS and looking into computer applications in Liverpool. He was championing the real-time reservations project in Aer Lingus, as the first really large-scale Irish computer application, and he needed technical support, so he head-hunted the present writer. So the allegations of Seán Mac Stiofain in his memoirs regarding our motivations in returning to Ireland are quite false(15).

The Mac Stiofain Memoirs

Seán Mac Stiofain had earlier encountered the Connolly Association. He was working as a shunter on the railways; he joined the Union and got on well with his workmates. The issue came up of paying the political levy with the Union dues. He refused, on the grounds that the Labour Party was supporting Partition. Encountering the CA and the Irish Democrat he discovered that their policy was that people should pay the political levy. I quote: 'it was then the policy of the Communist Party of Great Britain not to attack the Labour Party. Consistent with this policy, the Connolly Association was in effect urging Irish workers to subsidise a party that perpetuated partition.... the CA criticised the IRA and condemned the use of physical force against the British occupation forces in Ireland. At the same time it was supporting... revolutionary force in Malaya, where it hadn't a hope. I wondered if they thought the Russian revolution they admired so much had been achieved without physical force... the party line was whatever Stalin said it was from one week to the next. There was no way of balancing these double loyalties to ensure that Irish freedom would be put first ...'(p51).

We can see why the window of opportunity was closed. Greaves in his attempts to decouple the CA from the CPGB, and give it an independent Irish-oriented policy development procedure, had in 1949 not yet managed to do this at its grass-roots. The dead hand of Stalinism helped push SMacS away from political methods and towards militarism, at a critical juncture in his career, when he was an active trade unionist working in England.

SMacS goes on to give a critical analysis (p52) of the roles of the European CPs, with which the present writer would have been substantially in agreement at the time. This in fact had fuelled the latter's movement towards attempting to make intellectual contact with the early politicising tendencies in the republican movement, which began in the late 50s, as we saw in the previous chapter.

'Any revolutionary who expected Ireland to accept a Russian-type society would be wasting his time. The social system the Republican movement preached in those days was... distributive ownership or co-operativism, with some nationalisation of certain key resources...'.

This indeed sums up well what the present writer attempted to do in the 1960s, and it is a great pity that SMacS's obsession with weapons and militarism helped to undermine it.

Subsequent to his return to Ireland SMacS referred (p92) to welcoming Goulding's taking on the leadership, but rapidly became aware of the politicising trend, which was as expressed in the 1965 conference proceedings referenced below, the famous 'nine proposals'. *These proposals were before the present writer's time of active association with the movement; they represented basically Goulding's politicising agenda, supported by Costello, Mitchell and others.* SMacS was elected to the Army Council at the next Convention, which was in early 1965. He claimed to know where the policies are coming from, blaming '...a Marxist whom I knew to be Moscow-oriented, and who had been in the CPGB and the Connolly Association...'. He proposed that this person be expelled, under the anti-communist rule. Goulding however stood over the membership of the person concerned, saying that if this person went, he would go too.

Thus Goulding in 1965 was prepared to stand over the basis on which I became associated, namely constitutional change leading to total politicisation of the movement.

Justin O'Brien(16) quotes Seán Mac Stiofain to the effect that Goulding had talked about contacting Moscow when in jail with him in 1953. Goulding was then said to have contacted the Soviet Embassy when Chief of Staff, possibly in early 1963, and was told that they did not support revolutionary movements, only governments. A couple of months after this the present writer and Anthony Coughlan were said by Mac Stiofain to have '...returned to Ireland, and the connection was obvious'. Mac Stiofain it seems believed this, or propagated it, implausible though it was (could Moscow have fixed up a job for me in Aer Lingus, and one for Anthony Coughlan in TCD? !!), and subsequently based his quasi-politics upon it.

The foregoing must represent SMacS's perception of the present writer, whose motivation he had totally misinterpreted; I was fed up with the CP/IWL narrow sectishness, and wanted to distance myself from their Rome-like worship of Moscow. But at this time I had never met him. How did he know? Someone must have primed him and given him a particular 'spin' on my political position.

***

I remember the occasion of my return in September 1963. I drove our Morris Minor to Fishguard, saw it winched on to the Rosslare boat, with all our chattels in it. On the way over I retired to what must have been the old 'commercial room', a sort of saloon where one could sit down and write, a relic of old-time commercial travelling. I wrote some notes on how I saw the movement for Irish national unity and liberation of the Irish working people might be developed. I recollect that I was influenced by the Castro model, but not in its 'armed struggle' aspect; the key to its political aspect was how a broad-based movement of politicised working people, rural as well as urban, in the country as a whole, had absorbed, subsumed, upstaged (to this day I can't find a good verb!) a narrow doctrinaire urban 'workerist' party based on the orthodoxy of the Communist international movement. I had picked up the Cuban story from the special issue of the US-published Marxist *Monthly Review*, edited by Leo Huberman and Paul Sweezy, which had appeared shortly before.

JJ and the European Common Market

In 1962 JJ had published his *Why Ireland Needs the Common Market*(17) which he regarded as a sequel or update of his earlier *Irish Agriculture in Transition*. The title was somewhat misleading, as it was in fact a reiteration of his critique of the economic policies of the advanced industrial countries which had been subsidising their agriculture, and consequently lowering the prices available to fringe countries like Ireland that were trying to build up on the basis of agricultural exports.

I give some quotes from this epilogue, which summarise the message of the book as a whole. He does comparisons ranging from the 1920s to the 1960s, in the US, UK, Germany, Denmark etc. "..Ireland occupies an intermediate place between Denmark and the peasant counties of Eastern Europe..". He argues that subsidised agricultural production fuels inflation. The situation is however dominated by vast defence expenditures, which act as a stabiliser.

JJ concludes as follows: "...The supreme test for the statesmanship of the Western World will be in its ability to substitute a policy of economic 'brinkmanship' for a policy of strategic 'brinkmanship' without falling down on the job.... (involving) the overseas expenditure of billions of pounds and dollars in constructive investment, and establish the foundations for an international economy which will have a social and ethical as well as a merely economic stability....".

JJ, TCD and Agriculture

The TCD Kells Ingram farm in the early 60s had an annual gross output of about £17K and employed 10 men. There were 182 cattle (a mix of dairy and beef), 449 sheep, 178 pigs, and the main crops were barley, potatoes and wheat. They had tried peas unsuccessfully. Agriculture and veterinary students spent one day per week there. There were also 22 acres of woodland. This was basically JJ's model mixed farm concept, on a scale such as to enable synergies to be demonstrated, as described earlier in his 1942 SSISI paper on 'Capitalisation of Irish Agriculture'(18). The Farm issued a one-year certificate, which was the responsibility of the KI Farm Committee, and issued in its name. The College as such wanted nothing to do with it.

This was totally at odds with the Agricultural Institute model, which consisted of a dispersed set of specialised units. The analysis of how agricultural research developed under Dr Tom Walsh's leadership must remain for the present on the longer-term agenda.

I subsequently gave it a preliminary treatment in the 1970s in my Irish Times 'Science and Technology' column(19), in which I began to develop a critical analysis which in retrospect is not unlike that of my father; we will see this in the 1970s chapter.

JJ made occasional forays to the TCD Board meetings. On April 25 1962 he corrected an earlier minute done in his absence: the lecturer they recruited for the School of Agriculture was not in 'economics' but in 'farm management'. So although his appearance was sporadic, he remained alive to the issues.

However from this time on one gets an increasing impression that the Farm and the Agriculture School were losing the battle for survival; the strategy was taking shape whereby Agriculture went to UCD and the Veterinary College went to TCD. The farm struggled on until 1967, when finally they decided to sell it. Some attempts were made to develop Townley Hall as a conference centre, but on the whole without success.

JJ's decision to move from Grattan Lodge in Laois, where he had piloted his market gardening concept, to Bayly Farm near Nenagh, to be near my sister and her family, had been a conscious decoupling from College political in-fighting. His move back to Dublin(20), where in 1964 he took a house in Dundrum, corresponded to the revival of his interest in the Berkeley project.

JJ and Partition

There was among JJ's papers, dated September 1963, an outline plan for the 1963-64 season of the Irish Association(21). It is appropriate here to extract a few quotes from a document which foreshadows current all-Ireland aspirations under the Good Friday Agreement.

"...For the comfort of the Northern minority may I point out that there is a possible analogy between the present relations of NI with the Republic and those of Scotland with England prior to the 18th century? Highlanders and Lowlanders were not the best of friends and there were religious as well as racial conflicts and differences. The Union of 1707 gave political form to a single British Nation, but there remains a strong sense of national individuality in Scotland and England as well as Wales. The Northern minority should co-operate in developing a sense of a common Ulster nationality which already exists in more than germ..."

"...We may as well admit that both islands have lost something by the political separation of 1922, as well as gained something, we hope a great deal. Ireland has a kind of Siamese twin, or triplet, relationship with the larger island, but the present political set-up does not always ensure that the larger twin, or triplet, will behave with consideration to one of the smaller. Our problem is to create, on EEC lines, a relationship between our three political entities which will be more advantageous all round, without prejudice to national and cultural values, and without impairing the present constitutional position...."

"..A Common Market of the British Isles would imply agreement between the UK Government (in consultation with the Government of NI) and the Republic to make a rapid transition to a common tariff surrounding these islands. The proceeds of the tariff would have to be distributed on some statistical basis between the Exchequers concerned.

"That by itself would imply free access for NI exports (as also for British exports) to the Republican market. To temper the wind to the shorn lamb of Irish industry a 10% customs ring might be maintained round all Ireland against British imports of goods competitive with Irish industrial products - this on the analogy of the 1800 - 1820 position. Southern industry would have enough to do in competing with exports from NI, and both areas might need a little protection from high-powered British salesmanship in their home market. The Border as a customs phenomenon would go and we would revert to the position that prevailed in 1922-23 before it was decided (to my horror) to turn the present Border into a customs frontier.

"There are other implications of course. There could no longer be different prices for the same quality of the same agricultural product in a common market of the British Isles. If agricultural prices to the Republic farmers could be raised to the scale now enjoyed by farmers in GB and NI it would add about £60,000,000 per annum to the income of Republic agriculturalists or about £150 per person so occupied..."

The Wolfe Tone Bicentenary

Prior to my return to Ireland in September 1963, the republican movement had been feeling its way, under the influence of Cathal Goulding and others, towards politicising its approach to national unification.

A Wolfe Tone Committee had been set up to commemorate the 200th anniversary of his birth; Sinn Fein was aware of it. The Ard Comhairle meeting on Feb 3 1963 had submitted Seán Cronin and Brian O'Higgins as names for it(22). It is not clear from the Sinn Fein record who was on it, or by whom it was set up. Presumably it can be inferred that the 'other branch' (namely the IRA) established it; Tomás Mac Giolla considers that this probably was Cathal Goulding at work. Brian O'Higgins died shortly after this. The recommendation of Cronin would have been the influence of the IRA people on the Ard Comhairle. He had been Chief of Staff at the beginning of the 1950s campaign, had been interned, being replaced by Ruairi Ó Brádaigh, and as usual in the Curragh had become political-minded.

There had been a suggestion from Dublin Comhairle Ceanntar (Regional Council) of Sinn Fein to hold a meeting on Cave Hill, near Belfast, in memory of the Wolfe Tone / Thomas Russell 'oath' occasion which took place there, and it was agreed that this be passed to the Wolfe Tone Committee. This Cave Hill meeting subsequently took place, as part of the pre-history of the process of foundation of the Belfast Wolfe Tone Society; it would then have been organised by the Belfast Wolfe Tone 'Directory'.

There was a Convention of Wolfe Tone 'Directories' in May 1963 which took place in Dublin and included the following(23):

Dublin: Seán Cronin, Harry White, Dick Roche, Uinsean Mac Eoin, Lorcan Leonard, Cathal Goulding, Deasun Breathnach, Ciaran Mac an Aili and Terry Conneally;

Belfast: Fred Heatley, M McKeown, S Caughey, Jack Bennett, John Irvine and Liam Burke;

Cork: Rory Driscoll; Derry: Hugh MacAteer;

Newry: Dan Moore; Waterford: Al Ryan; Ballina: Greg Collins.

How was this group identified, selected, assembled? It was probably as a result of personal contact by Cathal Goulding. Apart from Seán Cronin it consisted of a mix of people with 1930s and 1940s republican backgrounds, supported by various professionals, mostly journalists, who were republican sympathisers willing to explore the political road, and unhappy with the Sinn Fein constraints. It had nothing to do with Sinn Fein; the Sinn Fein minutes at this time show only 'fuzzy' knowledge of it. It represented the measure of Goulding's perception of political reform potential, as seen from the perspective of the IRA, as it remained in vestigial existence in 1963. The word 'Directory' I suspect probably is Fenian/IRB usage, looking back to the United Irishmen and the French Revolution.

A Sinn Fein Ard Comhairle meeting took place on the same weekend 11/05/63, from which the following has been abstracted, as well as some items from subsequent meetings: '...there was a perceived need to clarify the WT committee position, and to get the *United Irishman* to publish a letter from the Secretary ...'

At a meeting two weeks later Éamonn Mac Thomáis reported to the Sinn Fein Ard Comhairle on proposed Wolfe Tone activities. The need to link with Sinn Fein must however have been recognised by Goulding, because Eamonn Mac Thomáis appeared in the Wolfe Tone Directory records for the first time on June 4, enabling him to report on June 5. Goulding must have invited him.

The Wolfe Tone Convention outlined an ambitious programme of events, pageantry, music, in various locations. The Cork events were to be associated with Thomas Russell's birthplace, Belfast events with the graves of Hope, Orr and Russell; there was a definite aspiration to reach out to the Protestant republican tradition: '...to use the Tone Bicentenary as a launching point from which the doctrine of Republicanism could be taught anew so that Tone's aim of a free, united Ireland, in which Catholic and Dissenter would work together in harmony and liberty, would be soon achieved ...'.

On July 26 the Wolfe Tone Directory finalised the plans for the Mansion House meetings planned for mid-September: Roger McHugh, a sympathetic UCD lecturer, to act as Director; lectures to be from himself, Hubert Butler, Ciaran Mac an Aili, Jack Bennett and Seán Cronin. Seán Bermingham and Terry Conneally were to be co-opted to the Directory. A letter went out seeking financial support for the series.

On August 24 1963 the Sinn Fein Ard Comhairle received a letter from TP Connealy seeking a speaker for a housing protest. John Joe McGirl proposed 'issuing a statement'.

Terry Connealy was active in the Wolfe Tone Directory (WTD) from the beginning, and in the Wolfe Tone Society (WTS) from June 1964 onwards, participating in the Housing Action Committee events; for example there was, circa 1965, a march on the Mansion House at which he and I met the Mayor. So Connealy in the WTD was part of the emergent left trend which saw the WTS as an outlet. Note that this episode pre-dates my presence in Ireland; I did not get back till September 1963.

On Oct 8 the WTD records note that the group now included Uinsean Mac Eoin, Lorcan Leonard, Harry White, Deasun Breathnach, Éamonn Mac Thomáis, Terry Conneally, Cathal Goulding and Dick Roche. An offer from Sairseal & Dill to publish the lecture series was considered. Hubert Butler had invited 'members of the Directory' to his home in Kilkenny; UMacE and LL went. Jack Bennett and Liam Burke were to speak at a meeting in Glencolumcille, Co Donegal. UMacE, LL and RR were to attend SF Ard Fheis in Moran's Hotel to sell literature. UMacE and LL were to survey Tailors Hall and liaise with Maire Comerford(24).

Thus the Wolfe Tone Directories were clearly set on the road to broad-based politicisation, taking on board the Protestant interests via Hubert Butler, before I had become involved.

A key meeting of representatives of the Wolfe Tone Directories took place in Dundalk on November 24 1963, involving Liam Burke, Tomás Mac Giolla, Martin Shannon, Uinsean Mac Eoin and Dick Roche. It was decided that the WT group would continue in existence under a new title, not as a political party, but to be 'agitational and educational' and to formulate a programme for the future.

Martin Shannon at this time was the Editor of the *United Irishman*. TMacG was standing in for Cathal Goulding representing the Army Council, which clearly regarded the Directory as its property. The concept of the 'think tank' to supply the UI and the movement generally with ideas was emerging. I was unaware of this meeting, though I remember meeting with TMacG around this time, and picking up indications that changes were in prospect; I had attended the Mansion House lectures, and been somewhat enthused by them.

On January 14 1964 the first WT meeting post-Dundalk took place; it included Uinsean MacEoin, Lorcan Leonard, Harry White, Richard Roche and for the first time the present writer RJ. There were reports on local meetings, and a draft plan by UMacE was approved for discussion at an extended meeting on Sunday January 26. This took place, with the above and Deasun Breathnach, E Mac Thomais, Seán Bermingham, Seán Cronin, Liam Burke, Jack Bennett and Terry Conneally also present. The meeting was inconclusive, except in that it was decided that the Cave Hill commemoration should continue.

At the February 11 WTD meeting there were present Uinsean MacEoin, RJ, Harry White, Cathal Goulding, Terry Conneally, Dick Roche, Padraig Ó Nuallain (an executive with the New Ireland Insurance Co, with a Clann na Poblachta background), Deasun Breathanach and one J Kennedy. An all-Ireland meeting was projected for Belfast. The Essay Prize was considered. A 'Ballad night' concept linked to a structured political mini-drama was projected; the sub-committee to run it included Máirín Johnston, my wife. A 'Who Owns Ireland' booklet was suggested by the present writer, and it was agreed to co-operate with SF in drafting their social and economic programme. Deasun Breathnach mentioned a co-op in Ballymena.

The experience of the Connolly Association and the work of Eamonn McLoughlin in structuring political mini-dramas based on ballads with interconnected scripting seemed to me to be relevant; ballad nights were all the rage at the time, with the revival of interest in Irish folk music, and Máirín was well established in the genre. The Ballymena co-op suggests the beginnings of an understanding of the need to build bridges into Protestant culture, though this was never followed up.

The Sinn Fein Ard Comhairle meeting on March 7 1964 dealt with the Ard Fheis resolutions: No 5 was to put in a new economic programme, and a committee working on this was said to include Rory O'Driscoll, Gerry McCarthy, Niall Fagan, Seán Corish, S Ó Cleirigh (Jackie Clarke), Tom Mitchell, Éamonn MacThomáis, Redmond O'Sullivan, Larry Grogan, Wally Lynch, Seán Ó Brádaigh, John Joe McGirl...

I have no recollection of any WTD or WTS interaction with this committee, but I seem to remember attending a Sinn Fein dinner in some place like Enniscorthy or Gorey in the spring of 1964, at which Rory O'Driscoll presided. This was my first official encounter, by invitation; it was probably an Easter event. I remember getting the measure of Rory as a classic, almost caricature, Fenian schoolteacher.

Chapter 7 Part 1: The Period 1961-1966

On April 22 1964 Desmond Greaves(25) attended an anti-apartheid meeting in the Mansion House, where he was impressed by the contribution of Barry Desmond (then an official with the Irish Congress of Trade Unions, whom CDG noted as Anthony Coughlan's friend). He commented '...the Labour Party would never dream of holding a meeting to protest against apartheid in Northern Ireland. ...'. Others present included Micheál O'Riordan, Justin and Loretta Keating and Justin's mother May, Johnny Nolan, Frank Edwards and Michael O'Leary (later Tanaiste). Anthony Coughlan (AC) was on the committee of the Irish Anti-Apartheid Movement which had organised the meeting, and Greaves noted that '...AC told me an interesting thing told him in Dublin, namely that Martin Ennals came back from the six counties two years ago with material completely condemning the six-county government.... but was prevented from publishing it on the intervention of Transport House as embarrassing to the Labour Party ...'.

Thus the early republican politicisation process, and the Civil Rights approach to the Northern Ireland question, were at this time on separate tracks. I had my feet in both camps. During this time however I was in the US on Aer Lingus business(26), but I was aware of the role of the Irish Anti-Apartheid movement led by the South African TCD law lecturer Kader Asmal and his wife Louise, and had recognised the relevance of its campaign to the Northern situation.

During this time there was tension between Irish Workers' League and the Connolly Association; Greaves had since the mid-1950s been leading the latter towards concentration of Civil Rights issues in the North, while the IWL emigrants were still organising, along with various ultra-leftist groups, to collect money in London for the IWL in Dublin, with the tacit support of the CPGB, an activity which had originated in the 1950s and still persisted.

These issues remained unresolved, being muddied by the theoretical confusion of the international movement, with Trotskyite and Chinese factions emerging to undermine the high church of post-Stalinist CP orthodoxy. The Greaves policy with the Connolly Association was being promoted largely in spite of the CPGB and the IWL. This had been the position since 1955, when it had adopted a new constitution, clarifying its independent role.

In Belfast on June 6 1964 CDG by invitation delivered a paper on 'British Policy Towards Ireland' at a weekend school organised jointly by the NICP and the IWL; there were 17 from the South and 25 from the North; the present writer was there along with George Jeffares, Sam Nolan, Johnny Nolan, Paddy Carmody and others; Betty Sinclair and Billy McCullough were there from the North. Greaves '...avoided (contemporary) policy like the plague ...' knowing the current differences of view. He sat in on the session the following day, listening to Carmody, whose talk was based on the Labhras Ó Nuallain economic analysis, and ignored CDG's own subsequent work critical of Barritt and Carter. Andy Barr spoke on trade unionism without introducing any political dimension, displeasing Betty Sinclair. O'Riordain enthused about the breadth of the participation (North, South and Irish in Britain) but showed no awareness of the potential role of the Labour movement in Britain, CDG's chief target.

On July 2 1964 in Dublin Greaves recorded attending a meeting of Sceim na gCeardcumainn, a trade-union based Irish language group, addressed by Micheál O'Leary. There was much reportage and controversy, and they got bogged down in electoral procedures. Packy Early, Barry Desmond, Máirín Johnston, Donal Donnelly, Des Geraghty were there among others (including the present writer). He concluded '...my impression is however that this movement will not come to anything as no person of much consequence in the labour movement is in it ...'. He attributed the origins and objective of the movement to '...Tony Coughlan, Packy Early and others for introducing the Gaelic language and "Irish Irelandism" into the trade union movement, and a very queer outfit it seemed. The chair was taken by the most incredible waffler I have ever seen. ...'. Later Máirín and I went up to Finglas to Cathal MacLiam's, with whom CDG used to stay on his periodic research visits to Dublin, and we spent the evening with CDG; we confirmed his negative assessment of the Sceim.

The Sinn Fein Ard Comhairle minutes of 04/07/64 contain a reference to my 'economic resistance' paper for the Wolfe Tone Society: it was agreed to pass it for discussion at cumann level. This was the present writer's first appearance on the minuted SF record. The paper was subsequently published in the October 1964 *United Irishman*(27); there was an introductory section which showed how imperialist economic forces worked within a unified financial system, with the partitioned State incapable of effectively controlling them in the people's interests. The task of the movement had up to now been seen as simply the ending of Partition, and in this we had not been successful. It would be necessary to give a lead to the spontaneous movement of economic resistance which was beginning to emerge in the West, in the form of co-operative organisations of small farmers, and small-scale local industrial initiatives, based on locally produced raw materials. Workers and management in the State sector of industry were identified as being part of the 'economic resistance', which also included primary producers, workers and traders co-operatives, locally based transport systems, with gombeen parasitic capitalism being replaced by community enterprise. The Ralahine model, as outlined by Connolly, was mentioned. Links between producers and urban consumers would require the development of a consumer co-op movement in the cities. The Credit Union movement was identified a means of organising a financial system supportive of local co-operative enterprise.

This is actually close to the thinking of JJ, Horace Plunkett and George Russell, viewed in retrospect. There certainly was an emphasis against the simplistic two-class model of traditional Marxism, and a desire to involve 'working owner-managers and self-employed' along with 'workers' among the progressive forces; also a feeling of the need to transform 'workers' into 'worker-owners' of their co-operatively owned workplaces. Industrial, commercial and social democracy would need a favourable environment within a framework of political democracy. On the whole I think it was theoretically a positive document, but perhaps the people who were influenced by it were too steeped in militaristic and elitist culture to interpret it validly, though as we have seen Goulding was supportive when I was being attacked by Mac Stiofain.

Thus for about a year after my return I was searching around for opportunities to broaden the movement, while staying in touch with the IWL. Then some time around June or July 1964 I decided to drop out from the Irish Workers League and throw in my lot with the politicising republicans, on the assurance from Cathal Goulding that he wanted help in converting the IRA from an illegal army into a democratically disciplined political movement reflecting the interests of the working people as a whole, broadly based on the socialist ideas of Marx, as adapted by Connolly to the Irish situation.

Foundation of the Dublin Wolfe Tone Society

On July 25 1964 at a general meeting of the Directory, RJ presiding, and Uinsean Mac Eoin, S Mac Domhnaill, Ethna MacManus, Seamus Costello, Deasun Breathnach, Richard Roche and Cathal Goulding present, a motion was proposed by Uinsean Mac Eoin, seconded by Deasun Breathnach and passed by five votes to one with two abstentions: 'that the Wolfe Tone Directories be wound up and their activities be terminated; that a new society, namely Muintir Wolfe Tone (Wolfe Tone Society) be formed and that all assets and liabilities of the Wolfe Tone Directories devolve on it.' The constitution was amended and adopted(28). RJ took on to be vice-chair and to handle publicity; Dick Roche remained as Secretary. Other posts remained to be filled.

Ethna MacManus, a pharmacist working in Dublin, at the time was one of my 'contacts' among whom were beginning to take shape strategies for the development of political left-republicanism. She had earlier been associated with co-operative developments in Killala, and had standing with the republicans, having provided a 'safe house' during the 1950s. She had when living in Killala been attempting to work 'bottom up', organising from the grass-roots, in association with the Mayo politicising republicans, and had had modest success.

An effort was made to recruit Michael O'Leary, then active in the Labour Party, but without success. Padraig Ó Nuallain agreed to act as Chairman, and Uinsean Mac Eoin as treasurer. The concept of 'economic resistance movement' was developed; there was contact with Fr McDyer the Glencolumcille co-operative priest, and with Peadar O'Donnell; the need for Donegal-Derry linkages was promoted(29). Some time after this there was a debate with Clann na Poblachta in Powers Hotel; this took place on November 2 1964. Justin Keating was present on the occasion, and was subsequently co-opted as a member.

We were making an attempt to build a group fit to involve people who subsequently became leading Labour Party intellectuals. Our re-think of the 'national question' in the Wolfe Tone tradition had aroused a flicker of interest. Anthony Coughlan at this time was supportive of his old UCC colleague and current flatmate Michael O'Leary.

The McDyer enterprise in Donegal was in touch with small farmers clubs in Mayo; a possible role for Sceim na gCeardcumann emerged; RJ was to speak to them(30). The key concept was the need to find means of linking urban workers with the projected rural co-operative movement revival. There were also notes towards the development of a 'co-operative congress', with urban, industrial and consumer dimensions as well as primary producers.

***

Greaves meanwhile in London was making attempts to develop co-operation with Clann na hEireann, the republican emigrant body. This was fraught with the usual tensions, with the Clann actively competing, and in some cases attempting to hijack or dominate Connolly Association meetings. His visits to Belfast, undertaken primarily in the context of his Mellows researches, also involved meetings with Jack and Anna Bennett (with whom he usually stayed when in Belfast), and with Seán Caughey, the Sinn Fein election agent. The latter's vision, CDG noted, was between elections in 1964 in the North and 1966 in the South to get the makings of an all-Ireland Dáil which would legislate for the whole of Ireland. CDG later agreed with JB that Caughey was 'bonkers'.

At the Wolfe Tone Society on October 20 1964 RJ was in the chair, present were EMacM, S Cronin, UMacE, A Coughlan, RR, TC, DB, J Keating and C Goulding. RJ was to meet with Peadar O'Donnell the following Saturday. JK reported on a meeting with a group from the USSR, in the context of trade development. There was talk of a 'freedom train' to run from Dublin to Derry, as part of a campaign against closure of the direct Dublin-Derry railway, then imminent.

This was Anthony Coughlan's first Wolfe Tone Society meeting. Nothing came of the 'freedom train' concept, alas. RJ's Peadar O'Donnell meeting was in the context of the 'economic resistance' concept, which had been promoted in the October 1964 United Irishman. In retrospect, this promotion was a mistake, in that it associated the concept with an explicit Republican ideology, this arousing suspicion in the mind of Peadar O'Donnell, whose experience of the movement was based on its form in the past, rather than the form to which we aspired.

The Peadar O'Donnell meeting subsequently yielded plans for a conference in the Gresham with Sceim na gCearcumann, County Associations etc, and an invited audience, including WTS representatives.

Uinsean Mac Eoin later proposed and Padraig Ó Nuallain seconded a motion calling on the Government to purchase the assets of the Northern railways should Stormont decide to close them down, and keep them going.

Round about November 1964 the present writer was considering changing his job, leaving Aer Lingus and going to work in the Institute of Industrial Research and Standards (IIRS). I had applied for, and had been offered, the job, but then later the offer was withdrawn. The Special Branch must have been active. There were various episodes around this time which suggested that Marxist-democratic politicisation of the republican movement was regarded by the Government as a real threat, and they were prepared to resort to dirty tricks to inhibit this process.

I attended some of the 1964 Sinn Fen Ard Fheis as a visitor, courtesy of Tomás Mac Giolla. I picked up some of the flavour of the situation, enough to suggest that there was indeed here some genuine radical democratic potential, despite the overlay of militarist irredentism. Seamus Costello and Seán Bermingham were elected to the Ard Comhairle. Motion 24, from Newry, urged the formation of Republican Clubs in the six counties, to overcome the problem of Sinn Fein being banned. This was passed with some amendment of wording. Motion 68 from Blessington was passed, calling for a national scheme of resistance to foreign take-over of land and industry, with a National Convention being convened to discuss the issue among concerned organisations.

The foregoing perhaps suggests that the October United Irishman article on 'economic resistance' had been read and was being taken seriously. We have summarised it above.

***

CDG on December 7 1964 recorded that Cathal MacLiam and he went to a Wolfe Tone Society meeting, where Ethna MacManus read a paper on Irish trade. '...Interesting things were said, and the representative of the big bourgeoisie present left the Sinn Feiners and IWL people without a stitch of policy. RHWJ brought in Partition effectively enough, and proposed a resolution for opening trade and diplomatic relations with all countries..... there is as much chance of Ireland abandoning Fianna Fail (or Fine Gael) in the near future as there is of water flowing uphill...'.

The next day CDG had lunch with the present writer; the penultimate paragraph in the December 7 entry is worth quoting in full: '...(RHWJ) said Cathal Goulding has gone to London (to look into) the demonstration which happened during the election, and that having heard I was in Dublin expressed a desire to see me. He is Cathal (MacLiam)'s first cousin so I suggested to Cathal we might invite him up. Taking all in all, things are progressing here as well as can be expected. The younger people with the Connolly Association experience are becoming personally acceptable to the Republicans, and after Monday's meeting RHWJ and Seán Cronin went off to AC's flat where the young Labour hero Michael O'Leary is sharing, and so all heads clarify each other by mutual interaction...'.

So on December 10 1964 Cathal Goulding arrived at MacLiams, and Greaves had the pleasure of introducing him to the cousin he had never met. CG had been supportive of Fitzmaurice and the joint Clann-CA demonstration; there was talk of 'pulling a fast one' on one O'Sullivan (who presumably was in the Clann leadership and hostile to the CA); CDG warned that such 'fast ones' usually slowed down genuine political development. He wanted to keep the door to co-operation open. Greaves noted: '...He said he and his colleagues were thinking in broader political terms than in the past. He struck me as a shrewd experienced revolutionary, but without much basic political knowledge... without a grasp of the laws of social evolution. The interesting thing is that he is prepared to support political action on matters of common concern. But like O'Riordain he appears to believe developments in Britain can be directed from Dublin...'.

Goulding was here trying, somewhat clumsily, to come to terms with the existence of the CA in London, and smooth its relationship with Clann na hEireann, in accordance with his policy of convergence with the Left.

Then on December 12 Greaves recorded an encounter with Peadar O'Donnell, Ethna MacManus and the present writer '...Roy pushing ahead quicker than things can go, and Peadar obstructing and driving Roy wild. I kept out of it...'. Peadar it seems wanted Sceim na gCeardcumann to push his Defence of the West ideas in Dublin, but found it somewhat of an amorphous body... 'they don't know what their aims are... there's a fellow from Trinity College at the top of it, and he's rather academic...', referring to Anthony Coughlan. Peadar later got his way with the Sceim through Donal Donnelly.

So we see at the end of 1964 the basis for left-republican convergence is being laid, and some elements perhaps capable of forming part of a broad-based movement for national unity, based on a co-operative philosophy, and with both urban and rural roots, were beginning to emerge. Desmond Greaves was observing this as a complementary progressive political development which could become 'all-Ireland' provided the Civil Rights issue in the North were to be resolved.

Survival as a Scientist

The move back to Ireland in September 1963 was as a consequence of joining Aer Lingus to participate in the real-time reservations system project. In this context I discovered that what I had been doing in Guinness had a name: it was in fact Systems Engineering, and this was a stepping-stone in the direction of Operations Research, which role crystallised out in the Aer Lingus epoch, via the techno-economic analysis of various projected systems with the aid of the computer.

This of course led straight back to Bernal, with his early association with Operations Research during the war, and the role of physics people in helping to transfer the art of mathematical modelling of systems towards the techno-economic and socio-technical domains. This was the means whereby I justified my existence in the context of the Aer Lingus 'real-time computer project'(26). I went on to identify the problem of how the likes of me, as a physicist, could make out in a relatively undeveloped socio-economic system, as Ireland was in the 50s and 60s, as being a 'science and society' problem. How could the Irish scientific community, such as it was, be motivated to consider it?

There were two channels that seemed to be open; one was to set up some sort of organisation for physics in Ireland within which physicists could interact and develop a sense of community, and the other was to help develop the Operations Research community to a level where it had some recognition in the Irish academic system. The airline OR community already had an international network, with an annual conference, and our work in applying computer-based modelling to the aircraft purchase process had achieved some recognition(26). We used this to help build an OR network within Ireland.

The first (physics) channel led to the setting up of the Irish Branch of the Institute of Physics. PMS Blackett came over from Manchester for the inaugural event, which was supported by ETS Walton the TCD physics professor and Nobel Prize winner, and by TE Nevin his opposite number in UCD. This Blackett contact constituted a (somewhat tenuous) link with the Bernal network of left-wing scientists, and with the origins of Operations Research in the work of physicists during the war. The second (Operations Research) channel led to an attempt to mobilise some pressure on the academic system to become interested in OR-type postgraduate work. This influenced FG Foster, the new Professor of Statistics in TCD, to initiate in 1970 an MSc in Statistics and Operations Research.

Earlier the OECD had sponsored a Report *Science in Irish Economic Development* of which the authors were Patrick Lynch of UCD and HMS 'Dusty' Miller, then head of R&D in Bord na Mona. This was, in effect, a Bernalist 'science and society' analysis of the Irish situation, as was subsequently admitted orally to me by Patrick Lynch, though Bernal at the time was unmentionable, being Marxist. Miller I understand had earlier had a left-wing background in England. Together they produced a document which was influential in turning the attention of the Government to the need to recognise science as a key factor in the national development programme. Miller however realised that if it was left to the Civil Service as it was then to take initiatives, nothing would happen; it was necessary to politicise the issues.

I later got to review the 1964 OECD Report(31) in the December 1966 issue of a monthly publication called *Development*, edited by Jim Gilbert, which was widely read in 1960s innovative management circles. Here are my contemporary comments via that channel:

"The survey team who have produced the White Paper on *Science and Irish Economic Development* are to be complimented on a comprehensive and courageous production which cuts across Departmental boundaries and exposes the lack of central responsibility for science policy or even means of formulating it. The changes it proposes are profound, some may say revolutionary. Justice cannot be done to it in a short article: however, some points can be picked out which will help to place it on the "must" list.

"The report finds that with few exceptions the Irish science '...effort is piecemeal, scattered thinly, not always related to national needs and so uncoordinated that it tends to undue overlap in some subjects and to an absence of activities in other important fields. Agricultural research is highly developed and organised, whereas Industrial research is relatively non-existent...'."

To follow up on the OECD Report 'Dusty' Miller called a meeting of people from the Dublin-based science and engineering organisations, and leavened this elitist mix with people from the Regional Science Councils, which had emerged to form the makings of a scientific community outside Dublin, based largely on the personnel of the State agencies. This led to the formation of the Council for Science and Technology in Ireland (CSTI) which was a loose federation of several science and engineering bodies based in Dublin, and the Regional Science Councils. It used to meet in the Institution of Engineers of Ireland premises in Clyde Road, and I became Secretary.

One of the objectives of the CSTI was to help in the formulation of a national science policy, with particular reference to the needs of the rapidly expanding applied science sector. Ray Keary, a geologist, wrote on May 26 1966 an article in the *Irish Times* entitled 'A Neglected Science' in which he castigated the Government for its neglect of the Geological Survey. This drew a response from PS Doughty of the Ulster Museum which referred to the 'futile retrospective tide of nationalism (sweeping all) rational thought away'.

This was an opportunity for me as Secretary of the CSTI to take up; I published a letter in the *Irish Times* on June 7 1966 in response to the Keary-Doughty exchange of *Irish Times* letters. Arising from Keary's reference to the Avoca mine closure I mentioned that I had heard from a number of reputable independent sources that it was not unconnected with the disclosure of the value of an ore concentrate cargo which took place when a ship ran aground and had to be salvaged. I had also heard from university geologists concerned that it was remarkably difficult for student groups to got access to the Avoca workings for educational purposes.

This prompted me to ask what was the true nature of the deal which has been done between the State and the foreign company that we are permitting at Tynagh to exploit our natural resources? Are we in receipt of royalties? If so, how are they calculated? Ray Keary had suggested that we should have a resident State scientific staff checking the exported concentrate so as to enable royalties to be calculated. Yet the history of Avoca and Ray Keary's article suggested that we were not. Dr O'Connell in the Dáil had attempted to have disclosed the terms of the contract between the State and the exploiting company. He was told that this was not available. Were we letting these people extract our mineral wealth in return for merely the wages of the workers?

I went on to comment that Mr Doughty had put his finger on the weakness of the type of 26 county nationalism that used the language as a shibboleth, and liked to think of a 26 County Catholic republic, with religious sectarianism built into its Constitution, and a partitioned university structure in Dublin. So emasculated had Irish science become under this dead hand that the situation so accurately described by Ray Keary had been allowed to develop in most if not all branches of science.

I criticised the Doughty response: the relative good fortune of Six County geology was, like the National Health Service, a product of a decision made in London that happened to benefit a part of Ireland. Suppose a London government were to decide that all geological work was to be handed over to the Americans?

I concluded by urging that we should plan our own resources without interference from outside, and without having to depend on hand-outs from any other nation. We could get by very comfortably if we devoted one tenth the effort per capita that the so-called advanced nations spend on rocketry and armaments to 'making two blades of grass grow where one grew before'.. Small-nation science, if imaginatively fostered by an enlightened government, could point the way to relieving the chronic famines of the '80s and '90s which will be with us if present population trends continue.

I conceded that Doughty's Unionism was right from the point of view of Science until it was proved wrong by the replacement of the Daniel O'Connell / Tierney / de Valera / AOH concept of the nation by that of Wolfe Tone and Connolly. On this unashamedly political note I closed....

I 'went for broke' on this, given that the CSTI had on the whole not worked as an active lobby to the extent that its founders had hoped. I hoped by this somewhat aggressive approach to provoke people to come to the AGM, but unfortunately the CSTI withered, and its constituent members dispersed to the separate camps, leaving their members dependent on the somewhat modest hand-outs from the National Science Council which in the end was established, on the traditional patronage basis with Ministerial nominees.

The historical parallel had been drawn between the CSTI as being to the Royal Irish Academy what the British Association was to the Royal Society in the mid 19th century. There was a grain of truth in this; the CSTI however was unable to become a powerful enough lobby. The experience did however generate a demand which fuelled the writer's 'Science in Ireland' series of articles in the *Irish Times*(32), the purpose of which was to indicate some ways in which science, technology and economic development interacted. This was commissioned by the then Features Editor Fergus Pyle as a consequence of the Ray Keary article and my subsequent letter.

1965: Republican Political Education Begins

Acting as Cathal Goulding's 'political education officer' on behalf of his 'HQ Staff', I had my first encounter with the Dublin unit of the then 'IRA', which took place in Howth, on March 7 1965, in the company of Ethna MacManus(33). This was my first attempt to feel my way interactively into the political thinking of the type of people who were motivated to join the Dublin unit at the time, mostly by some kind of romantic militarism, or a sense of adventure.

I tried to explain that the secondary effects of Partition generated problems that needed to be addressed, and by organising to do this, we come in contact with a wide variety of people, with whom we can build an organised approach to the achievement of desirable tactical objectives. In this process we had the opportunity of playing a leading role, but we would have to earn it. Father McDyer's 'co-operative of 10 subsistence farmers' had showed development potential for local leadership. Could this be replicated elsewhere, and also in an urban working environment? If so, there was the possibility of developing a 32-county Co-operative Congress, to which people would look for ideas, rather than to the two partitioned administrations.

I went on to generalise this to the existing 32-county Trade Union movement, within which organised approaches to local issues were feasible, ranging from worker co-operative takeovers of local mills, to lobbying the Dublin government to help keep the Shorts factory open in Belfast, and in general in support of the transformation of the Northern engineering industry away from imperial and towards national objectives. Why should the Sugar Company have to go to Germany to get its equipment? etc.

I was promoting a concept of an active politically conscious trade union and co-operative movement, which understood the importance of an all-Ireland approach to employment, market development, welfare etc, as a stage in laying the basis for a possibly future 1918-type election; this was of course the alternative to militarism. I went on to suggest that the 'army', if it were to take seriously its claim to be the 'legitimate government of the country', should go out and 'survey the battlefield'; in other words, get a feel for the local political, economic and social issues which have, however indirectly, an all-Ireland dimension.

During the next few months I met with various 'army' units, such as they were, throughout the country, and conveyed a message along these lines, with local variations. Those who took it up, and many did, remained with the movement in the 1970s and were not taken in by the 'provisional' nonsense. Some became co-operative and trade union activists, I have since gathered anecdotally, but I am unable to quantify the extent that this took place.

I put the 'army' in quotes because, as Mick Ryan(34) has since confirmed, the impression that I then picked up was that the IRA did not then exist as a serious military organisation; it consisted of a few groups of local activist visionaries held together by local O/Cs nominated by Goulding; I doubt if there were more that 200 in the whole country.

There was a Wolfe Tone Society meeting on March 9 1965, to which Cathal Goulding came (he had attended a few of the earlier meetings, but later attendances were rare). A meeting in Belfast was projected around Easter. A memo by Kader Asmal was noted; RJ had seen Edgar Deale and noted that his organisation, the Irish Association for Civil Liberty (IACL), did not take initiatives on the Offences Against the State (OAS) Act. Names were targeted for circulation of the Asmal memo, which related to civil liberties in the South.

We have here a clear indication of the beginnings of the Civil Rights approach, supported by Kader Asmal, who was then leader of the Irish Anti-Apartheid Movement. A copy of a letter from RJ to Jack Bennett has turned up relating to the projected meeting in Belfast; it was intended that the meeting should be supportive of the New University of Ulster being located in Derry, and urged that there be a Donegal dimension, and a proposal for it to be associated with a scheme for the integrated development of the North-West, a jointly-funded cross-border body. It was also suggested that a ballad concert should have an orange and green theme, with interspersed narrative. There was also a cryptic reference to Shorts, the Belfast aircraft factory and a Protestant stronghold, indicating an aspiration to achieve left-wing trade-union contact in the context.

***

Meanwhile in London the NCCL conference(35) had been planned for the small Conway Hall but they had to move to the larger one because Ulster TV had become involved, due to the interest in NI civil rights. Seán Caughey, Betty Sinclair, Dr McCluskey(36) and Austin Currie all contributed. The overall result of this was positive and a significant step in the direction of achieving a cross-community civil rights movement in NI, and of breaking down the barriers between the 'catholic nationalist' tradition and that of Marxist-democracy.

***

At the May 4 1965 meeting of the Wolfe Tone Society it was noted that the sponsors of the Asmal Civil Rights document included (UCD Professor) Roger McHugh, Hubert Butler, Joe Johnston and the new Professor of Law in TCD *(this must have been JD Morton, who had joined the College on January 1 1965; he would have responded to an approach by Kader Asmal)..* This document had been agreed at an earlier meeting on March 30, and was an attempt to get an effective civil liberties movement going in the South. Anthony Coughlan, Uinsean Mac Eoin and Kader Asmal were to meet Edgar Deale and Christopher Gore-Grimes to negotiate the formation of a new body. This was the genesis of 'Citizens for Civil Liberties' (CCL). There was here an inter-generational link; Edgar Deale's name has already occurred among the supporters of JJ's early co-operative campaigning, and JJ supported the current initiative. The fact that JJ had signed the document would have encouraged Edgar Deale to do business with the current generation of Civil Liberties activists. Nothing much came of this initiative however in the short term, though in the long run it led, via CCL, to the foundation of the current Irish Council for Civil Liberties.

***

Meanwhile in the North Greaves in his diary described a 'historic event' on May 6 1965 in the Belfast ATGWU hall: '...there were about a hundred present.... these included all political parties but Unionists and Nationalists.. It was interesting to hear the Catholic delegates of the ITGWU getting up explaining discrimination to Protestants who were listening for the first time. There was unfortunately no declaration against discrimination from a Protestant as such - though there were several speeches that assumed that attitude - and the strongest speeches came from people who described themselves as atheists, some from one side, others from the other. The republicans of course could not resist using the platform, and Seán Morrissey visibly squirmed, such is the duality of his position as an ex-republican. I had a talk with Andy Barr and Hughie Moore afterwards, and all agree it was a historic event, the fact that there was here a meeting of Protestant and Catholic workers under the auspices of the Labour movement directed to democratising the State...'.

Greaves subsequently held that this should have been the seed-bed for further developments, and that the NICRA, as it emerged from the War Memorial Hall meeting in 1966, was doomed to disaster due to its failure to develop organic links with the labour movement, and its inability to counter the influence of Ian Paisley on the Protestant working class; more on this later.

The initiative to set up the NICRA came subsequently via the Dublin Wolfe Tone Society, basically from Anthony Coughlan. It did not follow organically from the above May 6 1965 meeting. Had there been a follow-up from this meeting, the War Memorial Hall initiative would have not seemed necessary. The NICRA or its equivalent would perhaps have emerged with a stronger trade union basis. The politicising republicans would have supported this, without being able to project a sense of 'ownership', as subsequently happened with the NICRA, to the detriment of the latter. CDG at the time unfortunately was preoccupied with the terminal illness of his sister Phyllis, and it is tempting to conjecture how things might have developed had the civil rights movement emerged organically from the trade union movement, as CDG had hoped would happen, and as he might have been in a position to encourage, perhaps via the NCCL, had he been fully active.

Greaves recorded subsequently on May 9 1965 that '...Caughey had "felt there was something wrong" with the social and economic policy document ...' (which the present writer had drafted for Sinn Fein), suggesting '...it should be sent to the Catholic Church for approval. Ruane indicated that he disagreed with this (on the grounds that)..RHWJ... as a Protestant might object. But he showed evident satisfaction at the fact that after being studied for three solid weeks by an eminent North of Ireland Catholic philosopher, it was pronounced unobjectionable to the clergy, and politically "revolutionary". So Caughey was satisfied. There was much dissatisfaction with Caughey... who else had they in the North? When they went up for the election campaign they found a political desert. So they had to give Caughey a free hand ...'.

This shows the depths of the Catholic-nationalist mind-set of the Northern republicans, and the extent of the political vacuum that we needed to fill.

***

There was a Special Sinn Fein Ard Fheis on June 12-13 1965, the agenda(37) for which was the output of the 'conference of republicans' announced at the 1964 Ard Fheis in the Bricklayers Hall in the course of the Army Council Statement. It is to be seen as essentially an 'army' document, aimed at changing the politics of the more traditional Sinn Fein. The various clauses were put to the Ard Comhairle, which in some cases recommended them for adoption.

This was a serious attempt to initiate the transformation of Sinn Fein into a radical political force, taking full part in the activities of civil society in both parts of Ireland. It was the fruit of the politicisation process of the previous internment, and probably was drafted by Goulding and Costello(38) . I did not have any significant hand in it. It was an attempt to impose the 'advanced thinking' of the key 'army' people on the relatively reluctant Sinn Fein 'sea-green incorruptibles', at a rate somewhat faster than the latter were prepared to go. However some of the proposals did get past the Special Ard Fheis and the resulting atmosphere in Sinn Fein became more open to climatic change.

The key 'civil society enabling proposals' were in Section [8]:

(b) That the whole question of attitude to be adopted by Republicans in prison be reconsidered with a view to revision of same.

(c) That there be no obstacle placed in the way of Republicans writing to government departments in the 6 Counties, 26 Counties or in Britain seeking information or requesting that something be done, etc.

(d) That Republicans acting as members of local organisations and not simply as Republicans be permitted and encouraged to take part in delegations to Ministers of any of the three governments administrating in Ireland.

This opening up however was marred by an over-riding philosophy of aspiration to 'own' broader organisations, and steer them into 'national question' issues. This comes over in Section [1]:

[1] (a)That the essential work of the republican movement at present is the development of political and agitational activities and the infiltration and direction of other organisations.

Note the use of the word 'infiltration': this reflects traditional elitist 'army' thinking and I remember noting the need to campaign against the concept via the educational opportunities presented by the following sections. People should be active in organisations which genuinely reflect their broader interests as citizens or specialists of one kind or another, a process basically different from 'infiltration' as then perceived by the activists.

(b) That educational and training programmes in both organisations should be directed to this end. That one educational centre for all recruits to the Republican Movement be set up, details of organisation to be worked out by the executives of both branches.

(c) That closer integration of the executives of both organisations is essential. That this should be achieved by having the same people on both executives.

(d) That the structure and constitution of each organisation should be streamlined to provide for close co-operation between both at local level.

This was accepted by the Ard Comhairle, but at the Special Ard Fheis only (b) and (d) were carried; (c) was lost, and (a) was amended as follows:

"That the essential work of the Republican Movement at present is the development of political and agitational activities and the giving of leadership, internally and externally, and the involvement of other organisations in struggles for limited objectives as a preparation for an ultimate confrontation with the British Government on the national issue. This amendment does not accept Recommendation No. 9 as a logical extension of these recommendations."

Recommendation [9] was: "That the executives of both organisations give consideration to action within existing parliament(s) on a guerrilla basis as a logical extension of the activities outlined in Recommendation 1 re agitation." This was of course rejected by the Ard Comhairle.

The above amended 1(a) was inconsistent with the roles required for republican activists, in subsequent non-violent initiatives such as the NICRA, by those who were at this time promoting the politicisation process. It was closer to the Blaneyite approach which subsequently emerged post-1969, driving the Civil Rights campaign into the Catholic ghettoes.

***

The minutes of the October 12 1965 WTS meeting record the Belfast Meeting: '...It was reported that a successful launching meeting had been held in Belfast between Dublin delegates R Johnston, Peter Kerr, Tony Coughlan and Uinsean Mac Eoin, and Belfast delegates Liam Barbour, Michael Dolley, Alec Foster, Jack Bennett and Liam Burke. It was agreed that for the moment the new group should concentrate its attentions on the civil rights issue, particularly the question of plural voting...

'..Contact was made with Republicans working on the same issue and it was learned that a Committee for Democratic Elections had been set up. Fred Heatley was asked and agreed to become Secretary of the new Belfast group. It was also made known that Ciaran Mac an Aili was prepared to read a paper which he had done for the UN on 'Civil Liberties North and South', to a meeting organised by the WTS in Belfast. It was agreed that invitations be sent to the UN Association in Belfast and that Prof J McCartney be invited to speak to the paper. It was suggested that the Committee for Democratic Elections should get in touch with the Campaign for Social Justice in Dungannon and, with an official link already in existence with the republican movement, to form a broad common platform on this issue with all similarly-minded organisations in the North ...'.

It was urged that the Dublin WTS Constitution be adapted to serve the new group as the Belfast WTS.

***

The launch meeting of the Co-operative Development Trust (Comhar Linn)(39), chaired by Michael Viney, was reported in the November 1965 *United Irishman*. In the December issue there was an article by Hubert Butler reflecting on his own republican credentials. This also had an article by George Gilmore 'Gentlemen, you have a country', and one by Maire Comerford)(24) on Rhodesia.

At the Sinn Fein Ard Comhairle on 13/11/65 Seán Ó Brádaigh introduced his education plan. SF and the 'other branch' were supposed to be acting in tandem on this, with RJ supporting SOB in the 'other branch', as part of CG's plan to integrate both branches into a single political movement.

This, while well-intentioned, never worked. It was not clear who was taking initiatives.

***

Greaves on November 25 1965 recorded a meeting with RHWJ over lunch in Dublin; I was said to be in a state of enthusiasm '...over his co-operative pool and other activities, all of which will do some good... I was quite pleased, even if I do not have his expectations.... co-operative ideas are taking on. At the Sinn Fein Ard Fheis a motion referring to penetration by mysterious left-wingers was withdrawn...'.

This was Motion 46 which condemned Communism, opposed collaboration with Communist organisations, and called for expulsion of any member having known connections with communism. The Ard Comhairle record simply skips this, going on from 45 to 47. The number 46 appears in the minutes but is overwritten by 47. It is therefore not clear whether or how this was considered.

I suspect that this motion was aimed at getting rid of the present writer, and was prompted by the valid perception that Stalinist communism as practiced in the USSR was to be discouraged. The present writer had clearly dissociated himself, in his writings, from this position, promoting instead the Connolly tradition: economic democracy, with the Ralahine chapter in Labour in Irish History as model. Goulding accepted this, and was prepared to defend me from attacks from the right-wing traditionalist quarter.

I did not attend this Ard Fheis, which took place in Moran's Hotel. I had been working primarily with Cathal Goulding, in the 'other branch'. To establish my right to be involved with Sinn Fein required that various deadwood obstacles be removed, and this now took place.

Greaves was prepared to be supportive of my interest in this direction, regarding it as perhaps a good counter to the traditional republican 'stunt' culture, and a step in the direction of learning about the organisation of civil society. In hindsight, my perception at the time was indeed over-optimistic, and developments in this direction were rapidly overwhelmed by the developing Northern situation, as we shall see.

On December 2 Greaves encountered Tony Meade who enthused about Brian Farrington's essay on Yeats, published as a Connolly Association pamphlet, which the *United Irishman* was reviewing.

During this time I had been active in the West, and I regaled Greaves with the news, which he recorded, that Peadar O'Donnell's Mayo meeting had '...only 40 present.. bishops, priests and the Catholic quality (with General Costello prominent)... the ordinary people have grown quite cynical over these schemes... Viney, who tried to work with him, was asked to forward a list of republicans and the impression was given that Peadar would try to secure their election to the "Defence of the West" committees. Instead, Peadar blackballed them ...'.

I remember this episode well; in retrospect Peadar could perhaps be forgiven for being suspicious of republican credentials, given their elitist and stunt-oriented political culture, but the Mayo people concerned had actually successfully made the transition into good democratic procedures via the experience of the co-operative movement, and he was blackballing people who might actually have given Defence of the West an edge, and made it work. The generation gap between Peadar and the post-50s republican politicisers was alas too wide.

Greaves on December 10 1965: '...Roy says that there is no truth in the six-county rumour that a further disturbance is to be expected. He says "if the IRA didn't exist, the six-county government would have to invent it".'

These rumours originated with the RUC; they apparently were taken seriously by the British Government, according to a recent (2001) book by Peter Rose(40), which exposes the British attitude to Northern Ireland as being one of total incomprehension, blindness, not wanting to know, and when forced into a need to know, dependence on faulty sources. He points out that in 1966 the British government thought they were facing a threat of a new IRA insurrection, related to the 50th anniversary of the Easter Rising. Their source was the RUC; there were alleged to be 3000 IRA volunteers involved. This was of course a complete fabrication; the 'IRA' at this time was actively engaged, with perhaps 200 activists, in becoming political within the previously empty shell of Sinn Fein. The British had no separate intelligence that was in a position to tell them this; they decided not to set one up, but to continue to depend on the RUC for their intelligence. The motivation of the RUC and the Unionist establishment for promoting this deception was of course to keep in existence the excuse for their repressive regime, supporting the privileged position of the Unionist elite.

1966 and the Commemoration of the Easter Rising

A letter dated January 1 1966 went out, signed by Noel Kavanagh and Claire Gill, joint secretaries of the Economic Independence Committee of the Wolfe Tone Society, as from the present writer's address 22 Belgrave Road; it was sent to various people asking them to lobby the Dáil on Tuesday January 14 on the Anglo-Irish Free Trade Agreement, meeting in Buswell's Hotel for this purpose. Briefing material on the Agreement was enclosed. Politically this served to educate Sinn Fein activists, who had hitherto distained having anything to do with the Dáil, into the art of lobbying the de facto decision-making body. Politically it also can be regarded as a rearguard action in support of the remaining shreds of the de Valera protectionist policy, on the basis of which some industrial development had taken place. I recollect the 1916 veteran Joe Clarke participating.

Shortly after this there was the episode of the 'Captured Document'(41); this was picked up in January 1966 in the possession of Seán Garland, who had attended an Army Council meeting which had begun to address some problems of the politicisation process. It is accessible in the Department of Justice archive.

Motions 60 to 66 of the November 1965 Sinn Fein Ard Fheis had related to the *United Irishman*; I don't have the record of what was done with them, but they reflected unease on the part of the traditionalists about the *United Irishman* content, and called for tighter Sinn Fein editorial control. In fact the UI was regarded as 'army' property, and Goulding defended its role as a key agent of political change.

The 'captured document' consisted of a political plan which had some degree of credibility, a military plan of highly questionable credibility (put in presumably as lip service to the tradition, to keep hardliners like Seán Mac Stiofain and Ruairi Ó Brádaigh onside for the present), a document analysing critically the feedback from the 1965 Extraordinary Ard Fheis, and handwritten notes on the recent 'Army Council' meeting.

The Goulding political plan contained a declaration of intent to 'assume an organisational form that (would) attract back people of national outlook in the trade union movement so that their efforts can be co-ordinated'. Sinn Fein had failed to do anything like this, and the role of the 'army' people in this context was seen as to initiate the education and rejuvenation of Sinn Fein. This would involve reform of the structure of the Movement.

There was however strong residual attachment to the idea of supportive military-type action in guerrilla mode, given the existence of politically-initiated actions involving large numbers of people.

It is possible to see the positive role envisaged for the present writer, but also the pathological persistence of the military mind-set, with which Goulding presumably wished to keep Mac Stiofain and Ó Brádaigh onside, while playing down its significance in order to keep the present writer also onside, a basically unstable and contradictory position.

In a major section headed 'Organisational Principles' it was proclaimed that the basic movement should be '...a political national and social-revolutionary organisation with an open membership and a legal existence... recruitment to be to this alone ...'. The basic unit is the local or factory Cumann. Within each Cumann would be specialist groups looking to influence broader peoples' organisations, '...a training ground for revolutionary government; the transition from the gun to politics in the past has omitted this training procedure and has therefore resulted in the Fianna Fail and Clann na Poblachta processes setting in...'. Specialist groups should have the right to involve non-members in their activity.

The following two key paragraphs enshrine what the present writer was prepared to accept as the beginnings of Goulding transition programme for getting rid of the 'army' as such and going totally political. Mac Stiofain and Ó Brádaigh would undoubtedly have been opposed to this, and I interpret the latter half of the second paragraph as a sop to them.

"H. The Army has its own organisational structure and (is) to function within the revolutionary organisation as backbone. Army recruits to be chosen from the best and most conscious members of the organisation. Under no circumstances should the Army recruit from outside on the basis of the emotional appeal of arms. The Army to give leadership within the organisation by the fact of its being composed of the most advanced elements within it, rather than by weight of numbers.

"I. The Army Convention to continue as a policy-making body, but this role to be played down in proportion as the basic policy decisions are seen to be made correctly, openly and in unity by the National Conference. The current position that the Ard Fheis is a rubber-stamp for the Convention is an imposition on the many good people in SF. The role of the Army Convention should evolve towards that of a specialist conference of certain people in the Movement for examining technical problems connected with the military aspect of the revolution. The Army Council will continually review this position."

The document went on to suggest that the Movement in its new mode should encourage affiliations of friendly organisations having objectives that did not conflict, the germ of the 'national liberation movement' idea.

The foregoing leap of imagination was somewhat visionary, with its implied repeat of the 1918-21 model, and with echoes of the Bolsheviks in 1917. They clearly regarded the taking of seats in existing Partition institutions as anathema, and had not envisioned any creative national role for 'cross-border bodies' as have emerged in the Good Friday Agreement. It could be argued that the Provisionals with their current policies have gone much further than Goulding was prepared to go in this document. The present writer at the time, working in political mode, was however alive to the potential of 'cross-border bodies', as expressed in the motion which I attempted to introduce at the 1965 Irish Association conference in Derry(6).

The 'Military Plan' I put in quotes because its purpose in this context was presumably to keep the militarists busy while not doing too much harm, while the politicisers got on with the job. It was totally unrelated to the political plan as outlined above, in which the present writer had a role. It was however close to a blueprint for the way the Provisionals developed in the North under Mac Stiofain's leadership. There was explicit reference to Cyprus and to the conscious use of terror tactics and assassination. It is not unreasonable to attribute this document to Mac Stiofain as an early draft of the Provisional plan for a northern campaign.

The document continued with a 'Report on the Special Ard Fheis' which expanded on the perceived roles of the Wolfe Tone Societies as they had evolved from the 'Directories', and on the 'Joint Republican Education Centre' concept, which however never existed as a 'Centre' but did exist marginally in the form of a loose interaction between Seán Ó Brádaigh in the then Sinn Fein context, the present writer acting for the 'Goulding Plan' and Anthony Coughlan acting for the Wolfe Tone Society. It never assumed a cohesive existence however. The use of the word 'Joint' in the title was Goulding's attempt to invoke his political plan in the SF context. The then SF mostly traditionalist leadership, being basically crypto- or quasi-Fianna Fail, was suspicious of it, fearing leftward political development.

Several agitations were noted, including actions relating to housing in Dublin, the Castlecomer mines, and the Dundalk Engineering Works, and it was noted that these had been on the initiative of 'army' activists, and that Sinn Fein had stood aside or not wanted to know. This was the measure of the extent of the political education problem if an effective integrated movement were to be developed along the lines suggested by the Goulding Plan.

Note that the underlying political philosophy seemed to be based on the idea that people in trouble should seek support from the shadowy 'Republic as virtually established', perceived as a sort of Robin Hood State. This did not encourage the development of the autonomy of the peoples' own organisations. I was aware of this at the time, and conscious of the need to change these perceptions via the educational programme.

There was recorded in the associated notes an interesting remark by Goulding: '...intelligence report on NATO Free State Army officers briefing (which) revealed Americans worried about republican influence on TU movement, reckoned 500 dissidents in Ireland easily dealt with ...'.

This suggests US paranoia about a repeat in Ireland of the Cuban model; it also indicates, what we always suspected, covert relations between the Free State Army and NATO. We were of course a very long way from a Cuban situation, but the US paranoia appears to have spread to the Fianna Fail leadership, and to have influenced how they gave priority subsequently in 1969 to the undermining of political republicanism in the Civil Rights context, rather than to exposing the British Government and focusing international pressure on the need to disarm the B-Specials. Also Goulding must have had a 'mole' in the Free State Army officer-elite.

***

The Wolfe Tone Society met on February 1; the Kenneth Armour lecture was fixed for Feb 8 in Wynne's Hotel; an attempt was made to invite prominent Protestants (Tony Farrington, Muriel Gahan, Douglas Gageby were mentioned). Plans for the 1916 symposium were taking shape: Asmal was to set the Irish struggle in the context of other 20th century freedom movements, Brian Farrington to speak on Yeats, George Gilmore on Labour.

In the February *United Irishman* we had Frank McGlade elected as Chair of the Northern Directory; 200 attended a meeting in Dungiven; the objective was to commemorate 1916 in the North. There was a report of an article by RJ on 'economics for trade unionists' based on a Sinn Fein educational conference; the key issue here was to replace the 'workers vs management' paradigm by 'workers + management vs owners'. Joe McGrane of the WUI and Kader Asmal also spoke at the event. It seems also I was critical of the 'parity with sterling' principle, and called for an all-Ireland economic model for use in policy planning. George Gilmore in his series defended himself against right-wing attacks by one Seamus Ceitinn.

On February 17 1966 Greaves in his diary recorded that Cathal Goulding had been jailed for possession of a gun: '...they are like children playing soldiers ...'. This episode, which was quite indefensible, resulted in Goulding's loss of the leading position for a time.

At the WTS on February 22 the Armour lecture was noted as having been good; this was a nod in the direction of the Presbyterian Home Rule tradition. My recollection of it however is that it was poorly attended, having lacked good pre-publicity, due to the uncertainty regarding date and location. In the March *United*

Chapter 7 Part 1: The Period 1961-1966

Irishman there was a 'Free Trade Catechism' which was basically a WTS critique of the Free Trade Agreement. There was an IRA statement attacking Stormont for manufacturing phoney incidents. The April 1966 issue was special; it was the 'golden jubilee' of 1916; the GPO was on the front page; it contained a page and a half by the present writer entitled '1916 and its Aftermath'. In this I outlined neo-colonialism, and mentioned approvingly Conor Cruise O'Brien's role in the Congo. I called for intellectual support for the development of the 'half-baked ideas which constitute this article'. Why were we not like Norway? Partition was the obstacle; emigration of all the best brains. Gilmore also wrote on the Labour Movement and the Rising.

There is on record a printed card with the Wolfe Tone Society 1916 Lecture series in Jury's Hotel: May 9, Brian Farrington on the Literary Revival and the 1916 Rising; May 10, Cian Ó h-Eigeartaigh on 'an Teanga agus 1916'; May 11, Kader Asmal on 1916 and 20th century freedom movements; May 12, Jack Bennett on Connolly, Ulster and 1916; May 13, George Gilmore on Labour and 1916. *Of these the first and last were subsequently published as pamphlets.*

***

Greaves in his diary recorded that he had lunch with the present writer on May 16: '...both he and Cathal (Mac Liam) stress the great success of the Wolfe Tone Society lectures... disclosure of a great republican "blueprint for revolution" in Saturday's *Independent*. Micheál O'Riordan says "obviously RHJ's composition". RHJ says "a composite document lifted from RHJ's reports"...'. He goes on to give an assessment of Tony Meade the UI editor '...a somewhat intense young man... very serious in the dedication to his cause... a slightly cynical sense of humour... I would say that his outlook is entirely bounded by bourgeois horizons, though he can ask Cathal "what is the Marxist line on that?" as if it was only to be brought out of the right pillbox ...'.

In May 1966 in the UI there was a report of the mass rally in Casement Park, Belfast, addressed by Malachi McBirney and Seamus Costello. Denis Foley analysed the NI elections, as a 'rout'; a good argument but a bad vote, abstention being the implied problem. There was an article on Glencolumcille; the WTS Free Trade Catechism continued, as did Gilmore on Labour and the Rising. A Fishing Rights body was founded in Galway; this was the National Waters Restoration League; the key issue was seen as inshore fishing for salmon.

Given that we were still stuck with the abstentionist policy, we had been trying to find a credible progressive non-abstentionist candidate for Mid-Ulster; I have on record a letter dated June 27 1966 addressed to me from Alec Foster, of the Belfast WTS, who was Conor Cruise O'Brien's then father-in-law, indicating inability to get a response from Conor. This indicates that at the time we were trying to contact him to explore political options, given that the aura of his progressive role in the Congo still hung about him. I later shared a platform with him at Murlough, commemorating Casement.

Greaves recorded on July 16 1966 an encounter of Cathal MacLiam with the *United Irishman* editorial committee, which happened to be in session when he called at the Sinn Fein office in Gardiner Place. Tony Meade, Seán Garland, Tom

Mitchell, Cathal Goulding and Denis Foley were there, discussing whether to print a reply by Tom Mitchell to the present writer's famous 'rosary' letter)(42), to which Mac Stiofain had taken exception. It seems they got quite heated. CDG's comment: '...Roy should of course never have raised the question which is entirely speculative since there is no sign of any Protestant drift towards republicanism ...'.

Nor indeed will there be, as long as they feel they have to dress up political commemorations in religious garb. This is a 'chicken and egg' problem. Protestants must be made feel welcome in a united Ireland. I am quite unrepentant about this, and regard Greaves's remark as pussyfooting.

Meanwhile *Tuairisc*, the Wolfe Tone newsletter edited by Anthony Coughlan, had been making friendly overtures to Labour. I have on record a letter dated 14/07/66 from Proinsias de Rossa, then a Sinn Fein activist, relating to *Tuairisc* promotion, offering names. He was however critical at the way *Tuairisc* seemed to be sniping at Sinn Fein and preferring the Labour Party: '...Sinn Fein has a ready-made national attitude and with encouragement and additional capable personnel could become a strong force within a short period. The negative attitude towards Sinn Fein will have to be dropped...'.

On July 23 Greaves recorded in his diary some pub talk with Des Logan, Tadhg Egan (both Connolly Association activists) and Tony Meade, joined later by Tony Ruane (then a Sinn Fein Ard Comhairle member; he subsequently supported the Provisionals). The latter's Sinn Fein vision currently was to '...go in when they have an overall majority ...' to which CDG replied '...you ask the public to buy a pig in a poke, and they won't...'. Tony Meade it seems had been promoting the idea of the Wolfe Tone Society replacing Sinn Fein as the 'political wing'. CMacL it seems had achieved some sort of level of approval or recognition by the republicans, though a member of the Irish Workers Party. CDG wondered how this would stand up if the WTS became a political party in its own right.

Then on July 24 1966 Greaves picked up from Des Logan the latest news of the 'G episode', which involved a threat by one G that Richard Behal intended to put a hand-grenade through RJ's front window. This incensed my wife Máirín, who put her brothers on to complain to Cathal Goulding; the latter established with Behal that this threat was without foundation. CG then went to Micheál O'Riordain and demanded that G be disciplined (it seems he was a 'member' of the IWP). Máirín's brothers also, it seems, took suitable action themselves.

This G it seems was doing his best to sow confusion and dissention among those concerned with the republican politicisation process. He was almost certainly acting for the Special Branch, of which the policy, like that of their colleagues in Britain, was to keep the left weak and divided, and the republicans engaged in military futilities, to the advantage of the ruling establishment. Any trend towards a broad-based republican Left, with realisable political objectives, had to be nipped in the bud.

***

At the July 26 1966 Wolfe Tone meeting it was agreed that Alec Foster should chair the meeting in Kevin Agnew's house in Maghera; the main topic would be 'civil rights and discrimination' and 'trade unions and unity'; *Tuairisc* had been sent out. Ethna Viney (MacManus) raised the question of Nitrigin Eireann: the refusal of a seat on the Board to an NFA representative, and threatened US take-over; EV was to work with Derry Kelleher on this. A Symposium on PR projected for September; the suggestion came from Michael Dore *who had been Ethna's employer and who felt strongly about the issue, as a citizen.*

Thus was planned by the WTS the Maghera meeting at which the War Memorial Hall meeting was planned; it was one of many things the WTS was doing at the time.

The July 1966 issue of the *UI* reported the Bodenstown commemoration, including the strength of the martial air and the presence of wolfhounds. A 'TU' banner was carried by Sceim na gCeardcumann. The Belfast Trades Council was said to have participated *(this might have been based on the personal participation of Betty Sinclair)*. The oration was given by Seamus Costello. There was a report of the Kader Asmal lecture on 20th century freedom movement, being part of the WTS public lecture series. The August 1966 issue continued with Asmal, covered the Belfast 12th of July events, noted the takeover threat of Nitrigin Eireann, and took an interest in Richard Nixon. In September Fr MacDyer thanked Clann na hEireann for their vacation help.

At the August 23 WTS meeting 11 were present; there was contact with Paul Gillespie (of the student Labour group); Eoghan Harris resigned; the Dore letter re PR was considered; RJ was to contact Dusty Miller (a progressive-minded engineer, whom we have previously met, who had been a joint author with Patrick Lynch of the 1964 OECD Report *Science and Irish Economic Development)* re Nitrigin; RJ proposed the formal setting up of a 'planning committee' to project future activities more systematically. RJ and SMacGabhainn reported on the Maghera meeting, at which a Civil Rights Convention was projected to which various Northern organisations should be invited. *This was the seminal meeting mentioned above, at which the War Memorial Hall NICRA-founding event was planned.*

Daithi Ó Bruadair reported that some 300 people had been at Murlough commemorating Roger Casement. *This was a meeting at which I spoke, and was introduced by Eoin (the 'Pope') O'Mahony as my father's son, with my father having been the author of the 1913 book 'Civil War in Ulster'. The 'Pope' knew this, although I had not briefed him; at the time I had forgotten this aspect of my father's background. Conor Cruise O'Brien also spoke; at this time he was seriously considered in the context of Mid-Ulster, as a possible candidate by the republicans.*

The September 13 1966 WTS meeting had 17 present, including Cathal Goulding and Seamus Costello; also present were Maire Comerford, Derry Kelleher, Anthony Coughlan, Aine Ni Shuilleabhain (later Ann Harris), Ethna Viney. Proinnsias de Rossa was proposed for membership; Desmond Fennell was to be seen by a sub-committee. The Planning Committee report was discussed; people were allocated as convenors of sub-committees to come up with ideas for events targeting special areas.

A copy of this report is on record; it noted that the membership of the Society was approaching 40, and that the possibility existed of setting up working groups with convenors. The following groups and convenors were suggested:

Language: Micheál Ó Loingsigh; Literature and Drama: Noel Kavanagh; Music, dancing etc: Mary Cannon; Education and student groups: Daithi Ó Bruadair. The foregoing constituted a 'cultural' group of groups. A 'socio-economic' group of groups was also projected: urbanism, housing, local government: Proinnsias de Rossa; science and technology: Derry Kelleher; health and social services: Anthony Coughlan (this however was queried); national economics: Ethna Viney; Co-operative movement: Seamus MacGabhainn; Trade Union Movement: Terry Conneally; historical research: Cathal MacLiam. *This completes the list as on the 'planning committee' report, but there was added in pen: civil rights - Tony Coughlan.*

Some comment is appropriate: this reflects how the present writer, although aware of the Maghera meeting and its significance, had not identified it as the key issue, leading to the weakest points of the Unionist establishment. Anthony Coughlan, to give him credit, did this, and insisted on the twelfth topic, undertaking to develop it. My own vision was to try to develop a rich mixture of intellectual fuel for a broad-based national movement, which I had hoped the politicised republican movement would become. In this grandiose concept however, in the 'planning committee' report, I had missed out on the key issue which AC saw.

The projected mode of operation of the 'planning committee' was to meet between aggregate meetings, with all convenors invited, but urged not to come unless they had a concrete proposal. AC has a marginal comment: 'too many groups? strength dissipated?' I think he could well have been right, though in retrospect I think this approach was in principle worth trying out; it would have selected those who were prepared to work creatively.

On September 27 1966 some of the convenors reported, Micheál Ó Loingsigh on language mentioned the 'Language Freedom Movement' meeting in the Mansion House; a 'silent protest' was projected. The indications were that few had yet convened. Anthony Coughlan came up with a proposal for an alternative to Edgar Deale's Irish Association for Civil Liberty group. AC was to go to Belfast to evaluate progress towards the projected Civil Rights meeting planned at Maghera.

The WTS 'planning committee' met subsequently in 22 Belgrave Road on October 5. MOL came up with a projected paper by Fr Colman Ó h-Uallachain. It was noted that the coming Maghera Convention, with which AC was concerned, was aimed at the Republican Clubs, to persuade them that Civil Rights was the key issue; it involved a reading of a key issue of *Tuairisc*, no 7, which contained an explanation of a Civil Rights strategy for undermining Unionism, written by AC. But note the conflict of date; the WTS annual report in January 1967 (see Part 2) gives August as the date of this meeting. My recollection, and that of Anthony Coughlan, are in agreement that there were 2 distinct Maghera meetings, the second of which, in October, was a Convention involving the Republican Clubs, while the first in August was strictly WTS and initiated the planning for the War Memorial Hall event.

Greaves was staying in the present writer's place on October 15 1966; he recorded that I turned up the next morning unshaven and jaded. This was the occasion of the 1966 Army Convention. CDG noted that I was '...inclined to inveigh against the romanticism of this exercise. He said that there was talk of entering the Dáil... Tom Mitchell and Tony Meade were not opposed... as the voting repeatedly revealed. They had sent AC to Belfast ... to revive the Wolfe Tone Society there, which means he can't be at the Labour Party conference....'.

This relates to supporting the Belfast WTS in its planning of the War Memorial Hall meeting. While the leading lights were journalist Jack Bennett, Queens lecturer Michael Dolley, school principal Alec Foster and others, there were however no links with the Queens student movement. AC would have gone on behalf of the Dublin WTS.

This is also useful in that it enables the 1966 Army Convention to be dated exactly. The November United Irishman contains echoes of it. I remember feeling at the time that this was no way to be making serious political decisions, in an all-night session, without documentation. I was elected to the Executive, where there was a clear majority of politicisers. I declined to go forward for the Council, which consisted of Goulding, Garland, Costello, Ó Brádaigh, Mac Stiofain, and 2 others, who could have been Mitchell, Meade, or perhaps Mac Giolla, I am not certain of this. The sending of AC to Belfast was of course a Dublin WTS decision; Greaves noted it ambiguously.

In the same entry CDG went on to note the funeral of Walter Dwyer, who was a Mayo plumber with a background in the US-based 'International Workers of the World' (IWW, the 'Wobblies'), and a founder member of the Irish Workers League. Seamus Ó Mongain the Mayo republican and co-operative activist, and Micheál O'Riordan the Irish Workers League leader, both spoke, as well as the local priest. All the foregoing would suggest that Greaves accepted the existence of a 'left-republican convergence' process, and regarded it positively.

At the October 18 1966 WTS planning committee it was noted that some money had come in for an article in *Business and Finance* on Nitrigin Eireann *(this was a joint effort from Derry Kelleher and the present writer)*. Maire Comerford reported that funds were coming in for the campaign to renovate the Tailors Hall. The projected Dublin meeting with Mrs McCluskey on 'Democracy in Ulster' was planned in the context of a series including Enid Lakeman *(the British Electoral Reform Society leader)* in support of the retention of PR in the Republic, in face of the Government's attempt to abolish it; also 'Language and Democracy in Ireland'. Anthony Coughlan reported on the Belfast WTS meeting; all was in order for the War Memorial Hall meeting on November 28 or Dec 1; Ciaran Mac an Aili and Kader Asmal were to speak.

Present at the above meeting as well as RJ and AC were Maire Comerford, Derry Kelleher, Micheál Ó Loingsigh, Tony Meade, John Tozer. It was minuted that '...WTS people entitled to attend Regional Conferences of republican movement ...'. *This could not have been a WTS decision; could it perhaps have been an 'army' decision conveyed by Meade? The latter, according to Greaves, was at about this time promoting the idea that the WTS network should expand politically to supersede Sinn Fein as the Republican 'political wing', unencumbered by SF negative baggage. There was also a proposal to set up a WTS in Tralee, which would have been an echo of the 'Meade plan'.*

Around this time I received a letter from one John Mitchell of Perry's Ale, Rathdowney, outlining the basis for the closure of the brewery; I remember looking in around then, as my uncle Jack Young used to buy the barley. Staff were transferred to Kilkenny. A local committee was set up. This was the last of the old 'real ales', and unfortunately it died before the new-wave 'real ale' movement caught on. I would have made contact in the 'economic resistance' context.

The October 1966 issue of the UI reported Mac Stiofain in Belfast, speaking in the Milltown cemetery. Labour Party Secretary Brendan Halligan lectured on Connolly, in the WTS series; this was a Labour-Left link; Mac Tomáis spoke on Casement.

In the November issue the farmers' protest continued. There was more from Brendan Halligan in the WTS series. Goulding was reported at the Seán Tracy commemoration at Feakle. There was a *Tuairisc* reprint on Unionism and Paisley. Tony Meade responded to the 'discovery' of the IRA by Hibernia. There were references to Wesley Boyd and Michael Viney. Meade however claimed not to be relinquishing the use of force.

The present writer's interpretation of the above, and similar references, at this time was that they were sops to the traditionalists, to keep them on side during the politicisation process.

On November 14 1966 Greaves recorded an invitation from Micheál O'Riordan to address an educational conference in Dublin the following February. There is some uncertainty about the date. He then went on: '...last Thursday Seán Redmond was at the (British National Council for) Civil Liberties (to which the CA was affiliated, SR being their representative) and who should arrive but McCartney *the London-based NCCL activist.* He was expressing fears that some villains from Dublin were starting a Civil Liberties which was not a branch of the British one, and SR was speculating as to who it was. I told him that I had tried to put the Dublin republicans up to setting up an independent one and had tackled C(athal) G(oulding) about it. Tonight I rang JB to get Fitt's address: "...we've a key Civil Liberties meeting coming off. Of course a certain view wants it to be a branch of London, and we have to be careful about the link with Dublin if we want the Trade Unions. So we'll have a separate six-county one." So that was good...'.

This is a further reference to the seminal War Memorial Hall meeting from which the NICRA arose. It had come about, as already noted above in the WTS context, on the initiative of the Dublin WTS, via the Belfast WTS. Prior work had been done on the republican network at the two Maghera meetings in Kevin Agnew's house, the latter being a leading Northern Sinn Fein supporter, who had earlier served as Tom Mitchell's election agent in the Mid-Ulster constituency, when during the 1950s he had won the seat. The first Maghera meeting was to plan the November Belfast Civil Rights seminar with the aid of the Belfast WTS, and the second was to persuade the republican grassroots to support it, while keeping their heads down. The second of these meetings was the one referred to by Tim Pat Coogan as having involved Eoghan Harris. The role of the latter, who at the time was a somewhat uncommitted fringe member of the Dublin WTS, was simply to read the Coughlan script, Anthony Coughlan being in Cork that day because of his father's death. The present writer, who should ideally have read it being the Dublin WTS representative, was inhibited by his stammer.

Speakers at the War Memorial Hall meeting from Dublin included Kader Asmal, the leader of the Irish anti-apartheid movement, and Ciaran Mac an Aili, who was explicitly a supporter of non-violence, and had played an earlier Civil Rights role in the republican interest. So it seems CDG was aware of the War Memorial Hall meeting and was supportive of the initiative, which must be credited to Anthony Coughlan, who produced the seminal Tuairisc paper for the Dublin WTS, as read by Eoghan Harris on my behalf at Maghera.

On November 15 a general WTS meeting was addressed by Fr Colman Ó h-Uallachain on language learning techniques; John Tozer's minutes summarise what he said. *From this emerged a campaign for text-books in Irish for schools, a neglected area.* There was a vote of sympathy with the widow of founding member Lorcan Leonard. A Meeting in Ballina on Sunday to discuss small-farmer co-ops was announced.

On November 18 the WTS public symposium on 'Bunreacht na hEireann and Irish Democracy' took place in Jury's Hotel; a resolution was passed supporting the retention of PR. It urged revision on the Constitution in matters relating to birth control and divorce, recognising these issues as being obstacles to national unity. It urged that the European Convention on Human Rights be embodied in law. *The text of the resolution is on record.*

At the December 6 general meeting UMacE reported on the Cork WTS meeting in the Munster Hotel. Some 60 people had been present; speakers were Cork WTS activist Uinsean Ó Murchú and Anthony Coughlan. The Belfast meeting had taken place in the British Legion War Memorial Hall; some 70 were present; John D Stewart, a veteran Protestant journalist, was in the chair; McNally and Asmal were the main speakers; an ad-hoc group was set up, not the WTS itself. The planning of the WRS AGM was referred to committee; projected topics include the alternative to the Common Market, the Casement Diaries, regional planning and the Gaeltacht, science and technology, labour and republicanism.

At the December 20 planning committee the WTS AGM was scheduled for January 21; the Common Market and Casement were to get priority. A letter(43) to prospective members was sent out, signed by Anraoi de Faoite (Harry White) as Chairman, on behalf of the planning committee.

The Ard Fheis (1966) in Moran's Hotel

I certainly remember this one in Moran's; there were two in successive years, with the present writer not attending the first one in 1965, though I had looked in on the Bricklayers Hall one in 1964. Goulding discouraged me from going into Sinn Fein before a credible support network had been built up there among the 'army' politicisers.

At the Ard Comhairle on 5/11/66 there were preparations for the Ard Fheis in Moran's Hotel; The American historian Bowyer Bell(44) was given permission to see records.

The 1966 AF records are relatively complete. There was a Secretaries Report, signed by Máirín de Burca and Ualteir Ó Loinsigh (Wally Lynch) which stated that the AC had met 17 times; Seán Ó Brádaigh was in charge of publicity; Richard Behal had been dismissed for unauthorised actions over Easter. It had been decided to context five seats in the Westminster elections. The candidates were Tom Mitchell in Mid-Ulster, Rory Brady in Fermanagh / South Tyrone, Neill Gillespie in Derry, George Mussen in South Down and Charlie McGlennan in Armagh. It had been difficult to rally the support of the movement behind the campaign. The results showed drops compared to 1964 in Derry, South Down and Fermanagh / South Tyrone, and increases in Armagh and mid-Ulster; in the latter they nearly won the seat.

I recollect that the feedback from the Republican Clubs was that if abstention had been abandoned they would have won easily, and the poor turnout was due to abstentionism being in discredit. This 'near miss' came back to haunt them subsequently when Bernadette Devlin won the seat.

The secretaries' report went on to record the poor attendance at a meeting of existing SF local government representatives, and to express dissatisfaction at the level of coverage of SF affairs by the *United Irishman*. It was noted that the 'joint educational centre' had been set up, but that it had fallen through for lack of support.

During this period the writer was being introduced by Cathal Goulding to various OCs throughout the country, and some sort of network was established for political education, with encouragement to actually join and participate in SF activity. The United Irishman and its rapidly expanding circulation became the key factor in this process. Local seminars were organised, but the 'joint educational centre' concept had never been high on the agenda, its practical value being questionable.

Mick Ryan recollects that at this time he was appointed O/C of Dublin, with the objective of activating the IRA politically via Sinn Fein, and installing a more politically aware and effective Dublin SF leadership.

The Report noted the continuing harassment of the head office by the Special Branch, and interference with the post. It was also recorded that they had protested against Irish people being recruited to the US army to fight in Vietnam. They had attempted to get the Hierarchy to support this position. The US ambassador replied to the effect that the Irish in the US were treated like everyone else. The Hierarchy had not acknowledged their letter.

A drive to bring back the remains of Dunne and O'Sullivan, Barnes and McCormack, and Daly had been initiated, and a committee set up for this purpose(45).

The Secretaries' Report has a complete list of all people who attended the 1966 Ard Fheis, typed out, with cumann name and location. The present writer's name is added on in pen, as representing Cumann Piarsaigh.

This indicates that by the end of 1966 the present writer was just about beginning to be accepted in the SF context, somewhat grudgingly. Despite this, the incoming Ard Comhairle included the present writer. This is an indication of the role of the 'army' vote in the SF Ard Fheis. One would not normally expect to get elected to the national executive at one's first National Convention. There had been an 'Army Convention' shortly before this, the effect of which would have been to reinforce the process of integration of the movement, and this certainly showed after the 1966 Ard Fheis.

Motions passed included a call for an updated reprint of the Constitution, ratification of more of the 1965 Special Ard Fheis 'civil society' procedures such as to encourage open activity, a call for the Ard Comhairle to shadow the Cabinet, and a detailed one from the Pearse Cumann, in which the present writer's hand can be detected. I give it in full, as it indicates the strength of the 'civil society' aspiration of the 'army' left-modernisers.

"That this Ard Fheis notes with concern (1) the continued deterioration of the housing conditions in Ireland; (2) the apparent ease with which demolition of sound property can be carried out for rebuilding in their own time by foreign speculators (3) the continued failure of the Corporation of Dublin to use its power to direct rebuilding to vacant central sites in depressed areas of the city; (4) the high rents paid by tenants of furnished rooms, their lack of security of tenure and the increasing dependence of working-class families on this type of accommodation. An Ard Fheis therefore calls upon the Corporation of Dublin to require that the demolitions be subject to planning permission and that vacant central sites be used for all types of development (housing, shops, offices, factories) immediately, using if necessary compulsory purchase. It calls on the Government in Dublin to legislate to give security of tenure to tenants of furnished rooms, with families subject to appeal to a tribunal. It calls on all Dublin Cumainn to agitate and organise the people to support demands along these lines.
Pearse Cumann, Dublin."

Motions were passed urging an organised approach to the coming local elections, with a raising of the public profile in selected provincial centres as well as in Dublin.

There were however many motions critical of the *United Irishman* from a 'sea-green incorruptible' traditionalist position. These would mostly have been referred to the incoming Ard Comhairle.

There was a report by Seán Ó Brádaigh as Director of Publicity, and he also had negative things to say about the UI, which had been critical of SF. He had issued 21 press statements during the year, on topic which included the Rhodesian crisis, the Free Trade Agreement, Ireland and Europe, the Royal visit to Belfast, labour legislation and the so-called 'Language Freedom Movement'. He had hoped to have the Social and Economic Programme ready, but this had got bogged down in statistics, and they had felt the need for expert advice.

Mick Ryan in his capacity as O/C of Dublin, by arrangement with the Irish-language writer Máirtín Ó Cadhain, had organised the disruption of the Language Freedom Movement meeting in the Mansion House. *The LFM was an ephemeral anti-Irish Language lobby.*

The Sinn Fein Ard Comhairle met on 26/11/66: as a result of the Moran's Hotel Ard Fheis, both the present writer and Cathal Goulding were members, along with Costello. Then on 11/12/66 the idea of a Coiste Seasta (CS) emerged, also the need for a revision of the Constitution. On 19/12/66 a meeting took place with the

Central Council of Tenants Associations. Support was sought for their national campaign against the increase of rents in local authority houses.

Finally on 31/12/66 at the SF AC the Coiste Seasta (CS) was set up: TMacG, CG, SO'B, M de B, Tony Ruane, Seán Mac Stiofain, Seamus Costello and RJ. RJ was appointed Director of Education.

In subsequent records this CS seems to have been a somewhat fluid body, augmenting itself according to the needs of the occasion. In fact it became increasingly indistinguishable from Cathal Goulding's 'HQ Staff'. We take up the sequence of events in the next section.

***

Greaves had a long entry on December 8 1966, in the middle of which the following occurs: '...the *Irish Times* had a report that Fitt was speaking favorably of the EEC. I had a letter from Art McMillan and mentioned this in my reply. I also wrote to JB and suggested a campaign to lift the ban on the UI so the people on the Falls Road can see the case against entry...'. The background to this was Prime Minister Wilson's revival of Britain's application to join the EEC, which has hitherto been blocked by de Gaulle.

The next day Greaves continued: '...there was a letter from McCartney (a leading NCCL man) reporting on the Belfast meeting which complained that "too many republicans" were there, and what was as bad, Jack Bennett seemed to be running things. Some of them had objected to taking up civil liberties other than political ones. Tony Smythe disclosed that when the meeting was announced the NILP had rung NCCL to ask if they were running it. They replied in the negative. Now they want Tony Smythe (the NCCL secretary) to go over as quickly as he can. ...... One of McCartney's complaints was that "too many people from Dublin" were at the meeting - they were indeed McAnally who defended Smythe after he had been bitten by the police dog that took a snap at Dr Browne, and Kader Asmal whose father-in-law is on the same EC *(ie Louise Asmal's father was on the NCCL EC with Smythe)*. But Seán Redmond had the response that there had been fierce battles on the Irish question for a long time past. We decided to urge JB to meet Smythe, and thus to spike McCartney's guns...'.

On December 31 1966 CDG recorded: '...AC.. told me about Cathal Goulding who requested space in the Democrat and then didn't want it. "Then" says Tony "they came to me and said Goulding wanted to write in the Democrat but didn't know what to write about. So he asked me if I'd write it for him." I said I had heard that that the republicans decided that no "message" should be sent to any paper but their own, and, pointing out that no question existed of a "message", expressed the view that they "muddled it up". "He always does" says Tony...'. *This would suggest that politically Goulding was somewhat at sea without a compass, while apparently wanting to encourage the movement to evolve towards the left. I am surprised that CDG does not comment to this effect.*

The *United Irishman* of December 1966 contained Mac Giolla's oration to the Ard Fheis, confirming non-participation in Leinster House. Cathal MacLiam defended the anti-apartheid movement. Seán Gault in Kildare wanted agitation not a lottery. *This was a valid criticism of the way Comhar Linn had evolved.* Noel Kavanagh wrote on cultural participation. *This was a further WTS initiative.* Meade wrote about Seán South, whom he knew personally. *Another nod to keep the traditionalists on-side.* Anthony Coughlan, who had attended the Social Studies Congress in Limerick, wrote on 'the Christian and the Social Services'.

According to Mick Ryan, in the 1966/7 period the Dublin IRA used regularly to steward the Housing Action marches. Also, Mick Ryan at about this time organised, in a Leitrim farmhouse, the first ever IRA training camp which had a political dimension. The present writer attended this, observing with detachment some war-gaming, but basically attempting to foster the primacy of the political role. I remember helping to upgrade the diet with dried apricots, and sleeping somewhat uncomfortably on the floor. To convey ideas to activists effectively it is necessary to share their hardships.

JJ in 1966

In August 1966, at the age of 76, my father published a short booklet of essays and collected newspaper articles, entitled *Irish Economic Headaches: a Diagnosis(46)*. The publisher was the Trotskyist intellectual Rayner O'Connor Lysaght, under the imprint *Aisti Eireannacha*, and JJ's booklet was no 2 in a series of which the first was a polemic by Máirtín Ó Cadhain *Mr Hill: Mr Tara* which was concerned with the politics of the language movement. I think he must have been motivated by the 1916-1966 commemoration, because it is critically retrospective as well as being forward-looking. Lacking a supportive movement to promote it, he depended on the bookshops, and I don't think many were sold. It contains echoes of what I had been attempting to do, as regards revival of the economics of the West via the co-operative movement, as well as a reiteration of his critical analysis of the negative effects on Ireland of protected agriculture in Britain.

Notes and References

1. The sequence of steps in the decline of the Agriculture School can be followed in my abstracts from the TCD Board minutes in the hypertext.

2. After his 'Consumer Demand' rebuff (see note 5 below) JJ lost interest in the SSISI, but he did attend, on April 3 1967, to comment on the paper by EA Attwood, on the comparative development of agriculture, north and south (Vol XXI, part V, p9). JJ had played a somewhat nominal role as Attwood's supervisor for his PhD. His last contribution was on January 26 1968, when he spoke to JJ Scully's paper on Pilot Area development (Vol XXI Part VI, p51). In the 1960s module of the SSISI thread in the hypertext my own and JJ's contributions are about equal in volume.

3. I have overviewed in the 1960s Barrington module JJ's last three attempts at economic commentaries oriented towards a lay readership. These were his *Why Ireland Needs the Common Market* (Mercier Press 1962), an article published in the *Irish Press* on April 20 1966 entitled 'The Relevance of a Berkeleyan Theory of Credit to the problems of Today', and his pamphlet *Irish Economic Headaches: a Diagnosis* (Aisti Eireannacha 1966).

4. In the 1960s academic module I review JJ's *Hermathena* publication ;Monetary Manipulation: Berkeleyan and Otherwise; (CX p32, 1970). He wrote this in 1964 but it did not get published until 1970. He included it as a chapter in his unpublished monograph *Consumer Demand as a Basis for Credit*. I also comment on the work of Salim Rachid in Illinois; I am indebted to Collison Black, late of Queen University Belfast, and who served with my father on the Council of the SSISI in the 50s, for drawing this to my attention. In a *Manchester School* paper (Vol LVI no 4, December 1988) Rachid mentions JJ's Berkeley work in support of his thesis regarding the existence of an 'Irish School of Economic Development 1720-1750', which included Berkeley, Molyneux, Swift, Dobbs and Prior, and was closely linked to applied-scientific development activity via the Dublin Society. I suggest that there is perhaps some raw material here for exploitation by scholars interested in the historical roots of development economics. I would go further and suggest that, in the composition of this group, with the strong scientific component as expressed in Dobbs and Prior, we have a good model which in current development economic thinking is lacking and needs to be recaptured. The key to economic development is technical competence in the useful arts, and this was the Dublin Society's prime objective.

5. JJ submitted his 'Consumer Demand as the Basis of Credit' to the SSISI and it was rejected as being too 'philosophical', the trend being towards econometrics. I have reproduced it in full, and it is accessible from the 1960s module of the SSISI thread in the hypertext.

6. The Irish Association was potentially an overlap area between my father's and my own interests, but this overlap never took place directly. For the background see the 1960s module of the Irish Association thread in the hypertext. He produced a paper for the Irish Association Council to consider, in confidence, an outline plan for 1963-64. This is worth reproducing in the hypertext, as it foreshadows they type of developments which might have emerged out of the Lemass-O'Neill meeting, had the politics of that event been allowed to develop without forcing the pace. It also foreshadows what has come out of the Good Friday Agreement of 1998. An additional key specific event was the June 1965 Derry meeting, planned to celebrate the founding of the New University of Ulster, focused, it was hoped, in Magee College in Derry. In the event it went to Coleraine. I attended the meeting; JJ had registered for it, but did not in the end attend.

7. We have encountered MacManus in the context of the Thomas Davis Society in TCD in 1920. In 1965, in his retirement, he gave a paper to the Harrogate Literary Society on 'The Irish Literary Revival 1890-1935'. JJ sent a copy to TR Henn in Cambridge, who was then involved in the start-up of the Yeats Summer School. Henn replied encouragingly, and there is a possibility he helped to get it published, but I don't know if this was successful. The paper has much anecdotal material about key figures, and in the form it exists in JJ's papers I am making it available, along with another MacManus paper on the poet Raftery and his association with the MacManus estate at Killeaden Co Mayo, in the hypertext support material of this work.

8. I have expanded on this aspect in the 1960s Science and Society module of the hypertext.

9. This issue has arisen repeatedly over the decades, but I can find no specific text related to it. Nomination to State Boards by the Minister is so much the norm that no-one questions it. The related organisations having access to specialist knowledge seldom if ever get 'nomination from below' rights, though a sensitive Minister might consult with them.

10. I have expanded on the technical description of our pilot plant and our various development projects in the 1960s socio-technical hypertext module.

11. For more on these patent specifications see the 1960s techno-economic module of the hypertext.

12. The London political period sources include, apart from my own papers, the *Irish Democrat* files and the Greaves journals, from which an abstract primarily relating to Civil Rights and the North is accessible; see Note 13.

13. Greaves Journal, Volume 14. I have abstracted a selection of Greaves material relating to Civil Rights in Northern Ireland, and this is available in the hypertext. Anthony Coughlan who owns the copyright has agreed to waive rights provided he is satisfied that the abstracted material is accurate.

14. Jim Fitzgerald had been in the 1940s on the fringe of the Promethean Society; he had become a talented theatrical director, and at the time was Head of Drama in the then new Radio Teilifis Eireann (RTE). He had been renting our house in our absence.

15. Memoirs of Seán Mac Stiofain, published by Gordon Cremonesi, London, 1975. I have an extended commentary on this, accessible in the hypertext.

16. Justin O'Brien, The Arms Trial, Gill & Macmillan, 2000, p19.

17. *Why Ireland Needs the Common Market*, Mercier Press, Cork, 1962. I have abstracted the chapters of this book in the hypertext, and given one chapter in full, where JJ outlines his pilot experience with market-gardening on the fringe of a small farm. This work relates to the Barrington-type outreach thread of the hypertext.

18. JJ still clung to his model of agricultural development as expressed in his 1942 SSISI paper. He continued to promote the TCD Kells Ingram farm as a centre for innovative agricultural research, and he attempted through his Irish Association contacts to give it an all-Ireland dimension.

19. Some commentaries on the Agricultural Institute as it had developed in the 1970s are accessible in the hypertext, where I have reproduced an edited version of my 1970-76 *Irish Times* Science and technology Column, under the title *In Search of Techne.*.

20. See the 1960s family module of the hypertext, where I expand to some extent on the family interactions during this period.

21. This document is available in full via the hypertext, both directly and via the 1960s module of the Irish Association thread, which gives the context.

22. Ard Comhairle minutes, 23/02/63; I have abstracted these in the hypertext. In general I have overviewed the 1960s political process primarily from my own papers of the time, and from the Wolfe Tone Society minutes which are, at least partially, in the Coughlan archive. The Wolfe Tone Societies were the key influence behind the 1960s attempted politicising of the Republican Movement. The attempt to develop a radical democratic political party out of the SF/IRA is documented in the archive of the then Sinn Fein, for access to which I am indebted to Tomás Mac Giolla, Seán Garland and the current Workers Party staff. There is also much material in the Greaves Journals, which I have abstracted in three detailed modules covering the 1960s decade; these however are currently under embargo but will eventually be made available when the Greaves diaries are deposited in the National Library by their custodian Anthony Coughlan. I have however produced an abstract containing excerpts of some Greaves material relating primarily to the NICRA, and Anthony Coughlan has agreed to waive the embargo in respect of this, so that it can become a referencable source on the current context.

23. The Wolfe Tone records have been preserved by Anthony Coughlan, since the demise of the Wolfe Tone Society at the end of the 1970s. I have with his permission embodied some abstracts of records of key events in the political thread of the hypertext, including the May 1963 Convention. The Hubert Butler lecture on the occasion of the Mansion House commemoration has been preserved in his collected essays, published by Lilliput.

24. Maire Comerford needs definitive biographical treatment; she was a friend of Constance Markeiwicz, had been secretary to Alice Stopford Green, and had served as Secretary to the First Dáil, of which episode she published a history in 1969. The publisher was Joe Clarke. She had remained on telephoning terms with de Valera. At the time of the death of Michael Collins she was with the 'irregular' unit said to have been responsible for the ambush, claiming that it was elsewhere. She dedicated some effort to the problem of the death of Collins, being convinced that the British were in some way responsible. I have touched on this question in my Atlantis review of the Tom Jones Diaries.

25. I have abstracted the Greaves Diaries, and these are available in the hypertext in 3 modules. This Mansion House meeting reference in the first.

26. The first IBM proposal for the Aer Lingus 'real-time reservations system' had stalled; the American Airlines version, of which we were to have had the European pilot version, had saturated at a third of its planned capacity, and we were trying to find out why. I developed a model of what was going on, using the theory of queues, and we were over in the IBM development labs in Kingston NY checking it out. This enabled me to get into computer-based problem analysis, at quite a detailed hands-on level. I go into this in some depth; it offers a handle on the inductive approach to organisational learning. The 'analytical simulator' of the real-time reservations system is described in the 1960s module of the techno-economic thread. Subsequent work on the 'what if' evaluation of the fleet planning options is also on record there. This work was reported at the 1965 Chicago conference of AGIFORS (the Airline Group of the International Federation of OR Societies).

27. I have taken a copy of the microfilm, but the quality is poor, and it is not feasible to scan it in. A more extensive abstract is available in the first 1960s module of the political thread in the hypertext.

28. The constitution of the WTS as adopted is on record in the hypertext, as well as extended details of the WTS events which are summarised here.

29. I subsequently managed to introduce a Donegal-Derry linkage concept (ie a cross-border development agency) at the June 1965 meeting in Derry of the Irish Association; this must have been the origin of the idea.

30. I have found my notes for this event, which took place on 24/10/64, and have included them in the WTS folder, currently in the Coughlan archive. I have included this and other related material in the hypertext, as an outline of my 1964 aspirations. I have also summarised there some of my contemporary notes on the 1964 Sinn Fein 'social and economic programme'; among other things these echo JJ's analysis of the role of the large-scale commercial farm.

31. The review is available in full in the 1960s module of the 'Science and Society' thread of the hypertext; additional background on the CSTI is also given, supported by some of the associated political arguments. The OECD Report was also discussed in the SSISI in December 1966, and its consequences were also discussed at a further meeting of the SSISI in 1970, to which I contributed; there was a symposium of the 'Science Budget' and I have summarised it in the hypertext.

32. The *Science in Ireland* series of articles which appeared on the *Irish Times* on January 9-13 1967 were part of the fruits of the earlier 1965-66 CSTI work; they also laid the basis for the 1970s *Science and Technology* column treated in the next chapter.

33. Ethna MacManus, now married to Michael Viney, had been influential in introducing co-operative principles to some Mayo farmers groups in the 1950s. She was among the group which founded the Wolfe Tone Society in 1964, and was an active supporter of the Goulding politicisation programme.

34. I have had this from Mick Ryan orally, and he has also gone on record to that effect in an article which was published in a special bicentenary issue of the *United Irishman*, revived for the bicentenary occasion in 1998 by Harry Donaghy, 27 Poland St, Belfast BT12 7EX, who now owns the *United Irishman* Publications imprint.

35. I give more detail from Desmond Greaves's March 13 1965 diary entry in the first 1960s political module in the hypertext; he goes into the anti-communist undercurrents.

36. Dr Con McCluskey and his wife in Dungannon were pioneer campaigners on civil rights issues, and were among the early supporters of the NICRA. See also the Greaves diaries, 8/6/64 and 13-16/3/65.

37. The agenda for this special Sinn Fein Ard Fheis is accessible in the hypertext.

38. According to Mick Ryan, militarism was still strong at the time; MR and Malachi McGurran were distrustful of Costello. The basis of this distrust was probably Costello's vision of combining the ending of abstention with what amounted to a Stalinist or quasi-militaristic political model. Some notes on the November 1965 Sinn Fein Ard Fheis, in Moran's Hotel, are embedded in the first 1960s module of the political thread in the hypertext.

39. The Co-operative Development Trust initiated a disastrous project called Comhar Linn, modelled on Gael Linn, which consumed resources and effort and never came to anything. I have written some critical notes on this episode in the 1960s module of the Plunkett thread of the hypertext.

40. Peter Rose, *How the Troubles Came to Ireland* (Palgrave, Contemporary History in Context series, 2001). I reviewed this for Books Ireland and have reproduced the review in the hypertext.

41. I comment on these documents elsewhere in more depth in the hypertext.

42. I had earlier written a letter to the *United Irishman* querying the use of the rosary at republican commemorations, which I felt should be projected as political rather than religious events. Seán Mac Stiofain took great exception to this. I considered it important then, and still do, to decouple totally all politics from any religious sectarian tinge.

43. This letter enshrines the then philosophy of the Society, and is worth reproducing in full in the hypertext, along with the Constitution.

44. The question of Bowyer Bell's terms of reference, and to what did he get access, remain on the agenda. I have seen him, and he said he was not encouraged to see me. Whom did he see? Mick Ryan finds this intriguing and feels it should be explored further.

45. The first two were the assassins of Sir Henry Wilson in 1922 on the orders of Collins. The second two were executed for bombing in Britain in 1939. The 'return of the remains' process had commenced with Roger Casement in 1966, on government initiative. The writer has often wondered whether the timing of the releases of these post-Casement remains might perhaps have been selected by the British to undermine the republican politicisation process. At the times of the releases the focus on Civil Rights in the North was beginning to take effect. Did they perhaps need to divert the republican movement back into military mode, which they knew how to handle? The Dunne and O'Sullivan funeral took place at Deans Grange and gave a high-profile public platform to Seán Mac Stiofain. The Barnes McCormack funeral took place at Mullingar in 1969 at a time when the NICRA was in the ascendant, and Jimmy Steele was the main speaker. The Barnes McCormack Committees were the skeleton of the post-split Provisional Sinn Fein.

46. This was JJ's last attempt at economic outreach polemic. I have abstracted it in the hypertext; it is accessible via the 1960s Barrington module.

Chapter 7 Part 2: The Period 1966 to mid-1969

As in the first part, I have kept the RJ and JJ stuff interspersed. The mainstream of the RJ material is abstracted from the 'political' stream of the hypertext. I intersperse material from other streams chronologically where appropriate. This section runs up to the period of tension leading up to the August 1969 crisis. I begin with some further 1966 JJ episodes, and then take up with RJ in 1967.

JJ and the Theory of Credit

There is among JJ's papers a preprint of an article published in the *Irish Press* on April 20 1966, entitled *The Relevance of a Berkeleyan Theory of Credit to the problems of Today*. This is the germ of the *Consumer Demand as the Basis of Credit*(1) monograph rejected by the SSISI, which JJ subsequently published in mimeographed form. It is an essay on the nature of money, and how it relates to credit. 'Any theory of credit that is concerned with the mere monetary aspect of things, and ignores the commercial aspect, bears a certain resemblance to pre-Copernican astronomy'.

The core idea of the essay is that producers should be credit-worthy if there is a demand among consumers for what they can produce, and this '...requires a determined effort by the public authorities to strengthen the bargaining power of useful producers whose bargaining power is weak.... Credit in the true sense is intimately bound up with the social and economic welfare of consumers as a whole. Since this also depends on specialisation of production and freedom of exchange we must regard freedom of commerce and flexibility of price relations, in conditions of social justice, as necessary conditions for the soundness of the credit structure...'.

Also in 1966 he published, with Aisti Eirennacha, a pamphlet *Irish Economic Headaches: a Diagnosis*. This represented a radicalisation of company, in that the publisher was Rayner O'Connor Lysaght, and the pamphlet was the second in a series of which the first was Máirtín Ó Cadhain's *Mr Hill: Mr Tara*, a language-movement polemic. It was also JJ's last attempt, at the age of 76, to popularise his ideas with a lay readership. In it he tried, not very successfully, to link his Berkeleyan ideas of credit with the development of small-scale high-value-added production systems of a type relevant to the needs of survival of the Gaeltacht(2).

JJ and the TCD-UCD Merger Debate

In 1966 JJ attended the TCD Board meeting when on May 18 they finally got around to sanctioning the election of women to Fellowship. JJ's maiden speech in the Lincoln College debating society in 1911 had been on women's rights. He must have enjoyed that Board meeting.

The issue of the TCD-UCD merger became important in 1967, as did the issue of Catholic participation in TCD, with the increasing opposition to the policy of Archbishop McQuaid. On February 22 with JJ present they discussed a submission from the Laurentian Society (this was the College society serving the needs of TCD Catholics) regarding the position of Catholic students. David Thornley, who later became a Labour TD, was involved. There was also a resolution from the UCG students expressing regret at McQuaid's statement. The TCD Board issued a statement on March 2, and there was an open discussion on TV as a result.

On April 26 1967, again with JJ present, the Board welcomed the Government's statement that there was to be one Dublin University with constituent Colleges. The 'merger debate' became intense, and this kept JJ's interest in Board meetings alive. There were resolutions from the Junior Fellows (May 10); the question of Irish being essential for Matriculation was a problem for the many Northern students in TCD (June 21). The sale of the Kells Ingram Farm involved the need to consult with Mitchell (who lived there), the Department of Agriculture, the Veterinary College, the Agricultural Institute and the users of the radioactive source (ie for experiments in plant genetics). Mitchell did not object to the sale of the farm, but in view of the merger politics the decision needed to be deferred (May 22). They had difficulty in meeting with UCD. The Board was addressed by the Minister on June 7(3).

By the end of the year the issue was moribund, but it had prompted many people to look at how closer relations could be developed, and contacts opened up, which continued. It encouraged TCD to think that even it they sold the farm, they could still have a role in agriculture.

RJ and the 1967 *Irish Times* Science articles

The experience with the Council for Science and Technology in Ireland, described earlier, generated a demand which fuelled the writer's 1967 *Irish Times* *Science in Ireland* series of articles(4), the purpose of which was to indicate some ways in which science, technology and economic development interacted.

The series began with a tentative outline of how science had influenced the course of history and how science in Ireland had been of a provincial rather than a national character, though on occasions it had achieved world stature.

It continued with an examination of some of the growing points of post-war science and technology, suggesting that the policy decisions which allocated resources to the various growth areas were dominated by factors which needed critical examination, especially by a small nation with limited resources.

A further article examined the role of pure research and its interactions with applied research and economic development, in particular dealing with the potential role of pure research as a training ground for people who would afterwards become highly productive assets to the economy.

The last two articles examined the contemporary Irish scientific scene, searching for any hint of a 'science policy' emerging from the existing structure, and making recommendations how a viable small-nation science policy might be evolved.

I have a feeling that these January 1967 *Irish Times* articles may have been influential. Derry Kelleher and I, in the Wolfe Tone Society, started a 'science and technology sub-committee'; it was just us, but it was useful when writing letters to have the WTS standing. We had the idea of perhaps coming up with ideas which might be implemented via the Council for Science and Technology in Ireland (CSTI), despite its cumbersome federal structure with affiliated bodies, some of which increasingly looked at it askance. In the event, the CSTI folded its tent when the National Science Council was set up in 1970, and Derry and I went on later to set up the Kane-Bernal Society.

RJ and the Dublin Wolfe Tone Society

The Dublin Wolfe Tone Society(5) Annual General Meeting took place on Saturday January 21 1967; this constituted a showcase event; the various current areas of interest were all covered by specialist reports, and there was a review of the previous year's work. This contained a reference to the setting up of the Cork society. It also expanded on the Maghera conferences: that with the Belfast WTS on August 6, and the second one in October. Both conferences were attended by Dublin and Cork WTS delegates, the second one also by Republican Club delegates from Tyrone, Fermanagh and South Derry. A document was discussed in depth at the second conference, which was based on the editorial of *Tuairisc* no 7. The following is from the Annual Report:

"The first step (towards the formation of the NICRA) was implemented in Belfast on November 28 when a symposium was held in the War Memorial Hall. The audience represented all shades of anti-unionist opinion, including nationalist, NILP, Social Justice, trade unionist, socialist and republican. The symposium was organised by an ad-hoc group consisting of Belfast WTS and trade union representatives. No elected committee was set up, but the ad-hoc committee was extended by calling for voluntary support for the purpose of organising the next meeting, which would be addressed by an NCCL speaker from London... It was considered unwise to establish a Civil Rights Convention under circumstances in which it would be rapidly torn asunder by political rivalry; the goal was a strictly non-political Convention. This could clearly not have been achieved at the first meeting..."

The formation of the Cork WTS had begun with an informal encounter between RJ and a group of UCC graduates '...known to a member of the Dublin society of Cork origin ...' *this of course was Eoghan Harris*. A meeting subsequently held in June 1966 was aimed at making a link in Cork with the republican movement, but this proved abortive due to internal problems in the Cork movement. *These relate to the anti-political militaristic mind-sets of Mac Stiofain and Mac Carthaigh who then dominated the Cork scene.* "..a preparatory committee was set up which held a number of meetings, expanding the membership to include individuals prominent in the trade union movement, in Dóchas, in the West Cork small-farm co-operative movement and in amateur drama. The Chairman was Dave O'Connell and the secretary Brian Titley. The inaugural public meeting was held on December 3rd and featured a review by Anthony Coughlan of Ireland since the Treaty, as well as shorter talks by Uinsean Ó Murchú (Cork WTS) on the language movement and by Uinsean Mac Eoin on the situation in the North. The second public meeting was held on Friday December 16 and was addressed by Jim Fitzgerald of Dublin on the National Theatre..."

Specialist reports to the Dublin WTS AGM covered Housing and Town Planning (UMacE), restoring the Tailors Hall (Maire Comerford), Micheál Mac Aonghusa on the Irish Language, Derry Kelleher on science and technology (unrecognised by the Government as a factor in economic development), Anthony Coughlan on Civil Liberty. Máirín de Burca reported on the changes occurring within Sinn Fein, and Fred Heatley reported on the Belfast WTS. Eoin Ó Murchú spoke on the development of the TCD students republican club, and Paul Gillespie spoke on behalf of Labour students. Dave O'Connell outlined the development of the work of the WTS in Cork. Seán Ó Cionnaith on behalf of the Sinn Fein leadership appealed for support in the coming local government elections.

Cathal Mac Liam was elected Chairman, Roy Johnston vice-chairman, Noel Kavanagh secretary, assisted by John Tozer, the treasurer remained Uinsean Mac Eoin.

This clearly represented a milestone in the development of political left-republicanism, with signs of growing influence and acceptance, and increasing friendly links with the labour movement. It was reported at length in the February United Irishman. In the coming period, we must try to establish 'what went wrong' such as to neutralise this promising renaissance.

At the February 28 1967 WTS meeting it was agreed to attend an Irish Socialist seminar in the Moira Hotel on March 11-12(6). Kelleher reported on the Connolly Association conference, which had been attended by young liberals, labour and trade union groups; Gerry Fitt had addressed it. A 'Protestant patriots' booklet was being promoted by Uinsean MacEoin. Micheál Ó Loingsigh reported back from a Cork WTS meeting, and urged starting a society in Tralee. A Limerick society was also proposed by Noel Kavanagh. UMacE reported in a meeting of the TCD Republican Club which he had addressed, noting the absence of any SF participation. There was a proposal to meet with the SF Ard Comhairle. Noel Kavanagh reported on setting up a Folk Council *(Dúchas I think it was called)*.

At this meeting also Anthony Coughlan reported on his Common Market document and called for a special meeting on March 7, with on the agenda the document to be published in a special issue of Tuarisc, number 8 in the series. This is on record in the WTS archive: it consists of a 16-page document covering all aspects of the EEC, and promoting the 'Association' process as an alternative to full membership. It got full treatment on the April 21 issue of *Business and Finance* and can be regarded as constituting the founding document of what later emerged as the Common Market Study Group, the CM Defence Campaign, and eventually the Irish Sovereignty Movement, in all of which the leading light was Anthony Coughlan.

The *Irish Socialist* seminar on March 11-12 1967 included some Dublin Trades Council people as well as republicans, and indicated that the left-republican convergence was very much still alive, at the level of mutual recognition and willingness to exchange ideas. But in practical terms the choice of dates for events was uncoordinated, so that mutual participation was subject to constraints. I had been able to attend only partially, due to attending an Ard Comhairle meeting.

Left and Republican Politics in the North

Meanwhile in the North, the Republican Clubs had decided to defy the ban and hold a convention(7). This was supported by observers from the NCCL in Britain, who had agreed to go, at the suggestion of Seán Redmond the Connolly Association representative on their National Executive. The CA had been tipped off about this event by Seán Garland, who visited London for the purpose on March 16-17. Tony Smythe agreed to go on behalf of the NCCL. There was also to be an Amnesty International representative, and Anthony Coughlan attended on behalf of the Dublin Wolfe Tone Society. It emerged from Jack Bennett in Belfast that the convention had been 'cleared' by the police. As Greaves succinctly put it: '...in other words an illegal organisation had asked police permission to hold a meeting of its entire membership, and had obtained it.... Kelleher was in the office at the time and told us that AC was going. But he entirely agreed that we would be wise not to do so, as we would hardly be classed as disinterested observers, and would be fulfilling the purpose the republicans wanted us to fulfill rather than the one decided at our own conference...'.

Then later JB rang from Belfast to the effect that Craig had announced on the radio that the convention was after all banned, whereupon the republicans announced that they would hold it in a 'secret place'. JB was left with the problem of how to get the observers there, which presumably was resolved; in his March 20 entry CDG noted that there were 80-100 people present, including Betty Sinclair and Anthony Coughlan. Six resolutions were passed. The preamble had involved the Trades Council, to which Betty Sinclair objected, as they had not been consulted in advance. '...They cannot involve organisations through individuals ...'. In the aftermath Tom Mitchell was arrested; people went to enquire about him were told he was not there, though they could see him. Greaves: '...The second in command, who is to take over shortly, showed visible embarrassment - and spoke with an impeccable Oxford accent ...'.(8).

The culture-gap between the Belfast Left and the politicising republicans was encountered by Desmond Greaves, when he went on April 20 1967 to Belfast from Glasgow, meeting with Betty Sinclair in her Trades Council office: '...She told me that she discovered that when she (had been) prevented from speaking at Casement Park it was not the fault of the GAA but that the republicans had cold feet at the last minute. How she found this out was that on the way to Murlough last year Seán Steenson *(not to be confused with Mac Stiofain)* drove her up in his car. "I believe you objected to my speaking last year" she remarked. "Not a bit of it". The republicans had told her they would be delighted to have her but they had been threatened that if she spoke they would never get the Park again. Even when she got to Murlough she was left off the agenda and the chairman was closing the meeting after S(ean) R(edmond) spoke. But one of the officials ran to the chairman. Betty wondered if a fight would ensue. Then the chairman, a local man, said "Miss Sinclair wished to say a few words". Such is the fear of Communism...'.

Later the same day Greaves got to talk to Liam McMillan, Art's brother *(and at that time O/C of Belfast)*: '...he showed me an exercise book in which he was endeavouring to get to grips with political ideas. He said "the Army would like to co-operate with everybody, including Communists, but there is a strong group of old-fashioned Sinn Fein in the way". He asked if I thought Betty Sinclair would co-operate in a campaign against unemployment. I said I was sure she would provided they did not attempt to usurp the functions of the Labour Movement. For that is the danger. She thinks they are all very suspicious of Protestants, and that the Protestants feel lost, not knowing what nationality they belong to, or having any history or culture. But he did not show signs of this. He is probably the most thoughtful and broadminded though the brother is more forceful...'.

Here Greaves was getting to grips with the width of the culture-gap between the left-politicising Belfast IRA and the Protestant radical tradition which was expressed in the CP. I was of course aware of this, and was similarly feeling my way towards bridging it. He went back across the water on April 21, after a brief encounter with Seán Caughey, who expressed a high opinion of Gerry Fitt, and was optimistic about the way things were going...'.

The EEC and Politics in the Republic

During May and June of 1967 there was the beginnings of public campaigning on the question of the European Economic Community (EEC). The issue was complicated by a decision of the Wolfe Tone Society to try to organise every second meeting in Irish, and to do its business through Irish. In the letter context Greaves remarked that '...whether they should do this before they have brought the Northerners in is doubtful.. the main thing is not to go too far. When the language is under such assault it is impossible to counsel caution in its defence...'. I recollect this period; the prime movers were Uinsean Mac Eoin, Deasun Breathnach and Micheál Ó Loingsigh; I must say I found it a constraint on the process of development of ideas which we could at the time have done without. But it was impolitic to say so.

On May 26 1967 Greaves(9) remarked that '...Cathal (MacLiam) and I... walked in the protest march against the Common Market sell-out. Sinn Fein had organised it, but if they had not invited the Irish Workers' Party they would have had nobody ...'. Derry Kelleher was there and I understand spoke.. *after some comments on wage levels etc CDG concluded:* '...so this movement is in a rather confused state.'

Viewed in retrospect it may seem strange that the EEC issue should have been so high on the agenda so early, while the Northern situation was developing so . rapidly. The UK application however had just been renewed, and it was just before de Gaulle's second veto. So at the time the EEC was beginning to assume the status of a threatening 'Greater Act of Union'.

There is a letter in the WTS archive dated June 3 1967 from Fred Heatley regarding Belfast participation in the proposed conference; this expresses some unease at the emphasis on the Common Market issue, and seeks more information. It was followed by one dated June 7 seeking to co-ordinate Belfast WTS participation in the Bodenstown commemoration.

Then on June 9 1967 CDG lunched with AC and Alan Heusaff the Breton; they discussed the Common Market and the various fringe national questions,

Heusaff being despondent. Heusaff wanted AC to speak on the EEC at a meeting *organised presumably by the Celtic League, with which Heusaff was associated.*

On a subsequent visit to Dublin on June 25 1967 CDG arrived at CMacL's house, where there was a gathering of Wolfe Tone Society representatives from Dublin and Belfast, the objective of which was to persuade the Belfast people to oppose the Common Market, and not to be embarrassed by the fact that Paisley was doing the same.

There is in the archive considerable correspondence relating to this meeting of Dublin, Belfast and Cork Wolfe Tone Societies which took place on June 24-25, on the fringe of the Bodenstown Wolfe Tone commemoration event(10). There was student republican club participation, and the booklet on Ulster Protestant patriots was on the agenda. The agenda is on record, which included a proposal to set up a 'central committee' of the 3 societies, meeting regularly. A document from the Dublin WTS analysed the roles of a range of organisations in Ireland, classified on the basis of:

(a) degree of opposition to the 'neo-unionist drift',
(b) whether political, economic or socio-cultural, and
(c) degree of involvement of their members in decision-making.

It is not clear whose document this was, but I recognise some of it has having been mine, and some of it could have been Anthony Coughlan; it would have been amended in the light of discussions at a Dublin WTS meeting.

It was agreed that a liaison committee for the 3 societies be set up to meet quarterly, the first meeting to be before the end of August. There was a distinct difference in attitude to the EEC as between Belfast and Dublin, and the complexities of the relationship between the EEC and the national question began to be probed.

On the Sunday the Civil Liberties question was discussed, again bringing out the differences between North and South; an all-Ireland movement would not be appropriate. It was the priority issue in the North, rather than the EEC. The assessment of the Left, in the 'analysis of organisations' document introduced by RJ, is worth quoting: "Both CPNI and IWP remain in relative isolation due (a) to the negative tradition of Stalinism and consequent foreign orientation, and (b) to failure to come to grips with the existence of the national question and the rule of British imperialism in Ireland, which led to their condemnation of the '50s campaign on the Border. The CPNI and the IWP have not succeeded in working out an agreed joint national strategy and remain organisationally distinct. Both groups have, however, a wealth of trade union experience and a number of members with considerable influence in the trade union movement. Theoretically speaking, the CPNI, half-heartedly, and the IWP, in full, accept the republican classics as an essential part of our revolutionary heritage..".

On June 28 1967 I wrote to Betty Sinclair seeking feedback on how the NICRA was functioning; I must have picked up some indications of feedback from the Republican Clubs which suggested that Civil Rights issues were occurring locally which were not being dealt with; I noted that Fred Heatley had been 'chafing at the delays' and warned of the danger of '...a return to the mental ghetto on the part of the dispossessed ...'. Betty relied pleading that she had been in Hungary (!) and was trying to catch up. She felt that the NICRA '...had not been able to attract the right kind of people.. too much in the way of groups and not consolidated enough to do its job properly ...'. We planned to meet at the end of July.

The foregoing I think must have been on behalf of the Sinn Fein Standing Committee, of which at this time the record is missing. Note how the East European connection of the CPNI was in practice impeding the development of common experience and procedures, at a time when there were crucially necessary.

A document 'The Case Against the Common Market: Why Ireland Should Not Join' was produced by Anthony Coughlan subsequent to the foregoing conference, and it was circulated on June 29 1967 to all TDs and Senators with a covering letter. A handful acknowledged. This was basically the conference document as discussed; it marks effectively the beginning of the anti-EEC campaign.

Marxism, Science and Society

In May 1967 I was invited by *Hibernia* to review a computer book(11) which had a social dimension. I identified many issues which subsequently became important in the socio-technical analyses of the 1980s and 1990s, particularly in relation to the impact of a computer project on the structure of an organisation.

At about this time, mid 1967, I was also actively involved in trying to analyse the nature of the information flows throughout the Aer Lingus management system, and I participated with others in one of the 'innovation groups' which they set up, as a sort of brain-storming process. During this I worked up the makings of a theoretical model for the role of the computer in the management process, defining the role of a manager as a 'reducer of entropy'(12) and attempting to define 'entropy' as a generalised measure the type of multi-dimensional uncertainty with which a typical manager had to deal. This pointed in the direction of what could become a theory of management costs, provided a 'temperature' could be defined for the management process. This I felt would be useful, because in classical thermodynamics, whence the concept of 'entropy' as generalised uncertainty had emerged, the product of the measures of temperature and entropy has the dimensions of energy, which of course can be directly related to cost. I felt we were on to something.

I discussed this with Desmond Greaves in June of 1967; we had set out on our bikes towards the north Dublin countryside; I recollect this occasion, and I remember distinctly trying to interest him in the above theoretical ideas on how a State firm should be managed, keeping track of the management costs. I had in mind the problem of how to manage a State firm under socialism, bearing in mind the (by then increasingly negative) experience of the USSR. I had hoped to get a discussion going with Greaves around the foregoing theoretical approach, with which he as a combustion technologist might perhaps have been familiar. He was however totally dismissive, along the doctrinaire lines that 'there is no basis for a theory of management overhead costs in Marxism'. I felt the existence of an intellectual gulf; we were not on the same theoretical wavelength. This I think was a turning-point in our relationship; I had tended to regard him as a mentor. From then on I became critical.

I began around this time to reflect on the nature of the problem of how to relate intellectuals in left-wing movements with working people in a meaningful way. The scientist-technician relationship is a possible model; I had observed this very positively earlier in France, and in my Dublin Institute of Advanced Studies epoch. I felt however that we were a long way from having a good model for the development of a consistent political party based on Marxist principles, within which a creative scientist-technician (thinker-doer) interaction might be actively encouraged.

Round about this time the PhD thesis work of Rex Cathcart on Berkeley(13) came to the attention of Desmond Greaves, who referred in his diaries to Cathcart's '...valuable thesis on Marx and Berkeley...'. Rex Cathcart was a historian, one of the 1940s Promethean stalwarts; he had been introduced to Marxist history by John de Courcy Ireland in St Patrick's Grammar School. After periods teaching in Sandford Park and later in Raphoe Grammar School, he later headed the educational programmes in BBC(NI). I chased this Berkeley hare, in case it interfaced with what JJ had done. Regrettably it is purely Marxist-philosophical, and has no interface with Berkeley as pioneer development economist, in which role he was of interest to JJ.

Politics and the North

On July 4 1967 Greaves recorded an encounter with Uinseann Mac Eoin, in which the latter expostulated about the present writer's 'hare-brained schemes' for various committees to do this and that; CDG commented that '...Roy can of course be mechanical to the point of utter impracticability...'. He picked up however from Mac Eoin that '...he thought that the south side (of Dublin) was the revolutionary centre from having the intelligentsia. But he agreed that the classes involved were broader, and that the activists were the intelligentsia of the newly rising nationalist small business people ...'.

This indeed corresponded to my then view; it had motivated me away from dependence on Marxist orthodoxy and the Irish Workers' Party (which the Irish Workers League had by now become). I don't think Greaves ever appreciated the basic weakness of the Irish working class as a source of Marxist organisation, let alone Marxist theoretical analysis. As for the 'hare-brained schemes', this suggests the conflict between simplistic centralist ideology-driven organisations and the need for working analytical groups to explore in depth various aspects with a view to uncovering opportunities, and I was pursuing the latter course. If UMacE regarded this as 'hare-brained' and CDG as 'mechanical', well then, those were their opinions, let the reader judge.

On July 31 1967 a meeting of Dublin WTS members with the SF Standing Committee took place; there is alas no record of this in the WTS archive.

Nor is there in the SF archive, as the Standing Committee was not then keeping proper records. It is highly probable that the question of how the WTS 'liaison committee' would relate to existing SF structures was discussed. There was an undercurrent in the 'army' (expressed among others by Tony Meade) which wanted the WTS network to leapfrog Sinn Fein, making a new political start without negative baggage, so this was a sensitive issue.

The question of the editorship of the *United Irishman* came up; according to Greaves in or about August 1967 an approach was made to Anthony Coughlan, who however declined. This indicates however that Goulding was keen to improve the political content of the paper, and saw Coughlan as the person to do this. Tony Meade had resigned, on the grounds that (according to Greaves via MacLiam, who was close to Meade) '...the paper is not taken seriously. There is talk of O'Toole doing it. He is not a member of Sinn Fein...'. MacLiam went on to suggest that the present writer was '...preparing his own exit ...'.

I certainly was not in 1967 'preparing my own exit', as the republican politicisation process was going well, the NICRA was in existence, and the Clubs were supporting it. Mac Stiofain was intriguing against this process; I was aware of this in general terms, but seriously underestimated his specific influence, as Director of Intelligence, with the Northern IRA units, which we were trying to transform into political clubs.

Around this time I wrote to the NICRA on behalf of the SF Standing Committee, of which at this time the record is missing. I have however a copy of a letter written by me to Derek Peters dated 4 Sept 1967, in response to receiving a copy of the NICRA newsletter, in which procedures were proposed for dealing with 'arrest without charge' situations. We were aware of how this procedure was used to harass those trying to develop the Republican Clubs politically. I was seeking to establish procedures to convey to Club members for use in such situations, involving contact with the NICRA: '...what to do so as to get the maximum embarrassment for the authorities out of it.. it will mean that we will be able to build a self-maintaining federation of Clubs with a life and communication system of its own; in fact a forum in which political ideas can evolve. They are of course doing their best to stop this; they want to keep the rebels in their ghettoes and without influence ...'.

Derek Peters was a CPNI member and was the NICRA Secretary. He replied by return on Sept 9 1967; they undertook to get an authoritative legal opinion; in the meantime we were warned that the Act does not require the police to invoke it when arresting, but unless they do they could be charged with illegal arrest. Their experience was that they went to extremes of provocation before invoking the Act.

The 'Three Wolfe Tone Societies' meeting, agreed on June 24-25, took place on October 15 1967. The Dublin agenda prioritised economics and the EEC (the Wilfred Beckermann lecture, and the development of the Defence of the Nation League), but was also active on language, history, theatre (Jim Fitzgerald and TP McKenna addressed a meeting in the Moira Hotel) and trade union history (Joe Deasy). Belfast had published a Life of Henry Joy McCracken, and was developing a Connolly centenary programme for 1968; a lecture series was projected for January on a range of topics: Irish music, the EEC, the Protestants and the nation, theatre in Ireland, the Anglo-Irish literary tradition etc. The Cork society was into urban preservation, trade union law, the EEC (a lecture by Coughlan was planned) and the need to promote discussion in Irish of things other than Irish itself.

This indicated that the lobby within the 'army' which wanted the WTS network to leapfrog Sinn Fein had been sidelined; Sinn Fein was the political organisation, and the WTS network remained an outreach body, for ideas development.

There are hints from this period of positive action to re-invent the IRA in its military mode. Greaves on November 24 1967 reported an encounter with one Ben Owens in Central Books, London, who reported contacts with the police and alleged IRA bomb threats.

This story needs further elucidation, but it suggests to me that the British dirty tricks department were prepared to re-invent the IRA for their own purposes, just as the B-Specials were with the Silent Valley incident, in order to try to prevent the development of progressive Irish political republicanism allied to the Labour Movement in Britain. Could this have been connected with the work of Mac Stiofain, who in his memoirs claims at this time to have been active in military mode? I leave this as a challenge to future historians.

The next day November 25 Greaves recorded a Manchester meeting commemorating the Martyrs, at which Jimmy Steele spoke, attacking the 'New Departure' of Davitt and Devoy; then '...someone plucked the chairman by the sleeve and he called Mr Fitzmorris to speak. That gentleman then announced that the Manchester Martyrs Committee had no connection with another committee purporting to commemorate Allen Larkin and O'Brien. "We are Catholics first and Irishmen afterwards" said he "and we do not want our freedom given us by Moscow" ...'.

Here we have evidence of a conscious attempt by elements who subsequently helped engineer the emergence of the Provisionals to subvert the republican politicisation process, from the angle of the Catholic Right, using the alleged 'Moscow threat' as a weapon to undermine the work of the Connolly Association, then concentrating on drawing the NI Civil Rights issue to the attention of the Labour movement in Britain.

The 1967 Sinn Fein Ard Fheis

At the Sinn Fein Ard Comhairle on 14/10/67 there was a further reference to the chronic 'social and economic policy' question; positions to be taken for the 1967 Ard Fheis motions were proposed. Then at the Ard Comhairle on 4/11/67 a steering committee was set up for Ard Fheis motions: RJ, Seamus Costello and Tony Ruane.

The idea was to get the motions into a logical order, so as to encourage a sensible discussion of the issues, and to do compounding where appropriate, in accordance with democratic conference practice. SC however took it as a 'licence to rig or railroad'; he issued voting instructions on bits of paper to trusties who were in the 'other branch', thus trying to use what remained of the military command structure(14).

At the Ard Comhairle on 18/11/67 the report of the steering committee was adopted, after a long and heated discussion, centred round Costello's motion on abandonment of 'abstentionism as a principle'.

This Ard Fheis took place at the end of November in the basement room of Liberty Hall. Unfortunately the agenda is not readily accessible, though I do have two key composited motions, and a long amended version of one of them, proposed by the Ard Comhairle. The key one, Group 2, was a call for principled participation in assemblies, to be decided on tactical grounds by the Ard Comhairle. It concluded:

* to examine and analyse the most suitable basis for convening such a 32 county national assembly and of bringing about the appropriate conditions for revolutionary parliamentary action referred to,
* to evaluate in so doing the experience of national revolutionary movements in other countries, and
* to report back on this matter to the next annual Ard Fheis or to a special Ard Fheis, whichever is considered suitable.

This compromise motion did not attempt to amend the Constitution, but set up procedures for the incoming Ard Comhairle to take a hard look at the whole philosophical basis of abstentionism.

If Costello had got his way, the Provisional split would have taken place at this 1967 Ard Fheis, or perhaps at the next one, in the Ó Liatháin Hall, when the Garland Commission was set up, in a further split-avoiding procrastination. It could be argued plausibly that the split, had it occurred in 1967 or in 1968, would not have given the Provisionals the initial momentum generated subsequently by the 1969 events in Belfast, and would have enabled the politicising movement successfully to contest and build on the mid-Ulster by-election, thus keeping at bay the Queens ultra-left which generated Bernadette Devlin. This is one of the crucial historical 'might have beens'.

It is evident, in retrospect, that this repeatedly postponed sanctioning of the politicisation process had been initiated too late, and was too indecisive and uncertain, to enable a strong, principled and united movement to be developed, fit to face with political weapons the armed B-Special counter-attack of August 1969.

Seán Ó Brádaigh's Publicity Report is on record; 18 statements were issued, on matters which included the Belfast shipyard dismissals, the EEC, the farmers agitation, the Potez closure, factory closures in the North, the Dundalk shoe factory, etc. The Defence of the Nation League was commended for its anti-EEC work. Support from Cumainn for the sale and distribution of printed material however had been minimal; notes on SF cumann activity fit to report in the *United Irishman* remained scanty.

On the whole we get the impression that a lethargic membership was reluctantly following, with heavy hearts, a basically modernising leadership. The 'socio-economic programme' mentioned in 1966 seems however to have sunk without trace(15).

***

The post-Ard Fheis AC met on 9-10/12/67; present were the President TMacG*, Vice-Presidents Larry Grogan and Joe Clarke; Tony Ruane, Máirín de Burca*, Walter Lynch, Tom Mitchell*, RJ*, Monica Ui Riain*, Mick Ryan*, Seamus Costello*, Éamonn Mac Thomáis; S Ó Brádaigh had sent apologies.

In this situation the VPs both were representatives of 'SF3' as defined by Laffan. If we define the emergent politicising Sinn Fein as 'SF4', I have marked the proto-SF4 Cathal Goulding supporting group with asterisks. It was somewhat uneasily divided at this point. Monica Ui Riain was Mick Ryan's mother; she lived in the East Wall area, and had good local standing.

Specialisations were agreed for AC members: Tony Ruane Finance, Seán Ó Brádaigh Publicity, RJ Education. On the proposal of SC seconded by RJ the post of Director of Industrial Activity was created, with a view to cultivating relations with the Trade Union movement. This was taken up by SC. Goulding proposed Seán Garland as National Organiser, with terms of reference to act '...on behalf of the Army and the UI...assist with the educational programme...and the director of industrial disputes... to sit in on CS meetings and be co-opted to the AC. This was proposed by CG, seconded by EMacT and passed unanimously.

Note the explicit reference to the Army, rather than the 'other branch'. This suggests that its priority politicising role was recognised, and its military role increasingly regarded as evanescent. There were however differing perceptions as to its role. The old military / IRB tradition would have seen it in terms of 'infiltrating' trade unions and 'assisting' industrial disputes with various kinds of quasi-military direct action. The politicising people would have seen it in terms of participating in the democratic organisations of the working people, and giving a lead where appropriate. The divisions between these perceptions however were somewhat fuzzy.

Seán Garland was then co-opted; also the regional representation was ensured by co-opting Eddie Williams from Cork and Paddy Kilcullen from Mayo, both of these being Goulding supporters. It was also agreed from then on to record the minutes in English, recognising the de facto situation regarding the need for accurate and transparent record-keeping. The Coiste Seasta was then elected: it consisted of Walter Lynch, Máirín de Burca, Tomás MacGiolla, RJ, Cathal Goulding, Tony Ruane, Seán Garland and Seán Ó Brádaigh.

The motions from the AF which had not been discussed there were dealt with. All those leading to actions in favour of working people and their organisations were adopted. They also adopted the aim of Sinn Fein as being a Socialist Workers Republic, with the intention of taking up appropriate international affiliations. This motion was from Bray, and originated with Costello. Motions to do with taking seats or otherwise were referred to the next Ard Fheis. There was a discussion on the Mid-Ulster question and it was decided to hold meetings in the constituency with the Clubs as a matter of urgency, and to delegate this to the Coiste Seasta.

The voting for the Ard Comhairle in the 1967 Ard Fheis is on record. Goulding topped the poll at 95, Seán Ó Brádaigh came next at 71, and then the present writer, at 70, followed by Costello at 67, Éamonn Mac Thomáis at 64, Tom Mitchell at 51, Frank McGlade 44, Mick Ryan 41 and so on.

I feel the relatively high vote for the present writer needs explanation. I was not all that well known, and did not have any track-record of having 'gone to jail for Ireland', military service or other conventional popularity qualification. It could simply be that Goulding, as the leading politicising moderniser in the movement, ordered the 'army' people to vote for me, and they obeyed. On the other hand it could be that there was a genuine perceived need on the part of the rank and file to support the sort of approach I had been advocating via the United Irishman and via the various educational seminars which had taken place in the previous year or two. Or it could have been a bit of both. MR tends to agree with the latter; it was a combination of the two factors.

Some Theoretical Issues: Socialism and Republicanism

Greaves noted in his diary a contact with the present writer on February 10 1968; it seems I was trying to track down some Clann na hEireann contacts; I was in London for a weekend break.

I recollect this weekend; there were other non-political priorities and the contacting of the Clann was somewhat peripheral. There was I believe something on, but if I had been there it would have been informally as an observer. I must have phoned CDG in the hopes of an encounter with him, to tease out the theoretical implications of the way things were evolving. But he was, I think, putting up the barriers; he had written me off as some sort of apostate.

In retrospect what must have been on my mind was the nature of the distinction between 'labour movement' and 'petty-bourgeois' modes of organisation, and whether the distinction was as black and white as he seemed to want to make out. Scratch a Dublin 'proletarian' and you find a 'petty-bourgeois' not very far below the surface. The Irish Workers' League in the early days had used Party funds to buy equipment for one of its EC members, to set him up in business, as an alternative to chronic unemployment. Most bricklayers were 'on the lump'. I was critical of Marxist orthodoxy, and anxious to explore how 'workers, working managers, working owner-managers and self-employed' could be brought into the developing movement for all-Ireland national democracy, and brought around to accept something approximating to a co-operative or democratic socialist vision as the follow-through.

The Belfast WTS in February 1968 ran a symposium on the Irish language, which was organised jointly with the New Ireland Society, and took place in Queens University. Micheál Ó Loingsigh from the Dublin WTS spoke at short notice, replacing a speaker who had let them down. He made the case that the language revival must be accompanied by 'the spirit of social revolution'. Flann Ó Riain and one Tomás Ó Muimhneachain also spoke, accusing the Dublin government of insincerity. Gogarty mentioned that 12 bodies in NI political and cultural fields had notified the Belfast WTS of their willingness to attend 'Connolly co-ordinating committee in the Presbyterian hostel on Monday next'.

The 1968 AGM of the Dublin WTS(16) took place on Saturday March 15, being convened by the Secretary Anthony Coughlan in a letter dated March 6. Cork and Belfast representatives were expected and would report.

Returning to practical politics to keep the sequence, at the SF Ard Comhairle on 23/03/68(17) Frank McGlade was now included, co-opted to represent the NI Republican Clubs, which were the legalising SF cumainn under a new politicising banner.

Costello felt let down over the lack of support he got in the Wicklow by-election. Clearly the movement was voting with its feet on the matter of contesting elections under abstentionism. Mick Ryan was appointed organiser for the whole of

Leinster, including Wicklow, Costello's weakness having been exposed. Malachi McGurran was appointed organiser for Ulster, and an educational conference was arranged for Belfast.

Stormont Intervenes

On this matter I can interpolate my own memoir. The objective of this educational conference was to introduce the Belfast movement, which hitherto had been dominated by considerations of illegality, to the opportunities for working in open political mode, once the Civil Rights issues were addressed, and concessions won. It was therefore necessary to give total priority to open work under the Civil Rights banner. I was to attend it and make this case.

The NI authorities however acted first. They had their spies, and knew our movements, which in any case were quite open. In the context of a visit to the Belfast Wolfe Tone Society prior to the planned conference, I encountered a gentleman who subsequently turned out to have been a 'plant'. He said he wanted to join Sinn Fein, and proffered a membership application form, which I accepted, not smelling a rat, though with hindsight I should have done. I did not take seriously enough the actual illegal status of SF in NI.

Subsequently I was picked up by the RUC and held in the Falls Road police station. They went through nearly every bit of paper I had on me, but by sheer good luck failed to pick up the SF application form. Betty Sinclair, the secretary of the Belfast Trades Council, and a leading member of the CP, got wind of my predicament, via Fred Heatley, of the Belfast Wolfe Tone Society, with whom I had been when picked up. She came with her NICRA and Trade Union auras, and argued forcefully that they had no reason to be using their Special Powers in my case. So in the end I was released, but the Belfast meeting was aborted, and the understanding of the opportunities presented by the opening up of Civil Rights, in the case of the Belfast Republican Clubs, was delayed.

Definition of Socialism

Returning to the minutes of 23/03/68: I am on record as having proposed setting up a sub-committee to examine the Sinn Fein Constitution. This was referred to the CS.

There was a draft article on the 'Sinn Fein Definition of Socialism' which had been asked for by the Irish Democrat. Costello insisted that this be circulated to Cumainn rather than sent to the Democrat.

This brings us back to the theoretical issues, as they arose in practice. I have a copy of this draft document(18), which amounts to over two pages of foolscap, duplicated, impossible to scan in. I will try to summarise its essentials:

It begins by referring back to the 1967 Ard Fheis amendment which refers to a 'Democratic Socialist Republic in accordance with the 1916 proclamation', and the key concept is 'cherishing all the children equally', this being inconsistent with large-scale inheritable private property. Connolly's formulation is suggested: 'the application to the ownership of the means of production of the democratic principle of the Republican ideal'. What follows expands on this.

The 'democratic socialism' as defined in the context of the British Labour Party is rejected as a phoney facade. We need to make our own definition, in terms of how to democratise the production process, seen as comprising 4 elements, supply, production, distribution and management, the latter being an essential part. There is a fifth element, ownership, which is in a different category. When this is under capitalist rules, ownership has over-riding rights, and sets management against the rest with orders to maximise profits, under criteria which ignore the social investment in the skills of the work-force.

Socialism rejects private ownership of the means of production, counter-posing social ownership. This can be municipal or co-operative in form, with decisions taken by elected management committees, from groups of those directly concerned. Examples are given. Large firms would function under policies decided by delegate conferences. Small family retail outlets would own collectively their wholesale supply systems. Managers would implement policies defined by management committees, in the interests of the people co-operatively owning the firm: workers, consumers and suppliers, in due proportion, depending on the nature of the business and its environment.

The State as known today would no longer exist; it would be replaced by federations of peoples' organisation. Parties would exist, uniting common-interest groups; three such groupings were suggested, with an 'activist group' catalysing the interaction between the other two, but without a dominant role.

Anthony Coughlan in May 1968, in a letter to Máire Bean Mhic Giolla, suggested a definition of socialism in terms of social ownership of the means of production and distribution by the central state, local government, regional organisations or co-operatives. He distinguished it from communism by the latter implying State support for an atheistic philosophy. He also wrote to me outlining the principles governing a revolutionary movement such as to enable it to survive exposure to parliament, and suggested that he considered that the republican movement was not yet in fact ripe to be able to take this step, and that I should not be trying to rush the process. The key issue was the quality of the candidates, and the nature of their relationship with the organised political decision process.

I was of course aware of these arguments and had been propagating them internally through the educational conferences. In retrospect however I think he was perhaps right to warn me that the process would be slower to ripen than I was at the time expecting. Some feedback came in during June on the 'definition of socialism', and this is on record with the present writer(19). People preferred co-operative rather than municipal ownership, and were uneasy about the potential for evolution into a 'one-party State'; a 'no-party state' was preferred, with elections to management committees of individual citizens known to electors. I have however no record of an integrated amended document having been prepared or agreed. I think we regarded it as an educational or consciousness-raising procedure, rather than a decision-making procedure.

The April 1968 WTS Plan

Issue no 9 of *Tuairisc*, the Dublin WTS newsletter, for April 1968 was the first for over a year, a re-launch, in the then current intensifying political environment. It was unsigned, but the indications are that it was edited by the present writer rather than by Anthony Coughlan. We called for a publication fund, to launch a publishing venture, and we outlined four documents which we felt we had ready to go out in the form of pamphlets:

[A] The New Republic: this was an outline of the social and economic structure of a model 32 county Republic, based on the ideas of Connolly's socialism, under the headings the State, Culture, Social Services, Production, Trade, Finance , Defence and External Affairs. Tuairisc went on to outline this: **it was in fact basically the Eire Nua document**, subsequently hijacked by the Provisionals after the split. It was strong on the 'Regional Government' concept, with the Capital moved to Athlone, cutting the link with Dublin perceived as the legacy of the Pale, the imperial focus, the centre of British influence.

[B] The Movement and the People: this was aimed at people '...who are actively concerned with building a conscious united revolutionary movement for a Socialist Republic in Ireland today ...'. This covered definitions of political terms, evaluation and classification of various existing organisations, enumeration of the main issues, an outline of methods of awakening people's understanding of the issues, analysis of the special conditions in the Six Counties, and an outline of the structure of the movement. *NB there was absolutely no military dimension in this context; this was the blueprint for the movement to 'go political' definitively.*

[C] The Technology of Independence: the *United Irishman* from September 1967 and January 1968 had published a series of articles on this theme, from Derry Kelleher and myself; it called for being printed in a more permanent form, '...for use in propagating the idea that there is no need for basing our industrialisation plans on the employment of the foreign expert and that Ireland is technologically quite capable of developing an advanced economy, provided we use correctly our assets of talented manpower ...'.

[D] Ireland and Europe, the Historical Links: This was the material presented at the Wynn's Hotel meeting in November 1967. '...It shows that there are two Europes: the Europe of the monarchists and monopolists and that of the ordinary working people. The main Irish historical links are with the latter, and the modern neo-Unionist trend, centred round the EEC and free trade with Britain, is a reversal of this tradition and an attempt to put us under the hegemony of the former.'

I don't think this publication project got off the ground. If it had, it would have constituted a valid theoretical basis for the development of an all-Ireland democratic revolution with social-revolutionary content, along the lines to which we had aspired in 1964. Its publication was pre-empted by the pace at which events developed, and the diversion of the attention of the movement towards the sterile issues of abstentionism, and its associated threat of re-emergent militarism.

Left-wing Undercurrents

On May 4 Greaves in his diary recorded an indication that the 'old Dublin crowd' were planning on the assumption of the demise of the Connolly Association, and on initiating fund-raising in London among the emigrant Irish for the Irish Workers' Party.

On May 12 1968 he recorded further that Micheál Ó Riordáin had been lobbying various East European embassies seeking to get goods for his fund-raising sales of work, with the support of Jim Prendergast, whom CDG labelled '...something of an embassy-fly ...'. CDG noted with disapproval that '...they still have the conception of a subsidised movement, with a low-priced paper and literature...'.

Prendergast and O'Riordan were of course both International Brigade veterans, and as such they had status of sanctity with the 'international movement' of post-Stalinist orthodoxy. It could credibly be argued that a military background is incompatible with good Marxist democratic politics in peacetime, and Greaves, and indeed the present writer, were up against this on the one hand with Prendergast and co, and on the other with Goulding and co. Prendergast, it seems, according to Betty Sinclair, had been influential in getting an 'English-type' public house set up in Moscow, which he frequented when there.

There is on May 14 a reference by Greaves to a meeting in Nottingham, with its Fergus O'Connor connection, at which the question of a Joint Council between the IWP and the CPNI was discussed. Greaves attended in his capacity as the Irish expert on their international affairs committee. John Gollan, the CPGB chief, very sensibly did not want the CPGB represented. The question arose of CDG or J(oe) D(eighan) going in their individual capacities, as neutral observers.

There are complex issues here, arising from the delicacy of the relationship between the CPGB and the movement in Ireland. The CPGB would undoubtedly have wanted discreetly to catalyse the process of formation of an all-Ireland 'official' Marxist party as part of the 'international movement'. Greaves with his Connolly Association and Irish Democrat roles would have wanted to maximise support for Civil Rights in the North from the organised labour movement. The CPNI - IWP joint meeting could perhaps be helpful in this context. This was of course a distinct process from the present writer's aspiration to develop the republican movement into an all-Ireland democratic Marxist party having broad-based support from 'workers, working management, working owner-managers and self-employed'.

Politicisation and the North

The question arose of finding a means for ensuring the legal existence of the Republican Clubs in NI, with SF banned, such as to enable them to participate in the Ard Fheis as affiliated cumainn. I undertook to draft a Constitution which would serve this purpose.

It was reported that sales of the *United Irishman* were on the increase. This was a consequence of secret meeting of 'army' unit OCs, which had taken place earlier in a 'safe house' north of Nenagh, at which this task was accepted as part of the 'army' politicisation process(20). Increasingly it was the accepted duty of 'army' people to give priority to activating SF cumainn, and making things happen at the political level. There were however those who accepted this role grudgingly, or simply withdrew, to come out of the woodwork later when the Provisionals emerged.

I was present at this meeting, which took place under conditions of the usual 'military' discomfort, people sleeping on the floor and suchlike macho cultural procedures. There was however no evidence of any actual military plan in the background; this aspect at this time was confined to the thinking of Mac Stiofain, who was not present on this occasion.

Connolly Commemoration

On June 9 1968 Greaves gave an account of the Connolly commemoration meeting in Dublin, which took place in Moran's Hotel. It was due to start at 10.45 a.m. and to CDG's surprise the meeting was already crammed; 150 people at least. He noted some names: '...Peter O'Connor *(from Waterford, another ex International Brigade man)*, Maire Comerford, RHJ *ie the present writer*, AC, Mrs Tom Johnson who is 93, Ina Connolly, Desmond Branningan, Donal Nevin, Barry Desmond, Seamus Costello, C(athal G(oulding), Seamus O'Toole (sic) (Ó Tuathail), Vincent MacDowell, John Swift, Micheál O'Riordain, Seán Nolan, P(acky) E(arly), indeed the whole of the progressive movement of Dublin... Carmody took the chair - needless to say the IWP were cock-a-hoop. And they were well received what was more ...'.

Subsequent to this it emerged that Greaves had been under false impressions(21) regarding the membership status of myself and Anthony Coughlan; he seemed to think that dual memberships were involved, whereas in fact while I was a member of the republican movement I had long since ceased to be a member of the IWL, and Coughlan had never in fact been a member of either, preferring to act as an independent source of political ideas.

Republican Movement Integration

In June 1968 the Sinn Fein Coiste Seasta started keeping proper minutes. The first minutes available are for 13/06/68. The Connolly Youth requested a representative to attend their annual convention. There was a call for protests relating to the contents of the proposed Criminal Justice Bill, which had been drafted in response to the situations created in the 'Housing Action' campaign, dealing with squatting etc. Then at the 01/07/68 meeting TMacG CG SG MdeB RJ were present: the political transformation is moving things in the direction of the CS basically being CG's 'HQ Staff', with the latter ceasing to meet as such. There were contacts with Melbourne and the Scottish Nationalists. Industrial issues existed at the de Beer diamond factory at Ennis, and with the proposed closure of the Potez aircraft factory. TMacG agreed to take RJ's draft Republican Club Constitution and filter it for issues that needed to be addressed via Ard Fheis resolutions. The Ard Fheis (1968) was fixed for November 31/Dec1.

At the SF CS on 08/07/68 TMacG reported on the Scottish Nationalists' Convention. Copies of the Republican Clubs constitution were to be printed and distributed in the North. Then on 15/07/68 it was noted that the status of the Republican Clubs Constitution was that it was a facade for public consumption in the North, given the legal situation there; the real Constitution was that of Sinn Fein. A meeting was to be called of all SF Councillors to prepare resolutions for the General Council of County Councils (GCCC).

The Ard Comhairle meeting on 20/07/68 decided to go for Liberty Hall for the Ard Fheis; Seán Ó Cionnaith was to be Organiser for Connaught. There was support for Austin Currie and civil disobedience in the North. There was a report of an Educational Conference held in June. There was concern about local councillors. It was agreed to write to local cumainn urging that they write to TDs about local issues. The question of how to commemorate the First Dáil (1919-1969) was referred to the CS.

At the SF CS on 29/07/68 progress on the PR referendum was reported; also on the campaign on the Potez closure. Seán Garland reported on a Belfast meeting at which it was stated that Betty Sinclair had disagreed with 'holding it under NICRA'.

I suspect this was a reflection of a situation where Garland had planned to meet with BS as a contact between the Republican Movement and the Communist Party, but somehow the wires had got crossed, and it had ended up as an NICRA event. Such contacts were going on fairly regularly, with a view to trying to ensure that the NICRA was kept 'cross-community', in the sense of having a Protestant trade-unionist component. This was regarded as important, the CP being seen as a useful window into Protestant radical activism.

A committee for the 1919 First Dáil commemoration was set up; this included Greta Ryan (Mick Ryan's sister, now Ui Murchú) and Éamonn Mac Thomáis; it also brought in Cathal Mac Liam, who by then was Chairman of the Dublin Wolfe Tone Society, and Seamus Mac Riocaird. *The latter was a 1930s stalwart, who had become politicised post-Curragh via the co-operative movement; he ran the Howth Fishermens's Co-op, and had been an active supporter of attempts to develop a new wave of co-operative organisation in the West, as part of the process of development of the social concerns of the Movement.*

At the SF CS on 12/08/68 it was noted that the Proportional Representation (PR) campaign was in progress; there was mention of PR Society literature via May Hayes, who was their contact in Dublin. *May Hayes had been a Connolly Association stalwart in London; she had retired on pension to live in Dublin (She had been secretary to Captain Harrison, who had been secretary to Parnell, a sort of apostolic succession on the constitutional side.) She was however not active and proved elusive.*

The Mid-1968 WTS Programme

I wrote to Anthony Coughlan on 24/07/68, referring to a WTS meeting the previous day which Tony as Secretary had been unable to attend; it conveyed from the meeting a vote of sympathy on the death of his father. I went on in the letter to fill him in on what had happened; we went on with the meeting because Maire Comerford had plans well advanced for her 'Aeriocht' and needed support (this was an open-air political-cultural event, in a mode pioneered earlier by Constance Markiewicz, which Maire was resurrecting).

I mentioned also in the letter about our move to collect signatures of notables for publication, in support of a campaign against the Criminal Justice Bill, then a Civil Rights issue in the Republic. I later sent out a circular convening a WTS meeting for August 13; this is annotated from the meeting itself, of which however I do not have minutes. It was proposed to re-examine the 'specialist group structure' of the Society with a view to reconstructing it.

The circular outlined an approach to specialist group project procedure: define the scope, allocate research to people, draw together the results and draft a paper, discuss this before the Society as a whole, revise the draft in the light of feedback, publish the revised draft, in *Tuairisc* or elsewhere, in preliminary mode, publish finally in referencable print, and then implement to the extent of getting it adopted as policy by a national organisation. '...This represented a steady systematic development of theory into practice, involving ever widening circles of people ...'.

The circular then went on to list some current issues lending themselves to the above 'project group' approach:

A: To develop the Criminal Justice Bill critique into an effective Civil Rights organisation;

B: To develop the current discussions about the TCD-UCD merger into a consistent national higher education policy covering various regional and specialist aspects;

C: To come up with a unified comprehensive education policy for second level which would be acceptable to teachers and parents;

D: To examine the question of State finance for the Arts;

E: To initiate some regular cultural event having a 'national cultural consciousness' aspect;

F: To address the question of birth control and divorce in the context of the requirements of a projected 32-county Constitution;

G: To address the question of a national health service taking on board the problems which had arisen in Britain in that context;

H: To produce a history of the First Dáil and its Democratic Programme in time for the 50th anniversary.

Of the above aspirations: A became the Citizens for Civil Liberties, later the Irish Council for Civil Liberties (ICCL); B contributed via press-controversy to the emergent 3rd-level politics of the 1970s, C later generated the 'Association for Democracy in Education' which campaigned, unsuccessfully, for comprehensive schools to be under the VECs rather than under the religious denominations, D was stillborn, E generated some poetry readings between Ireland, Wales and Scotland which have persisted, being eventually taken over (I think) by Comhdhail Naisiunta na Gaeilge, F laid the basis for the Divorce Action Group, G was stillborn, and H helped to produce Maire Comerford's book on the First Dáil.

This broad-based approach remained the present writer's aspiration for the development of a theoretical basis for a projected democratic movement for national unity, some time in the future, and I was pushing it on the eve of the Coalisland-Dungannon march, which attacked the Achilles heel of Unionism, and triggered the subsequent rapid and increasingly chaotic developments. There was thus a clear mismatch between the present writer's strategic vision of a broad-based radical democratic movement capable of picking up some Protestant political support in the North, and the Greaves-Coughlan tactic of going for the Unionist underbelly via the Civil Rights demands.

It is quite clear from the above that we had not put these together. We were not acting in concert; we each did what we thought it best to do at the time, in our respective areas of influence. The consequence was that when the NICRA demands began to be realised, and the situation opened up politically in the North, there was not in existence enough of a broad-based non-violent democratic movement, with an all-Ireland structure, to take advantage of it. Fianna Fail irredentism took over, with a strong Catholic-nationalist flavour, and the basis for the armed B-Special pogroms of August 1969, and the subsequent emergence of the Provisionals, was laid.

Filed with my 1968 WTS material is the last 4 pages of a 5-page letter, probably from Tom O'Connor of Coalisland, a leading member of the Dungannon Republican Club. In it he outlined the view from below of the various organisation in Dungannon concerned with the housing issue: the Homeless Citizens League, the Campaign for Social Justice and the Dungannon Housing Association. This was in the lead-up to the famous incident where a Council house was allocated to a single Protestant woman, while families were in the queue, triggering the Coalisland to Dungannon march led by the NICRA. This letter supports our contention that the Clubs were active in the grassroots, and were in a position to give local support to the march, ensuring it went off peacefully.

The Dungannon NICRA March

There was, at the SF CS on August 12 1968, talk of a Potez workers' meeting. The 1919 Committee was not yet set up. The US embassy was to be picketed, over their base in Derry. There was mention of a 'Human Rights' demonstration on August 24; Tom O'Connor was to speak on behalf of the Republican Clubs. This would have been the Coalisland to Dungannon march, the first major public demonstration.

I feel I should intersperse here a recollection, as I was there, and so was Anthony Coughlan. The latter, working via the Wolfe Tone Society, was much more actively committed than I was to the specific NI Civil Rights situation. He had produced a written statement for the occasion, and I remember someone, I thought AC himself (though he does not recollect it), trying to get it 'read off the platform', or into a situation where it could be read, if there were to be a meeting, with a platform, and words said. The approach was via Fred Heatley, who was an NICRA activist, and a member of the Belfast Wolfe Tone Society. Fred objected strongly, as it had not been discussed in advance. He later claimed, and to the best of my recollection published, that the paper was a 'statement from the Army Council', and that he was right to block it for this reason. I feel I need to go further into this episode.

The paper was Coughlan's own, and he intended it as a genuine attempt to capture the sense of the occasion. It has turned up in my own papers, and I am certain that Fred Heatley was mistaken in his attribution. The Army Council at this time was politicising as hard as it could, and would have had no interest in issuing public statements in such an environment, realising full well their potential for damage, if claimed by the Army Council as source.

The copy I have is not fit to scan, but I summarise it here. It is entitled 'Declaration.... Dungannon August 24 1968', and begins: 'To our fellow-countrymen, to the people of Britain and to all democrats and democratic governments everywhere ...' continuing with a lengthy introduction listing the grievances, which concludes with reference to Section 75 of the Government of Ireland Act under which Westminster has the right to legislate to give equal civil rights in Northern Ireland as in the United Kingdom. It then goes on to list the items which should be in a Bill of Rights, including the lifting of the ban on the Republican Clubs and the repeal of the Special Powers. It calls on the Parliament in Westminster to act, and on that in Dublin to press the former to act, and to raise the matter at the UN. It is an exemplary document as regards content, though unimpressive in presentation, being duplicated in rather small typescript on two sides of a foolscap sheet, so many copies must have been produced and some distributed. It was however not read off the platform, at the meeting which took place at the road-block near the hospital, which was addressed by Betty Sinclair on behalf of the NICRA.

The foregoing shows how the leadership of the NICRA, and those actively promoting the process and supporting the demonstration, were relatively unorganised and unprepared, because if this document had gone through the appropriate channels, it undoubtedly would have been adopted by the demonstration with acclamation. It is one of history's 'near misses'.

Dungannon Impact on the SF Leadership

It is noteworthy how in Dublin Sinn Fein circles it was 'business as usual'; the significance of the Dungannon meeting was not immediately picked up. At the CS on 19/08/68 it was noted that the Proportional Representation campaign was developing, without May Hayes. The Dublin Comhairle Ceanntair was seeking to build support via the Dublin Trades Council. There were however moves to try to co-ordinate the Republican Clubs in the North; a meeting was arranged for Derry on Sept 14, followed by an all-NI meeting, to be held in Monaghan (due to difficulty in getting a place in the North). CG was to contact Anthony Coughlan.

Note that there is a continuing clear acceptance of Anthony Coughlan as a source of advice to the Northern Republicans about how they should relate to the developing Civil Rights campaign. There was an acceptance of him as being virtually 'part of the movement' via the Wolfe Tone Society, with Cathal Goulding, Malachi McGurran and Liam McMillan as the personal links.

Regarding 1919 it was noted that Maire Comerford was writing a history. There was some contact with the Basques. Then however at the CS on 26/08/68 they decided to take no action on the Basques, due to splits. The PR referendum question continued. There was finally, after some delay, a report on the NICRA Dungannon meeting. This had ended with the march being blocked, where the Coalisland road came in, near the hospital; they had a token sit-down; there was some speechifying; it all ended peacefully.

The Irish Left and the Czechoslovak Crisis

Greaves on August 21 1968 noted in his diary how the Czechoslovak situation became acute when the USSR invaded; Des Logan, a Connolly Association supporter, phoned CDG early to get a reaction. Pat Devine submitted his Irish Democrat copy, in support of the Russians. CDG had to edit it down. Questions came in; what did the CA think? CDG took the line, we don't know, we have not yet discussed it. Des Logan was indignant, '...this will split the Party ...'.

In CDG's August 29 entry we have an account of the CPGB meeting at which the Czechoslovak crisis is discussed. It is beyond our scope to analyse this. It is possible to make out that he prefers the Irish to the narrow parochialism of the English. He remarked that apart from Des Logan all the Irish tended to be pro-Russian. The overall impression is that CDG took up a position of defence of Soviet intervention, regarding it as politically necessary.

Then on September 5 1968 it seems I was in London; I phoned CDG and then looked in. While I was there MOR phoned, congratulating CDG on his stand on the issue; there had however been complications in Dublin, and a statement critical of Russia had gone out, despite MOR, who now wants to get CDG to '...knock sense into people's heads ...'.

A leading group of IWP activists, including George Jeffares, Sam Nolan, Joe Deasy, Paddy Carmody and a few others, later broke with the IWP on the Czechoslovak issue, mostly ending up in the Labour Party. The attention of the IWP leadership was concentrated on this issue for many months, extending to years, while the Northern situation developed its positive potential. My evaluation of their minimal utility in the developing Irish situation, as outlined above, was on the whole confirmed.

In the same entry CDG went on to record a long conversation with the present writer, whom he regarded as being '...largely at sea... wondering if he had been wasting his time with SF... he had opposed the burning of the ship at Galway... he was not.. persuaded that the Russians might have a case in Czechoslovakia.. AC had drawn the conclusion that the Russians must be mad... Cathal thought that they could do no wrong... others filled into other parts of the spectrum...'. Joe Deighan turned up, he also was seen as '...very confused ...'. He went on: '...he told me the republican clubs were about to launch a grand civil disobedience campaign in the North. Now that in itself would not worry one. But I asked him if they had consulted the Trade Unions or the Labour Movement. Of course they had not. So they learn nothing and forget nothing, and are liable to go off on any tangent ...'.

Greaves overestimated the practical possibility of the republican clubs engaging in consultations with the Trade Unions or the Labour Movement. The channels did not exist, except very marginally via Betty Sinclair and Derek Peters in the NICRA leadership. The latter however were out on a limb, acting as individuals, without having their Party behind them.

In the Sinn Fein leadership the Czechoslovak crisis barely caused a ripple; at the CS on 09/09/68 there was no word from the 1919 committee; the Proportional Representation campaign was still going on; the projected meeting on Sept 15 was taking shape (Maghera, not Monaghan); 80 delegates were expected; TMacG, CG, TM and Anthony Coughlan were to go. This was for the purpose of ensuring that the Clubs understood their role in relation to the broad-based NICRA movement, and the need to keep to restricted CR objectives (no nationalist sloganising or flag-waving etc)

There is an entry by Greaves on September 11 which fills in some detail on the IWP meeting which decided about Czechoslovakia, O'Riordan being voted down 18 to 13, Nolan being away. There was also a second-hand description of the present writer's behaviour on the day of the invasion, indicating the extent of my upset.

Post-Dungannon Sinn Fein and the Left

The uptake of the significance of Dungannon remained dormant. At the Sinn Fein Ard Comhairle on 21/09/68 the attention was on the Criminal Justice Bill, and on the 1919 project, for which the Mansion House had been booked for June 21 1969. It was agreed to hand it over to the National Commemoration Committee (the ad-hoc committee referenced earlier having apparently not delivered).

Cathal Goulding laid down an ordinance to the effect that Cumann na mBan was no longer part of the Movement(22). This had resulted from the development of feminist equality all round, and a sense that there was no need for a special group reflecting traditional female roles. The shell of the organisation at the time was occupied by a traditional apolitical group, regarded by CG as a source of right-wing intrigue.

Note that this was CG acting as the 'Government of the Republic', as embodied in the Army Council, rather than making a contribution to a Sinn Fein leadership decision. Political integration of the movement was far from complete, and the old procedures persisted.

CG then went on to give an account of a meeting of Republican Club activists which had taken place the previous week at Maghera. The activists had objected to the failure at Dungannon to break the police barrier; military-type thinking was still the norm. It was agreed that the Republican Club representatives on the NICRA Committee should put their views, but then accept and implement majority decision. A Regional Council was set up, chaired by Malachi McGurran.

At the CS on 30/09/68 the Proportional Representation campaign was discussed. The Irish Congress of Trade Unions had produced a leaflet; this was to be distributed by the Cumainn. Attempts by the Pearse Cumann in Rathmines to contact local Fianna Fail, with a view to public debate, had been blocked by FF HQ. External Cumann contacts in this context were to be encouraged. There was a call by Seamus Ó Brogain the Cumann secretary for a more comprehensive registration, so as to identify hidden talents.

Greaves on October 9 1968 discovered that Anthony Coughlan had been drenched by water-cannon in Derry, at the October 5 civil rights march there. He asked Tony '...if they stood for socialism why didn't they join the working-class movement? AC: The unions and Labour party would never do anything. CDG: so you have a short cut? They said they had. It is to be hoped it proves shorter than their cut to the United Irish Republic...'. Cathal Goulding it seems had been on the way to Derry but his car broke down. CDG: '...I said I thought they should all keep away. But you might as well talk to the table. CG then yanked AC off to an editorial meeting of the *United Irishman*(!).

Anthony Coughlan was advising the republican movement how to relate to the civil rights movement through personal contacts with key people. In the context, 'joining the working-class movement' was irrelevant. The disastrous nature of the USSR's action was indeed showing up across the board. What chance was there of getting any sensible approach to developing a broad-based politicised left-republican convergence in this situation? At least the republicans were not allowing themselves to be diverted by it, but the Left, such as it was, was effectively neutered.

The next day October 10 Greaves went to Belfast, failed to find Betty Sinclair, and went on to Derry, where he met with Ivan Cooper, picking up the impression that they were all under the influence of McCann and the Trotskyite element, though Cooper told him of the new committee from which McCann had walked out. He had no contact addresses in Derry and was depending on contacts made via the Derry Journal.

Meanwhile at the Sinn Fein Standing Committee (CS) on 14/10/68 the final rally of the PR campaign was supported, though it was in effect run by Fine Gael. The verdict of the Irish electorate in this case was masterly: they elected de Valera to be President, but rejected his party's attempt to copper-fasten its rule on the Irish people, by retaining proportional representation for the electoral system.

On the Civil Rights question: it was noted that there was a new group in Derry.... *This must have been the middle-ground committee from which McCann had walked out.*

There had been a march in Dublin on the British Embassy and it was agreed that this had been a mistake. It was agreed to write to the 'other branch' to ask for an explanation, to see what thinking had motivated the idea. *Yet Cathal Goulding was on record as having been at this meeting. Why did he not explain there and then? Probably because due to his recent spell in prison he was no longer actually in the leadership.* It was felt that the Wolfe Tone Society should be in a position to initiate the setting up of some sort of Civil Rights group relevant to the situation in the 26 Counties, which included the Criminal Justice Bill issue. It was agreed to combine meetings of Regional Executives with educational conferences on the same weekend.

The pressure to link NICRA with the national question, even among the vanguard of left-republican politicisers, was very strong. Janice Williams, who participated in the Embassy demonstration, recollects it has having been quite small. She had no idea it was 'disapproved of'. She went in the company of Seamus Ó Brogain and other members of the Pearse Cumann, of which she was a member.

Later on October 19 1968 Greaves recorded encountering Betty Sinclair, who regaled him with the '...sharp internal differences within the Civil Rights Committee.. the anti-communism of Heatley.... the refusal of the CP to participate effectively. At the Political Committee when she raised the question the Chairman Andy Barr looked at his watch. She said that both he and Graham wanted TU jobs, and Barr particularly will fight strenuously any line of policy that would lose him ground in the trade union. Thus Party policy is made subordinate to the Sheet Metal Union - the old old story, the unholy alliance I have been battering my head against for twenty and more years... Of McCann she says if he was on the platform she would walk off... she has high praise for McAteer who... stood by her side through the meeting. We discussed the republicans who she says are very difficult to work with. They invited her to one of their committee meetings, secret no doubt, but she did not go. I said I thought she was right ...'.

A proposal had arisen, initiated by Heatley, to the effect that those who had participated in the 'illegal march' at Derry should sign a paper saying they had done so. Betty agreed initially to this at the meeting, then went home and had second thoughts, conveying these to McAnerny the secretary, who also began to have doubts. Together they went to a third, who felt the same. Heatley was indignant. Some compromise formula was agreed.

Betty, whose heart was in the right place, was thus being left out on a limb by her Party. Her wavering on the signing issue must have been influenced by her relative exposure. The inability of the most advanced sections of the Northern Labour Movement to take up the issues, in the manner that CDG had hoped, must have been increasingly obvious.

At the Sinn Fein CS on 21/10/68 Tom Mitchell reported on the Derry events(23); some 3000 had participated. It was agreed to leave discussion of their significance until the next AC meeting scheduled for 26th. There was a march on US embassy planned for Nov 2, organised by Irish Voice on Vietnam *(this was an informal group involving Peadar O'Donnell and George Jeffares; the latter at this time was the Irish Workers Party foreign affairs expert, and he had successfully focused broad-based public opinion, including many religious groups, against the Vietnam war)*. Mick Ryan was to organise the stewarding of the march. A statement on the government defeat in the PR referendum was to be issued. The Republican Club in UCD had requested Goulding and Costello to speak. At this time both in TCD and UCD student republican clubs were flourishing, fruits of the politicisation process.

The Ard Comhairle meeting on 26/10/68, despite the decision of the previous CS, was concerned mainly with consideration of the draft constitution which was to come before the coming Ard Fheis. It paid no attention to the opening up of the NI situation arising from the Derry Civil Rights events. Various amendments to the draft were considered, the key one being to make participation in Assemblies (ie Stormont or the Dáil) an AC decision on tactical grounds, rather than a 'principle' enshrined in the constitution.

Representatives of the Connolly Youth, the Workers Party and Connradh na Gaeilge were to be invited to the Ard Fheis.

There was an extended meeting of the Sinn Fein CS on 28/10/68 at which CG's regional organisers reported. This was part of the process of CG's 'HQ Staff' being subsumed into the political shell of the reforming Sinn Fein. The core-CS group was all there and consisted of Tomás MacGiolla, RJ, Tom Mitchell, Seán Garland, Seán Ó Brádaigh, Wally Lynch and Máirín de Burca. Mick Ryan, Bartley Madden(24) and Malachi McGurran were brought in their capacities as regional organisers for Leinster, Munster and NI (nominally 'Ulster' but NI de facto) respectively.

MMcG's report is recorded in most detail: a regional executive was to be held in Maghera; TM or WL to attend. There were 5 clubs in Belfast, 6 in Armagh, 5 in Tyrone, 7 in Derry. The next NICRA march had been fixed for November 16 in Armagh.

Then at the CS on 04/11/68, with TMacG CG WL TR SG RJ SO'B TM MdeB present, TMacG and WL reported on the Maghera meeting; all areas had been represented; they wanted to push for a CR march in Derry on November 16 and Armagh November 23 or 30. There were 22 clubs and 4 regional executives. An educational conference was planned for Armagh on December 1. The commemoration at Edentubber on November 10 was to be used as a means of handing over Ard Fheis papers.

This sort of arrangement was still considered necessary, given the illegality of Sinn Fein in NI. Edentubber was considered a convenient near-border location to which people came annually to commemorate a 1950s tragedy. There is however an implied contradiction here. People attending an event linked to 1950s militarism would tend not to be in tune with 1960s politicisation.

There was a court-case involving one McEldowney in the North; this was innovative in that the movement up to now had not defended itself in court, refusing to recognise its legality. They decided to ask Geoffrey Byng QC to defend; this was a significant nod in the direction of linking with the Left in Britain, and cultivating pro-Irish elements with it. Byng had written extensively on Ireland, Partition and the Special Powers.

It was agreed that MMcG would instruct the Clubs not to support in NICRA any move to dislodge Betty Sinclair from the chair. The link with the Belfast Trades Council, and Protestant radical activism, as expressed via the CP, was to be maintained. The NICRA must not be allowed to become simply a protest organisation of the Catholic ghettoes.

Mick Ryan has commented retrospectively to the effect that McGurran felt that the movement went too far into embedding itself in the NICRA and lost its own political identity. My own impression is that from here onwards the IWP and the CPNI, and the 'international movement' generally, were in effect so shattered and divided by the events in Czechoslovakia that they increasingly became irrelevant in the developing Irish situation. Their original relevance was as a window into the thinking of the Belfast Protestant working-class; this window became closed off in proportion as the NICRA was forced into the Catholic ghettoes.

In London on November 9 1968 Greaves recorded receiving a letter from the present writer indicating that I was '...mending some of my ways ...'. He also receives one from MO'R to the effect that I had been to see him. He thought it might be to renew my membership. He also recorded that C(harlie) C(unningham) has noticed '...an improvement in morale; since 1962 we have not had a victory; now at last ...'.

I recollect this episode. I was indeed uneasy about the way the republican movement was going, and had made an informal approach to O'Riordain to seek his views. But no way could I at that stage have re-joined his party. I felt that the politicisation process among the republicans had been started, had momentum, and needed to be completed as far as possible. I had no inkling of the impending Provisional threat. Mac Stiofain was playing his cards close. Although critical of Greaves, especially his hard-line Czech attitude, in line with that of O'Riordain, I felt I needed to keep up the contact. There were signs of internal reform within the 'international movement'; I had not totally written it off. Maybe if the politicised left-republican project succeeded, there would be a place for it in a reconstructed international movement, without the heavy centralist hand of Moscow, then dominated by the so-called 'Brezhnev doctrine' which justified intervention.

We may have on December 10 in the Greaves Diaries the beginnings of doubts about the integrity of the USSR-dominated 'international movement'; he recorded a conversation in CPGB circles about a 'spontaneous' meeting in Moscow in support of some proposal, with the result appearing in print within a few hours: obviously a 'put-up job'. He went on to note the opinion of a Hungarian, to the effect that differences between 'socialist' countries arose from competition for the West German market. The Czechs with their reforms would have been well positioned to improve their market share. CDG concludes '...I did not feel that this was an adequate explanation for the gigantic sledgehammer taken to this nut ...'.

In Dublin on December 13 1968 Greaves recorded seeing Seán Nolan and lunching with Anthony Coughlan, without comment. The next day he showed up at the IWP Christmas bazaar, where he discussed the Czech situation with Carmody: '...there is nothing for us in an anti-Soviet campaign ...'. Carmody agreed. CDG also encountered the remains of the IWL group who had been so destructive of the CA a decade previously (see Note 35, Chapter 6).. Carmody wanted to talk with them, expressing sympathy with Pat O'Neill who had been 'crucified' while in the Electrical Trades Union. CDG: '...the "crucifixion" consisted of touring England in a motor-car posting bogus election papers for Haxell. It would be impossible to have the slightest sympathy for anybody involved in that discreditable operation ...'.

The evidence of the deep-rooted corruption of the USSR-dominated 'international movement', extending right down to the membership and practice of its component member-parties, as observed at first hand by CDG, was visibly accumulating. Carmody was apparently prepared to defend O'Neill's actions even in 1968. The role of Greaves in the Irish context was consistently to focus on 'civil rights in Northern Ireland' as the essential next step, and to try with fact-based Marxist rationality to reduce the impact of ideology-driven ignorance, whether from the Stalinism of the international movement or from the Fenian adventurism of the republican political culture.

Greaves also recorded a meeting on December 16: '...some kind of Wolfe Tone Society caucus.. which had not been properly convened... this was the plot, revealed by Ó Loingsigh after complaints that the IRA took every major policy decision themselves without consulting the Wolfe Tone. Mac Eoin added that he did not think anything of Sinn Fein either. The decision in question related to Mid-Ulster ...'. It emerged that Tom Mitchell resigning from Sinn Fein to take his seat, and inviting Conor Cruise O'Brien, were considered as options preferable to Austin Currie. Greaves disapproved of both.

I recollect various discussions along these lines. I was never happy with the antagonism to Currie, which was based on traditional republican distrust of the nationalist Party. In the end we were usurped by Bernadette Devlin, who succeeded, and fuelled the anarchist fringe. The incubus was of course abstentionism. We were still stuck with this, though we were working on it via the 'Garland Commission'. The frustration was palpable.

At the Coiste Seasta (CS) meeting on 11/11/1968 there was a complaint from Donegal that they had had no contact with the Ulster organiser. This was an indication of residual grassroots opposition to the leadership's de facto recognition of the anomalous political position in the 6 Counties. The Ulster organiser was concentrating on Northern Ireland where the problem was. There was a decision to issue a statement on Civil Rights in response to the remarks of Neil Blaney, the Donegal Fianna Fail TD. *The first explicit linking of Civil Rights to the national question came from Blaney, and this was rightly regarded as counter-productive, an assertion of Catholic-nationalist irredentism.* The Dublin Housing Action Committee was seeking for SF to affiliate and it was agreed to do so. The DHAC was a broad-based group. Earlier references seemed to indicate that SF members outside Dublin thought it was a SF-owned body. Sinn Fein was going through a process of learning how to deal with bodies which it did not own, the NICRA being a key contributor to this learning process.

At the CS on 18/11/68 the idea of civil disobedience in the North was discussed. It was agreed to urge the Wolfe Tone Society to look into how best to set up some sort of civil rights movement in the 26 Counties(25). The Ard Comhairle meeting followed on 23/11/68. On the face of it, the leadership group seemed strong enough to have recommended constitutional change to the Ard Fheis, but for some over-cautious reason at the previous meeting on October 26 they had hesitated. Costello, on the Minutes, objected to the record of the final resolution on October 26, claiming it had been put to the meeting and passed. He was over-ruled, and Costello wanted his objection recorded. The resolution had been passed for submission to the Ard Fheis, but not with the AC recommending it, which Costello had wanted.

Malachi McGurran, reporting from the North, was critical of the proposed O'Neill reforms; one man one vote and repeal of Special Powers not yet in sight. The central NICRA body was regarded as lacking in initiative. It would be necessary for the Republican Clubs to get PROs and make contact with local press, radio and TV. A march was planned for Armagh on November 30, and this was on Republican Clubs' initiative. It would be necessary to get the clubs to set up local broad-based CR committees.

Costello wanted the Wolfe Tone Society to press for a Civil Rights conference in the 26 Counties, to focus on the Offences against the State Act, and the Criminal Justice Bill. *The perception here, from the 'militarist wing' as embodied in Costello, is of the WTS as a tool, to be told what to do. In fact it was not like this; the WTS took its own initiatives, but tended to defer to Goulding's suggestions when these occurred. Costello, in fact, was a contradictory character, who wanted to get rapidly into front-line politics, from his local power-base in Bray, and was prepared to use the military command-structure to help him do so. This became evident at the next meeting . MR is supportive of this assessment.*

There were organisers' reports from Mick Ryan (Leinster) and Bartley Madden (Munster), no details given. Paddy Kilcullen reported that there were now 5 cumainn in Mayo and 4 in Sligo. The Ard Fheis was confirmed for December 8; the Workers Party, Connolly Youth, Gaelic League and Misneach were to be invited to send observers. Misneach was a radical language movement, associated with Máirtín

Ó Cadhain. There was a clear perception of an emerging broad left, with a cultural dimension.

The Ard Fheis (1968) in the Ó Liathain Hall

The last Coiste Seasta before the 1968 Ard Fheis took place in the Ó Liathain Hall on 02/12/68. Tomás MacGiolla, RJ, Walter Lynch, Seán Garland, Tony Ruane, Seamus Costello, Máirín de Burca were there. There was support for the Irish Voice on Vietnam. It was agreed to discourage the Tenants Organisations from entering the election. The public sector of the Ard Fheis should be dedicated to Civil Rights in the North, the Criminal Justice Bill and the Anglo-Irish Free Trade Agreement. I had declared my intention of not going forward for the Ard Comhairle, preferring to concentrate on the Wolfe Tone Society and research. Costello urged me to go for the AC but to step back from the CS, which in the end it seems is what I did.

The voting analysis sheet for the 1968 Ard Fheis, and most of the relevant records, have become available, and my name is not on it. Yet I am on record as having attended subsequent meetings. So I must have been, in effect, co-opted. There were press reports to the effect that I had been 'defeated', and I have a copy of a letter I wrote dated 9/12/68 to the effect that for personal reasons I did not stand for elections, despite considerable pressure. I was consciously trying to pull back from a leading position, although in the event, in effect, I was not allowed to do so. The results in order of preference were Goulding 109, Costello 94, Seán Garland 78, Máirín de Burca 70, Seán Mac Stiofain 67, Larry Grogan 61, Derry Kelleher 61, Éamonn Mac Thomáis 60, Tony Ruane 58, Joe Clarke 58, Seán Ó Brádaigh 55, Frank McGlade 53, Parry Kilcullen 53, Mick Ryan 49, Seán White 49, Des Cox 46, Malachy McGurran 45, Marcus Fogarty 45... etc. This gives a good measure of how a vote on a serious constitutional amendment would have gone. They would have been just short of their 2/3 majority. Someone must have done a head-count, and the Garland Commission fallback procedure was adopted.

In the 1968 Ard Fheis the general political flavour was positive and forward-looking; most if not all of the politically progressive motions were carried, and the 'sea-green incorruptible' ones rejected. Tomás Mac Giolla's presidential speech exuded optimism as a result of the Civil Rights events at Derry and Armagh which had exposed the ugly face of Orange hegemony embedded in the State machine; he went on to refer to the east-west economic partition of the country, and to invoke James Connolly, drawing attention to the fact that the year was the centenary of his birth.

The Constitutional motions were however referred to the Commission. The key one which they had hoped to pass was No 17: '...to contest all elections, and allow its elected members to take their seats in Leinster House...'. This was proposed jointly by 5 cumainn, including Pearse (Rathmines), Connolly (Arklow), and the Belfast and Donegal Comhairle Ceanntair. Similar motions were tabled from Galway, Limerick and Glencolumcille. None however addressed the question of Westminster, despite the looming by-election in Mid-Ulster.

I have the impression that perhaps again Costello fouled things up(26) by trying too hard, issuing voting instructions on bits of paper to the 'army' people who were present. This was again picked up and queried, poisoning the atmosphere. In the end the motion was not put, due to fear of it being defeated in the aftermath of the Costello attempt to rig it.

Instead Seán Garland proposed an amendment that a Commission be set up to go into the question in detail, holding meetings all over the country, and report to a special Ard Fheis. This was the origin of the 'Garland Commission'; it was an attempt to rescue the movement from the day's failed attempt to legalise political participation.

The failure to reform Sinn Fein in the direction of acceptance of political participation in the Dáil and Westminster, at the 1968 Ard Fheis, had disastrous consequences. The incoming Ard Comhairle had a substantial majority of politicisers, on my reckoning 16 to 7. It was immediately faced with the mid-Ulster by-election, which was winnable, and had in the past been won by Tom Mitchell. However its hands were tied, and it had to resort to all sorts of devices and intrigues to find an 'agreed candidate' who could pull Republican support.

In the end Bernadette Devlin won the seat, enhancing the adventurous and inexperienced ultra-leftist trend which had emerged via the Peoples Democracy (PD) movement among the Queens students. This tended to look to Paris; they thought the socialist revolution was round the corner. They did not defer to the broad-based NICRA, which in December 1968 called off all marches, to allow time for O'Neill to deliver, and a breathing-space to organise properly on a regional basis, preserving the cross-community focus on civil rights issues, with trade union, tenant association and other community group links where feasible.

Instead the PD marched from Belfast to Derry, through a series of small Protestant Antrim towns, leading eventually to the ambush at Burntollet, where they were clobbered by the Orange heavies. This coat-trailing exercise was disastrously counter-productive. It certainly exposed the true face of Orange thuggery, but were we not already well aware of this? It helped reduce Civil Rights to a Catholic ghetto movement, and made it difficult for Protestant trade-unionists to rally in support of local government electoral rights ('one man one vote'). After Burntollet, Civil Rights became a crypto-Nationalist issue.

1968 Ard Fheis Aftermath

The first post-Ard Fheis Ard Comhairle took place on December 22 1968. It analyses into the following composition:

Left-republican politicising core: Cathal Goulding, Tomás Mac Giolla, the present writer, Seán Garland, Seamus Costello, Tom Mitchell...

In what capacity was I there? I must have been co-opted, and agreed to serve, given the stresses of the developing situation, despite my desire to pull back, and my precarious employment situation.

Active followers of this trend, who had been engaging in socio-political actions in various parts of the country: Seamus Rhatigan, Máirín de Burca and Gabriel McLoughlin in Dublin; Paddy Callaghan in Kerry, Derry Kelleher in Wicklow...

A strong Northern contingent associated with the emerging Civil Rights politicisation: Tom O'Connor, Dennis Cassin, Liam Cummins, Des Long, Malachi McGurran, Kevin Agnew..

Marcus Fogarty: at present I can't place him. Mick Ryan suggests he may have been a subsequent Provisional supporter from Cashel, though his subsequent voting record does not support this.

A group who subsequently supported the provisional split: Tony Ruane, Seán Mac Stiofain, Joe Clarke, Seán Ó Brádaigh, Larry Grogan and Éamonn Mac Thomáis.

Joe Clarke, the old-timer who had defended Mount St Bridge in 1916, from this time on felt he had to use his Vice-President status to attend not only the Ard Comhairle meeting but also the Coiste Seasta meetings. He was resolutely opposed to any practical politics and a dedicated worshipper of the Holy Grail of the abstract Republic 'as by law established'. His role was an additional and unwelcome brake on the politicisation process.

Kevin Agnew was a solicitor in Maghera; many of the key meetings had taken place in his house. He had been Tom Mitchell's election agent.

Larry Grogan was another old-timer, who had been active in the 30s; also judged by MR to be very conservative. Mac Stiofain was primarily a military man; he had been invoked in the Sinn Fein context earlier by Gerry McCarthy, as a conscious right-wing militarist counter to the Goulding left-wing political trend. He subsequently became Chief of Staff of the Provisionals. His English accent and background was rendered acceptable in some quarters by doctrinaire insistence on the use of Irish on all possible occasions.

This was the AC which had to steer the Movement through its most difficult period. The minority which subsequently became the core of the Provisionals was vocal and influential. Its first task was to address the Mid-Ulster election question. There had been planned a Convention in Cookstown on the next day (Dec 23) to select a candidate. The northern consensus was that if an abstentionist candidate was selected, there would be no Movement within a month. Names of possible 'agreed candidates' came up: Fred Heatley and Frank Gogarty, both of whom had NICRA public standing.

Éamonn Mac Thomáis, true to form, wanted Tom Mitchell to stand as an abstentionist candidate. The Dublin 'sea-green incorruptible' had learned nothing from the NICRA and Republican Club experience.

Seamus Costello proposed a special Ard Fheis to decide on abstention, thus pre-empting the Garland Commission. Derry Kelleher and Paddy Callaghan supported this. Both were active in local politics, the former in Greystones and the latter involved in Killorglin where he had pioneered a shell-fish production and marketing co-operative.

After a long discussion, it was proposed by Seán Garland and seconded by the present writer that 'after the Convention in Cookstown we issue a press statement to the effect that Convention had been held and election machinery set up, but that we were anxious to preserve the unity of anti-Unionist forces which had been demonstrated in the Civil Rights Campaign, and that we were prepared to meet other interested parties before announcing the name of the candidate and policy ...'. A sub-committee was set up to negotiate an agreed candidate with other groups. This consisted of Tom Mitchell, Cathal Goulding, Malachi McGurran, Liam McMillan, Tomás Mac Giolla, Francie Donnelly (South Derry) and Pat Coyle, plus the right to elect two others at Cookstown.

This was basically a Goulding IRA politicising group, with a nod in the direction of the Cookstown meeting. Billy McMillan was O/C Belfast.

This was put to the meeting. EMacT's amendment was defeated 5 to 13. The original proposal was carried 12 to 5. Costello then had another go at undoing his recent Ard Fheis blunder that had lost him his anti-abstentionist motion and led to the Garland Commission; seconded by Paddy Callaghan he proposed that if the Cookstown meeting asked for an extraordinary Ard Fheis to disown abstentionism, that this be done as soon as possible. This was lost by 7 to 12.

Implementing the Garland Commission Procedure

There were then steps taken to set up the 'Commission of 16', whose task it was to deal with the Garland amendment. The following names are on record as having been proposed for it: Tomás Mac Giolla, Seán Ó Brádaigh, Éamonn Mac Thomáis, Derry Kelleher, Paddy Callaghan, Dennis Cassin (identified by MR as 'ultra-left', now in the US), Tom O'Connor, Gabriel McLoughlin, Liam Cummins, Kevin Agnew, Seamus Costello, Brian Quinn, Malachy McGurran, Marcus Fogarty and Seamus Rhatigan.

Here some uncertainty develops. There are only 15 on this list. The minutes go on to say the 'eight were to be elected and the following were successful'. What I suspect this means is that this was an Ard Comhairle panel, with the other 8 being nominated by the Army Council.

An election took place, by secret ballot, and the following emerged as the Sinn Fein component: Tomás Mac Giolla, Seamus Costello, Seán Ó Brádaigh, Derry Kelleher, Liam Cummins, Paddy Callaghan, Dennis Cassin, Malachy McGurran. Of these all but 2 were IRA politicising activists, Goulding followers. Of the other two, one was a left-republican of long standing. The other was Seán Ó Brádaigh, and he resigned at the next meeting, being replaced by Seamus Rhatigan.

I have not yet tracked down who were the other 8 to make the 16; perhaps this will emerge in due course. The present writer must have been among them, as he undertook to prepare an agenda for the first meeting of the Commission scheduled for 05/01/69. It is appalling to contemplate in retrospect how the movement had 'shot itself in the foot', the consequence of Costello having tried to railroad the December 1967 Ard Fheis.

Here we had the Northern scene exploding politically, with a chance of an early election win, and an emerging Republican Club political machine, supportive of a mass civil rights movement which crossed sectarian barriers, involving Belfast trade unionist support. In this context we had had to dedicate our leading people to a laborious internal reform of the Sinn Fein Constitution, when they should have been steering the movement to hold the NICRA middle ground and prevent it being hijacked by ultra-leftist adventurism and Catholic ghetto-nationalism. The 1968 Ard Fheis was indeed the key turning-point where things began to go badly wrong.

In the January 1969 *United Irishman* I had a critical comment on the role of Conor Cruise O'Brien in the Labour Party: active branches were needed if socialist policies are to be developed; this was not helped by a cult of prominent individuals. Kevin Agnew was to stand in mid-Ulster, Currie was attacked as a spoiler. There was a 'Protestant view of Civil Rights'; there was a series on the 1939 IRA; Mac Giolla's Ard Fheis remarks on the 'crisis of capital' were reported; there was a note on the Goulding (fertiliser) empire. There was a reference to the Garland Commission which arose out of the 1968 Ard Fheis. Issues treated included Criminal Justice, Taca, Galway fisheries, Eoin Harris in RTE.

The SF Ard Comhairle met again on January 4 1969, primarily to elect officers. Vice-Presidents were Joe Clarke and Cathal Goulding. Secretaries were Mick Ryan and Máirín de Burca. Treasurers were Tony Ruane and Éamonn Mac Thomáis. Organiser was Seán Garland. Publicity was offered to Seán Ó Brádaigh but he declined. Finance was with Seán Mac Stiofáin. Education remained with the present writer. Local Government (linked with the labels 'agitation and economic resistance') was with Seamus Costello. Mick Ryan had to be co-opted, and this was done on the proposal of Joe Clarke seconded by Tony Ruane. On the Commission it was noted that Seán Ó Brádaigh had declined to act, and he was replaced by Seamus Rhatigan, so that the Ard Comhairle component of the Commission was totally composed Goulding-supporters.

It is evident that his proposers perceived Mick Ryan as being basically 'hard-core militarist', despite his energetic espousal of the politicisation process. It is perhaps worth noting that those who subsequently were associated with the Provisional split had homed in on the financial roles. Seán Ó Brádaigh was clearly distancing himself from the politicising process.

The Mid-Ulster Election and the NICRA AGM

On Mid-Ulster it was reported at the January 4 AC meeting that the Cookstown meeting had decided to contest with Kevin Agnew as abstentionist candidate, with a view to using him as a lever to get the type of agreed candidate they wanted; he would resign in favour of a suitable person. Austin Currie had been seeking the nomination, and he was regarded as unacceptable. The SDLP was not yet in existence.

Currie's credentials were based on his role in the Dungannon local authority housing scandal. The hostility of the Republican Clubs to his candidature was based on what to my mind was a mistaken identification of Currie with traditional sectarian Nationalist politics. He subsequently was an effective SDLP politician for many years, but in the end came south, and became a Fine Gael TD. He would have been a more effective and principled MP for Mid-Ulster than was Bernadette Devlin. So this rejection of Currie must be seen, in retrospect, as another key political blunder.

I have a copy of a paper from the NICRA dated January 5 1969 entitled 'Explanatory Memorandum on Proposed New Constitution'. A copy of the original

Constitution is associated with this. I must have received this in my capacity as a paid-up member. The main purport was to introduce the idea of a broad-based mass local membership, with a regional structure, represented on the central executive. Criticism of the earlier unrepresentative character of the latter body was being taken on board. The memo was signed by the outgoing executive members Kevin Agnew, John MaAnerney, Liam McMillan, Aidan Corrigan, John D Stewart, Malachi McGurran, Peter Cosgrove and Kevin Boyle. There is a note to the effect that LMcM was replacing Malachi McGurran, while the latter was in jail under the Special Powers Act for political work in support of the Republican Clubs.

During this time, it is noteworthy that Seán Mac Stiofain was left at large. Did the Special Branch perhaps know his role as Director of Military Intelligence, and tacitly approve of it, as the key to their 're-invent the IRA' strategy?

At the Jan 19 meeting of the Sinn Fein Standing Committee it was agreed to work for a full attendance at the AGM of the NICRA on February 15, and to get good radical people elected to the Executive. *This suggests that there was pressure from the republican activists to get rid of the broad-based moderates who had given the original Committee its strength: a drift into ultra-leftism.* Issues left for further discussion included the attitude to the new Derry Action Committee, Peoples Democracy and such; the emerging student left was perceived as being inexperienced and undisciplined. The general Civil Rights development strategy needed to be worked out; we needed more marches, and to keep them peaceful. In the background to all this we needed to establish a distinct Republican Club identity. *(Mick Ryan in 2001: 'Yes, but we didn't')*

Then on 27/01/69 a proposal for a march from Dundalk to Belfast was rejected, as being not in accordance with NICRA policy, this being to keep the issues related to civil rights in the North and to keep clear of any all-Ireland nationalist-looking dimension.

This tactically impeccable policy was viewed with total incomprehension by the 'sea-green incorruptibles', who felt themselves increasingly isolated, in a process with which they were politically at total variance. Catholic-nationalist irredentism, of the type pioneered in the current context by Blaney from Donegal, was closer to their way of thinking than was that of the current Ard Comhairle majority. The possibility of winning some middle-ground Protestant support for democratic reforms within Stormont, such as have now at last begun to be achieved under the Good Friday Agreement, and which were within reach in 1969 thanks to the NICRA, never occurred to them.

There was a letter from Limerick looking for a speaker from the Dublin Housing Action Committee to help set up a similar body in Limerick. No action was taken.

This again shows the then local 26-county republican grass-roots mind-set: the perception of the DHAC, and other such broad-based bodies, as being somehow Sinn Fein property, had continually to be countered. This was one of the roles of the 'educational conferences' which we organised from time to time; these promoted a vision of a bottom-up association of peoples' organisations, for which the Movement would help focus a political lead, helping them to formulate demands on Government for legislative change.

On Mid-Ulster: one Frank Morris *(according to MR he was from Convoy, Donegal; an ultra-right nationalist)* was seeking the nomination as the 'agreed candidate'. This did not meet with support. Seamus Costello and Malachi McGurran were to meet a potential 'agreed candidate', who was not named, but referred to as 'she'. Kevin Agnew was to hold an initial meeting. This was the first time Bernadette Devlin entered the arena. She was perceived, correctly, as being associated with the Peoples Democracy group, and therefore somewhat unpredictable.

The target was to ensure that the NICRA after its AGM would remain under republican 'control' (this word was used, and it reflected the perceived need) and would take initiatives.

Seán Ó Cionnaith, who now was organiser for Connaught, was to call a meeting to explain the meaning of the developing process of 'co-operation with radicals'. Máirín de Burca had urged the need for a 'labour-republican alliance' in a public statement and this had caused unease among some purists.

This would have been one of the series of educational conferences which were organised in the context of the Garland Commission. Regrettably I don't have a record of these in detail, though references crop up peripherally in various sources.

There is no record of the 1969 AGM of the Dublin WTS which apparently took place on January 24-26. There is however in the archive a record of some comments on the documentation by Uinsean Mac Eoin. There seems to have been a fairly comprehensive national development plan, covering housing, physical planning, the building industry, accommodation (ie rented flats etc), rents and purchase, land, finance, rural services, and regionalisation. It would seem that the document on which he was commenting was strongly regionalist, with a 9-region map.

The Wolfe Tone Society and the Sheelin Shamrock School

There is in the WTS archive a document which is undated, but seems to be an outline by the present writer of the concept that later led to the Sheelin Shamrock School. This was the makings of another high point in the process of convergence of the Left with the politicising left-republican movement. It took place in the autumn of 1969, and was an attempt to strengthen the analysis of the politicisation problem in the context of the work of the 'Garland Commission'. It is noteworthy that the document was not strictly a WTS document, more a 'republican movement' one, but at this time we were working hard to develop the broad inclusive 'National Liberation Movement' concept, in which I would have seen the WTS embedded. I give below an outline of this document, for what it is worth:

Topics included 'Ireland and the World' (Kader Asmal), 'The Irish revolutionary tradition and the lessons of history' (de Courcy Ireland); the class structure of Ireland today, the way forward and the 'radical alliance' concept, parliamentarism and the lessons of local government, trade unions and industrial democracy, democracy in a disciplined movement, civil disobedience, a critique of the Labour programme, the experience of the Stormont elections. A library of supportive documentation was specified, including the 'Commission documents'. Projected speakers included Coughlan, Asmal, Mac an Aili, Costello, Ó Riordáin, Roche, Noel Harris, Ó Tuathail, Mac Giolla, Goulding, Greaves as well as RJ. *This list looks aspirational, but in fact good coverage of the radical spectrum was obtained in the event, including O'Riordan, Asmal and de Courcy Ireland. Greaves around this time recorded receiving an invitation from the present writer, and was encouraged to accept by Micheál Ó'Riordan, but declined.*

The February *United Irishman* led with 'Civil Rights or Civil War'. Uinsean Mac Eoin wrote in objecting to the smear on Currie, but calling for the seat to be contested by a 'good Protestant to show the republican flag at Westminster' *(this would be representative of the progressive inclusivist views being promoted by the Dublin Wolfe Tone Society, of which UMacE was a stalwart supporter).* The 1939 IRA historical series continued. There was a further critical analysis by RJ of Labour Party policy; the latter ignored the North totally, except for a trivial remark about comparative Irish Sea transport costs. There was a call from Derry Civil Rights for the campaign to become civil disobedience; marching was not enough. The 'who owns Ireland' series continued with a look at Guinness. Topics included buying a house and the effects of land speculation, ground rents.

The call from Derry to escalate the campaign would perhaps be an indication of the influence of McCann and the PD, arising from the Burntollet events. The NICRA leadership at this time were increasingly concerned not to raise the pressure too rapidly, for fear of Orange backlash. There were increasing indications that this, if and when it occurred, would be spearheaded by the RUC and the B-Specials, as indeed it was in August.

There was a full meeting of the new Ard Comhairle, with its regional representatives under the revised Constitution, on Feb 10(27). Tomás Mac Giolla presided and the attendance included the present writer, Malachi McGurran, Dennis Cassin, Mick Ryan, Caoimhin Campbell* (from Mayo), Larry Grogan*, Seán MacStiofain*, Derry Kelleher, Joe Clarke*, Seamus Rhatigan, Paddy Callaghan, Tony Ruane*, Éamonn Mac Thomáis*, Seán Ó Brádaigh*, Máirín de Burca, Seán Gormley, Des Long*, Marcus Fogarty(?), CG, Gabriel McLoughlin, SG and SC. Of this group of 28 the 8 marked with * subsequently 'went Provisional'.

It is necessary to comment here that the 'Holy Grail' purist attitude to the abstract Republic could sometime be combined with a progressive attitude to local community development work, on co-operative principles. Caoimhin Campbell was representative of this trend; he and the Mayo republicans in the 50s had helped re-develop the co-operative movement among the farmers, in association with Seamus

Ó Mongain, Cathal Quinn and Ethna MacManus (who later married Michael Viney). I had used the experience of this group, with their philosophy which they had developed under the name 'Comhar na gGomharsan' (community of neighbours), in spreading the social-republican message elsewhere, in 'educational conference' mode. It came as a surprise to me that, despite their grass-roots practicality, the Mayo social-republican activists mostly supported the Provisionals. This basically contradictory position to my mind needs analysis and explanation.

At the Coiste Seasta meeting on 10/02/69 TMacG as usual presided; SMacS, TR, CG, MR, SC, SG and MdeB were there, as well as the present writer; Joe Clarke glowered at the proceedings, exuding disapproval, having painfully come up the stairs on his crutches. It was agreed to ask Mrs Dempsey to be Trustee. The editor of the *United Irishman* should sit in on meetings. SC and MMcG were still on the trail of the elusive Bernadette Devlin. A Tyrone meeting had shown little support for Tom O'Connor and some support for Austin Currie. Regarding the Peoples Democracy programme it was agreed to issue a statement of support '...with qualification on their outlook on Partition ...'. The *United Irishman* was urged to take up the question of the ESB maintenance strike, and TMacG agreed to put to the Wolfe Tone Society the idea of a 'joint committee'. This latter point was a reflection of an acceptance that Anthony Coughlan and the WTS were a key source of insight into the Civil Rights situation in the North.

Greaves on February 13 received a letter from the present writer wanting him to '...address a school for the republicans. They are on to prepare the way for taking seats in the Dáil. He said MOR was in favour of my going. But I told him that I thought it unwise to (work) in that particular garden, and anyway I was not free at the proposed time ...'.

This was the Sheelin Shamrock School, one of the series of educational conferences which were organised in the context of the Garland Commission. It took shape along the lines suggested in my earlier memorandum, quoted above.

Local Work in Rathmines

I have found among my own papers a copy of a press-release dated 19/02/1969 which arose from a routine meeting of the Pearse Cumann in the present writer's house. It reads as follows:

Second-Class Citizenship in the 26 Counties

Speaking at a meeting of Cumann Mac Piarais, Sinn Fein, Rathmines, the Rev EVC ('Ned') Watson, Rector of Rathmines parish (C of I) stated that there was a definite implication of preferential recognition for the Roman Catholic Church in Article 44 of the Constitution, and that this had legal effect in that the *Ne Temere* Decree was held to be binding in State law as well as Church law. The rigorous enforcement of the Ne Temere Decree was an important factor in the decline of the Protestant population, especially in rural areas.

Article 44 gave freedom of conscience subject to public order and morality; the latter came in effect under the jurisdiction of the RC Church due to the 'special position' of the latter.

Rev Watson criticised segregated education on the grounds that in applying for a job this provided a basis for discrimination. If he were living in the Six Counties today he would not with clear conscience advocate Irish unity subject to the 1937 Constitution.

Arising from Rev Watson's remarks, Mr George Gilmore stated that when de Valera drafted the 1937 Constitution it was worse, but it was improved on by some of the more republican elements of the Fianna Fail cabinet. Dorothy MacArdle, the historian of the Republic and till then an admirer of de Valera, broke with him on that issue. Mr Gilmore expressed surprise that there had been no response from the C of I leaders to the opportunity presented by the All-Party Commission, and at the cold response of the latter to the letter in the press from Professors Johnston and Luce. He suspected that the Church leadership was essentially conservative and realised that the present sectarian set-up was a good defence of property against radical thought.

Dr Roy Johnston, Chairman of the Cumann, presided.

The foregoing constitutes additional evidence of my attempt to re-assert the traditional inclusive non-sectarian republican political position, in the developing situation. I knew Ned Watson, though I did not attend his Church, having dropped out in the 1940s. He had been the scout-master in 1939 in Avoca School Blackrock, on the occasion when Erskine B Childers and I staged our protest against the use of 'God Save the King'. He had, I think, addressed the Cumann on an earlier occasion, at my request, and on this occasion took up the opportunity for an encounter with George Gilmore. A decade later, when he heard that Janice and I had joined the Quakers, his comment was 'God moves in a mysterious way'!

The NICRA, the PD and Republican Politics

Greaves in his diary in Belfast on February 26 1969 noted that he had met McAnerny the NICRA secretary who filled him in on how the student movement was being taken over by 'manipulators' who are no longer students themselves. '...A carefully packed meeting, poorly attended by the ordinary members, was called, and the candidates went up... The "manipulators" will not allow properly constituted committees of officers. The world and his wife can come in... these "scuts" as McAnerny calls them are trying to oust Betty Sinclair from the chairmanship of the NICRA. The Derry pair, Hume and Cooper, disaffiliated from the NICRA so as to be able to pursue their political ambitions ...'. He then went into the origins of Hume and his role in ousting McAteer. CDG went on: '...McAnerny is not a republican. He is not even anti-partitionist. He wants to remain with the UK and continue to receive British subsidies. But he is a level-headed rational small businessman, very solid, sociable and broad-minded. He has no objection to the students preaching "Trotskyist communism" but objects to its being done under his banner...'. Later he saw Hughie Moore who predicted Betty was in for a tough time.

The March *United Irishman* focused on Civil Rights for the South, Dáil repressive legislation etc. RJ continued his critique of Labour policy. Tactics were outlined for stewards at demonstrations. The Galway fish-in was reported. There was a feature on the Independent Orange Order and Lindsay Crawford.

It is a not unreasonable conjecture that because of the Joe Clark and Seán MacStiofain presence, Cathal Goulding tended to absent himself, and take key decisions elsewhere, reviving the old 'HQ staff' procedure. This if true reflected another negative consequence of the 1968 Ard Fheis indecision, and the 'Garland Commission' fudge. If the constitutional amendment had gone through, and the core Provisional group had walked out in December 1968, they would not have had the August 1969 events initially to fuel their renascent militarism. With a unified political-republican leadership, the NICRA would have held the middle ground, and perhaps August 1969 would have passed off without an armed Orange pogrom. Mid-Ulster could have been won by a politicising left-republican, holding out a hand of friendship to the Protestant working-class, in the Wolfe Tone tradition, and the anarchist ultra-left would have been contained. This was the vision we had been playing for, and we were close to achieving it.

The perpetrator of the debacle, Seamus Costello, in a subsequent split founded the 'Irish Republican Socialist Party' (IRSP) and the 'Irish National Liberation Army' (INLA) which had a destructive record of splinter-group activity over the years, including the Airy Neave assassination in the House of Commons. Bernadette Devlin was associated with the IRSP. Costello himself was assassinated, under circumstances as yet unexplained. The 'INLA' has since descended into drug-dealing and criminal-fringe activities.

On the whole the 1969 leadership of the movement was not in a healthy state, and our failure was inevitable. I hope this record will help people to learn something of the futility of military structures in politics, and of the difficulty of getting rid of them once they become embedded in the culture. I must admit that at the time I had totally under-estimated the cultural strength of the IRB military conspiratorial tradition, although open democratic-Marxist politicisation was nominally on top of the agenda.

Returning now to the March 3 1969 SF CS meeting: there was trouble at the Dun Laoire cumann (Joe Nolan); this was an indication of proto-Provisional rumblings. The meeting planned for Feb 28 had been postponed perhaps to Derry on March 16, or (preferably) in Monaghan on 23rd. Breasail Ó Caollai was appointed organiser for West Ulster *(to keep the Donegal activists happy and in the picture; BOC was the brother of Maolseachlainn Ó Caollai who headed the Gaelic League; BOC subsequently became an influential journalist and special-interest magazine entrepreneur)*.TMacG reported that the first meeting of 'Citizens for Civil Liberty' had taken place, consequent on the WTS initiative.

Greaves in his diary noted that, after some contacting of historical sources, on March 4 he arrived back at Cathal MacLiam's to find '...C(athal) G(oulding), S(eamus) C(ostello) and another republican drinking with Tony... there was a great argument. I find them personally very modest but politically very arrogant. I was trying to head them off this move that is being planned for creating a breakdown of law and order that will compel England to abolish Stormont. "But that would be no harm" says CG "it would show it is Britain's responsibility". I had great difficulty in persuading him that this was now admitted (and) we must move on to the next stage - working out a policy. I don't know whether much was agreed, but they will think over what has been said, and, what I forgot to say at the start, they had come up so as to find out my views on matters in general ...'.

On March 6 Greaves recorded Anthony Coughlan's opinion that CG was no longer Chief, and that younger men in their thirties, SC and Mick Ryan '...are prepared to depart even further from traditional practices ...'. Later he saw Asmal and Ron Lindsay; the latter had been writing for the *United Irishman*, opposing the 'breakdown of law and order to invoke British intervention' theory, and AC had been composing draft editorials to this effect, but Ó Tuathail had cut it. '...This is just what annoys me about the position where AC and RHJ work for the UI instead of the *Irish Socialist*, providing the republicans with a socialist screen which they discard when it suits them... one never gets thanks for helping people like this ...'.

If AC and RJ had confined themselves to 'working for the Irish Socialist' there would never have been a Wolfe Tone Society or a Civil Rights movement in the North. However CDG had a point; there was indeed a cultural gap between the socialist and republican traditions, and in some situations this could be destructive.

In New Books later on March 8 CDG picked up from Seán Nolan that '...the development in Belfast is about as bad as could be.. Betty Sinclair had gone up for the chairmanship of NICRA and received only two votes. One of the PD people got it *(Frank Gogarty)* and the vice-chairman is Vincent McDowell, who doesn't even live in the six counties, but in Dublin! The republicans voted against Betty. I was talking to MOR about this....' It seems that MOR had been on to CG and had been reassured that the republicans would support Betty; in fact it had the status of an "order", but they disobeyed...'.

This was the crunch issue; Betty would have helped keep the NICRA on a constitutional path avoiding adventurism; the new leadership represented a move towards the 'abolition of Stormont via breakdown of law and order' policy. The republican vote was crucial, and indicated that the Republican Clubs where perhaps increasingly following the policies being promoted by Mac Stiofain, with armed insurrection in mind. The chain of command emanating from the Dublin politicisers no longer worked.

Evidence of contemporaries however, picked up retrospectively in January 2002, suggests that Betty being voted down was in response to her actual performance; she had been increasingly unreliable due to the influence of drink. He went on to suggest that she had probably been over-optimistic in her earlier conversations with Greaves regarding the existence of her diaries, perhaps with the intent of keeping records, but never getting round to it. So the influence of Mac Stiofain, while real, might not at this point have been decisive. The failure of the CPNI to give consistent support to Betty in her NICRA situation would have increased the stress on her situation, and made the drink problem more acute.

At the SF CS 11/03/69 the Pearse Cumann (of which the present writer was a member) was calling for the Dublin Comhairle Ceanntar to meet monthly instead of quarterly, thus increasing the political awareness of the Dublin movement as such. A national consultation conference on Civil Rights in Northern Ireland was called for London on March 23. This was the Connolly Association taking the initiative in support of the developing situation. Mick Ryan and the present writer were to go, and Clann na h-Eireann in London were to send 2 delegates. The barriers between the left labour movement activists in Britain and Sinn Fein were by now nearly completely broken down. On Mid-Ulster: TMacG reported that Bernadette Devlin had again declined to stand as a 'republican agreed candidate'; a meeting was planned for Carrickmore. Republican Club members were to attend in their personal capacities, and a statement was to be issued to the effect that 'we had not been invited and were not taking part'.

Thus BD got nominated, basically with PD activist support, filling the vacuum left by persistent Republican abstentionism. Her subsequent success pumped up the anarchist ultra-left beyond their capacity to deliver.

Greaves, back in London on March 19 1969, recorded a phone-call from Noel Harris, a leading NICRA member at the time, over on union business, who confirmed that the Belfast situation was due to the failure of Andy Barr and the others in the Party to back up Betty Sinclair, with which CDG agreed. On March 23 the CA conference took place; it seems I attended it, in the company of Pat Ó Suilleabhain from the Clann. I gave out that I was coming as the latter's guest, but according to CDG he picked up from other sources that I had sought out POS and brought him along. There was a 'dissident United Ireland Association (UIA)' presence. Afterwards Joe Deighan, who had been to Belfast, filled in CDG about the NICRA scene: Gogarty on amphetamines, and various 'Peoples Democracy' lunacies. Also '...this woman the republicans are trying to push instead of Currie is somewhat unstable to put it mildly...'.

I am on record as having attended the above London meeting; there had been 130 present, from 61 organisations, and a committee was to be formed. The Clann people attended, and I had attended a Clann meeting afterwards; there had been about 15 present; organisation was poor, and they had a lack of sense of direction.

At the Sinn Fein Coiste Seasta on 24/03/69 for once we did not have the glowering presence of Joe Clarke, who no doubt reported every move to the proto-Provisional core-group waiting in the wings. A meeting was planned for March 14 for the organisers, to deal with the expanding of the *United Irishman* circulation(28).

Regarding the NICRA, a meeting was planned with 'interested parties' to discuss the resignations from the NICRA Executive. The AGM had taken place, and it looked as if a railroading job had been done, somewhat heavy-handedly, with the result that some middle-ground, and perhaps Protestant, leading members had felt squeezed out.

The 'interested parties' would undoubtedly have been the Communist Party trade union activists, on whom we depended for the preservation of the fragile cross-community composition of the NICRA executive.

On Mid-Ulster it was agreed to withdraw from the election and say nothing. Republican activists on the ground would have supported BD with heavy heart and a sense of frustration; a classic opportunity missed.

In the April *United Irishman* it was noted that 1000 B-Specials were called up arising from the Castlereagh explosion, which turned out to have been an RUC special branch job, a provocation to justify the existence of the B-Specials. The IRA claimed a role in a Meath land dispute. There was a critical analysis of how the PD worked which exposed the fact that it had no consistent membership, election or policy development procedures; it was all done ad-hoc with whoever happened to be there. Michael Farrell and Kevin Boyle were elected to the NICRA executive, and as a result some of the older leadership, who had been counselling caution, resigned; these were Kevin McAnerney, Fred Heatley, Betty Sinclair and Ray Shearer. There was a survey of County Cavan; there was an article on policy regarding foreign fishing-boats; notes on agriculture policy and small-farmer co-operation; the Poacher's Guide; in the 'Who Owns Ireland' series the Building Societies were treated.

Note the tendency for the IRA to give itself a quasi-political role; this was a source of tension between the present writer and Goulding; it interfered with the programme of subsuming all political activity into an activated and disciplined Sinn Fein. But Goulding, feeling the pressure from Mac Stiofain and co, felt he had to 'keep the lads happy' with quasi-military activity having a political flavour; this was an ongoing and increasingly intense internal contradiction in the republican politicisation process.

A general meeting of the Dublin WTS in 24 Belgrave Road (Mac Liam's) on April 15 1969 had Kader Asmal speaking on Trade Union Law. Seán Cronin's pamphlet on *The Rights of Man in Ireland* had been published by the *United Irishman*. Associated with Anthony Coughlan's circular for this is an m/s letter from me to AC as input to the WTS meeting; I would be late, due to a Trades Council meeting. *At this time I represented the Aviation Branch of the Workers Union of Ireland on the Dublin Trades Council.* The 'RTE affair' was on the agenda. *This had to do with the resignation of Lelia Doolan, Jack Dowling and Bob Quinn, as outlined in their book 'Sit Down and be Counted'.* I urged attempting to get together a group of radical media people to tease out the implications of this, perhaps via a symposium on 'Democracy and the Mass Media'. I included Jim Fitzgerald and Eoghan Harris in the list of target people. I also urged that a 'witty' article on the 'Twelfth of July' be developed, for suitably timed publication, leaning on the Brendan Behan angle, 'to torpedo the Dungiven events'. Call for the parades to be welcomed, and supported with fiddlers and pipers. We need also a civil rights demo in Sandy Row. *(This was a last-ditch attempt to de-fuse the threatening sectarian explosion).*

In connection with the 1969 elections in the South the WTS ran some meetings arranged by a 'voters advisory group' in various shopping centres in Dublin. Not much came of this; it was a gesture in the direction of broadening the experience of the movement in the context of the Garland Commission process.

With hindsight, and in overview, I am inclined to think that the Commission episode was a disastrous diversion, which prevented the attention of the politicising leadership from concentrating on the developing Northern situation, where it belonged. I recollect Anthony Coughlan remarking to this effect at the time, and being unable to escape from what was a procedural straitjacket. Mick Ryan is supportive of this assessment.

In the May *United Irishman* it was noted that Wilson had sent 500 extra troops to Northern Ireland. *This was presumably a response to the Castlereagh deception; the British had no intelligence of their own and depended on the Stormont Special Branch.* The Silent Valley event was covered, and identified as another loyalist provocation event (the B-Specials had blown up the Belfast water supply, and blamed it on a mythical IRA). The 1939 story continued. Fermanagh county was analysed, in the county series. There were reports of Easter statements: Derry Kelleher spoke in Dublin, Goulding at Burntollet, Seán Keenan in Derry.

Greaves on May 8 1969 noted a meeting of the 'NICRA' at the Irish Club, with the '...embassy-controlled United Ireland Association very much in evidence... the republicans are completely untrustworthy and cannot keep out of intrigue. Their connection with the Embassy is quite noticeable over a period...'.

This merits further investigation. I suspect this may have been an early indication of what later became a concerted Fianna Fail intrigue to take over the NICRA, rather than actually a republican initiative. I am surprised that CDG does not pick this up. A republican initiative involving the embassy in London is somewhat incredible.

The June UI was to be sold in the North, flouting the ban. It contained a Galway IRA claim of a land war action. The Palestine situation was analysed. There was an article 'Civil Rights: What Next?' *(from internal evidence this was probably from Anthony Coughlan; it talked of 'putting Westminster on the spot' and called for Westminster to legislate, under pressure from the Irish in Britain).* Kelleher began a series on ideologies. *This appeared subsequently as his 'Republicanism, Marxism and Christianity' pamphlet.* The Citizens for Civil Liberties was founded in Dublin. A new EEC threat was noted. RJ reviewed the Dorothy Robbie play about Constance Markiewicz, produced in Greystones. Housing Action demonstrations were reported.

Greaves visited Belfast on June 5 1969, and then went on down to Dublin. In Belfast he had met Betty Sinclair, who had been near a nervous breakdown: '...she felt naturally displeasure at Moore and Barr who showed no interest in her work, and they listened to ... McGlade's chatter passed through CG and MOR back to Belfast. She was surprised to have annoyed some of the republicans... she was also upset that MOR had not come to her first, and rightly so. She says she has kept a full diary of all the events in the past few months and it should be an interesting record. She criticises H(ughie) M(oore) and Stewart. They cut out of one of her articles a derogatory reference to Chinese policy because it might offend the young people who are pro-Chinese. They are boosting Peoples Democracy in their paper because it has certain support ...'.

Talking to O'Riordan on June 7 1969 Greaves picked up the Dublin version of the Betty Sinclair story; it seems she got drunk at a CPNI party and insulted some republicans who blew in. The Party dismissed her from the executive, and banned her from the paper. MOR disagreed with this. CDG: '...time we all grew up ...'. After some days, mostly in the national library, he encountered the present writer on June 14, it seems I told him of my 'impossible position'.... I was however optimistic about changing electoral policy.

The foregoing would appear to support the evaluation of Betty Sinclair's condition, reported earlier. It also indicates that cross-links between republicans and CPNI in Belfast were somewhat undeveloped. I had earlier tried to set these up, but apparently without success.

On June 18 1969, travelling to make contacts on the historical trail, CDG encountered one EC, who it seems was on the Limerick Comhairle Ceanntar of Sinn Fein, and was currently engaged in discussing '...RHJ's long document on revolution without the working class(29). Their whole conception is that of "taking over" the labour movement. No doubt it is with that in mind that CG and others consulted the CPNI on how to "work in the Trade Unions" ...'. *CDG went on with what I suspect could be an admission of his own doubts:* '...in these days when masses of people fear the irrevocability of communism, there are strange phenomena of attraction and recoil ...'.

At Bodenstown on June 22 1969 CDG encountered all the leading elements of the 'republican-left convergence', but couldn't refrain from commenting: '...Tom Gill made the "oration". It was full of socialism, but nowhere did the workers emancipate themselves... RHJ - socialism through the petit-bourgeoisie, and of course it is not socialism, at all ...'. Later he encountered Tom Redmond who was then in the process of setting up a branch of the IWP in Bray; Costello was trying to persuade them to "stand for physical force". This would imply acceptance of IRA hegemony.

Costello I had counted among the leaders of the politicisation process, yet according to this, of which I was unaware at the time, he was even then still steeped in the 'physical force as principle' culture, so derided by Connolly. I had hoped in the 'Garland Commission' process to replace this pathology with some sort of democratic political culture, based on class alliances and common interests.

This is a good break-point; in the next section I take up the narrative where pre-August tensions begin to emerge, and the situation then becomes dominated by the August 1969 crisis.

Notes and References

1. I have made JJ's unpublished work *Consumer Demand as the Basis of Credit* available in full in the hypertext. It is also accessible from the 1960s SSISI module, in which I give it an introductory overview.

2. This I have also abstracted in the hypertext; it is accessible via the 1960s Barrington module. JJ's attitude to EEC accession had been initially in favour of it, publishing a book *Why Ireland Needs the Common Market* (Mercier Press, Cork, 1962) and then later, in his final years, he was critical with articles and letters to the newspapers.

3. The details of this proposal, in which lurked the proverbial devil, are outlined in Donal McCartney's *UCD a National Idea* (Gill & Macmillan 1999) p314ff).

4. The *Irish Times* series *Science in Ireland* which ran on January 9-13 1967 arose as a result of the earlier CSTI experience. I have put it into context in the 1960s module of the 'science and society' thread of the hypertext.

5. I overview the 60s political process in such depth as I am able to do, primarily from my own papers of the time, and from the Wolfe Tone Society minutes which are, at least partially, in the Coughlan archive.

6. Correspondence about this Irish Socialist conference is in the WTS archive; a note from RJ mentioned that the Editor of the *United Irishman* was going, and that it was by invitation only; the emphasis was on Anglo-Irish relations and the EEC, and speakers were Desmond Greaves (representing the CPGB), Joe Deasy (IWP) and Andy Barr(CPNI).

7. This episode is described with great detail and humour in the Greaves diaries, which I have abstracted in one of the 1960s political modules of the hypertext.

8. Greaves Diaries 20/03/67. Regrettably the record of this episode from the SF side is missing, but it gets a mention in the Wolfe Tone record; Sinn Fein had after the 1966 Ard Fheis set up a Standing Committee to work between Ard Comhairle meetings, and did not get round to minuting it properly until the following June. It was clearly a seminal event. Yet its impact was already being undermined by Mac Stiofain, who claimed in his memoirs to have been organising the Northern IRA units from the angle of military intelligence, in a role given him by Goulding, at this time. The process was riven with contradictions.

9. Greaves Diaries 26/05/67. I have expanded on the detail of the Greaves visit in the integrated chronology module of the hypertext.

10. There are extensive notes in the WTS archive on this conference of the three Wolfe Tone Societies, by Noel Kavanagh the Dublin Secretary, and a list of the participants. I have abstracted these in the 'integrated chronology' module.

11. *The Computer in Society*, Brian Murphy, published at 12/6d in the Great Society series by Anthony Blond, 50 Doughty Street, London WC1. In the script I sent in I tried to put computing into the overall context of the history of technology, but the editor cut this introduction. In the hypertext version here I restore it.

12. I have discussed this substantively in a subsequent paper in Physics Today. I also made use of the experience for a seminar in the Irish Management Institute in 1968, and this is on record in the 1960s module of the socio-technical stream.

13. I have summarised the Cathcart thesis in the 1960s module of the academic stream of the hypertext.

14. According to Mick Ryan, Costello was court-marshalled and suspended for this. MR was O/C of Dublin at the time, and the Dublin Comhairle Ceanntar was actively political. Costello's voting instructions for elections to the AC it seems were Goulding and Costello plus about 10 straw men supporters of Costello. MR was not on Costello's list. For more detail on this Ard Fheis see the 1967 political module in the hypertext.

15. Mick Ryan, interviewed by the present writer in 2001, is inclined to agree with this. Given that a split was imminent, whoever controlled the timing of it has the advantage. This advantage was left to the Provisionals, who waited to vote at the 1969/70 Ard Fheis in Jury's Hotel, and then walked out, leaving the movement crippled politically for another year. Costello on this occasion wanted to force a walk-out before the vote, by suitably amending the standing orders, tactically a good move. The development of such a tactic in 1967 or 1968 however was prevented by mutual distrust between the key actors (Goulding, Garland, McGurran, Ryan and Costello). Mick Ryan around this time became organiser (IRA/SF) for Dublin and Leinster except Wicklow, the latter being left to Costello. In his memoir, published in 1998 in a commemorative *United Irishman'* issue produced in Belfast, he recounts how he had to struggle to get Cathal Goulding to understand the extent to which the organisation was moribund.

16. I was not present, but had submitted a memorandum to Anthony Coughlan. I was obviously attempting to develop a broad-based radical-democratic intellectual leadership of a national-democratic movement, at a time when the students were occupying, or were about to occupy, UCD.

17. It was noted that the Coiste Seasta had handled the correspondence, and there was a CS report, but we will have to await archive access for this, if it exists.

18. I have been able to identify a full version of this document, or perhaps a later adaptation of it, as published in *Nuacht Naisiunta*, the Sinn Fein internal newsletter, on April 27 1970. It is accessible in the integrated chronology in the hypertext.

19. It is in a folder containing a limited amount of 1967-68 Sinn Fein-related material, including correspondence with Derek Peters and Betty Sinclair about the NICRA and how to improve its relationship with the Republican Clubs, primarily regarding arrest without trial etc. It also includes letters from Anthony Coughlan on the abstention question, 'Definition of Socialism' material, draft recruiting leaflet material for the 26 and 6 counties, and miscellaneous correspondence relating to educational conferences etc. Box RJ5, RJ collection, Linen Hall Library, Belfast.

20. Mick Ryan has filled in that this meeting was in Andy McDonnell's house near Pallas; he agrees it was a turning point, being a recognition of the key role of the *United Irishman* as an organiser and purveyor of political ideas, on the Leninist principle. He expanded on this in his 1998 published memoir.

21. This misunderstanding on the part of Greaves is treated in more depth in the 1967 political module of the hypertext. Greaves had not grasped the extent to which the Irish Workers Party vision and mode of operation, rooted as it was in the by then totally corrupted and Moscow-dominated 'international movement', was a political cul-de-sac in the Irish context.

22. Mick Ryan adds some background to this. He had been chief marshal at Bodenstown. The CP had been there, and had wanted to carry a banner. This was a political decision, and MR referred it to CG, who was indecisive and referred it back to MR, who said OK carry it, whereupon Cumann na mBan refused to march.

23. I had been in Princeton at an AGIFORS meeting when the Derry events took place. I remember seeing the Derry events on TV in the US. The result was that I was not in on the 21/10/68 meeting. I get the impression from the record that the SF leadership was too obsessed with its internal reconstruction problem to appreciate the full significance of the developing Northern situation. I was at the 26/10/68 meeting, and had to go along with its priorities, as I had been in on the drafting process of the constitution.

24. Mick Ryan retrospectively regards choice of Bartley Madden for Munster as having been a disaster; he was quite unsuitable for the job, leaving Munster full of Provisional raw material, through lack of political impact.

25. This in the end happened; there emerged Citizens for Civil Liberties; we treat its foundation in the Wolfe Tone Society theme of the hypertext. Also, the possibility of inviting Conor Cruise O'Brien as a possible successor to Tom Mitchell as mid-Ulster candidate, which was discussed around this time, is confirmed in CCO'B's *Memoir: my Life and Themes*, Poolbeg, 1998.

26. Mick Ryan is uncertain whether this episode happened twice, or just once, with him wrongly attributing it to an earlier Ard Fheis. It could have happened at both 1967 and 1968 Ard Fheiseanna, or just at the first, when it was associated with the initiation of the 'steering committee' procedure.

27. This meeting dealt with the Ard Fheis resolutions, which in the minutes are referenced by number. We must await the archive access process before analysing this, but for the record I note that numbers 7, 14, 15, 16, 17, 18, 19, 20, 23, 35, 36, 37, 73 were referred to the 'Commission of 16'. Although I am on record as having attended, I have no recollection of this meeting. When I see the texts of the resolutions perhaps my memory will be stimulated.

28. The UI circulation, under Ó Tuathail's brilliant editorship and later under <u>Mick Ryan's management</u>, was becoming a significant success-story, and the movement needed to adapt to the increased demand for its ideas as expressed in the paper.

29. CDG's idea that somehow the vision which we projected 'excluded' the working class is difficult to explain, unless he was going on indications from the republican political culture seen in practice, in which case he undoubtedly had a point. The '<u>Commission Report</u>' embodied the vision, but the implementation of the vision would have had to pass through the filter of the republican political culture, which we had set out to change, but had grossly underestimated the size of the problem.

Chapter 7 Part 3: The Period mid-1969 to end-1970

I continue in this part to intersperse remaining JJ stuff. The mainstream of the RJ material is abstracted from the 'political' stream of the hypertext. I intersperse material from other streams chronologically where appropriate.

Pre-August Tensions

At the Sinn Fein Coiste Seasta meetings on 16-23-30/06/69 there were increasing echoes of the Barnes McCormack funeral, which was emerging as a source of tension. There was on June 30 talk of a 'civil rights split' emerging, in speeches in Strabane; sales of the *United Irishman* at NICRA events were taking place, strengthening the irrelevant and unwanted link between CR and the national question.

Meanwhile the Civil Rights movement in the North had got out an 'Ultimatum to Stormont' dated June 1969, in the form of a 4-page printed leaflet, listing the civil rights demand, and indicating the extent to which they had up to then in effect been blocked by Stormont. *This was a well-reasoned and devastating indictment, and constituted a good basis for developing the campaign on a broad base, and was a powerful counter to all talk of 'civil rights splits', which probably originated from hostile sources.*

The July *United Irishman* printed a letter from Betty Sinclair critical of the June 'Civil Rights' article, though on minor points, like the use of the word 'reformist'. The 'Belfast Letter' noted that an attempt to run a cross-community Connolly Commemoration was ghettoised. Farrell, McCann and Toman opposed the flying of the tricolour as being 'bourgeois'. Kelleher on ideology wrote about Teilhard de Chardin. Ó Caollai wrote about Connradh na Gaeilge. A fish-in article was headed 'Reconquest'. The Zambia situation was analysed. Mac Giolla's Bodenstown speech was given. We got the Barnes McCormack background story; this was part of the 1939 series. There was a call for the Orange parades to assume the status of folk festivals; it was noted that we too objected to Rome Rule and Article 44 of the Constitution.

There was no sense here of awareness of acute danger signals from Belfast. The present writer went to Belfast and observed the 1969 12th of July in Belfast at first hand; I enquired about the personalities depicted on the banners, and no-one knew who they were. I enquired 'why Finaghy' hoping to get some sense of history, but was told 'because the Orange Order owns the field'. I got talking afterwards to some who had walked, and they enthused about having gone to Dublin for the Horse Show, and met with Brendan Behan. There was no sense of impending pogrom, fuelled by any burning sense of political grievance at grass-roots. This reinforces my impression that the August pogrom was planned and engineered top-down by some ultra-'loyalist' core-group associated with the RUC and the B-Specials, continuing the momentum of the Silent Valley affair, with the objective of provoking the IRA into military confrontation.

At the Coiste Seasta on 07/07/69 there was a Cork letter (according to Mick Ryan from Jack Lynch, not the then Taoiseach, but the Cork republican old-timer) objecting to red flags at Bodenstown. It was agreed to promote the Plough and the Stars as the labour symbol. Cathal Goulding proposed that Jimmy Steele, who had given the Barnes and McCormack oration in Mullingar, be removed from the panel of republican speakers. MMcG reported policy of getting republican club people to steward Civil Rights marches, and prevent sectarian clashes developing.

Mick Ryan recollects (2001) attending an HQ meeting in or about July 1969, with Goulding, Garland, Ó Brádaigh, Mac Tomais; it was in Grogan's house. Ó Brádaigh asked Goulding had he a plan to defend the people in the event of a pogrom, of which he had picked up early warning signals. Goulding said 'yes' but not convincingly. Goulding's QM was one Pat Regan. On the day of the pogrom the latter was nowhere to be found, MR was appointed QM. Oliver McCaul was practically in tears for lack of weapons. Goulding had put total trust in the political process.

This poses important questions to historians. Who planned the pogrom, and at what level was it planned? It involved B-specials and armoured vehicles, and was implemented by agencies of the British state against defenceless people. Ó Brádaigh had advance warning of it. Was this a deliberate attempt on the part of the British State to provoke an armed response, so as to allow them use traditional repressive methods, internment etc? Was the leak to Ó Brádaigh and co deliberate? Ó Brádaigh in a recent (2001) conversation with the present writer insists that there was no leak, they were just reading the signs.

The political response to the pogrom would have been to let it run its course and turn all attention to getting the world media to report it, and thereby show up the nature of British rule; to get the democratic forces in Britain out on the streets; to get the Dublin government to get at the British and to complain to the UN, with US support. To go for guns was to do what the enemy wanted. We fell partially into the trap, falling between two stools; the Provisionals fell into it whole-heartedly, while we fell into it half-heartedly, but enough to divert our attention to issues like getting prisoners out, and rendering ourselves liable for internment when it came. Anthony Coughlan and I resolutely held out for a totally political response, but increasingly no-one was listening.

At the Sinn Fein Ard Comhairle on 19/07/69 the first three recommendations of the Commission Report(1) were considered.

The first recommendation was passed for submission as an Ard Fheis resolution by 10 votes to 8; this projected the vision of a broad-based movement, involving many organisations, political, economic, social and cultural, with the politicised SF playing a leading role. It was agreed not to name names, simply to project the concept in principle. Amendments from the proto-Provisional people present, which projected 'loose associations' and the banning of association with any other political groups, were rejected.

This illustrates the difference between the proto-Provisional approach, which had more in common with Fianna Fail and, indeed, Stalinism, with their aspirations to a one-party State, and on the other hand the emergent democratic-Marxist approach of the Goulding vision, with its aspiration to a broad-based multi-party national movement.

It was agreed unanimously to drop recommendations 2 and 3. *I don't as yet have on record what these were.*

Recommendation 4 was considered subsequently on August 23; this contained the policy on parliamentary participation, and was passed by 11 votes to 8, the names being recorded. It was hoped to call an extraordinary Ard Fheis shortly, to which a motion would be put, enshrining the proposals of the report as amended at these meetings.

The August 1969 Crisis

In the August *United Irishman* the main headline was 'The North Began'. *This was ambiguous, as it referred back to the IRB welcoming the Larne guns as a signal to arm.* There was a call from Derry for UN troops to defend them from the RUC and the B-Specials. McCann defended his attitude to the Tricolour. The Dublin Housing Action and the Ground Rent campaign were mentioned. The Barnes McCormack funeral was reported: *this was addressed by Jimmy Steele and amounted to a Provisional call to arms.* The Devenny death in Derry, consequent on the April RUC attack on people's houses was noted, increasing the tension. There was more about Zambia. Kelleher wrote on ideology. Neutrality and the EEC were treated, as was beach access at Brittas.

There was no sense of giving a lead to people, what they should do in the event of a pogrom, though the Derry call was the beginnings of what might have been a good policy. Goulding had had warnings of an impending pogrom from Ó Brádaigh and Mac Stiofáin. According to Ó Brádaigh he had told an all-Ireland meeting of OCs that it was up to the British to impose reforms on Stormont, including the disbanding of the Specials and the disarming of the RUC, which they would be forced to do if a pogrom was visibly started by the local Crown 'forces of law and order' and it was exposed and known to the world. Politically the Dublin Government should demand this, and call on the UN to intervene. This, if true, was an exact reflection of what Anthony Coughlan was saying at the time, as I recollect it. It was 'theoretically correct', but far from credible to the people on the ground who were at the receiving end of the pogrom, and needed guns to defend themselves and their houses.

Goulding had, apparently, bought (currently and in detail from Coughlan, and earlier in principle from the present writer and the Wolfe Tone Society) the essence of the Civil Rights political approach, but did not know how to motivate people to act upon it in the presence of a military-type threat from the 'loyalist' Establishment. It should have been possible to break through to the British Government, under Wilson who already was beginning to be aware of the RUC and B-Specials problem, in such a way as to pre-empt the pogrom. Why did this not happen?

At the Coiste Seasta on 11/08/69 it emerged that Bernadette was proving elusive. More organisers were appointed (this was rubber-stamping an 'army' decision process). TMacG reported on the Maghera meeting at which 70 or 80 had attended, but no-one from Derry. It was agreed that if there was trouble on the 12th, then a meeting on the 13th should demand that the State move in to defend the people.

There is ambiguity here: did they mean the British State? Or the Irish State? I seem to recollect that the former was intended, in accordance with the policy of separating out the civil rights issues from the national unity question. Haughey, Blaney and Boland later emerged as proponents of the latter course, and it is probable that this would have been the thinking of most republicans on the ground.

The next AC was fixed for August 30, and Anthony Coughlan was to be invited to the next CS meeting to discuss the NI civil rights situation and also the looming EEC issue.

On August 16 1969 Greaves phoned Jack Bennett in Belfast to get a report on the situation: '...he expressed the opinion that the IRA was operating in such a way as to bring about a breakdown of "law and order" so that British troops would be brought in ...'. *He echoed Goulding as evidenced in the arguments of March 4 noted above.* CDG went on: '...but you don't mean to say that they've risked raising this sectarian frenzy? ...'. JB, somewhat irritated, supposed they had, but it would '...break the deadlock ...'. CDG swore he would not go to see JB when next in Belfast.

This seems to support the hypothesis that the Northern IRA units had been re-organised as such, and were under the influence of Mac Stiofain, who wanted to provoke a military response, and that the trend into politicising via the Clubs had gone into reverse. On the other hand, JB could have been absorbing disinformation spread by those planning the pogrom. The lack of arms in Belfast seems to support the latter hypothesis.

On August 22 1969 Greaves arrived in Belfast; despite his earlier resolve he rang Jack Bennett, who '...had his bellyful of "breaking the deadlock" ...', but was helpful; they went to see Andy Barr: '...he was quite shaken..... I told him we intended to pursue the encouragement of reconciliation between the two religions. He said that perhaps he had gone too far in trying to keep open relations of co-operation with Protestants. The trouble was now that men he had known all his life would no longer talk politics with him. The events of the past few weeks had converted the moderates into bigots...'.

Later he saw Gerry Fitt, who described the desperation on the Falls Road and the demand for arms. He had rung Callaghan and got a secretary; finally he got through to the man himself, and soon afterwards the troops came in. Presumably Callaghan had consulted Wilson. Subsequently Callaghan promised to disarm the B-men, and assured Fitt that the reason he was not doing it at one blow was that the arms would then mysteriously disappear. Fitt was on top of the world, and quite convinced that what had happened was a result of a 'plan' that CDG and he had hatched in the car on the road between Liverpool and Manchester. The next step was to get the B-Specials to fire on the British troops. '...Between you and me that's being fixed up now...'.

I have looked back at this Greaves diary entry, which was on May 26 1968, and I can see no evidence of a 'plan' as such, but some evidence that Fitt was in a position to influence Wilson to be critical of the RUC and B-Special situation.

The same day he toured the Falls area with Jimmy Stewart, observing the barricades, and how they had defended themselves against the pogrom. There were 75,000 people behind the barricades. CDG concluded that '..this was no spontaneous pogrom, but a highly organised and well prepared attempt to drive the Catholics out of the city and set up a Paisleyite dictatorship to forestall the introduction of democratic rights ...'. He went on down to Dublin and observed the 'Solidarity' movement beginning to emerge from the general confusion.

The SF Ard Comhairle on 23/08/69 was called early, due to pressure of events. There were only 13 people there; CG, SMacS and MR sent apologies; MMcG and DC were absent in jail. I don't seem to have been present either. EMacT wanted recorded the names of those who had voted on Section 4 of the Commission document recorded. The situation outside was in crisis and this was all the 'sea-green incorruptibles' could think of.

Those for recommending at the Ard Fheis the abandonment of the constitutional ban on electoral participation were: Tomás Mac Giolla, Kevin Agnew, Seán Ó Gormaile, Derry Kelleher, Mick Ryan, Seamus Rattigan, M Fogarty, Seamus Costello, Denis Cassin, Cathal Goulding and Liam Cummins. Those against were: C Campbell, S Mac Stiofain, Tony Ruane, Joe Clarke, Des Long, Oliver McCaul, Éamonn Mac Thomáis and Máirín de Burca.

Those who rejected accessing the parliamentary process should be seen as unable in any parliamentary role to distinguish themselves from Fianna Fail. Those who accepted the parliamentary role were prepared to do so with a distinctive programme of legislation directed at democratising the ownership of productive property. The latter amounted to an emergent democratic-Marxist approach. The anomalous member of the second group is Máirín de Burca; she did not go 'Provisional', and is now, as she was then, a militant pacifist.

TMacG outlined the northern situation; we needed to maximise pressure on the Government; raise the issue at the UN; the Free State army was moving to the border. Our people were on the barricades, but we were not getting credit; we needed good TV and radio spokesmen. There had been no NICRA meetings since the 12th; conflicting statements were being issued.

In Dublin a 'Solidarity' committee had been set up, which included SF, LP, WTS, ITGWU, Dublin Trades Council and the GAA. It was important to keep the response political.

Yet in the background the response was being conceived in military terms; the old channels of influence and command structures were re-emerging.

The Sinn Fein Response to the August Crisis

At the Sinn Fein Coiste Seasta on 25/08/69 present were TMacG, Seamus Rattigan, Seamus Costello, Joe Clarke and Máirín de Burca. Arrangements were made for full-time office presence, M de B and SR being available. Eddie Williams was appointed full-time organiser for Munster. Anthony Coughlan was to be invited to attend a CS meeting, in the context of the emergent 'Federation' proposal and its perceived relationship to the Common Market.

The northern crisis was turning people's attention away from local political work all over. There was a civil administration emerging behind the barricades in Derry; this was real and effective; I had occasion to observe it in Derry the following weekend. I also met with Bernadette Devlin, and she had agreed to come to Dublin on September 13. The 'Federation' concept was beginning to be identified at this time, as a perceived 'political solution' by agreement between London and Dublin, in the context of both States joining the EEC.

In the September *United Irishman* the main headline was 'Blame Britain!' and the main political threat was seen as the Dublin government being manoeuvred into a 'federal solution' in which in effect they whole of Ireland would come back into the UK. Dublin was called upon to take a hard line with Westminster. The need for leadership in the 'defence enclaves' was recognised, and the slogan was 'defend the enclaves until Civil Rights is imposed on Stormont'. The Civil Rights demands were given as: one man one vote, end discrimination in jobs and houses, disarm and disband the Specials and disarm the RUC, abolish Special Powers, introduce Proportional Representation, and grant the right to secede and join the Republic should the people so decide.

Note that this is more or less what currently exists under the Good Friday Agreement.

The overall strategy was 'no direct rule, impose Civil Rights on Stormont, PR elections under UN supervision' and it looked as if the Coughlan influence was continuing. There was however an IRA statement published, signed by Goulding: the IRA was said to have been mobilised and was at the service of the defence committees; the Dublin Government should be prepared to use the Free State Army, and should seek UN Security Council support; there should be 32-county elections under UN supervision.

Mac Stiofain attributed this statement to the influence of Coughlan, I think mistakenly, and certainly for the wrong reasons. More likely it was Goulding attempting to hold the 'army' together, and give it a political role, though it had the negative effect of apparently justifying the RUC's world-view in which the IRA existed as a military threat, which view they had been feeding the British, fortified by events like the Silent Valley deception. They could say to the British, 'now you see, I told you so'. The fact that Goulding signed the statement himself however suggested political motivation; he wanted to reassure the defence committees that their immediate needs had not been forgotten, while keeping the overall thrust political and UN-oriented.

At the Coiste Seasta on 1/09/69 TMcG, RJ, JC, SRR, MdeB, Tony Ruane were present. A Federation statement had been issued by the Republican Clubs. The Coughlan meeting was long-fingered. The weekly newsletter was initiated. Seán Ó Cionnaith reported from Connaught that the effect of the Northern crisis had been to cause all local work to be abandoned. Local meetings to explain the political position were needed. TMcG reported from Derry; civil administration existed; RJ was to go there the following weekend; feasibility of worker-co-op initiatives against unemployment would be examined.

During the next period the SF minutes become unreliable; most of what happened was as a result of ad-hoc decisions made in a confused situation. The Ard-Fheis date was repeatedly postponed. Nuacht Naisiunta(2) becomes a useful source. My wife Janice Williams, who returned from Wales in August, found that the whole structure of Sinn Fein had changed, and was working in quasi-military mode, with people being expected to obey top-down orders. An all-Dublin meeting took place which was chaired by Seamus Costello.

The initiation of Nuacht Naisiunta was an indication of a realisation on the part of the leadership that they had a long way to go before the membership, all over Ireland, could be got to understand the unfolding events in the North in its complex political context, rather than in a simplistic irredentist military mode. It was, viewed in retrospect, a rearguard action against the Fianna Fail supported 'provisionalisation' process, which was aimed primarily against the role of political republicanism in exposing of the dependence of Fianna Fail on shady property deals and political corruption.

The first issue of *Nuacht Naisiunta* (NN) is undated, but it was probably around September 1 1969, and its content was related to the Callaghan visit. It contains:

- a statement from Frank Gogarty, the NICRA Chairman, backtracking from the misunderstood demand for 'direct rule from Westminster'; they wanted Westminster to intervene to clear up the mess and to impose reforms on Stormont;
- an admonition to the Irish Labour Party to drop the 'Direct Rule' demand;
- a call to the Trade Unions in the North to distance their members from what was identified explicitly as a genocidal attack;
- a call for support from the Arab nations;
- the text of a letter written to Home Secretary Callaghan which re-iterated the demands for the disarming and disbanding of the B-Specials and the disarming of the RUC, an amnesty for those who had defended their homes and manned the barricades, release of political prisoners, an end to the Special Powers Act, and the implementation of the basic demands of the NICRA: one man one vote, outlawing religious discrimination, impartial electoral boundaries, proportional representation etc. The letter was signed by James Gallagher, provisional secretary of the Republican Clubs Northern Executive; it also contained the demand that their existence should be legalised.

A Constitutional Convention?

I have an M/S copy of what seems to have been a draft for an internal newsletter, though I can't trace it in *Nuacht Naisiunta*. It must have been intended for internal 'army' distribution, though I suspect it may not have seen the light of day. It is however a good summary of my then thinking.

The draft paper admitted our being unprepared, but stressed that this puts us in a good political position; we were not part of a plot preparing an armed insurrection. The mobilisation order went out only after the people had turned to us in despair seeking physical defence. There was a huge response, but most had to be sent home, as it was impossible for people unfamiliar with the terrain to be militarily effective at short notice. Support eventually being given was under the control of local defence committees.

The main priority at the time was political: we needed to make the case for an all-Ireland solution, not a Council of Ireland, nor a repeat of the 1st Dáil, but some sort of peoples consultative convention on the Constitution, not yet practical politics, but we must make it so. '...It could be constructed from representatives of peoples' organisations; this would have the advantage that the 6-county Protestant workers would be represented through their trade unions, rather than through the MPs they elect, the latter having in the face of the world forfeited their right to rule ...'.

Recommendations from such a Convention might include abolition of the special role of the Catholic Church, and concessions to regional interests by decentralising government (the 'Eire Nua' concept). To lay the basis for such a Convention required that all Cumainn develop local links with the people's organisations, initially via the organisation of a relief fund, setting up local Solidarity Committees. Demands on the Dublin Government should include getting the issue regarded internationally as all-Ireland and not internal UK, active support for local defence committees against B-Special-organised pogroms, no obstacles to be placed in the way of direct peoples' aid channels to defence committees. Demands to be pressed within the peoples' organisations should be to channel aid within their all-Ireland networks eg via the trade union movement, involving Protestant workers, and to seek north-south exploratory meetings to explore the constitutional needs.

'..The more joint all-Ireland meetings occur within the framework of the peoples' organisations, the more "direct rule from Westminster" will be seen for the retrograde step that it is, and the easier it will be to call an all-Ireland Convention...'.

At the SF Coiste Seasta on 8/09/69 TMcG, JC, MdeB, SR, RJ were present. There had been a statement issued on Article 44 of the Constitution; one was in preparation on the Federation proposals. RJ complained that *Nuacht Naisiunta* (NN) had no number, date or address on it. This would be remedied from now on. RJ and Seamus Rattigan were to attend the Connolly Youth conference as observers. A Clann na h-Eireann recruiting leaflet was rejected as unsuitable.

All-Ireland Solidarity

The second issue of *Nuacht Naisiunta* is dated September 9 1969 and began with a call for financial support for the Bogside people, the contact being Mrs Dempsey at 44 Parnell Square. *This contact and location subsequently became 'Provisional'.* It was noted that the Defence Committee was in process of becoming a mini-government, and contacts were being established with similar bodies in Belfast; Malachi McBirney and Paddy Devlin had spoken to a Bogside meeting on behalf of the Belfast people.

Bernadette Devlin was admonished for going to the US without consultation, and for coming out with the 'direct rule' demand. The strategic options were discussed, 'direct rule' from either Dublin or London being dismissed, in favour of an 'interim arrangement in the national interest'.

The 'all-out war' concept, with intervention by Jack Lynch's Army, was dismissed as being at best liable to give a 29-county Free State, labelled the 'Fennell/Bunting Solution'(3). It was regarded as preferable to hold out with the 'mini-republics' until substantial political reforms were granted along the lines of the Civil Rights demands.

"In order to make Irish-oriented politics practical in the 6 Counties we would need (1) PR at all elections (2) the right to secede the whole 6 Counties from the UK should a majority wish it, and (3) the right to make trade agreements. Under such a system the days of Unionism would be numbered. They know it; that is why they oppose even ordinary civil rights. If secession were constitutional the whole 'disloyalty' element would be removed..."

The foregoing situation approximates what currently exists under the Good Friday Agreement.

The sale of the *United Irishman* was urged; Liam McMillan had been released but Malachy McGurran was still held, on a charge of possession of illegal documents. Yet UVF men were out on bail on arms charges.

There was a Sinn Fein Coiste Seasta statement calling for the removal of the Rome Rule threat implied by Article 44 of the Constitution. It was noted that this call was beginning to be broad-based. They also opposed talks of 'federation' of Britain and Ireland which were beginning to be voiced by Dublin and London politicians, with in effect re-opening of the Treaty talks.

Condolences were sent to Vietnam on the death of Ho Chi Minh.

The closure of the Seafield Gentex factory in Athlone was noted, and trade union action was called for; issues like factory closures and housing for the people were not to be forgotten due to Northern pressures.

There was no reference to the IRA statement(4). signed by Goulding, which appeared in the September United Irishman, outlined above. The significance of this needed to be explained to the members, and it wasn't.

In the September 16 1969 issue of *Nuacht Naisiumta* there was a lengthy analysis of the 'Solidarity' ad-hoc group which originated from meetings at the GPO during the August crisis week. It was noted that the call for intervention by 'Jack's Army' has ceased to dominate. There was now an address, 94 St Stephen's Green, and a phone. There was a steering committee of republicans, trade unionists and other radical groups. A meeting was held in Jury's on September 14, and a limited consensus was achieved, along the lines that:

(a) it is still strictly a civil rights issue, though Britain is responsible and the national question underlies it, and

(b) the religious-sectarian aspect of the 1937 Constitution should be amended.

People named as being present included Rev Terence McCaughey of Citizens for Civil Liberty, Barry Desmond and Justin Keating (Labour TDs), Ivan Cooper and Bernadette Devlin MP, Tomás Mac Giolla, Seamus Costello and Micheál O'Riordan. This was a broad-based centre-left grouping.

This was a challenge to the 'Direct Rule' demand which was now associated primarily with Conor Cruise O'Brien and Noel Browne. The Labour Party was thus not monolithic in support of the latter position.

On the North it was urged that the barricades must stay; Chichester Clarke was resisting the 'political demands', though promising reforms such as a points system for housing. The key demands, eg reform of the RUC, remained. There was a guarded welcome given to the Cameron Report, which had actually commended the role of the republican clubs in the Civil Rights movement. They objected to smearing of the young left agitators as 'international conspirators', and to the 'puffing up' of John Hume.

The issue concluded with references to the Dublin Housing Action Committee, Citizens Advice Bureaux, and the Ground Rents issue.

Defence Committees and the NICRA; the 26-Co Response

At the Sinn Fein Ard Comhairle on Sept 20 1969 there were present were TMcG, C *Campbell, Tony *Ruane, RJ, Larry *Grogan, Joe *Clarke, Seán Mac *Stiofain, Éamonn Mac *Thomáis, Denis Cassin, Des *Long, Seamus Rattigan, Liam Cummins, Paddy Callaghan, Seán Ó Gormaile, Derry Kelleher, Marcus Fogarty, Gabriel Mac Lochlainn, Máirín de Burca.

*The *proto-Provisionals were all there, making no contribution, but observing the scene and preparing behind the scenes for the walk-out, no doubt noting our total rejection of any military option.*

It was noted that the citizens defence committee was no longer under republican control; this was due to co-options *(by its proto-Provisional and Blaneyite leadership, Seán Keenan, Paddy Doherty etc)*; the barricades were coming down; the NICRA however was again emerging. Dalton Kelly was PRO and the AGM was planned for January. A meeting was planned for the 26th at which the Republican Clubs would organise activities relating to the CR issue, including a civil disobedience campaign. Paddy Callaghan reported that the Federation of Co-ops had met the Minister and the possibility existed that the Federation if developed could control the sea fishing industry. The Ard Fheis was again postponed *sine die*, due to the 'unsettled state' and a perceived threat of violence; it had been arranged for October 19. This was proposed by Seán Mac Stiofain *(no doubt because he needed time to organise and schedule his walk-out for maximum impact and harm to the politicisation process).*

There was a substantial change of emphasis in Issue #4 of NN dated September 23 1969, with topics like the Galway fish-in and a new Cumann in Sligo on the front page. Dublin homeless were jailed. On the North it was noted that the barricades had mostly come down, due to the combination of the British Army and the Catholic clergy. The Citizens Press, which the NICRA published, was commended and support urged for its Covenant campaign. Open UI sales and political activity were called for.

The Solidarity group was seen as presenting scope for doing spade work towards a constitutional referendum on Article 44, contacting Protestant communities tactfully, bearing in mind the negative effect of the Ne Temere decree in generating ghetto-consciousness.

The indication here however is that the Solidarity group was becoming evanescent; the foregoing looks somewhat aspirational.

The 'Federation' concept was decoupled from the 'British Isles' dimension and the concept floated at the level of devolution of Connaught away from total Dublin top-down control.

There were hints here at constitutional reforms of the 26 Counties such as to make a transition to an all-Ireland solution seem more acceptable and less threatening to Northern Protestants.

The Northern crisis took front-page priority again for issue #5 of *Nuacht Naisiunta* (NN) on September 30 1969: the Citizens Defence Committees had re-erected the barricades; the Republican Clubs were urged to meet and establish their own identities, and to help to make the Defence Committees truly representative of the community as a whole.

This good advice I suspect was largely ignored on the ground; Head Office was not enough in touch; republican activists tended to prefer their 'defence committee' type roles, and to ignore the need to stoke up their collective political consciousness. This led to the domination of the defence committees by the type of Fianna Fail-like people cultivated by Captain Kelly. Not enough social-republican spade-work had been done. I picked up this impression during the time on several occasions with trips North.

The remainder of the *Nuacht* was taken up with the Conradh, the Land League, Housing Action and fisheries; the Common Market began to make an appearance as an issue to think about.

***

I have on record a copy of a letter I wrote on 24/09/69 to Justin Keating, arising I think from a 'Solidarity' event at which he had spoken. I was attempting to develop a local basis in Rathmines for a 'Solidarity' event, on the neutral ground of the Connradh na Gaeilge hall in Observatory Lane. We had links with local Connradh and local tenants organisations, but no links with Labour. Anthony Coughlan was to address a meeting, which we wanted to be broad-based, and to accept a suitable message to try to convey to the Government indicating what they should be pressing on Westminster. The key demand was '...to implement rapidly and with no nonsense the CR Charter; also to press that there be no backing down by Lynch into any Commonwealth-type pseudo-unity deal ...'. I went on to suggest that 'PR plus CR plus the right to secede' in the North would transform the situation, with the UI legalised etc. I had tried to get Noel Browne to accept this, but he had refused to listen. I have however no record of any reply from Keating. There was later some contact, on similar lines, with Brendan Halligan on the Solidarity network.

On the same day I wrote to Anthony Coughlan, stressing the importance of trying to develop local broad-based links around the 'solidarity' demands. I also declared the intention of pulling back from the 'front line' of the movement, in order to write stuff which might be useful in a broader-based 'liberation movement' context: '...Liberation Tracts that would give guidance to those people who were working in the mass-organisations... not specifically Sinn Fein policy... spell out the steps from here to national independence and socialism in the form of a sequence of concessions to fight for, such that the people can understand them ...'.

I went on: '...I would like this to appear more or less as from your group (this was the Common Market Study Group), which seems to be the group which spans most effectively the radical spectrum. I would like on the whole to play down my identification with the republicans, except in the broadest sense. I feel there is now much work to be done in teaching the Left how to speak the language of national liberation (especially in the North), more than to teach the republicans the ideas and organisational principles of socialism. I am inclined to accept Desmond's criticism that the former should have come first, and I want to back-track (or advance) myself into that position over a period without rocking the boat of radical unity. A transition period like this, in an environment accepted by both sides, would I feel do the trick; also I want to hedge myself against the possibility that the work on the Commission may have been a waste of time, due to the danger of the movement reverting to type in the possibly coming military situation (of which don't underestimate the danger). In this case the movement will collapse and split and we must establish as many national links of a positive character under the Solidarity banner so as to be able to pick up the bits and weld them into a genuine national movement without the mythology...'.

I concluded by mentioning that '...from Jan 1.. I will be trying to earn a living without benefit of a job... I will need a period with as little public activity a possible, until I get my existing reasonable reputation for professional competence a bit better known... I'm not out to make a lot of money, just enough to keep me and the family going, and perhaps give Máirín a little less to crib about ...'.

The foregoing, seen in retrospect, is a valid representation of my then thinking, under the pressures of the crisis and the impending split.

***

At the SF Coiste Seasta on 29/09/69 TMcG, TR, SmacS, SR, RJ, JC, MdeB were present. Dalton Kelly attended from the NICRA. It was reported that the meeting of Republican Clubs had been poorly supported; the plan to get active clubs in every county, with a 6-county executive to handle publicity remained unfulfilled. Dalton Kelly reported on the Citizens Press; it was hoped to get the Defence Committees to adopt it, while keeping policy under control of the movement.

I have a copy of a duplicated leaflet issued by the NICRA in September 1969, which calls for civil and political rights to be legislated by Westminster, as the alternative to Direct Rule and the abolition of Stormont. It is labelled 'draft' in m/s, so I don't know if this ever became the official policy. It was clearly an attempt to defeat the PD direct rule demand politically. It refers to a Covenant for people to sign. The political rights were '...explicit recognition... of the right of the people of Northern Ireland to political self-determination ...', and the right of Stormont to negotiate trade agreements with other countries. The civil rights were votes for all at 18 in all election, a boundary commission to define local government areas, Proportional Representation, freedom of assembly and expression, anti-discrimination legislation, and an impartial police force.

The relationship between the Defence Committees, the Republican Clubs, the NICRA and the Citizens Press during this period needs to be analysed, perhaps with the NICRA records as additional source. What I suspect is that the first were increasingly under Blaneyite / proto-Provisional control, and were subverting the membership of the second, and keeping the third and fourth at bay. The foregoing SF minute is ambiguous.

The 'Federal Deal' Concept; the role of Fianna Fail

In the October *United Irishman* Britain was seen as fomenting a civil war so as to be able to come in as the saviour, and impose an all-Ireland federal deal (a 'federation of these islands'). The UN approach was half-hearted. Faulkner's new local government proposals were denounced as a new gerrymander. There was a promotional review of Coughlan's pamphlet 'The Northern Crisis, Which Way Forward?' published by the Solidarity group against the 'abolition of Stormont' call. The main British objective was seen as federation of Ireland with Britain in the projected EEC context. The trail had been blazed with the Free Trade Agreement. Economic resistance issues: ground rents and fishing.

At the Sinn Fein Coiste Seasta on 6/10/69 Mac Stiofain was present, along with TMcG, SR, MdeB and JC, also RJ. RJ reported on Housing Action Movement feedback from the Left: it was rumoured that SF was withdrawing from active participation due to a secret agreement with the FF government, relating to the Northern question(5).

During the rest of October one gets the impression here that the lines of communication with the Northern leadership people, and their contacts on the ground, were becoming eroded through the Defence Committee system, under increasingly proto-Provisional and Blaneyite influence. Most of the Nuacht Naisiunta content was 26-county parochial.

I have a copy of the London *Evening Standard* dated October 14 1969 which contains an article by Tom Pocock attempting to make sense of the Northern scene. I remember encountering him, and he did make an effort to report fairly the aspirations of the republican left, which he linked with my own name and those of Cathal Goulding, Seán Garland and Anthony Coughlan. '...Against the advice of the Left, the Right began a crash programme of re-armament and military training, with the active help, so I have been told, of three members of the Irish government and some factions within the Army... military-type camps... the Donegal Mafia... radio station beamed on Ulster... Indeed, my most alarming memory of this visit to Dublin is not of inflammatory talk over Guinness but of a charming member of the Irish Cabinet remarking over coffee in a luxurious restaurant that he has been in favour of ordering the Army to march into Ulster. Odd that the most rational and least bloodthirsty Irishman I met should have been a Marxist ...'.

At the Sinn Fein Ard Comhairle on 18/10/69 TMacG, CC, SC, EMacT, TR, LG, JC, SMacS, GMacL, DC, RJ, DK, SR, DL, KA, OMacC were present. Republican Clubs were to support Kevin McCorry or Dalton Kelly for the NICRA full-time organiser. Citizen Press was to remain under republican control, but with Belfast Central Citizens Defence Committee (CCDC) represented on the management committee. The Regional Executive of Republican Clubs had been set up, and clubs re-activated. The Clubs legality case had however been defeated in the

Lords; people had been therefore convicted, but given conditional discharges. A campaign to release Malachi McGurran and Prionnsias Mac Airt (Frank Card) was initiated. Seamus Costello gave a list of current active regional organisers. Ard Fheis date was fixed for January 10-11. Mac Stiofain proposed that the 2 main resolutions be circulated in advance with information as to their timing on the agenda. This was accepted.

Mac Stiofain obviously had in mind the need to drum up maximal attendance at the crucial times. If his military plan was to be developed, the political plan needed to be stymied with maximal disruption.

Issue #8 of NN on October 21 1969 opened with the Hunt Report, using the text of a speech given by Tomás Mac Giolla in UCD. He was critical of the Report, which appeared to concede the NICRA demands, but in fact side-stepped them, with reforms which were nominal and cosmetic. McGurran and McAirt were still imprisoned, despite the Special Powers being supposedly abolished.

The ban on the Republican Clubs had been upheld on appeal to the Lords. The local courts however were not willing the sentence those accused of membership.

Pre-Split Intrigues

On October 23 Greaves in his diary noted an attempt to recruit Peter Mulligan, a CA stalwart, into the IRA(6). It was indicated that there apparently was an intention to resume military action in 1971.

It seems I had been over in London on business, and had been staying with Seán Redmond. CDG recorded an encounter in the Lucas Arms on October 24. I was somewhat self-critical, but was inclined to be dismissive of the projected 1971 resumption of hostilities, though aware of the possibility that I might be kept in the dark. The Kerry republicans had broken with Dublin, and now there was a meeting in Belfast; Jimmy Steele was involved. I was in two minds about going forward for the Ard Comhairle. The question of 'petit-bourgeois organisational pre-suppositions' came up; I had earlier been aware of this as a problem and had wanted to discuss it with CDG, but he had been dismissive. We concluded, good-humouredly, that I was, like JJ, before my time, too impulsive, too talkative, and too keen on print.

At the Sinn Fein Coiste Seasta on 27/10/69 TMacG, JC, TR, RJ, GMacL, MdeB were present. *Note that the CS meetings during this period were basically being carried by RJ and TMacG on behalf of the leading politicisers. The role of Joe Clarke was to put a glowering negative presence on the process, backed by Tony Ruane, and fortified by SMacS from time to time.* TMacG reported on the 6-Co Regional Executive: five areas were represented; people had in most cases been absorbed into CRA work and club work had been dropped. Billy McMillan was elected Chair, Liam Cummins secretary, Kevin McCorry press officer and Oliver Frawley treasurer. The first meeting was fixed for Belfast on November 2 and there was to be a motion proposed by J White and seconded by R MacKnight 'that a revolutionary front of all radical groups be set up for the purpose of organising the youth into a revolutionary movement and to press the social objectives of the movement now'.

It is far from clear what the philosophy of, or strategic thinking behind, this motion was; it seems to have come bottom-up from the people concerned, and to have reflected ultra-left PD-type influence; it certainly was not a reflection of leadership thinking.

Thirteen regions were defined for elections to the incoming Ard Comhairle; these were realistically based on the known distribution of Cumainn and Clubs, and defined in terms of ease of access to a regional centre. It is not clear who drew up the list; it could have been from Goulding, who would have had a feel for the main foci of politicisation. They were 'all-Ireland' in structure, eg we had 'Donegal/Derry' and 'Fermanagh / West Cavan / Leitrim'.

Issue #9 of *Nuacht Naisiunta* on October 28 1969 opened with an accusation that the Fianna Fail leadership were actively engaged in colluding with the British in a scheme for a Federal Union of 'these islands'. The source of this was, it seems, statements by Terence O'Neill and Eddie McAteer, along the lines of 'a little United Nations in the British Isles'. There was an attempt to trace this back to the Lemass-O'Neill meeting. Fianna Fail were challenged to decouple themselves from this concept.

It was noted that the Northern Committee of the Irish TUC at its meeting on October 22 had demanded the reorganisation of the RUC and the abolition of the Special Powers Act. Republicans were urged to seek TU support for the release of McGurran and McArt.

The November *United Irishman* featured the exposure of the 'Haughey, Blaney and Boland' (HB&B) attempt to take over the Civil Rights movement. It was not clear whether it was Government or Fianna Fail; there was money involved. They plumped for FF; Brady and Corrigan were involved; what was the role of Lynch? O'Neill and McAteer had issued jointly a statement calling for a federation of these islands, a re-invention of the old 'Home Rule All Round' concept from the 1900s, though with Partition. The role of the Republican Clubs in support of the Civil Rights was highlighted, in defence of the political role, and in answer to those who were saying 'where were they?' when the people needed defence from pogroms.

At the SF Coiste Seasta on 3/11/69 TMacG, SR, TR, Mick Ryan, Seamus Costello were present; Seán Dunne and Andy Smith attended as from the Dublin CC, and Joe Nolan from Dun Laoire. It seems I was not present at this one, unusually. This was to resolve the Dun Laoire question. The Dublin CC position was that the Tracey Cumann promoted by Joe Nolan was 'paper', and a new active Cumann had been set up in Sallynoggin; Joe Nolan could join this if he liked. Joe Nolan was challenged to produce the minute book. Mick Ryan reported complaints that CS business had been discussed outside the CS; this was aimed at Joe Clarke but no names were mentioned.

I have among my papers a copy of 'Notes for Organisers Meeting' dated 3/11/69. This was aimed at organising the regional conferences, and ensuring that the Ard Fheis papers were distributed. Thirteen areas had been defined, each with some degree of geographical unity, each with 10-15 cumainn. The 'report on the work of the movement' which they were urged to deliver was summarised; it covered the role of the Civil Rights movement, public opinion in the world, the Belfast and Derry situations, local work going on with housing and trade union groups, the Fianna Fail attempt to take over Civil Rights and to isolate radicals, while working a deal with Wilson on the EEC, Free Trade and NATO. The role of *Nuacht Naisiunta*, the weekly newsletter to cumainn, was highlighted.

This political message was however not well adapted to the state of political development of the movement at the grass-roots, which was rapidly lapsing into a militarist mind-set. There is also a 'draft note on the job of organiser', defining weekly and monthly cycles, based on the United Irishman, and a suggested daily routine. There was, on some occasion about this time, a session with the regional organisers, and some of the regions were re-defined on the basis of their local knowledge.

There was a WTS meeting on November 4, at which Manus Durkan spoke on 'The Power of the Insurance Companies'. There was also a poetry reading in Jury's Hotel, with Seán Ó Tuama, on November 15.

Manus Durkan was a Fianna Fail trade union activist who had helped the IWP activist Noel Harris organise the ASTMS in the insurance business. The poetry reading was part of a series organised by Meryl Farrington to make cultural links with Irish, Scottish and Welsh poets.

One gains the impression that WTS momentum was declining, and that it was unable to respond to the Northern crisis, given the way it had developed.

During November 1969 a campaign developed for the release of McGurran and Mac Airt (Card), while the Fianna Fail takeover of the Civil Rights movement proceeded apace, funded by business supporters. There was a bomb provocation at Bodenstown. There was some proto-Provisional rumbling in a few cumainn. There was increasing concern about Standing Committee business being openly circulated, aimed at Joe Clarke. *The Voice of the North*, edited by Seamus Brady, was acting for the Haughey Blaney Boland consortium. The perception was that £400 per week was being contributed by the HBB consortium '...to help in harnessing Civil Rights to the Fianna Fail star ...'.

Republicans were urged to sell the *United Irishman* to counter this subversive ploy by the 26-county Establishment. There was some diversion of effort over a matter of a primary school closure at O'Brien's Bridge (Montpelier). There were indications that HQ was uneasy about the ability of local republicans to express national policies with any consistency, in a situation increasingly dominated by the Fianna Fail proto-Provisional position. Bernadette Devlin had approached the Movement to organise meetings for her in the 26 Cos. It was agreed to seek a meeting in advance to agree policy positions: UDR, British interference, sectarian strife etc.

Regional conferences to elect regional members for the incoming Ard Comhairle, under the revised regionalised constitution, were announced. The full Ard Comhairle would be elected at the coming Sein Fein Ard Fheis ('1969'), planned for January 1970. The regional meetings would double as educational conferences, to update members on the developing Northern situation. The 6-co executive was now meeting regularly and club members were being encouraged to join the NICRA.

The Wolfe Tone commemoration oration was reported in Issue #13 of NN on November 24; the occasion was the 171st anniversary of his burial, and it was a response to the blowing up of the grave-stone, as reported earlier. Liam Ó Comain, secretary of the 6-county Republican Executive which united the Clubs, recalled the guiding principles of Presbyterianism, civil and religious liberty, the rights of the common man and true democracy. He reminded his audience of the simultaneous foundation of the Orange Order and Maynooth College, in response to the threat of non-sectarian democratic unity. There was however an explicit nod in the direction of the use of force to dislodge Britain, though in a projected context suggesting unity of Catholic and Protestant workers.

There was a Strabane demonstration for the release of Mac Airt (Card) and McGurran, and a defence of the RTE programme exposing money-lenders, which had been attached by Minister for Justice Ó Moráin. It was suggested that the money-lending fraternity was extensive and influential in the local management of the Fianna Fail vote in working-class areas(7).

Thus not only was political left-republicanism exposing the top-level corruption fuelled by developers' land deals in local government, but also the mafia-type local control system for the urban Fianna Fail working-class vote. One can, in retrospect, understand the viciousness with which the Haughey group at the top moved to marginalise the influence of politicising republicans. Not only were they opening up the possibility of real reforms in the North such as to enable cross-community democratic politics to unite working people, but in the South they were exposing how democratic politics was being subverted by moneyed mafias. We had touched many raw Fianna Fail nerves.

The Connolly Association conference met on November 30 1969; Greaves characterised it in his diaries as a '...recall of the one wrecked by NICRA'. There were delegates from Birmingham, Coventry, Manchester, Oxford and London; the Movement for Colonial Freedom was there, and a few Labour Party and Trade Union people. Hume it seemed was in favour of people joining the Ulster Defence Regiment. Greaves regarded the formation of latter as an 'astute move' on the part of the British, going on to remark that '...the absence of theoretical clarity in Belfast Left circles seems to prevent their extending influences on the nationalists, who are heavily divided... the IRA members of London NICRA were at the NICRA conference in Belfast ...'(8).

In the December *United Irishman* the Special Powers was the target, the continued holding of McGurran and Card being the key issue. There was a review by the present writer of Bernadette Devlin's book; her policies were attributed to Farrell, McCann and Toman. The EEC threat was again mentioned, along with Building Societies and Land Leagues.

The year ends with a confused rearguard action on the part of the paper, to re-assert, somewhat half-heartedly, the political republican agenda, in the context of the impending Ard Fheis.

Bernadette Devlin

In December 1969 meetings were arranged for Bernadette Devlin, on the initiative of Sinn Fein in Limerick. She had avoided a prior meeting by the expedient of flying to Shannon. She was reported as having spoken well and been co-operative. Collections went for the Northern relief fund.

In retrospect, I must say I never fully understood how these meetings had come about, by whom or how they were initiated, what their objective was. I was inclined at the time to attribute them to the initiative of the Limerick politicisers, but from the Coiste Seasta record it seems the initiative came from Bernadette. Were they perhaps a diversion? Who was taking whom for a ride? It seems I did not voice my unease at the CS, though I remember distinctly being uneasy, and critical of their lack of political focus.

There were meetings at Ennis, Nenagh, Tipperary, Cashel and Thurles. She then flew back from Shannon to prepare questions for the next weeks Westminster session, including the issue of the McGurran-McAirt imprisonment.

It is noteworthy that the only leading republicans to be imprisoned where those who were in the lead of the politicisation process; this supports the long-standing Greaves hypothesis that there was an influential back-room group in the Home Office which actively wanted to encourage the re-emergence of a sterile non-political military IRA. They arrest McGurran, but not Mac Stiofain.

Issue #14 of *Nuacht Naisiunta*: "It is evident that the Irish people have adopted Bernadette as a figurehead, whether they agree with her or not. In her speeches she stressed, correctly, the Lynch-Wilson machinations and the danger of a Federal fraud. She also stressed the need to build an all-Ireland movement with social-revolutionary objectives, so as to help persuade the Northern people that national unity under Fianna Fail was not the issue..".

She was '...complimented on doing a good job of combining agitational work with the occasional use of the parliamentary machine so as to express its inadequacy....' (and was) '...developing her ideas away from the rather arid doctrinaire student socialism and towards a more national-rooted revolutionary tradition...'.

I attended the Thurles meeting. She drew a crowd. I remember thinking at the time the meeting lacked political focus. She concentrated on the conditions of the working people in the North, and the need for social reform. These meetings were apparently a bottom-up Limerick initiative, part of the internal grass-roots Sinn Fein campaign against parliamentary abstention with a view to influencing the coming Ard Fheis. They had little relevance however to the actual Northern situation.

More 'Federal' Hints

The Ard Comhairle on December 6 concerned itself with Ard Fheis preparations, ratifying the regional structure. McGurran was released. There was reported on December 9 a response to a kite flown by Quentin Hogg, the British Shadow Home Secretary, in Trinity College, who proposed 'three-level dialogue (ministerial, parliamentary and executive) between Stormont, Dublin and

Westminster, in the form of a 'dry run' for future European integration. This 'federal' concept was rejected with a call to '...clear up the mess... in the Six Counties by:

(a) imposing a Bill of Rights on Stormont

(b) imposing PR in elections

(c) granting explicitly the right of democratic secession, so as to make all-Ireland politics non-subversive, and then withdraw completely from any further interference in Irish affairs...'.

This indicates that strategic Head Office thinking(9) was still in terms of the need to sustain the momentum of the NICRA, despite all the Fianna Fail machinations in the North and the increasing domination of local politics there by 'defence committees' and the like, and to oppose any steps towards an effective absorption into the UK via a 'federal' process, in the EEC context. He key intellectual influence remained Anthony Coughlan.

The Year 1970 and the Split

The *United Irishman* began the year with a reference on the front page to an IRA statement, signed by 'JJ McGarrity', of which the main thrust was against the *Irish Press* group and its attempt to split the movement.

There is an agenda here for historians: to what extent were Tim Pat Coogan and the Irish Press *directly involved, on behalf of Fianna Fail, with the process that led to the emergence of the Provisionals and the isolation of the politicising Left? It certainly was our perception at the time that this was their agenda.*

There was also a review by RJ of Michael Farrell's *Struggles in the North*, along with George Gilmore's *Republican Congress*: Gilmore found the basic politics of FF and the IRA in the 1930s identical. In the Republican Congress the premature support for the 'workers' republic' vision led to leakage of support to FF. Farrell's chronology was accurate but the analysis faulty; he has a 'moderates' group with Hume et al wanting Catholic concessions within the UK, a 'militants' group with Blaney et al wanting a 32 county FF republic, and socialists attacking capitalism so as to win Protestant workers for a workers republic. There was no mention of the Republican Clubs and their mobilising support for the NICRA. I went on to suggest that the Congress error was being repeated: attacking capitalism before getting rid of the imperialist-imposed partitioned structure.

This issue of the United Irishman pre-dated the January 1970 (postponed 1969) Ard Fheis, where the split occurred publicly. This has been widely described. The proto-Provisionals remained in the hall long enough to vote against abandoning abstentionism, and then staged a walk-out, with various incidents guaranteed to attract journalistic attention. Among the visitors associated with the walk-out was Gerry Jones, a prominent Fianna Fail supporter on the Taca network (the Fianna Fail financial support mafia). They had a hall booked ready to meet in for the purpose of founding the Provisionals.

According the Greaves the split occurred because of the outmanoeuvring of the Civil Rights movement in the North, and the consequent discredit of the republican policy of political action. He attributed it to the folly of the present writer, and undertook not to take sides. The London republicans were supporters of

Mac Stiofain while Goulding's support was in Birmingham. The Huddersfield arms episode was 'official' and Goulding stood over Smullen and co.

In other words despite the best politicising efforts of the present writer and others, the movement on both sides of the split was reverting to traditional mode, under the pressure of the Northern events. Also it seems that Goulding had been keeping the present writer in the dark regarding the Smullen episode.

Greaves had hopes that Labour in Ireland might now take a strong national stand. In Dublin he picked up the impression that Meade and the present writer were happy with the situation, regarding the Provisionals as lacking in people of ability. I conveyed the impression that the 'official' politicising structures were holding, and that the Northern Executive of the Republican Clubs had replaced the 'Northern Command' structure. CDG however picked up the impression that I was not told everything; I was not aware, for example, that Costello had been in London. I was, it seems, unable to give a satisfactory account of Belfast, and was under the impression that Jimmy Steele had no influence(10).

He was of course quite right. We had totally underestimated the extent to which Mac Stiofain had been actively building the Northern Command structure, outside of the political process.

The Ard Comhairle met on January 17, with Tomás MacGiolla, Malachi McGurran, Seán Ó Cionnaith, Cathal Goulding, Liam Ó Comain, Oliver Frawley, MJ Dunfy, Ivan Barr, Tom Mitchell, Frank Wogan, Frank Patterson, Oliver McCaul, Seán Dunne, Seamus Costello, Mick Ryan, Máirín de Burca. There were apologies from RJ, Paddy Kilcullen, Tom Kilroy, Sylvester Doolan. Éamonn Mac Thomáis had been elected but had walked out. Regional representatives who had walked out were Peter Duffy, JJ McGirl, Ruairi Ó Brádaigh, Des Long, Ned Bailey. The position of George O'Mahony of Cork was not known.

The present writer had agreed to continue as Director of Education. MdeB and Sean Ó Cionnaith were secretaries. Seamus Rhatigan and Derry Kelleher were treasurers. The Coiste Seasta was to include as well as the officers MR, CG, TM and SD.

I did not want go forward, having just then left Aer Lingus(11). and being faced with survival in self-employed mode; I definitely felt I had to get more into a backroom situation, and out of the front line. But I was stuck with the education job and felt that somehow I had to continue with it. This meant that I continued on the CS.

It seems that one Jerry O'Keefe, who was a visitor representing the NAIJ, had assaulted Sean Mac Stiofain, so they agreed to complain to the NAIJ. The issue was raised by Tom Mitchell.

Why should a visitor take such an action? Could this be part of a prior arrangement to generate 'news'? The media would assume it was a delegate, and help to promulgate an aura of 'injured innocence' around Mac Stiofain.

Publication of the social and economic programme was to be prioritised. This appeared in the February *United Irishman*(12), under the title 'Freedom Manifesto'. *Insofar as there was a focus for the 'National Liberation Front' concept, this was it.*

Issue #16 of *Nuacht Naisiunta* on January 19 1970 contained a barebones account of the Ard Fheis; it was noted that the broad-based 'National Liberation

Front' motion had been supported, but the electoral policy one had been defeated, not getting the required 2/3 majority. Both these motions had come out of the work of the 'Garland Commission'. There was no reference to the walk-out.

Other topics included the EEC (Coughlan's *Case Against the Common Market* being promoted), the *United Irishman* (current sales were at 45,000 but there were problems in getting the money in from the cumainn), the Springboks tour and the proposed Trade Union and Industrial Relations Bills. The issue of all-Ireland sporting organisation in the cycling context was treated, a matter dear to the heart of Seamus Ó Tuathail, the Editor of the *United Irishman*.

At the Coiste Seasta on 26/01/70 there were TMacG, Derry Kelleher, CG, RJ, TM, Seán Dunne, Sylvester Doolan; also Seamus Ó Tuathail. The Labour Party had invited TMacG to their Annual Conference; Sean Dunne was to go. The Connemara Cearta Sibhialta movement had written supporting the 'National Liberation Front' concept. No reply to the statement issued by the 'breakaway group' but errors of fact were to be corrected with the UI and NN. The Westminster election was discussed, and the coming NICRA AGM. Tom Mitchell was to meet with Bernadette. Malachi McGurran as a candidate for the NICRA Chair was considered but no decision was taken.

Issue #17 of *Nuacht Naisiunta* on January 26 1970 contained an overview of what happened as regards the walk-out. They had all stayed together until after the elections to the Ard Comhairle. While the votes were being counted, a delegate got up to propose the continuation of support for and co-operation with the IRA. At this point 'an altercation then arose' and a number of delegates and visitors walked out. The event had been pre-planned; they went off to the Kevin Barry Hall. Some of those who had opposed the electoral policy resolution remained behind.

The remaining body of Sinn Fein was thus in a constitutionally anomalous situation, lumbered with the electoral debris of those who had walked out.

The February 1970 issue of the *United Irishman* led with 'Hold Firm - No Civil War'; the British were standing aside and encouraging it, all-Ireland Federation with Britain being the perceived prize. The 'Freedom Manifesto' was published. This was our attempt to put some flesh on the bones of the 'National Liberation Front' concept which had crept into the discussions; this choice of labelling was elsewhere criticised as being derivative and misleading; it certainly gave rise to great confusion in the Ard Fheis debate. Mac Giolla in his speech at the Ard Fheis had accused Jack Lynch of promoting a new Act of Euro-Union.

The Coiste Seasta met on February 2; TMacG was to speak in Cork on March 6, and RJ was to go with him, to run an educational conference on that weekend. We had earlier had an encounter with Ciaran Kennedy, the Economic and Social Research Institute Director, who was systematically talking to all Parties. There was also reported a meeting representative of all Republican Clubs in the Brackareilly Hall, Maghera on February 1; it was addressed by Billy McMillan from Belfast and Anthony Coughlan from Dublin, with the latter stressing the need for the avoidance of sectarian clashes and the development of the role of the NICRA. Malachy McGurran presided, and Tomás Mac Giolla also spoke.

Issue #18 of *Nuacht Naisiunta* attempted to survey nationally the effect of the walk-out. Support for the leadership in the Six Counties was seen as solid, this comprising the republican club activists who had been supporting the Civil Rights approach. *Others who subsequently emerged via the Provisional process would simply not have been on record with Head Office.* Support for the 'breakaway group' was seen as emanating from Cavan and Monaghan. In Dublin six out of ten cumainn, representing 80% of the membership, were seen as 'loyal'. The picture elsewhere however was confused, due to the conflation of two totally distinct issues: electoral tactics and support for trying to keep the Northern issue on a political road.

The unifying philosophy was seen as the need to develop a broad-based popular anti-imperialist movement for the re-conquest of Ireland, the 'National Liberation Front' concept.

A protest outside the British Embassy about the banning of the Republican Clubs and the sale of the *United Irishman* was reported as having taken place on February 2; there was music and songs.

The February 23 1970 issue of *Nuacht Naisiunta* reported a Liberty Hall conference which had been opened by Cathal Goulding. It was addressed by Kader Asmal on imperialism, Oliver Snoddy and Eoin Ó Murchú on the 'Cultural Revolution', Tom Kilroy and Seamus Ó Tuathail on farming and land issues, with Brian Heron (a Connolly grandson) giving the progressive US angle. Tomás Mac Giolla declared the intent of running similar conferences regionally.

The Ard Comhairle met on February 28 1970 with TMacG, Liam Cummins, M Dunphy, Mick Ryan, Oliver Frawley, Cathal Goulding, Seamus Rattigan, Ivan Barr, Tom Mitchell, Seán Ó Cionnaith, Paddy Kilcullen, RJ, Tom Kilroy, Derry Kelleher, Donnchadh MacRaignaill, Oliver MacCaul, Seamus Costello present.

This was the makings of an effective post-split national leadership, of what was the makings of an effective all-Ireland political republican movement. What went wrong? Were there avoidable blunders committed? Or was the initiative marginalised by external 'force majeure'? I hope to be able to tease this out in what follows, or at least contribute to helping others to do so(13).

Seán Keenan in Derry 'did not want an enquiry into his dismissal'; ie he was registering his opting out in favour of the Provisionals. Local Derry activists threatened to withdraw support from NICRA street protests, seeing 'education in ideology of revolution' as an alternative. They were instructed to persist with public support for NICRA events. Church gate collections were called for the Bombay Street Housing Association.

On my various visits to Derry to interact with the activists, I had marginally encountered Seán Keenan, in a house where we met; he tended to be passively in the background, watching TV, while we tried to develop some degree of political understanding.

There was a discussion on whether a membership fee should be made a condition of membership; it was left that the Comhairle Ceanntar had the power to waive it. The prisoners release campaign was to be intensified. Frank Patterson was agreed as a unity candidate for South Down. Unity candidates to be discussed by the Clubs Executive. Tom Mitchell to go to Belfast to discuss current policy.

The March 1970 issue of the *United Irishman* continued on the 'No Civil War' theme, a divisive civil war still being perceived as what Britain wanted, with all-Ireland Federation with the UK as the strategic vision. The 'Abolish Stormont' demand was countered by 'only when the alternative is the Republic'. There was an

NICRA group to go to the US: Denis Cassin, Malachi McGurran and Brigid Bond. The fisheries campaign continued. There was however an extended report on the 3rd AGM of the NICRA, which took place on February 14-15 in Belfast, attended by 500 people. The secretary Peter Morris reported the formation of 8 regional groups. Ivan Cooper promoted continuing extra-parliamentary action, around a demand for a Civil Rights Charter. Gerrymandering required re-drawing of boundaries. The report was proposed for acceptance by Daltún Ó Ceallaigh and passed unanimously.

The UI report of the AGM then went on to report on some emerging divisions: Con McCluskey it seems objected to the NAIJ in the USA being the contact-point; there was said to be a Black Panther connection, which Michael Farrell supported, leaving McCluskey isolated. Farrell went on to propose the development of a Civil Rights movement in the 26 Counties. There were attacks by PD people on 'Catholic bigots'. The Farrell motion was referred to the incoming executive, and it was recommended that the Citizens for Civil Liberties should be the contact-point, also the Article 44 campaign. The PD element in the conferences seems to have been a source of ultra-leftist disruption.

I feel I need to comment with hindsight on an aspect of the foregoing: I find it remarkable that we were dedicating so much energy to peripheral issues like ground rents and fisheries, relics of evanescent landlordism, at a time when the situation was so explosive. The explanation perhaps is that this was intended as a means of keeping activists in the 26 counties doing something of local interest, so as to divert them from madly rushing North and fuelling what was verging on a civil war situation. It probably had the opposite effect, however, as many were motivated to join the Provisionals by what they perceived as lack of leadership attention to the exploding Northern situation.

The IRA statements also perhaps were intended to serve the same purpose. The movement was imprisoned by its historical structures; the process of transforming it into a broad-based political movement of the democratic left was far from complete, so that in the end the Provisionals were clearly were the winners in the competition to pick up the loyalties of the activists. Enough people remained with the 'officials' eventually to achieve some Dáil representation, which however later split away from the Workers Party rump, forming the Democratic Left party, which eventually merged with Labour. The basis of the DL split was the perception of the residual existence of an 'inner group' having continuity of experience with the 'official IRA'. The Fenian-IRB tradition dies hard; it has been a powerful influence on the political culture.

In Belfast on March 15 1970 Greaves attended the conference which marked the unification of the CPNI and the IWP into the CPI. He was on the IWP invitation list but not on that of the CPNI. There were greetings from some 20 CPs in various countries. When it was over Seán Nolan asked him if he had any misgivings. He said he had: '...but it is done. The problems you haven't solved before reunification you will have to solve after it ...'. Then he went down to Dublin, in the company of AC, who it seems had been present as an observer, presumably in his capacity as the Dublin correspondent of the *Irish Democrat*. The next day, March 16 1970, he spent some time with Cathal Goulding, who called in to MacLiam's house. '...Some of the bounce had gone out of him. He was more inclined to be self-critical... too busy in his business to get around to see people ...'. The Belfast events did them terrible harm, specifically '...having no guns ...'. CG tended to blame the lack of guns on the Belfast people themselves: '...the test of a man when the movement is broke is how deep he'll dig into his own pocket ...'.

Note the apparent assumption that lack of Falls Road guns was the problem, rather than the existence of the armed Protestant B-Specials as a component of the Crown forces. Thus the pogrom succeeded in its objective, of making everyone think in terms of guns for 'defence'.

CDG went on to remark that the difference between the UI and the Poblacht did not warrant a major split. Goulding responded: '...Stephenson wanted the abstention issue discussed so as to kill it quickly. When we proposed delay as there was no election in sight, Costello challenged him "are you afraid to fight it out?" So it was discussed, and the result was the split ...'.

The indications are however that Goulding wanted Belfast to be undefended, and to use the ensuing situation politically to get the B-Specials disarmed. This however gave the Provisionals the role of 'defenders of the people'.

CG went on to discuss Costello, the North, British policy, Federation etc. There was a mention of RHJ in this context. CDG concluded '...one gets the impression of a very imperfectly centralised organisation ...'. CG had been invited as a 'fraternal delegate to the CPNI conference. He asked CDG had he misgivings about this CP reunification; he said he had, but asked CG for his: '...I saw the CPNI as a door to the Protestant workers, if they become anti-partitionist they may close it ...'. CDG replied that he thought that in that case they would have to make the trade union movement the door.

Then, on the question of the 'Irish Republic Now Virtually Established' CG was dismissive: '...revolutionaries must work from things as they are. For my part I cannot see any broad basis of politics being evolved from anybody but dedicated Marxists. They will show the way to the future...'. CDG goes on: '...it struck me that CG is now in a transitional phase. Joe O'Connor in London expressed the opinion that the Goulding IRA will go CPI and the other become the recognised IRA. It would be a pity in ways. But I think this might be true of Goulding. That he has enormously matured is certain...'.

Later: '...I saw RHJ again for a few minutes. It struck me that he was conscious of having lost influence. CG goes to MOR now not to him. As I left the house he said "I want to talk with you - about philosophy". It was because I had accused him of following Fanon...'. The next day he recorded that I had pointed him in the direction of Ned Byrne, Kevin O'Byrne's father, who knew Mellows. Then he went back to London to work on the paper.

At the Dublin Wolfe Tone Society on March 24 1970 Joe Deasy spoke on 'The Independence of Small Nations'. There is on record a copy of the notice for this meeting, signed by Anthony Coughlan, secretary. "..The speaker will be examining, with particular reference to Ireland, the problems which a small nation has of maintaining its independence and identity under the political, economic and cultural pressures of imperialism. This has special relevance at a time when the twenty six county State is seeking to obtain membership of the Common Market under precisely such pressures..". He went on to give notice that "...the Society intends organising a Conference on the subject and related matters in the near future..". The circular also promoted a poetry reading on March 22 by Dic Jones the Welsh farmer-poet, in the series produced by Meryl Farrington.

In *Nuacht Naisiunta* on March 31 1970 Tomás Mac Giolla in the Derry Easter Commemoration responded to the presence of British troops; they were there to defend the RUC. He attempted to promote the vision of common interest between working people whether Protestant or Catholic, calling on the former to reject their propertied Unionist Establishment leadership.

Then on April 7 1970 Goulding, speaking at Glasnevin, began by taking up a basically Connolly position, but then in the latter part of his speech lapsed into a contradictory position in which he promoted the ('official') IRA as an essential factor in the revolution, while advocating the recognition of 'all forms of struggle and not confining ourselves to the form of struggle inherited ...'. He was struggling with the transformation problem in the presence of pressure from the traditional 'physical force' cultural mind-set. He felt the need to raise the profile of the 'official IRA' enough to keep the waverers on the agreed political track.

On April 14 1970 an article on the North condemned sectarian attacks on Orange marches which had led to confrontations with British troops. Attention was drawn to the prospect of talks between Dublin, Stormont and London regarding possible new constitutional arrangements, with London seeking more control over Dublin (reinforcing the 'federalism' threat). Support was urged for the NICRA Bill of Rights Campaign.

At the Ard Comhairle on April 17 1970 TMacG, MdeB, DK, Padraig Maloney, DMacR, SC, MR, LOC, OF, MD, TM. A Ó hAnnracháin, Frank Wogan, SR, SOC, CG were present. Belfast affiliation fees were handed in. Bombay St collections were unsatisfactory. Educational conferences had taken place in Limerick and Cork and were planned for Tyrone and Waterford. A prisoners protest meeting had taken place in TCD (SOC). Eoin Ó Murchú was appointed Organiser for the Gaeltacht. A meeting fixed for Maghera on May 10 to organise a new 6-co Executive. Bill of Rights campaign support was to be urged on Clann na hEireann at their Birminghan AGM.

Arising from this meeting the Coiste Seasta issued a statement on 17th April 20 1970 which analysed the role of the Nationalist Party, Blaney and Fianna Fail in the engineering of an approach to local leaderships offering aid on condition that they break with Republican leadership in Dublin, perceived as a political threat from the left. A 'red scare' tactic was used. People were urged to forget about political issues and concentrate on military defence against organised pogroms. Military intelligence officers from the Free State were involved: Kelly, Drohan and Duggan. A 'Civil Rights Information Office' financed by the Dublin Government was set up in Monaghan, with Seamus Brady in it, producing the *Voice of the North*, defined as 'a Fianna Fail paper masquerading as Civil Rights'(14).

The April 20 issue of *Nuacht Naisiunta* contained in its education section a continuation of a paper on 'Imperialism and the Irish Nation'; I have located what I think is the earlier part published subsequently in Issue 31 on May 5. It was unsigned but clearly by Anthony Coughlan and represented the classical Connolly Association position, emphasising the need to develop support from the labour movement in Britain. It was also visibly a dry run for Coughlan's later contributions to the anti-EEC campaign.

The education section on May 5 contained the introductory section of the 'Imperialism and the Irish Nation' paper, of which what appeared to be a continuation had been published in issue 29. It outlined the classical Marxist analysis of what Imperialism is, in terms of the European imperialist States and their empires in Africa and Asia. It linked into Irish history via the setting up of the Free State as a pioneering 'neo-colonialist' venture, with the handing over of power in the ex-colony to a government favourable to the continuation of imperial economic domination.

The April 27 1970 issue of *Nuacht Naisiunta(15)* had a report of the sentencing in Mold of people, one a British Army sergeant, for causing explosions in Wales between 1966 and 69. The report appeared to indicate sympathy with them, without analysing the possible role of establishment agents provocateurs in attempting to discredit Plaid Cymru. This ill-advised report I suspect could have initiated the line of thought that led to the subsequent canard about the 'official IRA' having given away its guns to the 'Free Wales Army', which body, insofar as it existed, was most likely an invention of the British 'dirty tricks department'. There are perhaps issues here requiring further elucidation.

At the Coiste Seasta on May 11 1970, attended by TMacG, DK, SD, CG, TM, SR, MdeB, it was noted that meetings on the Westminster elections had taken place. CG reported on Belfast; 5 points were agreed:

1) FF agents to be opposed wherever identified.
2) 'Well-known people such as Gerry Fitt' should not be opposed, but movement should put forward its own policies.
3) Contest one trial seat on the abstentionist policy.
4) Circulate a questionnaire seeking views on abstentionism or attendance.
5) Attend 'unity conventions' in strength, get republican policies accepted, and our candidates where possible accepted as unity candidates.

South Tyrone urged getting NICRA policies agreed by the unity candidate. SR reported from Armagh; it had been a badly organised meeting, with small attendance, no unified decision were taken. There was however said to have been a 'successful educational conference' on the Sunday. In Derry they did not want a republican candidate, nor to attend any unity convention. They wanted to march on the American base protesting about Cambodia. There had been a complaint about picketing in connection with squatting families, without informing the action committee.

Here we again have evidence of a pincer movement on the exposed position of the Republican Clubs: ultra-leftism in Derry, and probably Provisional recruiting in Armagh. Electoral strategy was crippled by the residual abstentionism imposed by the January Ard Fheis.

TMacG reported from Mid-Ulster; they did not want an abstentionist candidate. They could select a republican abstentionist candidate and use this as a lever to get a preferred unity candidate.

At the Ard Comhairle on May 16 TMacG, RJ, SOC, SC, PK, IB, DK, DMacR, MMacG, SR, FP, FW, TM, OMcC were present. Kevin Agnew and Kevin Murphy were also present as visitors. There was a re-run of the Westminster election discussions as at the Coiste Seasta, dominated by the abstention incubus. It was agreed to try to recruit Labour Party drop-out dissidents. There were positive results from the organising effort, and UI sales were increasing. It was agreed to call a meeting of republican NICRA activists with a view to enhancing the Bill of Rights campaign. The Estate Agents conference was to be leafleted with housing action material.

On May 26 1970 *Nuacht Naisiunta* noted that the British Embassy had been peacefully occupied by members of the movement during the previous week. The politics of the occupation were related to what was going on in the North, but the precise nature of the demands were not made clear; it was assumed readers all knew. In fact this issue was a demand for the release of Eamonn Smullen and others who had been arrested seeking to obtain arms, in the August 1969 aftermath, in a 'sting' operation. Those concerned in the occupation were arrested and remanded in custody. Janice Williams, who later became my legal wife after a lengthy period as 'common-law' wife, spent a week in Mountjoy over this episode, earning the credit of having 'gone to jail for Ireland', this being considered a political asset in some quarters. This episode perhaps also contributed to the growing unease of the Government regarding the role of the post-split IRA in the 26 Counties.

There was also a lengthy continuation of the 'Imperialism' paper, which set the stage for later arguments about the Common Market, confirming the authorship of Coughlan. It raised the following issues:

(a) Exploitation of Irish agriculture by the artificial rigging of the British market, favouring the store cattle trade and 'dog and stick' farming. *The arguments presented here closely follow those of JJ in the 30s and 40s.*
(b) Increasing domination of imperial capital over Irish capital in the Irish economy.
(c) Outflow of Irish capital abroad, mainly via banks and insurance companies but also privately.
(d) Political subservience to British imperialism in the field of foreign policy.
(e) Cultural domination by Britain.

Republican Clubs in the North (Newry and Coalisland) were reported as selling openly the *United Irishman*, and were campaigning for the release of Republican prisoners in Britain. Presumably what they were imprisoned for actions related to the August 1969 events, and it is assumed everyone knows what these were, as we are not told.

Coiste Seasta June 2 1970: TMacG, SR, SOC, Seán Dunne, TM, CG, SD, RJ, SC. There was a report of a very negative meeting in Derry by TMacG; it was badly organised, and indecisive regarding election policy. Coleraine Club was missing. Seamus Rattigan and RJ were to monitor the Common Market Study Group. RJ presented an agenda for an Organisers' Conference, planned for June 22/23. SOC to meet with LP dissidents. Seamus Costello and Jim McCabe to meet with Fermanagh South Tyrone republicans to discuss candidate selection.

Dublin Comhairle Ceanntar were to issue a statement on local democracy, in connection with the Commissioners meeting. *This was to do with the then suspension of local democracy in Dublin; it sank without trace; there was no subsequent sign of it in Nuacht Naisiunta, that I have seen. This indicates that attention was on issues like prisoners and the key issue of local democracy had slipped down the agenda. According to Janice Williams they did try to organise a public protest event, and to get Labour supporters to speak, but were unsuccessful.*

Greaves on June 2 recorded receiving from Anthony Coughlan a Hibernia article which contained '...the story of Fianna Fail's negotiations with the IRA, and the subsequent decision to split it. .... AC says the article is substantially accurate. He speaks of great political confusion in Ireland. He goes on to assign responsibility to the unprincipled intrigues the republicans themselves resorted to. It looks as if they are repeating 1948, a la Clann na Poblachta. The entire direction is to discredit Fianna Fail ...'. Later on June 6: '...I think the split in the movement (product of Roy's nonsense) has deeply demoralised the Irish left ...'.

The next day June 6 1970 he has the following to say: '...they never succeed in anything. They belong to a class that cannot win. And yet the glamour surrounds them. For all the talk of "socialism" they are clearly opposed to it. They make blunder after blunder... talking about a "National Liberation Front"(16). That is RHJ's invention. I am inclined to think the IWP are foolish to change their name to CPI and have this non-organic amalgamation, or shall we say, incompletely organic. Clearly the masses are miles away from them...'.

We were never very specific about the 'National Liberation Front' process, but the feeling I had was that the IWP-CPNI amalgamating into the CPI was politically a non-starter, and would be moribund due to the dead hand of Stalinism. People disillusioned with this might be able to think their way into joining an expanded, integrated and politicised republican movement which, as well as the primary objective of national unity through democratic reform in the North, had the core democratic Marxist objective of attaining democratic control over the capital investment process, and creating a friendly environment to co-operative enterprise. The 'NLF' was, for a time, a convenient in-house label for this concept, which we used during internal discussions. We never managed to think of a good name for the concept, although viewed retrospectively it was perfectly valid, taking on board as it did a recognition of the developing crisis in post-Stalinist Marxist orthodoxy, which came to a head subsequently in 1989.

There was a series of Coiste Seasta meetings in June(17) which dealt with EEC controversies, Northern conventions, analysis of 'hawks and doves' in Fianna

Fail: Lynch was regarded by Mac Giolla as leading a sell-out to Britain: '...the new constitutional arrangement which the British Government now has in mind for Ireland is a federal arrangement, which would end partition as such, but would keep all of Ireland firmly under the political and economic control of Westminster...'. The present writer tried unsuccessfully to make the case for a Special Convention in time for a possible Autumn election combined with a referendum.

There was a report of a resolution from the Whitehall-Santry branch of the Irish Labour Party in support of the release of the prisoners in Britain, suggesting that this campaign was broadening, as the reasons for the arrest were beginning to be understood.

Janice, who (as we saw above) herself was jailed in Dublin over this issue, recollects that it arose because some Irish activists, mostly of the political left, some with republican backgrounds (Eamonn Smullen being one), had been arrested in London and imprisoned on what was visibly a trumped-up conspiracy charge. This I must say I tend to interpret as another indication of the workings of the British 'dirty tricks' department: the intent was clearly to isolate political republicanism, encourage the movement to revert, both 'officially' and 'provisionally', to its traditional militarist mode, and draw attention away from the Civil Rights issue in the North.

The July 1 1970 issue of *Nuacht Naisiunta* featured the 'official' IRA again 'coming out of the closet' and issuing a further statement, attempting openly to play a political role, taking away from the leading status of the NICRA in the northern situation.

This I must say, with hindsight, counts as an appalling blunder. I personally had no role in it.

The statement condemned the sectarian fighting, and attributed it to British manipulation. Orange parades were forced through republican areas with the support of the British Army. Bernadette Devlin had been arrested. Northern units were encouraged to co-operate with defence committees, 'giving military aid.. for the adequate defence of peoples lives and homes ...'. While doing this they were urged to 'contain sectarian strife'.

There was a final paragraph based on the perceived threat of the 'federal solution' based on the foregoing analysis of Lynch's dealings with the British. The thinking behind this must have seemed obscure to the activists in the North, some of whom still saw the NICRA and the Bill of Rights as the key issues.

This statement must have emanated from Goulding who was feeling the strength of the politicisation process wavering, with half-baked recruits wondering which way to turn; should they go 'provisional'? The political alternatives were looking increasingly obscure. He felt he had to issue what amounted to an 'official' call to arms, to keep them onside. But at the same time the 'call to arms' was fudged, with somewhat fuzzy politics, enough however to fuel Government paranoia about a threat from the Left.

The political influence, such as it was, I am inclined to think was primarily from Anthony Coughlan. The present writer was increasingly taking a back seat, having taken on an innovative self-employed role, which included the Irish Times *science and technology column, to which I was giving some priority.*

Popularising Science

The mid-year of 1970, when I was trying to distance myself from the catastrophic Northern developments, is a good time to introduce what became increasingly my main interest in the 1970s. After resigning from Aer Lingus, and setting up as a technology consultant, increasingly on the fringe of Trinity College, I approached Douglas Gageby, the then Editor of the Irish Times, and sold him the idea of a regular 'science and technology column'. I suggested a need to keep a watching brief on the actions of the new National Science Council, then recently set up under the chairmanship of Colm Ó h-Eocha, as a result of the Government taking on board the recommendations of the Lynch-Miller OECD Report of 1964, noted earlier.

In the early 1980s, during the phase-out of my TCD consultancy work, I got the opportunity to edit the material of the column into a book(18). It is appropriate here to quote from my introduction, which outlines the philosophy:

"This is a record of a personal crusade. The object was to try to bring about a situation in Ireland such that the best scientific brains would be permitted both to fulfil themselves scientifically and to earn a living in their native country, contributing to its technological and economic development. Prior to about 1970, the normal career-pattern for the young Irish scientist involved emigration, in many cases (most cases in some disciplines) permanent. The best-known Irish emigrant scientist was, perhaps, John Desmond Bernal, to whom can be attributed the identification and naming of the 'Brain-drain' process as a characteristic of the imperial-colonial relationship.

"The raw material of this book appeared in the form of a 'Science and Technology' column in the *Irish Times* which ran from the beginning of 1970 to the end of 1976, a period of seven years.

"This was a time when the Irish State was beginning to recognise that science and technology were important factors in the national economic development process. The Lynch-Miller report *Science and Irish Economic Development* had come out in 1964, recommending the setting up of a National Science Council to advise the Government. This took place, let it be said, as a result of the outside influence of the Organisation for European Co-operation and Development (OECD); there was no way whereby such an innovatory approach could have been developed within the impervious walls of the Civil Service without a strong external influence of some kind.

"The Column, while it existed, had a philosophy which can perhaps be summarised by asking the question: 'How best can scientific discoveries be creditably transformed into useful and appropriate technology, in the context of a small developing nation attempting to assert its identity in the neo-colonial aftermath of a global imperial system?'

"By a process of continuous critical chipping away at the pillars of the imperial legacy, a certain amount of consciousness was aroused in the Irish scientific community, to the extent that when the Column terminated in January 1977 its lack was noticed and commented upon. These comments continue to this day, in a high proportion of encounters by the writer with people whom he has not met before, in which his role in the Column period is looked back upon with nostalgia. This restructuring of the Column material is an offering to these sometime readers, in the hopes that they may find it useful or stimulating. It may also prove to be of interest to those concerned elsewhere than in Ireland with the initiation of creative State policies for science and technology in developing countries; where possible this has been borne in mind when selecting and structuring the material.

"All I have done is picked out sequences of contributions to the contemporary discussions which took place within a set of themes or channels as suggested by the chapter headings. In some cases a coherent evolving picture emerges, in others a sequence of loosely-related snapshots..

"In most cases the problems treated are still with us, so that I think I am safe in saying that the material has not become dated. Readers can amuse themselves by updating the record mentally in the fields that they know. Mostly they are likely to share my impression that the basic rate of change, in spite of activity which in some cases seems frenetic, is really rather slow.

I have tidied up the stylistic infelicities which resulted from the need to meet a weekly deadline and have corrected errors drawn to my attention at the time. I have not done any more research into the topics covered; to do so would have been prohibitive, as well as changing the whole character of the exercise. It does not claim to be a scholarly work and should not be regarded as such. If there are errors of fact which escaped the contemporary control-loop, I apologise for them. They can, if necessary, be cleaned up in a second edition, if such turns out to be merited.

"Where I have amended substantively the text, it is in the light of information available to me at the original time of writing; I have avoided retrospective cheating. Where retrospective comment is called for, I have added it via the explanatory notes at the end of each chapter. I have also sometimes used the latter as an aid to generalising the experience outside the Irish context.

"I must take the opportunity of thanking Mr Douglas Gageby, who as Editor of the *Irish Times* provided me with the chance to begin the regular column at the end of 1969. This, for him, was a 'shot in the dark'; there was no precedent in Irish newspaper tradition. The cross-channel precedent (Crowther and the Manchester Guardian in the 1930s) was unknown in Ireland.

I am also indebted to Trinity College for the period of funded research leave which made this possible."

Thanks to the foregoing, I got to review a book by Dr Michael Woods(19), then in charge of the Agricultural Institute horticulture unit at Kinsealy, and subsequently (2000) Minister for Education. I was somewhat critical, accusing him of being unduly influenced by the vision of the Harvard Business School, but supportive of his proposition that the researcher should have a hand in the dissemination of the results.

Also in 1970 I was invited to contribute a paper to *Léargas*(20), the journal of the Institute of Public Administration, in which I showed, using Aer Lingus experience, how in the economic planning and operations research domains the use of the computer in mathematical analytical mode was making the bridge between its scientific applications and its use in routine data-processing.

It is appropriate here also to mention the initiation in 1970 by Gordon Foster in the TCD Statistics Department of the MSc programme in Operations Research(21), with which I became associated after leaving Aer Lingus, as an extern supervisor, with academic 'Research Associate' status. This helped contribute to my economic survival in this difficult period, and I develop this in the next chapter.

The Political Mess Worsens

Malachi McBirney's Bodenstown speech was reported on July 6 in *Nuacht Naisiunta* as being a statement from the IRA which attempted to discourage violent attacks on provocative Orange marches, leading to sectarian strife between Protestant and Catholic workers. It was becoming evident that the British Army was actively encouraging Orange marchers to go through republican areas, seeking to provoke an armed response. The emphasis in the references however is to 'Citizens Defence Committees' and the Civil Rights agenda had apparently been dropped.

The Dublin Wolfe Tone Society record takes up again, after a gap, on July 7, when typed minutes of committee meetings begin; Uinsean Mac Eoin took over being secretary, with Anthony Coughlan bowing out with a view to concentrating on the Common Market Study Group.

The July 13 1970 Coiste Seasta noted that one Joe Sweeney in Clonmel had resigned; he was to be told that Anthony Coughlan was not a member of the movement.

It is not clear how this resignation was related to any act of Coughlan. It could be Sweeney reacting against the emphasis being given to the EEC campaign. The content of the letter illustrates the perceptions underlying the leakage of support to the Provisionals: SC, CG and TMacG were seen as apparently being led astray by the likes of the present writer and Coughlan.

On Belfast TMacG reported back; there were 6 active clubs; the Falls Citizen Defence Committee was un-elected; they wanted to broaden its base and give it a local government function. 5000 copies of the UI had been seized; CG wanted to have it bought up at Westminster.

Michael O'Riordain (CPI) had tried to set up a unity meeting in Dublin and had asked the Provos to send a speaker, but they had refused, even for Éamonn Mac Thomáis in his personal capacity. There was considered to be no point in TMacG going.

The hard-left, in well-meaning ignorance, wanted some sort of abstract 'unity' with people who even at that moment, it turned out later, were planning a campaign of divisive terror.

Greaves in Belfast on July 15 1970 observed the increasing militarisation of the scene. Betty Sinclair thought it would be better to have the 26 counties united with the six and federated with Britain than to have this go on. He encountered Madge Davidson and Dalton Kelly in the NICRA rooms, along with a Connolly Youth lad from Dublin; the latter became his '...guide around the ruins ...'. The CY were meeting with the British YCL at the weekend; they were critical of the CPGB. CDG tried to explain some of the problems. They observed lads playing football, and soldiers looking on.

Back in the NICRA offices Jimmy Stewart arrived and took CDG up to the '...Defence Committee rooms. There were moves on foot to transform it into a

Catholic Defence Committee. The priests were coming in, and NICRA is being denounced as "communist". I felt uneasy about the whole position...'. There was discussion about the Ardoyne proposal to re-route Orange processions; CDG's demand would have been to ban them.

The Wolfe Tone Society committee met on July 17 1970. It was agreed to try to organise a 'solidarity-type' conference in Dundalk in mid-September. UMacE announced that a WTS had been started in Newry. RJ and CMacL were to visit Limerick; poetry readings were to be abandoned. The AGM was fixed for November 7. UMacE read a paper giving his assessment of the North.

The Mac Eoin paper (1.5 pages) is in the WTS archive: he saw control as now being with the Army and Westminster; federal settlement with pretence of national unity were seen as a possibility. In this context Fianna Fail would move in on Nationalist ground; radicals like Bernadette would be isolated. NICRA was now outdated; a moderate nationalist umbrella group was required, to express minimum requirements for a federated republic, avoiding radical rhetoric such as to drive moderates into the arms of Fianna Fail. He calls for a new role for a Northern WTS (the old Belfast WTS being defunct) with the objective of trying to win the middle ground.

There is also in the WTS archive a copy of an interview by Jack Dowling of Cathal Goulding, done for *This Week* on July 31 1970. *This was when Goulding was trying to hold the movement together after the split, and build up the 'officials', which later became the Workers Party.* He outlined the then thinking of the leadership of the movement regarding how to achieve a socialist republic, and how the movement had attempted to go political, with parliamentary participation, to the extent that they were not in a position to supply 'defence' in August 1969, though they had put up armed resistance to the July 3 1970 re-occupation of the Falls by the British. He gave his views on the basis for the split. He defended the organisation from the charge of being anti-clerical and 'red'. He claimed to have persuaded US supporters that parliamentary participation would be useful if guided by revolutionary principle.

Coiste Seasta meetings in July covered regional reports, attitudes to provisional meetings, educational conferences (with the present writer participating as from the Common Market Study Group; I was consciously back-tracking, and the movement accepted it). I had however drafted a new members pamphlet, which was read and approved.

The Ard Comhairle on August 8 1970 was attended by TMacG, FW, MR, IB, TM, RJ, DK, LOC, DMacR, SR, MMcG, SOC, OF, SD, AOhA, SC, OMcC. Breasail Ó Caollai attended as visiting Connaught organiser. TMacG gave an overview report of the work of the movement in support of the NICRA. There were detailed regional reports, showing a consistent high level of activity by many cumainn, all over, reflected in high UI sales. Thee were 10 active Clubs in the 6 Counties, taking up trade union and housing issues. A committee was set up to draft a short-term policy document for the movement, with a resolution, proposed by SC and seconded by MR: 'recognising that the ultimate objective of the Republican Movement is the establishment of a Democratic 32 county socialist republic....

taking into account the existing political, economic and military position in the 6 and 26 counties...'.

A drafting committee was set up consisting of TMacG, SR, RJ, CG, MR, OF and OMcC; this was to meet local and middle leadership N and S, and to report back to an AC meeting on the 22nd.

This initiative seems to have sunk without trace; the next AC meeting was on November 7, and I can find no mention in Nuacht Naisiunta.

Coiste Seasta on August 17 1970: present TMacG, MR, DK, SOC, SR. The sub-committee was working and had reported; two drafts had emerged; both were to be presented on 22nd. AC members were to be contacted. The new 6-co regional executive was: Malachi McGurran Chair, Liam McMillan vice-chair, Liam Ó Comáin Sec, Francie Donnelly Treasurer, Oliver Frawley PRO, with Peter Morris, Malachi McBirney and Tom French as publicity committee. There were 25 clubs represented at the Brackereilly meeting at which the new executive was set up.

There seems then to have been a long hiatus, and the August 22 event remains unrecorded. Politics however was still struggling to continue.

Some WTS correspondence from RJ dated August 21 1970 is on record; I can fill it in by recollection. Cathal Mac Liam and I went to Limerick; we met with Jim Kemmy, but the contact network was fouled by our encountering a hack journalist of the Fianna Fail persuasion, with whom Kemmy had had negative experience. The mission came to nothing; we had insufficient local knowledge to enable us to avoid the pitfalls.

It seems also we were supportive of the City Quay housing protest, which we attempted to link politically with the 'Battle of Hume St'(22); this also was unsuccessful, because the City Quay people, whose community was being demolished, could not identify with the Hume St issue, which was basically architecture and urban planning in the abstract, related to office environments. There was also currently a housing protest going in Pembroke Road, with squatters in occupation.

It seems that about this time I had considered going for the Seanad, Owen Sheehy-Skeffington's seat being up for grabs, due to his illness. In the end I decided against it, and the seat went to Mary Robinson, who later became President. Greaves it seems would have regarded this as a positive move on my part. Skeffington had had a heart attack; I had been to see him, and there was some rapprochement; I might even have had his 'blessing', which would have picked up a few votes. I was however too concerned with the problem of how to make a living as an applied-scientific consultant, and this would have been a diversion(23).

There was a WTS committee meeting on September 15 1970. It was agreed to co-operate with the Newry WTS in a 'concerned citizens' conference on October 3, on the North. It was urged that about 6 people should prepare papers, and that it should not be open to the press. It was agreed to try to re-activate Alec Foster with a view to trying to re-convene a Belfast WTS. A general meeting of Society fixed for October 6, to discuss the current position in the North.

In the WTS archive there is a copy of a letter dated September 17 which went out to selected people as from the Newry WTS, signed by Geraldine McGuigan, inviting them to '...a small conference sponsored by us, and supported by a countrywide group of concerned citizens who have been directly or indirectly involved in events... October 24.. Derryhale Hotel, Dundalk. She went on to list an initial group of invitees: Margo Collins, Madge Davison, Bernadette Devlin, James Donnelly, Jack Dowling, Sam Dowling, Mike Farrell, Frank Gogarty, Brandan Harkin, Fred Heatley, Ciaran Mac an Aili, Oliver MacCaul, Terence McCaughey, Kevin Boyle, Eamonn McCann, Kevin McCorry, Uinsean Mac Eoin, Malachi McGurran, EK McGrady, Frank MacManus, Eamonn Melaugh, Terry O'Brien, Emmet O'Connell, Roy Johnston, Edwina Stewart.

There appears to be nothing on record to confirm that this actually happened; it is a group spanning officials, provisionals, communists, PDs, Trotskyists and various WTS contacts from the middle ground, from which an agreed position would be somewhat unlikely to be forthcoming. It looks like the Society was grasping at straws, in a rapidly worsening situation.

Nuacht Naisiunta on September 22 1970 with its Nixon statement placed the movement firmly among the international consensus of opposition to the Vietnam war, and urged local republicans to associate themselves with various demonstrations against it.

The NI Republican Clubs statement, issued from the Regional Executive, with Malachi McGurran in the lead, attacked the Public Order Act and the Criminal Justice (Temporary provisions) Act as being in effect the re-introduction of Special Powers. They were trying to resurrect the Civil Rights agenda, in the face of increasingly militarist oppression by the British Army.

At the Coiste Seasta on Sept 28 1970 a meeting to exchange ideas about anti-EEC actions was planned among representatives of 'radical groups'; this should not initiate actions 'as itself' but maybe a joint group could come later. A pamphlet on the EEC and Neutrality was in preparation, by Kader Asmal.

The 'radical groups' label is a euphemism for interaction with the Communist Party in the context of the emerging 'national liberation movement' concept. The barrier posed by the existence of the Stalin incubus was however palpable. While the movement valued and respected the ideas and actions of local CP activists, we were acutely aware of the Stalinist label as a political liability. Whence the perceived need for keeping such meetings discreet.

On October 5 1970 TMacG reported at the Coiste Seasta on a meeting with the Dublin Regional Council of the Labour Party, a radical focus, which was keen to get joint internal meetings going to co-ordinate anti-EEC actions, for example public meetings at factory level. SOC reported on anti-EEC meetings with the Connolly Youth, and with Sligo and Bray campaign committees. Meetings with broader representation were planned. The question of a Cumann commission on collections for the NICRA arose; it had been reported to the NICRA in Belfast by Eddie Glacken the CYM Secretary.

This was a cause of friction, representing as it did a basic difference in approach to money as between SF and CP activists, illustrating, perhaps, the 'petit-bourgeois' status of the former in the eyes of the latter, who were dominated by a sort of 'Stalinist puritanism'!

On October 6 1970 a general meeting of the Dublin Wolfe Tone Society took place, which was minuted by Uinsean MacEoin(24). Cathal MacLiam was in the chair. RJ reported on the aborted Limerick project; Micheál Ó Loingsigh reported on plans for an anti-EEC meeting there. Anthony Coughlan traced the origins of the NICRA, and criticised the role of the 'Peoples Democracy'; he called for a Bill of Rights; direct rule was not a solution. RJ stressed that the Belfast WTS should have remained in existence and not allowed itself to be absorbed into the NICRA. Dick Roche called for the WTS to create a role for itself as a bridge between people of differing religions, and the reconcile the 'two wings of the republican movement'. Con Lehane stressed the deep fears of the Northern Protestants. Maire Comerford praised the way the NICRA had split the Orange movement. Other speakers included Alan Heussaff, Brendan Ó Cathaoir, Staf van Velthoven, Uinsean Mac Eoin. The AGM was fixed for November 3 in 20 Marlborough Road; a weekend conference projected for later.

In *Nuacht Naisiunta* on October 7 1970 it was reported that the Nixon visit had been duly demonstrated against, and a large Dublin SF contingent had marched behind the Vietnam war protest banner *(led incidentally by Peadar O'Donnell, with George Jeffares doing most of the organising)*. This had prompted Provisional elements to accuse them of 'being more interested in Vietnam than Derry', but the newsletter defended stoutly the internationalist tradition of small-nation solidarity.

There was an advance notice of a meeting to be held in Rathmines organised by the Pearse Cumann, which it seems I chaired. An attempt was made to have it broad-based, and the target was the EEC. I have no recollection of this meeting; perhaps it happened, but it probably was a damp squib. This again must have been Coughlan influence; he seems to have been attempting to find something for the Dublin movement to do, which would point in a good strategic direction, recognising that there was little they could do in Dublin to affect the deteriorating situation in the North. He had recently published his pamphlet *Why Ireland Should Not Join*, and *Nuacht Naisiunta* 52 promoted it with a review.

Meanwhile in the Falls Road the Ulster Defence Regiment had seized 7000 copies of the *United Irishman* and burned them in Ross St. The seizure was under Regulation 8 of the Special Powers Act. The UI was avowedly non-sectarian, while sectarian papers like Paisley's *Protestant Telegraph* and Seamus Brady's *Voice of the North* were free to circulate. In the UI statement the key quote was "..both the Unionist Party and the British authorities fear the acceptance by even some section of the Protestant community of the non-sectarian philosophy of Republicanism ...'. A reprint was promised, in greater numbers, to profit from the publicity generated by the seizure.

The Coiste Seasta on October 12 1970 agreed a donation of £5 for the Irish Voice on Vietnam.

This again was an aspect of the 'NLF' concept. George Jeffares was the prime mover in the Vietnam context, fronted by Peadar O'Donnell. GJ subsequently became the prime mover in the Labour Party Dublin Regional Council, which he tried to develop as a Left-political think-tank and ideas-forum. He had by then dropped out from the CPI over the question of Czechoslovakia, along with Sam Nolan, Joe Deasy and others who subsequently contributed to the 'Labour Left' tendency. It was natural for an emerging 'democratic left' tendency, wishing to escape from the dead hand of Moscow domination, to move closer to the politicising republicans. At the same time, it was natural for those among the politicising republicans who had residual military mindsets as baggage, to want to move closer to the 'official CPI', Moscow domination notwithstanding. There is an empathy between Stalinism and top-down military-type organisation. These were two contradictory aspects of the republican politicisation process, which ultimately destabilised it.

Then at the Coiste Seasta on October 26 1970 there was planned an anti-Manshold week of lectures, being organised by an ad-hoc committee of CYM, CP and Labour Left. The Hilltown Co Down meeting planned for November 15, mentioned earlier by Rhatigan, was to be focused on the EEC.

The underlying strategic thinking behind all this I attribute to the influence of Anthony Coughlan, who was promoting the 'Federation' model: ie the British were perceived as using the leverage of the Northern situation to influence the Irish government to come into the EEC along with them as some sort of federated close-knit unit. This concept surfaced repeatedly. The result was that the politics of Northern reform was half-hearted, leaving open a political vacuum later to be filled militarily by the Provisionals .

Then on October 26 1970 it was reported in *Nuacht Naisiunta* that a meeting was held in O'Connell St, organised by Dublin SF, to call for the release of the prisoners in Britain. This for the first time went into who they were and what they were in for. They had, it seems, in the emotional atmosphere of August 1969, attempted to get hold of arms for the people of Belfast. In some cases maybe only talked about it. This episode had provided a focus for the British militarising (trend? campaign? conspiracy? how does one label a situation where the British establishment reacts instinctively to Irish events?)

The episode had generated a number of occupations, stunts etc to draw attention to the prisoners, but these had been mostly unsuccessful in doing so. In contrast, '...we have now witnessed the spectacle of mass hysteria and hero worship of Mr Haughey and three others who have been found not guilty of failing to import a comparatively useless consignment of pistols... sheer incompetence... comparatively simple task... did they really want to import the arms, or only want to appear to... are they to be regarded as national heroes while six young men are ...forgotten in British prisons?'

It is remarkable how destructive the presence of the gun is to the development of sensible politics. The degeneration of the political situation must be attributed to the key mistake of allowing the August 1969 pogroms to trigger the militarisation process. It should have led politically to the disbandment of the Specials, and to sweeping reforms to Stormont, had the political path been followed consistently.

There was a call to develop a campaign for the restoration of local democracy in Dublin, with setting up a Citizens Committee, supported by representatives of tenants and residents associations, to monitor the decisions of the Commissioner and publicise them, particularly in relation to speculators and landlords.

Cathal Goulding's oration at Edentubber was given in full in *Nuacht Naisiunta* on November 3 1970. In it he attacked the 'five points of difference' promulgated by the 'loose association of individuals and splinter-groups which give its allegiance to what is generally styled the "provisional army council"..'. He turned round the question, to ask what were their points of difference with the 6 and 26 county establishments? He took his stand robustly on the left, 'placing the common people... as masters of their own destiny... making and maintaining contact with the disunited masses of the discontented... weak because they are disunited ...'. He did however speak on behalf of the IRA, and predicted that before the 70s were out the British right to rule Ireland would again be challenged in arms.

He clearly felt that having adopted an IRA position he had to compete with the Provisionals in military mode, or at least to threaten to do so, verbally, to try to hold his own supporters, an inconsistent political position.

The AGM of the Wolfe Tone Society took place on November 3 1970. There is in the archive no record of this directly, but there exist what looks like notes for an annual report by RJ of 1971 activities, which commences with a note as follows: Chairman Cathal Mac Liam, Vice-Chairman Micheál Ó Loingsigh, Joint Secretaries Derry Kelleher and Dick Roche, committee Dermot O'Doherty, Seamus Mac Gabhainn, RJ and Joy Rudd.

The Sinn Fein leadership continued to be distracted by the local O'Brien's Bridge / Montpelier school issue; Eoin Ó Murchú was to get out from this and go back to trying to organise the Gaeltacht. The contact pattern with various support organisations remained fuzzy, and was tending to include the Peoples Democracy as well as 'English radical organisations'. Plans for the Sheelin Shamrock educational conference were firmed up. A 'Freedom Manifesto'(25) was to be prepared for the Ard Fheis (RJ's motion); regional meetings to take place beforehand.

The Sheelin Shamrock conference took place towards the end of November 1970, and was memorable as a relatively high point in the political development of the post-split left-republicans. Topics for Sheelin were planned to include '19th century revolutions', 'significance of the TU movement', 'history of class struggles', 'decline of socialist movement after 1921', 'the Movement in the 40s and 50s', 'small farmers and the CR movement'. Speakers would, it was hoped, include de Courcy Ireland, Kader Asmal, Noel Harris, George Gilmore, Tom Kilroy, Dalton Kelly and various AC members. This plan was largely fulfilled, and some 50 people attended. Janice Williams, who participated, recollects that Ruth First of the ANC spoke, along with Asmal.

The event was however subject to stress from the military tradition, in that the selection of personnel to attend it was actually an 'army' function. Janice Williams shared a room with 2 other women, one of whom had a gun in her possession (she said she was 'minding it' for one of the lads), and the other of whom was subsequently convicted of a serious offence involving firearms. Despite Goulding's declared policy of avoiding recruiting people on the basis of the 'romantic appeal of the gun', this was apparently continuing to happen, and of course the August 1969 events reinforced the process, strengthening the mind-set of the middle leadership who would have been doing the recruiting. the event was organised militarily, and orders were expected to be obeyed. Those of us who were concerned with trying to fuel the political process at the top in fact had little control over what went on in the undergrowth. Much recent Army recruitment had inevitably been in response to August 1969.

In *Nuacht Naisiunta* on November 16 1970 Seamus Ó Tuathail, editor of the *United Irishman*, reminded the Queens students of the origins of 1790s republican philosophy in the continental Enlightenment, and went on to attribute the religious mania a partition-time to the industrialist of the North defending their access to the markets of the Empire. Carson sent 100,000 to defend the Empire and Redmond sent 170,000. He went on to draw a parallel with Chichester Clark and Jack Lynch, with Ireland being led back into the Empire via the Common Market. In passing he mentioned the 1932 'outdoor relief' riots when Catholic and Protestant workers united.

No clear currently relevant political message emerged from this, or from the Goulding oration at Edentubber. The militarisation of the situation had allowed the Bill of Rights and the NICRA objectives to sink without trace in the movement's perceptions. They clung to historical analogies, worthy but impractical.

Mac Giolla in Oxford had a better-constructed, though still historical and ideological, message, where he attempted to counter Jack Lynch's statement that the Northern trouble was an Irish problem: Britain saving Ireland from the Irish, like America saving Vietnam from the Vietnamese, and Russia saving Czechoslovakia from the Czechs. He went on to attack the sectarian barriers erected by the British ruling class. The barriers would crumble when the British rule was destroyed. Republicanism he defined as separatist, socialist and non-sectarian. The mantle of de Valera over which Lynch and Haughey were fighting was not, and never had been, a republican mantle. Socialism, in the Irish republican context, he claimed as the native growth through Connolly, repudiating current factions looking to Lenin, Stalin, Trotsky and Mao.

A meeting, called at Swatragh co Derry by the Connolly Republican Club, included Kevin McCorry (NICRA organiser), Oliver Frawley (Belfast Republican Clubs), Máirín de Burca, Kevin Agnew (NICRA Chair at this time) and Seán Ó Cionnaigh as speakers as well as Bernadette Devlin.

The focus however had been displaced towards the issue of the republican prisoners in Britain (see above) and away from the potential for local community development offered by the existence of the Swatragh co-op.

On November 22 1970 Greaves noted in his diary that the Belfast NICRA had endorsed the McRory report, of which he did not approve, writing so to McCorry. Effective local government was gone. The next day he noted that the WTS and the CCL in Dublin had endorsed the draft Bill of Rights. Then on December 1 he learned from Seán Nolan in Dublin that Anthony Coughlan was coming to London to attend an EEC meeting; it turned out the next day that AC was to speak at the meeting, filling in for Justin Keating, who has cried off.

Anthony Coughlan was increasingly putting his efforts into the anti-EEC campaign, the Northern question having become intractable due to the developing Provisional militarism.

This anti-EEC campaign was increasingly being taken up by (official) Sinn Fein; they were to approach small-shopkeeper organisations urging measures such as co-operative purchasing, to enable them to compete with supermarkets, while pointing out the EEC threat. Eoin Ó Murchú was to speak on the EEC at Ennistymon Macra na Feirme. Tomás Mac Giolla was reported as speaking in Clontarf at a Dublin North-East Anti Common Market Committee, along with

Dalton Kelly of the TCD Republican Club. There was much Northern Republican Club activity reported, including the first anti-EEC meeting in the North.

A letter by RJ on the question of the dissolved Dublin Corporation was accepted to be sent to the Dublin Comhairle Ceanntar and to the Dublin Trades Council.

This emphasis on the EEC at this time, and the attempt to develop the wider European view of the national question, undoubtedly was the continuing influence of Anthony Coughlan. Any analysis of the development of the thinking of the left in Ireland during this period would be incomplete without input from the Irish Democrat, of which AC was the Dublin correspondent.

At the WTS on December 1 1970 Antonia Healy gave a Humanist view on Freedom of Conscience. There was another attempt to re-activate Belfast.

At the Sinn Fein Ard Comhairle on December 5 1970 Malachi McGurran reported that CRA march in Enniskillen had gone off without incident, but they were expecting summonses. Regional meeting fixed for Dec 13 to discuss future march policy. Ard Fheis resolutions on electoral policy were agreed. Anti-internment meeting fixed for Dec 12, with broad platform including civil rights organisations, tenants, trade unions.

MMcG proposed 4 regional groupings of the 24 Clubs, for election of regional delegates to new Ard Comhairle. There was also proposed a 6-cumainn regional grouping in North Leinster. All were agreed.

It was agreed that all speakers at educational conferences should be first approved by AC or CS. *It is not clear if this was just precautionary, or if some specific speaker was being objected to. I don't recollect any tension on this issue; there was general agreement on the need to promote the intellectual unity of the broad left.*

The December 8 1970 issue of *Nuacht Naisiunta* was dominated by a perception that internment was on the agenda in the 26 counties. A series of anti-internment meetings was projected. The Ard Fheis was projected for Liberty Hall on January 16-17. The Manifesto set the agenda for the regions: get to understand the specific needs of working owner-managers, self-employed and unorganised workers which were not catered for by the current Fianna Fail hegemony.

It is far from clear what was the trigger for the perception that internment was on the agenda in the 26 counties. It could have been that Lynch, having put Haughey Blaney and Boland in their places, was expected to turn on the Provisionals, and in doing so take up the 'officials' for good measure, as the Special Branch records would have difficulty in distinguishing. At national level 'repartition', the 'federal solution', and 're-opening the Treaty negotiations' seem to have been in the air. In this context the emphasis on the EEC seems to have been a diversion. The full analysis of the early post-split days must remain on the agenda.

An anti-internment march by Northern Clubs was planned. Derry Kelleher was to speak in Dublin at a Barney Casey commemoration, organised by left-wing groups. Barney Casey had been shot in 1940 when in internment, and the inquest had been adjourned sine die; Kelleher had witnessed the event. MdeB urged that the re-opening of the inquest be made an issue.

There is an extensive minute of this issue in Derry Kelleher's handwriting. The issue must have been raised at this time because internment was felt to be on the agenda, this being the way in which the Northern government was reacting to the NICRA campaign; they were trying to provoke an armed response to the 1969 pogroms and their aftermath; the Provisionals were in process of organising to oblige; the left-politicisers would of course also be interned; many of the latter were also beginning to react by reverting to their earlier military mind-set.

This concludes the year 1970; there were no more meetings until after the Ard Fheis. We take up the thread in 1971 in the 1970s context, the year 1970 being taken as being the last one of the 60s decade.

JJ and the EEC

I have not touched at all in this section so far on what JJ was doing; basically he was working over his Berkeley material, and I reference this in the next chapter. He did however develop an increasingly critical view of the European Economic Community (EEC)(26), based primarily on his global view of primary-producer economics. In this context he took an interest in the work of Raymond Crotty, and had several meetings with him.

Notes and References

1. I have a copy of these minutes in full, and I will expand on them if and when I can resurrect the internal draft version of the Report; the version which is here accessible would have edited in the results of these discussions. A version of the Commission Report has come to hand via an Ulster Quaker source: a historian Roy Garland who has been studying loyalist-republican political interactions. This is available in full, but I have yet to authenticate it against my own records. I suspect it may be the version as amended by the Ard Comhairle. It looks to me quite credible; I have corrected a few errors which were due to typing or the scanning process.

2. I am indebted to the late Derry Kelleher for drawing my attention to a file of *Nuacht Naisiunta*, the internal Sinn Fein newsletter which commenced in September 1969 in response to the August events, and continued from some years. This remains accessible in the Workers party archive.

3. The writer Desmond Fennell and the Orange leader Major Ronald Bunting, who had led the violent ambush of the People's Democracy marchers at Burntollet. Both had in differing ways had argued in '2-nationist' mode for re-partition to concentrate the 'Ulster British' more compactly in the north-east.

4. In his memoirs Mac Stiofain took great exception to this statement. He was of course then preparing his own military campaign.

5. This would appear to be an echo of proto-Provisional intrigue, supporting the Justin O'Brien thesis in his *Arms Trial*.

6. This must be an indication of Mac Stiofain's followers already active, prior to the split. It is basically confirmed in *Mac Stiofain's Memoirs*, in principle, though not in detail. He was engaged in active military planning from 1967, either under the false impression that this was what Goulding actually wanted, or, alternatively, with the intention of actively restoring the military agenda, despite the then Goulding Army Council policy.

7. This is referenced in the November 24 1969 issue of *Nuacht Naisiunta* in the hypertext.

8. The latter would not have been 'IRA' as such, but proto-Provisional or Blaneyite supporters of the attempt to take over the NICRA in the Fianna Fail interest. Greaves, at a distance, found it difficult to distinguish.

9. In the background there were moves afoot to amalgamate the Irish Workers Party and the CPNI, and this is treated in the Greaves diaries, who observed it in the context of the ongoing attempt of the left-republicans to find common ground with them. I have abstracted some of these insights in the integrated hypertext chronology; they suggest that the motivation was to think through the various national policy issues arising from the current crisis.

10. The foregoing is distilled from a more extensive series of abstracts from the Greaves diaries which feature in the hypertext 1970 integrated chronology during January.

11. I had resigned from Aer Lingus, and was beginning to work as a scientific consultant, in self-employed mode. To ease the transition I had done a deal with Douglas Gageby, the *Irish Times* editor, to provide him with a weekly 'Science and Technology' column, which was for him something of an innovation, though I had earlier, in 1967, provided some features on this theme. I have been able to edit much of the material of this column into a publication *In Search of Techne* which constitutes a critical view of 'science and society' issues in the first half of the 1970s. This is available in the hypertext. See also the 'Popularising Science' section of this chapter, below. It will also form an important source for the next chapter.

12. The essentials of the results of the Garland Commission were published in the February 1970 *United Irishman*, under the title 'Freedom Manifesto', and this is accessible in the hypertext, as is the Garland Commission Report in full.

13. The Ard Fheis resolution overflow was dealt with; I have recorded their fates by reference number in the integrated chronology, but lacking a copy of the agenda this is meaningless. It must await the sorting out of the Workers Party archive.

14. Most if not all of the foregoing, recognised at the time by the Movement, has been substantially confirmed by the analysis of Justin O'Brien in *The Arms Trial*, reviewed in the hypertext.

15. The Education section of the April 27 1970 *Nuacht Naisiunta* contains a short paper 'Socialism - a Definition' which we have encountered before (March 1968). I recognise this as having been my own production; it represents a good summary of my thinking at the time, and it is worth reproducing in full; see the 1970 integrated chronology on this date.

16. The 'National Liberation Front' canard had assumed, to my mind, an undue importance in people's minds. It was never intended as a slogan or a name of a confederating body, or a real movement involving any formal amalgamation. It was used by Mac Stiofain and others to imply the existence of a 'communist threat'. Insofar as I ever used it, it was to connote a process of expansion of the movement to soak up a broader range of progressive forces than Sinn Fein itself, and the embedded politicising IRA who were activating Sinn Fein. The 'Freedom Manifesto' as published in the February 1970 *United Irishman* was an outline of what we then had in mind for a broader movement.

17. These meetings are reported in more detail in the 1970 integrated chronology in the hypertext.

18. *In Search of Techne* was the title; the publisher was to have been Tycooley, and I had in mind that it might be of interest in the context of the UN Development Programme. Unfortunately the publisher, who specialised in the UN market, went out of business, and I was left stranded. I have therefore added it in full to the hypertext backup of this book, and will find it useful to reference from time to time from now on.

19. The review was published in the *Irish Journal of Agricultural Economics* (July-August 1970); the book was *Research in Ireland* by Dr Michael Woods, Institute of Public Administration, 1969.

20. 'The Computer as an Analytical Management Tool', in *Léargas*, the journal of the Institute of Public Administration, August 1970.

21. Some of the background to this initiative is given in the 1960s module of the Science and Society thread, which builds on the Bernal influence.

22. Plans to demolish most of Hume St and rebuild were being resisted by a group of young UCD architects: Duncan Stewart, Deirdre Kelly and others. Students were in occupation. This was based on support for the conservation of Dublin Georgian architecture, against the depredations of philistine property developers, who visibly had bought political influence in the planning process, mostly via the Fianna Fail party. We as the movement attempted, with only partial success, to relate this the 'housing action' agenda. The Hume Street battle was partially successful, in that in subsequent developments the facades were retained, but much sound Georgian property was needlessly gutted.

23. I am not going to pursue the analysis of the transition of Official Sinn Fein to its eventual Workers Party status; this is perhaps partially illuminated by Derry Kelleher in his memoirs. During 1970 I increasingly distanced myself from the process, under pressure of work. I did however contribute an article to the September 1970 *United Irishman*, on 'The Future of the Agricultural Subsidies', in which I reviewed a Government report. I made the case that subsidies should be social and not volume-dependent on commodities, and that co-operative groupings of farms could become large-scale commercial units.

24. There are some notes by the present writer in the WTS archive, also dated October 6 1970. They are worth reproducing, and they are accessible in the hypertext in the integrated chronology.

25. *Nuacht Naisiunta* at about this time was promoting the 'Freedom Manifesto', published in the February 1970 issue of the *United Irishman*, and subsequently reprinted as a broadsheet for wide circulation. It represented a reasonably definitive statement of the post-split 'official' republican position, developing somewhat the 'national liberation movement' concept, with separate demands relevant to the existing 6 and 26 county situations.

26. JJ's attitude to EEC accession was initially in favour of it, publishing a book *Why Ireland Needs the Common Market* (Mercier Press, Cork, 1962) and then later, in his final years, he was critical with articles and letters to the newspapers.

Chapter 8: The Period 1971-1980

Introduction

The 1970s for the present writer were a constructive period scientifically, but depressing politically. I cultivated an Operations Research problem-solving consultancy on the fringe of TCD, with the support of Gordon Foster in the Statistics Department. Some of the projects which we analysed using computer-based models were actually close to the type of pilot-project which my father had been promoting(1).

I continued to develop the *Irish Times* Science and Technology column, which ran weekly from 1970 to 1976(2); initially it was a 'feature' and then later it moved to the financial page, becoming in the context more applied-scientific. This was stimulating and to this day is remembered with nostalgia by many people I have met since, including industry leaders, who read it during their student days.

I went on to generalise the OR and Statistics experience via the Industrial Liaison Office, from which I initiated the TCD Applied Research Consultancy Group. This survived up to 1980, and employed up to 8 people. It turned out to be primarily a fringe enterprise generator, rather than a problem-solver, though valid work was done. The College however stood it down, and went for a model where the spin-off enterprise was the main output.

Politically, I continued to fight a losing rearguard action against the rising tide of 'official IRA' militarism, which increasingly was trying to compete with the Provisionals. When they went into political assassination, with Senator Barnhill, this was the last straw, and I resigned, though without rancour, as I wanted to keep the lines of communication open. I made an attempt to re-establish a working relationship with the 'orthodox left' (the CPI), but this proved totally barren, the pathology of the latter having gone beyond redemption following the Soviet invasion of Czechoslovakia.

A subsequent period with the Labour Party proved to be equally barren, in that procedures for policy development, and analysis of problems in terms of feasible routes towards solutions, with membership participation, and a learning mode, were largely non-existent.

During the 1970s the family scene(3) was dominated by the death of JJ in 1972, and my setting up home with Janice. Towards the end of the decade my elder daughter Una went to the US; my son Fergus went through College and became a composer; Nessa was born to Janice and me.

The *Irish Times* Science Column

I have introduced this in the previous chapter, and mentioned it in the introduction above. It is appropriate here to select a few samples which show how I tried to develop the 'science and society' aspect.

March 24 1971

The Regional Scientific Councils were founded... to provide a meeting-ground for the exchange of ideas between scientists of various disciplines in centres other than Dublin; they were conceived as a means of establishing an intellectual climate, a stimulus to the imagination, for those condemned by their employment to rustication or exile from the heady atmosphere of the Metropolis.

They have a historical precedent in the 18th century: the Lunar Society in Birmingham united in monthly philosophical dinners a small group of innovators, craftsmen and scientists who were at the centre of the technology of the first Industrial Revolution. They were practical men and they questioned the dogma that all good must flow from London. They used to meet at the full moon, the better to see their way home on horseback, whence the name.

The Cork Council... is in a sense the leading one, in that it has a broader base from which to draw its membership. The scope of its activities includes popularisation, by means of lectures on topics of interest, to a mixed lay and specialist audience; it also provides a career guidance service, does regionalist political lobbying and holds exhibitions.

This pattern has tended not to include the reading of learned papers and the publishing of proceedings, which on the whole is all to the good.

Nor has it led directly to the development of interdisciplinary work among scientists; this however may occur as a result of chance contacts or conversations at Council events.

There is no Scientific Council in Dublin, fulfilling any analogous function. If there were to be one, it would be likely to have a rather different emphasis, as many of the functions carried out by the Regional Councils are already catered for by the specialist bodies and by old-established bodies such as the Royal Dublin Society.

These reflections are stimulated by a visit to the Carlow Scientific Council's exhibition which took place on March 9-11. Carlow is an expanding technological centre, with some 100 or so qualified professionals. The Regional College of Technology is due to open this year *(1971)*, providing courses in industrial chemistry (among other things)... with emphasis on natural products and on the needs of local applied-scientific research, which is centred in the Oakpark centre of the Agricultural Institute, and in the research laboratories of Erin Foods ltd and the Irish Sugar Co, of which Dr Tadhg Twomey is the Director.

There is little evidence so far of local science-based industry 'spinning off' from either of the main research centres. The main obstacle to this, possibly, is the existence in the semi-State bodies of a civil-service approach to pension rights; the latter would be forfeited by anyone leaving a research-centre to start a science-based small enterprise......

May 5 1971

A word is perhaps necessary on the question of whether to have an Irish (scientific, voluntary-membership) Institution, or an Irish section of a UK one. This is a highly political question, which is not helped by communications barriers which are placed sometimes by the London HQ, and sometimes by the Dublin Government, in the way of Irish specialists (organised in UK-based Institutions) talking to the authorities.

There are no political boundaries among working scientists. The natural interaction crucible for Irish scientists and technologists is the island of Ireland for cross-fertilisation and interdisciplinary work, while for specialist work within the discipline the natural crucible is the British Isles, Europe, the US and the world.

We need to organise so as to have access to both types of network. Thus any attempt to have a 26-county 'national' body which cuts off our Northern colleagues is basically negative, though it may sound 'patriotic' to some to counter-pose such a body to one with London HQ. On the other hand, London-based bodies, for which Ireland is a region, can be negative if they discourage autonomy.

To build a national scientific consciousness under these circumstances is decidedly tricky, requiring tact and diplomatic ability of a high order. No wonder we have so far been unsuccessful....

October 20 1971

The death on September 15 of J D Bernal FRS has passed without comment in Ireland (to my knowledge), apart from one or two minor obituary notices. Readers [of this column] will have noted that from time to time I have invoked his name in connection with the idea of social responsibility in science. I take this opportunity of paying tribute to a remarkable Irishman, who ranks with Joyce and O'Casey as a world-figure in human culture. The fact that his career was constrained to develop outside the mainstream of Irish life has resulted in most Irish people being unaware of his existence. That this is not the case for emigrant writers of equivalent stature constitutes a measure of the relative status of science in the Irish consciousness.

Bernal, if he had remained in Ireland, would be unlikely to have become a world-figure.... an unfortunate truth that has to be reckoned with. Science in Ireland, though now beginning to know itself, is still stunted by decades of impoverishment.

Bernal was educated in England and went to college at Cambridge. On completing his Tripos he got the opportunity of going into research under Sir William Bragg, of X-ray crystallography fame *(this physical technique enables spatial structures of molecules to be elucidated).* He was from a land-owning family near Nenagh, Co Tipperary: the same class of 'minor landed gentry' that has contributed Parnell to politics and Yeats to literature. His principal contribution to science was his development of the technique of X-ray diffraction analysis to the extent that it could be used to unravel the structures of large and complex molecules. He can therefore be counted among the initiators of the currently booming science of molecular biology. If Watson and Crick are counted as the founding fathers, then Bernal was the grandfather.

However, he was far from being the ivory-tower purist; he was an all-rounder, working at all levels. During his 'fundamental' period in the thirties, he was active in the foundation and organisation of the Association of Scientific Workers, the first scientists Trade Union.

(The latter has recently merged with a number of other 'white-collar' unions such as ASSET and the Insurance Guild to form ASTMS, of which the general secretary is Clive Jenkins.... The Irish section of ASTMS organises the staffs of the IIRS, the Agricultural Institute and other Irish scientists and technologists. The Bernal 'social responsibility' tradition persists...there are plans for expert working groups.....to develop an informed view on questions such as technology-based redundancies.....)

Then during the war, along with the generation of basic scientists who evolved into technology via radar and nuclear weapons, he became associated with what became subsequently known as 'Operations Research'. As scientific adviser to the Chief of Combined Operations (Lord Mountbatten) he was actively involved in the research background of the Normandy landings; this despite his political reputation as a Marxist.

His most significant contribution to what has come to be known as 'the science of science' was perhaps his 1939 book *The Social Function of Science*. Such was the impact of this that on the 25th anniversary of its publication a tribute to it was organised in the form of a book of essays by leading scientists, mostly FRS, who had been influenced by Bernal's work. Entitled *The Science of Science*, it is compulsory reading...... The editor was JG Crowther. Few people can have had the satisfaction of a pre-obituary tribute of this calibre.

I had a brief exchange of letters with Bernal in 1967. This was when, in the pre-National Science Council days, we had a voluntary federation of most of the specialist associations, known as the 'Council for Science and Technology in Ireland'. We had big ideas, but, of course, no resources. We thought, at one stage, of trying to put on the pressure for the siteing of a major international laboratory in Ireland, as a stimulus to Irish science. We had in mind molecular biology, as the front-line where the most rapid and spectacular advances were being made.

I wrote to Bernal, hoping that he might come over. But by then he had had the second of a series of cerebral haemorrhages, and he was unable to take the invitation up. Despite his condition, however, he showed an informed interest and '...would have been delighted to contribute most actively because it is a scheme that is near to my heart...a sign of a scientific renaissance in my native country...'

He then went on to cite a list of possible international contacts which would need to be lobbied, and to stress the need for '...ample connections with agriculture and medicine...'

It seemed to him '...to be worth connecting it with the International Biological Programme under the ICSU, though this would require considerable negotiation...'

I have heard no more of this project. The CSTI didn't have the resources to lobby for it. The ball passed to the feet of the National Science Council......

There is scope, I feel, for an interdisciplinary lobby of active scientists to take up questions like this in an informed manner. The CSTI was a non-starter, because it was a federation of existing bodies.. Like a convoy, it was limited to the speed of the slowest.

A society with an individual (rather than corporate), active, socially conscious membership, devoted to the organisation of pressure for socially desirable objectives in Irish science, would have a positive role to play. Derry Kelleher (of the Chemical Engineers) and myself in November 1968 attempted to found such a body; we got virtually no support. We were disgusted at the way in which the CSTI, in which both of us had been involved, had folded up without even a whimper when the National Science Council was established, despite the fact that the CSTI recommendation regarding the NSC structure had been ignored.

Possibly now the time is ripe for re-examination of the need for a gadfly-society of the type we had in mind. We wanted to call it the Kane-Bernal Society, after Sir Robert Kane and Desmond Bernal. It could fulfil a function, by the physical presence of its members at events, [analogous to what this column is trying to do via the printed word]. It could research and publish pamphlets developing specific proposals for science policy in Ireland in more depth, and in a more permanent and effective form, than can this column.

What better means of inaugurating it than at a meeting to commemorate J D Bernal?

RJ in post-split Sinn Fein

Post-split 'official Sinn Fein' did its best to hold the remains of the movement together by using the threat of the European Economic Community (EEC) as an Act of Greater Union. There was a perception that the Referendum was due the following April in 1972.. The state-church issue in the schools was taken up, with support for community and vocational schools. There were letters from detainees and internees in Crumlin Road. The O'Brien's Bridge / Montpelier school project dragged on; the movement had actually attempted to supply a series of volunteer teachers to keep it going, one of them being Eoin Ó Murchú, who had given up a job in the management of a Gaeltacht factory in Tourmakeady.

This abuse of educated volunteers in the movement having leadership potential was to my mind a highly questionable practice, suggesting a perception that people were expendable. The Montpelier episode, with all its ramifications, needs analysis by local and political historians.

There were no drastic post-split changes in the main objectives of the Dublin Wolfe Tone Society. There was to be a more open membership, but no party political affiliation. Current areas of interest were declared to be civil rights and constitutional reform, North and South. Irish language and culture, the co-operative movement, science and technology, and educational reform remained on the agenda.

The Dublin leadership, and the present writer, remained in touch with what was going on in the North, as best we could. The NICRA was trying to keep going in the increasingly polarised post-pogrom situation, with the support of the politicising republicans, and partial support from the CPNI, with Betty Sinclair continuing to play a key role, supported by Joe Deighan and John McClelland, CPNI members who had Connolly Association (CA) background. There was however a London 'NICRA' which was presenting itself as an alternative to the CA, under Blaneyite influence, and in the general confusion the NICRA proper was not alive to this danger. Greaves remained in touch, attending the NICRA annual conference in January 1971, and subsequently meeting John Hume in Derry, whom he suspected of drafting a 'Bill of Rights' as '...an alternative to the thing those Reds have prepared ...'. This however turned out to be simply a submission to the Crowther Commission; John Hume made him welcome and showed him round(4).

Greaves in Belfast as usual went to see Betty Sinclair, who had been at a meeting of West European CPs, and had '...expected to see me there ...'. She gave her impressions: '...the old camaraderie of pre-war years has gone... the Dutch will not sign anything... the Italians did not seem to care about anybody but themselves ...'. She went on to tell him '...that whereas the Republicans for all their faults would be glad to have Joe Deighan and John McClelland on the Civil Rights executive, the

Party (which means the Stewarts) has vetoed it. I was unable to get any closer to the problem ...'.

It seems we were increasingly up against the rampant theoretical confusion of the West European post-Stalinist Left, which popped up with depressing regularity to frustrate Greaves's attempts to develop a broad consistent movement for the limited objective of Civil Rights in Northern Ireland

There was on January 24 a meeting, organised under NICRA auspices, which however Greaves regarded as the result of an 'orange-communist cabal .. analogous to the NILP ...'. Speakers at the meeting were Kader Asmal, Greaves, then Hume. Greaves spoke with a 'strong republican bias' given the situation. He suggested that 'they *(the CPNI)* were at their old trick, to demand something and then object to it when they got it, to pose as great reformers before the republicans, but by doing nothing decisive, to hold the Orangemen and the NILP. Hume had been brought in, in an effort to confuse the issue ...'.

CDG here was attempting to develop a critique of the CPNI, whose role in the development of the NICRA had been ambiguous. In fact the conference seems to have been a genuine though somewhat confused attempt to develop public support for the Bill of Rights approach, which they were trying to extend to economic questions. There was however an undercurrent of anti-communism against which they had to try to swim.

There was a sequel to the foregoing, which Greaves picked up from Anthony Coughlan in London on January 31 1971: it seems that Micheál O'Riordan and Cathal Goulding were busy discussing an 'anti-imperialist conference' which might be called jointly by the Belfast and Dublin Trades Councils. They had brought in Peoples Democracy (PD), it was understood at the Republicans' request, and had decided not to mention Civil Rights but to discuss only the EEC and economic matters. Coughlan thought that the omission of civil rights was partly a sop to PD and partly in accordance with the 'orange communists' that were in the North; it was all confusion; they had no general perspective except with regard to their own small groupings.

I don't recollect anything ever coming of this; it is a reflection of the general level of disorientation and confusion of both the Marxist left and the republican left, in response to the perceived current threats of the provisional campaign and the looming concept of the EEC as the new Act of Union.

The role of the British Army in Belfast was treated in the February 10 issue #62 of *Nuacht Naisiunta*. Belfast republicans were increasingly divided between the 'official' and 'provisional' positions. All eyes were on the possibility of a 'federal solution', with Callaghan, working closely with the Tory Home Secretary Maudling, in Dublin, to discuss a Lynch-Heath deal which nominally ended the Border but in fact gave Westminster a role in Ireland as a whole. The situation continued to deteriorate, with shootings in Belfast, and anti-red witch-hunting. There was an instruction to Cumainn to avoid contact with the 'breakaway group'. Conor Cruise O'Brien challenged Tomás Mac Giolla to a debate on the North. This took place subsequently, in Newman House. It was well attended, and chaired by Fr Austin Flannery. It received some publicity, ideas were exchanged with suitable rhetoric. It could perhaps be regarded as a stepping-stone in the rise of CCO'B to prominence as a Northern 'expert'.

During the first quarter of 1971 the split situation became increasingly embittered, with continuing concern with the EEC issue, and the perceived threat of a British-dominated all-Ireland 'federal arrangement'. The principal theoretical influence would appear still to have been Coughlan, whose explicit agenda at the time was along these lines. It became evident however that from this time on the influence of myself and Coughlan were in decline, though the momentum of political convergence(5) of the 'broad left' continued for a time; in the end it was undermined by the increasingly militarised situation.

Meanwhile, according to Greaves(6), in the North there was increasingly evident a '...carve-up ...' of the NICRA executive positions between the '...IRA and the CP ...'. *he meant the CP and the Republican Club representatives, some of whom may residually have considered themselves as the 'official IRA' but whose motivations were still political; the leading person in this context was Malachi McGurran. The 'primarily IRA' element had by now gone 'provisional', and would end up suppressing NICRA meetings.* Joe Deighan and John McClelland, who were ex-CA stalwarts with long experience of democratic lobbying in the London environment, were sidelined.

This reflected a 'Left-Republican convergence' in the worst sense; and it persisted later with organisations like the Resources Protection Campaign in the south: the heavy-handed Stalinist top-down tradition and the Fenian conspiratorial top-down tradition were the key converging philosophies, both being pathological sources of party-driven 'machine-voting', in a context where a broad knowledge-based movement was needed. In such a situation there was no room for ordinary civil rights activists.

During the second quarter of 1971 the Dublin Sinn Fein leadership was concerned with the Forcible Entry Bill, political prisoners in Britain, the Guinness and Whitegate Refinery disputes, unemployment, the National College of Art crisis, Bodenstown, pub bombs and sectarianism, local government, fishing rights, tenants rights, feminism, and the EEC. On April 13 1971 there was an Easter statement from the IRA, calling for confrontation on social, economic and political issues, and avoidance of military confrontations, while helping people where necessary to defend their homes. *Thus Goulding still felt he had to retain the IRA persona when making political statements.*

On April 19 1971 there was a call in *Nuacht Naisiunta* to open up meaningful discussion with 'other left groups', referencing current published material in the *Irish Socialist* and the *Irish Democrat*. '...To dismiss the old-established Marxist left as "a bunch of academics" or as "pure trade unionists" is to underestimate seriously the degree of theoretical and practical development... with regard to the national question ...'. The *Irish Socialist* contained an article by Betty Sinclair which pointed out that the use of force by '...extremists among anti-Unionists... serves to unite Unionism ...'. The *Democrat* attacked the *Tribune (the London left-Labour periodical)* for their support of 'Direct Rule', and called for a Bill of Rights giving republicans in the 6 counties the right of organisation and propaganda; also to disarm the Orangemen and close down the 'gun clubs'. A draft Bill of Rights, as an Amendment to the Government of Ireland Act, had been tabled.

This was identified as the last chance perhaps for decades to make use of constitutional reform procedures with some chance of being listened to.

At the WTS on April 20 the committee discussed the Gaeltacht radio, and a collection of Tone's writings. Derry Kelleher resigned as joint secretary and I succeeded him.

I went to Bodenstown for the unveiling of a new monument (to replace the one blown up by the loyalists). Moss Twomey (a veteran republican who had been active in the 40s and 50s) spoke, and both 'official' and 'provisional' groups were there. There was an EEC aspect, and a Breton, the sculptor Yann Goulet, was there, who walked away when they played the Marseillaise. Kelleher went with him.

The foregoing was noted by Greaves(7), who went on to '...suggest that the EEC opposition send a delegation to London to get big money off the sugar planters. They are thinking of employing a man at £10 a week to work in Cathal's spare room. I told them I would advise him not to consider it. A £10 man would make no impression. Crotty has been at it full time for six months, living on his savings, but must soon stop ...'.

There is an echo here of JJ; protected sugar from beet in France was, and still is, a relic of the Napoleonic wars, defended by vested interests ('les bettraviers'). It is economic nonsense where tropical producers of cane sugar can produce under favourable conditions at low cost and need to export to develop their economies. CDG, like JJ currently and earlier, had in mind the overall iniquity of European protected agriculture, seen in global terms. The 'sugar planters' were of course the British sugar giants, like Tate and Lyle, who depended on tropical sugar. These would have been strongly anti-EEC.

The Wolfe Tone Society on May 4 1971 held a general meeting. It was supposed to be 'as gaeilge', but turned out to be 'gan cainteoiri', and so was a flop. It had been projected to relate to the need for a radio in the Gaeltacht, and speakers were to include Eoghan Harris and Breandán Ó h-Eithir; there is a notice to this effect.

Around this time, or perhaps earlier in 1970, I remember attending an Oireachtas event centred in Rosmuc, organised by Cearta Sibhialta na Gaeltachta, and a pirate radio was run for the duration, using equipment lent by the republican movement. This created political pressure for the official setting up of Radio na Gaeltachta. The above projected meeting would have been in this context.

The WTS May 18 committee meeting considered the use of Irish language at meetings. Issues relating to the Tailors Hall, Community Schools, Planning Acts, the Liberties, the Dodder and the SF leadership came up. Tomás Mac Giolla, was invited to address the July meeting on 'short-term political alternatives to Fianna Fail in the context of the EEC threat, what role for the republican movement?' It was suggested that the feedback from this event would be helpful in drafting a political manifesto.

At the WTS general meeting on June 1 1971 Uinsean Mac Eoin read a paper 'Watchdog on Developers'. The idea of an All-Dublin federation of amenity groups was suggested, as part of the battle for the restoration of local democracy.

Issue #77 of *Nuacht Naisiunta* on June 13 contained a statement opposing the proposed Church domination of the boards of the projected Community Schools, and defending the secular democratic composition of the current Vocational Education Committees.

Malachi McGurran's Bodenstown speech was reported in the June 21 1971 issue; he aspired to working-class unity across the sectarian barriers in the North, and attempted to link the Northern situation to the impending EEC referendum. Then on June 28 there was a further attempt to define what was meant by the 'national liberation movement' in terms of a multi-class, multi-organisation anti-imperialist alliance with the working people in the lead. After the removal of alien imperial influences it would then be possible to build a socialist society. A follower was promised for the next issue, but this never came.

We have here increasing evidence of ideological confusion and political floundering. The shots were increasingly being called by the Provisionals in the North, and the attempted political road was being marginalised. The present writer was no longer in a leading position, but he contributed to the development of the 'Mornington School' during the following summer.

Nuacht Naisiunta in the 3rd quarter of 1971, as well as the internment question, covered issues which included existing prisoners, the EEC, Radio na Gaeltachta, fishing rights, housing in Dublin, and the CIA.

The Mornington School was announced in the July 5 1971 issue, initially from July 4; there would be sessions on 'Imperialism and the Irish Nation', on 'the Cultural Revolution', and on the Northern situation. The School would be open for August and September also, in proportion to demand. *I remember contributing to this school; we built up quite a good library of relevant Marxist literature, and held group discussion sessions around readings.*

There is in the WTS archive an m/s paper by Uinsean Mac Eoin, dated 'Sept 6' annotated 'discussed 14/7/71'. It is concerned about the politics of a federal agreement thought to be on the agenda between Heath and Lynch. It is not clear what its standing is. From the date September 6 it would appear to have been produced prior to the (projected and perhaps apocryphal) October 1970 Newry meeting of 'radical groups'.

Greaves in July 1971 came up with the idea of making the Connolly Association conference educational, and moving in the direction of an 'Irish Democrat Supporters League' to strengthen the paper, and to get Trade Unions to join(8). The entry continues however as follows: '...today the devil Heath announced his EEC plan. The shadow of a West European Fascist Empire hovers over us, and I wonder how well the Celtic peoples, leave alone the working class of England, fare ...'. *I recollect this perception existing among the Left, perhaps a war relic.*

Nuacht Naisiunta issue #81 on July 12 1971 claimed Martin O'Leary as the first martyr of the new phase of struggle. His funeral in Cork was reported, Seamus Corry of the ITGWU laid a wreath. He had lost his life at the Mogul mine at Silvermines, in an IRA action in support of the striking miners.

According to local lore this action, which involved disabling an ESB sub-station (a hazardous operation), had a positive political effect. The present writer however wants to place on record that he had nothing to do with it, and would have opposed it had he known it was in prospect. It illustrates perfectly the nature of the problem of dealing with the still dominant culture rooted in the traditional military nature of the IRA, which had persisted despite our best efforts since 1965. The elitist role of the IRA, in acting 'for' the workers from outside, is the antithesis of that projected for the type of left-wing democratic activist organisation we had being trying to build. This was the beginning of the end of my association with the movement.

There is in the WTS archive a document written by RJ entitled 'Notes on the Northern Situation'; it is worth reproducing in full, as it summarises the present writer's then perceptions. It would have served as input to the August 3 1971 meeting of the Society.

Notes on the Northern Situation / RJ 25/07/71

Westminster wants Ireland at peace and with a satellite government in Dublin who will vote under her control in the EEC Council. She is prepared to consider a political solution. British policy on Ireland is bi-partisan, she is prepared to use the Labour network to fly kites. Paul Johnson's article in the *New Statesman* is such a kite. She is prepared to influence the Irish situation using civil service contacts, diplomatic influences, the press, the Labour network, as well as direct policies in the six counties.

There are signs that the form of the political solution is taking shape. The 'two-nation' idea of O'Brien is more than a theory. It is fast becoming a reality, thanks to the worsening sectarian situation in Belfast.

Consider the following steps from the point of view of Britain:

1. Draw out the republicans into an insurrectionary position in Belfast and Derry. In Belfast, this has the effect of causing pogroms, splitting finally the trade unions, rendering any idea of working-class unity impossible. In Derry this has the effect of putting pressure on Lynch to intervene militarily.

2. Arrange with Lynch that this military intervention when it takes place will look like a withdrawal in the face of a provisional campaign, and that Lynch will recover more national credibility, thus gaining support for his EEC referendum.

3. Arrange a political leadership for the 'liberated area': this is the group which has withdrawn from Stormont. The factors involved in the setting up of this group were (a) the external affairs people in the Arts Club meeting (b) O'Leary. In other words, the civil service and the Labour Party channels of influence.

The form of the political solution is therefore a 29 county Free State, with movements of populations out of Belfast, and a split in the Trade Unions. This will look sufficiently like a step towards the Republic to gain Lynch some kudos, or maybe the alternative leadership which is waiting in the wings, if Lynch is not the man to do the job.

*This at the time was our perception of what was going on behind the scenes, in the background of the 'arms crisis', with Haughey in the wings. We were convinced that the over-riding issue was membership of the EEC, that there was a Lynch-Heath understanding, and that re-partition was the goal. This perception has been dismissed as fantasy. But there **was** a plan to arm the Provisionals, and to do military training in Donegal. We were aware of numerous intrigues which were going on, all over. Who connived? Do we yet have the full story? The paper went on:*

How is this strategy to be countered?

[A] Preserve working-class unity in Belfast. This is a tall order, but may possibly be approached by the Belfast Executive (of the official republican movement) approaching the Trades Council, in writing, backed up by leaflets, press statements etc, repudiating the deeds of unknown arsonists, probable agents provocateurs, and bombers, on Protestant shops, especially co-ops which are the property of the workers. This repudiation should be accompanied by an offer to support local vigilante groups, set up under Trade Union control, to defend initially co-op property, ultimately peoples property from arson by these unknowns. Also to urge that the Trades Council, once these Peace Corps were set up, should press the military to confine their attention to protecting public property and to leave over patrolling of streets where the workers live, law and order being taken over by the Trade Union Peace Corps. Make it known that the official movement will give unconditional support to a Workers Peace Corps organised under TU control.

[B] Take the initiative in pressing the MPs who have withdrawn, into a new position, different from the 'Catholic liberated area provisional government' position that they have got themselves into. Press them to bid to form an alternative government in Stormont on the common programme of opposition to the EEC with the anti-EEC elements in the Unionist Party. Try to convert the withdrawal into something different from a link in the Lynch-Westminster chain. The exact nature of this bid has yet to be worked out, but it must be such as to split the Unionists, and it must come with pressure from below, from trade unionists worried about EEC effects. And it should not look like a 'challenge to the Constitution', or the alliance with the anti-EEC Unionists is a non-starter. Again, a tall order, but it should at least be called for, so that some people in retrospect may see we were right.

There is no record of the status of this document; it probably is analogous to that of Uinsean MacEoin as discussed on 14/07/71, though from a more left-wing perspective. The Provisionals were seen, correctly, as a totally destructive influence on the embryonic working-class unity we had tried to nurture, with some initial success. It was of course hopelessly unrealistic, grasping a straws, in a disastrous situation. The starting-point, the 'Heath-Lynch collusion' in an EEC-oriented strategy, deserves the attention of critical historians. How much substance did it have? How important was strategy relating to the EEC in the minds of the Government, in the context of the Northern crisis?

Nuacht Naisiunta in issue #83 dated July 27 1971 recorded that there were raids on the Sinn Fein Head Office and on peoples' houses, to coincide with raids by the British and RUC in the North. The raids in the 26 counties were associated with acts due to agents provocateurs, and there were indications that all Dáil groups had agreed on a procedure for introducing internment, based on an alleged discovery of a plot to stage a coup d'etat. There was of course no such plot, but the situation illustrates the extreme paranoia of the Fianna Fail government regarding left-wing actions to draw attention to the failings of its social policies, and domination by speculative urban development interests. Ivan Cooper in Derry was highly critical of these actions, on the grounds that they increased the danger of internment dominating the scene in the North.

At an extended committee meeting of the WTS on August 3 1971 a memo to Jack Lynch was projected, to be drafted by a sub-committee consisting of RJ, Oliver Snoddy and Manus Durcan. The September meeting 'as gaeilge' was to be on the North. Kelleher would speak on the Guinness run-down. The committee met again on August 8 and issued a statement to Press from which is worth reproducing the concluding summary:

WTS Open Letter to Jack Lynch - August 9 1971

1. The claim that civil rights for the Six Counties within the UK constitutes the 'Achilles heel' of Unionism stands vindicated.

2. Crude nationalistic statements from 26-county political ends by spokesmen close to the Government have helped identify undeservedly the civil rights movement with the partition question and to drive it into the ghettoes, giving rise to the present danger of civil war in which the prime sufferers would be the divided working people.

3. The onus is in Westminster to undo the damage done by the Carsonite rebellion. This is possible if it (a) abandons all claim to rule Ireland (b) announces a programmed disengagement (c) disarms the Orangemen and bans the Orange parades (d) imposes a Bill of Rights on Stormont and concedes enough independence to Stormont to enable it to take its own EEC decision and to deal with Dublin as it wishes.

4. The onus is on Dublin to secularise the Constitution and to provide for an Irish federal regional structure.

5. Any talks between a reformed Stormont and Dublin to be entirely a matter for the Irish and without interference by Westminster.

6. No internment, whether as part of a package deal or otherwise.

7. No political settlement involving re-drawing the Border, movements of populations, 'Catholic areas' or any principle which questions the Irishness of Protestants.

The 'Letter to Jack Lynch' got substantial coverage in the national press, and some congratulatory letters came in. I wrote also to Paul Johnson in the London New Statesman, thanking him for the coverage of the issue in terms of the need for a phased withdrawal, and enclosing a letter for publication; I also enclosed a copy of the foregoing 'Open Letter to Jack Lynch', giving it the status of a draft yet to be agreed, but published as a discussion document; also a copy Anthony Coughlan's EEC document. The letter for publication covered much of the ground of the 'Letter to Jack Lynch', and added in also the following:

"The 32-county Irish Congress of Trade Unions is already waking up to the EEC implications. The first significant resolution, calling on the Congress Executive to meet the Dublin Government to discuss the implications and to examine alternatives, came at the 1970 Congress from the largely Belfast-based Sheet-metal Workers and Coppersmiths.

"There are apocryphal stories about, of anti-EEC meetings organised by republicans in Protestant areas of County Down, where after being duly jeered by the Paisleyites a special EEC edition of the *United Irishman* was nonetheless bought and read.

"If any shock treatment exists capable of making the Northern Protestants realise that they must face the world as Irishmen, this is it...".

The ICTU opposed EEC entry in 1972, but to no avail; the referendum was carried by a massive 73% majority. Our attempt to use the EEC as a unifier for perceived working-class interests across the sectarian divide was, on the whole, wishful thinking. For more extensive coverage of these and related political issues, see Appendix 10.

***

There is a gap in the *Nuacht Naisiunta* record from July 27 until August 16, when there was a statement from Northern Command, describing what amounted to a battle between the 'official IRA' and the British Army, in an attempt to resist a swoop leading to internment. They called for a political solution, but not the one in prospect in the current Heath-Lynch talks.

In the subsequent commentary, *Nuacht Naisiunta* attacked the Provisional bombing of Protestant halls and premises, and the black-and-tan role of the British Army backing up the armed Orange mob. Under a sub-head 'what Heath wants' it was suggested that the role of the Orange mob had killed the 'new Union via the Lemass-O'Neill road'. His alternative was (a) to provoke sectarian strife to the extent of movements of populations (b) pull in the Border to include a 90% Protestant area and (c) do a deal with Lynch handing over some 'Catholic' areas. This was regarded as giving Lynch enough political capital to win the EEC referendum, and to give Heath an Irish puppet vote in the EEC Council.

Clearly the WTS analysis of the Heath-Lynch negotiations had been taken on board. The arguments were developed along the lines of the 'Letter to Lynch' above. This analysis has been dismissed as fantasy by some commentators, but does it not begin to look familiar when we contemplate the recent history of Bosnia? We were aware of the possibility of such a scenario developing when we were attempting to demilitarise the situation and develop a political approach via Civil Rights.

It was basically the then thinking of Anthony Coughlan, perhaps with some input from Greaves, in desperation, under the pressure of a situation rapidly descending towards what we would now recognise as Bosnian. I had little to do with it, apart from my July 25 memo above. My attention at this time was on the Mornington School, where people were trying to absorb some of the historical background, including European political experience, and the experience of the Labour movement in Britain. We built up quite a useful library, which went historically back to the English Republic (as analysed by Rodney Hilton), included most of the Irish republican classics, also TA Jackson, Greaves etc, and most of the works of Connolly. Immediately after internment however it became obvious that the activists, however much they aspired to take the political road, could think of nothing but internment and all background political education was increasingly seen as irrelevant.

I as WTS Secretary wrote on August 16 to the New Scientist congratulating them on their 'riot control' article which had emphasising the political rather than the technical aspect. I followed up with an outline of our current position, summarising past history.

There were extended WTS drafting committee meetings on August 17 and 23 1971 on the North, with inputs from Daltun Ó Ceallaigh and Anthony Coughlan, the key concepts being a 'reformed Stormont' and 'imposition of democratic constitution from Westminster'. An attempt was made to get into dialogue with the Provisionals, but the outcome of this is not on record.

The revised and expanded Coughlan draft was in the end issued as from the Society, and is on record. It covers 3 foolscap pages of single-spacing small type, covering much the same ground as the foregoing, in more depth. It drew a response from Garrett Fitzgerald, who '...found much to agree with in it, although there are some points on which I would put a slightly different emphasis. I should like to congratulate you on having prepared a rational policy statement at a time when so many people are reacting irrationally ...'. He supported our opposition to 'direct rule'.

Nuacht Naisiunta in the August 23 and 27 issues gave details of a battle of press statements between Head Office, the Provisionals, Conor Cruise O'Brien, and a bogus statement issued by the Special Branch purporting to be from the 'officials'. These present a challenge to aspirant historian-interpreters; it is clear that once we get into a military situation deception is the order of the day. The emphasis changed on September 7 when the Republican Clubs commented on the scene, the target being the Provisional bombing, and Blaney. On September 20 Northern Command, while visibly on a war footing, and claiming British casualties, attempted to dissociate itself from the 'lunatic bombings which have affected the livelihood of the working people ...'.

During August 1971 John Miller in TCD wrote to the Wolfe Tone Society seeking to organise a quarter-page ad in the London Times signed by members of TCD staff. Desirée Shortt for the Tailors Hall Directors wrote confirming the letting to the Society of the musicians gallery room above the main hall, and naming it the 'Wolfe Tone Room'. The Society occupied this for a time, and held its meetings there regularly on the first Tuesday of the month, starting September 7 1971.

The first Tailors Hall meeting of the WTS was on September 7 1971. It was one of the 'as gaeilge' series; Maolseachlainn Ó Caollai and Risteard Ó Glaisne spoke, on the general theme of the Aug 23rd statement.

A copy of the invitation to this meeting is on record; it was in support of the Civil Rights demands in the North; projected speakers also included Janice Williams *(she maintains however that she did not speak, and was not even asked, suggesting that the sub-committee organising the meeting was not functioning properly)* from the South, while from the North there were projected Jack Bennett, Joe Deighan, Bernadette Devlin and Frank MacManus. In the event, Padraig Ó Snodaigh, Ó Caollai and Ó Glaisne spoke, and a letter from the North by Joe Deighan was read (the Northern list of names seems to have been somewhat aspirational). The 'August 23 Statement' was supported by a resolution. A statement by Maolseachlainn Ó Caollai on behalf of Connradh na Gaeilge was issued to the press, in English, giving some historical background on the use of Irish by Scottish Presbyterian settlers in the 18th century.

On September 10 1971 again in the Tailors Hall there was a book-launch for Greaves to promote his Mellows book, and to present Maire Comerford with a copy.

Chapter 8: The Period 1971-1980

It seems also around this time we tried to get 'prominent people' to sign the letter to Jack Lynch; George Gilmore wrote in declining, and David Thornley, then in controversy with Cruise O'Brien, felt it would be impolitic, while agreeing with the letter privately. There is in the WTS archive a Hibernia cutting dated September 24 on Thornley's political position.

The September 28 1971 *Nuacht Naisiunta* issue referenced a document from an un-named source which reported a CIA secret meeting in Washington, indicating a serious interest in Irish internal affairs, with roles for executives of US-based companies in Ireland.

The WTS October 5 general meeting held a post-mortem on the attempt to get the Irish-language group working for September *(ie we explained the weakness of the September meeting by the failure of the Irish Language group to deliver)*. Successive North memoranda were considered. A tax and social reform group was set up. Finally at the October 19 1971 committee the need to loosen up the Irish language constraint was recognised.

There was an attendance analysis; the consistent supporters were said to be RJ, Cathal MacLiam, Derry Kelleher, Alan Heussaff and Joy Rudd. Occasional were Uinsean Mac Eoin, Dermot O'Doherty, Seamus MacGabhainn, Micheál Ó Loingsigh. *Janice Williams was also a consistent supporter at this time, but she seems to have been overlooked.* Richard Roche had dropped out(9).

The *Nuacht Naisiunta* then resumed, after a gap in the record, on November 9 1971, the Sinn Fein Ard Fheis having taken place in the interval. Elected to the Ard Comhairle were Máirín de Burca, Seamus Costello, Cathal Goulding, Tony Heffernan, Derry Kelleher, Malachi McBurney, Malachy McGurran, Liam McMillan, Donnacha Mac Raghnaill, Seán Ó Coinnaith, Eoin Ó Murchú and Mick Ryan. There was provision for regional representatives from 13 defined regions, 4 of which were in 9-county Ulster.

There was a reference to an educational conference in Greystones, to be held on November 21 1971, as an open event. Outside speakers included Matt Larkin, de Courcy Ireland, Oliver Snoddy and Tom Redmond, indicating a conscious aspiration towards a 'broad left' programme.

There was also a report of Malachy McGurran's speech at the Edentubber commemoration; by using this event they were asserting continuity with the 50s tradition, while changing the political message and distancing themselves from the Provisionals: '...can they justify their sectarian attacks on the Protestant workers, and would they agree with ...their leader when he says that if the Protestant people don't like the Provisionals' Irish Republic then they can get out?'

The November 16 issue focused on visits to Dublin by British politicians; they urged no talks while there was internment in the North. It was reported that Ó Brádaigh and Mac Stiofain had admitted that they were prepared to meet in secret with the 6 Tory MPs. There was also an evaluation of the Ard Fheis suggesting that with the increased scale of the event there had been trouble over democratic procedures; they had attempted to concentrate discussion into 6 main resolutions.

The call for 'no talks with the British until internment is ended' was re-iterated on November 22 1971 in connection with the visit of ex-Prime Minister Harold Wilson. This issue also contained a statement from the 6-county executive of the Republican Clubs which was supportive of the Civil Disobedience campaign being promoted by the NICRA. The latter was exposed to a takeover threat, associated with Aidan Corrigan, an attempt to develop a 'Provisional' political base (the 'Northern Resistance Committee' set up in Omagh on November 21). The article went on to accuse the Peoples Democracy of '...courting the Provisionals in an attempt to win the influence that they had failed to do within the NICRA ...'. There had earlier been a Dungannon NICRA conference which had resisted this Provisional or perhaps Blaneyite takeover threat; the people concerned had retired to Omagh to set up their rival show.

These manoeuvrings need further analysis, perhaps in the context of the history of the NICRA and its attempts to keep the campaign broad-based political despite the developing Provisional campaign, with the 'officials' also being active militarily.

The relative political positions of the NICRA and the 'officials' was illustrated in the November 30 1971 issue of *Nuacht Naisiunta*, in which they published in full the NICRA demands (effective local democracy under PR and reformed Stormont, not 'direct rule'; legislation against discrimination and sectarianism, and the ending of internment) but then went on to assert the demand for the all-Ireland Republic, and to highlight the role of the 'official IRA' which was then actively at war with the British. Seán Ó Cionnaith in the US had been experiencing trouble and misreporting in his attempts to explain this complex situation, with the Provisionals also being active.

The December 7 1971 issue opened with an attempt to get Hillery in Foreign Affairs to take up the case of the internees, but then went on to publish a 3-page manifesto signed by Eoin Ó Murchú, with the title PRO. This attacked the 'Wilson Plan': a Commission drawn from the 3 parliaments in Dublin, London and Belfast, to draw up a new 32-county constitution, for an Ireland within the Commonwealth, with retention of Special Powers and internment. The statement countered by urging the development of workers' unity across the sectarian divide in the political struggle against the Common Market, which was opposed in the Protestant community by Boal and Paisley(10).

Leading off with a partial list of prisoners and internees, and a listing of actions in Galway, the main content of the December 14 1971 issue of *Nuacht Naisiunta* was a report of an anti-internment rally in the Mansion House organised by the Dublin Comhairle Ceanntar. The speakers were Seamus Ó Tuathail (the editor of the *United Irishman*, who had happened to be in Belfast in a sporting capacity and had been picked up, but subsequently released), Malachy McGurran, Tomás Mac Giolla, Bernadette Devlin and Micheál O'Riordan. The principal message was supportive of the NICRA demands, as noted above, but the press it seems picked up on a remark by Bernadette relating to the assassination of Senator Barnhill, and the overall message was lost.

It was becoming increasingly clear that the role of the 'official IRA', in the context where the NICRA was attempting to develop a mass campaign of civil disobedience against internment, was totally counter-productive. The Barnhill episode was among the final factors which triggered my own withdrawal from membership of the movement. The embryonic *left-wing unity suggested by the above Mansion House event was tragically aborted by the persistence of the military mind-set; this pathological tradition, fuelled by competition with the Provisionals, subsequently was siphoned off and flourished with Costello and his 'INLA', after the 'officials' in the end got sense and called a cease-fire.*

The final *Nuacht Naisiunta* issue of 1971 was on December 21; it reported the names of the officer board of the new Ard Comhairle: Secretaries were Máirín de Burca and Tony Heffernan, vice-Presidents were Malachy McGurran and Derry Kelleher, Treasurers Donnacha Mac Raghnaill and Janice Williams, Organiser Seán Garland, Publicity Eoin Ó Murchú, Education Derry Kelleher. It contains also a statement from 30 internees in Crumlin Road supportive of enhanced political actions to counter the negative effects of the Provisional bombing campaign, and to counter the threat of internment in the 26 counties.

The Year 1972, Bloody Sunday etc

The January 2 1972 issue of *Nuacht Naisiunta* led off with an account of Seamus Costello's speech at the Seán South commemoration in Limerick. *Note that it was still policy to maintain continuity with the 1950s military tradition, presumably in the hope that by this means they would keep at least some of the activists from leaking away to the Provisionals.* The content of his speech however was basically broad-left political, seeking the Bill of Rights, and joint actions between the British and Irish Trade Union movements. Subsequent issues concentrated increasingly on the EEC as well as the anti-internment campaign, the civil disobedience campaign in the North.

Bloody Sunday was covered in the February 7 1972 edition, calling for unity behind the NICRA banner, but also acting as a political outlet for the South Down / South Armagh command of the official IRA; '...the whole world (was) looking on in disbelief ...'.

Shortly after this I resigned. I felt that, given my precarious self-employed situation, I was no longer in a position to contribute anything, though I had hopes that the emergent 'left-unity' situation as indicated at the Mansion House meeting might consolidate, with the leadership in what appeared to be good hands. This hopeful situation was however killed by the further descent into militarism, stimulated by the Bloody Sunday events and internment.

Nuacht Naisiunta however apparently had nothing to say about the Aldershot incident, where the 'official IRA' attempted to 'retaliate' for Bloody Sunday. Maybe one or more issues are missing from the record; there is no way of knowing, as the sequential numbering had been abandoned. The present writer went to see Goulding after Bloody Sunday, urging restraint, so as to keep the attention of the international media on the exposure of this British act of barbarism. The Aldershot event was however, it seems, already set up; Goulding said nothing.

Tomás Mac Giolla on March 13 speaking at the UCC Republican Club attributed responsibility for the violence and terror in the North to all three governments. He included Dublin '...because of its deliberate, calculated campaign through 1969 to split the Republican Movement and divert the Civil Rights struggle into a military campaign. Mr Lynch and his government were deeply involved in this as was Mr Tim Pat Coogan and some of his staff on the *Irish Press*. Their activities were documented in the pages of the UI in 1969 and 1970 and recently were again exposed by the London Times "Insight" team in their book "Ulster" ...'.

Concluding Remarks on RJ's SF Period

In January 1972 I formally pulled out of Sinn Fein, and, indeed, from the so-called 'official IRA', which had been showing signs of re-emergent militarism, consequent on the August 1969 events. I remained however in reasonably good standing, and was in a position to continue to help them with their internal education programme during the summer of 1972, at the 'Mornington School', although the environment was increasingly becoming poisoned by the internment process, with peoples' thinking totally dominated by perceived military objectives, and being 'on the run'.

Janice remained on the Ard Comhairle until the next Ard Fheis, at the end of 1972, after which she also bowed out.

Nuacht Naisiunta continued up to June 1976, constituting a record of the ongoing attempts to keep political republicanism going on a 'broad left' basis, the IRA remaining in existence even after it called a ceasefire in mid-1972. The political movement's attempts to survive, with sales of the *United Irishman*, distribution of anti-sectarian leaflets, support for the residual Civil Rights campaign etc, were increasingly restricted, being caught in the crossfire between the Provisionals and Costello's INLA(11).

It is important to put on record how in those days we did our best to transform the Fenian conspiratorial tradition into an open principled democratic one, using the best aspects of the Marxist democratic-revolutionary tradition, and trying to avoid top-down Stalinism, though this kept surfacing via Costello and those for whom the military tradition was dominant.

I remember Costello expressing admiration for Stalin, because he used to rob banks for the Bolsheviks!

Greaves never forgave me for making the attempt as I did; he wanted to let the Fenian tradition die, for lack of intellectual resources, and rebuild a movement from scratch, based on the organised working-class, with in mind Micheál O'Riordan as focus. He had had a hand in setting up the Irish Workers League in 1948 with this in mind, but he had illusions about its potential. It was a basically flawed concept. No way would this have been possible, given the dead hand of Stalinism, which to my mind was much more of an incubus than that of the Fenians and the IRB, though the latter of course had the potential to become a native Irish Stalinism, as indeed they did.

My judgement at the time was that there was more democratic potential in moderating and upgrading the Fenian tradition into a new-wave political force, capable of uniting broad strata of working people, including working owner-managers and self-employed, on an all-Ireland basis, than there was in narrow 'workerist' Marxist orthodoxy as embodied fundamentally in MOR, and perceptibly in CDG and co.

I hoped later to develop this thesis with as much evidence as I could muster, and try to build a neo-Marxist 'market socialism' model, of which the central ideas was 'direct democratic control over the capital investment process by the people concerned', the State being the referee and not a player. The apostolic succession is Marx Engels Connolly, but we have, as yet, no credible follower of Connolly of the same stature. Maybe we can provide the raw material to help one emerge, and I look to the left-green convergence to pick this up(12).

The germ of this idea is in my father's interactions with Plunkett House in the period 1913-1933, and this has been described in the earlier chapters. There is actually some degree of continuity of philosophical position between my father and myself, which I did not recognise when he was alive. I have in Chapter 3 presented evidence that he was promoting the writings of Connolly in the 1920s, on the international network, and that during 1921 and 1922 he was giving lectures on economics in the evening to working people in TCD, more or less unofficially, with the support of Tom Johnson.

JJ's Last Act: the EEC and Berkeley's *Querist*

JJ at the end of his days was a supporter of the anti-EEC campaign, attending its rallies when he was able to. His basic objection was due to the workings of the Common Agricultural Policy, which subsidized European production in volume-dependent mode, generating powerful vested interests in agri-business, and inhibiting access to European markets by products from outside. He saw the analogy with the way British subsidies had strangled Irish agriculture in the previous decades. Ireland becoming a beneficiary of the policies of the in-group he saw as a short-term benefit but long-term disaster.

I give here one of a series of letters(13) which JJ wrote to the *Irish Times* some time before he died:

JJ in the *Irish Times*, December 18 1970: 'The Invisible Coalition':

Sir / One is sometimes tempted to join one of our left-wing revolutionary organisations in the hope of teaching them a little sense. Many of the ends they have in view are highly desirable but the means used to further them are deplorable. An outstanding example is the destruction of the Nelson Pillar. A well publicised movement to have Nelson removed and Wolfe Tone substituted would have commanded widespread sympathy and the significance of the change would have been obvious to everyone. Many similar more recent episodes could be referred to.

Watching the political game from the outside one cannot help being amazed that so many of the personalities concerned cannot see the obvious. The political Labour party which has not the remotest hope of ever becoming a majority party in the life time of most of us, is hopelessly divided on the question for or against coalition. The real coalition is staring us all in the face but we do not see it. That is the de facto coalition between Fine Gael and Fianna Fail to land us all in the EEC with our eyes shut.

The greatest betrayal of our national interests and freedom since the Act of Union in being openly planned by the major parties, and the general public silently acquiesces. The Labour party, instead of wasting its energies in a dispute about a coalition with Fine Gael, should consciously adopt the cause of an all Ireland radical party that is determined to keep all Ireland out of the Eurocrat Empire by every legitimate means.

Many people up north have grave misgivings about the EEC but they lack organisation and leadership. The Labour party can make no more valuable contribution to the cause of natural freedom and self determination on an all Ireland non-sectarian basis than this. If they fail to adopt this obvious cause in my view, they should have not only their eyes, but their heads examined.

***

In the last few years of his life JJ pulled together several of his published papers and re-worked them into chapters supporting the projected 'definitive edition' of Berkeley's *Querist*. Some correspondence he left suggests that he had some difficulty in finding a publisher interested in this *Querist* project. In the end it was published in 1970 by Dundalgan, with some TCD sponsorship. Some copies were taken up by libraries; it got few reviews, and was remaindered(14).

He submitted it for the degree of DLitt by extern examiner, and the degree was awarded in May 1972, on the same occasion as the composer Shostakovitch was awarded an honorary degree. I had to help him up the steps to receive it.

Shortly afterwards he went into Limerick hospital (he was then living in an extension of my sister's house near Nenagh) for a minor operation, to do with what the surgeons laconically call 'the plumbing'. He made heavy weather of the anaesthetic, and died as a result. When last I saw him he was in intensive care, and we held hands. Before the operation I recollect seeing him sitting up contentedly in bed, reading something lightweight, perhaps PG Wodehouse, or a detective story. Once he had put his Berkeley book to bed, he felt he had done all he could. He had shown up at a meeting in Athlone in early 1972, which was attempting, against the tide, to persuade Irish farmers that the EEC was to be viewed critically. He was however content; he had published his book and got his Doctorate.

Coincidentally, perhaps by way of epilogue, the Dublin University Co-operative Society, which JJ and others had founded in 1913, died shortly afterwards(15).

Operations Research

The timing of JJ's death for me was unfortunate, as the International Federation of Operational Research Societies conference was taking place in Dublin (August 21 to 25), and I was scheduled to give a critical response(16) to a keynote paper, on the topic of 'simulation', by Professor TH Naylor, of Duke University, a leading world authority. I had written the paper, and Maurice Foley, then a member of the Council of the ORSI, delivered it on my behalf.

I had established my credentials with the Operational Research community when working with Aer Lingus in the previous decade; the Airline Group of IFORS the international federation used to meet regularly, and the modelling work we did on the performance of real-time computing systems, and on fleet planning, had given us in Aer Lingus some standing with the international community. As a result I was asked to be a member of the international programme committee, and I found myself in the front line at conference-time.

The IFORS conference was influential in raising the profile of Operational Research in the Irish context; I had been working with Gordon Foster in the TCD Department of Statistics on developing an MSc programme, and I was able to contribute to the utilisation of university based research results in industry, as well as to getting 'real-world' problems for the MSc students concerned(17).

Post-resignation Politics

After my resignation I had some time to give active support to the Common Market Defence Campaign, which was led by Anthony Coughlan, Micheál Ó Loingsigh, Raymond Crotty and others. The campaign had gathered a mixed bag of supporters from a wide-ranging political spectrum, some of whom subsequently became supporters of the political parties which had opposed entry, to a greater or lesser degree. For example, my sister Dr Maureen Carmody chaired the campaign in Nenagh, where quite a high anti-EEC vote was obtained, due to her succeeding in making the various supporting political activists keep a low profile, and stick to the issues, which included a threat to local industry. I and various others did our best to get the few members of the farming community we were in touch with to adopt the global economics view, as my father was doing, and to be critical of short-term dependence on the artificially high price structure. We were mostly unsuccessful, despite a last-ditch rally of some small farmers in Athlone, which my father attended, where some historic Land League banners were on display, and courageous speeches were made.

The Campaign used to meet in various scattered locations, and eventually, when it had become the Irish Sovereignty Movement, in the basement of a house owned by Uinsean Mac Eoin in Mountjoy Square, which he was engaged in re-developing. This was also the venue for the meetings of the then declining Wolfe Tone Society. It was a cold and uncomfortable location, and did not help our public image. I recollect an occasion when we had caught some mice, and had lit a fire, and a leading member of the group, who incidentally was a schoolteacher, came up with the question 'do mice burn?'. Subsequently reflecting on this, I had occasion to use it as an example of the gulf between the culture of the Irish aspirant political elite and the culture of technical competence(18).

The interactions generated by the anti-EEC campaign were diverse and creative in their own way. We were supported among others by Seamus Deane, then in UCD (he is now in Notre Dame). He then edited a periodical called *Atlantis* which was an attempt to fill the gap left by the demise of Seán Ó Faolain's *Bell*, and indeed the earlier *Irish Statesman*. It was a critical review at a high intellectual standard, in a format such as to remain vertical on the bookshelves and be referenced. I had previously done a review for *Atlantis* of the Irish volume of Lloyd George's secretary Tom Jones's *Whitehall Diaries*. In this context, wishing to capture some of my Sinn Fein experience, Seamus Deane asked me to contribute a paper on a critical analysis of the various visions of the 'New Ireland' which had been floating around during the previous decade or so. This I did with alacrity, being then in an unattached political state, searching to make meaningful contact with the Left, such as it was. The paper was developed initially at a Wolfe Tone Society event which I outline in what follows.

Desmond Greaves recorded attending a conference organised by the Dublin WTS in the Nuremore Hotel, Carrickmacross, in November 1972(19). This was a significant attempt, on the part of the Society, to focus on Northern issues, and some of the papers were subsequently published. Maire Comerford, Jack Bennett, Kader Asmal, Derry Kelleher and the present writer were also there, as well as Liam de Paor from UCD. Anthony Coughlan was not present, being then pre-occupied with the post-Referendum transformation of the Common Market Defence Campaign into the Irish Sovereignty Movement. When he got sight of Jack Bennett's paper however he took steps to publish it, and there was some dispute over how the proceedings of the conference were to be published. In the end some of the papers appeared in various separate publications, but I don't think the conference was ever published as an integrated proceedings, under the WTS imprint, which is a pity, because in my recollection it was a significant event.

The people opposed to the EEC included, as well as 'official' and 'provisional' Sinn Fein, the Communist Party, the Labour Party, the Irish Congress of Trade Unions and a good few non-political 'concerned citizens'. These held together for a time in the Irish Sovereignty Movement, the objective of which was to keep a watching brief over the way the Government related to the EEC. They considered at one time attempting to become an electoral force, but drew back, preferring to remain as a cross-party political lobby. The active politicals concerned attempted to develop activities of their own, under the label 'Left Alternative'.

The existence of the latter was the basis for some organised Irish participation in the 'World Congress of Peace Forces' which met in Moscow in October 1973(20). This was attended by a group of 30 rather disparate people from Ireland. There was a strong journalistic contingent which included Donal Foley from the *Irish Times*, Carmel Duignan and Seán Ó Mordha from RTE, Liam McGowan from the *Sunday World*, Prionnsias Mac Aonghusa and his father Criostoir and John Mulcahy of *Hibernia*. As a result there was quite good coverage of the event in the *Irish Press*, including a series of articles by Liam McGowan which contrasted his experiences with those from his earlier visit in 1955, when along with Anthony Cronin and Peadar O'Donnell he had been demonised by the *Catholic Standard*. Brezhnev gave a lengthy keynote speech on the Yom Kippur middle-east crisis, being reported at length by Donal Foley on October 27.

The group also included some Trade Union people: Robin Joseph, secretary of the Scientific Staffs Branch of ASTMS, Betty Sinclair of the Belfast Trades Council, and others. Seamus Scally was there from the Labour Party, Kevin McCorry from NICRA, Brigid Wilkinson from Amnesty International, Con Lehane from Citizens for Civil Liberty, John McGarry from the Irish United Nations Association. The present writer was there representing the Dublin Wolfe Tone Society. One Joan O'Brien was there from the Language Freedom Movement; this was a cause of some tension in the group.

There was a group of Communist Party of Ireland people, including Micheál O'Riordan and Edwina Stewart; also Betty Sinclair as above, and Frank Edwards of the Ireland-USSR Society. The group also included leading left-oriented politicising republicans Tomás Mac Giolla, Seán Garland and Dessie O'Hagan. The present writer, having resigned from the republican movement, subsequently for a brief period re-joined the Communist Party, with the aspiration to help along the convergence of the republicans with the left, which seemed to be beginning to develop some dynamics. This Moscow episode seemed at the time to be an indication of some degree of philosophical convergence between the two traditions, and the fact that a reasonably broad-based group could be assembled and persuaded to go to view the Cold War issues from a Moscow perspective, seemed to augur well.

A highlight of the plenary sessions was Salvador Allende's widow's account of her husband's overthrow by the CIA-engineered coup in Chile; this was then recent history. Donal Foley reported these in the *Irish Times* on October 27. (Shortly afterwards in Dublin, with Jim Fitzgerald I helped organise a concert of Chilean music by Isabel Parra, in aid of the refugees.)

Overall however the conference was a top-down railroading operation. There were various working groups set up, to discuss previously prepared documents. I attended the one on 'Economic, Scientific and Technological Co-operation', and contributed a prepared position paper, in which I attempted to develop a role for smaller fringe-countries in the 'east-west' in helping to transfer scientific know-how to the 'south'.

I had recently completed the preliminary analysis of the 1971 Census which gave for the first time a head-count of people having qualifications in science and engineering(21).

It was evident that there was a reserve of qualified manpower available in Ireland, and that this tended to be exported to the already-rich core of the post-imperial world. I was then also building up the TCD MSc programme in Statistics and Operations Research, and we had experience of practical techno-economic development work with graduates from various scientific disciplines.

Some of the TCD projects(22) on which we were working seemed to me to be models relevant to the development economics of the 'third world'. There would perhaps be scope for an internationally-funded development agency to locate in Ireland, and/or in one or more other European 'fringe' countries, for the purpose of training a cadre of graduates from third-world countries in techno-economic analysis relevant to their development programmes, with emphasis on a co-operative approach to adding value to products of primary producers.

I attempted to develop a correspondence with various people I had met at the conference who were concerned to influence the fate of any 'peace dividend' which might emerge as a result of the 'detente' process in the direction of suitably located postgraduate programmes addressing the development economics environment. Regrettably this did not succeed. This particular conference did not enable the necessary related networking to develop.

I was attempting to use the 'international movement', in the form it had assumed under Soviet domination, as a vehicle for bottom-up networking among people who were prepared to adopt a democratic, bottom-up approach to the transfer of technologies relevant to the development-economics of the third world. I was, perhaps, attempting to build on a development philosophy which I had earlier encountered peripherally at an Irish Management Institute conference in Killarney: that of ('small is beautiful') Schumacher, who had addressed the conference but had been totally sidelined(23). I did however spend some time with him at the conference, and we exchanged ideas.

Very little, if any, of the contributions of the Moscow participants, many of whom were dedicated experts of international standing, were embodied in the final documents, and this was remarked upon by perceptive participants, with whom I subsequently corresponded. It was a classic top-down, railroaded, Stalinist affair, geared to the propagation of Soviet foreign policy.

On returning to Ireland I found myself in the position of acting secretary to what became known for a period as the 'Irish Peace Group'. It was, presumably, hoped that there would be some cohesion, and some continuity of effort, but despite some efforts on my part, nothing ever came of this. It must go down in history, from the Irish political angle, as an interesting 'junket', from which some people perhaps may have gained some experience of the state of the 'international movement'. Those perceptive enough may perhaps have seen some early warnings of the subsequent demise of the USSR.

The Kane-Bernal Society Mk 2

Round about 1972 Derry Kelleher and I attempted to resurrect our earlier concept, and we had a series of meetings in the basement of 190 Pearse St, in the building occupied by Professor FG Foster's Department of Statistics in TCD. During this time I had attached myself to Foster's Department, and was helping to supervise some of the MSc projects in Operations Research(17).

The group, apart from Kelleher and myself, included Myles Parker, Robert Blackith, Martin Speight, Paul Dowding, Noel Murphy and others; the latter was a UCD chemical engineer, while most of the others were basically environmentalists from TCD. We identified various problems and opportunities in the general area of the interface between research and the implementation of its results, mobility of people between teaching and research, the human aspects of implementation of innovative systems, problems of man-machine relationship, definitions of 'growth', planned obsolescence, urban planning, supply and training of technicians.

We got as far as drafting a constitution, and I have a copy with amendments in pen. The 'Methods of Work' section called for '...a periodic meeting to hear progress reports from problem-area groups, and the reading of papers by people of suitable standing, either in public events organised by the Association, or on the grounds of other societies..... the encouragement of interdisciplinary and inter-institutional contacts... publication of a newsletter.'

I also have copies of drafts of articles written by me and by Kelleher on the analysis of the Guinness crisis; I have no evidence or recollection however of their being published. The thrust of the analysis was directed at the nature of the Guinness management structure, and the opportunities presented for diversifying with the support of the available bio-technical know-how into areas other than the fermentation of sugar to get alcohol.

There are records of various meetings throughout 1972, and interactions with the Biomedical Engineering Society (via Noel Murphy) and the Industrial Archaeology Society, with Dr HS Corran, and I seem to have been able to use the contacts to generate related published material via the *Irish Times* column(2).

After the end of 1972 the trail goes cold, and I suspect that the network continued informally as an ideas-supply source for the Column. It is appropriate to resurrect some of these *Irish Times* articles, and I have made them available in Appendices 11 and 12, as they relate to the 'science and society' and socio-technical' streams.

The Wolfe Tone Society in Decline

The records are sparse, but in May 1974 there was an issue #2 of the new series of *Tuairisc*, bound, with a cover, in a handy size, priced at 20p. Issue #1 in the new series had appeared some time previous, in March 1973, and had been entitled 'Democracy and Local Government', but alas this is not on record.

Issue #2 contained an article based on a paper which my sister Dr Maureen Carmody read to the Society, entitled 'Protestants in the Republic', from the perspective of a medical doctor who had raised her family in the Protestant community of Nenagh, where her late husband Dermot Carmody had been the Vicar. It also contained a critical paper on the educational system, presumably by Joy Rudd, which focused on the question of denominational control.

Reaction to the Energy Crisis

Consequent on the 1972 energy crisis much attention was directed at influencing the Government to take the question seriously, and allocate resources into the necessary supportive research and development. In due course I initiated and serviced a small pressure group of engineers and concerned citizens called 'Conserve'. Together we drafted a memorandum to the Government, which we circulated among the TDs during 1975. It is possible that it may have had some influence on subsequent energy policies, but it is hard to say.

The memorandum outlined the dangers involved in nuclear power production, leaning mostly on the Brown's Ferry experience in the USA. It noted the aspirations of the physicists to produce fusion energy, but set this aside as being long-term (the date post-2000 was suggested!). It then went on to develop a strategy for conserving fossil fuels, while various forms of solar energy were developed to the extent of becoming economic. A key concept in the conservation plan was the development of the gas grid to feed a multiplicity of small local combined heat and power systems, rather than to convert the Kinsale gas to electricity in a large generator, in a location where the waste heat would have to be thrown away. Proposals for a nodalised system of public transport were also outlined(24).

Brief Encounter with the CPI

Some time after the Moscow conference, perhaps unduly encouraged by what I picked up regarding the 'detente' atmosphere, and the broad-based nature of the group which went, I joined the CPI(25). I must at the time have been a believer in the positive potential for convergence between the CPI and the 'official' republicans, with whom I had remained on communicating terms, my resignation having been accepted. Disillusion however set in rapidly.

Greaves visited Dublin on March 22 1975 to attend the CPI congress, which took place in Liberty Hall. Support for the 'declaration of intent' was on the resolution. There were some 120 people there. He noted that '...they had a number of resolutions and adopted the somewhat unusual procedure of debating them one after the other and voting on the whole lot tomorrow ...'. I too had noted this, being present, and marked it down as another piece of Stalinist procedural pathology; voting after the debate has been forgotten encourages machine-like voting in support of the leadership's position on each issue. Greaves however seemed optimistic about the prospects: '...many new recruits and promising young people... new branches springing up all over the country, thanks to their having the right policy ...'. MOR in the closing session paid a warm tribute to CDG for his '...40 years stand for Irish independence in Britain ...'.

In June 1975 Greaves claimed to have received a phone-call *(in fact, she had written to him, and spoken to him subsequently in Cathal McLiam's place)* from Janice Williams, then Secretary of the Wolfe Tone Society, asking him to speak at a meeting, in the context of its policy of fostering the convergence of the Left with the 'official' republicans, along the lines suggested in the 1970 'Freedom Manifesto'. It seems they had sought permission to reprint his Marx House pamphlet on the national question, but now wanted to print an edited version of a tape recording of the talk which he was invited to give. This he declined to have anything to do with, writing to the Chairman Cathal MacLiam to that effect.

Greaves was, it seems, content to let the WTS run down, and was unsupportive of our efforts to keep it going. My vision when with the republicans had been to transform the movement into one which would be primarily political, and represent the common interest of workers, working managers, owner-managers and self-employed, conceived consciously as a class alliance around common class interests in a national liberation context, and in that sense being basically Marxist. Greaves always dismissed this as 'making the revolution without the workers' and as 'petty-bourgeois', the latter being a dismissive label. He was of course himself petty-bourgeois, and most of the working class has petty-bourgeois aspirations, aspiring to own its own business. His dismissal of his own roots, and his failure to recognise the unrealistic nature of the aspiration to working-class purity, was a barrier to his total understanding of the Irish situation, though he did understand it better than most Marxists in Britain.

Greaves had positive insights, like (on November 29 1975) '...the Irish proletariat is not revolutionary at all, and does not recognise any such vanguard ...'! Of course! This was precisely the reason that I had attempted to develop the broad-based class alliance concept, on rational grounds, avoiding jargon labels like 'revolutionary vanguard', or indeed 'proletariat'. This sort of language however crept into the 'official Sinn Fein' after I had resigned, under the influence of ultra-leftist elements who joined, filling the intellectual vacuum. My resignation had been caused by the re-assertion of the militarist culture in the movement, perceived as being the way to compete with the 'Provisionals'.

Greaves visited Dublin again on February 10 1976, primarily for a meeting with the ITGWU executive about his projected history, which seemed likely to proceed. From his political contacts he picked up the way official SF had infiltrated and taken over the Resources Protection Campaign, as they had done with the

NICRA. He concluded with a revealing passage: '...I notice on all sides the same impatience with SF that I feel myself. This claim to national decision-making without popular mandate is objectionable, and I think that there is an element of it inherent in the idea of a Communist Party with a special status in a socialist state, which requires serious examination, though it is not a subject I have ever given much thought to ...'.

SF at this time under Eamonn Smullen's guidance was attempting to upstage the CPI and become the recognised Irish embodiment of the 'international movement'. It is interesting that this was a trigger for Greaves's implied questioning of the 'dictatorship of the proletariat' principle, the article of faith on which the 'international movement' placed so much weight.

However pathological the situation is where there is one highly centralised Stalinist top-down organisational claiming 'revolutionary vanguard' status, the existence of two such is indeed a recipe for disaster, with each claiming to control broad-based bodies by the exercise of disciplined infiltrating voting machines. This was a long way from the situation envisioned in the 1970 'Freedom Manifesto' as published in the United Irishman, which, though flawed in its ambiguity regarding the IRA, enshrined the pinnacle of the present writer's influence.

The *Irish Socialist* around this time was edited and largely written by Eoin Ó Murchú, who had been active in SF in close association with Eoghan Harris during the latter's period of intellectual dominance. The circumstances of his move from 'official' SF to the CPI remain obscure to the present writer. At the time of my resignation from SF in 1972 EOM was seeking to issue a damning statement but was over-ruled by the then leadership, who respected my integrity.

In July 1976 according to Greaves there was a complaint by SF against the present writer, calling on Micheál O'Riordan to discipline him for exposing to key leading people in the Resources Protection Campaign that the left were at war within it, fighting for take-over(26).

This was indeed true; I had been present at a broad-based meeting in Athlone, attended by ASTMS and other trade union people with strong technological skills, with standing and influence, some of whom I knew personally thanks to the *Irish Times* 'Science and Technology' column; it looked like the Resources Protection Campaign was beginning to attract technological heavyweights.

I was however appalled by the way the meeting descended into a slanging match between rival voting machines on some motion, the purport of which I forget. I attempted to generate a knowledge-based compromise consensual amendment, but was shouted down by both sides. This was, if anything, evidence of an ignorant petty-bourgeois struggle between two so-called 'working-class' voting machines, in a contest for the ownership of an organisation which neither of them understood. Greaves did not have a clue about this, and added some pejorative remarks about the present writer.

Science and Marxism

In or about October 1977 an episode occurred which is worth recording. Helena Sheehan, now on the academic staff of Dublin City University, was then doing her PhD in the philosophy of science in TCD, and I was in the TCD industrial liaison office, at the science-technology interface, acting on behalf of the College. I made an effort to build bridges.

Helena was associated with the TCD Communist Society, which ran occasional political events of student interest. I attended one at which she spoke on the 'scientific revolution'. While much of the discussion was somewhat 'up in the air', I felt it no harm to encourage the idea that mastery of science was an important aspect of social change. So when Helena came up with the idea of an invited speaker from the USSR with a science background, I was prepared to make an effort to ensure that the event was supported by at least some members of the College science community, and I made this known. This however turned out not to be welcome; I was accused of 'wanting to take over' the meeting. So I did little, but I did turn up to hear what the USSR speaker had to say. She had presumably got him to come over via the Party network.

The meeting was not very well attended; she had apparently made it an event to which outside political people came in, rather than as a promotional event relating Marxism to the student and College environment. The USSR guest speaker (I forget his name) turned out to be a tired hack, for whom this presumably was a trip to the West as reward for loyal service. However I took him as a possible source of insight into current USSR developments, and I asked a question about the Lysenko episode, which had earlier been a crunch issue at the interface between science and politics. The speaker however brushed aside the question, on the grounds that Lysenko, being by then discredited, was not a fit subject for study in a science context.

In other words, the problem of the dialectics of the interaction between science and society, including the analysis of historic pathologies, had not been identified in the USSR, and was being simply ignored. We had here an example of the atrophy of critical thinking under Brezhnev. However I did not get the impression that any of the Irish Marxists of the 'high church' picked up on this.(27)

Tensions with the CPI

I had in 1973 become secretary of the Irish Peace Group, and had with increasing difficulty been attempting to make it work. Greaves in September 1977 claimed that it was '...now undertaking initiatives first thought of by the ISM ...'. So he called in to Seán Nolan in the bookshop and asked if he '...approves of RHWJ's new position.. "the difficulty is lack of personnel" said SN ...'. Well they have been caught once ...'.

The Irish Peace Group, as we saw above, had emerged out of an attempt to set up a broad-based peace lobby based on a group of politicals and journalists who went to a World Peace Council conference in Moscow in 1973, at one of the high points in CPI-republican convergence. It included Tomás Mac Giolla, Micheál O'Riordan, Betty Sinclair, Robin Joseph (then Secretary of the ASTMD Scientific Staffs Branch), Cristoir Mac Aonghusa and his son Proinnsias, Donal Foley of the *Irish Times*, and a few others, including Irish CND people. It had a tenuous existence for a while, but lacked cohesion. During my secretaryship I attempted to make some things happen, but without much success. It was basically a postal address for receiving masses of World Peace Council published material, which was of questionable value. Here was Greaves on the CPI network making the case against my attempting to develop any sort of positive role for myself on the fringe of 'high-church left orthodoxy'.. I subsequently discovered that O'Riordan had been leaking the highly libellous internal character-assassination document he had prepared in support of my expulsion to journalist members of the Peace Group. I am not surprised nothing came of it.

On December 1 1977 Greaves went to Dublin, basically to work in the National Library, but the timing was coincidental with a reception at the Soviet Ambassador's house on December 2. Micheál Ó Riordain was to be invested with the Order of the October Revolution, and had secured an invitation for Greaves, who heard this at the last minute via Betty Sinclair. It was an event for the Party leadership and their friends, and a few other key people, among them Seán MacBride. A copy of Greaves's *Life and Times of James Connolly* was presented to the Ambassador, which Greaves autographed. Con Lehane and Cathal Goulding were present.

This would appear to have been an event which in effect asserted CPI priority on the international network, in front of selected other observers. No-one from England was there, apart from Greaves himself. He made no comment on the event in his Diary.

There was a reference in his Journal by Greaves on December 11 1977 to the present writer's expulsion from the CPI which managed to avoid any serious explanation of the issues involved, and to add in various 'negative spin' comments. My expulsion was consequent on a public row I had with a leading Party activist. I had had negative experience of the latter when we were both in the republican movement. After I resigned on the militarist issue, he wanted to issue a damning statement, but was prevented by the leadership from doing so. It seems they wanted to retain ongoing good relations with me, and to accept my reasons for resignation in good faith.

Later this particular activist took up with the Eoghan Harris group who was then advising Goulding, initiating the policy move away from republican objectives and towards support for international capital, welcomed as a 'generator of an Irish proletariat' . When he later made the transition to the CPI, under unexplained circumstances, he was made welcome and lionised, rapidly becoming a guru of the Stalinist political culture which still remained in fashion in the CPI.

In this capacity the activist in question spoke at a meeting in November 1977 on cultural issues, as part of the 60th anniversary celebrations of the October Revolution. He defended the repressive Zhdanov cultural policies of the USSR, which had led to the isolation and persecution of numerous globally-famous Russian literary and scientific figures, and had stifled critical comment. I quite rightly attacked him for this, pointing out that if the Party was ever to have any influence it would have to decouple itself from this sort of carry-on, and learn to apply Marxism creatively to specifically Irish problems. For this I was expelled, with a duplicated libellous character-assassination document being circulated by O'Riordan. This event showed up the total political bankruptcy of the CPI, and its inability to read the signs of the coming disasters, which were then increasingly apparent(28).

Brief Wolfe Tone Society Resurrection

On January 12 1978 there was issued a WTS press statement supporting Taoiseach Jack Lynch who had reaffirmed national unity as the aim, and called for practical initiatives directed at breaking down partition mentality on the South, and for developing areas of north-south co-operations. *This was Sunningdale-time.* The WTS statement included the following: '...in the area of cross-border co-operation it should never again happen that a body like the EEC Commission would have to show us the way ...'.

I read a paper entitled *On the Problem of Democratic Unity* to the Dublin WTS on January 24 1978 which was subsequently published in the anarcho-trotskyist periodical *The Ripening of Time*, Issue #9, March 1978. This was associated, in a subsequent Ripening of Time Issue #13 evaluating our earlier contributions from their particular political angle, with a paper in Issue #11 by Derry Kelleher critical of the evolution of 'official Sinn Fein' towards the 'Workers Party' labelling. In this I attempted a class analysis of Ireland, distinguishing between North and South, and identifying the type of parasitic bourgeoisie which is currently (2002) being exposed in the Tribunals. I went on to analyse how these classes were represented in a complex political structure, mentioning particularly the mafia-like control of the working-class exercised by Fianna Fail. I attempted to map out how a new left might emerge in the undergrowth, with a convergence of progressive elements currently working in the Labour Party, Sinn Fein and the Communist Party. I tried to analyse the cultural obstacles to this, which included divisions in attitudes to the Provisionals. I compared the process to small-shopkeeper competition; this had showed up in the EEC Referendum. I suggested how a convergent political line might be developed, along the lines of a 'Co-operative Democratic Federation'.(29).

This 'Ripening of Time' paper would perhaps have had more impact had it been published under the auspices of a journal having a wide readership among the people concerned, but none existed. We were reduced to dependence on an ultra-left splinter-group for publication outlets. We should of course have developed Tuairisc to an appropriate level as the vehicle for material of this nature, but alas the energy was gone out of the Wolfe Tone Society, and it died.

***

There is on record (in the WTS archive, though Anthony Coughlan is 'fairly certain' that it relates to the Sovereignty Movement) a Programme for 1978 which has the following items: Jan 24: AGM; Feb 14: 'British Attitudes to Irish Unity' (C Desmond Greaves); March 14: 'Attitudes to Irish Unity' (Fr McGreil); May 9 'EEC - a Step towards Irish Unity? (Micheál Ó Loingsigh); it then goes on suggesting titles without speakers, implying aspirations to cover areas like 'citizens rights', 'Labour and Irish Unity', control of education as an obstacle to unity, the political impact of religious differences, cultural diversity in a united Ireland. It is perhaps worth remarking that the lack of reference to the various electoral events which took place during the decade suggest a certain detachment from current politics in the 26 Counties.

There is no mention of this WTS meeting in Greaves' diary, though he was in Dublin for some time around this date; this suggests he did not set store by it.

Chapter 8: The Period 1971-1980

During the 1970s I recollect that the membership of the Society became extended and somewhat diluted. The meeting-place in Mountjoy Square contributed to its negative image. It attempted to provide opportunities for the 'left alternative' network, which included the Labour Left, the CPI and the 'official republicans'. The latter evolved into the Workers Party via a period as Sinn Fein the Workers party. This trail was mostly sterile and I am not going to pursue it. The brief renaissance in 1978 was intended to develop something around the opportunities presented by the Sunningdale Agreement, such as it was. I don't recollect any event at which the WTS was formally wound up, but the records remain with Anthony Coughlan, and we are indebted to him for their preservation.

***

The Applied-Research Consultancy Group in TCD

The following note is adapted from the May 1980 issue of the monthly journal Trade and Industry:

"The TCD applied research and consultancy group was set up in 1976 with the help of a £25,000 training grant from the IDA, after a period of operation of an Industrial Liaison Office financed by the National Science Council.

"During the preliminary period it had become apparent that the gap between research done in the academic environment (no matter how 'applied' in nature) and the problem-solving needs of industry was too wide to be bridged by academic staff in marginal time aided by research students.

"The 'ARC Group' formula was developed during 1976 in discussion with the IDA, which was interested in strengthening the linkages between Irish third-level education and the rapidly developing high-technology sector of industry in Ireland. It consisted in taking in full-time junior consultants having applied research experience at post-graduate level, who would be capable of taking industrially sponsored projects to completion within a deadline, with the aid of some co-ordinated support from academic staff members having relevant expertise.

"These 'project officers' were, so to speak, amplifiers of academic expertise, rendering it available for industrial problem-solving to a client's deadline, rather than within an academic schedule.

"At the conclusion of the third year of the ARC Group enterprise (in which an estimated £102,000 revenue was generated, years one and two having shown revenues of £16,440 and £43,475) there are employed a manager, secretary, eight project officers, two technicians and the equivalent of 2 or 3 more graduates in the form of part-time support from about 10 academic staff whose expertise had been found useful and who were willing to work as internal consultants, taking their reward either as personal income or as additions to their personal research funds.

"The group currently consisted of four units relating to ten or more academic departments:

1. the micro-computing laboratory, specialising in dedicated application of microprocessor technology (hardware and software);
2. the bio-systems unit, specialising in software developments for special-purpose data-banks, mainly in applied biology and agriculture;

3. the applied physics unit specialising in the development of innovative instrumentation for industrial quality and process control;
4. the environment / applied biology unit which was engaged in doing base-line surveys, environmental impact analysis and monitoring, as well as general-purpose problem-solving where there was a biological factor (e.g. spoilage).

"Charges depended on the length of the project, level of required expertise, amount of special services required etc; they ranged from £15,000 to £25,000 per man-year, or £100 to £150 per day. Project sizes range from a man-day to a man-year; the average was about two man-months.

"The ARC Group on the whole tried not to compete directly with the State applied research institutes, though in some cases a competitive role was thrust upon it. It preferred to see itself as a specialised sub-contractor to the State research institutes, as well as a supplier of services not available elsewhere in the country. Nor did it wish to compete with existing commercial suppliers of services; it preferred to develop systems and licence them out.

Its main stock-in-trade was the expertise of those academic departments where the research was relevant to industry. The main advantage to the college was an in-house window into industrial problems, providing ideas for basic-applied research of academic interest.

"The current year's academic MSc project could, if set up with insight, turn out to be the solution to next year's industrial problem. "

***

The ARC Group was discontinued at the end of 1980, with the present writer's contract continuing, at the level of 'research leave', for some years subsequently. It did not succeed in covering its costs and making a profit for the College, though on total-cost accounting it did so to the extent of about 85%, paying for services (eg computing time, office space and staff consultancy) received from the College. The IIRS at the time supplied a service to industry which was subsidised by the State to the extent of the order of 50%. It was constrained in the type of contract it could offer to junior consultants, with the result that there was a turnover; it was in effect a training ground for people who subsequently contributed to the development of the then nascent high-tech industry.

The College subsequently set up procedures for encouraging and spinning off high-tech enterprises, and this on the whole has been successful. The ARC episode can perhaps be seen as a pilot for the subsequent model, from which lessons were learned. Some work of significance was done during the ARC period, and I look upon it as relatively speaking a success story(30).

George Jeffares and the Labour Party

My attempt to get the Communist Party of Ireland to abandon its uncritical support for the USSR, and adopt a critical Marxist philosophy related to the current needs of Irish politics, was unsuccessful and led to my expulsion. I was again in the political wilderness. George Jeffares had for years been trying to do the same, from a position of long-standing loyalty to the cause. He was a TCD graduate of slightly earlier vintage than our cohort, in modern languages, primarily French and Spanish. After a period teaching in England he returned to Ireland, along with his wife Marion, an artist, and long-standing member of the CPGB. We have already encountered them during the early 1950s in this narrative. After a period spent in China, teaching languages to Chinese trade specialists interested in Latin America, George returned and assumed a leading role in the Irish Worker's League in the later 1950s, and attempted to help build its intellectual base. His own economic base was a used car business, which he carried out successfully, establishing a reputation of reliability and integrity, in a trade where these qualities tend to be rare.

Since 1969 George had been trying to get the Party to stand aside from the disastrous policies of the USSR as implemented in their intervention in Czechoslovakia. He was supported in this by a group which included Sam Nolan, later Secretary of the Dublin Trades Council, Mick O'Reilly, later a leading ATGWU activist and others. In or about 1977 things came to a head, and this group resigned en bloc, leaving the CPI denuded of any critical intellectual ability. The vacuum was filled by Stalinist doctrinaire elements, leading to the situation which forced my own resignation.

George joined the Labour Party, and ran a local branch from his house in Rathgar, where I attended the meetings. He also resurrected the Dublin Regional Council, and attempted to develop it as a focus for in-depth political discussion of key issues, with expert speakers, attracting support from a handful of critically thinking members of the party in Dublin who aspired to influence party policy. He contributed to a Foreign Affairs Committee, to which I was also eventually recruited.

I have no records and few positive recollections of this political period, which lasted about a decade, ending in May 1987 with the Single European Act debacle, which I describe in the next chapter.

Notes and References
1. JJ's death occurred in the middle of the 1972 IFORS (International Federation of Operations Research Societies) conference, which took place in TCD. I was on the international programme committee. I contributed a response to one of the keynote speakers, on the topic of 'Simulation'. This paper was read on my behalf by Maurice Foley of the Operations Research Society of Ireland (who subsequently became Chief Executive of Guinness Peat Aviation), as I was at the funeral. For more background on Operations Research, see also Notes (17) and (22). Some of the work done in this period has been written up in a book by Julian Mac Airt, *Operations Research in Ireland* (Mercier Press, Cork, 1988).
2. I edited the material from the *Irish Times* Science and Technology column into a book *In Search of Techne* during the early 1980s, for publication by Tycooley, a firm specialising in servicing the UN development agency market. Unfortunately the firm closed down. I am taking this opportunity to publish the material in the present supportive hypertext It relates primarily to the 'science and society' and 'socio-technical' streams of the hypertext, which are referenced primarily from Appendices 11 and 12.
3. I treat the family developments in the 1970s in more detail in the family module of the hypertext.
4. See the Greaves Diaries, January 22, 1971 for more detail on these episodes.

5. For example, at the Wolfe Tone Society on March 2 Joy Rudd spoke on Community Schools. The paper in full is on record in the WTS archive. There is also a copy of a memorandum and resolution attacking the undermining of the concept of the 'community school' by handing over ownership and control to religious denominations, and for dealing only with the Catholic Hierarchy. This was on the agenda on April 6.

6. Greaves Diaries, April 11, 1971.

7. Greaves Diaries April 24-26 1971. In Belfast on April 26th CDG met with Hughie Moore and others, urging them to produce an anti-sectarian pamphlet. Joe Deighan had become more active, and Bobby Heatley was noted has having been making mincemeat of the PD. Back in London on April 28 1971 it turned out that Fenner Brockway's Bill of Rights was again on the agenda. This occupied much time and space, culminating in a lengthy account of the lobby on May 5. The Bill went to the Lords on May 12. CDG had been working on this for years, but Labour was now in opposition, and the Bill was rejected.

8. Greaves Diary July 7 1971. Hostility to the EEC was evidently becoming an increasing factor in CDG's thinking, expressed here in somewhat exaggerated wording.

9. There is a hiatus in the WTS record after this; meetings in the Wolfe Tone Room of the Tailors Hall continued for a time, and then later the Society started meeting in the basement of a house owned by Uinsean Mac Eoin in Mountjoy Square. We were there for some years, and various events took place, but the role of the Society became increasingly marginalised. The location was against it; once a visitor from the North spoke at a meeting, and his car was stolen. There are however a few relevant documents on record, and with luck more may turn up.

10. In the perception of the Left, including Greaves, the Wolfe Tone Society and the politicising republicans, there was a strong conviction that the Heath-Lynch talks and the thinking of the Government had linked joining the EEC with a political solution to the Northern problem involving re-partition and a re-writing of the Irish Constitution. We were being brought in to into the Commonwealth, and also with Britain into a Greater Act of Union, we being in Britain's pocket. Analysis of the State papers (c.f. the 2002 release, Taoiseach papers) however suggests that the EEC and the North were quite unrelated issues, in the minds of both parties in the Heath-Lynch talks. The Wilson plan for a revision of the Constitution however had substance. The indications are that Lynch's opposition to it was more based on defence of the Roman Catholic clauses in the 1937 Constitution than on the Commonwealth issue, on which he stood publicly. The opposition of the extreme Unionists (Paisleyites) to the EEC was on the basis that they regarded it as a Roman plot. The aspiration of the Left to ally with them on the issue, based on their regarding the EEC as a German neo-imperial scheme, was ill-founded and illusory.

11.. I leave the analysis of this period to others; Derry Kelleher perhaps can be said to have made a start, though much remains to be done to counter the various dismissive Unionist academic analyses of the politicising republican left, such as that of Patterson.

12. The 1970s module of the political thread of the hypertext contains some of JJ's last letters to the press as well as an account of my own post-republican evolution in search of sensible politics in various areas of the 'left'. I have also overviewed the continuing post-split evolution of 'official' Sinn Fein, based on further analysis of *Nuacht Naisiunta*, their internal newsletter, which ran from September 1969 to June 1976. This is currently accessible in the Workers Party archive in their Hill Street headquarters, Dublin 1. The high point of the evolution of post-split 'official Sinn Fein' is perhaps represented by Tomás Mac Giolla's July 1972 Carrickmore speech, at a Northern Republican Clubs conference. This was re-issued in 2000 as a pamphlet.

13. I have selected this from the series given in the beginning of the 1970s political module of the hypertext. The others deal with the same problem from different perspectives, and include some critical notes on Garrett Fitzgerald's economic statistics. He also in March

1971 contributed to the debate on Northern Ireland, referring back to his *Civil War in Ulster.*

14. *Bishop Berkeley's Querist in Historical Perspective,* Dun Dealgan Press, 1970. I have abstracted JJ's *Querist* chapters, and put them together with some background correspondence, and a review, in the hypertext. It is accessible from the 1960s module of the academic thread. This work has since been referenced in the context of the 'development economics' domain by Salim Rachid in the University of Illinois, who has identified an 18th century 'Irish School of Economic Development' which included Swift, Berkeley, Molyneux, Dobbs and Prior, the latter two giving the group an important applied-scientific dimension.

15. The obsequies of the DU Co-operative Society took place shortly after JJ's decease. By the 1970s it has become an anachronism. If it were to upgrade itself to modern retailing standards, it would have required substantial capital investment. The procedure for keeping track of member purchases in books was cumbersome. It was difficult to recruit and maintain staff to service the required opening hours. On top of all this, the Students Union, which had expanded with the quasi-political wave of the 1960s, and was making money in the travel business, decided to go into retail trade, in competition with the Co-op, which was perceived as being part of the 'old Establishment'. These factors all added up to a death sentence.

16. Professor Naylor's paper is in the *Proceedings of the 1972 IFORS Conference* in Dublin (North Holland, 1973) p205. I have embedded an overview of the paper and my response in the techno-economic stream, and my response is accessible in full.

17. I expand on the techno-economic modelling experience gained with Professor Foster's Masters Degree in statistics and Operations Research' in the 1970s module of the techno-economic stream in the hypertext.

18. I used this episode to illustrate some issues relating to education and the practical arts in a paper 'Science in a Post-Colonial Culture' published in a somewhat mutilated form in the *Irish Review* of Spring 1990. I have given the original paper, over which I stand, in the hypertext. The published version I repudiate, in that in the editing it lost its principal message.

19. Greaves diaries November 1972; it is regrettable that the record of this potentially important event, which brought together a group of experienced and influential people to focus on the Northern Ireland question, is missing from the WTS archive. The event would perhaps have assumed greater significant had the proceedings been integrally published. My paper and that of Greaves were published in *Atlantis* 5, April 1973; this was a half-yearly scholarly journal edited by Seamus Deane. I had established standing as a contributor to this with my earlier review of the Irish volume of *Tom Jones' Whitehall Diaries* in the previous issue, *Atlantis* 4, September 1972. This stimulated me to contribute to the subsequent issue, which was dedicated to a vision of a 'new Ireland', and in this context I persuaded Greaves to contribute his November 1972 WTS paper. Both were opportunities for political reflection, and they are available in full in the hypertext, along with my Tom Jones review. See also *The Irish Crisis*, C Desmond Greaves, Lawrence and Wishart, 1972 for CDG's contribution to the analysis.

20. I give some more detail on this in the 1970s module of the political stream in the hypertext.

21. This was subsequently published: 'An Approach to National Manpower Planning in Science and Technology', Journal of the Statistical and Social Inquiry Society of Ireland, Vol XXIII Part II, p21. The completed paper was delivered on January 9 1975 by RJ, co-authored with Genevieve Franklin. I had occasion to deliver some lessons from this paper at a seminar of the Society of College Lecturers in 1975, for the benefit of the Industrial Development Authority.

22. Some of the TCD projects on which we were working have been referenced by Julian Mac Airt in Chapter 6 of his book *Operations Research in Ireland* (Mercier Press, Cork, 1988). I expand on the projected 'technology transfer to the third world' concept, as adumbrated in the Moscow working group, in the 1970s module of the techno-economic stream.

23. Such was the extent of his isolation that I had found myself unable to report on him in the 'innovation' stream of my *Irish Times* column, in which I evaluated the IMI event critically. I was however able to write at some length about the Moscow conference in the 'third world' stream of my column at the time.

24. A copy of this memorandum, dated May 1975, is available in the hypertext.

25. In my initial encounter I agreed to attempt to do some backroom work on economic modelling of the two parts of Ireland separately, and to compare their performance with the performance of a united economy. I had done some macro-economic modelling work with Crotty, and had a feel for how it might be done credibly, without however getting bogged down in detail. This actually turned out to be a tall order, due to incompatibility of economic data-sets in the two parts of the country. I wrote some notes on how the problem might be addressed, and these are accessible in the 1970s module of the political stream of the hypertext.

26. Constructive democratic political work in 'broad groups' has always been bedevilled by political ideologues behaving sectishly, and I wrote some notes for internal use in the CPI addressing this problem. Regrettably I don't think they had any impact or influence. I tried to behave in the Resources Protection Campaign according to my own guidelines, and was censured for it; I was supposed to have voted mindlessly with the 'voting machine'.

27. This episode made my expulsion inevitable, although I tried to develop some rational discussion around the issues, and I have made available copies of related correspondence. I never managed to get the issues discussed openly.

28. The period with the CPI in the mid-1970s was largely unproductive, a painful lesson in the pathology of decline. Some of the episodes I have described are partially documented in the Greaves Diaries covering the period; these give the dates reliably, but the comments are mostly my own. The Diaries however would in this period constitute a useful source for a student of international relations within the international Communist movement. The stresses within the CPGB and their relationship with the evolving Irish situation are documented with insight.

29. The paper by RJ 'On the Problem of Democratic Unity' from Issue #9 of *The Ripening of Time* is available in full in the hypertext; it is summarised in Appendix 10.

30. The present writer found the ARC Group experience a stimulus for the development of an integrated philosophy of techno-economic (e.g. biomass energy systems) and socio-technical (eg global genetic resources in support of the food crops, marine database development) modelling. I embedded something of this philosophy in a Technology Ireland paper of January 1978.

Chapter 9: The Period 1981-1990

Introduction

After what looked like a promising start with the UN Conference on New and Renewable Energy Sources, in 1981 in Nairobi, which I attended representing the World Federation of United Nations Associations, thanks to Seán MacBride, the 1980s subsequently became a nadir-period for the present writer. I worked out my contract with TCD in various processes of attempted re-invention, with occasional bits of consultancy from State agencies(1).

The 'Techne Associates' concept evolved out of this re-invention process. This was an attempt to develop a science, technology and innovation 'brokerage' as a commercial operation, initially in association with TCD, and eventually in its own right(2).

The relationship with the Labour Party made it easier to get consultancy projects out of State agencies where Labour in government had influence: in particular the Youth Employment Agency, which sponsored my exploration of the Regional Technical Colleges as local enterprise generators(3). This work I understand has since proved useful.

I spent some time in Brittany, with some French government support, looking a small innovative high-tech enterprises, from the angle that they might be targets for synergetic commercial agreements with comparable firms based in Ireland. This aroused the interest of Shannon Development, and some further work along these lines ensued(4). A further related project (in 1987) involved looking at the role of the Innovation Centre in Limerick and its relationship with the National Institute of Higher Education (NIHE), which had hitherto been somewhat abrasive. I proposed a model, based on the development of the NIHE postgraduate process as the prime innovation contact-point, which has since become the norm.(5).

The foregoing work enabled me to make a useful contribution to some work the National Board for Science and Technology had contracted with the EU to do, exploring the potential for inter-regional linkages between 'less-favoured regions'(6).

While all this was going on Janice and I were involved in the Strasbourg case on the 'right to re-marry', which we had agreed to take up, at the suggestion of the Divorce Action Group. The case was handled by Mary Robinson, who subsequently became President of Ireland.

Relations with the Labour Party became strained as a result of the way they handled the 'Single European Act', stifling debate at Conference by highly questionable methods. I therefore made the transition to the Green Party, and began to contribute to the development of their policies, procedures and organisation.

Retaining an ongoing interest in international affairs and the peace movement, I participated in a 'floating conference' in a boat on the Dnieper, which led to some further insights into the way the USSR was going into crisis.

Critical interaction with the economic Establishment continued via the SSISI(7), at the level of comments on various papers on industrial policy etc, which are on record.

The UN Conference in Nairobi on 'New and Renewable Energy Sources'

The Irish United Nations Association, on the initiative of its President Seán MacBride, organised on May 13-14 1981 a conference which was attended by most if not all Irish researchers in the renewable energy field. The *Proceedings* of this were published, edited by the present writer(8), and this is on record in the Trinity College Dublin library, and perhaps elsewhere.

With the money raised by organising the conference, the IUNA was able to fund the participation of the present writer in the UN conference, a memorable experience, some aspects of which I have recorded, and summarise below. I give first a brief outline of the Irish contributions, as recorded in the IUNA conference proceedings.

I briefed MacBride for his preface to the Proceedings; in fact I took over the whole organisation and management of the conference, which I did from the TCD Industrial Liaison Office. In the initial Liberty Hall meeting which MacBride had called, it became apparent that he did not have a clue whom to invite.: It was dominated by aging Clann na Poblachta supporters, whom he felt he needed, to bolster his ego. I laid it down as a condition of my participation that it should be handled strictly as a techno-economic exercise, and I produced a list of the people who should be invited, whom I had mostly got to know as a result of my earlier renewable energy work, which had arisen out of my treatment of the energy crisis in the *Irish Times* column. He had to back down and accept this.

The preface concluded: "...High powered propaganda and salesmanship very nearly persuaded our own establishment in Ireland to push the country into the adoption of nuclear energy as an alternative source of energy. Luckily, a healthy and informed public opinion reacted vigorously against this trend. It was realised that there were many other sources of renewable energy available to us, and indeed to many other countries of the world which were not being adequately availed of. These included:

> Solar energy,
> Wind energy,
> Wave and Tidal energy,
> Peat, Biomass, and Timber.

"These were all freely available to us in varying degrees. But they had no powerful transnational financial interests to promote them. It is in these circumstances that the United Nations, with constructive foresight, took the initiative of convening the World Conference on New and Renewable Sources of Energy, which was held in Nairobi in August 1981. As soon as the United Nations had taken the decision to convene the world conference at Nairobi, the Irish United Nations Association took the initiative in convening a preparatory conference in Dublin so that Ireland would be in a position to make constructive contributions to this great world problem..."

"...The Preparatory Conference was duly held, through the hospitality of Carroll's Theatre, in Dublin on 13 May 1981. It was a most useful and constructive conference in which all those involved in the production of energy, both in the private and public sector, participated actively. In this connection, great tribute must be paid to both Mr Terence Gavaghan and to Dr RHW Johnston for the input which they both made in the preparations for the Preparatory Conference, and in the follow up. It was their untiring energy and organising ability that ensured the success of the Preparatory Conference.

"As a result of the Preparatory Conference we found it possible to be represented at the United Nations World Conference in Nairobi by Dr RHW Johnston. His contribution at the Conference itself, and the many contacts which he made there, have proved of very considerable value....".

Objectives of Preparatory Conference in Ireland

A national paper surveying new and renewable energy activity in Ireland had been prepared for the UN Nairobi Conference by the National Board for Science and Technology. In support of this contribution, IUNA had undertaken, with the backing of three United Nations bodies, to organise a Preparatory Conference in Ireland :

(1) to ensure that interested organisations and the Irish public are made aware of the scope of the UN Conference in Nairobi;

(2) to ensure that the NBST paper to be presented in Nairobi is backed by appropriate supplementary briefing material, particularly where Irish experience has relevance to developing countries.

The response to the conference call, in terms of contributed papers and attendance, was considerable; the 1970s energy crises were fresh in the public memory. I summarise this below; there is no point in giving the papers in full, as the proceedings are available, and anyway they would need updating in the light of subsequent developments.

Norman L Brown, former energy advisor to UNAID, in a keynote paper gave a global overview of the energy scene, with particular reference to developing countries. He stressed the high proportion of energy which was dependent on firewood, and the consequent threat to forests. He made the link between fossil fuels, atmospheric CO_2 and global warming, the relationship between which were already common knowledge in the scientific community.

Dr Keith W Robinson, of the National Board for Science and Technology, overviewed the Irish contribution to the UN conference. Giving a passing reference to peat, an effectively non-renewable resource, in terms of the forestry potential of cutaway bog, he gave priority attention to wind and biomass, and mentioned wave and tidal power, small-scale hydro, geothermal and direct solar conversion, in all of which areas research was ongoing, though on a small-scale. He stressed the importance of energy system analysis in the context of selection of strategic options. Overall Irish work in this field was poorly developed and needed attention.

Contributed Papers

Dr Denis Mollison, from Heriot-Watt University, Edinburgh, gave some estimates on wave power; Brian Hurley (Bolton St College of Technology) and Annraoi de Paor (UCD) reviewed the field experience of the Wind Panel of the Solar Energy Society; Professor GT Wrixon and Dr SB McCarthy (UCC) outlined an approach to powering a dairy installation with photo-voltaic cells, at the 50kW level; Owen Lewis (UCD Architecture) outlined various approaches to solar energy applications at the domestic level; Ian Cowan (IIRS) reported on heat pump work.

There were three papers on mini-hydro topics, from Richard Flaherty on run-of-the-river schemes, Paddy Belton (who manufactured mini-turbines), and BM Kelly on modular design.

There were peat papers from J Cooke and J Martin, both of Bord na Mona. Short-rotation forestry was covered by Dr Michael Neenan of the Agricultural Institute (Oakpark, Carlow) and Dr Trevor Gibbons of TCD, who outlined approaches to the techno-economic analysis of production systems *(to which work the present writer had earlier contributed)*. Michael Jones of TCD (Botany) outlined tropical biomass options, and Jerry Healy reported on some EEC-funded biomass developed using cutaway bog as site. Chris Shouldice (Agricultural Institute) surveyed liquid fuels from biomass sources, including rapeseed oil. Frank Lunny went into biomass combustion problems in boilers.

There were contributions from Dr CT Isolani (the United Nations University European representative) outlining the global research position, and from several Irish-based institutions with an interest in export of know-how: Michael O'Donnell for HEDCO (Higher Education for Development Co-operation), Michael Maloney for DEVCO the state agency export development service, Bill Jackson for APSO (Agency for Personal Services Abroad), Tim Cahill O'Brien for IDA (Industrial Development Authority), and Gerry Murphy for Coras Tractala the export trade promotion agency.

This completes the listing of the contributions; one can perhaps comment in retrospect on the nature and extent of the co-ordination problem if we were to 'get our act together' in an energy crisis situation. The present writer at the time made an effort in this direction, going on to outline some conclusions reached as a result of the preliminary Irish conferences, followed by some conclusions reached following the experience of the Nairobi conference itself:

"It is appropriate to supplement this message by a reference to current UN Industrial Development Organisation (UNIDO) policy, which is to collaborate with the UN Food and Agriculture Organisation (FAO) on the production of wood-based charcoal for industrial purposes, including smelting (cf Rome meeting 15-16 January 1979). This technology, if successfully introduced into tropical countries having forest reserves, could sound the death-knell of the latter. The primeval forest of Ireland was largely wiped out in the 17th and 18th centuries by smelting with charcoal, as if it had not already been enough plundered in the interests of the British Navy. Modern charcoal production involves pyrolysis of wood, with gas and oil as by-products, these also being fit for local industrial energy and transportation needs. It can be an efficient process and is seriously under consideration as one of the energy conversion options for use with managed biomass plantations in developed countries. If this technology is unleashed in developing countries lacking energy other than forest reserves, it could be a recipe for world ecological disaster, unless accompanied by a massive re-forestation programme....

"Peat technology tends to be somewhat site-specific. It overlaps with biomass in that in some cases (eg papyrus) the possibility exists of harvesting the current annual production, while in other cases the accumulated biomass, when removed, can be replaced by a renewable system There is export potential in both cases for special-purpose harvesting machinery, or the know-how for its local production....

"Biomass, like peat production, is very site-specific. In this context, biomass does not only refer to short or long rotation forestry but to non-woody biomass which may be more suitable under some conditions. Examples of non-woody biomass are sugar cane and beet production on agricultural-quality land and papyrus in more marginal areas. The guiding principle for biomass production should be high yielding renewable resources occupying land not required or unsuitable for food production.

"Questioning the thermal efficiency of 'wet' processes, Mr JF Kelleher (Owen Kenny & Partners) pointed out that power alcohol production from molasses, a waste by-product (except where it can be used as cattle feed) from raw cane sugar manufacture, was providing a substitute for petrol in certain Third World countries. However, about 75% of the energy realisable in the power alcohol had to be provided by the fuel input to the distillation process...".

This of course is the redoubtable Derry Kelleher whom we have met in the Kane-Bernal and Wolfe Tone Society context.

"In photo-voltaics, the design and construction of a 50 kW pilot power station near Cork (Wrixon) will enable valuable systems experience to be gained in a pre-economic full-scale operation, during the period immediately prior to the mass-production of low-cost photo cells.

"In the capture of diffuse solar energy, despite the adverse seasonality factor, there were indications that solar panel technology was already cost-effective in new housing... In wind energy, the elements of a viable system exist.... In the field of small-scale hydro-systems, similarly, the elements of a viable system exist...

"It was generally conceded that the Conference was useful in that it enabled those concerned with renewable energy technology to interact with those concerned with development co-operation in the context of a specific problem common to Ireland and other energy-deficient developing countries. An impression of fragmentation among the agencies emerged...."

It was the intention of the writer, when at Nairobi, to act on behalf of those of the supporters of the IUNA Preparatory Conference who were not directly represented in the Government delegation, along the following lines:

1) To keep in touch with the Government delegation and to exchange relevant information during the course of the Conference.

2) To seek informally to cultivate contacts with new and renewable energy experts in other countries, both developed and developing.

3) To ensure that the experience of the Nairobi Conference is appropriately made available in Ireland to those working in the field and to the relevant agencies concerned.

The following section gives some conclusions drawn from the Nairobi experience:

"...Networks have been set up among non-governmental organisations, and between the latter and key governmental contact-points, which are likely to lead to significant opportunities for increased funding for renewable energy work in one form or another.

"...The status and role of relevant NGOs in the UN decision-making procedure has emerged strengthened and with enhanced experience.

"...There is emerging an embryonic appreciation of the common interest between the disarmament lobby (which is active in 'east-west' UN negotiations which are centred in Geneva) and the 'orderly energy transition' lobby which has initially been focused at Nairobi. It is increasingly evident that the resources soaked up in the arms race, if diverted towards the energy transition problem, would enable the latter to he resolved within a decade or two. At Nairobi, this emerged strongly from the NGO people (who were all 'south' and 'west'; there were no 'eastern' NGOs in the political sense) and also from the 'eastern' governmental delegations. These two political forces, however, showed no signs of being aware of each other, though they were saying the same thing.

"...There is an enhanced understanding of the crucial role of **local** energy availability in the development process; the concept of the 'autonomous community renewable energy centre' as the development-focus for the future has gained respectability and now ranks in importance comparable with traditional large-scale centralised urban-based systems, particularly where 'national grids' are non-existent."

In conclusion, it is worth while placing on record that the Irish governmental contingent consisted of a 'front-line' group (Mr Conor Murphy, Department of Foreign Affairs; Dr Owen O'Neill, Department of Energy; Dr Keith Robinson (National Board for Science and Technology) backed up by a support group consisting of Mr Scan Tinney (ESB), Mr Maurice Keane and Mr Val Martin (Bord na Mona) and Mr Tim Cahill O'Brien (IDA).

The objectives of the support group were promotional, and significant success was achieved (a) by the ESB/Bord na Mona team in selling 'electricity from peat' technology (b) by the IDA in selling a crash-course in renewable energy technology assessment.

In addition to the above, the writer set up some contacts which could perhaps have led to the establishment of postgraduate programmes in renewable energy systems engineering, on a collaborative basis between Irish and Third World universities. Such a training programme would have been in a position to attract such finance as does become available for the promotion of 'north-south' technology transfer procedures on the higher education network...

On the whole, the impact of this conference was minimal; oil prices declined, and the sense of urgency evaporated. The various people went their separate ways. In retrospect, however, it must be said that the conclusions were valid, and remain valid to this day. Wind energy in Ireland is beginning to become a significant source, belatedly. In Denmark they took it seriously in the 1980s and they now export standardised wind-turbines to service the wind-farms of the world. On the whole, we can perhaps claim to be creative innovators and adapters, but must admit to being weak on the organised follow-through.

Chapter 9: The Period 1981-1990

The Institute of Physics (Irish Branch) Technology Group

During the period 1981 to 1983, with the TCD contract coming to an end, the writer tried various approaches to enhancing the market for private-sector scientific expertise. One such was an attempt to develop the interface between physics in Ireland with engineering, and with industry located in Ireland; this took the form of the Technology Group(9) of the IP(IB), initiated by Dr Norman McMillan in 1981.

We attempted to identify people doing physics in Ireland which had industrial relevance, and we ran some seminars, mainly in Cork and Galway, at which we attempted to interface the industrial engineering fraternity with the physics which was going on in the RTCs and university colleges. On the whole however we were not very successful, though perhaps we were influential in the promotion of applied-physics courses whose graduates were more employable in industry.

The Institute of Physics however never managed to pick up as members the industry-based people who had emerged from these courses, and the problem of how to balance the academic orientation of the Irish Branch of the Institute of Physics remains with us.

Left Politics and the Patronage Process

On December 30 1981 I went to Betty Sinclair's funeral. Her career was an indicator of the failure of the Left to pre-empt the 'Provisional' process. This was a sort of Left-nostalgia trip; Desmond Greaves was there. There was little or no intellectual contact with him, or with any the Irish Left, on the occasion. The question of her memoirs, said by Greaves to be relevant to the NICRA period, remained then and still remains unresolved.

On November 20 1982 there was an Irish Sovereignty Movement seminar in the Shelbourne, addressed by Greaves, which I attended, perhaps nominally on behalf of the Labour Party International Affairs Committee, but I don't recollect what the impact was, if any. It would have had to do with the neutrality issue, in the context of the Falklands war.

The 1980s were spent initially in the Labour Party, with subsequently, at the end of the decade, a transition to the Greens. Most of the effort however went into socio-technical consultancy(10), where this could be picked up, and this had political undercurrents. In this context I had the problem of finding a means of economic support when the TCD contract came to an end in 1984. I found the Labour Party contact useful in this context, Ruairi Quinn, our local Dublin SE TD, being then the Minister in charge of the science and technology, innovative enterprise development and suchlike. This led eventually to some contract work with the Youth Employment Agency, which helped keep the wolf from the door in a very lean period. The concept originated in terms of a projected venture-seeding process, which I called Techne(2), generating some contact with the Minister, and with Niall Greene, a Labour Party influential who headed the Youth Employment Agency.

It is worth remarking on the importance in Irish culture of political networking in the obtaining of jobs or contracts with State agencies. I found myself at the receiving end of what amounted to favours, engaged in a process of which I had been critical.

There was a socio-technical episode with a political dimension which took place in Carlow, in March 1984. Greaves mentioned it in his diary. It seems I had saved a factory in Carlow, organising a meeting of Trades Council, Chamber of Commerce, Agricultural Institute (Oakpark) people and the Regional College people, who did not otherwise know each other. We produced a paper which seems to have been influential. Padraig Ó Snodaigh in the National Library, having Carlow contacts, had tipped me off about the problem. Regrettably I do not recollect the details, but I would not have been able to call the meeting were it not for the extent I had established myself in the 1970s as the spokesman of the applied-science community, via the *Irish Times* Column.

Science and Irish Culture: the Historical Background

In the early 1980s I found my self doing reviews for Books Ireland(11) which had a 'science in Irish history' flavour. This reminded me of an earlier concern: the cultural status of science in the Irish context. Hamilton, Tyndall, Fitzgerald and others are household names in the science context, internationally, but no-one in the global science community associates them with Ireland. Similarly, only a few among the scientific elite in Ireland are aware of them as global figures with Irish roots. Contrast this with the international status of Joyce, Yeats etc as generators of international scholarly networks, summer schools etc.

Richard Kearney was then editing the *Crane Bag*, which was a critical cultural review(12), one of the many subsequent attempts to fill the niche vacated by *The Bell* which had pioneered the role in the 1940s, with Peadar O'Donnell in the lead. I remember going to Richard's place in Pembroke Cottages, Donnybrook, and discussing the question in some depth. The result was an analysis of the impact of the 'British Association for the Advancement of Science' meetings in Ireland, which took place in 1835, 1843, 1853, 1857, 1874, 1878, 1902, 1908. This provided a series of snapshots of the cultural evolution of science in Ireland, prior to the first world war. The scene was dominated by colonial culture, and the events were triumphal celebrations of the scientific and technological might of the Empire.

The emergent Catholic bourgeoisie had been largely excluded by Cardinal Cullen's ban on the 'godless colleges', but people like Callan (of induction coil fame; he was physics professor in Maynooth), Kane (best known for his 1943 *Industrial Resources of Ireland* book), Hennessy and a few others were gaining recognition. Callan had studied under Galvani and Volta in Italy, and Kane with Liebig in Germany. Kane became the 'token Catholic' heading Queens College Cork, in an attempt to beat the Cullen ban. Thomas Davis, then editing the *Nation*, attended the Cork meeting in 1843, but failed to appreciate the essential nature of the problem of how to relate mastery of scientific technology with the Irish republican vision. He did however pick up some potentially innovative publishing procedures, relating to reproduction of photographs.

De Valera attended the 1908 meeting, along with David Houston, a College of Science lecturer, who subsequently taught science for Patrick Pearse in St Enda's. The latter went on to develop milk quality control procedures for the dairy co-ops. The remainder of the participants were representative of the elite at the time, their names being mostly unmemorable. Thus the links between the emergent Irish national elite and the imperial and global science scene were somewhat tenuous.

JD Bernal FRS and Ireland

In 1984 I came across a biography of JD Bernal FRS(13) by Maurice Goldsmith, entitled *Sage*, which I had occasion to review somewhere (regrettably I have lost track of this episode). I felt that the author had not done justice to Bernal's Irish background (he was from Nenagh, Co Tipperary), for which he had depended mostly on Bernal's own subsequent reminiscences, which seemed to me to be somewhat romanticised. I looked into the matter, and found that the book had been written without the co-operation of the family and friends of Bernal, and that another multi-author biography was in gestation, edited by Brenda Swann and Francis Aprahamian. I made contact with this project, and undertook to contribute a chapter on the Irish roots, emphasising the political angle.

The present writer had encountered Bernal's writings in the 1940s, in the context of the developing Marxist thinking among the student left. I had subsequently been in touch with Bernal himself before he died, in the context of my attempts in the 1970s to initiate some 'science and society' studies and activities, with Derry Kelleher and others under the banner of the 'Kane-Bernal Society'. This contact continued virtually, via the Bernal biography support group, during the lengthy gestation of the projected book which did not finally get published until 1999(14).

Bernal was initially educated locally; he and his younger brother Kevin went first to the Nenagh convent school, then to the Protestant school in Barrack St, this being regarded as preferable to the boys school run by the Christian Brothers. The building once occupied by this school is the prime candidate for locating the Bernal plaque.

Bernal picked up locally an early interest in science. In his teens he was aware of the Birr telescope, with which the Earl of Rosse had some 60 years previously pushed forward the frontiers of telescope design, and was in touch with several other local gentleman-amateur scientists, one of whom, Launcelot Bayly, introduced him to crystallography; with another, one Parker, Bernal went geologising. He developed a feel for industrial technology though contacts with local industry, and the mine works at Shalee.

His mother (who was American) had wanted to support his scientific inclinations, and researched the Irish educational opportunities. In the end she sent him to boarding-school in England, initially to Stonyhurst, then later to Bedford, whence in 1919 he went to Cambridge. There was family religious pressure (they were Catholic 'minor landed gentry') to take him out of the Protestant school, and the level of teaching of science in Irish Catholic secondary schools, even in the elite Clongowes immortalised by James Joyce, was not up to the standard required by his mother. Boarding-school in England was considered necessary.

Bernal was however acutely aware of what was going on in Ireland, and observed it during his vacations, keeping a journal, which is archived in Cambridge. He recorded his support for Redmondite Home Rule, and subsequently for Sinn Fein, which position later under the influence of Cambridge colleagues, primarily Henry Dickinson and Alan Hutt, evolved into Marxism and support for the Bolsheviks. The influence of his mother's Protestant background, and early exposure to interaction with the Nenagh Protestant community, helped him to avoid identifying the Irish national question with Catholicism, as many had done. During his Bedford period he had been devoutly Catholic, but in Cambridge he recorded how he lost his faith sequentially: '...first God, then Jesus, then the Virgin Mary, and lastly the rites... now I had a quarrel with the Church because I could not help seeing it as an active agent of political reaction ...'.

His Cambridge work on crystallography drew him to the attention of Sir William Bragg, who was then setting up his research team to take advantage of X-ray diffraction techniques. He worked with Bragg in the Royal Institution until 1927, contributing to the experimental technology by the design of the X-ray photo-goniometer subsequently to be produced by Pye of Cambridge as the standard tool of the domain.

Bernal then went back to Cambridge in 1927 to a lectureship in structural crystallography, where for the next decade he worked on the structure of liquids, inventing the 'statistical geometric' approach to liquid modelling, and on solids of increasing complexity: pepsin, proteins, viruses, identifying the type of helical structures which subsequently led to the discovery of DNA.

Politically Bernal's student Marxism, picked up in the immediate aftermath of the Bolshevik Revolution in Russia, evolved into an increasingly positive attitude to science and the role of scientists as a political force. He retained an interest in Ireland, and his brother Godfrey recollected, for the present writer, his interacting with the German engineers who in the late 1920s were working on the Shannon hydro-electric scheme, which was planned to supply an Irish 'national grid', then an innovative concept.

This project has received global recognition, with an international award, on the occasion of its 75th anniversary in 2002. It was a key component of the infrastructure of the eventual industrial development of the Irish Free State.

During his Cambridge period he had, thanks to his political activities, picked up much experience of the interactions between science and government, with Marxist insight into the historical background. This led him to publish his seminal *Social Function of Science* in 1939, which was celebrated in the 1964 festschrift *The Science of Science*, edited by Goldsmith and McKay as the founding text of the thriving scientific study of science itself in a social context, which by then had begun to thrive(15).

Politically after the war Bernal was increasingly isolated by the 'cold war' environment. He put much effort into the World Peace Council and to the nuclear disarmament movement. He was among the prime movers in initiating the Pugwash conference, which was an important communication channel between the USA and the USSR at leading science and government level during the worst period of the cold war. In this process he kept in the background himself, not wishing to compromise Pugwash by his Marxist associations.

Bernal had a totally integrated and egalitarian approach to science and to politics; for him the works of the technicians and craftsmen were as important as those of the scientists. He regarded this egalitarian teamwork process as being a basis for his visionary model for the socialist society of the future, rather than the flawed state-centralist model in the east. He participated however in the Lysenko debates in the Engels Society, the forum for Marxist scientists in Britain, with JBS

Haldane and Hyman Levy, mostly at the philosophical level, but finding it uncomfortable turned his attention subsequently to the peace movement and to the promotion of trade unionism among scientists, having been a founder member of the Association of Scientific Workers. Successive editions of his *Science in History(15)* gave declining attention to Lysenko's significance.

Having burned his fingers with the Lysenko episode, in his review of Watson's *Double Helix*, and of the period, in 1968, Bernal concentrated on evaluating his own lab's relationship to the work, and how they had managed to 'miss the boat', despite having developed the key experimental technology. He was unable to make the leap into the ethical and political problems which subsequently have emerged on the fringes of molecular biology and its applications. It could be said that the 'Lysenko debate' has, in effect, re-surfaced, with a new twist.

Due to Bernal's relative isolation during the Cold War, many of his ideas were developed as a sort of 'Bernalism without Bernal' in various 'science policy research units' during the later 1950s and 1960s. They were taken, with acclamation, to the US by Derek de Solla Price, a Bernal disciple. These units now flourish, in Sussex, Edinburgh, Manchester and elsewhere, usually with some recognition of Bernal's influence. There is one in University College Dublin, in the foundation of which the late Professor Patrick Lynch had a hand. The latter was co-author, along with the engineer HMS 'Dusty' Miller, of the 1964 OECD Report 'Science and Irish Economic Development', which was consciously, though implicitly, Bernalist. The authors both on different occasions explicitly admitted to Bernal's influence in the OECD Report context to the present writer, though publicly due to his Marxism Bernal had then in Ireland somewhat the status of a 'non-person'.

Bernal in Ireland however enjoyed something of a 'posthumous rehabilitation', in the form of a Royal Irish Academy discourse by his colleague Dorothy Hodgkin FRS, which took place in 1980(13). The vote of thanks was proposed by Tom Hardiman, then the Executive Chairman of the National Board for Science and Technology in Ireland.

I have sometimes had occasion to ponder on what might have been my personal reasons for empathy with Bernal. We were both just too late to have had the possibility of being involved in a world war, and observed the war from similar situations: an upper-crust boarding-school, with vacations in a 'minor gentry' rural environment. During vacations the war imposed a need to improvise in all sorts of ways involving the need to understand technology, particularly that of energy. There was a degree of alienation in the neighbourhood network: Bernals as Catholics in a Protestant minor-gentry environment, the Johnstons as jumped-up Ulster peasantry.

Thus we turned our respective attentions to intellectual pursuits, and in both cases there were opportunities to become interested in science and technology. In both cases our university periods were dominated by world-shaking political transformation. Perhaps on another occasion I may explore this further..

In practical terms, I count the main influence of Bernal as being in fuelling my current concern with the cultural history of science and technology, in the peripheral, post-colonial, emergent-nation environment. Bernal touched on this, but left the analysis unfinished. He coined the term 'brain-drain' during the 1950s, but failed effectively to address the problem of how political movements for national independence might deal with the 'brain-drain' problem at source, in the process of revolutionary transformation of emergent nations. I have, to the best of my ability, despite overwhelming constraints, attempted to take this up, swimming personally against the emigration tide, and helping to contribute to the creation of opportunities for science graduates, to the extent that I have been able to do so.

Science in Ireland 1800-1930

There was a conference organised in 1985 by the TCD Physics Department, consciously to fill the gap left by the failure of the Academy to do justice to its 150th anniversary with a conference with milestone published proceedings. This attempted to cover the field, and the proceeding were published. I was asked by John Banville to review it for the Irish Times *later in the year, and I give here an edited-down version, so as to get some flavour of the importance of the history in the cultural context(16).*

Scientists in Ireland have an ongoing identity crisis, unlike the literary Irish, whose international recognition is usually unquestioned, even when, like Shaw or Beckett, they make their careers abroad. Visitors from abroad however usually express surprise when they discover that (for example) Hamilton or Tyndall were Irish.

This question was addressed in a modest preface by the editorial group, which included Dr ND McMillan of Carlow RTC, Professor DL Weaire of TCD and Professor Susan McKenna Lawlor of Maynooth, from which I quote: "why did Ireland, in those days more distant in practical terms from Britain and Europe, produce so many notable figures in the history of science? The question is at least as significant as its much discussed literary equivalent with which there is, no doubt, some subtle connection..."

The book falls into three sections: mathematics, astronomy and experimental science. Contributions from abroad tend to fall into the mathematics area; there is some concentration on the relationship between research and teaching, on the influence of the French mathematical revolution, and on practical 'hand and eye' instruction.

One can see national politics lurking in the French connection; this is a vein needing to be exploited within the paradigms of Irish national historiography....

Apart from the Dunsink, Armagh and Birr Castle observatories there were some half-dozen lesser-known centres of significance, usually run by gentleman-amateurs.

Dr JG O'Hara (who is working in the Leibniz Archiv, Hannover) had contributions on Humphrey Lloyd (who cultivated an extensive network abroad in relation to the measurement of the earth's magnetism) and on the correspondence between Hertz and Fitzgerald. This was in connection with the verification of the Maxwell theory of electromagnetic wave propagation, which is at the root of all modern radio communication, a key frontier area of physics at the time. The three world centres for the development of electrodynamics at the end of the 19th century were Berlin (Helmholz), Cambridge (Maxwell) and Dublin (Fitzgerald). The work of O'Hara, in establishing the international standing of Irish-based science in the

19th century, is helping to lay the foundation for the future approaches to Irish history which are needed to give Irish science the place it deserves.

Other contributions are on 'Samuel Haughton and the Age of the Earth' (by Norman McMillan), John Joly on colour photography, radioactivity and (again) the age of the earth (by John Nudds), on the transatlantic cable (by Dr D de Cogan, from the Nottingham Engineering School), and two biographical studies: 'Mary Ward, microscopist 1827-1869' (by Dr Owen Harry of QUB) and 'Robert Woods: biophysicist 1865-1938', (by Professor C S Breathnach of UCD).

Why is this important? I suggest that it is because in the history of science and technology in Ireland we have a unique laboratory within which can be analysed the tensions between the fundamental internationalism of science and the conflicting technological needs of the imperial State, in competition with those of the emerging embryonic nation. Overlay this with the cultural tensions arising from religious pluralism within the emerging Irish nation, and we begin to see a web of fascinating but possibly frightening complexity. No wonder traditional political, economic and social historians have shied away from it.

Yet the problem will have to be addressed, if Irish experience is to be used effectively in helping to form policies for using scientific technology in the contemporary third-world development process.

The present writer's outline solution, for what it is worth, is to create an academic appointment, for the study of the history of science and technology in Ireland, within a history department which is strong in economic and social history, and is alive to the need to enhance creatively the study of the nation-building process in a post-colonial situation. Do I ask the impossible?

Rural Technology

An opportunity to develop further the foregoing arguments occurred in 1987 with some review of books relating to the impact of technology on rural Ireland, viewed historically. Again I give edited-down versions(17).

Between Michael Shiel's history of rural electrification in the Republic under the leadership of the Electricity Supply Board and Wallace Clark's family epic of the linen-mills of Upperlands near Maghera on the Clady river, there is an interesting complementarity which may perhaps help to illuminate an aspect of the problem of Irish nationality.

Clark traces the history of his family firm from its origins in the 1700s to the present day. The key invention was the beetling-mill, dating from the 1730s: fine weaving may have been learnt from the French and points of bleaching from the Dutch, but harnessing of water-power to the processing of linen came from the Anglo-Irish inventors. '...Ireland is blessed, more than most countries, with rivers of fall of about one in thirty, and width around 30 feet; of a flow which a private individual could dam, ideal for waterwheels...'. The beetling-mill was an adaptation of the hammer-mill or the spade-mill to the needs of the linen process, replacing one of the more laborious operations.

Jackson Clark dammed the Clady in 1740 and initiated the development of an industrial complex which lived entirely from the water-power of the Clady right up to 1889, when the first steam-engine was bought to power a stenter-frame. Prior to this the power for the mills had come entirely from a series of water-wheels and, later, turbines (incidentally, for Clark's benefit, a Belfast invention first described by Thompson at the 1852 meeting of the British Association in Belfast, under the name 'vortex water-wheel'). The extra cost of steam, at £30 per HP-year compared to £3 for water, paid off by providing independence of the weather. Water-power remains, however, an important supplementary energy-source to this day. Indeed, it provided as early as 1908 a source of modern-standard 220-volt AC, when most municipal utilities were on the old Edison 110-volt DC standard.

Social historians will find useful material illustrating the paternalist company-town which arose as the fruits of Ulster Protestant rural enterprise. Written as it is from the angle of the leading family, it leaves gaps in the record to be filled by social (particularly labour) and political historians, although the period described so well by Michael Farrell in 'The Arming of the Protestants' is touched upon; one has to read between the lines here.

Once these limitations are recognised, we are left with an interesting and readable book, of significant interest to the economic historian and to historians of technology. It is a pity the author didn't give more attention to this aspect in the indexing, which is somewhat sparse.

Turning now to Michael Shiel, we have a well-researched and documented history of the ESB rural electrification scheme, which formally extended from 1946 to 1976, bringing electricity to 99% of the houses in the country.. There is scope for someone to develop the pre-history of electricity in Ireland; this is skated over in one short chapter dealing with the pre-ESB scene, in which credit is given to Callan in Maynooth for his early (1830s) work on electromagnetic induction, and to Parnell for switching on the first public lighting in Carlow in 1889. The latter was supplied from a flour-mill four miles away: is there a story here to parallel Clark's?

There were 161 separate electricity systems in the Free State in 1925. All these were subsumed into the ESB in 1927 and shortly after, and most generators were shut down. It would be interesting to know what was the statistics of the 161: how many were municipal, how many 'big-houses', how many industrial enterprises. I suspect that there was a strong Protestant component in this early electrification, associated with the process of 'improving landlords' transforming themselves into an industrial bourgeoisie; possibly there was a significant Quaker component: very much the southern analogue of the Clark process, but less concentrated and on the whole less successful.

(If credits are to be given in the pre-history, why only Callan? What about Parsons, the centenary of whose steam turbine was celebrated this year with an international conference in Dublin, and Purser Griffith, who not only pioneered peat production but systematically drew attention to Irish hydro-electric potential, providing a foundation for McLaughlin's subsequent successful assault on the Shannon? This is the type of touchy issue that underlies Irish nationality; an 'us and them' question. What do 'they' have to do before 'we' accept 'them' as 'us'?)

This was all leapfrogged by the ESB, which in a decade brought Ireland into the vanguard of European technology, with a copious supply via a national grid at 20% of the previous cost per unit. This was the most impressive achievement of the partially-complete Irish democratic revolution: cheap energy for the people, the Catholic peasantry triumphant breaking the monopoly hitherto held by the Protestant landlords and capitalists. By 1939 there were 170,000 consumers connected, rising (somewhat miraculously) through the war years to 240,000 in 1945. There remained, however, 400,000 rural dwellings in darkness.

Pre-war approaches to rural electrification had been limited to within 2 km of the existing transmission network; this had been laid out with the main towns in mind. Lemass in 1939 called for new plans, and by December 1942 the ESB had produced the essentials of what became the 1944 White Paper, which was substantially the plan as implemented. It was a very substantial scheme, involving 1M poles, 75,000 miles of new distribution-line additional to the 2000 miles then existing, 100,000 transformers. A special organisation was set up under WF Roe, which recruited raw graduate engineers, demobbed army-men and local trainee craftsmen into a quietly efficient organisation which gained universal respect. In the words of the Parish Priest of Carnaross, Co Meath, '...these nice people came amongst us, did their job with speed and efficiency......behaved quietly and decently and left without any fuss or display ...'

The firm of Unidare came into being to supply cable and transformers. Numerous small firms now exist in remote places, like Gweedore and Clontibret, due to local entrepreneurship doing what can be done with cheap power. In most cases the 'fixed charge' (or 'ground rent' as it was called in some places where it was a bone of contention) was recovered by simply replacing the old battery radio: in pre-transistor days these had vacuum-tubes and required two separate power-sources, both expensive.

Coasters were used to ship the poles and heavy equipment to small Western ports, especially Donegal. Most of the poles came from Finland, Irish forestry not yet being well-grown. There is a reference to the use of Irish in the negotiation of the contract, to financial advantage. This aspect of nationality needs to be sung louder. I have heard of other instances. It might even appeal to Wallace Clark, and help him and his fellow-Irish Protestant entrepreneurs to take positive advantage of the opportunities presented by the New Ireland Forum!

Towards the end of Michael Shiel's book there emerge signs of strain: has the ESB, under rural political pressures, over-invested in a dispersed system that will have difficulty in becoming economic? Small, decentralised local electricity generation is again in favour and many of the old mill-sites are being re-activated. Cost-conscious rural-dwellers turn to LPG for cooking. Microelectronics is beginning to be used to schedule the farm load and chop peaks that would overload the fragile network. We have yet to develop the full implications of the gas grid. We could be back to municipal generation, with combined heat and power, by 2000. *(Alas, this in 2006 remains on the agenda!)*. Maybe it will emerge that the isolated farm dwelling is an anachronism and we should be in villages, like the continentals. Sociologists in 50 years time may blame rural electrification for helping to perpetuate the individualistic tradition of dispersed high-cost living, where it would have made more technical, economic and social sense to have built up the villages.

Science Brokerage as a Business?

When my TCD contract came to an end in 1984 I tried various approaches to reconstructing it. One such involved an outline proposal for a national-based agency which would serve as a one-stop shop portal for entry into the totality of the applied-research consultancy and dedicated postgraduate research potential of the Irish third-level system. This was not viewed positively by the existing College industrial liaison offices, who saw themselves as competing rather than co-operating(18).

As an alternative step towards this concept I backtracked and produced the following paper 'Innovation, Enterprise Development and the 3rd-level Colleges' in October 1984, and it helped lay the basis for the subsequent work with Limerick and the RTCs.

Background

Recent years have seen the increasing acceptance of the importance of dynamic linkages between the college-based R&D, industrial product and process innovation, and new business formation processes.

The role of college-based industrial consultancy, fortified in the cases of the NIHEs (ie National Institutes of Higher Education, being prototype Universities of Technology in Limerick and Dublin) by the intelligence of industrial problems gathered by students in the course of their co-operative stages, is given explicit recognition and encouragement through the Industrial Liaison Offices.

Opportunities for serviced business start-ups exist in various innovation / enterprise incubator centres in proximity to college campuses.

There is stated to be no shortage of finance for taking marketable concepts to full-scale production, once they are market-researched, prototyped, production-engineered etc to the extent that risk is minimal.

Despite this the flow of actual viable venture-opportunities remains a trickle. There is a bottleneck in the system.

The Problem

There are some indications which suggest that the interfaces between the Colleges and Innovation Centres need lubrication; also, that the nature of the process is such that it requires more than just money; it needs management.

For example, it seems that where the enterprise centre depends primarily on the College (as with Dublin Institute of Technology and Prussia St) it operates well below capacity; also that where the centre is working at or near capacity (as at Limerick) the flow from the College is minimal.

A factor contributing to the low flow from NIHE (Limerick) is the matching problem (of conflict) between student projects (identified during the co-operative stage) and the interests of the academic supervisor.

A factor influencing both cases is the pull of the best students into existing jobs, to fill an already-defined role.

An additional factor, which favours the student's decision to opt for the 'easy' road if it presents itself, is the fact that most if not all student projects are within-discipline and individual (and thus a long way below the enterprise-threshold). Despite the clear message of the Deans' Conference there is no trend yet into team projects involving complementary skills from science, engineering and business.

We are clearly dealing with a high-entropy situation, where the lubrication-process needs to involve putting resources into the organisation of structured networks linking resources, needs and know-how.

Outline Solution

It is proposed to set up a 'dynamic interface' in the resources/needs area (ie in the Innovation Centre rather than in the College), with the objective of cultivating the College as a know-how- source.

The prime function of this interface would be to become familiar with the regional resources and needs, translating these into problems and opportunities, linking the latter with identified know-how-sources in the College, thus setting up an 'enterprise network' around each problem/ opportunity.

In some cases, the 'chemistry' of the network will 'work', and a project will specify itself, around which a group of students will gather, possibly under the leadership of a member of the 'network group' in the role of external supervisor. In such cases, the project will make the transition from the College to the Enterprise Centre with a forward momentum and a creative team structure.

This process will require seed-funding, supplementing the 'sweat-equity' of the participants, who will mostly have no actual cash to put in. The seed-funding will constitute an equity-stake in favour of the agency.

Thus we are talking of a hands-on managed venture-seeding processor catalysed by an active agency located in the innovation/enterprise centre, distinct from the College, but charged primarily with the conscious development of the College as a resource.

Immediate next step

Set up a funded project to pilot the above process, for a 5-year trial period, with the right to take an equity stake in the projects it seeds. The proposer is in a position to make this his sole task for the pilot period, and to implement the total operation with minimal administrative assistance, from a serviced location in an innovation/enterprise centre. It would he appropriate to set up a management committee and reporting procedure, but speed of decision-making and minimal bureaucracy is essential.

The above outline was a sort of manifesto which helped to sell the socio-technical consultancy work which followed, as described below, following the digression to Strasbourg.

***

Church and State: The Strasbourg Divorce Case; the Education System

Janice and I never ran into the slightest trouble with neighbours or others about our irregular 'marriage' arrangements. The Strasbourg case, which ran sporadically between 1982 and 1986, gained us nothing but respect. A consequence was that our daughter Nessa was no longer deemed 'illegitimate', the category being abolished legally as a result of the case. The detail of the case I leave to the legal text-books. I have commented on the case briefly in the context of my analysis of the Greaves diaries, with a view to countering any misunderstanding which might arise from the study of his journals, where he is in error(19).

The first divorce referendum was run prior to the conclusion of the case, and this of course contributed to the main case being lost, as the judges deferred to the verdict of the people. There was one judge who placed on record a dissenting verdict, and the legal opinion was that this was what the court really thought. If the referendum had been deferred, and the case allowed to finish without the explicit political message dominated by the Catholic view, it is probable that we would have won. A post-case referendum would then have enabled the constitutional change to have taken place earlier. In the event, however, we had to endure a further decade of anomalous marital status, which however we had no difficulty in surviving.

Nessa went to school initially in Scoil Bhride, the famous Louise Gavin Duffy foundation in Oakley Road, which was Irish-language based. In fact, she went initially to an innovative pre-school group on Scoil Bhride premises, which Janice succeeded in founding, and which has continued successfully since, contributing to the revival of the school, which prior to that had been in decline. Janice currently (2002) serves on the Board of Management.

There are political issues embedded here. The school was nominally attached to Rathfarnham Catholic Church parish, with the priest as manager, which of course was the initial anomaly, as the Irish language is not the property of the Catholic Church, which indeed during the 19th century did its best to suppress it. Under pressure from parents of all-Irish schools, the Department of Education had to accept a patronage procedure under Bord na Gaeilge, with management committees, on which however the Bishops retain nominating rights, so that the anomaly persists. At the time of writing (2002) there is a key case developing with a school in Dunboyne, with the Principal being sacked by the Board of Management over an issue relating to the teaching of religious doctrine in a multi-denominational context. Janice in the Scoil Bhride context remains alive to these issues.

Nessa then went in 1990 to the St Louis nuns in Rathmines, this being the nearest second-level school. Her Quaker status helped in both cases to ensure survival in the predominantly Catholic environment. Our preliminary enquiries with the school gave a positive impression which in the following years was vindicated. The alternative would have been some Protestant fee-paying school, and subsequent comparative anecdotal studies, on the family and neighbourhood network, were favourable to St Louis, which was non-fee-paying.

It emerged that most of the St Louis girls came from far-away places like Tallaght, reinforcing our impression that Dublin parents mostly are under the illusion that some school far away is better than the one available locally. The scene is dominated by petty-bourgeois snobbism, and much peak-hour traffic is generated. Ownership and management of the school system remains a key issue on the political agenda, the current system being socially divisive and economically costly, with its parasitic transport load.

Innovative Enterprise and the 3rd-Level Education System

In the period 1985-86 the present writer had the opportunity to take a close look at the role of the Regional Colleges, in the context of regional enterprise development. In this context, various versions of the 'Technopole Model' emerged, including one associated with the National Institute of Higher Education, Limerick (later Limerick University), associated with Shannon Development.

In the course of several consultancy assignments, sponsored by the Youth Employment Agency and the National Enterprise Agency, it was possible to develop a directory of people and centres available as local sources of consultancy expertise for innovative enterprise start-ups, and to outline a procedure where feasibility studies of marketable concepts were acceptable as final-year undergraduate or postgraduate projects.

This constituted as an exercise in socio-technical analysis(3), and as a result I built up some standing as a '3rd-level interface' consultant, so that in 1987, after the Brittany and 'linkage' episodes, I was asked to do some analysis of the relationship between the NIHE in Limerick and the Innovation Centre which had been located close to the campus, but which had failed to interact. We come back to this below.

Ireland and Brittany

The opportunity arose in May and June of 1985, thanks to a French Government Fellowship, to study the equivalent process in an appropriate French region. The writer chose Brittany, where there are many features comparable with Ireland: scale, dependence on agriculture, a well-developed 3rd-level education system, and, more recently, a rapidly developing electronics sector. There is also a sense of historic background and cultural identity which somewhat parallels the Irish experience, though without national statehood.

A strong maritime tradition in Brittany, and a prosperous fishing industry, constitutes a source of experience from which the Irish have yet significantly to draw; despite comparable or greater natural resources this Irish sector remains weak.

It was decided, given the time available, to restrict the scope of the study to a search for candidates for a 'binary twinning' process, this being defined in the following terms:

(a) twinning between research centres in Ireland and Brittany where in both cases there is a strong incentive to convert scientific knowledge into viable economic technology giving employment within the region;

(b) innovative enterprises, associated with the above centres and committed to growth in the region, might possibly provide scope for two-way licensing agreements, giving mutual access to each other's markets with complementary products, and to each other's R&D sources.

I wrote a résumé(4) which gave the basic statistics of the pilot-study, without specific detail, and concluded by suggesting a constitution for a 'technology transfer network', which if appropriately set up and funded might prove useful to innovative small and medium firms in Brittany and Ireland in strengthening their viability. It might also, for example, increase their access to such EEC project funding as was conditional on international co-operation.

As a result of the foregoing work the writer was asked to contribute along the following lines to a major European study of the process implemented by the National Board for Science and Technology.

1986: Inter-Regional Linkages

What follows is an abstract of the writer's contribution to a Report(6) prepared on behalf of the National Board for Science and Technology by Dr Stan Nielsen for the European Commission, in or about October 1986. It promotes a concept of inter-regional networking between peripheral regions of the European Union. RJ March 2001.

I attempted to identify a sub-set of regional activities or initiatives where the ERDF-enhanced (European Research and Development Fund) autonomous growth process may be further enhanced by deliberately fostered inter-regional synergistic linkages.

Typically one might expect such linkages to develop between:

(a) a 'Less Favoured Region' (LFR) engaged in initiating an integrated regional development plan, and another LFR (possibly having a cultural empathy) which had initiated such a plan some years previously and had gained some experience in surmounting cultural barriers etc;

(b) two or more LFRs having common access to a natural resource;

(c) several LFRs developing a common approach to a common problem such as to make it worthwhile to share a research and training facility.

I identified some negative experience, in that where major non-teaching centres of research (national or Community) have been implanted in an LFR (usually for political reasons), the spin-off in the form of linkages with regional industry, and related inter-regional linkages, is usually slight. Interaction via the 3rd-level postgraduate teaching system was crucial.

We defined a 'Technopole' as a managed complex having third-level teaching, postgraduate applied research and enterprise incubation facilities, acting as a focus for dynamic growth in an LFR.

We defined a 'Technet' as a specialist sectoral network, involving one or more technopoles, possibly inter-regional, having access to postgraduate research and enterprise incubation facilities appropriate to a particular sector or technology.

It was proposed that the basic policy for the development of LFRs should involve the identification and enhancement of appropriate 'technopoles' and 'technets', bringing together know-how and resources so as to generate autonomous enterprise and economic growth. It was further proposed to provide in the 'technopole' specification a functional unit whose task it would be to identify and support the development of inter-regional linkages (both with other LFRs and with the developed central regions).

To summarise, if the development of inter-regional linkages is to take place, it is essential that within each LFR there should be at least one pro-active unit, with adequate resources, knowledge and initiative, in a position to promote and maintain them.

Once there is in existence in an LFR a technopole with a pro-active linkage development unit, having the competence and ability to recognise potential synergies, there are various types of linkage opportunity which can be developed, for example:

(a) **Research Associations:** a grouping of firms in several LFRs using a particular technology, with support from local research centres, developing where necessary specialist facilities at an appropriate location. We are envisaging the transfer of the old-established RA principle as pioneered in Britain into a mode appropriate to LFR development.

(b) **Demonstration Projects:** one might envisage the establishment of projects, with an appropriate innovative technology implanted in an LFR environment, enabling hands-on experience to be gained in a variety of LFR environments.

(c) **Licensing and technology transfer** between an firm and an appropriate partner firm in a developed region, or an innovative firm in a developing LFR.

(d) Development of a rationale for the **implantation** of an appropriate JRC (joint research centre) into a particular LFR environment, for use by several LFRs sharing a problem, or having access to a common type of resource.

(e) Organising **trips abroad**, or periods of study and work-experience, with identified personnel appropriate to identified regional problems. NB: this process should not be dependent on an exchange process, as stipulated in (eg) the COMETT scheme; people in LFRs on balance need to spend more time abroad gaining experience than people in developed regions.

(f) Development of a positive **structured approach**, involving the postgraduate RTD personnel and SME management, to **language and cultural barriers**.

It was considered essential that decisions relating to ERDF funding applied to any of the above actions be made rapidly and with minimal bureaucracy, by an accessible agency within the LFR technopole, according to guidelines laid down centrally in the Community interest.

***

Political Transitions

Contact with the Labour Party during this mid-80s was minimal and led to little in the way of visible political achievements. I submitted a memorandum on the national question to a Commission set up to study it in January 1986, in which I outlined the opportunities under the Anglo-Irish Agreement and in the European context(20). I gave some prominence to the question of sectarian education, and the problem of local government reform. It had little or no impact at the time. It indicates my then current thinking on the North. (I developed this further in 1988, with a paper(21) for a seminar organised by the Ulster Quaker Peace Committee, in Lisburn.)

The Labour Party had planned its annual conference for December 1986 in Cork, in the City Hall. As a consequence of the Sovereignty Movement Campaign, led by Anthony Coughlan, there was a significant amount of informed opposition to the Single European Act (SEA), especially from the Trade Unions, and from residual elements of the Labour Left. The possibility existed of a conference decision against.

Coincidentally there happened to be an industrial dispute in Cork with the municipal workers, who manned the City Hall. This enabled Dick Spring to call off the Conference, in a pseudo-left act of 'solidarity'. He went on to make a personal television appearance, urging support for the SEA. This piece of political manoeuvring I found absolutely sickening. If they had wanted to defend party democracy and run the conference in the City Hall despite the strike, it should have been possible to do a deal with the municipal workers to come in for the necessary few days, to oblige the party, or some suitable agreement could have been made, such as to use the conference as a lever in support of the workers' claims. So in effect the Labour Party went into the ensuing referendum without any agreed policy, and with Dick Spring's TV appearance used as the means of establishing one, by default.

Shortly afterwards I met with Roger Garland, then the only Green Party TD, and a few others, and became convinced that the banner of non-violent social-reform politics was passing to the Greens, with the addition of long-term sustainability and environmental concern(22). This was a step in the direction of the type of integration of science with social concern which I had been seeking over the years, and which the traditional European Left, in all its forms, had ignored.

Greaves, shortly before his sudden death on August 23 1988 in the train on the way back from a meeting in Glasgow, wrote a lengthy entry(23) on July 4 where he looked back reflectively on the 1930s and Stalinism:

'..in a sense there had to be "primitive accumulation". This was achieved by Stalin, and people put up with him, when the alternative was to join the third world themselves. Stalinism led to stagnation because everyone's aim was to keep his head down. The result was a series of mistakes in which the western CPs were alienated - whether what he did was wrong was another matter; I think not. But there was a mass perception in the West that socialism didn't work, capitalism did. Now if Gorbachov succeeds in the economic field the western public will see an alternative to capitalism. The differences on the left may be healed; the Labour Party will relax its anti-soviet stance. Though by then the financial feudalism of the SEA will have been clamped down on us and we may spend thirty years in an "Austro-Hungarian Monarchy", reactions will be encouraged when this increasingly displays its contradictions and breaks up under the impact of revolt in the third world ...'.

So it seems Greaves had hopes of Gorbachov, as indeed we all did, or at least those of us who tried to build an independent Marxist movement based on bottom-up democracy. Most of the 'hard Left' in Ireland rejected Gorbachov.

July 12: '...This morning's *Independent* had a story about the split between Adams and the IRA. If Adams goes into politics he will take IRA arrogance with him, make all sorts of blunders and end up like Garland ...'.

His death was premature and tragic. Despite his latter-day coldness, I retained a high regard for him till the end, and I went to his funeral, which took place in Liverpool towards the end of August 1988.

Socio-Technical Issues within the Firm: the Mentec Project
From March 1988 I found myself working on the 'Mentec Customer Analysis System'(24). This system was developed at the personal suggestion of Mike Peirce the Chief Executive, an ex-colleague who had been supportive in the 1970s of the TCD Applied Research Consultancy Group when with the Engineering School. He resigned from TCD in 1979 to found Mentec, to supply with industrial market with production-oriented software systems. By 1987 when this innovative

system was prototyped the firm was well-established, employing perhaps 100 people, in the Dun Laoire Industrial Estate.

It was an attempt to combine relational database technology with the then fashionable 'expert system' approach, to build an accessible record of in-house sales and maintenance experience, with regard to customers and products, in several distinct business sectors. The 'expert system' aspect involved combining qualitative judgments of sales people with hard data, and it was somewhat naively assumed that these judgments would be forthcoming from the sales people who were seen as the end-users.

While a working version was built, the project stalled, and Mike Pierce, though the Chief, found himself unable to push it through against the resistance of his sales people, who had not been in at the initial basic conceptual design stage; this had evolved interactively between Mike and myself.

A salutary lesson was learned, on both sides, which was later developed in the 1990s, with IMS and the IT-USE project, described in the next chapter. It is also an illustration of the 'expertise elicitation problem' on which many 'expert system' projects foundered.

***

Last Days of the USSR and the role of Gorbachov

These notes, written in July 1988, arose from participation in the May/June 1988 Kiev/Odessa Peace Cruise and were prepared for the record of the Society of Friends. A variant of this paper was sent to the Soviet Peace Committee for their information. It seemed appropriate to do so, in return for their hospitality; among the objectives of the Peace Cruises was the trying out of new ideas. The Soviet Peace Committee was prepared to put resources into this 'market research' via the 'Cruise' process, and deserved feedback. I subsequently had occasion to write a contemporary note assessing the role of Gorbachov, using insights picked up during the Peace Cruise(25).

I had visited the USSR in 1973 (for a World Peace Council event, of which the value was questionable, being dominated by unreconstructed procedures inherited from the Stalin epoch), in 1979 (professionally, on behalf of the UN FAO) and in 1986 (for a World Federation of Scientific Workers assembly).

In 1986 it was possible to see the beginnings of a critical appraisal of the past, but the 'dead hand' was still in evidence. By May 1988 however it was evident that the flood-gates had opened, and we were dealing with a radical-democratic revolution, of the type which had tried to happen in the 1920s and been killed by Stalin, and then had again tried to happen in the 60s and been killed by the weight of Stalin's appointees. The 1980s re-think however was being implemented by people whose political formation were totally post-Stalin and who had no inhibitions.

The Peace Cruise itself

This section was submitted to the Irish Quaker publication 'Friendly Word'.

The 'Peace Cruise' was organised by the Soviet Peace Committee, who had invited representatives of peace organisations in the West to engage in an exchange of ideas with Soviet specialists, in a floating conference, punctuated by visits ashore in the main towns (Kiev, Kanev, Cherkassy, Zaporozhye, Kherson and Odessa).

Participants paid their own fares but once there were the guests of the Soviet Peace Committee. The Irish group consisted of representatives of Irish CND, the Irish Peace Council, the Irish Peace Institute and Centre for International Co-operation (Limerick) and Women for Disarmament; the press was represented by Maureen Fox of the Cork Examiner. I participated on the initiative of the Dublin Monthly Meeting Peace Committee, with the support of Dublin Monthly Meeting (Quakers).

The Soviet group numbered some 30 and was composed of academics and researchers of a high level of distinction in areas such as philosophy, history, politics and law. Their support for the politics of 'perestroika' and 'glasnost' was palpable; the Soviet Peace Committee was clearly a leading body in the radical democratic transformation which was in progress.

There was a group of comparable size from the USA, which included 22 peace groupings (represented in ones and twos) and 10 press people. The other participants were primarily from West European countries.

The conference broke up into 4 seminars: disarmament (primarily looking at what was going on in the UN), the peace movement (looking at problems of citizen diplomacy etc), spiritual life (this covered a wide area including the analysis of the 'image of the enemy', peace education, the Christian millennium in Russia etc) and innovations in Soviet society (the economic and legislative reforms underlying 'perestroika').

I participated in the fourth seminar and came away with an impression of the depth of the long-delayed democratic revolution that was then in progress. The key Soviet participant was Valery Savitsky, Deputy Director of the Institute of State and Law, USSR Academy of Sciences, who was an uncompromising critic of past practices, in a manner which left Western critics without arguments. I have kept notes of the proceedings and have produced a 12-page commentary of my own based on the discussion, which I have sent to the Soviet Peace Committee for their consideration. The main thrust of this was on the problem of using expertise trained in the military, space and nuclear programmes for the peaceful transformation of Soviet industry under perestroika, and it is aimed primarily at the economic specialists who were present.

Events of religious interest included a visit to the Kiev monastery, now handed back to the Church, which was the base for St Cyril's mission of a millennium ago, and to a seminary in Odessa.

Also of interest was a discussion which took place in the Odessa Hall of Sciences between some local academic Marxists and the cruise participants; included among the latter was an Orthodox prelate who had joined the cruise and was one of the key participants in the 'spirituality' seminar. There appeared to emerge a feeling that assertive atheism was 'passé' and that the role of Marxist academics should be focussed, not simply on 'non-belief', but rather on a philosophical study of the nature of belief and of existence, within which convergence between Marxism and Christianity might perhaps prove feasible, especially given the agreement on the need to change the world rather than simply to contemplate it.

On this theme there was a move made by Mikhail Zykov, a Cruise participant who lectures in philosophy at the Lunacharsky State Institute of Theatrical Arts, to set up a "World Spiritual Network" of correspondents who would exchange papers and ideas. This would appear to be an attempt to initiate a personal correspondence network, initially under the umbrella of the Soviet Peace Committee, which is a further innovative step towards the opening up of personal contact opportunities. I have added my name to this network and hope to initiate a correspondence. There is some unease among intellectuals that the perestroika process may be blocked by conservative forces, but momentum would seem to be building up so as to make it effectively irreversible.

I placed 20 copies of Richard Harrison's "Irish Anti-War Movements", courtesy of the Dublin Monthly Meeting Peace Committee, in school and community libraries along the route, via local-based interpreters, who were mostly English teachers in schools and colleges. These were received with interest and appreciation.

Perestroika politics.

There is a well-tried system, known to bureaucrats for centuries, whereby the innovating and well-meaning leader is foiled by the implementation on the ground of theoretically good reforms in a bad and insensitive manner, so as to discredit them. I have seen this process again and again in Ireland. It has been analysed in the British TV series *Yes Minister,* which has enjoyed mass audiences, primarily in countries which have inherited the bureaucracy of the British Empire. It would surprise me if it had no relevance to the problem of overcoming the legacy of the Imperial Russian bureaucracy, and I have recommended it to them as a possible cultural import.

Alcohol

An example of the above is the implementation of the anti-alcohol campaign. There is much here to be learned from the US Prohibition era, where the response was the development of organised crime around the production and distribution of illicit alcohol. There is danger of this experience being repeated in the USSR, and the disappearance of sugar from the market is a danger-signal.

It would appear that there was a problem of vodka being drunk by workers during the working day, and in excess in the evenings leading to subsequent absenteeism, and that this problem is now perhaps less acute. Its solution should however not be approached by closing down hotel bars and making people queue round the block for a Sunday bottle of wine.

I have instead suggested to them that it is better approached by (a) raising the price of vodka relative to beer and wine (b) encouraging a beer and wine culture as an alternative to a vodka culture (c) opening up the democratic process in the workplace, so that the type of frustration leading to alcoholism does not build up (d) development of social pressures towards sobriety in a manner which is visibly successful elsewhere (eg litter, bus-tickets etc).

If the USSR is to develop its vast potential for intellectual interaction via international conferences (incidentally a good earner of foreign exchange as a form of specialist tourism), it will be necessary for them to appreciate the key role of the talk among the specialists in the bar afterwards. This is where all the real information is exchanged; the papers and discussions are simply means of identifying whom one wants to talk to afterwards over a glass of beer.

In this context the existence of a segregated 'hard-currency bar' (as was the case in the Cruise boat) was a total disaster, as it put barriers between Soviet and Western participants. I understand that this procedure is on its way out, and not before time.

Personally I rejected the 'hard-currency bar' and spent my free time in the company of Soviet citizens drinking local beer.

Democracy

In the discussions in the Odessa Hall of Sciences the question emerged of the role of Pamyat in the development of a critical consciousness under perestroika, and the apparent reluctance of the authorities to act to suppress unhealthy racist tendencies.

It would appear that Pamyat itself has positive aspects, involving the conservation of aspects of the environment having historic or Russian cultural heritage value. However it would appear that some people interpreted Russian culture has being exclusive, and needing a perceived enemy to unite it, with the Jews playing that role. This of course is at the root of Fascist ideology, and is intrinsically anti-democratic.

In many, if not most, bourgeois democracies there are by now laws which forbid incitement to race hatred, with severe penalties. (They are not always implemented consistently, but at least they are there.)

In the Soviet Union there is excellent legislation against propaganda or incitement to war. This enlightened legislation should lend itself to easy amendment to include incitement to racial, religious or ethnic hatred, enabling the prosecution of those attempting to develop Pamyat into an organisation expressing racialist ideologies. (I made this point in the Odessa seminar.)

Failure to prosecute this tendency, on the grounds that this would be an infringement of the new perestroika liberties, would appear to be an example of the type of bureaucratic action (or inaction) referred to in the opening paragraphs intended to discredit perestroika.

It should be possible to quantify the rules for democratic enterprise management in specific cases, and this is a development area for study.

The rules of democratic procedure, applied in an economic context, have evolved usefully in the context of the co-operative movement in the West, from roots in 19th century England which were known to, and admired by, Marx. Because of the emphasis in recent times on the role of the State, they have had little chance to develop under socialism. Perestroika presents an opportunity for their resurrection.

The foregoing represents a summary of the present writer's contribution to the seminar, as it was contributed to the Soviet Peace Committee. Regrettably the politics of reconstructed socialism which seemed to want to emerge during the cruise did not materialise, and we now have a mafia-dominated capitalism of the worst description. The blame for this must be attributed to the residual Stalinist group which subsequently staged the putsch against Gorbachov, leading to his replacement by Yeltsin. The politics of this putsch must have been in preparation at the time of the cruise; I recollect the sensation caused by the 'Andreevna letter' which was published in the newspapers at the time. This threw down a renascent Stalinist gauntlet.

I went on to write the following notes on 11/02/89 during the emerging USSR crisis, and I think they may be worth placing on record as an indication of my thinking about the USSR at the time.

1. The historic agenda for socialism was defined by Marx and Engels at a period when the European nations were becoming established and their boundaries defined in a framework of bourgeois democratic revolution: a centralist nation-state, equality before the law for all citizens, one man one vote. Marx regarded the bourgeois-democratic nation-state as a stepping-stone towards socialism, the latter being characterised by the extension of the democratic principle to the ownership of capital, and the management of industry. This was the 1848 aspiration, which however was defeated. The European states in the aftermath of this defeat became defined on the basis of hegemony and imperialism, and were usually multinational.

2. A political party with socialist aspirations did not achieve state power until 1917, in an imperialist state without a democratic tradition, in the middle of an imperialist war. The early Soviet democracy which emerged was fragile and lacking in precedent (their sole prior experience was the 1905 Petersburg Soviet, and before that the Paris Commune). The Soviet state took over much of the imperial bureaucracy, which was accustomed to ruling by administrative ukase.

3. In this situation it is not surprising that the political differences between the ultra-leftist Trotsky and the moderate Bukharin led to the emergence of Stalin, who 'resolved' the political problem simply by exterminating both, and any followers who wanted to explore the road to socialism by political methods. Stalin operated a top-down Russian imperial machine, with appointed officials operating simplistic doctrinaire policies. He has left a terrible legacy, which Gorbachev is now facing.

4. Gorbachev is the first of the post-Stalin generation to achieve influence. He has to take up Marx's task of completing the democratic revolution, as it were, retrospectively, in a state where the socialist revolution has been (after a fashion) completed without it. He faces formidable obstacles, not the least being those in the bureaucracy who owe their careers to the unquestioning implementation of Stalinist methods of work. These are the direct inheritors of the old imperial bureaucracy; they are anti-democratic and Russian chauvinist. They stand behind such manifestations as Pamyat, which is a Russian nationalist movement of the right, with virulent anti-Semitic policies.

5. He also faces the task of modernising Soviet industry, and ensuring that the fruits of the high-technology efforts (hitherto concentrated in the military and space sectors) are generalised, by free mobility of trained personnel. The obstacles to this are formidable and rooted in traditional imperial bureaucratic practice.

6. The non-Russian Soviet Republics are another problem-area. Imagine if the British Empire in 1918 had been held together under a London government

seeking to build Socialism. Few if any of the ethnic groups of the old Empire would have accepted to see their social systems regulated by London-originating legislation, however well-intentioned.

7. The process of establishing democratic territorially-based national states, with equal rights for individual citizens irrespective of ethnic origins, has scarcely begun. The imperial system, whereby Russians have de facto priority rights throughout the USSR, has only now under Gorbachev begun to be challenged.

8. Gorbachev is addressing all these problems with energy and insight. He is likely to succeed, indeed he must succeed, as the consequence of failure is a reversion to something worse than Stalinism, characterised by paranoia and xenophobia, to which the response can only be reversion to the 'cold war' at best, and a shooting war at worst.

9. Success will be measured by the continued cohesion of the USSR, despite the increasing autonomy of its constituent states. Many different experiments are possible in structuring Marx's road to the democratic management of capital (ie socialism) within an economic system retaining some central planning of investment priorities. The results of these experiments will enable lessons to be learned at a rapid rate. A single unitary experiment which goes disastrously wrong is not a good school.

10. One of the most important forces in the new wave of Soviet politics is the green movement. In this there is a parallel with industrial western Europe, particularly Germany. There is on the horizon a common enemy, against which the human race can and must unite: our own ignorance and lack of foresight, which are now being recognised as the source of the threat of the 'greenhouse effect' and the 'ozone hole'. This 'common external enemy' (of our own making) must force some convergence in global thinking in economics and politics.

11. The socialist forces in the West are historically divided as a result of the legacy of Stalin. It is no longer relevant to defend the indefensible abroad against attacks by our oppressors at home. The problem of democratising the ownership of capital in the West (i.e. the aspirations of the Left) can be achieved through a convergence of the traditional sectors of the Left with the Greens. Reconstruction of the EC states under the influence of 'perestroika' is in sight on the political agenda, provided the Left-Green converging consensus can accommodate the aspirations of the submerged nations which have not yet achieved statehood.

12. The Irish have a special status as the sole ex-colonial state in the EC, and as such have an important potential role-model for other emerging nations. We also have special status in the EC as the only non-member of NATO. These qualities give us status as a location for events of international significance, with UN standing, not only for east-west events (where neutrality is important) but also for events addressing the outstanding problem-areas of ethnic nationalism, and the elaboration of solutions within a democratic framework. (I am thinking not only of the Irish, but also the Scots, Welsh, Basques, Armenians, Kurds, Palestinians, Esthonians ....)

13. A Gorbachov visit to Ireland could perhaps help to place the above problems on the global political agenda.

The foregoing constitutes a sort of manifesto for the type of politics which the present writer has tried to help to develop via the Green movement during the 1990s and into the new millennium. It is a matter for eternal regret that we do not have a reformed USSR under Gorbachov as an international bastion of support. However I suggest that the manifesto stands on its own; it does not depend on any external State power supporting it. An international movement based on the principles embedded in it, built from the bottom up, is beginning to look feasible.

More on Science and Culture

The opportunity presented itself to address the 'science in Irish culture' question in 1990 in the context of the Irish Review. I submitted a paper, but it was heavily edited down, and the notes and references were suppressed. I give here the introduction, and statement of the problem, which is still with us(26).

Introduction

The stimulus for this essay is a reading of the first six issues of *The Irish Review*, which claims on its title-page to be 'pluralist and interdisciplinary', and to include within its scope 'the arts, society, philosophy, history, politics, the environment and science'.

With the exception of a short statement of the problem by Dorinda Outram (IR 1), there has been no attempt to date to ensure that science is considered in the context of Irish culture. Nor is there any apparent awareness that the process of the transformation of science into useful technology, and the application of technology in the generation of utility, is itself a cultural phenomenon, subject acutely to the constraints of a post-colonial cultural environment.

The present writer attempted to rectify this omission from the Irish cultural canon with an article in *The Crane Bag* (12), which treated the series of British Association meetings which took place in Ireland as historic snapshots of science and its application in the colonial culture, raising a series of questions regarding the role of the colonial scientific elite in the context of the Irish nation-building process. These questions remain largely un-addressed by historians, or indeed by historians of science, despite their importance in other post-colonial situations such as India, Kenya, Zimbabwe etc.

This article is a second attempt to address the same problem, this time from a contemporary rather than a historical angle.

I propose to begin with two illustrative vignettes, which I hope will help to state the problem. I then go on to comb the issues of IR from the start up to now for illustrative references, or glaring omissions, which fill in the statement of the problem in more detail. I do the same for a recently published book (27) from Manchester aimed at the Irish Studies market.

Coming round to the search for an approach to the solution, I analyse the content of a quarterly published in Britain entitled 'Science as Culture', which addresses the problem as seen from the angle of the imperial heartland. Despite much interesting content, I conclude that this excellent journal has not addressed, and is unlikely to address, the problem as stated.

I go on to suggest that the seeds of the solution to the problem exist but are lying dormant within the sub-cultures of the specialist disciplines of science and technology in Ireland. These seeds need to be planted in the type of soil that *The Irish Review* is cultivating, and made known in the broad national culture, broadening and enriching it. I go on further to suggest how this might be done, with *The Irish Review* playing a seminal role.

Statement of the Problem

I promised two vignettes. Here is the first one. Think yourself into a company of radical activists, trying to organise a campaign for the defence of national sovereignty against erosion by joining the EEC. Trade unionists, language activists, teachers had come together with a sense of idealism, meeting in a damp basement, which had to be cleaned up and made habitable. There was a fire in the grate, in which we were burning rubbish. We had set mouse-traps, and caught some mice. The question came up, in all seriousness: 'do mice burn?' In other words, was the fire an appropriate place to put their dead bodies? It was, of course, and they were duly cremated.

Think about it, though. Here were people, of the intellectual calibre to develop as leaders of national political movements; some have in fact since become eminent. Mostly about 'two generations off the bog', and having lost the basic craft feel for the properties of organic matter known to their agricultural forbears, they would have been totally dependent on an urban educational system for knowledge, plus of course their own experience. Yet they were unable to make the simple inductive leap from the cremation process (known to them in human culture) to an obvious procedure for getting rid of a dead mouse. We would seem to have here an illustration of the width of the gap between the verbal and the practical cultures.

Second vignette: the present writer was in Kenya, attending a UN conference on 'New and Renewable Energy Sources' (8). This lasted several weeks, and there were weekends. On one weekend, he took up a contact with a mission school in a remote area, with a view to getting a worms-eye view of the post-colonial Kenya scene. The school, as well as teaching basic literacy, taught agricultural practice. Land had been transferred from colonial settlers back to African farmers. The colonial settlers had been competent agriculturalists, practising 'contour ploughing' as an anti-erosion device. When the Africans took over the land, they reverted to ploughing up and down the hills, with the result that the effects of erosion were already visible. Rejection of the colonial culture, it would seem, included blanket rejection of all its aspects, whether good or bad.

This then is the statement of the problem: in a post-colonial situation, how does a government, seeking to assert an independent lead in the development process, ensure that the 'practical arts', needed for mastery of the technology necessary for national survival, are effectively nurtured and embedded in the national culture, after transfer from the colonial elite?

The Problem as seen in *The Irish Review* to date

Dorinda Outram lectures in the Cork History Dept, and has a background in the history of science from a political angle, with her work on Cuvier and the French Revolution. She is the first academic historian in Ireland to draw attention to the fact that there is in the Republic no official academic recognition of the history of science as a subject. She suggests (IR 1, p45) that to admit to the relevance of history of science in the Irish contest would be '...to challenge the "deep structures" not only of Irish history, but of Irish historical scholarship and of Irish culture.

She goes on: '...the absence of science from the Irish political tradition as a source of ideology points up the isolation of even radical Irish politics from the continental mainstream, where science-as-progress/reason-as-justice has been present ever since the days of Condorcet...'

In reference to John Banville's novels Kepler and Copernicus: '...so peculiar is a culture which deifies history yet yields to literature the vital task of rendering visible heroic models of the scientific pursuit....'. She might here have added that Banville's heroes were mainland European.

She finishes by asking questions: what does it mean to make a career in Irish science? What substantive science has been produced in Ireland? She warns would-be scholars approaching this question that the Faustian paradigm with the 'military-industrial complex' at its core is hardly appropriate. She sketches an alternative paradigm, with 'flash-points' of genius at the European fringe, in the 'late-emerging' European nations; this she prefers to the colonial model appropriate to Canada or Australia.

To this excellent adumbration of the challenge I have not seen any response.

I attempted to respond, and the paper is accessible in full in the hypertext(25). I am not reproducing it in full here, as much of the ground has been covered earlier.

Epilogue to the 1980s: the Clifford Correspondence

I had an exchange of letters with Brendan Clifford in August 1990, after having reviewed his book(28) on the Belfast press in the 1790s. I was supportive of his analysis and interested to probe his views on the current scene. He was one of Desmond Greaves's 'betes noirs', to be classed dismissively among the 'Trotskys and Potskys and Maos and Bow-wows', and I wanted to get the measure of him as an egregious critical historian.

I wrote to him, touching on questions like the Campaign for the Separation of Church and State, Canon Sheehan and the All for Ireland League, and Horace Plunkett, Father Findlay and the co-operative movement, religious education and the technical competence question, on most of which he had commented earlier. I was increasingly of the view that critical views such as his, relating to Northern Protestantism and Catholic nationalism, needed to be taken seriously, and that there was an increasing need for a serious egregious critical journal.

I suggested that '...there was the makings of a technically competent and patriotic national bourgeoisie among the southern Protestants, typified perhaps by Purser Griffith, who pioneered much of the ground subsequently covered by the ESB and Bord na Mona. They are largely unsung...'.

'...No-one has analysed how the Ulster Liberal Home-Rule-supporting bourgeoisie was emasculated; it certainly existed and my father Joe Johnston would have counted himself among them. He wrote a pamphlet against Carson in 1913, exposing the disastrous consequences of the Larne gun-running, from a 'Home Rule within the Empire' position (which was the staging-post that the AFIL were promoting)...'.

'...Regarding the consequences of the Larne gun-running: have you ever looked into who the people were who did the Howth gun-running? Was it perhaps a foreshadowing of the way Mountbatten handled India: ensure a religious divide, and see that both sides are armed? I often wonder. Might not the Asgard crew be regarded as the sort of upper-class adventurer such as the British dirty tricks department might recruit for a nefarious purpose? And they ensure Childers gets killed in case he spills the beans? ...'.

Brendan Clifford replied on August 25 1990; I give the following extracts:

'...I seem to remember that we had some disputes about Connolly and about Marxist political economy in the late sixties. I think I have rescued Connolly from his 'interpreters' - Leninist, Social Democrat, or theological - and restored him to the position which he made for himself. Of course, CD Greaves' book is the one that is found in all the bookshops. Yet I think that my pamphlets have had more effect in the vital part of the world where things are done. I know that because of them a number of people who would otherwise be in the IRA are not in the IRA...'.

'...In the early seventies I became aware, through contract with some *New Left Review* intellectuals and a brief, though close, acquaintance with a Welsh professor whom I notice appearing much on television of late, Gwyn Williams, that I had always read Marx into a background of philosophical commonsense gleaned from Locke and Kant, and that I had discounted as mere flourishes of rhetoric passages which they spun into a comprehensive and systematic philosophy. I was certain that humanity could not live within a mere systematic elaboration of the *Preface to a Critique of Political Economy*. The *New Left* gave Marxism its highest development as a pseudo-science in the middle and later seventies. They did this with great commercial success, and their jargon saturated the British Labour movement, with the result that it became incapable of empirical thought and Thatcher took over. All I have heard in politics from the *New Left* since Thatcher took over has been silence. Gwyn Williams seems to have combined rhetorical Welsh nationalism with echoes of Marxist pseudo-science in order to become a TV personality...'

'...I know that for most of a century Southern Protestants have felt considerable antipathy towards Northern Protestants. I find the Protestant middle class in the North contemptible, but for the opposite reason to what might be supposed. As soon as they become slightly cultured, they become disdainful of the culture of the mass of the people, and they segregate themselves into Cultra or Malone Road or Hillsborough. They become nice people and wash their hands of vulgar practices. At the same time they remain Unionist. But they do nothing to make the Union civilised. And they leave it to upheavals of the uncouth masses to ensure that the Union stays. I'm afraid that the element that is unashamedly Orange is the only element I have a shred of respect for...'.

'...All the institutions of civil society have gone by default of the respectable Protestant middle class into nationalist hands. Since Protestant society remains thoroughly Loyalist - at the end of the day, even Cultra is found to be crudely Loyalist - that is a thoroughly unhealthy state of affairs. It means that the feelings of the mass of the people are given expression only in the demagogy of party politics. Virtually everything else in the institutions of society is manipulated against them. That would be well enough if there was a probability of their will being broken. Twenty years ago, in debates and private discussions with supporters of both wings of Republicanism, I disagreed with the view that their will could be broken by the combination of physical force and political cleverness. It was not broken. It was only made to turn vicious...'.

'...I am occupying that part of myself by producing a dispassionate history of Catholic nationalism from the heroic days of Walter Cox and JB Clinch, and of the two significant resistances to Catholic-nationalism, *The Nation* and *The Cork Free Press*. And I don't know there is much else I could do. It is Angela who has worked out a secular programme and given it political currency in the Church & State magazine during the past eight or nine years. It has been very interesting seeing the lines of thought she and others work out in the magazine make their way into the public mind at a lapse of about two years...'.

'...The campaign against the Godless Colleges must have had the effect you mention. I took it up last year in a debate with Bob Cooper *(the Fair Employment Agency executive)* as a factor leading to imbalance amongst employers in the North. And I asked why his FEA in its analysis of the "normal" factors in the causation of the differential employment pattern between Protestants and Catholics, so that the "discrimination" element could be specified, had taken no account of the lack of Catholic entrepreneurship. I said that discrimination could not account for the lack of Catholic entrepreneurship. All were equally free to be obsessed with industry and devote their lives and their savings to small business and dedicate themselves to making it larger. But, if virtually all the entrepreneurship came from one community and that community as a whole had an obsession with science, technology and thrift, one could not in the normal course of events expect the result to be an even distribution of employment in both communities. This point had been made a number of times in *Workers' Weekly* in comment on FEA reports. Cooper made no reply. But in live debate his failure to reply would be very obvious...'.

'...It's a long time since I read Plunkett's dispute with the Catholic clergy about the industrial consequences of Catholic education and culture, but I think his reasoning was essentially on the same lines as mine. And one of the things I liked about Canon Sheehan was his brisk attitude on this matter. He said that if Catholics didn't stop whinging and get on with doing they would continue to be the cause of their own misfortunes. And he pointed out how the Jews managed to do things under forms of oppression entirely beyond the experience of Irish Catholics. My debate with Cooper was a couple of days after I had spoken about Canon Sheehan down in Newmarket. And I began by quoting Canon Sheehan on whinging. Cooper, a good Protestant who beats his breast unceasingly for the sins of his people, has an adoring following of nuns. And they did not think at all kindly of Canon Sheehan that day...'.

'...What I remember about the Larne and Howth gun-running is that the former was done with the maximum secrecy and the latter with maximum publicity. The former seemed to be done for an absolutely earnest military purpose and the latter as a piece of Redmondite exhibitionism. Childers was an overt imperialist at the time of the gun-running. And he was obviously an imperialist in 1914-18. I don't know what he was at the end...'.

I have reproduced the foregoing extracts(29), as a partial guide to some areas needing further elucidation. I find it regrettable that a forum for the development of egregious critical ideas has never managed to survive in Ireland, with any continuity of experience, in recent decades.

Notes and References

1. This consultancy was mostly of a socio-technical character, resulting in reports which were not usually for the public domain; I have outlined some of them in the hypertext.

2. The 1984 'Techne' concept emerged as a distillation of the TCD experience. I give the basic inaugural document in the hypertext, in the socio-technical stream. I also give some notes in the academic stream on my relationship with TCD at this time, along with some references to scholarly-type publications.

3. An 'executive summary' of the *Regional Colleges* report is available in the hypertext. I have also expanded on this at some length, in sequence, in the 1980s module of the socio-technical thread of the hypertext, as overviewed in Appendix 12. There were two reports on regional colleges, and a user-manual for community enterprise activists who needed to access their local Colleges for support.

4. The concept of inter-regional linkage development I develop further in the hypertext, in the socio-technical stream. It led further to the related concept of a 'quad-linkage' between a high-tech firm, and its associated research unit in a college, in Ireland and Brittany. I reported on this for Shannon Development.

5. I have treated the NIHE(Limerick) and the Innovation Centre more fully in the 1980s module of the socio-technical stream of the hypertext.

6. I include an abstract of my *Less-Favoured Regions Report,* as prepared for editing into the Irish National Board for Science and Technology Report on this topic. An overview of the Report, somewhat expanded from the abstract, is given in the 1980s module of the 'socio-technical' thread as summarised in Appendix 12.

7. This SSISI interaction included industrial policy 1982, mergers 1989 and Newman 1990. This is overviewed in Appendix 6.

8. I make available some notes on the contributed papers, which were given in the Proceedings at the level of one-page abstracts. The 1981 UN conference, its political background and implications are treated in the 1980s techno-economic module.

9. I have the minutes of the Industrial Group of the Institute of Physics (Irish Branch), which met for a period in the early 1980s, and have outlined what happened in the 1980s module of the socio-technical thread.

10. I have treated extensively socio-technical consultancy in the 1980s module of this stream, which is overviewed in Appendix 12 (see note 6 above).

11. Among the reviews in with a science in history flavour were in 1981 a couple relating to Hamilton and Tyndall. See also the 'science and society' theme in Appendix 11.

12. The *Crane Bag* paper was published in Vol 7 #2, 1983, the 'Forum Issue'. I never got to see a proof copy, and it is full of misprints, which I have corrected in the hypertext version.

13. I have expanded on the Bernal influence in the context of the science and society theme as overviewed in Appendix 11 (see note 11). Dorothy MC Hodgkin FRS, who worked under

Bernal in Cambridge in the early 30s, has published a biographical memoir in Vol 26, *Biographical Memoirs* of FRSs, Dec 1980. She also read a paper in the Royal Irish Academy on Oct 28 1980, based on Bernal's *Microcosm;* this was published in Vol 81, B, No 3 of the RIA Proceedings on Sept 2 1981. Helena Sheehan in Dublin City University has a chapter on Bernal in her *Marxism and the Philosophy of Science, a Critical History* (Humanities Press International, 1985 and 1993). The biography entitled *Sage* (his nickname) by Maurice Goldsmith, published by Hutchinson in 1980 is based largely on secondary sources.

14. A multi-author biography *J D Bernal: a Life in Science and Politics*, with insights from people having first-hand experience of his multi-dimensional activity, edited by Brenda Swann and Francis Aprahamian, was published in 1999 by Verso. Authors include Ritchie Calder, Eric Hobsbawm, Chris Freeman, Hilary & Steven Rose and others; Chapter 2 on the Irish roots was contributed by the present writer. Abridged versions of the first two chapters, by Ann Synge on the family background and by the present writer on Irish political and scientific influences, were published in Notes and Records of the Royal Society, Vol 46(2), 267-278 and Vol 47(1), 93-101 respectively. See also P G Werskey, the Visible College, Allan Lane, London 1978, and EA Roberts, the Anglo Marxists.

15. Bernal's own publications, apart from his numerous scientific papers, include: *The World, the Flesh and the Devil* (Cape, 1929), *The Social Function of Science* (Routledge Kegan Paul 1939), *The Freedom of Necessity* (RKP 1949), *Marx and Science* (Lawrence and Wishart 1952), *Science and Industry in the 19th Century* (RKP 1953, Indiana University press 1970), *World Without War* (RKP 1958), *Science in History* (Watts 1954, 1957 and 1965), *The Origin of Life* (Wiedenfelt & Nicholson 1967), also posthumously: *The Extension of Man: Physics Before 1900* (W&N 1973).

16. *Science in Ireland 1800-1930: Tradition and Reform,* edited by JR Nudds et al, published in 1986 by the TCD Physics Dept £10. I was asked by John Banville to review it for the *Irish Times* later in the year.

17. Reviews, probably Books Ireland, circa 1987: *Linen on the Green,* Wallace Clark, Universities Press (Belfast), NPG; *The Quiet Revolution,* Michael Shiel, O'Brien Press, £15... See also JJ's contribution to the debate in the Seanad in 1945; he drew attention to the problem presented by isolated rural housing which has currently become acute.

18. This 1984 'Techne' concept is explored in some depth in the 1980s module of the socio-technical stream. An opportunity arose in January 1987 with the *Irish Times* to do a retrospective review of my earlier criticism of the Aer Lingus Young Scientists Exhibition, from the previous decade, specifically in relation to the 'Group Projects'. I used this to advocate a reorientation of the exhibition from 'seed corn for export' towards acting as a generator of innovative enterprise for the Techne venture-seeding process.

19. Greaves Diaries, Sept 14 1983; the reference to the Strasbourg divorce case is totally misleading. Janice and I allowed our case to go forward challenging the Constitution at the European Court of Human Rights, not the European Commission. We were selected from a panel of similar volunteers by the Divorce Action Group, on the grounds that we were considered the most likely to win.

20. This memorandum on the national question, to a Labour Party Commission set up to study it in January 1986, is available in full in the hypertext. I also made some efforts via the *Links Europa* network to arouse interest in the Northern Ireland question, and the implications of the Single European Act, among European socialists. I kept in touch with the *Links Europa* network during my transition to the Green party, and they published in 1990 some of my material relating to the 'Green-Left Convergence' process in European politics.

21. I have made available my paper to the Ulster Quaker Peace Committee in full in the hypertext.

22. The Green Party work of the present writer does not begin properly until the 1990s decade, but I record my positive thoughts on the first encounter at the end of the <u>1980s political</u> module, referencing the <u>*1989 Green Manifesto*</u>, which I uploaded to the GreenNet, a pre-Web Internet conferencing system which was beginning to be useful as a tool in support of international political networking.

23. Greaves Journal, Vol 38, July 4 1988.

24. The <u>1988 Mentec database</u> and its socio-technical implications are described in greater detail in the 1980s module in the socio-technical stream of the hypertext.

25. I have expanded in the hypertext on this assessment of developments in the USSR, as seen in the <u>Peace Cruise</u> of 1988. My contemporary view of the role of <u>Gorbachev</u> is also on record. Also worth a look is the record of the attempts I made in the late 1980s to resurrect de Valera's earlier scheme for developing a <u>Radio Eireann World Service</u>, using the short-wave bands. When in the USSR I was totally dependent for news on the BBC World Service via my pocket SW receiver.

26. The <u>*1990 Irish Review*</u> paper, as an outline of the 'science and culture' position as seen in 1990, is accessible in full, uncut, in the hypertext.

27. *Writing Ireland: Colonialism, Nationalism and Culture;* David Cairns and Shaun Richards, Manchester University Press 1985.

28. <u>*Belfast in the French Revolution,*</u> Brendan Clifford, Belfast Historical and Educational Association, £UK7.50. On this occasion I also reviewed *Artisans and Sans-Culottes,* Gwyn A Williams, Libris, £UK7.85; I mention this on foot of Clifford's mention of Williams.

29. I have reproduced the <u>correspondence in full</u> in the hypertext, in association with the <u>1980s political</u> module,

Chapter 10: The Period 1991-2002

Introductory overview

The 1990s are rich in raw material, thanks to the existence of the personal computer. The problem is to select from the mass of material available that which may be of more lasting significance, and which contributes to the development of the overall philosophy, building on the experience of the previous decades. I have produced what will appear as a somewhat scrappy chapter, basically a series of abstracts of underlying documents, mostly available in the hypertext, with some linking commentary.

I have selected what seem to me to be the highlights of the final decade of the century: interaction with an increasingly influential Green Party, the final collapse of the USSR and discredit of the central-State model of socialist planning, episodes at the interface between science, technology and business, mostly related to the innovation process, the Maastricht referendum, the increasing importance of the Internet, the ongoing Northern problem and the roads leading eventually to the Good Friday Agreement, the ongoing role of science in society, the crisis in the Left and the perceived need for a 'left-green convergence'. Some related issues of specialist interest are touched on accessibly via the Appendices.

The Irish Green Party: Initial Contacts

By the early 1990s the Green Party had emerged into existence, and while it was initially somewhat 'crank fringe', it seemed to have enough going for it to enable a constructive interaction to take place.

I early got involved with aspects of policy development, after contacting Roger Garland, at that time their only TD. I attended local Green party events, and National Council meetings, where policy was discussed, though indecisively. I contributed my Regional Studies Association (1) paper to this process. This made some international comparisons, and leaned heavily on the earlier work by Tom Barrington.

I was additionally concerned that the party should make the best possible use of the Internet, in particular the GreenNet conferencing system, which I had been exploring. Here are some extracts from a letter I wrote to Roger Garland on February 23 1991, in response to an enquiry from him relating to some European Green initiative:

"....The process of achieving an all-European Green consensus on key issues involves 2 stages: (a) each national group working out its own assessment of the key issues and their prioritisation (b) all groups interactively by negotiation agreeing what are the key priority issues for action at EC or CSCE level; this will be a sub-set of the issues as seen by each group.

"For example a key issue in the UK is electoral reform and the abolition of the antiquated English system which blocks new parties emerging. A key issue in Ireland is the upgrading of local democracy and the establishment of an effective regional dimension, with the emergence of Limerick, Sligo etc as integrated government centres, with all functions except defence and foreign affairs. Neither of these however are key issues at the EC level, unless it becomes possible for the European parliament to legislate to over-ride national legislation in favour of a standard approach to local government and electoral democratic practice. The elevation of these issues to EC level is itself a key issue: do we value democracy imposed by the EC above sovereignty at the level of the national State? ...

"....A key issue at the EC level is the arms industry; this tends to be considered by the defence integrationists as the Trojan horse for achieving a common defence policy. The Gulf war is going to provide all sorts of arguments; the one we should be leaning on is how to prevent the arms industry from becoming regarded as a prime export-earner. The EC should not be arming dictators, and then profiting when they have to be contained. They make profits from arming both sides. This will mop up all peace dividend from the end of the cold war, unless it is put down, and the resources diverted to civil utility.

"....I envisage a system in which every national Green centre has at least one computer-literate PC-owner who is registered with GreenNet. This person, whom I label the 'GN Window', should ideally be on the national executive and deputed to implement the networking function, reporting to a networking committee at national level. Alternatively, someone on a networking committee at national level should be deputed to liaise with the computer-literate PC owner who acts as the technical support service for the GN window.

"These 'GN windows', one per State, or one per nation where there are several nations within the State (eg the UK), should set up a private electronic conference, in which would be available for general circulation all policy documents judged to be of EC, CSCE or UN significance. There should be a second private electronic conference devoted to proposals for, and planning of, co-ordinated international actions aimed at focussed EC, CSCE or UN events (eg the coming Luxembourg EC Summit). There should be a third conference, aimed at the media (ie a public conference) in which actions would be reported and agreed policy documents made available to the public....."

This was before the Web had captured the public imagination; the vehicle was a conferencing system called GreenNet, to which I had subscribed, and of which I was exploring the utility. It was a good system in its time, but lacked consistent uptake, and was superseded by the Web.

Socialism and Democracy: Some Notes Towards a Re-Think

This was written under the influence of the collapse of the USSR, and circulated to various contacts on the Left; there was no suitable publication outlet.

It is evident that the central political problem of the Left is how to bring about democratic control over the capital re-investment process, and how to mobilise people to this end, without generating a bureaucratic monster.

The following is a summary of some preliminary ideas on this topic which are currently the subject of an ongoing research program. I would welcome some preliminary feedback on these ideas, as an aid to the analysis of the problem, and the choice of direction of the research.

[A] Capital

1. Marx called his big book *Capital* for a very good reason: it is because the accumulation of capital for re-investment is the determinant of economic growth, and the direction of the growth determines the nature of society.

2. How capital is invested for economic growth depends (a) on the interests of who owns the capital and (b) their level of know-how. (The latter factor is increasingly important, as the technology of production becomes more and more sophisticated.) Because more people are concerned with the effects of capital investment than those who actually own it, the investment of capital becomes a social issue, and this is what socialism is all about.

3. There are two contrasting approaches: (a) the 'capitalist' approach, which says 'leave the investment decision to the owners of capital acting according to their perception of the market, and all will be well'. This is the classical 'Adam Smith invisible hand' concept. There is also (b) what up to now has passed for the 'socialist' approach, which says that social control over investment must be imposed by the central State.

3a. There is a need to re-examine the trends of socialist thinking which hitherto have been marginalised: the anarcho-syndicalists, Guild socialists, co-operativists etc, in the light of the collapse of central-Statism.

Connolly has been criticised for his failure to address the problem of the State, which was held to have been done successfully by Lenin. Perhaps in the year 2100 it will be apparent that the mainstream of Marxist thinking flowed via Connolly, and the principal application of Marx/Connolly thinking will be seen to have been in the context of the development economics of emerging democratic nation-States, in post-imperial situations. The attempt to apply Marx's thinking, top-down, in a centralist imperial system, will be seen to have been a disastrous aberration.

Marx's own practical political period, when he edited the *Neue Rheinische Zeitung*, was in the context of attempted emergence of a democratic Germany at the economic fringe of the first Industrial Revolution, then spreading from Britain and beginning to enter the continent via Belgium. Germany was emerging from the aftermath of the Napoleonic imperial period, and had not established a national-democratic State. Marx's primary political objective of the 1840s was to do just this.

4. Where the central State has been democratic, as in most western European countries, some limited democratic control over capital in certain key sectors has been achieved, in the national interest. The form of this control is similar to the private sector: a firm is set up, which has to operate according to commercial criteria, the principal shareholder being the State. Where such a State firm has an incentive to innovate, it is often successful. There are several examples of this model in Ireland.

5. Where the central State has been dominated by bureaucracy and in effect 'owned' by a 'party machine', the effect has been disastrous, leading to the crisis which we are currently observing in the USSR. We have had, in effect, one big

monopoly capitalist, without competition, and no incentive to innovate in order to re-invest capital more effectively.

5a. The current privatisation crisis in Ireland suggests that there may be an analogous process at work, the full implications of which have yet to emerge. It would appear that although there is in the Irish State sector a substantial creative know-how component, which has up to now been the secret of its success, this in recent times has been offset by the destructive type of 'know-how' which empowers a political, or politically connected, 'nomenclatura' to enrich itself personally, at the expense of the peoples' property, without adding real value to the social product.

6. The key to successful re-investment of capital is the link with the innovation process, and it is necessary in the current crisis to find means of combining this with the introduction of democratic control by some means other than the central State.

7. Given that the basic economic unit is the firm, then the problem is to ensure that those who control the re-investment of the surplus it generates are
    (a) socially responsible and
    (b) aware of the potential for innovation available in the current state of technology.

[B] The Firm

1. The group responsible for re-investment of the surplus generated by a firm is usually the Board of Directors. Under 'capitalism' it is responsible to the owners of the capital, who put up the original money to start the firm, to those who helped fund its subsequent expansion by investing additional capital, and to no-one else. Yet there are many other people whose lives are bound up with the survival of the firm: not only the workers and the management, but also the suppliers (for whom the firm may be the only market, as in the case of farmers supplying a creamery) and the consumers (for whom the firm may be the only accessible source of a key product or service).

2. A socially responsible Board of Directors should therefore look after the interests of owners, workers, suppliers and consumers, to the extent that the firm survives, making the necessary innovations to adapt to changing technology and market conditions.

3. A mechanism for ensuring that the Board of Directors became and remained responsive to these social interests would be to open the capital fund to access by them, and to provide means of ensuring that their share was in proportion to the extent of their interest. Thus the Board would still represent the owners, but the owners would be composed primarily of the worker, supplier and consumer interests. Thus a supplier, to ensure the future of the outlet, might be prepared to accept some % less, the balance going into the capital fund in the suppliers name. A consumer, similarly, might be prepared to pay a % more, into the capital fund, to ensure ongoing supply. And a worker might be prepared to accept a small % of wages in the form of shares (equivalent to a pension fund deduction).

4. In a vibrant, free-competition situation, these options need not be taken up, as the market would see to it that there were always alternative sources and outlets. A perfect market enables the 'perfect democracy' of consumer/producer choice to exist. Such a situation however is theoretical; the market is always imperfect; there

are local and sectoral monopolies etc; workers can't always easily move. In the real world of imperfect competition it would seem that some such mechanism for democratising the ownership might represent a possible approach to ensuring the long-term viability of a particular firm in a given situation. The so-called 'perfect democracy' of market choice under capitalism usually tends towards a monopoly of the 'most popular' choice, so that the 'democracy' of the market, while it works transiently, is in the long run negated. This was one of Marx's key points.

5. Under capitalism, it is already the case that a significant proportion of the available capital is concentrated in workers' pension funds. We are simply generalising this concept into a possible model for a 'privatisation' process which is also a 'socialisation' process, operating at the level of the firm, without heavy-handed interference from the central State.

6. Under the 'democratised ownership of capital' system the innovation process would be likely to work without tending towards monopoly for the successful innovator. If, for example, a consumer discovered a better product elsewhere, there would be 2 options: (a) buy it, and abandon the interests of the original supplier, or (b) put pressure on the Board of Directors to produce the better product, licensing in the know-how if necessary. The 'capitalist free market' would tend to take course (a) and allow the local firm to decline and ultimately collapse. The socially responsible course is (b). Those who are pressing for a 'market economy' as an alternative to central-State management should be aware of this option.

[C] The State, Democracy and the Nation

1. The role of the State in the foregoing scenario should be to make the laws and collect the taxes necessary to enforce them. It should not be interventionist, except to set the system up and monitor it.

2. An important role for the State might be to legislate for the transition of an innovative small firm, founded privately by an individual (this is usually the best way to innovate), into a fully-structured firm with Board of Directors responsible to an appropriate social mix of shareholders. The stage in the evolution of the firm at which this takes place should be the stage at which under capitalism the firm 'goes public'(2).

3. Tax law could be used to ensure that large shareholdings did not accumulate under the control of individuals who might then exercise undemocratic power (this is the central problem of western capitalism; it is especially acute when such power is exercised without competence, environmental sensitivity or social responsibility).

4. Apart from the democracy of the firm via the spread of share-holdings, there is also the fundamental democracy of the district and the region, and of course the nation. It is a good principle that the person elected should be known personally to the elector and this means that the basic unit should be small. This is high of the agenda of the 'Green' component of European democratic radicalism, and needs to be taken on board by the 'Left' component.

5. In the region and the nation there is the question of ethnicity; there should be no discrimination against any ethnic group, and some form of proportional

representation. Democracy must be inclusive and sensitive to minority interests; it is not good practice to structure things so that one group is always 'voted down'.

6. Typical multi-ethnic situations have urban groups of extern origin embedded in an aboriginal rural hinterland. The key to democratising this system is in the development of a common perception of economic interest. (This of course was the Connolly approach to the problem of multi-ethnicity in the North.) The foregoing model for democratising the firm may help to develop this common perception. To tear an urban centre apart from its hinterland is a recipe for disaster (e.g. Derry and Donegal), and we are seeing many such disasters in contemporary European history (e.g. the Serbs in Croatia), which mirror the problem in Northern Ireland with which we are familiar.

I am putting forward the above 'theses' in the hopes that they may generate some analytical and creative discussion among those of the democratic political community who are concerned with the problem of social vs private ownership.

Any critical comments which I take on board I will acknowledge and attribute to their source, in the event that these initial ideas ever develop to the extent that they become publishable in a more elaborate form.

I am not aware of any echoes which arose from these theses. Reviewing them now after over a decade, I consider that they remain a valid statement of the problem, and an indication of steps towards the solution. The lack of good publication outlets for innovative political and socio-economic ideas was a barrier, and this remains the case.

***

Operations Researchers, Engineers, Management

In 1991 I assumed the Presidency of the then moribund Operations Research Society of Ireland, at the suggestion of the few remaining supporters, and we set up a few events in the hopes of focusing scientific know-how into the area of management and innovation. We ran an inaugural seminar, in the DIAS, at which Fred Ridgway, who had started life as a physicist, outlined his progression into servicing the Bank of Ireland with internal problem-solving consultancy, in the OR tradition.

I attempted during my Presidency to make bridges into the Regional Studies domain, the common ground being the use of the computer in spatial planning, and into the Engineering domain, where the IEI at the time was toying with the idea of a Management Division(3). In the end the consensus was to try to keep the ORMSI going with John Cantwell in the chair(4).

The Society retains a tenuous existence, on the fringe of Cathal Brugha's work in the UCD Business School in Carysfort. International contacts are being kept up and people attend conferences. On the whole the OR paradigm seems to have run its course, and most of the innovative analytical approaches pioneered by OR in the 1960s have become routine. The sensitive management of innovation, taking into account both the human and the technological dimensions, remains a problem area, where activists tend to trade under the name of 'the socio-technical approach'.

The Need for a History of Science Centre

In the 1990s I found myself increasingly concerned to get the history of science in the Irish context recognised as important, as a resource for the education of humanities and business studies people. Teachers and decision-makers increasingly exposed themselves as having little insight into the importance of science in the culture. The issue has global relevance in the analysis of colonial to post-colonial transitions, science being seen by liberation movements as an imperial tool rather than as a development resource.

I produced some documentation in support of an approach along the above lines to Prof Gerry Wrixon, then Chief Executive of Eolas the science funding agency which had by this time taken the place of the National Board for Science and Technology.

I suggested terms of reference for such a new foundation. It should not be labelled 'history of science', but should have some name which conveyed its full scope, which would be to identify, chronicle and understand the processes at work whereby scientific discoveries take place, and scientific knowledge is transformed into technological know-how of economic significance in the specific Irish nation-building process, and to relate this to other post-colonial situations.

The first step towards setting up such a foundation might be some quite modest funding, on a project basis, with a co-ordinator who understood the terms of reference, and acted as extern sponsor of a number of projects in various university departments. Some projects might involve postgraduate students, others marginal-time work by motivated individuals, such as exist in all branches of science and are interested in the history of their discipline. There is also a fund of expertise and goodwill among retired people with scientific knowledge and background, but who are currently in isolation.

Little came of this at the time, though I was able to promote the idea in a 1991 meeting with recently-elected President Mary Robinson, who took an interest in a commemorative event dedicated to Robert Boyle at his birthplace Lismore. I supplied her with some historical briefing material appropriate to the occasion.(5).

The Maastricht Treaty and Referendum

I interacted with Anthony Coughlan in relation to this topic, helping to fuel the internal debate in the Green Party. The following extracts from a letter to AC dated 14 February 1992(6) summarise what I thought then, and still do:

"...The perception of most people is that the financial discipline imposed by monetary union is a good thing and to be encouraged, in that it will make more difficult for irresponsible governments to indulge in uncontrolled spending sprees, as has happened in the past. The argument of the Left that government spending, if investment-oriented, is a 'good thing' has fallen victim of the track-records of the centralist States of the East, supported by the Greencore experience on the home ground. State/Party mafias sugaring themselves etc.

"...There is a new ball-game, which the Left will have to learn: the key politico-economic concept is to leave investment decisions with the firm, but democratise the composition of the Board of Directors, without direct intervention by the central State. This is a tall order, and until it has been demonstrated in pilot mode, the left does not have a leg to stand on in matters economic. Economism as a leftist weapon is a dead duck.

"...The nation-province argument is more complex than you appear to perceive. There is no such thing as a nation-state, pure, and without ethnic minorities. If there were such it would be either boring or an abomination. The old imperial States of Europe (Britain, France, Spain) are breaking up, with Scotland, Brittany, Catalonia emerging. The people concerned with these movements welcome the idea of a European Confederation, as a larger version of the Swiss model, as it weakens the power of their old imperial centralist oppressors. If we are to participate meaningfully in this politics, we should be seeking to weaken the old imperial centralist States, strengthen the emerging proto-nations, and oppose the development of too much power at the Confederation centre. Talk of the Austro-Hungarian 'prison-house of nations' is facile.

"...The key issue, which should be in the front of the shop window, is neutrality. In the confederation, all armed force should be territorial, except a small central core on standby for UN type activities, with UN recognition as a regional peacekeeping force. This is the primary ground we should be fighting on, as it is in accord with our existing position as an emerging post-colonial nation, with a positive UN peacekeeping record. The WEU and NATO are anachronistic and should be dismantled, as has been the Warsaw Pact.

"...If Ireland were to give a lead in this politics, and were to combine it with a positive policy of active aid to the 3rd world, and indeed to East Europe, with transfer of relevant technological know-how and associated educational and training services (such as we are doing already on a small scale), we could assume a leading role in the world as catalyst of the resolution of the north-south conflict, AND into the bargain generate work for our own people in supplying the necessary goods and services.

"...So you need to reverse the order: put neutrality up front, and develop its potential as a generator of economic activity at the interface between the first and third worlds."

The Maastricht referendum was carried, but less overwhelmingly than in the case of the previous Single European Act. This gave heart to the No campaigners, who hoped that the next referendum might be lost.

More on Green Networking in 1992

Much updating of Green policy was going on during 1992. Topics included Institutional Reform and Forms of Government (treated by Donal de Buitlear, John Goodwillie and others), Northern Ireland policy and cross-border bodies regenerating the pre-Partition hinterlands (this relates to the Andy Pollak initiative below), Energy policy (largely via Brian Hurley and the Solar Energy Society), Marriage Laws policy, and so on. I felt that my main contribution should be to organise to make these papers accessible via the Internet, using GreenNet conferencing technology, the Web not yet being top of the agenda. I wrote to Roger Garland on March 14 1992, and I again give some extracts(7) as follows:

"...As you know I have been trying to develop the electronic networking system, with a view to helping to develop common Green policies throughout

Europe where these are of EC relevance (e.g. the CAP and organic farming, the Maastricht business, neutrality and the accession of Austria and Sweden, third world trade etc.). 1 have not been succeeding, because the key Green parties of Europe and the Green co-ordination processes are not yet over the computeracy barrier.

"...Of the European Greens the only parties showing any sign of computeracy are the Germans, the British, the Swedes and the Finns. I see no sign of the French. The USA, Canada and Australia are well developed into networking; indeed the network is dominated by the latter 3, and European input is negligible.

"...There was last week a meeting in London of the Green MEPs with the UK Green Party. This was supported by Willy de Backer, who is charged with developing electronic networking by the EPGG. I have been in correspondence with Willy, and with the GreenNet people, on this question. Willy and the GN people had a meeting, with my briefing. I have not yet had feedback as to the outcome; perhaps Patricia (McKenna MEP) has. It may be at the level that the EPGG is doing its own thing 'top down' and wants to use its networking ability for political advantage, in which case we have to try and develop a 'bottom up' ballgame with people we meet via the co-ordination events....

"...Also, on Northern Ireland: the network is dominated by a chap in New Jersey acting for the Provisionals, with the result that the overall Irish input on this issue is totally unbalanced. Can you perhaps let me have any stuff you can lay your hands on relating eg to the question of the SF Ard Fheis in the Mansion House, as this issue has been raised in an anti-Green manner on the network. Or indeed anything on the Peace Train, or other actions relevant to the ongoing situation.

"...I have all of our basic Green policy documents uploaded into a reference knowledge-base, with an indexed structure, as a sort of demonstration model of what should be accessible from all Green Parties in Europe ..... This however is not yet properly developed; I had hoped that the EPGG people might be able to encourage this, so that we can see, for example, what is the French Green policy on nuclear energy, with a view to being critical of it. It would also be useful to see what is the German policy on agriculture, and how it relates to the CAP crisis.....

"... However there are other questions, like economics, the social wage, the crisis in the West, the meat crisis (Goodman, Halal etc) where I feel I have something to contribute. Like for example how much of the meat and general agricultural crisis is due to the seasonality problem? Unique in Europe we have a 15 to 1 seasonality ratio for milk.

"You can't have high added value products without continuity of supply. Meat similarly; they all calve in April and slaughter in October, like in mediaeval times. I did a report for Bord Bainne in 1972 on this theme, and developed a computer model of the industry and its supply base which enabled the 'added value' aspect to be quantified. It was shelved because all they could think of then was the milk price rise on EC accession; they didn't think it through.

"(Indeed, my father Joe Johnston in 1932 did a paper in the Stat Soc on precisely the same issue, exposing how we had lost the UK market to the Danes because we only condescended to supply butter in the summer. The key was then, and still is, to grow crops for winter feed.)

"This is a key strategic issue, and it is linked up with organic farming and the premium prices obtainable in the German market. It could be the salvation of the West, and Irish agriculture in general. We ought to be mobilising the organic growers and providing them with a political voice...

"...We should be focussing on the agriculture and unemployment crisis with the next election in mind, and have the key candidates identified. The positive angle on the first is 'go organic' and the second is 'social wage, legalise the black economy; abolish income tax and put all tax on energy and productive fixed assets'. This could be done be re-defining existing cash flows, with no-one being worse off. In the aftermath of the change however, a firm would have the right to hire someone from the unemployed by paying a marginal economic wage on top of the social wage, and to pay overtime to met a deadline without taxing it. Business would be transformed overnight.

"This needs to be developed into a package which could be sold politically to the masses of unemployed and to the Trade Unions and to small business; it should be perfectly feasible, but needs careful marketing, so as not to appear 'crank'...."

At this time I had not resolved the problem of how to get close to the somewhat anarchic Green centres of decision. The response was disappointing. I was somewhat in advance of the posse. So I turned to the Northern Ireland question, and responded to Andy Pollak's initiative:

The 'Northern Initiative 92'

Andy Pollak, an Irish Times journalist, about this time began an enquiry which subsequently became the Opsahl Commission, and I made a contribution to it, which I give in full below. The Northern scene of course continued to dominate the public consciousness, and I was beginning to feel the need to research my father's role, which led eventually to the idea of this book(8).

Submission to the 'Northern Initiative' / Roy H W Johnston June 1992

This submission is based on nearly a century of family experience, and 45 years of personal political experience, in the attempt to establish a democratic pluralistic nation on the island of Ireland, as a framework for a modern developing economy.

I give as an appendix some notes on that background; I prefer to begin with the analysis of the situation and to outline a possible model for future development.

In the analysis I consciously adopt a European perspective, being painfully aware of how the failure of the Irish to develop successfully along democratic pluralist lines has weakened the supply of good models for the peaceful transition from colonial to post-colonial politics in a large number of situations in Europe, the most acute one currently being Yugoslavia.

So I begin by mapping out, in the abstract, two extreme 'malign scenarios' and one intermediate 'benign scenario' (if I may borrow Conor Cruise O'Brien's cliche).

Alternative European scenarios:

Let us consider first one of the malign ones, then let us look at the benign one, then the second of the malign ones. It becomes possible to understand the second malign scenario as a response the 'threat' of the benign one, as perceived by central imperial power in decline.

Malign A:

There is a strong central authority in Brussels; atrophy of the old States has taken place (these are mostly multi-national, the 'nation-State' being actually a rarity); there is complete mobility of people, goods and capital throughout the EC.

The leads to an 'ethnic melting-pot' situation, with some similarity to the USA, and a tendency towards de-cultured monoglot masses, concentrated in the main existing industrial areas, primarily Germany. It would differ from the USA in that the lingua franca of the business and scientific / technological upper crust would be English, while that of the masses would tend to be German.

Europe as a whole would develop on a macro scale along the lines exhibited within those existing States having strongly centralist structures (the most extreme being Britain and Ireland, the latter being a micro time-capsule of old 1920s imperial Britain): a dominating central core, with high property prices, attracting labour from a declining fringe; the labour when there being confined to ghettoes, and facing a high threshold before being able to influence core politics (examples: West Belfast Catholics, London Irish, Berlin Turks, Paris Bretons...).

The ultimate malignity of this scenario is the way it lends itself to the manipulation of the urban labour market, using exploitation of the ethnic tensions of the ghettoes, by a cohesive unified upper-crust. In the USA this model, classically described by Upton Sinclair, remains with us to this day, and is at the root of the recent Los Angeles riots.

This malign scenario is the one perceived by those who opposed the accession of Ireland to the EC in 1972 (the present writer included), and by their successors who are currently opposing the Maastricht treaty constitutional amendment. It has considerable force, and is inevitable unless the pure economic forces are somehow moderated and controlled by socially responsible forces under democratic control, as it is suggested might just be possible in the following 'benign' scenario.

Benign:

The central authority is minimal, and all power is devolved to cohesive regional governments (or perhaps cantons, in that we are to some extent leaning on the Swiss model, though not uncritically, as in the Swiss cases there is a democratic deficit in some areas such as, for example, votes for women), which are not necessarily coterminous with the present States.

A canton should not be smaller than a population sufficient to support a credible third-level education centre, capable of supplying a competent leadership for politics and business rooted in local resources, including innovative enterprise based on scientific know-how; say about 200,000 population. This, for example, is of the order of the size of the independent state of Iceland.

Cantons should on the whole be as small as possible, but where big cohesive units exist, as a result of past imperial structures (e.g. London) then it would make sense to accept their integrity, and think of the canton of (say) Anglia as London and its immediate hinterland, up to boundaries defined by the hinterlands of whichever cities emerge as the political cores of neighbouring cantons (Bristol, Birmingham etc; it is not relevant here to go into political details in the English context).

(The analogy between the projected Anglia and existing Austria is worth exploring: post-imperial London, relieved of the pathological pressure on house prices due to its current centralist State role, would become a pleasant place to live, an attractive international focus for science and the arts.)

All power of government would exist at the canton level, except defence and foreign affairs; there would also need to be a system of justice such that any perceived injustice to any individual or group within a canton could be referred to the central High Court for resolution, with binding authority (ie a Bill of Rights).

The central authority would be the executive of a European parliament with two chambers, one directly elected, and the other with representatives of the cantons (we are here thinking of something like the US Senate).

Cantons would have the right to, and in some situations should be actively encouraged to, federate between themselves, for cultural purposes (eg if the cantons in England want to pay to maintain the monarchy as an ongoing soap-opera, they are welcome to do so), or for specialist economic purposes (e.g. the maintenance of safety in sea travel, or the management of a major river catchment).

No canton would have the right to legislate in such a way as to curtail ethnic, religious or linguistic minority rights (e.g. 'a Protestant Parliament for a Protestant people', 'recognise the special status of the Roman Catholic Church' etc).

Procedures would need to exist to detect and positively prevent administrative practices which discriminate against minority rights outside legislation (e.g. administratively dispersing Breton-speaking teachers throughout France lest Breton culture should be supported by a viable education system etc).

Models for the peaceful democratic secession of smaller from larger units exist in European history e.g. Norway from Sweden in 1904; this was the model to which the Irish Home Rule movement, in the lead-up to 1914, was to some extent looking.

Models for the maintenance of cultural rights by minority groups also exist: the Swedes in Finland and the Germans in Denmark have a healthy relationship with their mother-cultures while being symbiotic with their hosts, though perhaps with the political battles over the Maastricht treaty the German situation in Denmark may become more tense.

There was the makings of a benign process in pre-1914 Ireland, with the positive participation of leading Protestant intellectuals in the national cultural and language movements, and in the economic development movement via the co-operatives, and in innovative manufacturing development.

(It would be interesting to analyse the extent that northern Protestant manufacturers participated in the trade exhibitions organised in Dublin by Arthur Griffith's Sinn Fein; I recollect reading in the memoirs of the late Mrs Czira about the Ferguson aircraft being centre-stage in the Dublin mansion House; this was shortly after Bleriot flew the English Channel; was this typical?).

Malign B:

I can perhaps label this the Enid Blyton model; all the toys in toy-land and all the goblins in goblin-land. It is no accident that this particular author of children's books flourished in the British imperial heartland. It is the model on which the decline of the British Empire would seem to have been managed; it could almost be said to be calculated to maximise the mayhem in the aftermath, leaving the declining imperial power still the main source of influence. (I am not suggesting an intentional conspiracy; just a cultural bias, resulting from generations of ruling elite reared on the classics and the history of the Roman Empire.)

After being piloted in Ireland, it would seem to have been perfected in India and Palestine, and is emerging as the 'standard model' for the self-dismemberment of imperial systems which have ceased to be viable, having the advantage that while the fringe tribes weaken themselves by wars to establish local hegemonies, the imperial core group can pull back to its heartland remaining relatively strong.

How else is one to interpret the thinking of Mountbatten, in engineering the pull-out from India, splitting the Indian Army on the basis of religion, and giving weapons to both? Literally, over Ghandi's dead body.

It is the model currently being operated, in its crudest form, in Yugoslavia, primarily it would seem by the Serbs.

It would not take much effort to convert the benign model outlined above into Malign B: all the central imperial power has to do is propagate the idea that the 'kith and kin' of the central imperial power would be discriminated against by the emerging fringe cantons. Where such people are in local concentrations, this destructive politics can be focused.

In Ireland, the central act in the malign scenario, from which all evil has since flowed, was the arming by the British Tory conspiracy of the Ulster Volunteers, with guns imported from Germany, in 1914.

This was analysed by my father Joe Johnston in his 1913 book 'Civil war in Ulster'(8), from the Liberal Home Rule angle. It was also analysed by Connolly from the standpoint of the European Marxist social-democratic tradition, which he had consciously espoused and was in process of adapting to the emerging Irish national question.

In Bosnia (I am here depending on the reports of Maggie O'Kane, who appears to me to be totally credible), it would seem that there were mass demonstrations in the streets, in favour of peaceful transition to independence, involving Bosnian Serbs, Croats and Muslims; these were broken up by Serbian snipers, members of Arkan's gang, sent in from outside. We have the extreme malign B scenario, masterminded so as to gain as much land as possible for an 'ethnically pure' Greater Serbia.

In Croatia, where the rot first set in, it would appear that independence was declared without setting up a system to ensure that Serbs in Croatia did not feel threatened, giving Serbia the pretext for intervening, and establishing the current pathological pattern.

Nor was there any attempt made, in the dismemberment of Yugoslavia, to see what the natural boundaries of the units should be, in rational economic as well as cultural and ethnic terms. The speed with which the seceding states were recognised, without effective provision for internal structuring embodying justice for minority groups, almost suggests a 'Malign B' scenario. Was this conscious? Is the EC to blame? Or was it just insensitive and unaware?

The importance of finding alternatives to the Malign B scenario, in the light of Irish experience, cannot be overestimated. The Northern Initiative is therefore of key current European significance. Can a model be found which encourages a benign scenario to develop, in a multi-ethnic post-colonial situation?

The Northern Ireland Problem

We are here dealing here with a situation which was set up in the period leading up to 1921, in Malign B mode. Political attempts to enable benign developments to take place were made in the 1960s, under the banner of the NICRA. These involved the first generation of University-educated Catholics, in loose and often edgy association with a handful of Marxist radicals of the Protestant tradition, who were consciously trying to rebuild the Connolly approach via the Trade Unions, and the politicising and disarming elements of the Republican Movement (who subsequently became the Workers Party). The present writer observed this process, and participated in it at first hand.

This benign process, which was totally non-violent, and was beginning to achieve political results, was again disrupted, and set into Malign B mode, by the armed attack of the B-specials on the Falls Road in August 1969. (The smashing of the peaceful demonstrations of multi-ethnic Bosnians in Sarajevo by the Serbian racialist gangs is the current analogue).

The emergence of the Provisional IRA was a response to this, just as the emergence of Muslim armed groups in Sarajevo was a response to the perceived need of the Muslim people to defend themselves and prevent their houses from being burned. One would almost think Arkan and co had studied the experience of how the Malign B scenario was initiated in Northern Ireland, and profited by it.

We are now in the second generation after the second Malign B scenario has been imposed in Northern Ireland.

The core of the problem is that the perceptions of the ghettoised peoples are so overlaid with the detritus of imperial decline, in Malign B mode, that it has become impossible for them to envision the alternative benign scenario.

In the core of the perceptions in the ghettoes are two remote enemies, on the one hand Dublin (with Rome lurking in the background) and on the other hand London and the dead hand of imperial Britain on Ireland, expressed in the very tangible form of (for example) the Paras in Coalisland.

No progress will be possible until both these perceived threats are removed.

Can this be done, with EC support, in a benign scenario of a new type? If so, the Malign A scenario for the EC can be avoided, and democracy will thrive in Europe, in a manner such as to enable its influence to be felt positively in economics as well as politics.

Some Basic Theoretical Concepts

Wealth is produced by the interaction of land, labour, capital and know-how. In the past, the land element has predominated, and possession of this resource is at the root of most tribal conflict. In proportion as the balance shifts towards know-how and capital, possession of land becomes less and less critical. How much wealth in Ireland directly accrues from ownership of land? 10%, perhaps? Tribal conflict is a total anachronism, once added value based on know-how becomes the main thing.

Labour and capital, the classical protagonists in Marxist theory, themselves become transformed, in proportion as know-how to do with the production, sourcing and marketing processes become of primary importance, rather than the ownership of capital.

Large chunks of individually-owned capital need to be re-invested with know-how of they are to be reproductive. Individual owners may think they can handle it, but can they? We have the Maxwell and Goodman debacles as object-lessons. They can up to a certain size, above which they lose contact with reality, lacking the ability to process simultaneously the necessary amount of information. There is a fundamental cybernetic problem.

Large chunks of capital, managed with know-how, in the Irish business culture tend to 'stick within the business they know': when they saturate the home market they tend to go to the largest anglophone market to hand, Britain or the USA, and to do what they know how to do. The first wave (Guinness, Jacob etc) went to Britain, the most recent wave (Smurfit, CRH etc) has gone primarily to the USA. Either way, they have reinforced the tradition of Ireland being a net exporter of capital, and fortified a business culture which is positively opposed to being entrepreneurial on the home ground.

The use of State funds to entice productive units of foreign firms to locate in Ireland is counter-productive, in that it is paid for by high taxation, which further depresses the environment for local entrepreneurship, and fortifies the tradition whereby the few successful local firms expand by investing abroad rather than by diversifying, and adding value with know-how, on the home ground.

The increasing dependence of all productive processes on know-how is however to the advantage of Ireland, which has a well-developed and competent 3rd-level education system. The skilled human resources produced by this system are currently being bought at a high price, appreciated and used productively by firms all over Europe and the USA which operate at the cutting edge of advanced technology.

If we can achieve a situation where capital and know-how can be combined in the adding of value in Ireland, to locally-produced (e.g. food) or imported (eg metal) resources, then it will be possible to give employment to an expanding workforce at an increasing level of skill.

Steps Towards a Benign Scenario in Ireland

In the foregoing I have suggested some concepts on the basis of which it should be possible to set up economically viable multi-ethnic political entities, or cantons. Let me now begin to get specific, and refer to the map, and to the historic pre-partition economic life of Ireland.

Starting with the Northwest, pre-Partition it was possible to get from Westport to Sligo and on to Omagh and Derry by rail; the system also interfaced with the light rail system in Donegal at Strabane and Derry. There was the makings of a viable economic hinterland in the Northwest, which extended down to the West. The possibilities presented by this were killed by partition; Derry was cut off from its natural hinterland; both Derry and its hinterland became declining peripheral areas of remote centralist capitals in Dublin, and in London via Belfast.

In the East, there was a rail complex linking Dundalk and Newry with the port of Greenore; Dundalk was linked directly by rail to Dungannon and Derry. We are talking of the 1921 situation, when rail transport, and connection to ports, was the key to economic development. The infrastructure was in place; given independence and a benign government close at hand, development of a vibrant economy was totally feasible. Partition killed all this, leaving Dundalk and Newry peripheralised.

Can these hinterlands be re-constituted, in the EC post 1992 situation, when there are supposed to be no physical borders any more?

Are there analogues in Europe, like on the French-Belgian border in the Ardennes, where the French side is highly peripheral as seen from Paris, but probably would benefit by association with the regeneration of the old Walloon industrial towns?

The town of Maastricht itself is said to be a model, with its hinterland in Belgium, Holland and Germany.

Let us think not of a central town and its hinterland, but a network of towns and their hinterlands, with some degree of specialisation between them. We should get away from the centralist model, even within the canton.

(In order to get a feel for what the natural flows would have been, it might be appropriate to refer to the records of the ill-fated Boundary Commission, in which my father, Ned Stephens and others catalogued where the farmers brought their produce, along the now-cratered roads of Tyrone, Fermanagh etc. On the other hand, this might not now be relevant; I just mention it as a possible historical by-way worth a look.)

A canton should be such as to support at least one viable 3rd-level education system, at least at the level of a Regional College of Technology.

The cantons would need to have devolved government, by agreement between London and Dublin, with the loss of 'sovereignty' from the centre being balanced equitably.

We are not talking about 'Dublin taking over Enniskillen' or 'London taking over Monaghan', but new political entities, formed as an EC project, with the blessing of London and Dublin, as steps in the direction of resolving the old and costly dispute.

Possible networks of towns at the cores of the regenerating cantons might be:
1. Derry, Strabane, Omagh, Donegal, Letterkenny.
2. Enniskillen, Ballyshannon, Sligo, Boyle, Carrick-on-Shannon.
3. Dundalk, Newry, Armagh, Dungannon, Monaghan, Cavan.

The first would in effect be the regeneration of the old Derry hinterland based on the Donegal light railway. It is already underpinned by EC-funded programmes in advanced communications (the STAR programme) which involves the RTC in Letterkenny and the Derry Technical College. It should be possible to develop a pilot political dimension, via the existing local government bodies, in the joint supervision of a network of College-related enterprise centres, and local business-funded College-based projects, in such a way as to give the initiative a positive image from the start, while the details of the cantonal political structure was worked out.

The second would be dominated by the tourist potential of the Shannon-Erne waterways link-up, fortified by the existing Yeats industry, and underpinned by the environment-oriented know-how based in the Sligo Regional College.

There is also an industrial tradition in the region, which is supported by the quality control know-how based in the Sligo College, which could be fortified by the linkage to Enniskillen, in which complementary technical college resources could be developed as part of the project, giving the canton a complete core of relevant developmental know-how.

Leitrim is more likely to turn around and develop a viable economy as the hinterland of the nearby Sligo-Enniskillen axis, than as a remote fringe of a centralist State based in Dublin.

The land-based bitterness of inter-tribal strife in Fermanagh can only be assuaged in proportion as local-based industry develops and generates jobs, to which well-educated young people have equal access.

The third canton requires further study; the Regional College in Dundalk would need to be complemented by another, possibly in Armagh, or Dungannon; the region is quite diverse; there is the potential for a link-up between Lough Egish / Killshandra co-ops and the Armagh apple-growers, to go for the high added-value European food market.

As in the first two regions, the pilot-step would be to get a Development Council into existence, to monitor the linkages between the 3rd-level Colleges and the innovative enterprise process, and to grant-aid this process, so that it was seen to be productive of local jobs, while the devolved cantonal political structures were negotiated between the two governments concerned and the European Commission.

This leaves a core-canton around Belfast, or perhaps two inner cantons, the second being based on the Coleraine-Ballymena axis. Both would be viable. Or you could put Coleraine in with Derry and Ballymena in with Belfast.

The preferences of towns at the fringe of two developing cantonal areas would need to be respected, by an appropriate democratic process. Cookstown would probably prefer to be with Dungannon than with Derry.

Thus we would have instead of a 6-county entity, we would have a 5-canton entity involving 12 counties, of which 6 from the Republic.

The steps would be initially a Development Council, with composition drawn from existing local political bodies, and access to development funding from Brussels, and the ability to deal direct without reference to London or Dublin, charged with encouraging know-how-based enterprise within the canton, and making links between existing enterprise and the sources of know-how in the canton.

The Development Council should go on to become involved in the process of defining the future role of cantonal government, and should be helped to do so by being given the opportunity to study and evaluate systems of government at the regional or cantonal level as they work in other European countries.

Law and Order

The above benign scenario is of course totally dependent on the removal of all arms from the situation. Cantons would need to become totally demilitarised zones, without British Army, UDR, IRA or UDA presence. This requires the concept to be sold politically to those concerned. It might be appropriate to provide for a nominal UN military presence.

What the British would get out of it would be the end of an ongoing nightmare, for which they would presumably be prepared to pay, by supporting the development funding via the EC.

What the IRA would get out of it would be the British Army out.

What the Catholics would get out of it would the ending of a situation where they were under any obligation to the IRA, and where they were effectively excluded from politics.

What the UDA and the Protestants would get out of it would be the ending of the threat of Rome rule via Dublin. (Would they feel a threat of Rome Rule from their neighbours via a local Catholic majority? The Bill of Rights aspect of cantonal law would have to take care of this, and this would have to be underpinned by European law.)

Implications for the EC and the Member States.

We are here suggesting a cantonisation process, with Bills of Rights enshrined in cantonal law, guaranteed by the EC.

This system, if it works in Ireland, should be perfectly well be generalised to all EC member States considering democratic reconstruction.

In the case of Britain, we have already touched on the Anglia concept; it is easy to envision a cantonal system where entities called England, Scotland, Wales might emerge as cantons or cantonal confederations.

In this case, the two cantons suggested for the north-east of Ireland might decide to opt to confederate with the Scottish cantons, and if this were to happen, I doubt if there is anyone in Ireland who would object. The 3 other cantons might or might not want to confederate with Dublin, and such other cantons which emerge in the present Republic: Cork, Limerick or whatever. This is another day's work.

The EC problem is how to make the transition, constitutionally, to a situation where there is enough devolved power at the level of the cantons to avoid the malign scenario of Type A, and where the old centralist imperial States, while possibly retaining ritual or cultural roles, do not block the process.

The other problem is how to prevent malign influences (e.g. arms manufacturers? Islamic fundamentalists?) from actively provoking incidents such as to transform the proposed benign transition into the malign type B model, with the 'cantons' all armed and trying to be 'ethnically pure', a process which we are seeing happening in former Yugoslavia and in former USSR.

The key therefore is the cantonal constitution, with Bill of Rights, and if this can be piloted with European support in the context of Northern Ireland, then the future of Europe is safe.

I added an Appendix to this, giving outlines of my father's career and my own. This I don't need to do here.

Science, Technology and Irish Culture

I had been active on this issue since the *Irish Times* epoch and earlier. Since the *Irish Times* my output had been mostly at the level of occasional book reviews. It must have had some slight impact, because in 1992 I was asked by WJ McCormack, who was editing a new edition of *Blackwell's Companion to Irish Culture*, to submit entries on 'Industrial Revolutions' and on 'Technology', which I duly did, and then forgot about, until they appeared in print some time around 1999. This domain became increasingly important as the decade evolved, so I introduce it here, at the level of 'watch this space'(9).

The 1992 Maastricht Referendum Aftermath

I wrote to Anthony Coughlan on June 20 1992, enclosing some money towards the campaign debt, and suggesting some pointers for the future. I again give some extracts:

"...Let me give you one or two post-mortem insights. The principal one is the impression that many informed political people who would have voted 'no' on questions of neutrality and sovereignty in the end voted 'yes' because that did not want to be in the same camp as the Hanafin gang and the ayatollahs. They voted for what they perceived as the European enlightenment against quasi-Muslim fundamentalism. This was reinforced by the appearance of fundamentalist youth rallies in the streets.

"...There were several good initiatives on the neutrality question, the best being from the Cork Quakers, which I had a hand in helping to promote and publicise. Jony Wigham ran a fringe event at the Yearly Meeting, at which a good few Nunan(10) books were sold, and there was serious discussion. I spoke to the Dublin Monthly Meeting on the eve of poll, and there was serious consideration given to it, and significant support for the 'no' position, but there were several there who had been supporters in '72 had reversed their position for the reason I indicated.

"...The Greens were campaigning actively, and they had the full political support of the European Green Co-ordination, which met in Dublin last weekend. This was somewhat to their surprise, as they had been inclined to write off the major European Green parties as being 'pro-European', and to vote to hobble the powers of the Co-ordination in its attempt to assume the role of a mandated body; this they are now on the road to becoming.

"...In the new ball-game which is emerging, the battle is going to be for local and regional democratic structures, which will enable the fringe to hold its own against the macro-economic forces leading to the reinforcement of the core. As I said before, the roles of central states and central super-state agencies are going to have to be curtailed, and we will have to find means of developing constructively the democratic forces at local and regional level, and weakening the centralist forces. The central state (of your so-called 'nation-state' model) is NOT a suitable vehicle for this democratic reconstruction, as it is mostly parasitic, especially in its Irish form (where it is a construct inherited from the period of imperial rule).

"...This parasitism it at its worst in the 3rd-world countries which have adopted the State structures of the imperial system; this is Crotty's 'un-development' scenario, of which the Irish are the pioneers.

"...The centralism of the traditional 'working-class movement', and the associated bureaucratisation, should be another indicator to you of the need for a new paradigm: the Trade Unions which were solidly 'no' in '72 came out solidly for 'yes', and what if any discussion was there within them?

"...The ultimate logic of the centralist 'nation-state', run by a centralist 'working-class party' is the use of the Russian colonists in the Baltic States to prevent the re-emergence of the latter, and, worse, the current 'ethnic cleansing' by Serbian gangs of Muslim villagers from Bosnian villages.

"...The democratic alternative scenario which I can see developing in the European reconstruction process is going to have to be 'bottom up', inclusive, and with democratic control exercised over economic decisions at the level of the community and the enterprise; we need to re-invent the co-operative movement.

"...The Irish Partition question is going to have to be challenged in this mode by the peoples living in the marginalised border areas, reclaiming the economic spaces weakened by Partition, and regenerating the natural hinterlands of the towns and urban networks. A theoretical basis for this can be found via Connolly in Marx, whose core-concept was the need for democratic control over the capital re-investment process. Connolly had the Ralahine model in mind for how this might work. Connolly never promoted State centralism; this was a construct which emerged in the USSR under Stalin. The whole political structure of the European Left has been poisoned by this pathology, and is on the whole beyond redemption, apart perhaps from some individuals."

The foregoing arguments, culled from private correspondence, deserved to be aired in a serious critical political journal at the time(10). They did achieve some airing in various Green documents circulated internally, but there was no access to the Left. The development of political ideas in Ireland has been seriously curtailed by the lack of such a journal. It remains so to this day.

Socio-Technical and Techno-Economic Issues

On the applied-scientific front in the 1990s, association with a young and vibrant software house enabled me to contribute to the development of a philosophy of knowledge-base development, and this work is ongoing, representing a culmination of a lifetime of dedication to science-based problem-solving.

The software-house work has been mostly socio-technical in its orientation, but I kept alive an interest in techno-economic work, and in the 'science and society' question, in support of the need to lobby for reforms within the political system(11).

Left-Green-Republican Convergence

There were many pointers during the mid-decade, in Ireland and more widely in Europe, suggesting common ground between the Left, the Republicans and the emerging Green movements.

The 1994 cease-fire gave an opportunity to open up communication with Gerry Adams again, reminding him of the internal British Army view of their role in the North, which was, and probably remains, that the top brass delights in it as providing a live training-ground enabling their lads to be 'blooded': I remember it being stated that 'the war in the Falklands was won on the streets of Belfast' by a British military man on a TV programme(12).

The May 1994 Gralton seminar, which I had registered to attend but was prevented by illness, was a focus for this process. Speakers included Éamonn Ó Cíosain on the 1934 Republican Congress, Seosamh Ó Cúaig on developing a rural renewal movement, Tom Barrington on decentralisation and local government reform; Declan Bree and Martin McGuinness spoke on 'Realising the Republic'. It was a constructive attempt at re-capturing the earlier left-republican convergence which had begun in the 1930s with George Gilmore and the Republican Congress, and which Goulding and I had attempted to rebuild in the 1960s, and extending it in the direction suggested by the Barrington *More Local Government* theses, essentially a Green dimension(13).

I had been in touch with Richard Douthwaite the previous weekend, in connection with his contesting the 1994 European election in 'Connaught-Ulster' for the Greens, and he was considering going to the Gralton event, combining the trip with lodging his papers in Cavan, but in the end he felt he had to support the local Afri famine march. I mention this because it underlines the potential for left-green convergence with the type of politics implied by the Gralton agenda(14). As regards the European dimension of the 'left-green convergence': European Socialism tends to be identified with State top-down centralism, in the minds of the Greens, and of those seeking democratic reform of Europe from the bottom up (eg the submerged nations, like Scotland, Wales, Brittany). The problems of the left-green convergence are:

(a) to get to Greens to appreciate the potentially positive and essential role of the State (e.g. in the enactment of property laws favouring democracy and the co-operative principle in business ownership, the right of workers to build up an equity stake etc), and

(b) to get the Left to understand the importance, not only of sustainable ecologically-benign development, but also of decentralised government (especially in Britain and France)(15).

The 1995 Divorce Referendum; Family Matters

I wrote to Patricia McKenna, the Green MEP, early in the divorce campaign, in February 1995. She had been campaigning, along with Anthony Coughlan and others, to ensure that the funding of referendum campaigns was 'fair', ie without State subvention in support of what a current Government wanted. This was indeed a valid consideration in the context of the various referenda related to the European Union and the abandonment of successive layers of national sovereignty. In the context of the divorce referendum however, there was an all-party consensus in favour of abolition of Archbishop McQuaid's ban on divorce, which had been inserted into the 1937 de Valera Constitution despite opposition from supporters of the genuine Enlightenment republican tradition. I give some extracts:

"....Divorce referendum..... where there is all-party Dáil unanimity in trying to reverse progressively a repressive constitutional provision that was imposed in the 30s by the undue influence of an undemocratic patriarchal multinational corporation, over the dead bodies of genuine Enlightenment republicans ....."

"...There are plenty of resources on the 'No' side; in fact, most pulpits, and a virulent fundamentalist element, funded from abroad. Progressives should not be seen dead in this company. This for me is a crunch issue. I look forward to be able to invite you to my wedding in the Churchtown meeting-house, if we get a yes. It we get a no, Janice will have to pay full inheritance tax, as if a stranger, on my decease.

"...Also, if there is a No majority again, the Northern Protestants will again say ha ha I told you so, Rome Rules OK. We simply can't afford not to get a Yes. Catholics, of course, who don't believe in divorce, can abide by their own church rules as long as they wish. They should not impose their church rule on others. I think you should come out publicly, and help to undo the damage Coughlan is doing. I am of course writing to him, but he is in my opinion beyond redemption, isolating himself into a corner..."

The campaign developed, with an increasing input from Catholic fundamentalists, to whom Anthony Coughlan appeared increasingly to be in thrall. I took this up with him:

"....For the first time we have what was the makings of a political consensus in the Dáil on the revision of a constitutional provision that was put in by de Valera under pressure from JC McQuaid, over the dead bodies of Dorothy MacArdle, George Gilmore, my father Joe Johnston (he wasn't then in the Senate because Dev dissolved it in the run-up to his constitution: I wonder why?) and all those who supported the concept of the secular republic in the Enlightenment tradition.

"The State is showing signs of standing up to the Church on a key issue on the 'liberal agenda', to bring us into line with the rest of European democracy, and removing rubbish that should never have been there in the first place. (Why is the 'liberal agenda' a dirty word with some so-called 'progressives'?)

"The last thing we want is for so-called progressives, who give out that they are concerned with valid issues like Maastricht, to be rocking the boat, and giving heart to the Catholic Right, that would, if it could, have us back in the old days of censorship, banned family planning, and running the Left off the streets. These people are no more interested in democracy than le Pen...."

I wrote again, on 14/11/95, to Patricia; she had not up to then been responsive, but I gained the impression that in the context of the campaign she did subsequently try to decouple the 'funding of referenda' issue from her own position regarding this one, and she did distance herself from the Catholic Right and the 'No' campaigners:

"...There is absolutely **no analogy** with the Maastricht situation. We here have a fragile all-party consensus, where an actual progressive lead is being given, on a key Church-State issue, against a well-funded international monopolistic corporation, the RC Church. In this context, it is totally **ridiculous** that you should be arguing for the Government to fund the Church.

"Especially when the 'no' gang is visibly well-funded (from where?) and well-organised (by whom?). Could it be that the Brits dirty tricks dept have a hand, in order to copper-fasten Partition, and torpedo the peace process, keeping their cosy live training ground, for to win their Falklands wars with? I wouldn't put it past them. Always ask 'cui bono?'...

"...Let the backbenchers of FF form a party of the Christian fundamentalist right if they want to, forming an opposition destroying the all-party consensus. If they do this, then they would have a case I suppose, but would they split FF on the issue? I doubt it. They will if they want to remain as the republican party have to accept that the separation of church from state is an essential part of the republican democratic process, firmly rooted in the American and French revolutions, to which we owe all of our political philosophy. Let them accept the lead of their front bench on this issue, and come into the 19th century from the 17th.

"....We will need every possible help if this referendum is to be passed. If it is not passed, we will sink into provincialism and be the laughing-stock of Europe. In fact Janice and I will have to think of emigrating, and writing off this benighted country as a backwater..... You have no idea of the pain this blasted referendum is causing to the many unfortunate people like us who were looking forward at last to regularising our situation. PLEASE take a PUBLIC STAND!!! "

She did, and the referendum was won, by a hair. We did in the end get married in the Churchtown meeting house, after I got my divorce. The latter was with the aid of template documentation supplied by Mags O'Brien, who had led the Divorce Action Group. The adapted documentation was agreed with Máirín my ex-wife; in court it took up some 5 minutes of the judge's time, and cost about £12 in a fee to a commissioner for oaths.

In the general family context, Nessa's post-illegitimate status, conferred by the Strasbourg case the previous decade, posed few problems; friends, neighbours and family all accepted Janice and myself without question as a de facto married couple. At Nessa's request we had earlier gone on a camping tour of Ireland, in the late 1980s, and in this context we had made contact with my father's home ground, meeting up initially with my cousin Alan and the Achesons, in Benburb and Killygarvan (between Dungannon and Cookstown). Alan subsequently went into an old peoples' home near Benburb, and we visited him there occasionally during the 1990s, using the occasion to look up other relatives. Alan died in August 2000, and was cremated in Belfast. We planted a tree fertilised by his ashes at Killygarvan, where he had worked, a year later; there was an extended family gathering on the occasion. We had to postpone it due to the foot and mouth disease. I had previously been able to use the occasion of his death to place something on record about Alan and his family background in the local press(16).

The Irish Green Party: Constitutional Reform

Initial attempts to identify policy development procedures proved elusive, the basic structure being somewhat anarchist. There was a perceptible constitutional problem, and it was increasingly being understood. A constitutional reform procedure was initiated, in which I was able to participate, and a new model emerged, which promised to be the makings of the necessary democratic vehicle for the development of radical conservationist policies, with full participation by a conscious principled membership(17).

The Constitution finally was adopted in 1997, after some tweaking. It has on the whole stood the test of time, though the question of the delegate representative character of National Convention still needs to be resolved. All members currently (2002) can go and have voting rights, and in practice about 25% of members go, which means that the Convention is dominated by the flavour of its location, an unhealthy situation. We will watch this space.

Reforming the Orange Order?

Early in 1996 (I have no record of the exact date) the Orange Order ran a sort of outreach meeting in Buswell's Hotel in Dublin, in which they made a political effort to justify their existence. One of the spokesmen was Henry Reid, a beef farmer in Fermanagh, and I had some talk with him afterwards. Subsequently Janice and I visited him on his farm, after attending a Quaker gathering in Lisnaskea. We had some talk about possible common interest areas, one being the need for an all-Ireland Department of Agriculture, to defend the island against imported animal diseases. I subsequently wrote to him, and here are some extracts:

"...I had yesterday an encounter with Stephen King who is a member of the Unionist Party and advisor to John Taylor. He was at the Buswells event, and yesterday read a paper to a conference in the Glencree Reconciliation Centre, organised by Servas (jointly between Britain and Ireland). Servas is a traveller-host network which is world-wide, with peace objectives, founded by an American ex-soldier after the last war. I listened to Stephen's paper, and formed the impression that there was a willingness there to consider all-Ireland institutions where obviously in the mutual interest, as in agriculture and tourism; also in cross-border regional development, where (as in Donegal and Derry) a natural hinterland has been carved up by Partition....

"...It seems to me that what we need .... is a constitutional settlement within the Union which will give enough autonomy to Northern Ireland to enable it to deal directly with Dublin on matters of common concern, without having to refer everything to London, and with a local/regional structure having the power to set up cross-border regional development agencies, with the right to refer to Brussels without reference to either London of Dublin. This should take care of the agriculture, fisheries, industrial development, tourism etc aspects of government with enough local and regional participation to ensure that no-one felt threatened. If investment pours in it can be a win-win situation; it is essential to get rid of the perception that a gain for Catholics is a loss for Protestants, and vice versa. There seemed to be the makings of an acceptance of this scenario in Stephen's paper.

"If such a constitutional settlement is to be acceptable to the hard-core Republicans, however, it would be necessary to include a proviso that it is politically legitimate and not 'subversive' to work politically within the system to persuade Protestants that it is in their interest to join in with the Republic, making it genuinely pluralist, and that if this were to be decided in a referendum, Britain would not stand in the way of the Irish re-unification process....

What I would like to know from you is: what acts on the part of the Dublin Government would reassure Protestants that in the event of such a process taking place, their faith would not be under threat? Would it, for example, be helpful if Protestants in the Republic were from time to time to parade publicly to celebrate their religion, and this were to be supported by prominent public figures of the Protestant faith (of whom there are many)?

"If such a parade were to take place in the Republic, it could celebrate the positive achievements of the Reformation, and also perhaps welcome the process going on the Catholic Church whereby in the end some aspects of the Reformation are belatedly happening (Mass in the vernacular etc), in the spirit of lending a friendly helping hand, rather than dismissing the unreformed elements as superstition.

"The Orange Order could perhaps form the focus of such parades if it were to drop its self-definition in terms of opposition to 'Catholic superstition and idolatry', and define itself in terms of religious freedom, civil rights and the rule of law. It could not hope to form the focus of parades in the Republic (outside the few areas where it has persisted) on its current self-definition....

"...The other aspect of the Orange Order that needs somehow to be moderated is the drumming, the objective of which is to strike terror into the hearts of Catholics; in this there is no doubt that it is successful. You have to ask, however, is it necessary, and is it Christian? Could not drumming be made into a competitive event, in a defined location, and the musical aspect played up, and the martial aspect played down?...

"...What is the chance of any of these proposals this getting on the agenda of an Annual Convention?..."

Unfortunately nothing seems to have come of this approach; perhaps it got discussed internally and dismissed; the evidence seems to be that the Order is increasingly being abandoned by the liberal element, and left under the control of the type of ignorant Protestant-hegemonists who appear to be behind the annual Drumcree provocations.

I did however make a further effort to reach out to the Orange Order, via their web-site. I contacted them through this channel, and they put me in touch with Cecil Kilpatrick, who fulfils an educational role within the Order. We corresponded for some time, and I went to see him, at his home near Hillsborough. Here are some extracts from my letters to him:

"....The contrivance of Northern Ireland, by shedding the more RC fringe of the more natural geographic unit Ulster, is historically well authenticated. Prior to Partition the industrialisation of the North-East was the key to the modernisation of Ireland as a whole. You only have to look at the railway map as it was then: the linking of Dundalk and Newry, both industrial towns, to Greenore as their export outlet; the linking of Sligo to Belfast via Collooney and Clones (in which enterprise the Gore-Booths of Sligo had a hand); the development of the Foxford woollen-mills (in Mayo) with expertise from Lurgan; the Donegal light railway system feeding Strabane and Derry. Protestant industry in the north-east was the engine for the modernising of the whole country. Harry Ferguson (of tractor fame) built Ireland's first aircraft, and exhibited it at the Sinn Fein Irish Manufactures exhibition in Dublin in 1912 or thereabouts. Home rule was an opportunity, and many Protestants supported it, including my father Joe Johnston. The Larne gun-running wrecked all that, and initiated the cycle of violence that is still with us. There would have been no 1916 if Carson and co had not initiated the arming process..."

"...The model for handling of cultural minorities in border areas is the Danish-German agreement about Schleswig-Holstein. The Anglo-Irish Agreement has some analogous features. It should however be possible for whatever political entity emerges in Northern Ireland for it to have the right to do business with the

Republic to the mutual advantage, and to respect equally the cultural rights of Protestants and RCs. It is my conviction that the Republic will in the end emerge as the best guarantor of the Protestant cultural tradition, and this sooner or later this perception will break through into the Northern Protestant consciousness, as the role of the English monarchy declines in the overall context of a disintegrating Britain. Where I fault John Hume is his failure to state the case openly that Protestantism does not need unionism. He defers to what he calls the 'unionist tradition', giving it a perceived priority over Protestantism. He forgets that it was the Protestants of the 1790s who invented the Republic...".

"...I often wonder if Mountbatten, when he organised the pull-out from India, was consciously modelling the procedure on the Irish experience, when he ensured that both sides of a religious divide (which divide the British had actively encouraged) were armed? The writings of Salman Rushdie, who is an Indian Muslim, some of which I have read (e.g. Midnight's Children), evoke for me a view not dissimilar to that of the Southern Protestants.

"...I am not going to take up the specifics, but simply to suggest that maybe the Irish Studies people in Britain could be persuaded to organise a conference, in some suitably selected location (why not Maynooth?! they feed you well there!), on the 'ethnic cleansing' theme in the Irish context. Or, indeed, Loughgall, or somewhere near it where there is a conference centre. I have recently attended a conference on history of science in Ireland which was split between Armagh and Benburb, with the latter as the residence location. Such a conference could treat the visitors from abroad to field trips. If you are interested in taking this up, I can put you on to the contacts...".

"...I could not agree more that the abolition of Stormont was a disaster. All the ultra-left and the Provisionals cheered, but there were some who disagreed, including myself; we said we did not want abolition, we wanted retention, introduce PR, and enact a Bill of Rights. I am glad you see the analogy with 1800, because this is exactly what we said. When I say 'we' I mean those of us who were trying to persuade the republicans to go political, and to support Civil Rights...".

Whither the Left?

In 1998 there was a celebration of the 150th anniversary of the Marx-Engels *Communist Manifesto*, which took the form of a large conference in Paris, under the label MCP98. I produced a critical paper(19) for it, and considered going. I would have gone if I had been able to go as part of a group, along with other participants from Ireland with Marxist backgrounds, making a collaborative presentation from a specifically Irish angle. I made an attempt to get together such a group, meeting however with apparent lack of enthusiasm. So I let the matter drop, but my paper for the occasion remains on record, and I consider it is a valid critical contribution, as far as it goes. To my surprise it turned out that there was, after all, Irish academic participation, by one of the people I had alerted. This confirms my impression that the idea of collaborative groups around a project, with people taking different aspects of an agreed approach to a problem, remains foreign to most academic work outside the sciences. Individualism remains rampant, even in a domain where one would have thought there might be emerging a sense of co-operation and community.

Notes and References

1. I had recently attended a Regional Studies Association conference to which I contributed a 'Regional Policy' paper.

2. I made a submission along these lines, in some depth, in the context of the 1991 Industrial Policy Review Group which produced the document known as the *Culliton Report*. In this I focused on the positive effects of the 'social wage' or 'guaranteed minimum income', and the process of getting rid of the 'black economy' by legalising it and making it the norm. This could be done by moving the basis of taxation from labour earnings to productive assets (land, buildings, equipment).

3. I served for a time on the Council of the Electrical, Electronic and Computing Division of the Institution of Engineers of Ireland. The 'computing' aspect at that time was aspirational, but we tried to make it happen, running a few events. It did not in fact emerge successfully until a decade later. During this period however we came up with some concepts which were feasible at the time, but were not implemented due to human and organisational barriers, as had been the earlier experience with Mentec. One such was the IEI expertise register.

4. I have expanded on this in the 1990s socio-technical module, with some subsequent correspondence. Most of what I did during the 1990s in the techno-economic domain was outside the scope of the Society, and related to political lobbying in 'sustainable development' domains of Green interest. I took an interest in the problem of the Dublin public transport infrastructure.

5. I used my May 1991 Books Ireland Review of the Academy *More People and Places in Irish Science and Technology* compendium as a starting-point for the Wrixon proposal, which along with one of the Mary Robinson letters is accessible in the 1990s Science and Society module of the hypertext.

6. The letter in full is given in sequence in the early 90s political module.

7. This letter in full is also given in sequence in the early 90s political module.

8. Echoes of JJ and the North: I had earlier made contact with the Albert Kahn Foundation in Paris, and remained in touch during the decade, sourcing material relating to my father during the war of independence and later during the 1920s, and donating a copy of the 1999 UCD Press edition of JJ's 1913 *Civil War in Ulster*. During his subsequent period of influence in the Statistical and Social Inquiry Society he had always kept the North on the agenda. John Bradley and Jonathan Wright presented a paper on May 13 1993 on 'Two Regional Economies in Ireland' (JSSISI Vol XXVI Part V p211), which I attended, contributing to the discussion. The opportunity also arose of reviewing the memoirs of James Douglas, with whom my father had worked during the 1917 Convention, and subsequently in the Seanad. It was edited by J Anthony Gaughan and published by UCD Press in 1998. The Irish Association, of which JJ was President from 1946 to 1954, continues in existence, and I again took up membership during the 1990s. I helped them develop a web-site archive. They continue to provide an all-Ireland platform for the now fortunately increasing numbers with an all-Ireland perspective.

9. I have reproduced the Blackwell Companion entries in the 1990s academic module of the hypertext, whence the 'Physics at the Fringe' paper (in *Physics World*, July 1992, Institute of Physics) and 'Biotechnology and Sustainability', published in 2001 by *Farm and Food* (ed Con O'Rourke), can also be accessed, along with other papers which are basically in academic mode.

10. Regrettably I don't have the exact reference to the Joe Nunan book; it was published in Cork in 1992 and was influential in the campaign. I had further critical interaction with Anthony Coughlan about this time, arising from his treatment of the Yugoslav crisis in the Irish Democrat. It would have been helpful to the development of ideas had these arguments been developed in a critical journal, rather than in private correspondence. The opportunity to develop such a critical journal existed, in the form of an annual commemorative Desmond Greaves weekend-school, with which I attempted occasionally to interact; some of the related material has been published by Daltun Ó Ceallaigh on an occasional basis. I refrain from chasing these hares now, but some of the arguments are on record hot-linked to the post-Maastricht analysis in the early 1990s political module of the hypertext.

11. Most of the work in the socio-technical domain with the software firm Irish Medical Systems is overviewed in Appendix 12. I have outlined some of it in the 1990s hypertext, in particular that related to attempting to understand the 'IT uptake' process as an aspect of innovation, and later the case-based reasoning approach to learning from prior experience. Some of the latter is included in the book by Bergmann et al, *Industrial Applications of Case-based Reasoning*, published by Springer Verlag in 1999. The 1990s techno-economic and the 1990s science and society activities complete their respective themes as overviewed respectively in Appendix 13 and Appendix 11.

12. I expand on this in the mid-90s political module of the hypertext, with my 12 February 1994 letter to Gerry Adams, and a reference to my April 6 1994 letter to the *Irish Times*, under the heading 'British Army's Role in the North', in which I drew attention to an item dated March 22nd by Colm Boland, in which Dr Philip Sabin, of King's College, London, is reported as reminding us that Northern Ireland "...provides a 'live training' opportunity for the British Army...".

13. More again in this in the Gralton section of the mid-1990s political module of the hypertext. See also my 'A Green Paradigm for Nationality' published in *Caorthann*, the Green theoretical journal, Issue 2, November 1994.

14. There is unfinished business here. In a follow-up letter to Declan Bree, the Sligo socialist councillor who had organised the Gralton event, I included my notes on the rail network which I had produced for Douthwaite. In my letter to Bree I also inveighed against the 'region' as defined artificially in terms of the strip of Border counties, counterposing the need to develop regional structures taking the Regional Colleges as foci and re-developing the cross-border hinterlands. For more on Green regional policy see my letter dated 19/3/94 to Bronwen Maher, in the mid-1990s political module of the hypertext. See also the record of my attempts to develop a Green science policy, which I have included in the 'outreach' theme pioneered by JJ under the Barrington banner, as accessed from Appendix 7.

15. I had encountered *Links Europa* when with the Labour Party in the context of trying to get a left-Labour network going at a European level. Rosemary Ross their secretary and I kept sporadically in touch. She is contactable at 21 Connaught Rd, Harpenden, Herts AL5 4TW, UK.

16. The obituary appeared in the *Dungannon Courier* on 20/09/2000, with the title 'The Johnstons of Tomagh'; it is in record in the hypertext in the 1990s family module. As regards the divorce referendum controversies, I have given my side of the correspondence in more detail (some of it was quite acerbic) in the mid-90s political module.

17. I have given an account of the intermediate steps in the development of the Green Party Constitution during the 1990s in the mid-1990s political module. In the further context of Green Party policy development I was motivated to attend the 1996 Amsterdam Conference of the International Network of Engineers and Scientists (INES) on Sustainable Development, and I was able to publicise this subsequently in Ireland, in the October 1996 issue of the Engineers Journal and elsewhere.

18. The 'orange order' letters are reproduced in full in the mid-1990s political module. I later got the chance to review Cecil Kilpatrick's book *William of Orange, a Dedicated Life 1650-1702*, published by the GOLI Education Committee, 1997, along with another group of books of Northern interest. There are further 'orange order' letters, relating to a projected Dublin event, in the end-1990s political module of the hypertext.

19. 'Updating the Manifesto: an Irish perspective', Roy Johnston; submitted to the 1998 Paris conference called to commemorate the 150th anniversary of the publication by Marx and Engels of the Communist Manifesto. I did not, for the reasons indicated above, get to deliver it, but it may exist in print somewhere in the voluminous proceedings of that conference. It may eventually even get published, perhaps with enhancement, if ever there gets to be published in Ireland a serious critical political journal, fit to take up the mantle of the *Irish Statesman*, the *Bell*, the *Crane Bag* etc. I look forward perhaps to helping to make this happen.

Conclusion: Reflections on the Century

In conclusion I try to summarise the development of JJ's economic thinking over the decades, focusing on the combination of liberal free trade with social control exercised via co-operative ownership of the means of production and distribution. I supplement this with an outline of my own evolving democratic political model, based on a requirement for democratic control over the movement of capital, with an explicit role for the support of science, technology and the innovation process.

It is necessary to consider the nature of the failure of the Irish co-operative movement, as exemplified in the Plunkett model, and the failure of JJ's analysis to have any impact upon it. The key issue here is the real-world drift towards commodity-based producer co-operatives, rather than the type of community-based co-operatives to which the early visionaries had aspired. This issue was addressed by JJ; he attempted in 1951, unsuccessfully, to revive the earlier community approach, in the form of a projected network of specialising family farms grouped around a central large-scale 'estate' under co-operative management, with the latter taking care of all marketing, including the strategic planning of production to adapt to market needs, servicing the whole group of farms associated with the central co-operative 'estate'.(1). He was attempting to democratise the working of the large-scale, labour-employing commercial manor-farm, of which he had shown the productivity to be far superior to that of the isolated family farm.

He had been attempting to promote aspects of this approach consistently over the decades, beginning with his 1913 promotion of consumer co-operation in TCD, followed by his exposure to experience of producer co-operation abroad, initially in his Albert Kahn analysis of experience in India in 1914-15, and then in France in 1916(2). This road of development, which he had hopefully envisaged taking place under all-Ireland Home Rule conditions, however was rudely interrupted by the 1916 Rising, and the Partition politics which followed. JJ's attention was diverted towards a dedicated but unsuccessful political campaign against Partition, and then to the long-term struggle to minimise its negative effects.

In this context, he made repeated efforts to defend and promote the co-operative movement. He contributed to the 1923 Agriculture Commission on the training of co-operative managers, and then extensively to the 1926 Prices Commission based on French experience of co-operative marketing picked up during his Rockefeller Fellowship(3). He had attempted to get the Plunkett House Library to set up as an Albert Kahn Documentation Centre(4). In all this however he was frustrated by the Civil War (eg the burning of Plunkett's house, and the transfer of Plunkett's attention to his Oxford centre), and by the effective partition of the co-operative movement, dependent as it was on State subvention, thanks to the way it had been related to Plunkett's Department of Agriculture pre-war, in a dependent mode.

He had attempted in the 1920s to use the Barrington Lectures in support of his co-operative development vision(5), during the period when they had been abandoned by the Statistical and Social Inquiry Society. He made an attempt to get into the Seanad in 1926, which was unsuccessful despite some cultivation of the rural Protestant vote. He then became active in the SSISI, and succeeded in getting the Barrington Lectures back under SSISI management by 1932, using his influence to keep them going on an all-Ireland basis. He began to gain first-hand experience of small-farm economics, in a process dismissed by his academic colleagues as 'hobby-farming': he employed a man to do the work, and kept the books, so that he developed a hands-on feel for costs and prices.

In the 1930s JJ began to pay attention to building up an academic reputation, with his work on Irish economic history, with particular reference to Berkeley's *Querist*, of which he recognised and promoted the role as seed-bed for ideas relating to the economics of development at the outer fringes of the English imperial system. He continued his polemical writings, criticising de Valera's policies(6), which he saw as disastrous for the primary producers, particularly the policy of attempted self-sufficiency in wheat(7), which he later identified as being a contributor to the wartime agricultural crisis, which generated near-famine conditions.

In the Seanad from 1938 JJ continued his gadfly role, urging the need to negotiate a win-win deal with the British, such as to build up Irish agricultural prosperity while effectively feeding Britain during the war(8). He made extensive use of his contacts with agriculture in the North for comparison with his own 'hobby-farming' experience, advocating, in effect, the development of an all-Ireland agricultural policy. He was involved from 1938 with the development of the Irish Association, in an attempt to keep all-Ireland intellectual contacts alive.

Post-war, after a period of actively contributing to the Agriculture Commission, and surveying what remained of the co-operative movement(9) as it had evolved, JJ again resorted to what his academic colleague again dismissed as 'hobby-farming', demonstrating that small-farm livestock production could profitably be combined with market gardening, in a farm in Laois. He developed further his north-south links via the Irish Association(10), of which he was President from 1946 to 1954, succeeding Lord Charlemont. Academically his work on Berkeley led to his giving the keynote paper at an international conference in 1953, in commemoration of the bicentenary.

In TCD JJ's main attention was on the campaign to defend the TCD role in agricultural education, the focus being the Kells Ingram Farm in Meath(11). This was an example of the large-scale productive labour-employing commercial enterprise that JJ had over the years attempted to get accepted as the norm, transforming the 'landlord's estate' perception by means of co-operative ownership. When this failed, in the environment dominated by inter-university rivalry and State centralist control of the agricultural research process, JJ turned his attention initially to his attempt to develop a Berkeleyan theory of credit, and then to his Berkeley *Querist* project(12), on which he spent his declining years, publishing finally in 1970. During this process he participated in the debates leading up to Ireland's accession to the European Economic Community, which he initially supported, but then opposed, on the basis that its volume-subsidised agriculture would undermine the third-world development process, just as British subsidies had undermined Irish agricultural development.

JJ's role as a 'one-man Agricultural Institute' in the decades before 'an Foras Taluntais' was set up was widely recognised in the agricultural research community; Dr Tom Walsh, who headed the Institute, turned up at JJ's funeral in 1972.

Conclusion: Reflections on the Century

***

My own political development was not consciously linked to that of my father, but there is no doubt that the family and educational environment was very much in the Protestant liberal tradition, with emphasis on technical competence and knowing how things worked, and how to make things that worked. The influence of the war, and the early use of electronics to pick up via short-wave radio what was going on globally, despite the Irish censorship, must have contributed to my taking up with the school group that became the Promethean Society(13) and subsequently the student Left in TCD.

The political model which we had worked at the micro level, in that we identified the need for student democracy, and we were successful in reforming the Student Representative Council, and giving it a variety of progressive social roles. Our perceptions of what was going on at the macro level, in the Irish environment, and in the global post-war environment, were both however seriously flawed. In the Irish case, the culture-gap between our attempted Marxist analysis of the situation and the then Irish political environment was huge, the majority of the group being of British origin. The bridging of the gap was attempted individually by the present writer, and by Justin Keating. As regards the global environment, the scene was increasingly dominated by the black and white characterisations of the Cold War, and the developments of Soviet foreign policy under Stalin.

(I was also conscious of the culture-gap between world-class science and the state of Irish economic development. I had encountered it initially with the Ecole Polytechnique laboratory in Paris, and later in the Dublin Institute of Advanced Studies. This was the 'science and society' problem(14), as instanced at the fringe of an imperial/colonial system, where the core was dominated by the military-industrial complex.)

In this political situation it is not surprising that the Irish Workers League, which emerged at the end of the 1940s and struggled on through the 1950s, remained as an isolated group without significant influence, somewhat like a religious sect, looking to a remote presumed utopia, dominated by politically unrealistic alien concepts like the 'dictatorship of the proletariat', in an economic environment dominated by emigration, or by the aspiration to start a small business or become self-employed(15).

Insofar as anyone was trying to do anything 'politically' in the black 1950s, it was the republican movement. We were of course critical of what they were doing, recognising the counter-productive nature of the 'politics of the gun'; we aspired to show the way to a genuine political road to Irish unity, beginning with the unity of the working class. Contact-points however were few. It was necessary for internment to run its course, and another republican generation emerge with the desire to 'go political', before there was any meeting of minds.

The meeting of minds began to take place in the late 1950s, with my articles in the *Plough*, and encounters with Seán Cronin. Then while I was in London, in the early 1960s, Cathal Goulding initiated in Ireland the process for commemorating the Wolfe Tone bicentenary, a process which led eventually in 1964 to the Dublin Wolfe Tone Society (WTS)(16). At the same time in London Desmond Greaves was independently laying the basis for the 'civil rights' approach to political reform in the

North, and I participated in this environment. So on my return to Ireland in 1963 the contact points and the organisational forms were there, ripe for the introduction of leavening ideas.

Scientifically my experience in London had enabled me to make the transition from the support-technology of high-energy particle physics, via systems engineering in an industrial environment, towards techno-economic analysis in an investment planning environment. This enabled me to contribute significantly to the understanding of the innovation process in the Irish economic development context(17), as well as to earn a living in Ireland.

What I had in mind politically was a democratic-revolutionary movement which would involve not only the 'working class' of Marxist tradition, but also wider groups of 'working people': working managers, working owner-managers, self-employed, all of whom seemed to me to have a potential common interest in democratic control over the capital investment process, and in building bridges with corresponding groups in the North, working politically towards an inclusive united Ireland, in a Northern environment where, given civil rights, it would be no longer regarded as being subversive and one could do so openly.

We were aspiring to a creative fusion of the Fenian and Marxist traditions, getting rid of the military aspect of Fenianism, substituting political education and intellectual discipline. We also wanted to get rid of the Stalinist incubus from the Marxist tradition, and we tried to do this by building on Connolly, and by attempting to regenerate the co-operative movement. In this latter aspect I was, unwittingly, following in JJ's footsteps.

The WTS enabled ideas along these lines to be clarified, and the problem arose of how to transmit them so as to be implemented by the activists in the movement. This process was rendered somewhat complex by the structure of the movement, consisting as it did of an active 'core' (the 'army') and a relatively passive and conservative shell (Sinn Fein). According to Goulding, the 'army' aspect was moribund, and the relatively few remaining activists in the 'army' were open to new ideas fuelling the politicisation process, and would be likely to respond by increasingly taking part in the Sinn Fein cumainn, and transforming Sinn Fein into a principled all-Ireland party of democratic social reform by constitutional means.

There were of course tensions within this projected process. For example, the concept of the Army Council as the Government of the Republic, with apostolic succession 'as by law established' from the First Dáil, was deeply rooted in the culture, and this was an elitist element in the philosophy. The Army Council felt it had the right to impose its will on the Ard Comhairle, and the latter felt it had to treat the former with respect. There were also elements within the 'army' for whom the military aspect remained sacrosanct, and who regarded Goulding's projected politicisation process with suspicion; in this context the prime mover was Mac Stiofain.

I was prepared to accept Goulding's plan, and to help him implement constitutional change in the movement from within. It was a gamble, but it seemed to me at the time likely to pay off, by enabling an effective broad-based political movement of the Left to be developed. The alternative process, based on the narrow 'Marxist' orthodoxy of the Irish Workers' League, isolated by the alien Stalinist influence, was in discredit. So I joined Goulding's 'HQ staff' and helped to set up a series of educational conferences, with which we hoped to enable the ideas emerging from the WTS to gain acceptance(18).

This process did not get under way sufficiently to enable the 1965 Ard Fheis to reflect the new progressive thinking, but by the 1966 Ard Fheis it became dominant, with Goulding himself elected to the Ard Comhairle, and the 'army' activists integrating themselves into a regenerating active Sinn Fein. The Republican Clubs in the North were set up and were beginning to assert a quasi-legal existence. The need for a Civil Rights approach in the North was beginning to be understood, so that when in 1966 the opportunity came to set up a broad-based Civil Rights movement, with the War Memorial Hall meeting planned for November, the Republican Club activists were prepared to go along with the idea, swallowing their unease at the name of the location, and keeping their 'united Ireland' ideas on the back burner. The 'educational conference' approach was beginning to pay off.

The momentum for the War Memorial Hall meeting had come from the Dublin WTS on the initiative of Anthony Coughlan, who had taken over the secretarial role, and was editing the newsletter Tuairisc. In retrospect it could be argued that he and I should have been better co-ordinated; we were working quite independently, with the present writer trying to build up a broad-based political understanding of non-violent political philosophy throughout Ireland, including an attempt to regenerate the co-operative movement, while AC was concentrating on the Achilles heel of Unionism, civil rights, setting up the June 1966 Maghera meeting which led to the War Memorial Hall meeting and the setting up of the NICRA(19).

Our thinking in mid-1967 is encapsulated in the reports of the June meeting of the 3 Wolfe Tone Societies, Dublin, Belfast and Cork, which was broad-based, had many visitors, and generated some political euphoria(20). With hindsight however, it is evident that the Northern Republican Clubs were not fully politicised to the extent of being ready to take up, with understanding, the challenge of how to support the NICRA actively, while keeping the national unity objective on the back burner. They were open to subversion by Mac Stiofain's militarism, which became easy once Unionism responded to the Civil Rights demands with guns and armoured vehicles, as they did with the B-Specials in August 1969.

In an almost incredible error of judgment, Cathal Goulding had in 1967 given Mac Stiofain a 'military intelligence' role in the North, in effect giving him carte blanche to undermine the politicisation process which was going on via the Republican Clubs, and lay the basis for the subsequent rapid emergence of the Provisionals, as a military response to the 1969 B-Special pogroms, which was of course exactly what the Unionist hard-core leadership wanted(21).

Our strategy might have succeeded had the build-up of the Civil Rights been allowed to proceed with a slow but steady strengthening of the organisation, cross-community, with Trade Union participation. Instead the pace was forced, a key factor being the January 1969 Peoples Democracy march on Derry, which 'trailed the coat' through a series of Antrim Protestant towns, and led to the Burntollet ambush. This polarised the situation into sectarian mode, pushed the Civil Rights demands into the Catholic ghettoes, and stimulated the August 1969 pogrom led by the heavily-armed B-Specials, which triggered the process that led to the

Provisionals, giving Mac Stiofain what he wanted, and incidentally what the Unionists and the British military establishment also wanted: a military campaign which could be contained, with the working people of the North increasingly divided on sectarian lines, perpetuating British rule.

In the event however the political process via Civil Rights was shattered, and the call went out for arms to 'defend the people', instead of a political call to disarm the B-Specials and enable a Civil Rights environment to be established. Voices such as mine, and those of Anthony Coughlan and Desmond Greaves, which called for the latter, were increasingly disregarded. The Provisional process set in inexorably, fuelled by fringe-Fianna Fail support, the key actors being Haughey, Blaney and Boland, supported by Dublin speculative property-developers, whose corrupt links with Fianna Fail politics Dublin left-republican activists were beginning to expose(22).

I have to conclude, self-critically, that I had totally underestimated the strength and persistence of the Fenian 'physical force as principle' culture, and likewise the strength and persistence of the loyalist culture of violence on which the maintenance of their hegemony depended. The people concerned were, and still are, all working people, whose objective interests, under normal circumstances, should coincide. Had we succeeded in building a Civil Rights environment in the North, without violent disruption, it would over time have been possible for working people irrespective of religion to identify their common interests. The Provisional decades have made this more difficult, but we must keep trying to identify areas of common ground, and build on them.

During all this period of intense political activity, I managed during working hours to contribute to the development of the use of the Aer Lingus computer in techno-economic analysis of projected investment decisions, and I discovered that this in fact existed as a discipline known as Operations Research (OR), which JD Bernal during the war had had a hand in initiating. In Aer Lingus we initiated the development of OR as a network within Ireland, and participated internationally, to the extent that we were able to pull the 1972 International Federation of OR Societies (IFORS) conference to Dublin(23).

After the movement was split at the (postponed '1969') Ard Feis in January 1970, I was increasingly marginalised politically, and I began to give priority attention to building up an applied-science consultancy business, working mainly at the interface between Trinity College and industry, initially with the Statistics Department, and then later across the spectrum with the Applied-Research Consultancy Group(24). This was a learning process, and it is possible to conclude that the creative role of the third-level system in economic development is concentrated in the postgraduate system, primarily at the MSc level, and that the uptake of creative graduates into economic life can be enhanced if small innovative firms are encouraged to start up, to take the results of college-based research towards effective implementation.

It was possible to keep in touch politically, with the Left and with the Labour Party, though these contacts on the whole were not fruitful. The Wolfe Tone Society went into decline. There was a dearth of publication outlets for critical or theoretical papers. Some reflective synthesis which I did, and presented to a Wolfe Tone Society meeting, were taken up by a Trotskyist gadfly journal; a reflective political publication by JJ had similarly been taken up by another Trotskyist publisher(25) in the 1960s.

Continuing in this mode in the 1980s and 1990s it became evident that the innovative enterprise process needed regional enhancement, if over-concentration of population in Dublin was to be avoided; concepts like the 'regional technopole' emerged into development economics thinking. This process however needs to be linked to genuine devolved regional government(26), and this issue remains very much on the agenda, being a major principled concern of the increasingly influential Green party, as well as a pragmatic requirement arising from the peace process in the North, under the Good Friday Agreement, with its provision for cross-border linkages.

The final collapse of the USSR and discredit of the central-State model of socialist planning was a focus of comment(27). There were many episodes at the interface between science, technology and business, mostly related to human aspects of the innovation process(28). The Maastricht and subsequent Nice referenda focused critical thinking on European issues(29), though the field was muddied by the increasingly strident intervention of the 'Catholic Right', on issues like divorce. The increasing importance of the Internet made it feasible to address more aggressively the 'science and society'(30) issue in the national context. The ongoing Northern problem and the roads leading eventually to the Good Friday Agreement were, I think, influenced by some of our analyses(31). The ongoing role of science in society, the crisis in the Left and the perceived need for a 'left-green convergence' remain top of the agenda(32).

Concluding Theses

What follows is my current (2005) summary of what I see as the lessons learned from the foregoing experience, and a few political suggestions which maybe our successors may take up.

1. The accumulated military experience of activists in an armed movement makes adaptation to subsequent democratic politics extremely difficult, though it can sometimes be done.

2. The State should be primarily a referee not a player in the economic game.

3. The players in the economic game can be individuals or organisations, but in the latter case the Board of Directors needs to be democratically accountable to all who depend on the firm, not simply to the owners of capital, a fortiori if the latter are remote. This is the central problem of the Left: how to bring this about politically.

4. Economic games can be played at the local, regional national and international levels, ideally under fair trade conditions, with democratic control by workers, consumers, suppliers, all being owners, at all levels. The 'core-fringe' development problem, in post-imperial situations, is how to set up the 'fair trade' rules, and how to foster the 'know-how', or 'enterprise', factor of production(33) in

'fringe' regions/nations. There is a role here for a co-operative approach to the availability of credit, in the manner foreshadowed earlier by JJ(12). Credit should be accessible, under locally-defined 'terms and conditions', on the basis of consumer demand and available productive know-how, rather than possession of land or capital as collateral.

5. Strong local and regional democratic government, within national and international frameworks, is an essential part of the State referee role, as a provider of education for cultural (including technical) competence, laws of contract, justice etc. Government by in-groups, defined in terms of religion, ethnicity or colour, are incompatible with justice: equal rights for all citizens is essential. Ireland, India, South Africa and Israel/Palestine share common features derived from pathologies rooted in British imperial culture(34).

6. Means must be found to prevent the above democratic process from being subverted by the type of corruption generated by private property in land, and the added value generated by re-zoning. As an interim measure, compulsory purchase by the local authority at the prior price, followed by leasing to the re-zoned users, would capture the added value for the community. In the longer term, the principle of private ownership of land needs to be questioned. Land should be owned by the whole people through the State, and leased out as a valuable resource for socially-defined use.

7. Economic development must increasingly become dependent on sustainable resources. This will require increasing scientific understanding of the properties of materials, of organisms, and of the production process, especially the interaction of the latter with human and organisational factors.

Notes and References
1. JJ tried to address this problem in his *Irish Agriculture in Transition* (Blackwell, 1951), in particular with his outline of the Orpen model in the final chapter.
2. See JJ's Albert Kahn Reports: the main one based on the 1914-15 work which concentrates on India, and the additional 1916 report on *French wartime food production*.
3. See JJ's addendum on co-op managers to the 1923 Agriculture Commission Report, also his addendum on the 1926 Prices Report on his French experience.
4. The background to this is in the 1920s Garnier letters.
5. Aspects of JJ's support for the co-operative movement are documented in the 1920s Plunkett House module of the hypertext, and in the 1920s Barrington module. See also his *Groundwork of Economics* which was distilled from his Barrington material. In Chapter 3 of this work JJ innovatively introduced 'know-how' as a key fourth factor of production, additional to the traditional 'land, labour and capital'.
6. JJ's 1934 *Nemesis of Economic Nationalism* emphasised the importance of the primary agricultural producer being adequately rewarded, thus generating a home market for industry.
7. JJ attempted in his 1938 wheat paper to argue against self-sufficiency in wheat, demolishing the then current arguments in favour which were based on a flawed analysis of late 18th century economics. This paper was unpublished, but he used it subsequently in his Seanad speeches during the war.

8. JJ's Seanad speeches from 1938 onwards are available in the 1930s and 1940s Public Service modules of the hypertext.

9. Aspects of his vision were to be found in RM Burke's co-operative estate and in the Dovea farm in Tipperary; he attempted to integrate the experience in his *Irish Agriculture in Transition*, particularly in the Orpen chapter.

10. JJ's relationship with the Irish Association is best overviewed from Appendix 9; it was his way of promoting an all-Ireland view in the North.

11. The Kells Ingram Farm saga is treated initially in policy terms via JJ's contribution to the post-emergency agriculture commission, and then later via the 1950s TCD Board records..

12. JJ's *Bishop Berkeley's Querist in Historical Perspective* was published by Dun Dealgain Press in 1970. JJ attempted to develop his *Consumer Demand as the Basis of Credit*, based on Berkeley, but this remained unpublished.

13. The emergence of the Promethean Society is treated in the 1940s political module of the hypertext.

14. The 'science and society' problem begins to be treated in the 1940s and 1950s theme modules of the hypertext. I also begin in the 1950s to recognise it in its socio-technical and techno-economic aspects.

15. The political isolation of the 1950s aspirant Left is treated in the 1950s political module of the hypertext.

16. My initial approach on my return from London is outlined in my 1964 memo. I have also abstracted the Wolfe Tone Society records in the hypertext.

17. I had occasion to comment on the *1964 OECD Report* in the December 1966 issue of *Development*.

18. I have recorded some of the details of this process in the 1960s RJ political module of the hypertext.

19. The basic Maghera agenda is outlined in *Tuairisc 7*; I have also abstracted the approach to Civil Rights via the Desmond Greaves diaries.

20. This is reflected in the June 1967 conference the 3 WTSs.

21. I have treated this in my notes on *Mac Stiofain's Memoirs* (Gordon Cremonesi, 1975) in the hypertext.

22. I go into some detail, as best I can, in a very confused situation, in the 1969 RJ political module, but perhaps the best insight into the Fianna Fail urban land speculation aspect is given in Justin O'Brien's *Arms Trial*.

23. I have made available some notes on the 1972 IFORS conference in the hypertext.

24. Some of this work has been described in Julian Mac Airt's book *Operations Research in Ireland* (Mercier, 1988).

25. My paper 'On the Problem of Democratic Unity' was published in *The Ripening of Time* #9, March 1978. Extracts are available in Appendix 10. JJ's *Irish Economic Headaches* had been published in 1966 by Aisti Eireannacha (Rayner O'Connor Lysaght).

26. I developed ideas around the 'Regional Technopole' model at a Constitution Club seminar in November 1986.

27. The crisis in the USSR in 1989 prompted me to record some thoughts on Gorbachov prior to his fall.

28. I have summarised some of the highlights in the 1990s socio-technical module of the hypertext.

29. It was impossible to decouple the divorce and Maastricht referenda, and this led to tensions among those critical of the trend into European integration. I have treated this in the mid-90s political module of the hypertext.

30. I develop this in 'outreach' mode, perhaps unconsciously in JJ's footsteps, and also in more specialised mode, in the 1990s science and society module of the hypertext.

31. My 1988 paper on Irish national identity to the Ulster Quaker Peace Committee may have contributed some leavening ideas; likewise perhaps the somewhat apocryphal 1986 Labour Party paper. More influential perhaps was the 1992 Opsahl submission, invoked by Andy Pollak's initiative.

32. Can the 'soft' Plunkett-Russell model, fortified by emergent regional policy ideas, be adapted to Green Party ecological thinking, and enhanced with understanding of the nature of the State to 'harden' it enough to be effective politically, without repeating the Stalinist/Fenian excesses? Could this perhaps be based on my Culliton critique, as submitted to the CII? Might the mcp98 paper be of use in developing the political angle?

33. See JJ's 1926 *Groundwork in Economics*, Chapter 3, where he (I think innovatively) introduces 'enterprise' as a 'factor of production' along with land, labour and capital.

34. See *Partition in Ireland, India and Pakistan - Theory and Practice*, TG Fraser, Macmillan, London, 1984. (TCD Library)

Appendix 1: The Family Background

The Johnston family in Tyrone goes back to the 1620s. My father JJ attempted to trace them in detail, and came up with a probable source in Scotland: Annandale in Dumfries. JJ claimed to have identified one ancestor who was involved inside the Derry walls in 1690.

In JJ's family research notebook(1) there is a family tree going back to Samuel Johnston, of Reskecorr (alternatively Reaskcorr, Drumnafern), Co Tyrone, born 1748, who married one Jean MacKeown on 9 May 1779. They had two sons, John and Samuel; the latter was my great-grandfather; he was born in 1789, and married Nancy McLean who died in 1850 aged about 50. They had a family of four, my grandfather John being the youngest, being born on 6 July 1834, according to my father's notes. The eldest, Alec, went to the USA aged 17. Then came Jane, who died unmarried. The third was Samuel, born 1831, died 1912, no issue. I can thus claim to be the fourth youngest son in succession, reaching back to 1748 in four generative steps.

There is a letter among JJ's papers from his Uncle Henry, dated October 2 1913, from an address North Arm PO, Vancouver, BC. It refers to the difficulty of getting agricultural labouring work; he had got 10 weeks work making hay; he had come to Vancouver the previous June to see his daughter, and then he had gone working on the railroads. He wanted a decent job at home or in Dublin. He must have got wind of JJ getting Fellowship in TCD and thought he could fix something. He said he was 'too old for this country'. This must have been a brother of my grandmother Mary Geddes. I have no record of any outcome.

My grandfather John Johnston retired from being a schoolteacher in 1897; my initial conjecture that he was born in the early 1830s is supported by my father's notebook as above. He spent most of his life in or near Donaghmore, and there is on record one of that name in the Presbyterian parish of Castlecaulfield. He would have moved into the neighbourhood from his father's place at Drumnafern when he became a teacher in Tullyarran in 1855, some 5 years after his mother's death.

Among the registered members of the parish in April 1855 in Castlecaulfield was one John Johnston, with an associated Mrs Johnston (no first name given)(2). There was also a Joseph Johnston, a Samuel Johnston and an Andrew Johnston on the same date, each associated with a Mrs Johnston. There was also a John Johnston a member of the Committee in 1878. Both these John Johnston entries are consistent with being my grandfather. The earlier reference, associated with a Mrs Johnston, suggests the possibility of a first wife, who died, before he married Mary Geddes. My father in his notes however has no reference to this possibility.

There was a John Johnston a teacher in Tullyarran school from 1855 to 1876, who also gave evening lessons to farm labourers. There is also a record of a John Johnston as the principal of Kilnaslee school from 1881 to his retirement in 1897. These were indeed the same person(3), but there is no record of how the gap was filled, though there is a record of a temporary John Johnston at the estate school at Parkanaur, during the Tullyarran period. Maybe he spent time at Parkanaur? Or went back to farming? The records, according to Rafferty, are somewhat incomplete. The most probable explanation is that he gave up teaching to concentrate on the farm for a time after he got married, and then went back to teaching when the need arose to support the education of his expanding family.

These schools are all in reach, by walking, of the Johnston home at Tomagh, the Kilnaslee school being the nearest. The Tomagh house still exists in part, as an outhouse on a farm owned by John Kelly. It is a typical earth-walled long cottage, with small windows, originally thatched, but later roofed with corrugated steel sheeting. The modern farmhouse is named Johnstonville, in honour of the earlier tenants of the farm, and the family is still remembered locally, though they moved elsewhere during the 1900s. I go into this further below. I am indebted to John Kelly the present owner for a photograph(4), which shows the house as it was in the 1950s, more or less complete, as an outhouse in the farmyard of the modern house.

In the Oxford University 1896 matriculation record for James, John's eldest son, the father's occupation is described as farmer, while for the later Oxford records of John (1901) and William (1907) he is described as ex- or retired teacher. He died, according to my father's notes, on 26/12/1909.

My grandfather married my grandmother Mary Geddes, age given as 20, of Skea, daughter of James Geddes, farmer, on November 28 1873. At this time my grandfather was 39.(5). This calls into question the 1855 Mrs Johnston who is in the Castlecaulfield record, though Mary Geddes could have been a second wife. I remember my grandmother in the mid-1930s when she was living in Dublin with my aunt Anne; she died on 13/03/1939. She was born on 24/08/1854 and so was 19 when she married my grandfather, and he was 39. He was thus much older, and could have been married before, though this is not in accordance with my sister's recollection of the family lore, nor is it in my father's notes. My sister was born in 1916, six years after he died, and never knew him.

The eldest son James was born on 24/11/1874 and the address where he was born is given as Donaghmore in the Oxford record, with the father living at Tomagh at the time of matriculation (1896); he was in Oxford as a postgraduate, having taken his primary degree in Queens Galway.

Elizabeth, a sister of my grandmother Mary Geddes, married Joe Loughrin; they lived at Killygarvan near Cookstown; there were 4 children of which two died; the survivors were Sophie, who ran the Killygarvan farm and remained in touch with JJ until she died in the 1960s, and Mina who married an Acheson. There were five brothers in the Acheson family, Douglas, Sandy, Harry, Morris and Walter, and one sister Winnie(5).

A sister of Joe Loughrin, Annie, married one Fred Hobson, and by that channel I believe there may be a family connection with Bulmer Hobson, though I have not traced this.

John Johnston of Tullyarran school, it would seem, had a radical outlook, in that he was prepared to give literacy classes to farm labourers, in addition to his work in the school(3). The school at Tullyarran is still standing, and is still in occasional use as a mission hall. It was closed as a school in 1904, having been open since 1824 or earlier. It was originally built by the landlord on the basis of subscriptions. It became part of the national school system in 1848, with Joseph Acheson the Presbyterian Minister as manager. John Johnston was the third teacher in the sequence.

Appendix 1: The Family Background

The Kilnaslee school was set up in 1820 and was connected with the Kildare Place Society. The school declined in the 1850s and was closed, but reopened in 1864 under the National Board, and John Johnston succeeded Samuel McCausland as Principal in 1881, retiring in 1897, although Rafferty seems to have some doubt regarding his Principal status. Maybe for a period it was a one-teacher school(3).

A possible explanation of the gap is that when he left Tullyarran in 1876, having married Mary Geddes, he decided to stay in Tomagh and work the farm full-time. This would tally with the Oxford record for James. Then when the boys needed schooling he went back to teaching in Kilnaslee.

The eldest son James was born on November 24 1874, then there was a daughter Mary Ann born on March 13 1877, but who died when small. The second son Samuel Alexander was born on December 25 1880, the third John on April 15 1883. Then came 'Harry' (William Henry) on December 17 1885, then William on May 13 1888. My father Joe was born on August 2 1890, and then Anne on November 10 1897. They were well spaced, which enabled the financial load of their education to be spread out over a long time, with the elder ones subsidising the younger from salaried jobs.(6)

According to my sister Dr Maureen Carmody they all went to Dungannon Royal School (DRS). They travelled in by train from Kilnaslee Halt; it is in walking distance of Tomagh. There was for a time a girls school associated with DRS, and Anne went to this for a time; the records however of this school are lost. She subsequently went to Alexandra College in Dublin, before going on to Trinity College.

Most if not all got scholarships, both to school, and on to college(7). Joe went to TCD, and John went to Oxford, as did William. James went to Galway and then to Oxford. Where did Sam and Harry go? Edinburgh, Dublin and Galway are all possible; JJ mentioned Edinburgh in this context, in one of his Seanad speeches, in support of the right to educate abroad. My sister however thinks one or other of them went to the College of Surgeons in Dublin. Both anyway did medical degrees; Sam went into practice in Newcastle-on-Tyne, where Harry joined him later. Harry moved to London after Sam's death from tuberculosis, in the early 1920s. The others, apart from Joe, ended up in Indian Civil Service.

Let me place on record here in outline some details of the Johnston uncles and cousins, and their locations, with a view to weaving them into the demography.

Indian Civil Service
James; died 31/03/37, was somewhat alcoholic and hypochondriac; married one Alma Sturton, known as 'Alma senior', who was upper-crust English. After retirement he wrote books critical of British rule in India, comparing it to pre-Reform England. There was litigation between him and the Indian Civil Service relating to this, according to my sister.

James's and Alma's eldest was Alan, who died in 2000, after a decade in a retirement home near Benburb. He had run a transport business in South Africa, served in the war, farmed in Laois, run a motor repair business, and ended his days again farming in Tyrone, helping his cousin Sophie Loughrin with the Killygarvin farm in her declining years(8). There were also Cynthia, Maurice, Alma 'junior' and

Anthony (Tim). Alan and Tim served in the 1939-45 war, the latter published a book, *Tattered Battlements*, on his experiences in the air defence of Malta.

John; married one Gladys Lullarbond (? I am here depending on my father's handwriting in his notebook), from the Isle of Man (according to my sister); he also died in the 1930s, or perhaps early 1940s; they had two daughters, Monica and Pam; after retiring from India they lived in Jersey. Monica was a ballerina with the Ballet Joos.

William; married one Ruby Mitchell, who (according to my sister) was Scottish; he retired in the 1940s; Ruby died, also their family Sheila and Peter when small. He lived into his 80s in Blackrock; died I think in late 1960s, before Joe. He lived with us in the Glen near Drogheda for a while in the 40s; Joe had the idea he might manage the farm, but William never took to it; and then fell out with JJ; over some issue which I never discovered. For a long time they were not on speaking terms.

Medical practice in England

Harry; married one Hilda Johnson who was English; they had two daughters Joyce and Christine.

Sam; died of TB circa 1923; my sister thinks perhaps earlier, when they lived in a house called Santoy in Ranelagh. I have no record of the widow, nor apparently had JJ when he did his 1945 notebook. However according to my sister, his widow Lizzie carried on working as a nurse, presumably in Newcastle, where Sam had practiced. The three sons (Tommy, Alec and Geddes) fostered with our family in the 1920s; JJ fixed them up with jobs as best he could; Alec joined the British Army in the 30s and had a 'good war' as a tank instructor; Tommy went into advertising, married one Dorothy Davis; there is a daughter Anne who went to Stranmillis. Geddes went to the Argentine, to a Mahaffey property, as a gaucho; came back for the war, joined the RAF and was shot down.

Careers in Ireland

My father Joe after Dungannon Royal School (DRS) went to Trinity College Dublin (TCD), where he studied classics and ancient history (1906-1910), winning two large gold medals for outstanding degree performance He became a Scholar in Classics in 1909. After taking his degree in 1910 he went on the Oxford, where he took a further degree in 1912. He then returned to Trinity where he successfully sat the Fellowship examination in 1913, being among the last to sit the difficult and broad-spectrum Fellowship examination. Subsequently Fellows were elected primarily on the basis of published work.

My aunt Ann went on from DRS girls school to board at Alexandra College in Dublin, from which she later went to Trinity College, studying law, entering the Civil Service in or about 1917. She is in record in a group photograph of the Gaelic League conference in 1912 which is on display in the Douglas Hyde centre near Frenchpark, which she attended perhaps as an undergraduate or from school.

My Mother's Family

My mother's father Robert Wilson, before he married my grandmother Jennie Dunphy, had been married to an Armstrong, by whom he had one daughter

Kathleen, who married George Harpur. There were six children, Ernest, Vi, Edith, Douglas, Grace and Brian; Ernest was an engineer in Mesopotamia; Douglas ordained as an Anglican priest; he and Grace went to England, and Vi married Billy Empey who farmed near Stradbally in Laois. Brian became a journalist in London, on the Daily Mail. Kathleen remained living in Blackrock until her death in the 50s. We remained reasonably well in touch with that side of the family.

Robert Wilson was a teacher in Keenagh Co Longford. He met my grandmother Jenny Dunphy, who was a civil servant in London, when she was on holiday in Longford. My mother in her papers had marriage certificates going back in matrilineal mode: Martin Dunphy, Jenny's father, married one Clara Cripps in 1850, and the latter's mother was one Jane Pond, who married Joseph Cripps in 1825 in Newington, Surrey.

There were three sisters, of which my mother was the eldest; Clare, Isabel (Isa) and Florence (Florrie). There were two brothers, Harry and Eddie. The former volunteered for the war on 10/09/1915 and died as a prisoner in Germany on 27/06/1916. My mother retained his voluntary recruiting record, which had been issued in a format suitable for framing and hanging on the wall. She had written a note of his death on the back. Eddie became an engineer, taking his degree in UCD, he married Dorothy Young, worked for a while in Rugby, but had a nervous breakdown, in the late 20s, and went into a mental home where he died.

Isa married Bob Nesbitt and they lived in Cookstown, and then later in Belfast, emigrating to Canada however in the 50s. According to my mother, as regaled by her to my ex-wife Máirín, they were under pressure from their neighbours in the Antrim Road area of Belfast, where they lived, due to the fact that my cousin Ian had married a Catholic. My sister however is inclined to dismiss this as apocryphal.

Florrie married Jack Young, Dorothy Young's brother. The Youngs were a landed family in Laois. Jack served in the war (he was at Gallipoli), and ended up working as a buyer of barley for Perry's Brewery in Rathdowney. When Uncle Jack returned from the war, he found the estate gone; his brother Frank had mismanaged it and sold it in Jack's absence.

There were contemporary cousins John Young and Ian Nesbitt whom I knew when small, unlike on my father's side of the family, where all the cousins were older and inaccessible.

My mother Clara, or Claire as she preferred, trained as a schoolteacher in the Church of Ireland training college, here she was a King's Scholar 1906-08; she taught for a time in the national school at Ballivor Co Meath, and was issued with her Diploma parchment in 1911; she kept this among her papers. I understand from her that she had attempted unsuccessfully to introduce some teaching of Irish, but was blocked by the rector, her manager.

The courtship and marriage between my father and my mother Claire Wilson took place while JJ was in College; they were married in 1914. Robert Wilson was a Mason, and during the courtship to please him JJ joined the Longford lodge, of which my maternal grandfather was the Grand Master. He subsequently resigned, in good standing, and never subsequently had anything to do with the Masons.

After they were married they went on a world tour, thanks to the Albert Kahn Travelling Fellowship(9). During this tour, they somewhat adventurously parted company, with JJ doing his socio-economic field-work in India, while my mother went from India to Australia, where she spent some time with her aunt Maude and uncle Harry, her mother Jenny's brother and sister(10). She then joined my father again in China. This all took place in 1914-15, when the First World War was raging.

My mother can I believe claim a distant relationship with President Woodrow Wilson, whose family came from Co Tyrone near Strabane. Robert Wilson had earlier Donegal connections (they were known as 'Wilsons of the Tops', but the background was never talked about; there was an aura of mystery). I believe that she got a visit to the White House during the Wilson presidency out of it, presumably at the tail end of their Albert Kahn world tour, but I have been unable to pin this down.

JJ's Family: My Sister

My sister Maureen was born in 1916; she was schooled in the Hall School, Monkstown, Glengara Park, Dundalk Grammar School, and then went to TCD where she studied medicine, taking a combined 'Med Mod' degree, which included Honours Natural Science. In 1939 she married Dermot Carmody, the second son of Dean Carmody, of Down. The latter had been a friend of Alice Stopford Green, and had a library containing most of the significant books relating to the national revival and Home Rule(11). Dermot studied divinity in TCD and had been ordained. For a while he served in Enniskillen Cathedral, and then served in Christ Church, Dublin, from which situation he married my sister. They lived initially in Sandymount, moving in or about 1942 to Ballinaclough, south of Nenagh in Co Tipperary, where Dermot had obtained the parish, along with that of the more remote and mountainous Templederry.(12).

In or about 1951 Dermot got the parish of Nenagh town, and they moved to the Nenagh rectory, which was initially an old terraced town house near the church; then later a new rectory was built in the church grounds. There they lived, until Dermot died suddenly, in September 1966, leaving Maureen a 'clergy widow', though with an extensive private medical practice. With great resilience, she built herself a house at Stoneyhigh, on the northern fringe of Nenagh town, from which she developed her practice for the next couple of decades(13). In 1970 she built an extension 'granny flat' in which my father and mother spend their last few years. This coincided with her active support for the 'Common Market Defence Campaign', which she chaired locally. This was the basis for the rebuilding of the Labour Party in Nenagh; there has been a Labour TD there for most of the time since.

Some time after my mother died in 1974, my sister moved back to a small town house in Nenagh, where she carried on her medical practice in semi-retirement, as well as a local political life with her Labour Party cronies, until in 2001 she had a fall, and had to go into sheltered accommodation in Dublin. In October of that year she had a stroke, and died in 2003.

Appendix 1: The Family Background

Conclusion: the Family Statistics

It is possible to compare the statistics of my father's generation and mine as regards where people end up living. Of my father's generation, the vast majority were associated with Britain and the Empire, some being 'empire-builders' in the classic mode. Of my own generation, there is just myself and my sister; between us we have 7 children, most of whom (five, or perhaps six) have made, or are in process of making, their careers in Ireland. Thus the decision of my father to make his career in Dublin in 1913, and to orient his thinking towards the needs of the emerging Irish nation, while taking an uncompromising Protestant stand, has paid off. This is a message perhaps worthy of consideration by contemporary Northern Protestants who are still paranoid about 'Rome Rule'.

Notes and References

1. This notebook, dated 16/08/1945, and entitled *History of the Johnstons*, is in folder 67 of JJ's papers.

2. Adrian McLernon the Presbyterian Minister has produced a booklet on the history of the parish of Castlecaulfield, in which this is to be found. He has also attempted to look into the question of the marriage and burial records of John Johnston, but without success, the records being incomplete. There are no relevant Johnston gravestones in the Castlecaulfield churchyard. It was often the practice to leave graves unmarked.

3. See *At School in Donaghmore*, produced by PJ Rafferty of the Donaghmore Historical Society. There is also a letter seeking financial support from one James Stern, of Balnagor, written to JJ in 1929, in which he claims JJ's attention by having been schooled by JJ's father in Tullyarran. This I have kept in Folder 66 of JJ's paper.

4. This photo, and photos of the remains of the other houses where the family lived after leaving Tomagh, are given both in hypertext Appendix 1 and in the 1900s family module.

5. I am indebted to William O'Kane of Heritage World (then at Dungannon, now moved to Donaghmore) for locating my grandfather's marriage certificate and death certificate. I am indebted to Winnie Acheson for most of this family background information; she got much of it from my aunt Ann in the 1960s; also to Sandy Acheson's widow 'Paddy', who lives in Benburb.

6. I am also indebted to Willie O'Kane and Eoin Kerr of Heritage World for these dates; they agree with those in JJ's notebook. More detail is also given in the hypertext 1900s module, in particular as regards the elder brothers.

7. I am indebted to Norman Cardwell (16 Trewmount Road, Killymahon, Dungannon BT71_6RL, phone 01868-722-510) the Dungannon Royal School archivist, for much of what follows elating to school careers.

8. I published an obituary for Alan in the *Dungannon Courier* of September 20 2000, in which I gave some of the family background. It was titled 'The Johnstons of Tomagh'.

9. See Appendix 3, and the related supportive background modules in the hypertext, for an outline of this tour.

10. My mother kept a diary of this epic journey. This and JJ's letters to her in Australia from India, Java and Hong Kong are preserved in Folder 68 of JJ's papers. I have abstracted my mother's diary in the 1910s module of this 'family' thread in the hypertext.

11. These Carmody books are mostly now with my nephew Pat Carmody, who is a Canon of the Church of Ireland in the parish of Mullingar, at the time of writing (December 2002). The Alice Stopford Green books were influential on JJ when young, and I have some notes on this aspect in the hypertext, beginning with a review of RB McDowell's biography (Allen Figgis, Dublin, 1967).

12. I have touched on this in the <u>1940s family</u> module of the hypertext.
13. I continue to treat the evolution of my sister's family in the <u>1950s</u> and <u>1960s</u> hypertext family modules; this constitutes an opportunity to comment on rural Protestant culture, its problems and opportunities.

Appendix 2: Trinity College Politics

To get the full flavour of the role of the Board of TCD in its long history, it is necessary to go to sources such as RB McDowells 'Trinity College 1592-1952'. In the current context I have scanned the Board minutes, which are accessible to readers in the TCD Library MS room, and identified references either to JJ directly, or to entities with which he was associated.

There is also a record of the meetings of the Junior Fellows, who were represented on the Board by two of their number, usually the most senior. I have scanned these minutes also, and interspersed some episodes from this source into the common chronology. It becomes apparent as the decades roll on that increasing frustration at the junior level leads to an enhanced role for the Junior Fellows meetings, leading eventually to the constitutional reform movement in the 1950s associated with AJ McConnell, subsequently to become Provost.

It will become apparent that JJ was in effect a pioneer or advance-guard of this 'new wave' of academic reform, though he was too early actually to 'ride it', and when it broke, he found himself sidelined.

JJ's first encounter with the TCD Board, apart from his undergraduate period, was in the context of the Fellowship examinations; he was among the last to become a Fellow by this mode. Shortly afterwards they changed the procedure, to submission of published work. There was perceived to be a glut of polymath Fellows, whose promotion prospects looked increasingly unrealistic.

The feeling of the Board at the time is summarised in a letter from the then Provost Anthony Traill (being ill in bed), urging that the Board '...give notice now that no examination for Fellowship will be held next year 1914... it is absolutely necessary to put a stop to the congestion of non-tutor Fellows...'.

There had been concern on this matter among the Junior Fellows, who in March 1913 had held a series of meetings at which concern was expressed at the excessive number of new Fellows coming in via the examination process. They wanted to get Senior Fellows to retire, and to reform the election process toward dependence on published work. There was also concern that the flow inwards via the examination process would be unrelated to the nature of the specialist teaching requirements: broadly speaking, too much classics and not enough science.

There are indications in his first decade as Fellow that JJ was someone who took up good causes, like student representation, a co-operative store for students living in College, and payment for the College servants ('skips')(1).

On October 18 1913 the question arose of having a co-operative food store in the College; JJ had a hand in this(2). JJ had by this time published his *Civil War in Ulster*; it is perhaps surprising that no echo of this seems to have reached the Board minutes(3).

JJ also is on record as applying for leave of absence to take up the Albert Kahn Travelling Fellowship, which he held in 1914 and 1915(4). Despite his active development of economics as his preferred discipline, his main academic role was as Assistant to Dr WA Goligher in Ancient History and Classical Archaeology. For a while he lectured the Indian Civil Service candidates. He was appointed a Tutor in 1917.

During his first decade he was a regular attender at the Junior Fellows meetings, and was associated with attempts to reform the tutorial system, and the process of election to Fellowship. There were links with politics outside the College in that the Fellows supported the Board in the latter's attempts to ensure that Government support for TCD was retained under the Home Rule Act.

Shortly before the Rising, on March 7 1916, JJ was mentioned as having put in an application that the Bursar should deal with the DU Co-op for groceries, and this was referred to the Bursar's discretion. The Co-op was clearly high on his current agenda, and there is evidence elsewhere that he regarded it as a pilot project in economic organisation(5).

The 1920s is a period when JJ was as yet not much into College politics, though he does get an occasional mention in the Board minutes, primarily in the context of his attempt to qualify himself for a role in the nascent School of Political Economy and Commerce. This however he did mostly by his extern work: service on Government commissions, the Barrington lectures and so on. He also tried to improve his academic qualifications, in that he attended a course in London School of Economics, for which he sought expenses at the November 21 1921 Board Meeting. This application was deferred until December 3, when he was re-appointed as Assistant to Professor Goligher (Ancient History and Classical Archaeology), while also receiving a slice of a supplementary grant, of which £60 went to Professor Bastable towards the new School of Political Economy and Commerce, and also £30 to JJ for work in this new School, as well as £5 to JJ for work in the History department.

As prospective input to the discussions on the supplementary grant, which was a spin-off from the Treaty negotiations, the Junior Fellows produced a report, from a drafting committee consisting of Canning, Luce and JJ. This was set up on a motion of JJ, seconded by Alton, at the meeting on Nov 27 1921, and reported on Dec 5, the report being adopted by the Junior Fellows, but apparently the Board had already on Dec 3 done the carve-up, so this work was in vain. This series of three Junior Fellows meetings in November and December were in fact all one meeting with adjournments. They covered a series of issues, including the problem of how to simplify the electoral procedure of Junior Fellows to the Board, and the role of Fellows in Honours teaching. These do not seem to have reached the Board. On can sense frustration(6) among the reformers.

In 1926 JJ got permission from the Board, slightly grudgingly, to take up a Rockefeller Fellowship, which brought him to France to study the price-differential between the farm gate prices and prices paid by consumers for food. He had in mind the need to develop an efficient co-operative marketing system, and this was the theme of much of his extern work(7).

In the mid-1920s there were again moves to set up a School of Commerce, and JJ by his outside work for the Government(8), and by research into retail pricing supported by the Rockefeller Foundation, felt that he deserved to be associated with this. Yet when the Board set up a School Committee in 1925, JJ was overlooked, in favour of Goligher, to whom he was still assistant lecturer in ancient history. He went on to publish his Rockefeller work in the SSISI in 1927. Nor did his *Groundwork in Economics*, a popularising book based on his 1920s Barrington Lectures, apparently count for anything.

Appendix 2: Trinity College Politics

Towards the end of the decade, in 1928, JJ was elected to represent the Junior Fellows on the Lectures Committee. I have not discovered what this implied, but I suspect it was a relatively routine process to do with scheduling and locations.

Then in 1929 the Board set up requirements for recruiting a Fellow in Economics, and arranged to do it by examination, imposing a strong theoretical bias. Extern examiners were selected, including initially Pigou, a world-figure in the domain, who however declined to act, being rightly suspicious of this obsolete procedure. The attempt to recruit for the Chair via a 'Fellowship by Examination' procedure then, rightly, sank without trace, but this episode introduced a delay in the emergence of a significant School of Commerce.

In the 1930s JJ became more involved in the College, eventually standing for the Senate and getting elected in 1938, but his relationship with the College authorities during the decade was under increasing tension. In 1932 they got around to setting up a School of Commerce, with JJ, Duncan and Constantia Maxwell lecturing, but as yet no Chair.

In 1934 the Commerce School Committee was extended to include outside experience, in the form of Dublin businessman JCM Eason, with whom JJ was actively involved via the SSISI. This I suspect represented JJ exerting his influence in making the School real-world oriented. It cut no ice with the Board however, because when he applied for a grant towards the publication of his critical *Nemesis of Economic Nationalism*, they cut back on his request, and imposed conditions. From correspondence which is on record in his papers, it is evident that to obtain even this, he had the threaten the Board with an appeal to the Visitors(9). He had aspired to publish his book with the weight of professorial status behind it; the Chair however went to Duncan.

During this time JJ had been farming near Drogheda; his ongoing economic laboratory was to run a 30-acre farm (the then norm), employing a man, and to keep the books. His insight into the economics of Irish agriculture gained by this means was unrivalled; he was recognised as a pioneering one-man Agricultural Institute by the professionals who followed in the 1950s and 60s (Dr Tom Walsh the Director of the Agricultural Institute showed his appreciation by coming to his funeral in 1972).

De Valera however had initiated the 'economic war', to the extent that some of the Irish people benefited from 'free beef' for a time, due to the collapse of the market. JJ's agricultural experiment was hit by this; he managed however to do a deal with the Board, based on actuarial calculations, to get an advance on his salary as Senior Fellow, to which he would be entitled from the time when two of his Board predecessors died off. There was a cryptic reference to this in the Board minutes, and I have a copy of the detailed letter which he submitted to the Bursar. He managed at the same time to link it with a criticism of the gerontocratic principle on which the College was run, and the iniquity of the promotional blocks put in the way of mid-career people.

As we have seen, Duncan got the Chair of Economics, and McDowell in his history assessed JJ as having fallen between the two stools of classics and economics, seeing his juniors get chairs before him, attributing JJ's incursion into farming to this cause. This is quite wrong; his incursion into farming was targeted at understanding real-world applied economics, and pre-dated his failure to get the

Economics chair by the best part of a decade. In the end a Chair in Applied Economics ('for present holder only') was created for him in 1939.

In 1937 and 1938 JJ took part in a series of Junior Fellows meetings which put on record a demand for a broadening of the basis for election of Provost; these later formed part of the basis for the McConnell Reforms of the 1950s. There was also at this time a hint of an abandonment of the seniority practice for co-opting Fellows to Senior status on the Board, and I suspect that this may have been encouraged by JJ's continuing 'enfant terrible' status, writing boat-rocking books and so on.

The 1940s began with JJ in the lead of the Junior Fellows, supportive of the democratic reform issues which came to fruition with the McConnell 'palace revolution' in the 1950s, but increasingly taking a back seat, as his accession to Board membership loomed on the horizon, finally taking place at the end of 1943 with the death of 'Matty' Fry.

In the late 1940s JJ's influence indicated the effect of 'new blood' in the gerontocracy; the first moves to develop a link with the Government took place, and money became available as a result of lobbying de Valera. The link with Magee was defended, despite obstructive moves by the Stormont Government. The School of Agriculture was strengthened, and staff was recruited in support of Statistics. There was a positive response to the national 150-year commemoration of 1798, and a proposal to form an Orange Lodge was rejected(10).

The Student Representative Council was strengthened by adopting a democratic constitution, which the Board accepted (the present writer RJ, then a student, had a hand in pushing this from below). There was continuing support for the all-Ireland Irish Students Association (in contrast to the grudging attitude of the NUI), and support for an all-Ireland Universities Council. Attempts by the British Colonial Office to gain access for recruitment were rebuffed.

During this, for JJ, 'golden decade' the basis was laid for what perhaps can be assessed as an important turning-point in his academic career: the Berkeley Bicentenary celebration, which was planned for 1953, and in which JJ gave a seminal paper on Berkeley as economist(11). Despite this, and his role of an advance guard of the 50s 'new wave' democratic reform movement, the next decade was to be one of increasing frustration, as the wave, in effect, broke over him, leaving him marginalised, though, as we shall see, he still had a positive role to play in the School of Agriculture, and in the episode of the Kells Ingram Farm.

The 1950s began with the Board responding to pressure from the Junior Fellows and taking further the negotiations with the de Valera Government. There were indications of Marshall Plan money becoming available for investment into agricultural research, and JJ had a hand in the early manoeuvrings of TCD to be in the running for a slice of the action.

This process however was interrupted by the deaths successively of Sir Robert Tate, being replaced by Parke, and then on February 19 1952 of Provost Alton, which opened up the battle for succession. This was won by AJ McConnell, from Ballymena, the Professor of Applied Maths, who was known personally to de Valera. The 'reform party' was now firmly in the lead, and proceeded to ensure that all the influential posts went to Junior Fellows and recent Board recruits, with the 'old guard' being sidelined, a source of experience perhaps to be called upon from time to time, but no longer calling the shots(12). .

In this context JJ got to be the keeper of the Board's minutes, which are in his writing for most of the decade. He contributed to the defeat of a proposal to force retirement on the old-timers, but a vote to abolish the fine for non-attendance slipped through, and this had the effect of slowly eroding the influence of the gerontocracy over the following years.

He attempted to get his lecture load reduced from 6 to 4, but was unsuccessful. He had earlier recruited Brian Inglis as a part-time assistant, to lecture in Economic Organisation. The Board now ruled that this had to come out of his salary. This rebuff was the trigger for JJ to pull out of Dublin and again take up part-time farming, this time in Laois, near Stradbally(13).

In June 1953 JJ again was passed over in the allocation of the key posts; he and Luce responded by writing a memorandum to the effect that it was bad policy to exclude the old-timers from posts of influence, as this would encumber the Professors with administrative tasks and prevent them from getting on with their professing, keeping their departments in the forefront of research etc. This memo was rejected, with Luce and JJ being consigned again to the fringe.

In June 1954 however JJ got to be Senior Proctor, a post carrying responsibility for validating degrees awarded. From here on the Board minutes refer to acceptance of the 'Proctor's Lists' on certain occasions; JJ felt the need to minute his own role. He continued to play a role in the ongoing negotiations involving TCD, UCD and the NUI and the Government in the setting up of the Agricultural Institute. These were protracted, extending over the best part of the decade, and are worthy of in-depth analysis, as a window into the slow learning process of the State about the role of scientific research, and into the negative effects of the 'intellectual Partition of Dublin' which mirrored the political Partition of the nation into rival hegemonistic-minded Protestant and Catholic components.

On November 2 1955 the College issued a press statement reminding the public of their role in agricultural education since 1906. In 1956 they decided to take steps to set up an enhanced School of Agriculture in association with the projected Agricultural Institute; they had also been strengthening their links with the Veterinary College, and JJ was on the School Committee. Then on March 14 1956 it was proposed to develop a School of Agriculture in association with the projected Agricultural Institute, and a printed memorandum was projected. The memo was critical of the Government proposals, which were described as vague. If the entity were to be centralised, TCD wanted unrestricted access. If decentralised, TCD wanted full faculty status. The memo suggested four university-based faculties, each tackling different research problems.

TCD was making a bid for soil science, with emphasis on upland soils. A location for a farm in south Co Dublin was sought, with access to upland. The farm was to be run on commercial lines. The other locations were to be related to UCD, UCC and UCG. The memo was presented to the Minister at the end of May by the Provost and Registrar.

In 1957 they decided to invest in Townley Hall, a Meath manor-house type farm of 300 acres, and develop this as the practical component of the School of

Agriculture. This issue was contentious, and the Board divided, the names being registered.

The Provost, Parke, Gwynn, Luce, Stanford, Wormell, Mitchell, Chubb and JJ were for; against were Thrift, Godfrey, Fearon, Duncan, Poole and Torrens. *There is digging to be done if we are to understand the political rationale for this division.* Both old-timers and 'new wave' are on each side. Opposition seemed to come from the science and medical faculties. Duncan, who held the Chair of Economics, was also opposed.

But Provost McConnell and Registrar Mitchell were supportive, and JJ for a time got to ride with 'new wave' college politics, until later when the project went sour under the stress of what perhaps can be identified as Government centralist institutional politics.

I can perhaps put forward as a working hypothesis that those against the Farm represented the old Protestant defeated-ascendancy view (keep your heads down, don't rock the boat, accept Catholic nationalist hegemony, and hope to survive unnoticed in the undergrowth) while those for the Farm represented a positive assertion of Protestant participation in mainstream national development. The Provost, Gwynn, Stanford, Mitchell and my father were certainly all of the latter view.

The TCD Agriculture School had earlier depended on students doing their practical work at the Albert College in Glasnevin, which has been set up by Plunkett under the Department of Agriculture and Technical Instruction. This was given to UCD in 1924, without consultation with TCD. A negotiated arrangement existed with UCD for continued access to the Albert College, set up under Coffey's Presidency. Townley Hall would give them an independent negotiating position in the context of the emerging Agricultural Institute structure.

The farm was to be called the Kells Ingram Farm, and this, in the context of the battle with UCD for slices of the Agricultural Institute cake, was a political act. Ingram was the author of the ballad 'Who Fears to Speak of Ninety Eight'. The naming of the farm was a bid to get the College accepted by Government as part of the national mainstream, and an act of defiance in the face of UCD's efforts to marginalise TCD, under the leadership of Tierney.

We had here a 300 acre unit, with timber, crops, livestock and a walled garden, an integrated traditional manor farm unit, supporting over 10 families and generating substantially more added value than 10 30 acre units would produce, if the farm were to be divided, according to the political objectives of Fianna Fail(14).

When the Annual Offices came around on June 19 1957 JJ managed, with the momentum of the Kells Ingram Farm victory, to get his way with regard to appointments. The Provost wanted Mitchell as Bursar and Chubb for Registrar, while JJ wanted these reversed; Mitchell had done a good job as Registrar along with JJ, representing the College with the Department of Agriculture, and JJ wanted continuity of experience with this role in the context of the Kells Ingram farm committee. JJ got his way. It was then agreed that Mitchell as Registrar should, as a routine role, represent the College in negotiations with external bodies.

Appendix 2: Trinity College Politics

The Farm remained contentious; in 1959 there was a bid to get rid of it, originating from Duncan and Fearon, but this was defeated, and the farm got access to more capital, and a direct link with the Finance Committee. This was stimulus to JJ to take a look at College investment policy, which he compared unfavourably with that of the Church of Ireland Representative Body.

The Farm, and its possible role in the still nascent Agricultural Institute remained high on the agenda of the academic leadership: Mitchell and Pakenham-Walsh were sent to attend a conference of Schools of Agriculture in Paris on July 27-31, under the OEEC (Organisation of European Economic Co-operation), the 'Marshall Plan' body which was funding the Irish investment in the Agricultural Institute.

On May 6 1959 the Board approved the initiation of an Honours course in Agriculture. On October 1, in JJ's absence, there was set up a School Committee for Agriculture and Forestry; Pakenham-Walsh became Registrar and the committee included McHugh the Manager, the Bursar, JJ, Mitchell and LG Carr-Lett. Much of the work within the TCD School of Agriculture was actually done in UCD under an old arrangement going back to Coffey's time; I interpret this as evidence of an attempt on the TCD side to further develop inter-university co-operation, in the context of the opportunity presented by the OEEC funding, despite Tierney's ongoing hostility, as documented by Donal McCartney in his 'UCD a National Idea'.

During this time my father remained active in defence of the TCD role in agriculture, insofar as he could, from his distant base in Bayly Farm near Nenagh. He was absent, during 1960, on February 10, 17 and 24. On the latter date the Board agreed to drop the Arts requirements for the School of Agriculture; this meant dropping the French and German options. JJ had I suspect had these requirements originally put in, on foot of his earlier experience of trying to get the Irish agricultural community to look to the Continent rather than to Britain for external experience.

On March 16 they decided to conclude an agreement with the new Agricultural Institute for setting up an Applied Genetics Unit. Then on April 20 they employed a Research Assistant, Saeve Coffey, and the following week they agreed to give Mitchell residential status there, while he remained Chairman of the Farm Committee. On May 11 it was agreed that George Dawson in Genetics should undertake work for the Agricultural Institute, and on June 1 they decided to expand the Veterinary College building into the College Botanical Gardens.

The TCD Board was still clearly aspiring to have an ongoing role for the College in both agricultural and veterinary science. Dawson's Genetics Unit was set up on June 29 at the farm, the agreement with the Agricultural Institute having been made successfully. By November however it became apparent that they needed to spend money on the farm again; they agreed to seek tenders for alterations.

On November 9, JJ being present, 5 students were excluded from the School of Agriculture, suggesting that the system was under some strain. JJ got to represent the College at the National Horticultural Research Conference to be held in Dublin in December. He was however absent on Saturday November 19, when the question of evidence for the Higher Education Commission is discussed.

To conclude the decade: one gets the impression that JJ's pet projects, the Kells Ingram Farm, and the Honours School of Agriculture, were under some strain, and he himself was losing interest, turning to the completion of his Berkeley book.

The 1960s decade(15) began however on an up-beat note, with JJ actively involved with the Kells Ingram Farm project, though living remotely, and with academic load decreasing.

The Farm and Agriculture School situation however soon began to decline; there were structural problems with Townley Hall, involving dry rot, which soaked up significant resources. Demand for the Honours Course in Agriculture declined; for a while there was a one-year certificate course, validated by the Farm Committee (the College itself wanted nothing to do with it). For a while they tried to develop Townley Hall as a conference centre, and occasional conferences were held there, for the Student Christian Movement and for the Fabian Society. JJ continued to take an interest; a lecturer in Farm Management was recruited.

A radioactive source was obtained and some work on plant genetics was done by Dawson and team, with a grant from the Agricultural Institute, which by now had become established as a centralist State research agency. By 1963 however it was clear that a strategy was emerging whereby Agriculture would go to UCD and TCD would get the Veterinary College. Despite this, the TCD Agriculture School, in a rearguard action, developed a course in agricultural microbiology, and they made an attempt to boost student numbers by recruiting from abroad.

Towards the end of 1963 the farm got a grant from Gouldings, the fertiliser firm, which enabled it continue for a while longer, though the emphasis in the coursework is increasingly in the direction of management, under Pakenham-Walsh; in 1964 the latter moved back to College to take over the Business Studies School, and it was agreed not to accept any more Honours agriculture students.

Thus it had become increasingly clear that the farm and the school of agriculture were being run down, and the College was counting on its Veterinary interest as its main link with the Agricultural Institute. JJ was again being marginalised, and his vision of a managed synergetic multi-enterprise large-scale farm as the model generator of rural wealth and employment was being eroded. Realising that he had lost the battle he turned increasingly to his last project, which was to pull together all is work on Berkeley into a publishable book.

Towards the end of 1966 JJ witnessed the ending of the Kells Ingram Farm episode. The Annual Report came on October 10; they decided to defer discussion until they saw the accounts on November 2. Then on November 9 they decided to sell the farm, subject to College agriculture policy and public policy; in other words they left the door open for a while to see if some deal could finally be done with the Government and the Agricultural Institute.

On April 26 1967, with JJ present, the Board welcomed the Government's statement that there was to be one Dublin University with constituent Colleges. The focus shifted to the 'merger debate', which became intense, and this kept JJ's interest in Board meetings alive. The sale of the farm involved the need to consult with Mitchell, the Dept of Agriculture, the Veterinary College, the Agricultural Institute and the users of the radioactive source. Mitchell did not object to the sale of the farm, but in view of the merger politics the decision needed to be deferred (May 22). They experienced difficulty however in meeting with UCD. The Board was addressed by the Minister on June 7. The details of this proposal, in which lurked the proverbial devil, are outlined in Donal McCartney's *UCD a National Idea* (G&M 1999) p314ff.

By the end of the year the issue was moribund, but it had prompted many people to look at how closer relations could be developed, and contacts opened up, which continued. It encouraged TCD to think that even it they sold the farm, they could still have a role in agriculture.

The 'merger' debate rumbled on for some time; there was a meeting on September 25 1968 at which the recommendations of the Merger Committee were discussed; JJ is on record as having attended. He was present again on April 23 1970; Watts and Dawson were also there; proposal were discussed arising from a meeting of TCD and UCD representatives.

JJ also attended on July 24 1970; there was no item I could see which might have been of special interest to him; perhaps he just looked in at random. He had, after all, not formally retired, being of pre-1920 vintage.

I may yet get some input from people who encountered him on these occasions, and pick up what angle he had on the merger, if any. David Spearman, Bill Watts and Frank Winder all overlapped with him during this period.

On previous form I conjecture that he would have held out for the interests of Magee College and of the Northern students. JJ is on record as having attended again on January 27 1971; the topic discussed was 'the future University of Dublin'; the merger debate was still smouldering. Watts and Winder were there. In 1972 he did not attend any meetings; he is recorded as absent up to February 23, when he vanished off the record; the Board accepted his wish to retire at a pension of £3207, with the status of Fellow Emeritus. The Senior Fellows met and co-opted TW Moody in his place.

The last act in the drama was played on May 3 1972 when it appeared in the Academic Council minutes that favourable reports from 2 external examiners on his Berkeley book enabled them to recommend that he be awarded the degree of D Litt. He received this at the June commencements, on the same occasion as when the composer Shostakovitch was awarded an honorary degree. I had to help him up the steps in the examination-hall to receive it. He died a few weeks later.

RJ and the TCD-Industry Interface

My own relations with the TCD Establishment can't be documented at the same level of detail, as the more recent Board minutes are not accessible. I can however summarise them from recollection.

When I left Aer Lingus at the end of 1970, I picked up some techno-economic consultancy, so I went to Professor FG Foster in TCD, and suggested I combine these with MSc project work, in a new programme he was developing, for an MSc in Operations Research and Statistics. I retained responsibility for delivery of a result to the client on schedule, while the students did some of the work, with me filling in if there were delivery problems. Academically I had the status of a sort of extern supervisor. This was eventually regularised by my being given the status of

'Research Associate' in the Statistics Department. There must have been a Board decision about this.

The projects involved team work, with a statistical data-gathering aspect, and then the building of a decision model, which used the statistics as part of its inputs, the rest of the inputs being conjectured values for parameters which enabled various scenarios to be explored, in a sort of 'what if' exercise. This type of procedure was becoming feasible for 'domain experts' using user-friendly high-level computer languages, typically Fortran. I found myself in with the extern examiner and the Prof carrying out the examination procedure.

The flexibility of TCD procedures are to be commended for making this possible, and I am indebted to Gordon Foster for knowing how to exploit them. The result was a programme based on good real-world problem-solving projects; these are described elsewhere, in the techno-economic stream(16).

While this was going on, the Industrial Liaison Office was initiated, and Justin Wallace was recruited, servicing the needs, as then perceived, for a while, without much success, so that he resigned, and the post was in danger of lapsing. I got wind of this, and put them the proposal that I would do it, part time, combining it with my own consultancy, and the arrangement with Foster.

In this context the opportunity arose to get seed-funding from the Industrial Development Authority for a proactive university-industry interface, supplying a specialist problem-solving service using project officers without academic priorities, working on the fringes of selected strong academic research groups, whose research results looked like they had good applications potential. This was set up, as an inter-departmental structure, the 'Applied-Research Consultancy Group', with the present writer as its manager.

The interest of the IDA was aroused thanks to an honorary degree being awarded to a leading Bell Labs researcher, an ex-colleague of Prof Vincent McBrierty in the physics department, who had worked in Bell Labs on nuclear magnetic resonance. There was a dinner, with IDA people present, and ideas were exchanged. At that time recognition of world-class research going on in Ireland by the IDA was non-existent; the civil service 'cult of the foreign expert' ruled supreme. This episode was perhaps among the beginnings of the process which in the 1990s led finally to some degree of State recognition of the utility of the Irish scientific research community.

Applied-research units were set up in association with the physics, electronic engineering, botany and genetics departments. Gerry Wardell worked on various advanced instrumentation concepts (eg measurement of uniformity of dispersion of filler in a non-homogeneous solid), some of which arose from McBrierty's work. Tony Moore pioneered some microelectronic applications, for example intelligent control of night storage heater charge, with Arthur Dexter. Daphne Levinge did environmental impact work, and Joan Ryan supplied a computer-based herd milk-yield analysis, at the individual cow level, for use in breeding, a spin-off from the genetic research of Padraig Cunningham.

The IDA funding enabled us to recruit good people from the existing postgraduate stock. For example, Daphne had done her PhD on the problem of re-vegetating mine tips. The group initially prospered; we doubled our revenue in three successive years, and covered our overheads(17). In the fourth year however we ran into a barrier; we went to the IDA for expansion funding, on the basis of our positive track-record, to invest in dedicated equipment (basically a PDP11 mini-computer) which would have enabled us to bid for some UN contract work, related to keeping track of genetic diversity in the world food crops. Our IDA proposal was blocked by a civil service ruling, that the IDA was not supposed to be funding academic institutions. As a consequence we ran into cash flow problems, and the TCD Board got worried. In the end we were stood down, but lessons were learned: the way to go for bringing research results to the market turned out to be the spin-off company. Mike Peirce's computer-aided manufacturing group, which had been associated with the ARC group, spun off and became Mentec ltd, one of the 'Celtic tiger' success stories.

The ARC Group records have been archived, and no doubt when the TCD records are available, historians of the 'science in society' and 'socio-technical' and 'techno-economic' processes in Ireland will perhaps find some footnotes from this experience. My contract came to an end in 1984 and I went back to the private sector.

Notes and References

1. As is the norm with these overview appendices I have divided the hypertext into accessible decade modules; the period 1911 to 1920 is abstracted in the 1910s TCD module.
2. I expand on this episode in the 1910s Plunkett hypertext module, overviewed in Appendix 4, where it emerges that Traill played a very positive supportive role.
3. JJ's role as a militant Home Ruler in the largely unionist TCD environment would have given rise to tensions, and it is quite possible that the Board were glad to see him disappear on his Albert Kahn world tour, hoping that it would settle him. I treat this in Appendix 10 which overviews the political thread of the hypertext; the book is accessible from the 1910s political module.
4. JJ subsequently, in a Seanad speech, acknowledged the influence of Mahaffey in persuading him to apply for the Albert Kahn Fellowship, as a means of extending his potential utility to the college; this theme is treated in Appendix 3.
5. He subsequently wrote up the experience in an article in the February 1921 issue of *Better Business* (vol 6 no 2) on 'The Trinity Co-op: Past present and Future'. This was the quarterly journal of the Co-operative Reference Library, Plunkett House. There was a forward by AE; it is available in full in the hypertext.
6. There is much detail about the politics of TCD and its relationship to the British and Free State Governments given in the 1920s TCD module in the hypertext, some of which affects JJ directly, and all of which is relevant background.
7. JJ's extern work was concentrated on the Barrington Trust lecturing as overviewed in Appendix 7, and from 1924 on the Statistical and Social Inquiry Society as overviewed in Appendix 6.
8. JJ's work for the Government included the Boundary Commission, the Agriculture Commission of 1923-24 and the Prices Commission of 1926; the detail of this is accessible via the Seanad and Public Services thread of the hypertext, as overviewed in Appendix 8. He had by his prior work in 1917-20 established his credentials with the Free State; this can be followed via Appendix 10 which overviews the political thread.
9. I go into this in more detail in the 1930s TCD module of the hypertext.
10. These and other related issues are treated in the 1940s TCD hypertext module.
11. This seminal paper on Berkeley as economist is accessed primarily from the 1950s academic module of the hypertext, as overviewed in Appendix 1.

12. The details of the McConnell succession, the Kells Ingram Farm and related matters are treated in the 1950s TCD module in the hypertext.

13. This gave rise to some pilot experience later recounted in the SSISI proceedings, in an economic symposium in 1959, dedicated to the Whitaker plan. JJ demonstrated the viability of combining market gardening with a few cows, provided organised access to a market existed. The College kitchen took his produce.

14. JJ had made this argument repeatedly in lectures and papers, typically in the SSISI where he had published 'The Capitalisation of Irish Agriculture' (JSSISI xvi, 44, 1941-2), and elsewhere, over the years from the 1920s.

15. The record of JJ's final decade or so, from 1961 up to 1972 when he died, is in the 1960s TCD hypertext module.

16. See the 1970s techno-economic module, also *Operations Research in Ireland* ed Julian Mac Airt (Mercier Press, Cork, 1988).

17. For some examples of the output of the ARC Group see the 1970s techno-economic and the 1970s socio-technical modules of the hypertext.

Appendix 3: The Albert Kahn Foundation and the French Connection

Background

The Deed of Foundation of the UK Centre for the AK Travelling Fellowships is dated 1910, and I have a copy. It is in the form of an agreement between Albert Kahn, of Paris, France, Banker, and the University of London, the latter being represented by a group which included HA Miers, the Principal of London University(1).

The Vice-Chancellors of all Universities in the UK, including the NUI and QUB and TCD, had the right to nominate candidates for the Fellowship. The 1911 Fellows appointed included Ivor Back; I have a copy of the *Ivor Back Report* (1911-12); it is an ill-structured chatty memoir, without table of contents or index, in the tradition of the English 'grand tour' traveller. I conjecture that the Albert Kahn Trustees would not have been pleased with it, and wanted to upgrade the standard.

The established emphasis on politics, economics and geography continued in 1912, when there were 10 candidates, including HAL Fisher, whom JJ knew in Oxford. I conjecture that it could have been Fisher who gave to JJ the idea that that he apply, though he subsequently attributed this to Mahaffey in TCD. The successful candidates in 1912 included GL Dickenson (classics, history, political science); I have also the *Dickinson Report*, dated October 1913. This is more scholarly in structure, with sections devoted to India, China and Japan, in the form of essays, in which he attempts to bring out what he sees as essential features in the culture.

In 1913 we have Douglas Knopp from Sheffield, and in 1914 Joseph Johnston, AJ Ogilvie and WT Layton. The latter two however joined up for the war. There is a long gap then until 1920, when we get John Ewing from Edinburgh and Eileen Power from Cambridge, and then in 1922 Leonard Halford and Dudley Baxton from Oxford. The record then ceases.

There are some further insights in the Meiers correspondence, which would appear to have commenced in or around 1907. It indicated that Albert Kahn had been running Fellowships along these lines in France, and aspired to set up centres in the US, Japan and Germany as well as in the UK. There had been 33 awards in France, which included Charles Garnier who went on to become the Executive Secretary of the Foundation in Paris. There is also a reference to five in Japan and two in Germany.

I have an example of one of the earlier Reports, in fact the first, published in 1914, but relating to 1909-10, by Tongo Takabe, Professor of Sociology at the Imperial College in Tokyo. This was published in French by F Rieder, rue de Vaugirard, Paris. It gives a page or two to most European countries, as seen through Japanese eyes. This and the two other Reports mentioned above were in JJ's possession, and I suspect he must have got hold of them in order to make his own proposal having seen the background.

I also have lists of the members of the Societé Autour du Monde for 1914, 1922 and 1931. The 1914 list while being mostly French has a strong German component, and includes members from Russia, the US and Japan. Post-war the German component vanishes. There is a thesis for someone in the elucidation of the significance of the details of this list, but the basic message is that pre-1914 it was the makings of a real international network, while after the war its scope and influence declined, though clearly Garnier did his best to keep alive the liberal-democratic tradition, with his support of Scottish and Irish national aspirations.

It would appear that Albert Kahn was consciously setting up to establish a network of people who he hoped would become influential in preventing war, and his method was to enable them to see how the world lived, learn from first-hand experience, and hopefully to set up correspondence networks.

JJ's World Tour (the Albert Kahn Travelling Fellowship)

My father's Report runs to 182 pages, and perhaps deserves eventual re-publication in its own right; it may perhaps primarily be of interest to Indian scholarship. It covers his travel round the world in 1914-15, but the bulk of its contents relate to India, where 3 of his elder brothers were in the Civil Service.

JJ had originally intended to travel through France, Germany, Austria and Turkey before going on to India. He had intended to take my mother with him; it had been planned as a sort of 'working honeymoon'. They landed in France, and then the war broke out, and they had to return. In the end JJ and my mother departed for India on November 21 1914, arriving in Bombay on December 19. My mother then went on separately(2) to Australia, to visit her mother's sister and aunt, with the intention of meeting up again with my father in Java, and going on to China, Japan, and back across the US. My father had therefore the chance to spend time in India in 'investigative journalist' mode rather than in tourist mode, and this adds depth to the Indian section of the Report.

In his introduction he declared that it had been written in 1916, and that his thinking had evolved considerably since then. Since it did not in the end get published until 1921, he doubted if it still possessed interest, due to the many problems with which the world was then confronted, consequent on the war. He indicated in footnotes areas where his opinions had radically altered.

(He was however able to use it in 1922 to persuade the *Manchester Guardian* to publish a series of articles of his on India, and this established his credibility as an investigative journalist to the extent that he was asked to do a similar series on Ireland in April of 1923, at the tail-end of the Civil War(3).)

The **Indian section of the report** contained the following sections, for each of which I give a brief outline:

India - Initial General Impressions: JJ sought in vain in Indian history for evidence for the type of political community with which we are familiar in Europe. The concept of family and kinship had not begun to be transcended by those of the citizen and the nation-state. An important obstacle to this was the caste system, which existed not only among the Hindus but also among the Muslims. He remarked acidly that among Europeans in India the caste system also de facto existed; they were far from giving a good example for the principle of egalitarian citizenship, to judge from the unwritten rules governing access to the 'station club'.

Spiritual Contrast between India and the West: ...the Hindu and Muslim religions were perhaps key factors. Islam JJ identified as standing in the same relation to Judaism as does Christianity, but Islam in India he found heavily influenced by the Hindu majority environment. Hindus were born not made; Hinduism did not claim universal status. There was an underlying monotheistic concept in the form of the impersonal all-pervading Brahma, of which the world as a whole as a material manifestation. JJ tentatively developed the parallel with the Christian concept of the Holy Spirit, and linked this with experience of the Christian missions. On the negative side however there was the doctrine of the Karma, which linked actions with the fortunes of the agent not only in the current life, but also in subsequent lives, through the process of transmigration.

Thus one's present misfortunes being a consequence of bad actions in a previous existence tend to encourage fatalism and submission. This in turn led to an aspiration to escape from the painful necessity of living for ever, and this is achievable by giving up actions and becoming an ascetic. This led to the statistic that in 1901 there were 5.2M religious beggars in India. He touched on Buddhism, the *Upanishads* and their interpreter Sarkaracharya, of the 9th century AD, and his *Path of Wisdom*, leading ultimately to the identity of the liberated soul with Brahma. In this context he popularised the doctrine of *Maya* or illusion. This highly philosophical religion is impossible to follow in detail except for a select few, but for purposes of popularising the concepts among the unlettered, Brahma was 'considered to have become incarnate in the god Krishna, who might be represented in the form of an idol and approached with prayer and sacrifice by even the humblest and most ignorant'.

Popular Hinduism: JJ went into the origins, dynamics and current statistics of the caste system. It is conjectured that it originated in the need of the Aryan invaders to differentiate themselves from their darker predecessors. There were originally four castes: Brahmans (priests), Kshatria (warriors), Vaisya (artisans) and Sudras (menials). These subdivided, and in 1901 there were 2358 distinct castes distributed among 43 racial or tribal groups, 1800 of these subdivisions being Brahmans. The complexity of the religious concepts imposes the need for a numerous and skilled priesthood. Sometime movements to eradicate the caste system emerge, but these simply tend to become new castes. It matters little what one believes, as long as one obeys the ceremonial procedures appropriate to one's caste.

Education: this question had first posed itself 100 years previously, in the form, should education be Oriental or Western? The first few existing colleges taught Oriental knowledge, but then Lord Macaulay in 1835 decreed that their 'absurd science, metaphysics, physics and theology' should be abandoned, that education should be Western, and through English (4). This restricted education to the upper castes. There was however resistance to education together of Hindus of different castes, and indeed Hindus with Muslims; in the latter case the opposition came primarily from the Muslim side, as the Hindus would accept a purely secular form of education. Under the *purdah* girls disappeared out of the system at age 10, when they were married off.

Administrative Machinery: there was no uniform system under the Indian Government, which was led centrally by the 'Governor-General in Council'. This included a few token Indians, but had a European majority. Bombay, Madras and Bengal had Governors with Executive Councils. The various Provinces had Legislative Councils with elected Indian majorities. Their administrative systems were however dependent on the dates on which they had been annexed. The fact that the police came directly under the Magistrate suggested to JJ that executive and judicial functions were somewhat unhealthily intertwined. The qualities expected of the District Magistrate included at least familiarity with, or even mastery of: law, economics, engineering, agriculture, archaeology, ethnology, sanitation, estate management, excise, police and local administration, supported by psychology and philosophy. JJ goes through a typical day in the life of such a paragon, presumably his elder brother, and it is possible to detect constraints on his objectivity, though there is perhaps a hint of 'tongue in cheek'.

Bureaucracy: this section is a sort of an aside, in which JJ compared actually existing bureaucracy on the British-Indian model with the then current situation in Ireland, unfavourably to the latter. In the Indian situation the impersonal and mechanistic aspect of bureaucracy, to which the central government aspires, was moderated by the existence of real power at District level, operated by real people who had to live there. A District Magistrate-Collector on leave in England encountered through his GP a local healthcare problem, involving an epidemic; local hospital resources were idle but could not be obtained without recourse to London; our Indian Civil Service friend (probably James or John) would have solved the analogous problem in India, had it occurred in his District, at the stroke of a pen.

The Work of the District Magistrate: JJ had some critical words to say about the Indian legal profession, which tended to be parasitical on the economic life of the people, and to seek to prolong and complicate disputes, viewing the bankrupting of their clients with unconcern. He gave some examples which suggested that legal practice in India was significantly dirtier than in Ireland. The District Magistrate goes on tour with a tent, and heard cases at a portable table. While on tour in this mode, the Magistrate picked up diverse bits of local knowledge; he **was** the government, accessible, and with a human face. This aspect of the government of India JJ identified as a desirable norm, absent in the UK itself, as instanced by the scandal of the starving soldiers wives during the War; they were advised to write to or call at the War Office for their separation allowances.

The Joint Magistrate (who is an Indian civilian): the Service was in process of apprenticing Indian assistants, and JJ sat in on one such court. One matter dealt with was the renewal of gun-licences, a process involving verification of a marking on each weapon. This process was necessary for Indians but not for Europeans; the latter could obtain and carry firearms without any formality. This opened up the possibility of Indians becoming armed unofficially through Europeans of like mind for revolutionary purposes. JJ remarks on the need to make the licensing system universal.

The Sub-Division: I quote: '...it is even said that a man has more power for good or evil as Sub-Divisional Officer (SDO) than he is ever likely to obtain again unless he becomes Lieutenant-Governor ...'. These were Indians or Eurasians of the 'Provincial' service, usually in their 20s or 30s; it was regarded as a training-ground for native recruitment to the Civil Service. One such had administered a major flood-control project on the Ganges, which JJ had compared to Irish experience of attempting to get things done with the Shannon or the Bann by remote and conflicting Dublin departments. JJ's support for strong local authority was reinforced by this Indian, and by subsequent French, experience. JJ went on to comment on problems connected with payment of rent in kind to landlords, and in this sort of situation the SDO tended to side with the landlords. We have here a sort of re-enactment of the scene in 19th century Ireland, with which JJ identified.

Judicial Procedure and the Law of Evidence: JJ gave some detailed accounts of cases where the application of the English laws of evidence constituted positive barriers to justice being done. He suggested that Japanese procedures might have been more appropriate, and stressed the importance of people in the judiciary having executive experience.

Agricultural Conditions and Agricultural Credit: JJ went into the historical background of land tenure and tax collection in India. Under the Moguls tax had been a proportion of harvest, and was farmed out to collectors, who took a cut. The British substituted a fixed rate per unit area, and recognised the Mogul tax-farmers or *Zamindars* as a sort of embryonic squirearchy. This made the villages more financially vulnerable in times of drought or flood. Under the Moguls the tax-farmers were supposed to keep back a 10% commission. Under the British this situation over time became reversed, and in effect a wealthy land-owning class was created. The government in the end had to intervene in the interests of the tenants, under the Bengal Tenancy Acts. This however had the effect of passing control from the landlords to the moneylenders, a consequence of the undermining of the village community by the process of encouraging individual peasant proprietorship. Credit had been handled at village level via the village *bania* who originally acted as a sort of community banker, without the bad odour associated with gombeenism. Once land-ownership at the individual level came in, credit became based on land as security, and to be in the form of a legal contract between individuals rather than a customary arrangement under common supervision. The *bania* became the usurer, who gained land by dispossession of its occupiers, who were unable to pay back loans under usurious interest, often as high as 75%. 'The village community was thus destroyed, and a regime of economic individualism was entrenched behind a barrier of law.'

The Co-operative Movement: this section takes up 17 pages and reflects JJ's enthusiasm for this bottom-up democratic approach to economic development. The movement went back to 1892, when the Madras government sent Sir Frederick Nicholson on a roving commission to Europe to study how the co-operative movement addressed the question of agricultural indebtedness. In this context he encountered Sir Horace Plunkett and the Irish Agricultural Organisation Society (IAOS), as well as the Raffeisen movement. It was soon realised that special legislation would be necessary. The first Co-operative Credit Societies Act was passed in 1904 when Lord Curzon was Viceroy, and JJ regarded this as being to his credit, however much he was execrated by articulate nationalist India. A further Act in 1912 provided for the appointment of a Registrar of Co-operative Societies by local government, and went further than the 1896 UK Friendly Societies Act, by providing for a propagandist and organising role for the Registrar.

In his subsequent 1920 note JJ referenced a book by HW Wolff on *Co-operation in India* and highlighted the process of political citizenship training in the co-operative movement, leading to the possibility of enhanced local government.

He contrasted the India situation with that in Ireland, where representative local democracy had fallen under the influence of gombeen-politicians, and co-operative initiatives tended to be attacked as conspiracies against trade. The State in India he regarded as a relatively benevolent bureaucracy, in a position to act progressively without gombeen influence. I quote: '...Imagine a Parliament consisting of John Dillons, Lord Clanrickardes, and Sir Edward Carsons, and you will have a faint idea of what an elected Indian political assembly would be like. A proposal to establish co-operative societies for the benefit of rural India would the strangled at birth by a Parliament thus constituted...'.

Comparisons between India and Ireland: JJ further emphasised the mutual support between the Indian Departments of Agriculture and the Registrars as being essential to the progress of the co-operative movement, and warned against the influence of the emerging gombeen political activists. Paradoxically, though JJ is a democrat in economic matters, in matters political he was convinced that representative democracy on the British model would throw up the worst type of self-interested gombeen element: '...The machinery of representative government does not work well in Ireland, and if the Irish people were to continue electing to the Irish parliament the same type of man they have been sending to Westminster, no scheme of Home Rule would work satisfactorily ...'(5).

Labour conditions and slavery: JJ went into some detail regarding how the labour market worked in India. Enslavement for debt, under the *harauri* system, was prevalent in Bihar and Madras. This relationship was supported tacitly under English law of contract, and the relationship in fact became hereditary. One way of escape for such slaves was to join a gang of coolies recruited for service in the tea plantations of Assam or Ceylon. This however was to suffer a similar fate. Recruits for coolie labour on these estates seldom if ever returned to their villages; it was a life-sentence.

Christian Missionary Effort: the four million or so Indian Christians tended, according to JJ, to belong predominantly to the lower end of the social spectrum, and this led to prejudice against them on the part of the upper-crust Hindus, especially the Brahmans. There had been up to the middle of the 19th century some recruitment from members of the educated classes into Christianity, but this trend had been diverted by the Brahmo Samaj movement, which was a reformed religion rooted in Hindu philosophy, but incorporating many Christian concepts.

Religious Movements other than Hindu: expanding on the philosophy of the Brahmo Samaj, JJ identified this as a progressive force, with its members prominent in social reform movements against caste, child marriage, right of widows to re-marry etc. There was also the Prarthana Samaj in Bombay, for which the social reform and nation-building aspects had priority. This movement attempted to show that the current abuses were not fundamental to the Scriptures, constituting a relatively recent corrupt imposition.

There was also a movement called the Arya Samaj was founded in 1875 by one Swami Dayananda Saraswati, against Hindu idolatry and back to Vedas monotheism. These ideas were further developed by Pandit Guru Datta, who was familiar with Western philosophy as well as Eastern. Despite a dogmatic appearance, JJ regarded the Aryans as a liberalising influence, and devoted 8 pages to them. Although it started in Bombay, its current strength was in the Pubjab, whose people JJ saw as somewhat similar to those of Ulster; he attributed the relative success of the co-operative movement in the Punjab to the character of the people there.

The Aryan approach to the caste problem was similar to that of the Prarthana Samaj; in other words, they sought to discredit it as a modern overlay which corrupts the pure Vedas. They organised educational missions in the villages. They claimed to be 'catholic' in the sense that they believed their message was not only for the Hindu but for Islam, the Sikh, for India as a whole, and indeed for the world. They had entered into competition with the Christians for the support of the 'depressed classes'. Their education policy was to use the vernacular, and to teach Western science through it, as part of a total curriculum. Although nominally non-political, the Aryan movement appeared to constitute a force supportive of the Indian National Congress. JJ regarded the Aryan movement as relating to Congress as the Gaelic League related to the Irish Parliamentary Party.

The Caste question: JJ picked up on the aftermath of a conference held in 1912 by an organisation known as the Aryan Brotherhood, which organised provocatively a multi-caste dinner in Bombay, including 'untouchables'. This led to much newspaper agitation, as a result of which some participants were 'outcasted', including one educated Gujarati, whom JJ quoted at length: '...castes are neither trade guilds or associations...they are simply based on birth....castes have become water-tight compartments disintegrating society into irreconcilable factions...the sole function of caste is to limit the area of dining and marrying relations...caste is not able to guide the social, economic, moral or religious live of its members... caste has been broken and is being broken on many sides, though it still has retained its outer shape.'

The Indian National Congress: JJ was critical of the policies of this body, particularly as regards its explicit inability to deal with problems of social reform, and as regards its failure to address the false educational policies which have evolved under the British, which have in fact formed the Indian political class in the image of their overlords. 'Measures of constructive statesmanship like the Co-operative Societies Act owe everything to the intelligence and common sense of an "autocratic and despotic administration", but little or nothing to the political advocacy of those who claim to represent intelligent and educated India.' If Congress is to be taken seriously, it needs to look into questions like the use of the courts in enforcing usurious contracts, and the 'harauri' system of slavery, as matters of pressing economic reform. Vested interests within Congress itself, as well as religious prejudices, are obstacles to this happening.

Concluding Remarks about India: JJ advocated that the Government should '...let it be known that it is quite prepared to consider the advisability of gradually resigning its functions when it is no longer in the best interests of India to retain them....it should realise to the full the enormous strength of its own moral position under present circumstances ...'. (JJ qualified this position by saying in his 1920 footnote that 'this was written prior to the Amritsar episode'. He went on to advocate that healthy local government should be built up on the foundation of the emerging co-operative movement, rather than on the basis of artificial 'electoral constituencies'. 'Representative bodies composed largely of members elected by co-operative federations might, perhaps, be trusted with legislative power...'. He concluded the India part of the Report with a statement that he has aimed to arouse curiosity rather than to satisfy it.

***

JJ then went on to give short accounts of Java, China, Japan and the USA; these, while being of interest as a record of travelling conditions for the European elite in 1915, a long way from the war, are nowhere near in the same depth as the Indian study, and it is the latter that makes this report worthy of reproduction in some detail, and perhaps eventually re-publication in full(6).

Post-Tour Contact up to 1920

Towards the end of 1916 JJ was enabled partially to fill in the missing European leg of his world tour, by engaging in a field-study of French agricultural production under wartime conditions. His Report(7) was published in Ireland and was widely reviewed, in the *Times*, the *Irish Homestead* and elsewhere. The key points were as follows:

1. The role of the Albert Kahn Foundation in enabling JJ to gain access to the Prefets.
2. The superiority of the French democratic republican State over the English Crown in organising in the common interest at local level.
3. The organised approach to the mechanisation of agriculture using existing local farmers' co-operatives; the superiority of American machinery.
4. The role of the *prefet* as co-ordinator at local level of all State agencies;

JJ took the opportunity to develop a critique of local administration in Ireland and the UK. He picked up much printed background material and this he deposited in the Co-operative Reference Library, 84 Merrion Square (now known as Plunkett House, the headquarters of the Irish Co-operative Organisation Society).

During his trip to France in 1916 JJ worked in journalistic mode, sending a report to the London *Times* which was printed under the header 'War Agriculture in France / The Benefits of United Action / A Lesson to British Farmers', from 'a Correspondent in France'. He also embodied his impressions of France in an imaginative series of articles in the *Irish Times*, signed 'Viator', entitled 'If France Ruled Ireland'(8); these appeared during September 1916.

***

From August 1916 JJ was in close touch with JG Douglas(9), AE and others lobbying for what subsequently became the Convention of 1917. He was continually in touch with Charles Garnier the Executive Secretary of the AKF, and it is evident from the Garnier letters in JJ's papers that he was feeding Garnier with material for propaganda in the Irish interest, the objective being to get Ireland on to the agenda of the Peace Conference. There are hints that JJ was in on the drafting of the Convention documentation.

The full analysis of the Garnier correspondence(10) must await access to the Foundation archive, which it seems has been recovered from Moscow, where it ended up after having been looted by the Nazis, and then liberated by the Russians.

Appendix 3: The Albert Kahn Foundation and the French Connection

Contact with JJ in the 1920s

There was a frequent exchange of letters between JJ and Garnier during the War of Independence and Civil War periods; it is evident that JJ briefed Garnier about what was going on, and Garnier publicised the Irish case in the French media(11). In this overview I pick out some of the highlights.

January 21 1921: Garnier acknowledged that they had received 100 copies of JJ's Report from University College London (UCL), for distribution to members of the Cercle. He complemented JJ: '...vous nous apportez une serieuse contribution a l'étude do l'Inde sociale et de la Chine ...'. He then went on to ask forgiveness for not having taken up JJ's offer of '...discussions amicales sur le Traité de Versailles ...'. This would have been at the time when the Irish independence movement was attempting to get itself on to the agenda, without success. JJ must have tried, unsuccessfully, to promote this via the Cercle.

February 25 1921: ....Garnier had found his earlier Irish experience (he had travelled widely there in the 1890s, during his period of study of Parnell and aftermath) in demand, and a series of travel articles was in process of becoming a book. He wanted to capture his experience of interacting with the 'young enthusiasts' and the poets: Yeats, Russell, JP Quinn, etc ...

June 12 1921: This letter of three pages, which occurred about 4 weeks before the Truce was declared on July 9, is almost totally dedicated to literary and academic matters: an honorary degree from TCD for the mathematician Borel (who it turns out is a member of the Cercle), the poetry of AE, which it seems has been studied in depth by Garnier's protégé Allarg. There is comparison with Shelley and Wordsworth. There is mention of a projected 'societé litteraire et scientifique franco-irlandaise'.....

August 20 1921: Garnier's next letter was from Engenthal (Bas-Rhin), where presumably he is on vacation; he acknowledged JJ's 'excellent letter of Aug 7' and then plunges into his book on Ireland of 25 years previous, three years after the death of Parnell, Home Rule accepted by the Commons but rejected by the Lords. He admits to having been totally Parnellite at the time of the split, and had nothing to do with J McCarthy, Tim Healy or TP O'Connor; he never understood how they could have abandoned their Chief under England's orders. Sigerson was on the fence, and he ranked him with the 'federationists' in favour of dominion status. Had Sigerson published anything since his 1893 *Revival of Irish Poetry*? He was attached in some capacity to the Catholic University; was he Catholic himself? When was this founded?

Garnier then got into the Dáil debates: '...where will it go in its intransigence?'; he regards public opinion in the Dominions as being the limiting factor. He regarded the move to bring the Dominions into the politics of the Empire as the most important event since the Armistice. It would appear that JJ's objective, as expressed in Civil War in Ulster, of all-Ireland Home Rule within the UK had evolved towards dominion status within an imperial confederation, and that Garnier had bought this idea.

Garnier went on to reflect on the importance of agriculture, and having the right agriculture-industry mix, as in France and Ireland, England having become over-industrialised, as Germany in 1914 also had become, '...et ce fut une raison de sa déraison'. He then mentions meeting Tagore who has joined the Cercle; the latter regarded Yeats and Russell as 'poetes freres'.....

January 31 1922: Garnier described his coverage of the 'congres mondial irlandais', encountering, as though in a dream, Yeats, Maud Gonne and Douglas Hyde (all of whom he had met in Ireland decades previously), and having long conversations with Miss McSwiney and de Valera, who '...'a l'air' (he puts 'seems' in quotes, as though sceptical) de saisir tres vite l'importance de questions pourtant éloignées de la politique pure comme celle des rapports intellectuels directs entre nos deux pays ...'.

June 8 1922: Garnier explained the arrival of a package which JJ should have received without explanation some days previous. It contained the proceedings of the meetings of a political and social studies group which met weekly, in the Cour de Cassation, under Albert Kahn auspices. This material is not commercially available, being reserved for 'centres de documentation' in educational and research centres. It seems Albert Kahn would like such a centre to be established in Trinity College, in a small reading-room, accessible to qualified researchers.

There is no reference in the TCD records of any attempt by JJ to set this up; it is probable that he felt he did not have the political clout in the TCD environment to take such an initiative. It seems subsequently he attempted to get this set up in Plunkett House.

Was there anything published about de Valera? What did JJ think of Joyce's Dubliners?

There is then a page added subsequently, in which he refers to '...les catastrophes publiques qui se prolongent de terrible maniere...si difficile a expliquer...mysterieuses et lamentables...'. We are now into the civil war. He sends a copy of his *Vie du Peuples* article on Arthur Griffith and he wants immediately to be briefed about Michael Collins. He asks JJ has he stopped writing in journals and revues, and asks him to think of the Cercle and the AK Bulletin for his writings. He invites JJ to come in the summer to Normandy with his family and his brother. *This must have been Sam, then dying of TB, and in process of leaving his family, Alec, Tommy and Geddes, for fostering with JJ in Stillorgan.*

July 3 1922: .... Garnier thanked JJ for taking up the Documentation Centre idea with the Co-operative Reference Library. *There is no trace of this in the Plunkett Foundation record in Oxford, nor is there in the Plunkett House library.* Garnier empathised with JJ regarding how the civil war has interrupted JJ's 'projects de conferences' by which he must mean the Barrington Lectures. A visit to Ireland remains on the agenda.

April 6 1923: Garnier referred to a postcard from the Midi, to which JJ probably replied. He returned a document lent him by JJ which contained background material on Michael Collins. The attention of the public was now turned away from Ireland.... He then went on to describe the French political scene, which was dominated by the conservative and reactionary 'Bloc National' elected in 1919 under the threat of Bolshevism. He regards Herriot as the man of the future, and the radical-socialist bloc....

Garnier then read JJ's letter, and was moved to add on the back of the envelope, in which he acknowledges JJ's concern with the economic depression in England and Ireland, but found it surprising that JJ held France rather than Germany responsible. This is Garnier's almost chauvinistic French response to JJ's economic analysis, which is under Keynes influence; all the gold is in the US and Germany is bankrupt, thanks to the 'reparations' aspects of the Treaty of Versailles, on which France was insisting. We have here what could develop into a break between JJ and Garnier, hitherto the best of friends.

June 22 1923: The storm hinted at in the previous letter blew over, as Garnier organised for JJ and family to have red carpet treatment at the Cercle, where they are soon due to arrive. Garnier planned to go to Dublin in September, thereby (he hopes) avoiding the elections.

August 31 1923: Garnier was present for the arrival of President Cosgrave, met by two government representatives and a sympathetic crowd. Cosgrave looked 'extremely young and smiling'. He went on with the 'caravane' to the Grand Hotel and had some talk with Dr Mac Neil (sic) whom he found friendly, and who undertook to facilitate him when in Dublin in September.

September 28 1923: Garnier wrote to JJ on his return to Paris after his trip to Ireland, basically to thank JJ for taking care of him when in Dublin, and for facilitating his subsequent stay in London. *It would appear that JJ had arranged for him to be met at Euston by 'M Nesbitt' who had arranged a place to stay. This was the family network; Bob Nesbitt from Belfast would then have been courting my mother's younger sister Isabel. He must have been in London at the time, and JJ would have produced him for Garnier, to help him get a feel for the Belfast Protestant world-view.*

April 16 1925: Garnier wrote to JJ from Strasbourg, thanking him for telling him about the death of Sigerson.....Garnier went on to mention Cosgrave's visit to Paris some three months previous. *(this is an indication of the extent to which they had lost touch)* and attendance at an event which was presided over by a French bishop. Garnier noted that he had '...eus surprise de voir le chef de l'Etat ployer les genoux devant le représentant de l'Eglise...'.

This must have alerted Garnier to JJ's predicament in what he now saw as a Church-dominated State, and the correspondence re-opens. There was a fragmentary letter which from internal evidence seems to be in 1925, and which suggests another visit. The following names and concepts occur in the fragmentary text, more or less in sequence: Arthur Griffith, the Collins article, a history 1895-1915, a projected history 1915-1925, 'does JJ think this feasible between Aug 25 and Sept 25?...' How much would it cost? possibility to work in the library? Garnier clearly wanted to pick up on his Irish contacts with a new publication in mind.

***

There was a gap then in the correspondence; there are some references in the AK record, and JJ visited Paris in 1926, my sister remembers it. It remains to piece together what happened; there was a link with the Rockefeller episode(12).

The next letter is dated **October 6 1928**, and seems to be subsequent to a real-presence encounter.

It starts off with 'je viens enfin de finir - et de vour renvoyer - le livre de James Connolly *Labour in Irish History*. Je vous remercie de me l'avoir fait connaitre. Il est clair, fortement documenté et bien écrit. Quel dommage d'avoir anéanti une intelligence pareil! He then goes on to reflect on the savagery of the Great War.

Garnier was still apparently struggling with his book on Ireland, being continually diverted by the need to travel for the Foundation. He mentions an invitation to lunch from one Ferguson which he had been unable to take up; he mentions that Ferguson was with Professor Henry 'de l'Evolution du Sinn Fein'. He goes on to ask JJ for anything he can find on the life of Connolly, and what is JJ's opinion of him.

JJ passed this letter on to someone, with the Connolly passages marked, asking the recipient to return it to him at 36 TCD, where he then had rooms.

***

There is again a long gap until **March 2 1929** when Garnier replied to a letter from JJ which apparently must have informed him about my mother's pregnancy with me. *This pregnancy came unexpectedly, and posed my parents with problems, in that they had moved some distance from Dublin, to Dundalk, in order for JJ to have hands-on access to an agricultural environment. JJ must have explained this to Garnier, who empathises.*

JJ must also have regaled Garnier with news of Irish political developments, which the latter found '...pas rejouissant ...', responding with some analogies from the 3rd Republic. He is however primarily concerned with the financial scene, where he estimates that 4/5 of all private investments have been annihilated, and '...la democratie chez nous comme partout est en sommeil, empoisonnée par les méfaits de la guerre ...'.

The next letter dated **August 29 1930** began with a reference to receiving a photo of the present writer, not yet one year old. After the appropriate family compliments, he gets down to business; JJ has sent him his paper on 'national transport'(13). Garnier accepted this as an addition to the raw material for his Ireland book (still chronically in gestation!) in which he had now begun to focus on the 'urban civilisation' aspect, with La Cité Irlandaise in mind as title.

Turning to global politics, Garnier noted the resistance in Britain and Ireland to the European Federation project; Garnier regarded this as necessary to keep Europe significant as between America and Asia (a foretaste of current EU thinking).

Garnier noted with regret the demise of the *Irish Statesman* and asks after 'le brave AE', hoping he remains a pillar of Plunkett House. In a footnote Garnier gave advance warning of a festive AK meeting on June 14, involving the British 'Boursiers', at which he hoped to see JJ.

Contact in the 1930s and later

For a time I thought that there was no Garnier correspondence on record in JJ's papers for the 1930s, though some must have taken place, because he visited Ireland in or about 1938 or 39; I have a distinct recollection of him visiting our then domicile in Newtown Park Avenue, Blackrock. He was, in the eyes of a 9 or 10 year old, a benevolent purveyor of exotic chocolate. However in the end the 1930s Garnier file turned up; the visit was in the context of his 'book on Ireland' project; it got published in 1939, and reviewed in the Irish Times, and TW Moody expressed an intention of reviewing it in Irish Historical Studies. I hope to be able to review it in the hypertext, when I can track it down(14). If in the end, also, we gain access to the AK archive, repatriated from Moscow, we will perhaps be able to trace something of JJ's contribution to the AKF in the 1930s.

At the time of Garnier's visit in 1938, JJ was campaigning for the Senate, and this flavoured the reopening of the contact. JJ however found time to set up contacts for Garnier with people who had known Kevin O'Higgins. On hearing of JJ's success back in Paris, Garnier invited JJ officially to join the Cercle Autour du Monde as a foreign member, and JJ accepted. His contact up till then must have been personal via Garnier, and with the standing of an ex Travelling Fellow. It seems perhaps that full membership was reserved to those who achieved public office.

There was some correspondence during and after the war. The first letter is dated **October 12 1941**, from Busnieres (Saone et Loire). Correspondence presumably took place via neutrals like Portugal, and took many months. Garnier thanked JJ for his letter of March 13 which took 3 months to come, and contained the news of my sister's first child Pat, making JJ a relatively young grandfather and 'le retour du senator Cincinnatus a la terre ...'. Garnier gave in return the sad news of the death of his wife at Busnieres, at the beginning of summer, indirectly a victim of the war.

He hoped in the next few days to get permission to go back to Paris to his old address '...pas de gaieté de coeur ...'. He mentions family matters, and refers in guarded language to '...l'aimabilité do notre ami commun ...' meaning the British, who had ensured delivery of Garnier's wedding present to my sister, after it had been salvaged from a sunken vessel; it was a painting by his wife. I remember it arriving, the worse for wear; we were at the time living near Drogheda. JJ must have written his March 13 letter to acknowledge receipt and to thank Garnier, who in his response remarks on the wedding present arriving after the first child.

Garnier went on to thank JJ for thinking of doing a review '...des Houles(?) du Pacifique' and he asked JJ to add to his copy a note of the date of going to press, which was April 24 1940, '...avant la catastrophe ...'. In view of the date, Garnier pointed out that the last two pages are of particular significance. *(There is a loose end here, the book not being available.)*

The first post-war contact came by diplomatic bag via JP Walshe in Foreign Affairs and Seán Murphy of the Irish embassy in Paris. JJ had put out feelers to try to trace Garnier, and Seán Murphy, who had been earlier known to both JJ and Garnier in the Paris context, obliged, having Garnier's MS neatly typed up. It is dated **March 23 1945** and acknowledges Seán Murphy as intermediary. He gives detailed family news: his nephew Daniel, a geologist, has found a petroleum deposit near St Gaudens. His daughter has been too occupied with the Resistance to make him a grandfather. Her uncle, Jacques Maritain, has been named as Ambassador to the Vatican; his mother was Protestant and his wife is a Russian Jew.

Garnier had just finished his history of Scotland. The Society Autour du Monde was asleep; the Rector of the University had dined with 'us' (presumably he means those who remained of the Cercle) in a restaurant, '...car les Huns ont vidé tout l'hotel que vous avez connu ...'. This presumably refers to the quai de 4 septembre building.

July 24 1946: Garnier wrote from Argyll, Scotland, where he was staying with the Michesons: GK, who is the MP, and Naomi his wife, who is a Haldane (sister of JBSH). Naomi was locally an activist in the Scottish Nationalist interest, and was a local councillor; she sought to support the establishment of a Parliament in Edinburgh. Garnier had known her for the previous 20 years or so and regarded her highly.

He declined with regret an invitation to come to Ireland. He mentioned receiving a letter from Douglas Hyde's sister, and urged JJ to encourage me ('le scientifique de la famille', then just about entering TCD to do a science degree) to go to Paris.

The last letter I have from Garnier is dated **April 25 1949**, and is from 35 rue de l'Arbalete. The occasion was the declaration of the Republic in Ireland; JJ had recently completed a 10-year spell in the Senate, and had a public profile thanks to his association with the Post-Emergency Agriculture Commission. Garnier conveyed congratulations on the Republic. He was now 80 years old, and not very mobile. His daughter was working with the Marshall Plan. His nephew the geologist has recently been drowned in an attempt to save a colleague. He ended by asking 'when will you send Roy to me?'.

Epilogue

When I went to Paris in 1951, it was not primarily at my father's suggestion, but at the suggestion of ETS Walton, the TCD physics professor, and Nobel Prize winner (later, in 1953, for his work with Cockroft two decades earlier, which has led indirectly to nuclear weapons). Walton sent me to Louis Leprince-Ringuet in the Paris Ecole Polytechnique(15).

In this context I went to see Charles Garnier, at my father's suggestion. He was living in reduced circumstances, in Rue de l'Arbalete, 5ieme, and we exchanged civilities over coffee and biscuits, without my understanding his significance or that of the Albert Khan Foundation. It is a pity that I had not briefed myself better on the Garnier correspondence, because I would have been able to pick up on the Mitcheson / Haldane connection, and we would have found common ground. I had encountered JBS Haldane, JD Bernal and others of the 30s Marxist scientific cohort, in the context of the 1940s TCD student left, via the Promethean Society. My failure to do this indicates the width of the then gap between myself and my father, and it is a matter for regret that I was unable to do justice to this opportunity to have a living link with the time of Parnell.

***

I had begun to pick up some understanding of my father's political role when in the early 90s I had occasion to be in Paris in connection with an IMS development project supported by the European Commission (I treat this in the socio-technical stream). I extended my stay, and made contact with the AK Foundation, primarily with Gilles Baud-Berthier, who has been helpful in enabling me to put this thread of the project together(16).

Appendix 3: The Albert Kahn Foundation and the French Connection

I hope eventually here to be able to give some more insights into the contemporary role of the AK Foundation, and to give contact-points. It seems they have an ongoing project to research the international liberal-intellectual network which they tried to set up before World War 1, and that this project extends to Tokyo, Moscow and other foci of 20th century tension. Watch this space.

Notes and References

1. I am indebted to the Librarian of University College London for a chance to examine the Minutes of the meetings of Trustees and associated correspondence, on May 7 1998. More detail is available in the 1910s Albert Kahn module in the hypertext. Gilles Baud-Berthier, the current Foundation librarian, has been researching the historical background, attempting to bring order into the confusion left by the Nazi theft of their archives and their recent recovery from Moscow. The 'Collections Albert Kahn' is located at 10 Quai du Quatre Seprembre, 92100 Boulogne, France, under the direction of Mme Jeanne Beausoleil.

2. I have recorded some extracts from her diaries in the 1910s family module.

3. There is a somewhat obscure reference to these articles in the Albert Kahn Foundation archive, together with other items of Irish interest e.g. a book by Simone Tery, who subsequently became the Paris correspondent to the Irish Statesman. See the 1920s Albert Kahn module. I have abstracted the articles in the 1920s political module in the hypertext.

4. It is perhaps worth looking here at the work of Zaheer Baber on Indian science, which I reviewed in the February 1997 issue of *Science and Public Policy* (International Science Policy Foundation). The book reviewed was *The Science of Empire* by Zaheer Baber, State University of New York (1996).

5. Remember that JJ wrote this in 1916, pre-Rising. In his April 1920 footnote he added: 'nowadays Irish MPs go to Wormwood Scrubbs, Dartmoor, or Mountjoy, and the fleshpots of Westminster are tabooed.' It is worth mentioning that in his *Civil War in Ulster* he had proposed effectively Proportional Representation for elections under Home Rule. In this Report he does not expand on this, though he concluded by hoping that '...Ireland...will intellectually emancipate herself from the traditions of British politics to which her existing Parliamentarians have succumbed...'.

6. A more detailed abstracting of JJ's Albert Kahn Travelling Fellowship Report is available in the supporting hypertext.

7. The Albert Kahn Supplementary Report *'Food Production in France'*, overviewed in the hypertext, was published in Ireland as a pamphlet by Maunsel, and was reviewed in the February 24 1917 issue of George Russell's *Irish Homestead*. In his review, which headed 'The Country of Clear Thinkers' (referring to France), AE hailed it as 'a most interesting and thoughtful pamphlet' and used it to bring French experience in to support his view that the co-operative society rather than the County Council was the appropriate unit in Ireland for the State's dealings with agriculture.

8. I summarise this in the 1910s political module, this being its orientation.

9. The memoirs of James G Douglas have been edited by JA Gaughan and were published by UCD Press in 1998. I reviewed them for *Quaker Quarterly*, published by Friends House in London.

10. There are some notes in the hypertext extracted from the incomplete AKF archive in Paris, courtesy of Gilles Baud-Berthier the librarian. I have also abstracted the Garnier letters up to 1920.

11. In JJ's papers there are six letters from Garnier in 1921, four in 1922, seven in 1923, and then the pace drops off. I have abstracted them in sequence in the hypertext, with comments where appropriate.

12. In his Rockefeller application JJ emphasised the French aspect, and he went to the trouble to get from the Department of Foreign Affairs a letter of commendation, specifically naming the Rockefeller Fellowship. This letter, written in French, and signed by JP Walshe, Secretary, dated August 18 1926, remains among his papers. In his SSISI paper on 'Distributive Waste', which appears to some extent to be based on the objectives of his Rockefeller Fellowship, there is in the full text only a passing reference to the French experience. He did however make extensive use of his French experience in his Addendum to the *Report of the 1926 Prices Tribunal*. These are accessible in the hypertext.

13. I have abstracted this in the 1920s SSISI module in the hypertext.

14. See also the 1930s Albert Kahn module, and also the 1940s and later AK module; also the 1930s Garnier correspondence.

15. I treat the scientific experience of my French postgraduate epoch in the 1950s academic module.

16. I made several trips to the Albert Kahn Foundation in Paris during the 1990s and I have included some notes on these in the 1990s AK module of the hypertext.

Appendix 4: The Co-operative Movement and Plunkett House

The co-operative movement had deep roots in Irish life and during JJ's youth it was thriving, under the leadership of Sir Horace Plunkett, RA Anderson, Father Finlay and others, after a major organising drive in the 1890s. Plunkett however decoupled himself from this process, and went on to work politically as a Unionist to set up the devolved Department of Agriculture and Technical Instruction, which he headed for a period. For the background to the co-operative movement, and its development during the fist half of the century, see Patrick Bolger's book(1).

My father's first venture into the politics of radical economic change was via the consumer co-op in Trinity College, which was registered in 1913, on the initiative of WJ Bryan, an active promoter of consumer co-operation, who went on to found a similar society in Oxford University.

Bryan had developed a cohesive philosophy for the role of university-based consumer co-ops, based on the idea that the university-trained elite, once they had been sold on the utility of the concept, could play a leading role in generalising it. This philosophy he expounded in an article in *Better Business*, the Plunkett House Library quarterly, early in 1916.

JJ was in at the start of the DU Co-operative Society, becoming enthused by the concept, and he carried it with him during his Albert Kahn world tour, which he used to gain insight into the co-operative movement in India, writing this up subsequently in *Better Business*, in support of Bryan(2).

JJ treated the DU Co-op as potentially a training ground for the students in a School of Commerce, yet to be founded; he hoped that when it did get set up it would be in a position to promote co-operative trading. He also regarded it as a pilot project for what might have been if Ireland had remained un-partitioned, and the producer co-ops of Munster had learned how to add value and service the consumer co-ops of Belfast and Britain. He used it as a window into the politics of the co-operative movement, attending the 1914 Conference of the Co-operative Union, as TCD Co-op representative(3). It was thus a part of his consistent campaign for an all-Ireland perspective, which he waged successively via the Barrington Lectures, via the SSISI and then towards the end of the 30s via the Irish Association.

The 46th Annual Co-operative Union Congress was held in Dublin, on the Whit weekend, 1914. The *Handbook* of this conference contains a review of the consumer co-op scene in Ireland, which was quite undeveloped; it would have been matched by one of the smaller English counties. The Congress was held in Dublin as a gesture in the direction of strengthening the Irish district, and mending fences with the IAOS, with which they had been in dispute in the 1890s. The Co-operative Wholesale Society had attempted to establish creameries in Ireland, but these had mostly failed, being superseded by the IAOS creameries, which depended on local societies appointing their own managers. The emerging Irish movement had found the Co-operative Union structures too inflexible.

The embryonic Dublin consumer co-ops however remained with the Union; they existed in Rathmines, Inchicore, Thomas St, Dorset St and Fairview. The Inchicore one went back to 1859, and serviced the railway workshop workers; it was criticised in the Handbook for being exclusive. The Dublin meeting of the Union in

1914 was thus a false dawn; it seemed to open for JJ a window into Irish co-operative politics, for which he then had hopes, but these proved illusory.

During JJ's Albert Kahn Travelling Fellowship, the co-op declined; it has obviously been dependent on his initiatives, and also the student population had been decimated by the war. At the meeting on November 22 1915, JJ on his return took over doing the minutes; he wrote marginal notes on the earlier minutes, realising the extent to which things had fallen apart in his absence. The agreed to take some trial copies of the *Irish Homestead*. Then at the December 3 meeting, with 10 present, JJ's detailed minutes include a decision to try to capture the trade of the College Kitchen for the IAWS, with some aggressive marketing. This came up at the Board, and the latter agreed to leave it to the Bursar's discretion, a rebuff. The decision to cultivate relations with the IAWS, which was related to the IAOS rather than to the Co-operative Union, was an indicator of a turn towards Plunkett House.

At the meetings in the first months of 1916, with JJ as secretary, there was evidence of a major effort to get more business; there was an attempt made to do a deal with the Dublin Consumer Co-op secretary to encourage non-College Dubliners to shop in the College, making postal or phone arrangement; this looked somewhat like grasping at straws. Business was in decline because of the decimation of the College population due to the war. Then came the Easter Rising, and the shop was occupied by the Officers Training Corps, which was defending the College against the insurgents. JJ as secretary was reduced to writing letters to the military HQ looking for compensation, which by the end of the year they received. JJ's last 1916 minutes were of the meeting on October 16. He continued to attend the meetings, with the status of Secretary.

At a meeting on December 14 1916 it was decided unanimously to record a vote of sympathy with Lt-Col Bryan on the death at the front of his son WJ Bryan, founder of the Co-op.

During 1917 JJ's younger sister Anne was in College, and she attended meetings, alternating with JJ, who was otherwise engaged, working on a committee with James Douglas, George Russell and others producing documentation for the Irish Convention. The co-op had slipped down somewhat in his list of priorities, but the minutes are mostly in his hand. The Bursar was continuing to deal for the College Kitchen with the firm of Andrews, and, according to a letter from HMO White, would use a co-op tender document to beat Andrews down, rather than to take it up. Hostility to co-operative retailing was, it seems, deeply engrained in the culture.

There were insights into co-operative politics: at a meeting on May 7 1917 the question came up of whom to vote for as the Irish representatives on the Board of the Co-operative Union (the all-UK body). It was agreed to vote for Smith-Gordon, Tweedy, Palmer, Adams and Fleming. Smith-Gordon had been encountered by JJ in Oxford, where he had shone as a socialist debater in the Union. RN Tweedy was an engineer who subsequently became a founder member of the Irish Communist Party. The co-operative movement in this period was a focus for those who wanted to democratise the economic system from the bottom up, and who identified with the politics of the Left in this spirit. At a subsequent meeting on February 26 1918 RN Tweedy was nominated to the Board of the Irish Section of the Co-operative Union.

Appendix 4: The Co-operative Movement and Plunkett House

There began to be echoes of the national struggle: on May 21 1918 JJ as secretary was absent; it was reported from the Chair that he had been detained at Baldoyle by the District inspector of Police.

In 1919 business began to take up again, with student war-survivors trickling back. Roles of committee members were defined: there was a sub-committee to keep in touch with the needs of the junior years. Then at the end of 1919 they pulled off the deal that set them up viably for the long haul: they established the Lunch Buffet, in the Dining Hall. This was an immediate success, and gave a good foundation to the wholesale purchasing operation, which they did via the IAWS. JJ then took over the Chair, which he occupied up to the end of 1922. He pulled out of active participation on co-op affairs once he saw it was on a sound business footing.

***

During this time Plunkett and the IAOS were inhabiting a different universe. The consumer movement, the Co-operative Union, was Manchester-based, and had not succeeded in making the bridge with the producers movement in Ireland. There is no record in the IAOS Annual Reports in the period 1913-1918 of any connection with consumer co-ops; they are classified as creameries, agricultural societies, credit, poultry and miscellaneous.

The Co-op Reference Library was started in Plunkett House in January 1914. The Annual Report in 1917 mentions the Library and its publication *Better Business*, but laments its lack of circulation. Then in June 1919 the *Irish Statesman* commenced, in its first existence; it incorporated the *Irish Homestead*, and attracted support from a galaxy of writers which included AE (who edited it), Stephen Gwynn, Henry Harrison (who had been Parnell's secretary), Paul Henry, JM Hone, Shane Leslie, Brinsley McNamara, Lord Monteagle, PS O'Hegarty, Horace Plunkett, Lennox Robinson, Lionel Smith-Gordon, James Stephens, WB and JB Yeats.

This continued up to June 1920, attracting additional writers like Erskine Childers, Captain JR White, Darrell Figgis, Aodh de Blacam and Bernard Shaw. There is no trace of any JJ contribution to this first *Irish Statesman* series, though he knew and socialised with many of the people concerned; he had been in Oxford with Smith-Gordon, and attended the AE soirées. *I find this surprising, because JJ had been supportive of the Convention process in 1917, and had been promoting the Commonwealth solution, with James Douglas and AE; the* Irish Statesman *had emerged specifically with this politics. It is perhaps necessary to explore possible reasons for this; it could be that he felt he had to give priority to building on his French connection, with Garnier and the Albert Kahn Foundation.* JJ did contribute later in the 1920s, to the second *Irish Statesman* series, which began in September 1923.

***

Decoupling himself from the detail of the DU consumer co-op project (he became Chairman for a while in the 1920s, after a long period as Secretary), JJ dedicated his 1920s Barrington lectures to the active promotion of the co-operative approach to economic development in the Free Trade environment, and there are pointers to this in his *Groundwork of Economics*. JJ's written record specific to the co-operative movement in the 1920s (4) is however sparse; he had high hopes of the *Irish Economist*, the successor at *Better Business*, and when this folded he lacked a suitable outlet. He did, probably, contribute to the *Plunkett Foundation Year-Book* on Northern Ireland during the decade.

There may be evidence in support of this in the Plunkett House archives, if I can find it, and in the local papers of the time; the trouble is that the Barrington archive has no record of locations or dates, so it is a matter of a random search. This remains unfinished business.

My father wrote an article in the February 1921 issue of *Better Business* (vol 6 no 2) on 'The Trinity Co-op: Past present and Future'. *Better Business* was an IAOS journal popularising economic concepts among the members of the co-operative movement. It was re-named *The Irish Economist* in February 1922, keeping the sequence numbering, but ceased publication at the end of 1923. JJ did several reviews in the Irish Economist, and contributed a polemical article in favour of free trade. This journal circulated widely among the member co-operative societies of the Irish Agricultural Organisation Society (IAOS) and it was clearly JJ's objective to try by example to help it promote the consumer aspect of the co-operative movement, complementing the primary producer aspect which had come into viable existence in the form of the co-operative creameries.

The first of JJ's reviews, in the February 1922 issue, was of *The Consumers' Co-operative Movement* by Sydney and Beatrice Webb (London, Longmans, 1921), followed in August 1922 by a review of *Money and Credit* by CJ Melrose (London, Collins, 1920), with an introduction by Prof Irving Fisher. Then in what proved to be the final issue in January 1923 JJ had a paper 'Free Trade or Protection for Irish Industries?'(5). In the 1930s JJ's economic writings, in the *Economic Journal* (edited by Keynes) and elsewhere, were used by analysts of the Irish scene in the *Agricultural Co-operative Yearbook*, published by the Plunkett Foundation in Britain(6).

In the 1940s JJ's main contributions were his attempt to influence Government policy, in the Commission on post-Emergency Agriculture, and some field-work in the late 40s which led to his book *Irish Agriculture in Transition*. The 1943-44 *Year-Book of Agricultural Co-operation*, still published by the Plunkett Foundation in Oxford, contains an overview by HF Norman, entitled 'Agricultural Co-operation in Ireland'. Unlike the mid-30s overview, there is no direct reference to JJ or his work, so he must by this time have faded from Plunkett Foundation consciousness somewhat.

There was however a reference in the Norman review to the need for active managed linking of groups of large and small farms together, as a synergetic whole, a foreshadowing of the concept introduced in the Seanad around this time by Richards Orpen. Norman mentioned Drinagh co-op, in Co Cork, which was one of the several co-ops visited by JJ in the field-work for his 1951 book, as a potential focus for the development of a pilot version of the Orpen model.

Norman in his paper drew attention to the way in which the movement in Northern Ireland had been undermined by Ministry of Agriculture policy. It is noteworthy that the view from Plunkett House remained 'all-Ireland' despite Partition.

I think it probable that JJ's exploratory field work, looking at situations where creamery co-ops had bought farms and were using them as demonstration units for upgrading agricultural practice, was under the stimulus of the Norman review. He saw in this a possible focus for the development of the Richards Orpen 'economic farm unit' model, embodying a managed cluster of farms with a common service centre. He wrote this experience up in his *Irish Agriculture in Transition*, published in 1951(7).

My father JJ in the 1950s remained concerned about the co-operative movement(8); he had the opportunity to look back on the foregoing experience in a 1954 publication by the National Co-operative Council which celebrated the Plunkett centenary. In this he wrote a paper entitled *Unfinished Programme*, of which the present writer at the time was not aware, but of which he now appreciates the significance(9).

There was a revival of interest in producer co-operation in Mayo in the 1950s, led by politicising republicans (Cathal Quinn, Ethna MacManus, Seamus Ó Mongain and others)(10); this set up milk production in Mayo for the first time, and even began to go as far as cheese, developing the local hotel market. This we regarded at the time as a pilot project for the left-republican political radicalisation of the 1960s, and there are some credit unions around which owe their existence to this process, though on the whole it was not significant, being sidelined by the developments in the North around the civil rights issue(11).

There is evidence in JJ's papers that he visited Mayo in the mid 60s; he left notes of a visit to Cathal Quinn, whom he regarded as a 'live wire'. The stimulus for the visit could have been the Dermot McManus correspondence at the time(12), and he probably visited the McManus estate at Killeaden, in what could have been a nostalgia-trip to try to pick up echoes of the (sometimes Gaelicising like Chevasse), improving, socially responsible landlord tradition exemplified by Standish O'Grady, Sir Horace Plunkett, Lord Charlemont, Bobby Burke and others, on which he based his promotion of the Richards Orpen model for rural civilisation(13).

The Dublin University consumers co-op, which had served the living-in students since 1913, was wound up in the 1970s; it had become hidebound and anachronistic in its methods of work, and succumbed to competition from the Students Union(14).

Some of the 1970s techno-economic work by the present writer for Lough Egish Co-op, and for Bord Bainne, has philosophical links with JJ's 20s work, and his 30s work on the 'winter milk' question(15). For example, the fact that Lough Egish, as a co-op organised by a group of 30-acre drumlin farms in Monaghan, were able to go for 'vertical integration' via leasing land in Meath to fatten their calves, would have pleased him.

The association of the present writer with the Green Party from the 1990s onwards has generated some re-examination of the Plunkett approach to the problem of organising agriculture for sustainability(16).

Notes and References
1. *The Irish Co-operative Movement, its History and Development*, Patrick Bolger, Institute of Public Administration, Dublin 1977. The recent conversion of several major Munster co-operatives into private limited companies, with global aspirations, suggests a need for a re-

examination of the history of the movement, and an analysis of its failure to develop a cohesive community orientation.

2. I have reviewed this material in the 1910s Plunkett module of the hypertext.

3. The souvenir handbook of the 1914 Conference contains a foundation photo of the TCD consumer co-op. Foundation details of the latter, and Bryan's *Better Business* article, are also on record in the 1910s Plunkett module of the hypertext.

4. I have made what I have found available in the 1920s Plunkett module. I am indebted to Kate Targett , the librarian in the Plunkett Foundation, Oxford, for unearthing several relevant JJ references.

5. The texts of these *Irish Economist* reviews are also accessible in the 1920s Plunkett module of the hypertext.

6. I have included in the 1930s Plunkett module a virtual reprint of *The Importance of Economy in the Distribution of Goods*, by J Johnston MA FTCD, published by the Co-operative Conference Association, August 1933. There is also, in the annual publication of the co-operative movement in Britain (1935 edition) on p67 an article by HF Norman headed 'The Irish Free State' in which JJ's analysis of the situation is quoted, based on his paper in the September 1934 issue of the Economic Journal. I have referenced this in the 'academic papers' stream, and given it in full in this 1930s Plunkett module.

7. The hypertext 1940s Plunkett module gives access to JJ's Post-Emergency Agriculture Commission work and to his *Irish Agriculture in Transition* where he develops the Orpen model.

8. JJ's expression of concern was via the Kells Ingram Farm, associated with the TCD Agriculture School, and there appeared to be an opportunity with the support of Marshall Plan money for the development of an Agricultural Research Institute. JJ hoped, vainly, that these might combine to show the positive socio-economic features of the Orpen model. I treat the background to this in the TCD Politics thread, which is accessible via the 1950s Plunkett module of the hypertext.

9. The Plunkett centenary paper by JJ is also in this 1950s module of the hypertext.

10. A note on a 1950s Mayo episode is also in this 1950s module of the hypertext.

11. I have embodied some of my own 1960s field-work experience in the 1960s Plunkett module of the hypertext, where it seems relevant.

12. This 1960s Dermot McManus contact was a result of a paper by the latter on the Irish literary revival, for the publication of which he sought JJ's support. JJ had been in political contact with MacManus in the 1920s and early 30s, but they drifted apart due to MacManus's Blueshirt politics.

13. The Richards Orpen model was outlined in some depth by JJ in his *Irish Agriculture in Transition* and also in a paper to the SSISI. Ideas similar to these had been previewed by Standish O'Grady in his 1912-13 articles for Jim Larkin's *Irish Worker*; see *To the Leaders of Our Working People*, Standish O'Grady, ed EA Hagan, UCD Press 2002, reviewed by the present writer in the December 2002 *Irish Democrat*.

14. I have recorded some notes on the demise of the DU Co-op in the 1970s Plunkett module of the hypertext.

15. I did some computer-modelling of possible winter milk scenarios when with the TCD Department of Statistics in the early 70s, and I have notes on this in the 1970s Plunkett module of this hypertext thread. I was aware of JJ's 1931 SSISI paper at the time, and referenced it.

16. See the Spring 2001 issue of the Teagasc periodical *Farm and Food* where I was invited to contribute an article on 'Biotechnology and Sustainability' by the Editor Con O'Rourke. This is reprinted also in *Organic Matters* the journal of the Irish Organic Fames and Growers Association.

Appendix 5: Academic Publications

Joe Johnston's published academic work tended to take second place to his polemical and outreach writings. He did however make a significant contribution to economic history, and the analysis of the origins of modern economic concepts. In the latter context he increasingly concentrated on the economic writings of Bishop Berkeley.

I have so far not found any publications in the 1910s decade (1) which count as 'academic' in the strict sense; his main output was initially via the Albert Kahn(2) Travelling Fellowship reporting procedure, and then later journalistically in national politics(3), into which mode the Albert Kahn work evolved naturally, via his 1916 work in France on the wartime agricultural production system(4).

In the 1920s JJ's main output was in the Barrington(5) direction, promoting co-operation among agricultural producers; there was some quasi-academic spin-off from this process, in the form of his book *Groundwork of Economics* (Educational Co, 1926)(6). He also served on the Prices Commission, and used its *Report* as an outlet for some of the results (ie the French sector) of his researches into distribution costs, done with the support of the Rockefeller Foundation. The Irish sector of this work appeared as his first paper to the Statistical and Social Inquiry Society in 1926(7).

In the 1930s JJ's academic output reached a peak, and much of it was concerned with his work on Berkeley, whose economic writings JJ increasingly regarded as seminal, a precursor of most if not all modern economic thinking. Most of this work was published in the TCD publication *Hermathena*. This somewhat restricted its international accessibility. He did however circulate reprints of *Hermathena papers* (of which small stocks remained among his possessions), and he began to publish in the mainstream economic publications in Britain, especially the *Economic Journal,* then edited by JM Keynes.

In a series of papers dealing with commerce, money and credit(8) in the ancient world, and in 18th century Ireland, JJ stressed the identity of money and credit as seen by Berkeley, relating this to Berkeley's promotion of the need for a national publicly-owned banking system. Private ownership of the banking system, as is has evolved, regarded the distinction between money and credit as being of great importance. For a modern financier, a debt is liquidated when money is repaid. For Berkeley, monetary obligations are only liquidated when transformed into solid goods and services. The latter was JJ's position, which he distilled into a 1938 paper for Keynes's *Economic Journal*(9).

My father also wrote extensively in academic mode on topics related to the world depression(10), and to the Economic War, in the latter case orienting his arguments towards distinct Irish(11) and English(12) readerships, and indeed audiences, in that much of the published material relates to lectures and seminars. Some of the papers published abroad are in fact Irish oriented, in that ideas published in a prestigious international journal would perhaps carry more weight in influencing policy(13).

After entering the Seanad in 1938 JJ had little time for academic publication, but he did contribute a further Berkeley paper to *Hermathena* in 1942(14). It had been written in 1937, and he had been diverted from completing it and submitting it by political pressures. It forms part of his continuing Berkeley analysis which he latter pulled together into his 1970 *Querist* book.

Also in 1942 he was accepted as a Member of the Royal Irish Academy(15). It is probable that he resurrected his 1937 paper and submitted it in order to strengthen his academic standing. The President of the Academy at the time was Eoin MacNeill; I suspect (without having hard evidence) that Eoin MacNeill may have encouraged JJ to apply at this time, during his Presidency, in recognition of his role in support of the Irish cause internationally, via the Albert Kahn Foundation(16). The politics of the foundation of the Dublin Institute of Advanced Studies, on de Valera's initiative, at this time involved the RIA, and was, I understand, somewhat complex. I have heard suggestions that the RIA had been distinctly unhelpful to de Valera in the context, in the late 30s and early 40s, when he required good academic advice. I conjecture that this 1942 Academy recruitment under MacNeill was part of that political process(17). In other words, Dev probably encouraged MacNeill to recruit national-minded academics to the Academy.

In support of his claim to academic distinction JJ listed his 1925 *Groundwork of Economics*, his 1934 *Nemesis of Economic Nationalism*, his *Hermathena* papers on managed currency in the 5th century BC, Irish currency in the 18th century, commercial restriction and monetary deflation in 18th century Ireland, Berkeley and the abortive bank project of 1720-21, the synopsis of Berkeley's monetary philosophy, Locke, Berkeley and Hume as monetary theorists, all of which are listed as his main academic works in the 1930s module.

The above suggests that he was proud of, and stood over, his *Nemesis* and this therefore gives it a place in the academic stream along with the *Groundwork*, though to my mind both are basically popularising polemical books rather than academic studies.

He also mentions, without detailed reference, papers in '...JHS, Studies, the Economic Journal and the Journal of the Statistical Society (sic) of Ireland, etc, etc ...' thereby indicating that he regarded these as part of the outreach programme rather than hard-core academic research contributions.

In November 1953 there was a special issue of *Hermathena* to commemorate the Berkeley bicentenary, which had been celebrated at an international conference held in Trinity College in July 1953. There were 70 universities present from all over the world. Éamonn de Valera, then Taoiseach (Prime Minister) opened an exhibition of Berkeleiana in the College Library. The delegates were received by the President Seán T O'Kelly. The keynote lecture(18) was given that evening by JJ on Berkeley's influence as an economist, with Professor GA Duncan in the chair, the vote of thanks being proposed by Senator Professor George O'Brien of UCD.

In the remainder of the 1950s JJ contributed further to the analysis of the performance of the Irish economy under the protectionist regime of de Valera, of which he was highly critical(19). This work however was done primarily in outreach mode, initially via the Seanad, and also via the SSISI and the Irish Association, rather than through the medium of academic papers.

Appendix 5: Academic Publications

***

My own published scientific work was concentrated in the 1950s(20), during the Ecole Polytechnique and Dublin Institute of Advanced Studies period. Some significant work was done both on the experimental detection and identification of 'strange' particles, and on the technology of the experimentation process.

Highlights included the discovery of the first sigma-minus hyperon and the measurement of its mass, and confirmation of the existence of an electron decay mode for the K-plus meson. Subsequent work, with Cormac Ó Ceallaigh, estimated the relative frequency of the various K-meson decay modes. We were able to use our analysis of the two-body modes as a means of increasing considerably the precision of using ionisation measurements for the estimation of particle velocity.

***

In the 1960s JJ, while in outreach mode being increasingly critical of the European Common Market, and in TCD politics fighting a rearguard action with the Kells Ingram Farm and the integrated large-scale commercial farm model, tended increasingly to concentrate on mining his own earlier ideas, with a view to linking them with a new annotated edition of Berkeley's *Querist*(21). This was published in 1970, and he submitted it for the degree of D Litt. It had always galled him that he had not done a doctorate during his earlier academic period, and this last fling in the academic world was his attempt to make belated amends.

The book had impact, and may yet have more. I am indebted to Collison Black, late of Queen University Belfast, and who served with my father on the Council of the SSISI in the 1950s, for drawing my attention to some work in the **University of Illinois** by **Salim Rachid**.

In a *Manchester School* paper (Vol LVI no 4, December 1988) Rachid mentions JJ's Berkeley work in support of his thesis regarding the existence of an **Irish School of Economic Development 1720-1750**. This included **Berkeley, Molyneux, Swift, Dobbs and Prior,** and was closely linked to applied-scientific development activity via the **Dublin Society.** Rachid distinguishes this group from the 'Mercantilists' with whom all economic thought prior to Adam Smith has tended to be uncritically identified by historians of economic thought, and shows how they were in fact Smith precursors. JJ went further and regarded Berkeley as being a Keynes precursor.

I suggest that there is perhaps some **raw material here for exploitation by scholars interested in the historical roots of development economics.** I would go further and suggest that in the composition of this group, with the strong **scientific component** as expressed in Dobbs and Prior, we have a good model which in current development economic thinking needs to be recaptured. The key to economic development is **technical competence in the useful arts**, and this was the Dublin Society's prime objective.

At this point it is appropriate to place on record that JJ in the 40s encouraged me to take up science as a career, and I now realise that this must have been as a consequence of the foregoing insights.

***

There was also some significant scientific work done by the present writer in the 1960s and 1970s, but in applied-scientific domains, where publication procedures are somewhat 'grey'. This work was increasingly in the various domains which were opening up to computer-based analysis, evolving in the 1980s increasingly into the commercial consultancy area. Then in the 1990s thanks to the EU-funded work which we did in knowledge-base development, using case-based reasoning, I did get my name on various team publications, including one done in hypermedia mode published by Springer-verlag(22).

Notes and References

1. I give in the 1910s academic module of the hypertext some insights into the Oxford environment (1910-12) where HAL Fisher would have been an influence. The influence via the student debating societies were primarily political.

2. For an overview of the Albert Kahn thread see Appendix 3.

3. JJ was quite prolific as a political journalist during the war of independence period; I have overviewed this aspect in Appendix 10.

4. For the European part of his Albert Kahn Fellowship JJ somehow managed to get to study the French wartime agricultural production system, as part of his Report. He also published it in Ireland, with Maunsel, in the form of a pamphlet supporting co-operative organisation.

5. I have overviewed the Barrington Lectures thread in Appendix 7, under the generic label 'Intellectual Outreach'.

6. I have attempted to pull together all references having some academic standing in the 1920s academic module, though they mostly border on other themes.

7. This paper was entitled 'Some Causes and Consequences of Distributive Waste' (J SSISI vol XIV p353, 1926-7). JJ was introduced as 'Fellow and Tutor of TCD, Rockefeller Fellow for Economic Research in Europe 1926-27, and Chairman ILO Committee, League of Nations Society of Ireland.'

8. The **Hermathena** papers were as follows: *An International Managed Currency in the Fifth Century BC*, XLVII p132, 1932; *Irish Currency in the Eighteenth Century*, LII p3, 1938; *Berkeley and the Abortive Bank Project of 1720-21*, LIV p110, 1939; *A Synopsis of Berkeley's Monetary Philosophy*, LV p73, 1940; also he published *Solon's Reform of Weights and Measures* in the Journal of Hellenic Studies, Vol LIV, p180, 1934.

9. *The Monetary Theories of Berkeley*, in **Economic History** (a supplement to the *Economic Journal*, edited by JM Keynes and EAG Robinson), February 1938. In this JJ identified in Berkeley forerunners of ideas expressed in Keynes' *General Theory*: "Berkeley anticipated Mr Keynes' view...that an increase in the quantity of money, if used for productive purposes, would increase the volume of employment."

10. *The World Crisis: Its Non-Monetary Background*, **Institute of Bankers**, Nov 17 1932. In this paper JJ focused on the disequilibrium between agriculture and industry, and on the various types of friction in the pipeline between the producer and consumer of agricultural goods. JJ used this Bankers platform as a means of launching his classic Free Trade onslaught on economic nationalism, later to be developed in his 1934 book *Nemesis of Economic Nationalism*.

11. *Agriculture and the Sickness of the Free Economy*, **Studies**, XXIV no 94, p295, June 1935. I count this among the academic stream, given that the Jesuit quarterly Studies is refereed and has a scholarly reputation. It is however polemic, and really belongs in the outreach category treated in the Barrington and Statistical and Social Inquiry Society streams. JJ got reprints for distribution. The de Valera 'self-sufficiency' policy was it its height, and agricultural exports were crippled by the 'economic war'. This was followed by *An Outlook on Irish Agriculture*, **Studies** XXVIII no 111, September 1939. This continued the arguments of the 1935 paper, in the light of subsequent experience. Aggregate money income in agriculture declined from £52M in 1929 to £29M in 1933 and by 1938 had increased again only to £38M. The increase in industrial production under protection had increased the wealth of the towns but had increased the prices of industrial goods bought by declining agricultural incomes.

12. The *Economic Journal*, edited by JM Keynes and EAG Robinson, in its September 1934 issue (Vol XLIV no 175 p453) carried a paper by JJ on *The Purchasing Power of Irish Free State Farmers in 1933*. This was a quantification of the catastrophic collapse of agricultural purchasing power consequent on the 'economic war' arising from de Valera's policy on the land annuities. Then we had *The Anglo-Irish Economic Conflict* in *Nineteenth Century and After*, DCCVIII, February 1936. This was a sort of 'think tank' or theoretical journal of the Liberal Party; the paper by JJ which is to hand is a reprint, and from internal evidence it was a public lecture read on an occasion, perhaps at his Alma Mater in Lincoln College Oxford, but this is a guess. Then in December 1937 we had *Price Ratios in Recent Irish Agricultural Experience*, *Economic Journal* (ed Keynes & Robinson); Vol XLVII no 188 p680. In this paper JJ developed a classical Adam Smith argument from the Wealth of Nations, regarding the need for a certain ratio between the price of cattle and corn to exist, if continuous improvement of arable and pastoral land is to take place. Then to summarise the Economic War experience we had *Irish Agriculture, Then and Now*, *Manchester School* of Economic and Social Studies; October 1940. This paper reviewed critically the 'economic war' period and analysed the relationships between cattle, pigs, poultry, milk, grass and cereals. JJ introduced it with an outline of his experience of farming and market gardening between 1928 and 1934, when he '...abandoned the unequal struggle and devoted his spare time to poltico-economic agitation ...' becoming a Senator in 1938.

13. The full sequence of academic and academic-type publications is abstracted in the 1930s module of the academic stream in the hypertext support documentation.

14. *Bishop Berkeley and Kindred Monetary Thinkers*; *Hermathena* LIX p30, 1942. "Whether money is to be considered as having an intrinsic value, or as being a commodity, a standard, a measure, or a pledge, as is variously suggested by writers? And whether the true idea of money, as such, be not altogether that of a ticket or counter?" *(Querist, p25, no 23)*.

15. Some details of this, as well as of the Berkeley paper referenced above, are accessible in the 1940s academic module in the hypertext.

16. There is a reference in the Garnier correspondence to a visit of Cosgrave and MacNeill to Paris on August 31 1923. JJ and Garnier, the executive secretary, were in frequent correspondence during this period, in the Albert Kahn Foundation context, with JJ briefing French public opinion through Garnier's journalism.

17. Dearly as I would like to, I am not going to try to tidy up this loose end now. It must remain on the agenda for researchers in the 'science and government' domain. or perhaps historians of the DIAS and the RIA.

18. *Berkeley's Influence as an Economist*; *Hermathena* LXXXII p76, 1953. This paper can be regarded as a review of all JJ's work on Berkeley to date, and I have therefore reproduced it in full in the hypertext. It can perhaps be regarded as the pinnacle of JJ's academic career.

19. Typical of his outreach work during the 1950s was his *Sickness of the Irish Economy* published by the Irish Association.

20. I have listed all my refereed scientific papers in the 1950s module of the academic stream, along with some expansion of the overview description given here.

21. More detail on JJ's academic 'last fling' is available in the 1960s academic module in the hypertext. JJ's *Hermathena* publication *Monetary Manipulation: Berkeleyan and Otherwise*; (CX p32, 1970) it seems he wrote in 1964, including it among the papers which he pulled together into his unpublished *Consumer Demand as the Basis of Credit*, which I have referenced in the <u>SSISI</u> stream. *Hermathena* in the end accepted it, perhaps because of his impending publication of his <u>Berkeley book</u>.

22. These themes are best overviewed from <u>Appendix 11</u> (science and society), <u>Appendix 12</u> (socio-technical) and <u>Appendix 13</u> (techno-economic) respectively. I can mention here however my 1996 review of <u>*The Science of Empire*</u> by Zaheer Baber, published in the Feb 1997 issue of *Science and Public Policy* (International Science Policy Foundation). The book reviewed was published in 1996 by the State University of New York.

Appendix 6: The Statistical and Social Inquiry Society

Background: the First Century

The Centenary Volume of the *Proceedings of the Statistical and Social Inquiry Society of Ireland (SSISI)* was published in 1947, edited by RD Collison Black, Lecturer in Economics in Queens University Belfast.

This, as well has details of the history of the Society, contains information about the background to the Barrington Lectures(1), which formed such an important part of JJ's activity during the 1920s, and which he continued to influence and participate in during the 30s and 40s.

Names associated with the foundation of the Society and with its outreach work included John Stuart Mill and Nassau Senior, and relations were developed with literary and other societies throughout the country.

The SSISI Today

The SSISI maintains an archive, which is accessible by arrangement in the Library of the Central Office of Statistics, by courtesy of the Director. I have scanned this and gained thereby some additional insights into JJ's work outside TCD, and identified also some material relevant to my own career. These are noted sequentially in the detail modules, which are organised by decade, and referenced from this overview.

The Society is still going strong, providing a regular meeting-place for Irish economic gurus and their critics, in the Economic and Social Research Institute, Burlington Road, Dublin 4.

I won't attempt to review Mary Daly's history of the SSISI (see note 1) here, but I take the opportunity to mention in passing that she identifies the leading lights of the SSISI before 1914, when JJ was forming his ideas, as being Liberal, typical being CH Oldham, also AW Samuels MP for Dublin University, the former being an explicit Home Ruler, while the latter in his SSISI papers was implicitly so, though labelled a Liberal Unionist. As late as 1917, when Partition was visibly on the agenda, Oldham remained an all-Ireland Home Ruler, reflecting what was then an important sector of educated Protestant opinion.

JJ and the SSISI

Charles Oldham was the first Principal of the College of Commerce in Rathmines, which was part of the system of technical education set up in Dublin in the 1880s under the influence of GF Fitzgerald, the TCD Professor of Natural Philosophy, and others, and which now forms the core of the Dublin Institute of Technology.

The philosophy motivating this foundation linked the Liberal 'free trade' ethos with technical competence as the best basis for industrialisation, in opposition to the protectionism then being promoted by the English Tories, and by Arthur Griffith in Ireland, under the influence of the German economist List. The SSISI in the 1900s and 1910s was very much under the Oldham influence, and JJ would appear to have been motivated to support it, especially because of its connection with the Barrington Lectures, which before the War had been a means of promoting Liberal Home Rule ideas publicly all over Ireland.

According to Mary Daly the Society took steps to revive the Barrington Lectures in 1919, but this fell foul of a dispute between the Council and its Librarian, Shannon Millin, who had entered into a correspondence with the Commissioners of Charitable Bequests without their permission. The result was that the matter was allowed to lapse, and they Barrington Lectures remained outside the ambit of the SSISI for the next decade or so. The Barrington Trust however appointed JJ as Lecturer, and he took over the task single-handed. This was outside the record of the SSISI, which at its meeting January 29 1920 declined to take on the administration of the Trust.

It would appear however that JJ had on his agenda the restoration of the SSISI Barrington link, and with this in mind he applied for membership and was accepted by the Council on Nov 14 1924, in a major cohort of 22 Oldham recruits, which included RJ Mortished, Prof John Busteed and a Plunkett House representative.

By this time JJ was beginning, at least outside TCD, to have a reputation as an economist, having served on the Free State Agricultural Commission. His membership of the Oldham-recruited 'group of 22', destined to revive the SSISI after its wartime decline, is in character.

During the first half of the 1920s the SSISI meetings were mostly in Plunkett House, and there was the makings of a linkage or at least a friendly understanding with the IAOS. The Plunkett House Library was supported by the Carnegie Trust, and the Librarian Florence Marks on Nov 22 wrote to the SSISI, transmitting a suggestion from George Russell that the Library be made available to SSISI members.

The sequence of meetings was as follows: May 28 and July 16 1920 93 St Stephen's Green, Jan 13 1921 RDS, Feb 4 1921 Plunkett House; there is a letter from Sir Horace Plunkett on record regretting his inability to be present to welcome them. The following 3 meetings in 1921 were there, then the last one on Dec 15 was at the RDS. In 1922 they oscillated between Plunkett House and Fitzwilliam Place. Meetings continued in 1924 and the first half of 1925, but then on June 19 1925 they accepted the invitation of the RIA, where they remained subsequently for many decades.

Mary Daly identifies the problem with Plunkett House simply as the timing: they were only allowed meet at 5pm, while they preferred 8pm meetings. It is possible however to put a deeper interpretation on this, given what is known about the background. If Sir Horace and the IAOS had been motivated to do so, they would have opened the place in the evenings, and helped to build up interest in, and use of, their library, which was dedicated to the promotion of co-operative principles of economic development.

Notoriously however Sir Horace's house was burned down in the Civil War, and he lost interest in Irish affairs, moving most of the assets of the Plunkett Foundation to Oxford, where it exists to this day as an important resource relevant to the world co-operative movement. The rupture of the embryonic link between the IAOS and the SSISI can be identified as one of the most tragic institutional casualties of the Civil War.

In the Albert Kahn sequence there is a reference in the Garnier correspondence to setting up a resource centre in Ireland, and JJ was advocating that this be hosted by the Plunkett House library(2). This was in mid 1922. I can find no trace of this either in Plunkett House itself or in Oxford. The use of the library for this purpose was undoubtedly on JJ's agenda, and the link with the SSISI would have been part of the ideas-promotional network which he aspired to develop.

Having accepted defeat in his Plunkett House plans, JJ turned his priority attention to the SSISI itself, and on October 19 1925, at the Society's first meeting in the RIA, JJ was elected to the Council, along with Dr Rowlette, T Barrington and RJ Mortished. At this same meeting of Council a standing committee was set up to make suggestions to the Government regarding the coming Census; this was chaired by the President (Oldham) and included JJ, Rowlette, Mortished and J Eason.

On May 6 1926 Tom Barrington read a paper on 'A Review of Irish Agricultural Prices', and JJ took part in the discussion(2). On October 26 Justice Meredith was elected President. Meredith was of the same Protestant Home Ruler tradition as Oldham and JJ; he had been associated with the Sinn Fein courts; there is a book on this topic by Mary Kotsonouris.

On February 24 1927 GA Duncan read a paper on *Rural Industrialisation*; Father Finlay and JJ spoke to it. This was JJ's network; Duncan was his colleague in TCD, Father Finlay was a legendary co-operative movement activist. JJ was clearly using the SSISI to promote Plunkett House economics, as best he could, despite the breaking of the link(3).

It will be seen from the TCD Board sequence that JJ would at this time have been pulling together a Report arising out of his Rockefeller Foundation project, in which he was studying the spread of prices between producers and consumers, using French and other continental experience(4). Taking producer co-operative control of the distribution system, and linking it with the consumer co-operatives, must have been his objective. His SSISI paper would appear to have been a 'dry run' for his Report, which however seems to have got lost, as the Rockefeller Foundation has no record of it, though they have record of his Fellowship.

During the years which followed JJ was a fairly regular attender at meetings, though living in Dundalk and Drogheda from 1928 to 1934, and then from 1940 to 1946. When there he often contributed to the discussions, and sometimes contributed papers. I list these below.

26/01/28 C Eason on the *Report of the Poor Law Commission*
26/04/28 'Health Insurance'
02/04/28 'Oireachtas as a National Economic Council'
30/05/28 'Exam Statistics'
15/06/29 JJ on 'National Transport' was accepted by Council for 1930
15/11/29 'Banks'
16/01/30 Thekla Beere on 'Language Revival in Ireland, Norway and Wales'

I put in the Thekla Beer reference because JJ must have been instrumental in inviting her, seeing as she was very close to his sister Anne, and a co-founder of the Youth Hostels Association; the two of them were Protestant language revivalists in the Civil Service.

At Council on 21/02/30 JJ proposed a motion that papers read at meetings should not be published without due authorisation. Then on 20/03/30 JJ read his paper on national transport problems(3).

JJ attended Council meetings on May 27 and then on October 10; at the latter a lunch was planned for November 22 or 24 in honour of Sir Josiah Stamp who would be in Ireland at the time, Ministers Blythe and McGilligan were to be invited, also Professor Joly the TCD geophysicist.(5).

JCM Eason the President delivered his inaugural paper on 14/11/30, the vote of thanks being given by the outgoing president Justice JC Meredith, and seconded by JJ. JJ attended the Council meeting on December 6 1930 at which he undertook to deliver a paper on March 19 1931 on 'Winter Dairying'(6).

At about this time the Barrington Trust again surfaces on the SSISI agenda, thanks to a letter from JJ which was on the agenda of the Council meeting on November 21 1930. It was agreed to refer the matter to an ad hoc committee consisting the JJ, Justice Meredith and the Officers of the Society.

The 'Winter Dairying' paper analysed the supply constraints on Irish dairy exports, which were dominated by seasonal effects, resulting in Irish produce being pushed out of the British market by the Danes.

The present writer had another run at this problem, with a computer modelling approach, for Bord Bainne in 1972. The problem is still with us, the summer peak milk production presenting a disposal problem, and the associated spring calving peak presenting a related problem as regards meat production in the autumn. JJ's analysis remains valid to this day, and the problem of consistent quality and smoothed supply of meat and milk products will remain with us until Irish farmers come around to a consistent winter feeding regime, as is the case for the liquid milk market.

JJ remained on the Council for 1931/32, and at the Council meeting on September 31 1931 the president JCM Eason opened up again the question of the Barrington Trust, the ad-hoc committee having reported. Manliff Barrington by this time was the only Trustee and he had declared the intention of continuing to consult the Society as he had done in the past. The JJ solo interlude was being post facto taken on board. JJ spoke to JP Colbert's paper on 17/12/31, the topic being 'Currency Problems in the IFS'.

At the Council meeting on October 12 1931 JJ made a proposal relating to the Barrington lectures, and then on February 4 1932 is was decided to seek press cuttings relating to the lectures. On April 7 the president JCM Eason '...stated that the position with regard to the Barrington lectures was somewhat unsatisfactory in the northern area ...'. On February 26 a paper by Justice Meredith on 'Separate Markets for the Unemployed' was delivered, and JJ spoke to it; it seems the meeting was lively and controversial, being adjourned to March 11.

There is then a long hiatus as regards JJ's participation in general meetings, but he was active on the Council in getting the Barrington Lectures upgraded and extended to cover all of Ireland. His next paper delivered to the Society was on the depressed state of Irish agriculture(7). The content of this paper was echoed in JJ's December 1935 Barrington lecture at Termonfeckin, and according to Mary Daly the press reports gave rise to controversy, and got JJ into trouble with the Barrington Trust. The objective was to end the economic war, and it was highly critical of the Fianna Fail government's policy(8).

JJ's participation in the SSISI Council in the latter part of the 30s appears to have been totally dedicated to ensuring that the Barrington lectures continued to exist and be taken seriously. There are regular references to 'reports' but these seem to have been lost. When JJ was elected to the Senate in 1938, his position was strengthened.

Issues addressed appear to have related to the Northern Ireland lecturer Lemberger; JJ seems to have wanted to get rid of him, re-advertising the position. JJ tried to get Duncan or Meenan to take it on, without success. Then in the end he succeeded in getting Lloyd-Dodd; the latter was elected to SSISI membership on 10/01/38, and a paper was projected for him. There was also a joint committee with the Engineering and Science Society(9) set up, to consider road transport; Shanahan was to act for the Society.

On May 17 1938 JJ and Dr Rowlette were congratulated on their election to the Senate. On November 25 1939 JJ attended a Council meeting and agreed to deliver a paper on 'Agricultural Prices and Costs in Eire and NI'. There is little record of JJ's participation during the war period, but then he was living in Drogheda, and depending on the GNR train and his bicycle. There is no record of his projected paper having been delivered. He did however keep in touch by correspondence, and was able to see to it that the Barrington lectures continued, on an all-Ireland basis.

On February 27 1942 JJ delivered a crucial paper(10) in which he challenged the then current conventional wisdom that small farms were intrinsically more productive per man and per acre than large; it all depended on the effective use of instrumental capital, organisational and management. He gave figures for large farms known to him which had achieved high productivity per man and per acre, and foreshadowed some of the arguments he used later in favour of managed large farms owned co-operatively by groupings of neighbouring small ones.

On April 27 1944 the SSISI held a session on Irish external trade, in an attempt to preview the coming post-war situation. The main paper was given by Dr Henry Kennedy, who drew attention to the low productivity of the land, and estimated how much it might be increased. There were contributions from others, including JJ who stressed our dependence on British policies over which we had no control(11).

Then in 1945, with George O'Brien as president, JJ went back into the front line of Barrington lecturing, continuing during 1946 and 47. He produced a paper which I suspect embodied some of the ideas he was attempting to promote(12). This was mis-titled in her index by Mary Daly, who referenced it as '...Irish Agriculture' (p233). She is not to be blamed for this, because the SSISI itself mis-titled the paper in the table of contents of its *Proceedings*. In fact the 'Rural Civilisation' label was significant and related to a preview of what currently is emerging as the 'eco-village' movement(13). JJ developed further the idea of an organised co-operative relationship between a group of farms of varying sizes, focused on a centre which made use of residual 'big-house' resources. This could well have been distilled from his current Barrington Lectures, though this is subject to confirmation, as I have not been able to find press reports of these. JJ did however set some store by this paper, as he ordered reprints to distribute, of which a small stock remains.

After something of a hiatus during 1948 (during which he moved house twice) he shows up again during Roy Geary's Presidency, contributing on 2/12/49 to Social Security symposium, in absentia, along with Eason, Mortished and others(14). He was critical of the way social security on the British model in the North had undermined the supply of farm labour. Then on 10/2/50 he spoke to a paper on 'Mid-Roscommon Farms', this indicating his growing interest in a micro-economic approach, later to be dismissed by the new wave of econometric and statistical-economic gurus as 'anecdotal'.

Then in 1950 it came to be JJ's turn to be President, having served his time on the Council for over two decades. Thekla Beere was Honorary Secretary. He continued up to 1953. During this period there were initially a rich crop of significant papers by people who subsequently became influential, though it might be said that towards the end of his second term he began to lose interest, when he made his post-war move back to the land, taking up a market-gardening enterprise near Stradbally in Laois. He was replaced by JP Beddy as President in June 1953. He continued on the Council, being re-elected on 11/06/54 along with George O'Brien and PS O'Hegarty. but he sunk into oblivion as regards Society decision-making after 1955, although they elected him a Vice-President on 16/05/58.

During his Presidency he attended and contributed regularly. Papers included John O'Donovan on 'State Enterprise' (12/05/50), James Meenan on the 'Universities' (26/05/50), TJ Keenan on 'Catholic Ecclesiastical Statistics' (6/10/50), P Brennan on 'Economics of Air Transport' 3/11/50), and then on December 8 1950 JJ gave his Presidential paper(15). Perhaps under some pressure from Geary and the incoming wave of econometric specialists, in this JJ abandoned his 'anecdotal' micro-techno-economic mode of analysis, and came up with detailed macro-analysis, supported by statistics, of the relationship between crops and livestock. His main message was to stress their interdependence, and the primacy of grass as a crop.

In 1951 then we have on February 15 Eason on 'Ten-year Comparisons', April 20 N Cuthbert on 'Income in NI', May 31 Hans Staehle on 'Irish Agricultural Statistics 1847-1913'. The autumn papers in 1951 however did not get organised. In the spring of 1952 there was a recovery, with a 'Symposium on National Income and Social Accounts', with Geary, Smiddy and Barrington. On April 28 we have Garrett Fitzgerald on 'Air Transport Rates and Fares', JJ contributing to the discussion, though alas the record is missing.

On May 23 1952 JJ was re-elected for his second term as President, despite his lapse of autumn 1951, which would have been associated with his move to Grattan Lodge. There followed RF Browne on 'Electricity Supply' (13/6/52), JJ contributing to the discussion; this was the early days of the rural electrification drive. There was a big influx of new members, mostly from the North. On 30/10/52 we had F King on 'Absolutism', and then on 17/12/52 Brendan Senior on 'Agricultural Education and Research', with JJ again contributing to the discussion(16). The basis was being laid for the development of the Agricultural Institute at the end of the 50s. (JJ's role in the politics of the foundation of An Foras

Taluntais was recognised positively by Dr Tom Walsh its first Director; he felt moved to attend JJ's funeral in 1972.)

Then on February 5 1953 JJ delivered his paper on 'Economic Leviathans'; Roy Geary spoke to it(17). This was subsequently published as a pamphlet. After this JJ disappears from view, being succeeded by Beddy. Dr McCarthy of UCC took the chair in JJ's absence for EA Grace's paper on 'Accounting and Economic Decisions'. JJ surfaced again however on November 30 1953 for BF Shields' paper on 'CIE and the GNR 1945-51', where he seconded the vote of thanks.

Under Beddy's Presidency there was a sequence of papers involving Bob O'Connor, Donal Flood, Geary, MJ Costello, CS Andrews, Ruairi Roberts, Donal Nevin and others. Then in 1955 there was a big influx of corporate affiliations.

In the Council record it becomes clear that JJ's main attention during his Presidency was to develop the Northern Ireland dimension, via the Barrington lectures, particularly with N Cuthbert, and with the recruitment of Carter and the Queens people, including Isles. The *Isles and Cuthbert Report*, which was the first serious critical look at the performance of Northern Ireland as an economy, was one of the results of this all-Ireland networking, in which JJ was the prime mover. He never lost sight of his roots, and always worked to keep alive the N-S linkages(18). There was also later a *Barritt and Carter Report*. The seeds of this critical work were sown by the NI outreach of the SSISI during JJ's period on the Council and during his Presidency.

He was also influential in attempting to resurrect his earlier Barrington work promoting the co-operative movement in Connaught; there was a paper by Stanley Lyons on December 2 1952 on this topic, based on his Barrington Lectures. The Lyons lectures had been arranged via the Young Farmers Clubs, Muintir na Tire and Parish Councils.

Despite JJ's declining level of attendance, due to his Laois interests, his NI influence seems to have persisted, with the momentum of his NI recruitment. There was a Report from the NI Branch on Sept 20 1958 in which a paper was projected by JW Garmany of Magee College on 'Training for Management'(19).

On May 1 1959 JJ surfaced again as a contributor to a session related to the Whittaker policy revolution(20). It was adjourned unfinished, being re-convened on May 22. Then on December 11 JJ spoke to Bob O'Connor's paper on 'Economic Utilisation of Grassland'. On foot of this revived activity he was re-elected to Council on May 13 1960. He was at this time living near Stradbally but staying in his rooms in TCD during the mid-week.

JJ's last encounter with the SSISI occurred when he submitted a paper in 1964 on 'Consumer Demand as the Basis of Credit'(21). Roy Geary and TK Whitaker both agreed that it should be rejected, on the ground that it 'pertained more to philosophy than economics'. In 1966 according to Mary Daly JJ explained to Attwood that 'the Society has gone all econometric and papers are usually incomprehensible...'.

RJ and the SSISI

I joined the SSISI in 1966. On December 16 1966 there was a symposium on 'Science and Irish Economic Development'(22) with papers from Prof Howie of

TCD, Prof TE Nevin of UCD and AV Vincent of Guinness's Brewery. I was present, and contributed, this being a primary concern of mine, then as now. The symposium was in response to the OECD Report, produced by Patrick Lynch and HMS 'Dusty' Miller, which laid the basis for the setting up of the National Science Council in 1969. This was a landmark event, in that it indicated that after a long period of neglect the Government was prepared to begin to take science seriously.

Colm Ó h-Eocha contributed a paper on *The Science Budget* on 20/3/70; this was one of his earlier contributions to the public debate about science policy, arising from his chairing the National Science Council. He defined what science policy was, and categorised it under several focused headers, against a somewhat diffuse background. He drew on international comparisons.

I participated in the discussion(23), having then just commenced producing a regular weekly column on 'Science and Technology' for the *Irish Times*. In my contribution I homed in on the economists' concept of 'residuals' and urged scientists to make known their work better, and to convey to the economics community the importance of science-based technological know-how as the major engine of economic advance. The 'residual' is the reservoir of human creativity. Patrick Lynch was supportive, pointing out that Adam Smith and Karl Marx had seen clearly the role of science in economic development, though in contemporary Britain the view was hazy. He castigated economists for their failure to analyse the 'residuals' where this type of know-how lurked.

I delivered a paper in on 'Scientific and Engineering Manpower in Ireland', based on the computerised analysis of the 1971 census(24). The work was done in 1973, but the paper did not get to be delivered until January 9 1975. It was co-authored with Genevieve Franklin. The reason for the delay was that the Census people did not get around to publishing what I had used until then, and they did not want me to upstage them.

This opportunity arose as a result of the inclusion in the 1971 Census of a question relating to qualifications in science and technology, a consequence of the setting up of the National Science Council (NSC), and the earlier 1966 OECD Report *Science and Irish Economic Development*.

The general background of graduates was analysed by sector and discipline, and projected taking into account the age-profiles as elucidated in the census returns. The model was validated by a process of estimating 1971 figures from a 1967 base-line.

A serious mismatch was exposed between the output of the higher education system and the needs of industry, especially for graduates having science qualifications. Procedures were suggested for encouraging young graduate uptake, such as encouraging mobility and entrepreneurship among experienced graduates employed in the State agencies, and developing masters-degree programmes to enable science graduates to achieve an industrial applied-science problem-solving orientation.

The paper attracted an audience which included the UCD and TCD careers officers (Derek Scholefield and Dermot Montgomery), Catherine Keenan of the National Economic and Social Council, Dr Diarmuid Murphy, Monica Nevin, Dr RC Geary, Paid McMenamin, Professor BM Walsh and AP O'Reilly. The responses were all substantive and reflected an appreciation that a significant problem had been identified and quantified. The consensus was not 'reduce output of graduates' but 'stimulate uptake by industry', and many of the people in the audience were in a position to influence policies in this direction, and did. Some of the seeds that led to the prosperity of the 90s were I think sown on this occasion.

The raw material of the paper had emerged from just such a 'problem-solving re-orientation' MSc programme (Operational Research and Statistics) pioneered in TCD by Professor Gordon Foster. Genevieve Franklin, along with Aoileann Ni h-Eigeartaigh, had earlier participated in this course, after completing honours maths degrees, and had gained some experience in computer-based modelling of techno-economic systems, in support of planning decisions.

It was hoped at the time that the result of this work might have become embedded somehow in a national 'skilled human resources planning' unit, perhaps in the IDA or elsewhere, but this did not take place, and it remained a 'one-off' exercise. The philosophy behind it however has subsequently gained general acceptance, and is now the norm.

I remained an occasional attender during the 1980s and 1990s(25), and on occasion commented, in a manner which indicated the evolution of my concerns.

On December 2 1982 there was a symposium on 'Industrial Policy in Ireland' with papers from Kieran Kennedy (ESRI), Frances Ruane (TCD) and Padraic White, then Chief Executive of the IDA. I am minuted as having contributed, along with Seán Cromien, Tom Higgins, Declan Cunningham, L Leonard, Hugh Logue. E O'Malley, Paul Turpin, T McCabe, E McCarthy, F Ó Muircheartaigh, PJ Drudy, Richard Humphreys and RC Geary. This was in response to the Telesis Report.

My own contribution was brief; I quote it in full: 'we need to develop procedures for realising the potential value of the third-level education system as a job-generating resource. The tradition whereby graduates expect to be offered jobs needs to be replaced by one whereby graduates create their own jobs.'

I went on to say that '...the science/engineering/business links within the colleges need to be strengthened, with a view to encouraging the transformation of student into entrepreneur. The 'Deans Conference on Education for Innovation' on March 30 1983 (sponsored by AIB and NBST) was a welcome step in this direction.'

At the time of this symposium I was fresh from the experience of the rise and fall of the TCD Applied Research Consultancy (ARC) Group and was attempting to generalise it, and in the process to re-invent my own entrepreneurial role. I had the feeling that there were opportunities associated with the process of high-tech firms spinning off from university-based research departments; Mentec ltd, founded by Dr Mike Peirce a short time previously, was an example. Dr Peirce had been a stalwart supporter of the ARC concept.

Dr RC Geary, who spoke as usual last among the commentators, enthused about the event. As usual he had incisive comments; this time he remarked that 'modern industry is antagonistic to employment', and viewed the socio-economic future with trepidation. I suspect that this may have been his last appearance at the SSISI, of which he reminded us on this occasion that he had been a member for 60 years, pre-dating the 1924 Oldham recruiting drive which brought in JJ. Geary was a quite remarkable internationally known figure, though mostly unsung in Ireland. He did however receive the Boyle Medal from the RDS, belatedly, in 1981, on the proposition of Cormac Ó Ceallaigh, who had been similarly honoured the previous year.

On March 2 1989 there was a symposium on 'The International Dimension in Corporate Mergers and Acquisitions', the speakers being John T Teeling and JJ Hayes. Both speakers were from the business world, the second being from Cement Roadstone Holdings (CRH). I am on record in the minutes as having contributed, along with some nine others, among whom, unusually, there was a significant business component.

I had been aware of the Nokia experience in Finland, where by employing development engineers they had diversified into telecommunications from having been in paper and pulp products, becoming globally significant in a know-how-intensive industry. I put this to the CRH spokesman, who replied along the lines that the well-tried culture was to support the 'stick to the knitting' strategy, accept the small size of the home market, and go abroad with what you know how to do. I had again run up against one of the main barriers to science and engineering graduate recruitment.

On March 29 1990, to celebrate the centenary of the death of Cardinal Newman, there was a 'Symposium on the Idea of a University' in the 1990s (Vol XXVI Part II p125).

Colm Ó h-Eocha, President of UCG, in a relatively short paper welcomed the new Office of Science and Technology, and the associated 'Programmes of Advanced Technology' (PATs). Daniel O'Hare, President of DCU, in a longer paper projected a model in which the gap between CP Snow's 'Two Cultures' would be bridged and gave some international comparisons. Norman Gibson, pro-vice-Chancellor of UU, harked back to Newman, with approval, and voiced some criticism of the then current Thatcherite philistine utilitarian attitude of government to universities.

This discussion included a contribution of mine, as well as ones from Roger Fox, AC Cunningham, Damian Hannon, P O'Flynn, Frances Ruane, Bob O'Connor and Dr C Fanning. Regrettably only Roger Fox's is on record. This is perhaps an indication of increasing pressures on the individual participants, who needed to sit down and put their contributions on record afterwards, and send them in. I regret that I failed to do so at this time; I was under pressure having taken up full-time employment after a bad period. However I have some recollection of what I probably said, having distilled the experience of the previous two decades working at the university-industry interface. What follows is a reconstruction:

Any university centre of research is associated with a teaching domain and generates postgraduate of two types: basically MScs and PhDs. The former tend to be partially taught and partially by project, and the projects are usually of a practical problem-solving nature, and in some cases are industrially sponsored. The PhDs on the other hand tend to look to develop the basic knowledge of the domain in depth. There is sometimes an 'us and them' attitude between these two streams, and little interaction.

I put forward a model in which there should be an MSc/PhD ratio targeted as a matter of policy, that the MScs should be funded by the State as part of the industrial innovation programme, with a related contribution from the sponsoring firm, measured in terms of time and attention from a key change-agent, who would have the status of an extern supervisor.

The PhDs on the other hand should be directly funded by the State (ie given a living wage, and the research unit or department given a contribution to overheads), in numbers related to the number of industry-sponsored MScs generated by the postgraduate system. It might be appropriate to fund say one PhD for every 3 MScs, based on a moving average over a few years.

A well-run department or unit would ensure that these streams interacted, via research seminars, and experience was shared in both directions.

The funding of this system would be State-dependent, but conditional on sponsoring innovative firms giving time to the supervision and problem-definition. This would be an indirect State support-system for the in-firm innovation process. The sponsoring firms would then have the option of recruiting the MSc when the project had been completed at the academic level, with a view to developing it further perhaps in the direction of a marketable concept. The PhD people in the background would be producing results perhaps relevant to future generations of MScs.

I had occasionally seen aspects of this vision working in my previous TCD epoch, but the episodes were sporadic, haphazard and tantalising. To make it happen systematically would require a totally different approach to funding of postgraduate research, and I put forward the above model with this in mind.

Notes and References
1. The Barrington Lectures are treated in Appendix 7, under the general heading of 'Intellectual Outreach'. They have for most of their lifetime been closely associated with the Statistical and Social Inquiry Society of Ireland (SSISI) of which the 150th anniversary was celebrated recently in a book *The Spirit of Earnest Inquiry* by Mary E Daly, published by the SSISI in 1997, ISBN 1 872002 29 3.
2. At the time of the war of independence and the civil war JJ was in frequent correspondence with the Albert Kahn Foundation in Paris, and there is reference in the correspondence with their Executive Secretary Charles Garnier to the setting up of a Resource Centre in Ireland, dedicated to the problem of the peaceful democratic transformation of conflict situations, and a co-operative approach to economic development. Garnier wanted this in TCD but JJ diverted it to Plunkett House, as he had no faith in the ability of TCD to service the type of users he had in mind, namely his visionary projected new breed of co-op managers. There is no trace of this in either Plunkett House or in the Plunkett Foundation records, that I can find. Not is there any trace in the Plunkett House records of the period when they hosted the SSISI. My conjecture is that JJ sought to cement the link between Plunkett House, the SSISI and the Albert Kahn Foundation, the focus being the Plunkett House Library. The rift between Plunkett and Ireland generated by the Civil War killed this creative initiative, which if it had succeeded might have transformed Irish economic policies in the 1920s and 30s.
3. JJ's own contributions are outlined in the 1920s SSISI module in the hypertext support material; they were 'Some Causes and Consequences of Distributive Waste' (J SSISI vol XIV p353, 1926-7) and 'National Transport Problems' (JSSISI XIV, 53, 1929-30). The first of these papers was a close follower to the Duncan-Finlay paper; Mortished and Eason spoke to it.
4. The French experience arising from the Rockefeller Fellowship surfaced in JJ's addendum to the 1926 *Prices Commission Report.*

5. It is on a potential future research agenda for someone to track down to what this related; there must have been some political objective.

6. The 1930s ssisi module in the hypertext contains abstracts of two papers by JJ: 'A Plea for Winter Dairying' (JSSISI XV, 33, 1930-31) and 'Aspects of the Agricultural Crisis at Home and Abroad' (JSSISI XV, 79, 1934-5).

7. JJ's paper 'Aspects of the Agricultural Depression at home and abroad' (JSSISI XV, 79, 1934-5) was read on May 23 1935; speakers included Duncan (TCD), Eason and George O'Brien; there was also Major Barrow, who was a large-scale labour-employing commercial farmer near Castle Bellingham, and a neighbour of JJ when he had lived near Dundalk from 1928 to 1932.

8. See the 1930s outreach module in the hypertext.

9. The Engineering and Science Society may have an archive, but I have not chased this hare. The society is moribund, having been upstaged by the Institution of Engineers of Ireland (IEI) and its precursors. There is some socio-technical history here perhaps worth looking into, in the context of the analysis of the evolution of the culture of science and technology in the transition to political independence. There may even be lurking a religious sectarian dimension in the culture.

10. 'The Capitalisation of Irish Agriculture', JSSISI xvi p44 1941-2.

11. 'The Future of Irish external trade' (JSSISI symposium meeting, April 27, 1944).

12. 'An Economic Basis for an Irish Rural Civilisation' (JSSISI Vol xvii, p1, 1947-8).

13. This movement, associated with architect Emer Ó Siochrú, environmental consultant Jack O'Sullivan and others, is a network of people who seek to organise and focus a drift away from metropolitan living towards economically rejuvenated villages, some of which might be in a position to export high-technology services via the internet.

14. *Social Security* White Paper symposium (JSSISI xviii pt 3, 262, 1949-50).

15. 'Raw Material for Animal Husbandry' (JSSISI xviii, 392, 1950-51).

16. In this session it was recorded that JF Knaggs joined; the latter subsequently became the Head of the CSO, and went on to head the European statistics office in Luxembourg. He had trained as a physicist along with the present writer, in TCD in the 40s. JJ's participation as President in the discussions is alas only partially on the record.

17. 'Economic Leviathans' (JSSISI xix pt 1, 42, 1952-3); this paper was the second of his presidency, and was delivered on February 5 1953. It was a monumental attempt to summarise the history of the interactions between the 'leviathans', Britain and the US, in the interstices of whose turbulent movements we in our small boat, and other European nations, have to survive.

18. See the Irish Association thread, for which the hypertext is overviewed (Appendix 9.)

19. John Garmany was among the active local organiser of the Derry conference of the Irish Association in 1965 which had been planned to welcome the New University of Ulster, in the company of John Hume and others including the present writer. The keynote speaker was Carter, then Vice-Chancellor of Liverpool University. It was expected to celebrate the upgrade Magee College was due, but in the event the New University of Ulster (NUU) went to Coleraine. To this rebuff of the people west of the Bann, the subsequent Civil Rights movement must be in part attributed. See also the 1960s Irish Association module in the hypertext.

20. Symposium on Economic Development. JSSISI 1959, or perhaps 1960; I have mislaid the reference.

21. I have abstracted this paper in the 1960s SSISI module in the hypertext, from which the text is available in full.

22. See the 1960s SSISI module in the hypertext.

23. See also the 1960s SSISI module in the hypertext.

24. RHW Johnston and Genevieve Franklin, 'An Approach to National Manpower Planning in Science and Technology' (Vol XXIII Part II, p21).

25. My 1990s contributions are partially on record in the 1990s SSISI module of the hypertext; they were primarily related to networking in the ongoing innovation consultancy context.

Appendix 7: Intellectual Outreach

I had originally labelled this theme 'Barrington' but it subsequently emerged, in organising the material, that JJ had many published works which were popularising economic concepts, or controversing on economic issues, which were not directly associated with his role as Barrington Lecturer. It seems to make sense to widen the scope of the Barrington label to include these. I hope the Barrington Trustees will forgive me for doing this. I think I can claim that his popularising and controversial published works were continuing the Barrington tradition after the role of the 'lecture' as medium had become increasingly marginalised, in competition with radio and television.

It then subsequently occurred to me that my own Irish Times *'Science and Technology' weekly column was in the same tradition, so I re-labelled the theme 'Intellectual Outreach' and integrated my father's role and my own, as successive popularisers of knowledge.*

JJ Background: the Barrington Trust - the SSISI Link

The Centenary Volume of the *Proceedings of the Statistical and Social Inquiry Society of Ireland (SSISI)* published in 1947 edited by R D Collison Black, Lecturer in Economics in Queens University Belfast, contains background information about the Barrington Lectures, which were initiated in 1849 as a consequence of a bequest from John Barrington, a merchant in the City of Dublin, for the purpose of enlightening the citizens of Dublin (4 lectures per annum) and the towns and villages of Ireland (24 lectures per annum) in the principles of Political Economy.

From the very beginning there was a strong link between the SSISI(1) and the Barrington Lecturers, the former advising the Trustees of the Barrington bequest regarding the choice of lecturer and topics of lectures.

There is given a complete series of Barrington Lecturers from 1852 to 1946 in Black's Centenary Volume. Prior to World War 1 there is a sequence of names, none of whom is known to the writer, but then I can't claim to be a historian of economics in colonial Ireland. No doubt they did their best to imbue the towns and villages of Ireland with the principles of the Liberal Enlightenment, and we can conjecture that they interfaced with the work of the co-operative movement in the 1890s and subsequently. The most notable of the Barrington Lecturers pre-war was C H Oldham, who was a prolific contributor of papers to the Society between 1895 and 1925.

There was a hiatus between 1913 and 1919, and then from 1920 to 1931, Joe Johnston was the only lecturer on record, 'intermittently'. He was active again from 1932 to 1935, and then again in 1946. His colleagues in his later period of activity were John Busteed 1932, 1935, 1946, J Lamberger 1932-36, F T Lloyd Dodd 1937-43, 1945, Liam Ó Buachalla 1937-40, 1942, 1944, James Meenan 1938-40, Denis O'Donovan and Michael Murphy 1941, BF Shields 1941-44, JJ Horgan 1944-45, Henry Kennedy 1943-45, M J Gorman 1946 and RD Collison Black 1946.

It would appear that JJ was instrumental in the revival of the series after the First World War, and that other lecturers came in after about a decade. According to Black during JJ's period the Council of the SSISI lost touch with what was going on in the Lectures, and only took control again in 1931. During the earlier part of this period the Society met in Plunkett House.

To get at the content of the Barrington lectures during the period would require a scan of the local papers, and it is only possible to do this where we can unearth dates and locations.

Minutes of the Barrington Trust

I am indebted to Ron Barrington the current (1999) Trustee for the opportunity to study these minutes. The earlier material must have been accessible to Collison Black in the 1940s for his work on the Centenary publication, but they seem to have vanished.

The 1896 Minute records a meeting in 35 Molesworth St with Richard M Barrington in the chair, with William Lawson and Jonathan Pim present. Minutes of three previous meetings, 17/01/93, 4/12/94 and 22/01/95 were approved and signed. It was agreed to appoint CH Oldham lecturer for 1896. These minutes were signed on 5/2/04 by RM Barrington.

This 1904 meeting was well attended: RMB in the chair, with present Manliff Barrington, JM(?) Shaw, Joseph T Pim, WF Bailey(?), TG Foley, CH Oldham, W Lawson, Sir William Findlater, Jonathan Pim, Arthur Samuels and WJ Johnston. This was an indication that the Statistical and Social Inquiry Society was taking an interest. The posts of lecturer were advertised in the Dublin, Belfast and Cork papers, and also in the *Times*, *Athaneum* and *Scotsman*. Four names were selected from the applicants. The minutes are scarcely legible, but it seems that they left it to the SSISI to make the choice. These minutes are unsigned.

The next minutes relate to 1909; on 15 Nov they advertised in the *Times, Athaneum, Scotsman, Spectator, Irish Times, Freeman's Journal, Cork Examiner, Northern Whig, Belfast Newsletter*. They also sent copies to TCD, Oxford, Cambridge, NUI, QUB, and to Profs Bastable, Marshall and Edgeworth in TCD, Cambridge and Oxford respectively.

As a result of this, 16 applications were received and these were considered on 23/12/09, at a meeting attended by AW Samuels KC, William Lawson, Ninian Falkiner, RM Barrington and Manliff Barrington. Four applicants were invited to address a meeting of the SSISI on 14/01/10 in the Leinster Lecture Hall, 35 Molesworth St, the President Justice Cherry in the chair. The lecturers and topics were:

JH Jones (Cardiff) 'Dumping and the Tinplate Industry';
Edward Kelly (RUI) 'Free Trade and Nationality';
HL Murphy (TCD) 'The "Infant Industry" case for Commercial Restriction';
WR Macauley ORR (RUI) 'The Individual and the State'.

On Jan 15 the Council met and recommended HL Murphy for 1910. There is a pencil note to the effect that he continued for 1911 and 1912.

Appendix 7: Intellectual Outreach

During this period Arthur Griffith was, on the whole, a hostile critic of the Barrington Lecturers, who were promoting a Free Trade ethos, and were critical of the type of economic nationalism advocated by Griffith.

JJ could have attended these meetings; he was in the final year of his Classics Moderatorship in TCD, and planning to go on to Oxford. The choice of topics reflected the concerns of the Irish liberal elite regarding the coming Home Rule situation.

There is then a note dated 1915 to the effect that the Trustees were now Manliff Barrington, Amy Barrington and Cecil Vivian Barrington. The lectures were in abeyance due to the war.

On Feb 20 1920 Amy and Manliff Barrington met the Council of the SSISI at 93 St Stephens Green, under the chairmanship of Sir William Thompson. Also present were Mr Wood, Mr Sparkhall Brown, Ninian Falkiner, CH Oldham and others. There were five candidates: Joseph Johnston FTCD, John J Walsh UCD, John J Clarke (Liverpool), JG Smith (Birmingham) and R Richards (Bangor). 'The qualifications of the candidates were carefully discussed, and on the Council's unanimous recommendation, the Trustees appointed Mr Joseph Johnston to be Barrington Lecturer for this year.' Manliff Barrington wrote to JJ accordingly. The SSISI however in its meeting on January 29 1920 decided against taking on again the administration of the Barrington Trust(2).

1921-22: 'Mr Johnston delivered lectures in these years, but owing to the disturbed state of the country in the latter part of 1922 and in 1923 (there were problems) in having regular courses, and in 1923 they were discontinued.'

1924: 'In this year Mr Johnston instituted classes in his rooms in Trinity College for working men. They were well attended and in July at a meeting which I attended papers were read by three members of his class, and a discussion followed. Mr Thomas Johnson, the Leader of the Labour Party in the Dáil, was in the chair.... The classes were continued in the autumn...'

The minutes, which appear to have been kept simply as notes rather than as signed records of meetings, presumably by Manliff Barrington, then go on to record the continuation of JJ as Barrington Lecturer for 1926 to 1928 (in pen) and then from 1929(3) to 1933 in pencil, with the indication that in 1932 and 1933 he was joined by J Lemberger MA of QUB. A couple of blank pages were left, in the hopes of infill, and then the record takes up again for the 1937-37 session, under the influence of the revival of interest on the part of the SSISI, as engineered by JJ.

Minutes of the Statistical and Social Inquiry Society (SSISI)

Turning now to the records of the SSISI, it turns out that JJ became a member in November 1924 and was elected to Council in December 1927. I conjecture that the Barrington Trustees abandoned their record-keeping during JJ's tenure of the Lectureship because they thought the SSISI was taking care of it. JJ meantime seems to have been struggling to get them put back on the SSISI agenda, and in this he did not succeed until 1932, when in the end, on foot of a letter, he got the Lemberger appointment, and also the Busteed appointment for Munster. Prior to this it is noted in the SSISI records that there had been only the one lecturer for the whole of Ireland (ie JJ).

In the SSISI records exceptionally there is some detail available for the 1932 programme. Lemberger lectured on June 18 at the Belfast School of Technology and on June 19 at Newcastle Co Down. JJ lectured at Carrickmacross on March 30, Ballybay March 31 and Bray on May 25, on' Ireland and the World Crisis'. Then on Sept 29 at Navan and Sept 30 at Wexford on 'The Place of the Cattle Trade in the Economy'(4). Busteed is said to have lectured at Newmarket, Ballyclough, Skibbereen, Cork, Clonmel, Thurles, Tralee, Limerick; no dates were given.

Mary Daly in her 1997 book records a lecture by JJ in Termonfeckin (near Drogheda) in December 1935, in which he attacked the 'self-sufficiency' concept, and got into trouble with the Barrington Trustees, to the extent that his lectureship was not renewed. The content of this lecture related to his then topical book *The Nemesis of Economic Nationalism*, which had evolved out of an earlier pamphlet of the same title, based on Barrington lectures delivered in 1933.

Subsequent to this the SSISI records confine themselves to the appointments, and there is no record of places or dates. There is reference to 'reports to the Trustees', which presumably contain this information, but this has alas been lost. There are in the Barrington archives two large volumes of cuttings for 1895, 1896 and 1904, which indicate what perhaps still exists somewhere, and the present writer would dearly like to find where they might be. Collison Black in QUB who wrote the 1947 centenary history has no knowledge of them, nor has Mary Daly in UCD, who wrote the 150th anniversary record of the SSISI as published in 1997. They may yet turn up in the recesses of the Barrington family, or in some university archive. I leave to others to pursue this trail.

When the record resumes in 1936/7 we have J Lemberger QUB for Ulster (no topics given), JF Meenan UCD for E and SE Saorstat (population, emigration, banking), and Liam Ó Buachalla UCG for W and SW Saorstat (Connemara economic problems, money, banking, industry, capital, labour, co-operation) Attendance at these lectures was in 100s.

In 1937-8 Lemberger (due it seems to pressure from JJ; see the SSISI thread) was replaced by FT Lloyd-Dodd (Principal of Belfast College of Technology) for Ulster (consumer co-operation, earnings and hours of labour, old and new industries, social and economic organisation in Germany, economic consequences of changes in population); Meenan remains but no topics are given; also Ó Buachalla remains and dedicates the majority of his lectures to various aspects of co-operation, with an incursion into the Irish industrial tradition; average attendance 216, in places like Rosmuc, Kilronan, Cloone (Leitrim) as well as Galway.

In 1938/9 the same team continued; only Lloyd-Dodd is on record as regards topic: shorter working week, hire-purchase, economic nationalism and self-sufficiency(5), raw materials and colonies.

1939/40: the team continued, with the war, social credit and agriculture as the main themes.

1940/41: four lecturers now, one for each province, though Ulster appears to mean Northern Ireland; Donegal is never mentioned, and Cavan is treated as Leinster. Lloyd Dodd continues, primarily on the war; for Leinster we have Denis O'Donovan, on the social and economic organisation of Germany, and a critical look at the social credit movement. (We can here perhaps detect the James Meenan influence; this UCD economist went on to write approvingly of Italian corporate state fascism, in a book published in 1944 by Cork UP; the author introduces it as a regretful post-mortem.) Michael Murphy of UCC took care of Munster mostly from the dairying angle, and BF Shields of UCD covered the West (vocational guidance, family allowances, the minimum wage, man and work...).

From 1941 onwards the record-keeping in the Barrington archive is meticulous; dates and locations are given. I am not here going to give details; it is for someone who works on the history of the Barrington Lectures to do this; I am primarily here concerned with the input from JJ. There is concern with agriculture, industry, the Beveridge Plan in Britain and its implications for Ireland, social security, the current issues of the day. It is recorded where the reports appeared in the local press. There is a thesis here for someone.

Then in 1945/6 JJ appears again as a Barrington Lecturer(6), this time in his capacity as a Senator, along with Prof John Busteed of UCC for Munster, Prof Collison Black of QUB for Ulster and MJ Gorman of Albert College for Connaught. The Black lectures were widely reported (dates given).

This detailed reporting continues for some years. In 1949/50 the Ulster Barrington Lecturer was N Cuthbert, who concentrated on the employment question. He subsequently was co-author of the Isles and Cuthbert Report, which was the first genuinely critical analysis of the NI economic scene. The role of JJ on the SSISI Council was consistently to ensure that the Society had all-Ireland vision, and that the NI scene was examined critically. He achieved this through influencing the Barrington Ulster appointments. Cuthbert continued for Ulster until 1951/52. In 52/53 he was replaced by AA Bath.

The detailed record, with locations, dates and names of local papers, continues until 1959/60. The names include many subsequently famous: Garrett Fitzgerald, Norman Gibson, Labhras Ó Nuallain, Micheál MacCormac and others. Then in 1960/61 there is simply a record of the names of the lecturers: Labras Ó Nuallain, T Raftery, JW Garmany and MJ Fitzgerald. The lectures were then suspended for a year.

I recollect that at a meeting organised by the Irish Association for Derry, in order to celebrate the new University of Ulster, then expected for Derry given the Magee College focus, John Garmany was present, in the company of John Hume. This was in 1965, and was the trigger for the Civil Rights movement, once the University went to Coleraine(7). The series continued in outreach mode during the 60s, but with declining audiences, due to the influence of television. Then in the 70s they drew back into the university campuses, and in the 80s to the Regional College campuses. Then in the 1985 the Trust decided to institute a prize for a good popularising lecture to be given in the SSISI, and that is how and where the Trust currently operates, hopefully with a benign influence on the economic gurus, to encourage them to make their output comprehensible to a lay public.

The only contact in the latter years between JJ and the Barrington Trust was via Dr EH Attwood of the Agricultural Institute, who had been a Barrington Lecturer in the 60s. Dr Attwood's PhD was supervised by JJ. This would have been JJ's last remaining contact with the SSISI scene, from which he had bowed out after his period as President, in the early 50s. In 1964 Roy Geary and TK Whittaker were responsible for rejecting his paper on 'Consumer Demand as the Basis of Credit', on the grounds that it was basically a philosophical tract, and not relevant to the SSISI. The econometricians were in charge, and JJ was a back number.

Post-Barrington Popularising Publications by JJ

Other than his many articles and letters to the press I have identified the following sequence:

JJ published a 30-page pamphlet(8) in 1957, critical of the then disastrous Irish economic situation, with the support of the Irish Association, and with a foreword by Sir Graham Larmour (Ulster Weaving Co) who had in 1954 succeeded JJ as President of the Association. The production of the pamphlet was supported with advertisements from Ford, Hughes Bros, Ulster Weaving, Gentex, Batchelors, Golden Vale, the Educational Building Society, the National City Bank, Pye, Wolsey, the ESB, Mattersons, Roadstone, Duthie Large and Hibernian Insurance, reflecting the channels of influence available to the then Council of the Association.

The earlier articles in the pamphlet had formed the subject matter of an address to the Irish Association in November 1955; the last was written after a discussion sponsored by the Association in Belfast on 12th November 1956, when Professor CF Carter MA, the Queen's University of Belfast, stated the implications for Northern Ireland, and Professor Johnston those for the Republic, of the European Common Market and Free Trade Zone proposals.

In 1962 JJ outlined the arguments about the European Economic Community (the 'Common Market')(9), with reference back to agriculture in the unregulated world of the 1920s, in which context he had served in 1926 on a Prices Tribunal, making a close study of the relationship between the prices received by the farmers and the prices paid by the consumers, as they varied over time.

The theoretical background at the time had been established by the American authors Foster and Catchings, and JJ had been able to crystallise his conclusions into a criticism of that book. The problem was that '...agricultural production is not integrated into the normal machinery of credit to the same extent as commerce and industry.... if the bargaining power of agriculture, suitably organised everywhere for production, processing and marketing, could be put on terms of economic equality with non-agricultural commercial and industrial concerns, one of the hidden causes of periodic depression would be alleviated if not abolished ...'. In other words JJ was re-iterating his classic 1920s Barrington Lectures position in support of the objectives of Plunkett House.

In chapter 7, which is given in full in the hypertext, JJ regaled the reader with some of his experience with horticulture as a supplementary small-farm activity. It is 'anecdotal', in the manner disparaged by the economic Establishment, but I prefer to describe it as an account of some pilot-projects which would have been generalisable, provided the marketing were taken care of by suitable organisation.

In 1966 JJ published a short booklet(10) of essays and collected newspaper articles which was his last attempt to address the lay public with economic arguments. I give the following extract from JJ's preface:

"Irish history is full of ironies, paradoxes and anomalies. With the establishment of a national government in 26 counties of our island in 1922 one would have thought that the future of the Gaeltacht was assured, and with it the possibility of restoring the language as a second vernacular in an increasing proportion of our total area. Actually, if statistics mean anything (and they sometimes do) the survival value of Gaelic as a spoken language was greater under alien rule than it has been under a succession of native governments. An attempt is made in the following pages to explain the forces which have operated to undermine the economic position of the small farmer in Ireland. The problem of preserving the Gaeltacht is part and parcel of the general problem of assuring the future of the small farmer. If one aspect of it is primarily concerned with preserving an essential element in our cultural heritage, another is concerned with maintaining (or restoring) a sound human foundation for our national economy as a whole."

By the end of the 1960s JJ had little time left, and there was unfinished academic business(11). His last years were spent with his work on Berkeley's *Querist,* which he submitted for his (somewhat belated) Doctorate, which was conferred in 1972, shortly before he died.

Intellectual Outreach Publications by RJ

During my undergraduate period in TCD I began to address the 'science and society' question, via discussions in the Promethean Society, in the Fabian Society, and on at least one occasion in the Dublin University Experimental Science Association (DUESA), where I attempted to put Newton's *Principia* into some sort of historical context(12).

Outreach work during the 1950s and 60s is perhaps best approached in the 'science and society' context(13). During the 1970s the *Irish Times* 'Science and Technology' column(14) was the principal outlet; in its time it as innovative in the Irish context and I think it was influential; it ran for seven years from January 1970 to December 1976.

During the 1980s I published some contributions to the analysis of the problem of public transport in the Dublin area, and also some critical comments on the Common Agricultural Policy of the European Economic Community. I also organised a JD Bernal Memorial Seminar, and published some notes on 'Systems Modelling in Management Science' in the niche *Operations Research Newsletter.* I began to address the 'Science in Irish Culture' issue substantively with a paper in the *Crane Bag,* a journal edited by Richard Kearney(15).

I put considerable effort in the 1990s put into attempting to get an organised academic historical centre for the study of the 'science and society in Ireland' question. I also developed my earlier critical analysis of European agricultural policy, culminating in my 2001 'Sustainability' paper, and contributed to the development of Green party science policy(16).

Notes and References

1. See also the SSISI thread, where I expand on JJ's role in domains other than Barrington-related.
2. This is on record in the SSISI Minutes, and Mary Daly mentions it in her 150th anniversary book *A Spirit of Earnest Inquiry* (SSISI 1997).

3. Much of the material of these early Barrington Lectures by JJ is embodied in his book <u>*A Groundwork of Economics*</u> published in 1926 by the Educational Company of Ireland. If any local press reports turn up I will record them in the <u>1920s Barrington module</u> of the hypertext.

4. I have managed to track down the <u>local press reports</u> of these lectures and these are available in the hypertext.

5. We have an echo here of JJ's <u>*Nemesis of Economic Nationalism*</u>; Lloyd-Dodd seems to have been a JJ follower on this issue.

6. The <u>JJ lectures</u> took place in Bagenalstown on Dec 12 1945, Kilkenny Dec 13 and Nenagh Dec 14; the topic was 'Our Agricultural Prospects'. Also in Athlone March 21 1946, Tuam Oct 21 1946 and Ballina Oct 22, the topic being 'Public Enterprise and Economic Development'. They were reported in the *Nenagh Guardian, the Western people, Irish Times,* and the *Tuam Herald.* Kilkenny local press thought it 'too dry' and declined to report. The material used in these lectures JJ subsequently worked up into his published book <u>*Irish Agriculture in Transition.*</u> The Tuam lecture was an occasion of contact between JJ and <u>RM Burke</u>, whose estate had become a co-operative farm; see the <u>1940s module</u> of this Barrington thread.

7. This cross-checks with the <u>IA records.</u> So the Barrington Lectures in their Ulster extension must have had some influence in the preservation of a residual, and the development of a new, all-Ireland consciousness, laying the basis for a new political approach to an all-Ireland vision, initially via the Civil Rights movement. This vision is currently embodied in the Good Friday Agreement.

8. <u>*The Sickness of the Irish Economy*</u> (Irish Association, 1957); the production of the pamphlet was supported with advertisements from Ford, Hughes Bros, Ulster Weaving, Gentex, Batchelors, Golden Vale, the Educational Building Society, the National City Bank, Pye, Wolsey, the ESB, Mattersons, Roadstone, Duthie Large and Hibernian Insurance, reflecting the channels of influence available to the then Council of the Association.

9. <u>*Why Ireland Needs the Common Market*</u> (Mercier Press, 1962).

10. <u>*Irish Economic Headaches: A Diagnosis*</u> (Aisti Eireannacha, 1966): the publisher Rayner O'Connor Lysaght accepted it as #2 in a series of which the first was a polemic by Martin Ó Cadhain *Mr Hill: Mr Tara* concerned with the politics of the language movement.

11. This included his last Berkeley paper 'Monetary Manipulation: Berkeleyan and Otherwise'; *Hermathena* CX p32, 1970, and his *Bishop Berkeley's Querist in Historical Perspective* (Dun Dealgan Press, 1972), as well as his unpublished *Consumer Demand as the Basis of Credit,* all of which are accessible from the <u>1960s academic</u> module of the hypertext.

12. This was broadly based on the Hessen paper of 1932 on the *Social and Economic Roots of Newton's Principia,* which had influenced JD Bernal to write his 1939 *Social Function of Science.* I seem to recollect that much of it was devoted to the problem of finding position at sea, and its influence on trying to understand the movements of the moon and the planets, in the context of the longitude problem.

13. The <u>1950s</u> period was one of absorbing the culture of science, and the working relationship between scientist and technician; there was little opportunity for outreach. There were more opportunities in the <u>1960s</u> to popularise 'science and society' issues, especially during the 'Council for Science and Technology in Ireland' episode, and in the Operations Research context.

14. I introduce this via the <u>1970s outreach</u> module in the hypertext.

15. The first set of topics are covered in the <u>1980s outreach</u> module of the hypertext, and the second set in the <u>1980s science and society</u> module of the hypertext. The *Crane Bag* paper, on the 19th century British Association meetings in Ireland, appeared in Volume 7, #2,

Appendix 7: Intellectual Outreach

1983, the 'Forum Issue'. It provided a series of snapshots of the state of science in Ireland over the century.

16. These topics are covered in the <u>1990s outreach</u> and in the <u>1990s science and society</u> modules of the hypertext. The paper '<u>Biotechnology and Sustainability</u>' was published by Teagasc in *Farm and Food*, Spring 2001 issue, along with some reports on the 1996 Amsterdam conference of INES (International Network of Engineers and Scientists) on this topic.

Appendix 8: Public Service and Seanad Éireann

My father is on record as being involved in economic research connected with the work of the Boundary Commission(1), in the Agriculture Commission 1922-24(2), and in a Prices Tribunal(3) in 1926 (sometimes labelled 'Profiteering Tribunal').

JJ made an unsuccessful attempt to get elected to the Seanad in 1926; I have some papers connected with that, and I put them on record here. He produced a canvassing postcard with his picture, appealing '...for the support of all voters who desire the reconstruction of the Nation's economic life on sound economic principles.' He gave as his qualification his status as a Fellow of Trinity College, Dublin, and Lecturer in the School of Commerce; also Barrington Lecturer in Economics, and Member of the 1922 Agricultural Commission.

The postcard continues, on the obverse side: 'In an effort to avert the serious consequences arising out of the Ulster situation, he published *Civil War in Ulster* in 1913. In *Groundwork of Economics,* recently published by the Educational Company of Ireland, Talbot St, Dublin (Price 2/6), he has sought to make the elements of this important science interesting and intelligible to all Irish men and women.'

JJ kept some records of the 1926 Seanad election in a scrap-book. There are cuttings referencing JJ's contributions to transport economics, making the case for common interest between railway shareholders and ratepayers *(the argument is based on the cost to ratepayers of damage to the roads caused by long-distance heavy loads which should go by rail, and which ratepayers were in effect subsidising).*

There is a copy of a newspaper advertisement, which JJ had put in: 'ELECTORS REMEMBER Economic experts will play an important part in moulding the economic policy of the State. Thoughtful electors will ensure that the Senate contains at least one TRAINED ECONOMIST by voting 1 JOHNSTON'.

There is a cutting which gives the complete panel to go before the electorate for the Seanad. This was made up of 19 outgoing Senators, 19 chosen by the Seanad, and 38 chosen by the Dáil. JJ's name appeared among the latter 38; his name was followed by (G.) which suggests that he had got a Cumann na Gael nomination. There were a few (F.)s listed: John Ryan, James Dillon etc which suggests that the F stands for Farmers. Other Gs were Henry Harrison, TP McKenna, Marquis McSweeney; the G's were dominant. JJ had, it seems, joined with Cumann na Gael to get on the panel, which would be voted on as one ballot nationally.

There is further cutting which gives an integrated list of all Seanad candidates, with a few words about each. JJ is given as Fellow and Tutor of Trinity College, with an address 9 Trinity College, (DN*) the latter meaning a Dáil nominee, with the * implying he was a Government candidate. Other candidates with whom his results may perhaps be compared were Douglas Hyde, Darrell Figgis, Sir Arthur Chance, Patrick McCartan, Marquis McSwiney, Liam Ó Briain, these being people of some intellectual attainment, associated broadly one way or another with the national movement, and credible 'specialist expert' types of Seanad candidate. Of these the only other DN* was McSwiney.

*It is perhaps significant that Marquis McSwiney had previously interacted
with JJ in the Albert Kahn Foundation context. JJ probably was in a position to use
his record, as a promoter of the Sinn Fein and subsequently the Free State interest
in France via Garnier, as a lever to get the Government nomination.*

There is a cutting giving some details of how the Dáil panel was selected; it
was quite complex, and JJ got on the panel on the 41st count. Topping the poll was
one Denis Houston, a Labour candidate, and JJ it seems benefited by his transfers.

There are cuttings referencing Oliver St John Gogarty, and a derogatory one
from a Dungannon local paper(4)

Then finally we get the Seanad election results, analysed by constituency. JJ
got a total of 1196 votes, and this compared with 1710 for Douglas Hyde, 601 for Dr
McCartan, 1066 for Liam Ó Briain, 788 for the Marquis McSwiney, 509 for Darrell
Figgis and 3722 for Sir Arthur Chance. The large numbers, leading to seats, went to
people with high local profiles in certain constituencies, rather than to people with
'specialist niche' profiles such as the ones listed, none of whom got in. Thus the
Seanad electoral procedure showed itself to be flawed, its aspirant role as 'panel of
experts' being frustrated by the electoral procedure.

It is interesting to identify the constituencies where JJ picked up votes. Most
were of course in Dublin, but after Dublin came in order of size of vote, Laois-
Offaly, Donegal, Sligo, Wexford, Carlow-Kilkenny and Cavan. This would suggest
that he had gone consciously for, or at least picked up, the Protestant vote. He had
subscribed to a press-cutting agency and this had picked up items in the *Church of
Ireland Gazette* advocating that readers should vote for JJ; there had also been a
review of *Groundwork in Economics* in that same paper, linking its publication to
his candidature in the Seanad election.

JJ finally, after the Seanad was reconstituted in 1937, got to represent Trinity
College on 3 separate occasions, from April 1938 to July 1943, when he lost in
Dev's mid-war election to TC Kingsmill-Moore. He got in again however in April
1944 and served up to June 1947. Then he served again from March 1948 until July
1949.

JJ's 1938 appeal to the TCD graduates who constituted the electoral college
was as follows:

"All thoughtful persons must admit that Applied Economics should be an
instrument of political as well as academic education. Since I am University
Lecturer in Applied Economics I appeal with confidence to the Electors of Dublin
University as a Candidate for Election to the Senate of Eire.

"If you elect me the Senate will contain a University representative who is
professionally competent to examine all public questions in a scientific spirit with
special reference to their economic aspects and implications.

"The Senate is being constituted on principles of vocational representation in
order that it should contain persons qualified to examine public questions in
precisely this spirit. In my present capacity I endeavour to further the welfare of the
University and of its Members, with which is intimately bound up the welfare of the
country, North and South ; if elected I shall be able to do so more effectively.

"As an Ulsterman who is also a citizen of Eire I regret the barrier that
separates North from South. I regret also the unwisdom of adding incompatibility of

economic structure to political and fiscal separation thus creating on our side of the Border. vested interests in the maintenance of Partition. It would be more statesmanlike so to order our affairs that our Northern fellow-countrymen might come to regard the idea of reunion with diminishing reluctance.

"An honourable settlement of the 'economic war' and a restoration of normal commercial relations with Great Britain and Northern Ireland are absolutely necessary if we would arrest the decay of our agriculture which must remain the foundation of our national economy."

He listed the following of his published works as being relevant to political image he wished to project:

Groundwork of Economics (The Talbot Press, Dublin), *The Nemesis of Economic Nationalism* (PS King & Son, Ltd, and The Talbot Press, Dublin), Articles in *The Economist, The Economic Journal, The Nineteenth Century,* and in the current (February, 1938) number of *The Fortnightly.*

He had got the support of a broad-ranging election committee which included Professors Broderick and McConnell (Mathematics), Stanford (classics), Walton and Werner (science), Duncan (economics), Curtis (history), Furlong (philosophy), Rudmose-Brown and Lidell (modern languages), Purser (engineering), Torrens (medicine), the Bishop and the Dean of Clogher (Enniskillen), Dean of St Patricks, and numerous others spanning the spectrum of leading active Irish-residing Protestant Trinity graduates.

He had a panel of honorary secretaries, who handled contact with graduates on the register, all over Ireland, mostly consisting of Church of Ireland clergy, teachers and academics outside Dublin (for example WH Porter in UCC, Rev AA Hanbridge in Dundalk Grammar School), with a core-group in Dublin consisting of WA Beers, RBD French and JM Henry; he has also LJD Richardson in Cardiff University whose role would have been to take care of the emigrants in Britain.

His first contribution(5) to the Senate debates was on the topic of the trade agreement which ended the Economic War; the motion was introduced by de Valera. In the lead-up to the War he used the Seanad consistently to outline his approach to how the coming emergency should be handled, emphasising the role of Ireland as a source of food supply for Britain, while consistently supporting neutrality.

During the War in the Seanad he consistently defended the interests of Irish agriculture(6), to the extent that he neglected the interests of his constituents, the TCD graduates, so that that he lost his seat in 1943. His 1943 electoral address attempted to put his work in context, and I give it here in full.

When de Valera called his mid-war election in 1943 my father was living in 'the Glen', a house near Drogheda which he had bought at the start of the war; there was a 20-acre farm attached, which he farmed, employing a man and keeping the books, as he had done over a decade earlier. This decoupled him somewhat from College politics, and he was not in such a good position to canvass and organise his support-group as he had been in 1938, though he had managed to add about 20 people to it. As a result he lost the seat, to TC Kingsmill Moore. His election address is available, and I reproduce it in full, as it summarises his then political position.

"In seeking re-election it is proper that I should give some account of my activities in the legislature during the five years in which I have had the honour to be one of your representatives. "In the course of the year 1938 I was invited, along with one other Senator of no party affiliations, to occupy a seat on one of the two Front Benches. I made it quite clear that I surrendered nothing of my independence, and that I did so mainly because it would add to the value of the service to my constituents and to the country. A Front Bench Senator has special opportunities for making his point of view effective. He can take part more easily in informed exchanges with the Ministers, and thus influence the course of the more formal proceedings. Needless, to say a Front Bench seat is no sinecure. One must be alert all the time, especially when some topic is under consideration with reference to which one has special knowledge or responsibility.

"My formal speeches occupy many columns of the Official Reports. In my maiden speech I stated that the Minority in Eire were not content to be regarded merely as guests, even if welcome guests, in the national household. I claimed on their behalf, as full members of the national family, the right to contribute to the "spiritual content of the national being" and maintained that our culture and our tradition should be regarded as Irish equally with that which derives from a Gaelic origin. Until we can create in Eire the concept of an Irish nation which transcends and yet embraces all its separate cultural, racial and religious elements, I held that the problem of Partition in the narrower sense must remain insoluble. Only thus could the "rainbow arch" of Irish unity and peace, of the poet's dream, be constructed, and in that sense I admitted that we of the Minority in Eire might be regarded as "rainbow-chasers," but in no other.

"When the present war broke out I took an early opportunity of pointing out that while neutrality was the only policy possible in our circumstances, it was nothing to be proud of and equally nothing to be ashamed of. If the war had originated as an effort by the League of Nations, of which we are members, to impose sanctions on an aggressor State we could not lawfully or honourably have remained neutral. If we choose to belong to whatever form of World Order shall emerge from the Present conflict, we shall have to accept its responsibilities and limitations, if we would share its privileges. In the meanwhile, we still retain, by our own choice, the privilege of membership of the British Commonwealth of Nations, which is so important to Irish University Graduates; it is to be hoped that this will become the basis of a better human understanding, as well as of more intimate commercial relations, with our British neighbours in the post-war era.

"Agricultural development, in conjunction with fully restored access to the British market, affords us the best opportunity of rapidly increasing the national income. Our general economic policy should have this main object in view, even if it involves some temporary slowing down of the rate of industrial development. I urged on the Minister of Finance that it should be part of an agreed national policy that the "agricultural horse" should be restored to his rightful place between the shafts of the "industrial cart" thus reversing the situation that has existed in recent years. The Government has recently appointed me a member of a small expert Committee of Inquiry on post-emergency agricultural policy, and I am now engaged in the study of the technical and economic questions involved.

"In the period of post-war reconstruction questions of general economic, as well as of agricultural, policy are bound to arise, and it is most important that the voice of a professional economist should continue to be heard in the legislature. The economic basis of any social security plan will also require close examination. In this and other connections the social and civic rights of women must be carefully safeguarded.

"In the matter of the Irish language I would have welcomed a policy of preserving the bilingual character of Ireland in the sense in which Canada is a bilingual country, it will be difficult enough to prevent Irish from dying out in what is now the Gaeltacht. Irish could have been used as an instrument of an education at once liberal and national in the rest of the country, but the teaching of other subjects through the medium of Irish to children whose mother-tongue is English is an educational monstrosity.

"In the matter of compulsory school attendance I shared in the opposition to those aspects of a recent Bill which seemed to give the State excessive power at the expense of parental authority, and the Bill has since been held by the Supreme Court to be unconstitutional.

"My views on these and other matters of public interest are on record, and have occasionally reached the wider publicity of the daily Press. I think I may fairly ask that every Elector should consider my public record before deciding the order in which he (or she) should cast his vote.

"My public duties were exceptionally heavy in the early part of this year, and my ordinary work was increased owing to the temporary absence of a colleague on war work. In the circumstances I did not feel justified in stating my case to the electors until I could do so without prejudice to public and academic interests. I hope that electors who have already been approached by other candidates, and who may have agreed to support them, will nevertheless regard themselves as free to vote for me.

"It is possible that one or other of the new Candidates would, if successful, advocate many of my political ideals with greater eloquence than mine, and equal sincerity. But it is quite certain that no such person could have, here and now, the experience and authority derived from five years' service at Leinster House in a most critical period in the history of the University and of the world.

"If I secure re-election I shall deeply appreciate the honour and do my best to be worthy of it. My re-election by an emphatic vote would also give clear proof that I have your moral support in the course I have taken in public affairs, and enormously strengthen my advocacy of all those causes and ideals which command our common loyalty."

Although he had in his nominating group some 20 more people than he had had in 1938, mostly clergy, whose support he had perhaps picked up through his son-in-law Rev Dermot Carmody, and there were no notable defections from his 1938 panel, he lost his seat to TC Kingsmill-Moore. I suspect his acceptance of 'front-bench status' might have told against him. While De Valera, in offering him front-bench status, apparently appreciated his critical feedback, the apparent approval of de Valera would perhaps have counted against him with the TCD graduate electorate.

After his defeat he was however recruited to serve on the Commission on Post-Emergency Agriculture(7), and his main work during the latter part of the war was in this direction, to the extent that his Seanad contribution became somewhat marginalised, though he did contribute substantively to the debates after 1944, when he replaced Dr Rowlette, and served with TC Kingsmill Moore and Professor Fearon. I don't have a copy of his election address on this occasion; he probably just fine-tuned his 1943 one.

The 1948 Election

My father had been re-elected in 1944, and so in 1948 he was in the position of defending his seat, in which however he was unsuccessful, losing out to the classical scholar WB Stanford. His election address was as follows:

"The recent General Election in Eire renders it necessary, in accordance with the Constitution, to reconstitute the Senate in full. In requesting a renewal of your confidence it is now possible to refer to certain matters which, on account of the censorship, it was impossible to mention when I had the privilege of addressing you in 1944.

"I have no military service to my credit, but I am proud of the fact that five of my nephews served in the armed forces during the recent World War. I am particularly proud of the fact that one of them was awarded the DFC for service in Malta in 1942.

"I am a citizen of Eire but I also prize my wider citizenship in the British Commonwealth of Nations. It is most desirable that Anglo-Irish relationships should rest on a foundation of mutual trust and friendly co-operation. To achieve this has long been one of my principal objectives in public life.

"Like many other citizens of Eire I am an Ulsterman by birth, and have many friends and relatives in Northern Ireland. All such persons have very special reasons for appreciating the fact that the "Border" constitutes an obstacle to social and cultural intercourse. To some extent it hampers the functions and limits the usefulness of our University. And yet, the direct approach to this problem is confronted by insuperable difficulties. In the meanwhile there are a variety of ways in which closer relations between North and South can be, and should be, cultivated. I welcome the fact that the Governments of Eire and Northern Ireland are co-operating in the development of the hydroelectric resources of the river Erne. Similar co-operation, for example, in the treatment and eradication of veterinary diseases, would be clearly desirable and should be promoted. When we have learnt to work together in neighbourly co-operation in all the ways now possible to us, it may become possible to approach the political question with greater realism and deeper understanding.

"As a member of the Post-Emergency Committee on Agricultural Policy I was able to collaborate in the production of its Majority Report on Agricultural Policy. This Report has helped to liberate our present Government from the dead hand of a narrow economic isolationism, and has been useful in the recent negotiations which have led to a mutually advantageous Anglo-Irish trade agreement. In the course of our deliberations in this Committee I kept constantly in mind the desirability of increasing the flow of commerce between Eire and the United Kingdom.

"In particular, the Majority Report laid stress on the fact that a considerable expansion of egg production, and of other forms of live stock products, was possible in Eire and desirable from the point of view of both communities. This view has now been publicly accepted by both Governments; in fact the principal recommendations of this Report are being implemented by the Government of Eire in consultation and co-operation with the Government of the United Kingdom. I feel I may claim to have contributed in some degree towards the development of this highly desirable situation. My personal part in connection with the work of this Committee was favourably referred to in the course of conversation by a member of the Government party, and, on another occasion, by a prominent member of the Opposition.

"A Senior Fellow who is also a Senator has special opportunities for safeguarding the interests of the University where otherwise they might perhaps, quite inadvertently, be ignored. When it was recently decided to raise to University status the professional education given in the Dublin Veterinary College it was found possible at my suggestion to arrange that our University should have a relationship to that College exactly analogous to that assigned to the National University. In this respect also a recommendation of the Post-Emergency Committee on Agricultural Policy has been carried out.

"The Dublin Veterinary College is maintained by the Department of Agriculture of the Eire Government, but it attracts many students from Northern Ireland, as it is the only institution of its kind in Ireland. Our interests with reference to it, and to the whole programme of education and research in connection with plant and animal diseases, are of no small importance to us and to the country as a whole. It seems desirable, therefore, in the interests of the country no less than in those of the University, that I should be enabled to continue my constructive and mediating work with the status and influence which membership of the Senate *as one of your representatives* undoubtedly confers.

"Nor is my Professorial work prejudiced in consequence. My membership of the Senate gives me a wider platform for the dissemination of knowledge, much of which it is my academic duty in any case to acquire and impart as Professor of Applied Economies. A close relation between the University and the State has, long before my time, become recognised as being of great value to the State. It has recently proved to be of great value to the University. The services of my predecessors, my colleagues, and myself, has helped to bring home to the Irish people of all classes the fact that our University is a great national institution whose welfare is inseparable from that of the nation. This has recently received tangible recognition, in the provision of a grant of £35,000, renewable annually, for the general purposes of the University.

"I have no affiliations with any political party. Nevertheless the policies which I advocate are seriously considered by members of all parties, as well as by the Government and the newspaper reading public. The fact that three times since 1938 I have been elected as one of your representatives (once without opposition), and the further fact that your representatives have always maintained friendly personal relations with members of all parties in Leinster House, are of material importance in this connection.

"As Chairman of the Governing Body of Drogheda Grammar School I have become conversant with the problems that beset many of the smaller Secondary Schools in Eire. If free secondary education were provided for all boys and girls likely to profit by it, the problem of "redundant" Secondary Schools might disappear. I hope to promote a discussion in the Senate in which the question will be approached from that point of-view.

"I welcome the decision of the Eire Government and Parliament to apply for membership of the United Nations Organisation, and I fully realise the international obligations and responsibilities, as well as the advantages, which such membership would entail.

"The liberty of the individual is the counterpart of responsible citizenship, and I have consistently opposed all applications of the principle of censorship and all extensions of administrative power which seemed to me ... incompatible with it.

"As to the Irish language, the real problem for Gaelic enthusiasts is to prevent its extinction, as the spoken language of any significant section of the .Irish people, and that is an economic rather than a linguistic problem. It is very desirable in any case that the economic conditions of the people of the Gaelic-speaking regions should be ameliorated. If this were successfully accomplished there might eventually be established a harmonious balance between Gaelic and Anglo-Irish Ireland. The examples of Canada and Switzerland would seem to indicate that different linguistic cultures can coexist within the framework of a united nation. In the meanwhile it is useless to pretend that any language other than English is the vernacular of the vast majority of the Irish people. I am altogether opposed to the policy of educating through the medium of Gaelic in cases where the language is imperfectly understood and the subject can be more easily taught and learnt through the medium of the vernacular.

"Needless to say, I am deeply sensible of the honour which electors have conferred upon me in electing me on former occasions. I seek re-election now because I believe that my capacity for service to the University has been enhanced by my record of former service. It is right that electors should regard the interests of the University and the country as of paramount importance, and ignore all personal considerations, in the exercise of their serious responsibilities. All I ask is, that they should estimate the claims urged in this address by reference to that standard before deciding the order in which they will cast their votes.

"I need hardly remind electors that promises of support, which concerned only the recent by-election, are subject to review now that the respective claims of six candidates are in question."

Despite this appeal, the TCD electorate went against him. I have no record of his support committee, but I conjecture that the developing internal College politics was hardening against the gerontocrats, with whom he had unfortunately become identified, as a Senior Fellow, despite his earlier support of electoral reform and various radical College causes.

The 1949 Election

My father must have considered standing, in that he went to the extent of getting a nomination paper signed by the necessary 10 people, but then he never lodged it, and it has remained among his papers. He was proposed by Duncan and seconded by McConnell; the others were 'Louis Bou' Smyth, Edmund Curtis, RJ Fynne, Jacob Weingreen, TS Broderick, JM Henry, RBD French and WB Stanford.

He must have been pondering how to get back, and wondering if he stood a chance on any of the so-called vocational panels, because there is a letter from Senator James Douglas among his papers, dated April 4 1950, which is critical of the Senate electoral procedures, and the lack of 'nominating committees' as provided for in the Act. He refers to 'vacancies' and the lack of procedures for filling them, until there is an amending Act.

The key paragraph is '...for personal reasons I would like to see you re-elected as you and I have many views in common, but I think your best chance of re-election is for the University. I am not impressed by your reasons for not standing again for TCD but doubtless you understand the position in the University better than I do.'

It is I think legitimate to conjecture that he must have seen the 'McConnell revolution' coming and felt he was no longer enough in tune with the academic Establishment to win an election.

***

His last spell in the Seanad was from July 1952 to June 1954, as a de Valera nominee, but I have been unable to track down how this came about.

In the modules of this Seanad stream I have outlined his contributions to the 1950s debates(8), in some cases in full. He consistently alluded to the Partition question, and to the potential for a constructive Protestant presence in a unified national State. In this context he worked closely with James G Douglas(9), the Quaker businessman who had been advising Michael Collins and organising war victim relief.

Notes and References
1. There is among JJ's papers a letter to the Times from one JR Fisher relating to the Boundary Commission and the 'alleged secret understanding' under which Collins and Griffith were induced to sign the Treaty. There is also a large cutting from the *Irish Times* of December 4 1925 headed 'Boundary Not To Be Changed'. JJ had worked on local economic analysis in support of the Free State input to the Boundary Commission, along with Ned Stevens and Kevin O'Shiel. There were papers connected with this work in JJ's TCD rooms when I helped him clear them in 1970, but these alas have been mislaid. The outcome must have come as a disillusioning blow; he had helped to establish that Partition would be crippling to Derry City which would be deprived of its Donegal hinterland.
2. James Meenan in his biography of George O'Brien (Gill and Macmillan 1981) refers (p126) to the latter's participating in the 1922-24 Agricultural Commission, along with JJ, Sir John Keane and Tom Johnson, the leader of the Labour Party; it was chaired by Professor Drew. It also included politicians and farmers' representatives. According to O'Brien, the main thrust of the Commission was in support of traditional Department of Agriculture policy, as it had developed prior to the foundation of the State, initially under Horace Plunkett. I have summarised these in the hypertext.
3. The Prices ('Profiteering') Tribunal was set up in 1926. Most of the cuttings JJ kept in his scrap-book subsequent to the 1926 Seanad election relate to this, and to his work on the economics of the distributive process, which he identified as being dominated by

'middlemen' who were instrumental in depressing agricultural prices. About this time he was awarded a Rockefeller Foundation Fellowship to study this process.

4. I give more detail of this background material in the 1920s public service module in the hypertext.

5. JJ's first contribution to the Seanad debates I have given in full; it is accessible from the 1930s public service module of the hypertext, along with those of his other speeches which I have been able to reproduce in full.

6. JJ's contributions during the earlier part of the Emergency were critical of the way that the 1930s agricultural policies had left the country on the verge of starvation. I have summarised these in the first 1940s public service module in the hypertext, and where possible given them in full; the yellowing paper does not lend itself to scanning.

7. This Commission produced a series of Reports which did in fact influence post-emergency agricultural policy significantly, and JJ regarded them as being among his most significant contributions in the public arena. I have summarised them extensively in the hypertext. The Commission was chaired by TA Smiddy and included RC Barton, C Boyle, Professor JP Drew, Henry Kennedy (Chief Executive of the IAOS), J Mahony and EJ Sheehy. Both Professor Drew and JJ had served on the earlier Commission from 1922 to 1924.

8. There are no signs of moderation or deference to de Valera in his final Seanad contributions, which I have abstracted in the 1950s public service module of the hypertext.

9. James Douglas's *Memoirs*, edited by JA Gaughan, were published in 1999 by UCD Press, and I have reviewed them for a London Quaker publication, and made the review available in the hypertext.

Appendix 9: The All-Ireland View and the Irish Association

JJ was among the founders of the Irish Association, the objective of which was and remains to keep alive all-Ireland intellectual contact, despite the political barriers.

The first decades of the Association are chronicled in a pamphlet(1) by Mary MacNeill. This goes in some depth into the early days and the war period, and continues up to 1953, with a mostly Northern perspective. Corresponding information relating to the Southern Committee of the Association remains to be located; it is explicitly assumed by Mary MacNeill to be in existence. The Northern material is in the Belfast Public Record Office. There is however very little mention of JJ's Presidency to be found there; it extended from 1946 to 1954. He had succeeded the first President Lord Charlemont(2). I have however been unable to ascertain the circumstances of his election to office; there is a brief retrospective mention by Mary MacNeill.

I have extracted some notes from the Northern Ireland Public Record Office (NIPRO) archive which seem to me to be relevant to this narrative, and I have collected them in decade modules in the hypertext, to which I hope to be able to add material relating to JJ if and when I find it.

The NIPRO 1930s record(3) contains some insights from the MacNeill and Montgomery correspondence relating to the foundation process. The origins of the Irish Association were rooted in the perceptions of the de Valera Constitution of 1937, as seen from the angle of the Northern Protestants. It was a conscious attempt to stem the increasing divergence of outlook, and to preserve the opportunities for all-Ireland interaction presented by the status of the Free State within the Commonwealth. Names associated with its foundation were Frank McDermot and General Hugh Montgomery.

The NIPRO record in the 1940s decade(4) is dominated by the war; Mary McNeill records with gratitude the unsolicited dash to Belfast of the Dublin fire brigade on the occasion of the blitz, and the support given in the Free State to refugees.

There is in JJ's papers a copy of IA Bulletin no 3 dated June 1941, which records these events; a meeting planned for Belfast, at which PT Somerville-Large was to speak about the Mount St Club and the Dublin unemployed, had to be postponed. Papers read to meetings of the Association were summarised: Constantia Maxwell spoke in Dublin on the 'Ulster Plantation'; Louie Bennett spoke in Belfast on 'Vocational Organisation'; Rev Robert Crossett spoke in Belfast on the work of Muintir na Tire; Major-General Sir George Franks KCB spoke in Dublin on 'Irishmen Abroad'. The latter paper on military history was supplemented in the discussion by references to the arts and medicine. William A Beers is listed along with Mary McNeill as being joint secretaries.

There was a Commonwealth Irish Association conference in 1943, with a keynote paper by Prof WGS Adams, Warden of All Souls, Oxford; the theme was 'Reconciliation with Ireland'.

In the aftermath of the war we had the declaration of the Republic, and Lord Charlemont's resignation, which was related to the move to promote the Council of Ireland. This was said to have been supported by JJ in the Seanad, along with James

Douglas(5). There are indications in the MacNeill letters that Charlemont was not in a hurry to find a replacement for himself after the resignation, and that the atmosphere in the Association had been rendered difficult due to the declaration of the Republic.

In Mary McNeill's paper, after her mention of JJ, she puts on record an attempt to associate Northern interests with a national post-war planning exhibition held in Dublin in 1946. Post-war planning was then a fashionable concept. An attempt was made to involve the NI Rural Development Council, the Ulster Planning Group, the Tourist Association, the Young Farmers Clubs and the Women's Institute. The then vice-chancellor of Queens was Chairman of the NI Advisory Planning Board, and the Irish Association approached him, but he blocked it. JJ then being in the Senate, and in the first year of his Presidency, would have been keen to make this all-Ireland episode into a significant happening.

There is practically nothing in the NIPRO archive relating to JJ's Presidency, which leads me to believe that he was, to an extent, *non persona grata* with the Northern Committee. There is however correspondence relating to Sir Graham Larmour's introduction to his pamphlet *The Sickness of the Irish Economy*, mostly with Eileen Calvert, then a Stormont MP, with whom he seems to have had a good relationship(6). There is in the NIPRO archive a letter from Irene Calvert to Jack Sayers, the editor of the *Belfast Telegraph*, urging that JJ's articles on 'Agricultural Anaemia', as published in the *Statist*, should be reprinted in his paper. JJ's paper to the Belfast Irish Association, planned for November 12 1956, was based on these articles(7) .

On the other hand however there was a debate organised in Kilkenny in 1954, in which Colonel Topping, then a Stormont MP, supported by William Douglas, Secretary of the Ulster Unionist Council, put the case for Unionism against Seán MacBride supported by Eoin (the Pope) O'Mahony. JJ and the Irish Association had a hand in setting this up, and there was local support from Hubert Butler and the Kilkenny Debating Society. There appears to be no record of this historic episode in the NIPRO Irish Association archive, which I find strange.

The 1960s decade is one in which there could have been an overlap between my own interest in the North and my father's. He was on the Council, as a Past President, and I remember him drawing the Irish Association to my attention, and was prepared to explore its possibilities.

There is a record(8) of a Council meeting on 6/04/64, at which JJ was present. A meeting had been planned for November on 'Science-based Industry'; CO Stanley and Armin Frank had been approached to speak, but had declined. The matter was then dropped. This must have been my initiative, through JJ, because I was then acutely aware of Armin Frank, an engineer, who was the Chief Executive of Standard Pressed Steel in Shannon. He had been actively promoting among the engineering fraternity the need for Ireland to invest its intellectual capital, in the form of scientists and engineers, into high-technology industry. I had been cheering him on, and using his arguments in left-wing and republican political circles. JJ must have picked this up, or maybe I gave it to him.

At this time my own (basically Marxist) project was to politicise the republican tradition, and to rescue its 'Democratic Enlightenment' core-philosophy from the subsequent overlays of 'Catholic Nationalism' and 'IRB elitism' with which it had been infested subsequent to its 1798 origins. It was in this spirit that in the 60s I had become associated with Cathal Goulding and the Dublin Wolfe Tone Society.

When I heard of the projected 1965 Whit Conference of the Irish Association, I discussed it with Goulding, and we agreed that it would be an interesting indicator of the internal democratic reform potential of the Northern Ireland environment. So I went along.

The Derry Whit Meeting in 1965

There is on record in the IA archive some material relating to the Derry Whit weekend in 1965: there was a civic reception on Saturday June 5; tour of the cathedrals, one could choose A or B. The AGM took place, in which I introduced a resolution (see below); this was discussed and referred to Council.

Speakers to the main conference included Rev J Shiels, on the Swatragh co-operative movement, and Prof CF Carter, Vice-Chancellor of the University of Lancaster (he had been Economics professor in Queens, and had co-operated with JJ via the Statistical and Social Inquiry Society, and the Barrington Lectures). The topic of Carter's paper was 'Founding a New University', and the occasion was quite poignant, because all Derry had expected the New University of Ulster (NUU) to be based on Magee, and the IA meeting had been planned on this assumption.

Shortly before the IA meeting it had been announced that NUU was to be located on a green-field site near Coleraine. The frustration of the Derry people was palpable. John Hume was there, and this event undoubtedly was a trigger for the subsequent Civil Rights explosion. Steve McGonigal of the ITGWU had accepted an invitation to speak also, and was present. All the forces which subsequently became the NICRA were there in embryo, including the present writer, then active with the Dublin Wolfe Tone Society.

Also present was John Garmany, the Magee economist, who had earlier interacted with my father in the context of the latter's efforts to keep alive an all-Ireland view via the Statistical and Social Inquiry Society.

There is on record in the IA archive in NIPRO a copy of a resolution which was presented at the Derry meeting, which took place on June 5 1965. It is in my handwriting, but there is no mention of my name. It was referred to Council for consideration. The resolution welcomes the Lemass-O'Neill talks, and supports the policy of regional growth centres. It calls on the Dublin and Belfast Governments to nominate Londonderry as a growth centre for the Derry Donegal Region. I had clearly in mind the type of cross-border regional development body which has in the end emerged under the Good Friday Agreement.

A Council meeting was called for June 23 or 24 1965, in Ballymascanlon, and I was invited to attend. I remember that meeting; my motion was considered politely, and they decided to do nothing, it was not their role to attempt to influence governments. I remember at that meeting how Sir Graham Larmour regaled the company, with glee, how he had observed a prime example of north-south co-operation, in the form of an episode in which Herdman in Sion Mills had sacked his Catholic workers, who had come across the border from Castlefin, Lifford and other places nearby, and then gone to the IDA to get grant funding to start a factory for them in the Republic.

This confirmed me in my opinion that Partition was a bourgeois conspiracy to use the two States proactively to keep the working-class divided, and that the Irish Association, despite the best efforts of my father, of which I had been aware, was, in effect, party to this conspiracy, in its then policies. I then therefore decided that it was not a relevant forum in which the 'politicisation of the republican movement' project could usefully be pursued.

On a subsequent occasion, in 1966, when in the North making contacts with politicising republicans and others, I attended the Rev Shiels's church service, and talked to him afterwards; I had encountered him at the earlier Derry IA meeting, and was aware of his interest in the co-operative movement. There was on the agenda the promotion of support for the co-operative movement, as a cross-community unifying process, in the common interest. I was attempting to sell this idea to republican activists as a mode of useful work, with possible long-term positive political effects. Some of them I believe may have bought the idea, but subsequent events made it difficult or impossible to develop.

Dermot MacManus

There are in JJ's papers some correspondence with Dermot McManus, and some papers by the latter on the co-operative movement and the literary revival, and on the history of his family estate at Killeaden Co Mayo.

I reference this(9) here, though it has no direct links with the Irish Association as such. A reading of the MacManus papers however will suggest that the MacManus family was part of the 'patriotic landlord' tradition to which Lord Charlemont, Standish O'Grady, Hubert Butler and others belonged, including the likes of Yeats, Synge and Lady Gregory. These would have been in the lead in an 'all-Ireland Home Rule' socio-political scene. The Irish Association can perhaps be regarded as the surviving shreds of this tradition.

JJ's Papers

I found among JJ's papers some files of 1960s material. It includes evidence of an attempt made by JJ to get Northern Ireland support for the TCD School of Agriculture and its Townley Hall farm. There is correspondence with the Provost, and with Irene Calvert, and an attempt to interest the Ulster Farmers' Union; this took place in late 1963. There is a 2-page memorandum in which JJ outlines a scheme for an extension of the work of the Agricultural Institute North, on the basis of a TCD - QUB joint project based on Townley Hall, in the form of an 'all-Ireland Land Utilisation College'. He had, it seems, corresponded with the Taoiseach about this.

He produced a paper for the Irish Association Council to consider, in confidence, an outline plan for 1963-64(10). This foreshadows the type of developments which might have emerged out of the Lemass-O'Neill meeting, had the politics of that event been allowed to develop without forcing the pace. It also foreshadows what has come out of the Good Friday Agreement of 1998. In a letter dated September 24 1963 Irene Calvert indicated that she had sent a copy to Professor Carter, and had arranged to have it duplicated for circulation. She added 'I think your synopsis is brilliant. You should provoke some thoughtful discussion.'

Appendix 9: The All-Ireland View and the Irish Association

There was a reception in honour of the incoming President, JF Dempsey, of Aer Lingus, followed by a 'discussion meeting' to which JJ's paper was contributed; the other main speakers were Professor CF Carter and Vincent Grogan. There is among JJ's papers a copy of the minutes of the Council meetings in March and July at which the foregoing discussion meeting was planned. The Council at this time consisted of JF Dempsey, Miss MA McNeill, Sir Graham Larmour, JJ, Edmond Grace, B NcK McGuigan, GF Dempsey, Irene Calvert and DR Reynolds (joint hon secs), Frank Benner, Capt Peter Montgomery and Tom O'Gorman.

There is a hiatus in JJ's record then until 1967, when there is a note from Sir Graham Larmour attached to a copy of a *Belfast Telegraph* article by Martin Wallace: "I think the enclosed article-copy will prove that our choice of President has been a wise one". The article attacks the Orange Order for their opposition to a proposed visit by the Bishop of Ripon: '...a few clergy are going to have to consider whether they should remain within the Order, whose devotion to civil and religious liberty is once more exposed as meaningless ...'.

By this time JJ seems to have become disillusioned with the Irish Association, because there is among his papers a letter dated July 28 1967, in which he pays up his subscription, and bows out, to give priority to his Berkeley work. He castigated the Committee for not taking any interest in aspects of this work which he had offered them. There is however no record of this letter in the minutes of the September 1967 Council meeting, which he had kept, along with a copy of the printed version to Professor E Estyn Evans' paper on *The Irishness of the Irish*, delivered at the Armagh conference of the Irish Association on September 22, 1967.

***

As we have seen above, the Derry Whit weekend conference in 1965, planned to welcome the NUU, was an episode with many link-points. JJ had planned to participate in this, but did not get to do so, I suspect on health grounds, but I did, and I attempted to get the meeting to support a motion relating to the opportunity for a cross-border body to engage in regional development in the North-West. John Hume and others subsequently associated with the civil rights movement were there. There is no doubt that the location of the NUU in Coleraine was a rebuff to Derry, and a deliberate downgrading of the long-term collegiate link between Magee College and Trinity College Dublin. This was one of the many triggers for the subsequent Civil Rights movement.

I had little to do with the Irish Association during the 70s and 80s; if I find any relevant linkages I will record them in modules for these decades. I began to take an interest again in the 90s, somewhat marginally, and have contributed to the development of their web-site archive(11).

Notes and References

1. *The Beginnings of the Irish Association* recorded by Mary A. McNeill, Hon. Secretary, Northern Committee, 1938-1953. This was initially produced for internal circulation, and printed in 1982 as a pamphlet which I have reproduced in the hypertext.

2. It is perhaps worth mentioning in passing that Charlemont was the landlord of the Johnston farm at Tomagh, near Castlecaulfield, where JJ spent his early years.

3. The NIPRO record contains a 1939 membership list, which includes JJ with the title Senator, and a record of a correspondence with de Valera in support of the foundation of an all-Ireland Students Association.

4. The record of Irish Association meetings during the war, such as it is, I have outlined in the 1940s module of this thread of the hypertext.

5. I have so far been unable to trace this in the Seanad stream of the hypertext; it may be that it occurred post-1948, when JJ was no longer in the Seanad, but Douglas was still in, and making the running.

6. I treat this, along with the Kilkenny Debates, in the 1950s module of this Irish Association thread of the hypertext, along with such additional JJ activity on behalf of the Association as I can track down.

7. A summary of this paper, probably a press release, I have edited into the hypertext, accessible from here and from the 1950s module of this thread.

8. The record is in Box 6 of the NIPRO archive. For a more extensive analysis of this 60s period see the 1960s module of this thread in the hypertext. The record of the Derry Whit meeting of 1965 is in Box 7.

9. I have reproduced this in the hypertext; it is available from here and from the 1960s overview chapter.

10. I have reproduced JJ's Plan in the hypertext, accessible from here and from the 1960s module.

11. The Irish Association web-site is publicly accessible at http://www.irish-association.org in its current evolved form. My earlier prototype web-site archive is accessible in the hypertext, at the state of development it had reached during 2001.

Appendix 10: National and Left-Wing Politics

Left politics does not begin with the present writer: JJ in his undergraduate days 1906-10 was supportive of progressive causes, on the evidence of his role in College Historical Society debates(1), and subsequently after 1910 in Oxford(2). When in Oxford he became a member of the Oxford branch of the Gaelic League, of which the President was Cluad a Chabhasa (Claude Chevasse, said to be the original of Monsewer in Brendan Behan's *Hostage*). This was the Gaelicising landed gentry.

When later in 1913 he became a Fellow of Trinity College he was, more or less discreetly, supportive of various aspects of the national movement, via various journalistic contributions to the post-1916 situation, particularly in support of the 1917 Convention. His main interest however was the introduction of democracy into economics via the co-operative movement(3).

JJ did however make an important contribution to Irish politics, with his *Civil War in Ulster*, published in 1913, in an attempt to mobilise Protestant support for all-Ireland Home Rule, and pre-empt the process that led to the Larne gun-running and the partitioning of Ireland(4).

By 1922 was giving lectures in economics to working men in TCD, supported by Tom Johnson the leader of the Labour Party, under the auspices of the Barrington Lectures. In his later Albert Kahn correspondence with Garnier he promoted Connolly. His political interests in the 1920s continued to develop; he stood for election to the Seanad in 1926, as a Government candidate, but failed to get in; he served on various economic commissions (agriculture, prices etc), but avoided full-scale party-political commitment, giving priority to the co-operative movement(5).

In the 1930s he was critical of the way the way Russia went in the direction of self-sufficiency, and used Russia as a counter-example in his 1934 *Nemesis of Economic Nationalism*, which as highly critical of de Valera's economic policies. Despite this he managed to establish some rapport with the Fianna Fail Government, and they asked him to join a Commission of Inquiry into the working of the Civil Service. He also at this time, somewhat discreetly, was adviser to the leadership of the opposition, on economic matters.(6).

In the 1940s(7) however he viewed my incursion into left politics with considerable sympathy, and he kept us on our toes by shrewd questioning.

***

There exists among JJ's papers a file of signed menus and seating plans of various dinners attended, over the period 1911 to 1960(8). These give some insight into the relationship between the TCD elite and the Free State and later the Republic elite over the decades, with the TCD people evolving into eventual acceptance and indeed celebration of the Republic under McConnell, when they honoured de Valera's Presidency in 1960. They also show the decline of the Plunkett 'improving landlord' and 'co-operative development' movement after the failure of the 1917 Convention. JJ initially identified with the latter, but transferred his support to the Free State when it became established. It is evident, not only from such dinner seating plans as are available, but also from his subsequent Seanad speeches, that JJ played a pioneering role in getting TCD accepted in the Free State context as genuinely part of the emerging nation.

***

My own development in the 40s and 50s from the student Left was somewhat egregious, as most of its members were eastern-oriented, thereby falling foul of Owen Sheehy-Skeffington, while I was among the few who tried to interface with the local situation in Ireland (Justin Keating was another). A key influence was Desmond Greaves(9). Some of this influence was negative, in that at a time when the post-Curragh republicans were attempting to politicise, he narrowed the scope by acting explicitly on behalf of the British Communist Party. I suspect that this episode, which took place in 1948 and which I witnessed, was instrumental in driving many away from the politicisation process, and into the arms of Gerry McCarthy and the re-emerging 50s-generation IRA, leading to another cycle of destruction.

The 1950s were dominated by the attempt to make the bridge between the left and the national question, and Greaves(10) played a positive role, perhaps conscious of the negative effect of his earlier intervention. There were attempts to analysis the ownership of the top firms in Ireland. There were also tentative contacts with the republicans via Seán Cronin. There were increasing tensions between the present writer and Marxist orthodoxy, as embodied in the Irish Workers' League; I recollect attempting, without success, to query what was going on in the German Democratic Republic with regard to people like Harich, and in the USSR with regard to Pasternak and others. These queries were brushed aside by the leadership, who considered any critical appraisal of the USSR as a mortal sin. I made my peace with Owen Sheehy-Skeffington, visiting him in hospital on the occasion of his heart attack. I had had prior correspondence, in which we had begun to identify some common ground(11).

The 1960s began with a period in London, working with Greaves and others on the campaign to get the prisoners of the 1950s released. Then when the chance to return came in 1963, with the Aer Lingus real-time project, I got in with the 1960s republican politicising process, initiated by Cathal Goulding via the Wolfe Tone Society.

This was successful, in that it led to rapid growth of what began to look like a real political movement, and people began to see the advantage of avoiding the encumbrance imposed by the need to take care of illegal weapons(12). Friendly relations were established with the Communist Party in Belfast (which was the radicalising road for the Protestant working-class), and the Civil Rights movement for a while looked like being successful, until it met up with armed counter-attack by the B-Specials in August 1969. The destructive role of the 'Peoples Democracy' as a coat-trailing anarchist body, in the lead-up to the 1969 debacle, needs critical analysis. Also the role of Fianna Fail and the Haughey / Blaney / Boland caucus in helping to arm the Provisionals needs to be analysed(13); the politicising left-republicans were perceived as a threat within the Free State by those who were engaged in funding Fianna Fail via a process of corrupt land deals.

Appendix 10: National and Left-Wing Politics

How the Sinn Fein leadership reacted to August 1969 can be traced to some extent via its internal newsletter, as well as in the Ard Comhairle minute-book(14).

Predictably the Provisionals emerged as a result of this, and the 'officials' (as they were known) reacted by trying to compete, at which point I pulled out. The process leading to the Provisionals has been described in Derry Kelleher's books(15).

***

I attended a conference in Moscow in 1973 as part of a 'broad left' group which included several journalists. The objective of the conference was to strengthen the global peace movement(16). I was encouraged by this to think that convergence of the 'old Left' with the 'politicising republican Left' might after all be feasible, and a brief, though somewhat uncomfortable, period with the Communist Party ensued(17). I was eventually expelled for publicly criticising their position on cultural matters in the USSR.

Analysis of this episode gives some insight into the processes of unreconstructed Stalinist thought. A period with the Labour Party followed, with George Jeffares and the International Affairs Committee, which proved to be a complete waste of time and effort, as it had no impact whatever on the policy of the Party. A critical look at how National Conferences are railroaded may be appropriate, but this is for critical Labour historians.

Political work continued in the context of what remained of the Wolfe Tone Society(18); there was a paper in 1974 from my sister Dr Maureen Carmody on Irish politics as seen from the angle of the rural protestant community, and I contributed a paper which attempted to analyse the way forward in 1978. *Tuairisc* was revived for a period, in an improved format, and my sister's paper is accessible in this mode. For publishing my own paper however, the WTS being moribund, I had to resort to a fringe-Left periodical which was well produced and was beginning to attract good critical papers: *The Ripening of Time.*

On the Problem of Democratic Unity

Extracts from the 1978 'Ripening of Time' Paper

"...We live in a multi-class society, politically divided into two regions, one under direct British rule, the other having political independence but without the political will to use it. The focus of this article is on the latter, but it will be necessary to keep the former firmly in mind . The class structure in the Republic may be described as follows...:

"*1 A parasitic bourgeoisie which makes its money by speculation in land, mergers, asset-stripping, fronting for multinationals and other devices which contribute nothing to the production of real wealth. This group pervades the financial bourgeoisie and is primarily responsible for the stifling of any State initiatives independent of the multinationals; it is influential in top State circles and dominates the formulation of economic and financial policies; its prime aspiration is to strengthen its links with its colleagues in Britain, in the EEC, in the US and elsewhere.

It has since emerged that this group has been busily engaged in ripping off the State via what has come to be known as the Ansbacher process.

"*2 An entrepreneurial bourgeoisie which fulfils a productive function; it usually owns its means of production and gives employment individually; its members have often evolved to this position by fulfilling a management function in a State enterprise, which they use as a starting-point for their own business, or from a self-employed situation. There is therefore a continuous recruitment into this class from the upper strata of salaried workers and from the self-employed; individual success is often registered by doing a deal with a multinational; this can sometimes, depending on the nature of the deal, bring a person out of the entrepreneurial and into the parasitic class....

"...Thus the 'national bourgeoisie' is not a stable group, but a highly unstable phase in the evolution of the entrepreneurial strata from a salaried or self-employed position towards a deal with the multinationals. This group may become stabilised partially, and given class and national cohesion, by direct State support, supplemented possibly by an organised co-operative approach to marketing, purchase of raw materials etc...

"*3 A substantial group of working owner-managers and self-employed, including the vast majority of farmers, from which the national bourgeoisie is being continuously replenished, and which replenishes itself continuously from the working class by various part-timing, lumping, moonlighting and other processes. This class, as well as recruiting from the working class, is also being decimated by shedding its failures into the working class, typical being the part-time farmer. This latter phenomenon however is complex, in that in many cases the wage is used as capital to develop the farm, and in such cases the role of part-time farming is to stabilise the role of small property in the economy.

"*4 A working-class which is stratified in a rather complex manner; for example, salaried workers owning their own houses (a numerous elite), wage earners depending on local-authority housing, public service employees ('permanent and pensionable'), etc. There is also a substantial difference between the mix of strata in Dublin and elsewhere; the numerical scale of the Dublin working-class gives it a special character, with greater opportunities for divisive sub-stratification, establishment of ghettoes etc by the local authorities under the control of the bourgeoisie. The working-class outside Dublin, being embedded in a sea of petty-bourgeoisie, has greater opportunity for itself evolving into a self-employed or small business situation.

"In the North, the same pattern reproduces itself, but in duplicate, in Protestant and Catholic versions. The difference being that in all cases the Protestants tend to be more numerous in the more favoured strata within each class, this being a consequence of the politics of Partition and the primary means of maintaining British rule.

"The above fluid class structure has reflected itself into a remarkably stable political structure, in which two main bourgeois parties dominate the scene: Fine Gael, representing primarily the parasitic bourgeoisie, Fianna Fail drawing support from most of the entrepreneurial bourgeoisie but with a strong parasitic element in key positions; each controls broad swathes of the petty-bourgeoisie by the exercise of patronage, Fianna Fail in addition controlling a large slice of the working-class by a refined mafia-type system with its principal basis in the local authorities.

"The Labour Party, theoretically the political voice of the organised working-class through the Trade Union affiliations, in fact attracts a mixed clientele from the three main classes, and has compromised itself by close political association with Fine Gael, thereby accepting the lead of the most parasitic sections of the bourgeoisie....

"The political structure in the North is similar in that it consists of two main bourgeois Parties and a weak, divided Labour movement. Insofar as the Civil Rights agitations which commenced in 1968 have borne fruit, it is in the weakening of monolithic Unionism of the Brookborough type and the exposure of the historical anachronism of a Protestant ascendancy based on British rule being used as a road-block to stop the march of a nation and its developing Labour movement This process is far from complete. The central problem for the democratic forces in Ireland is how to gather together the forces necessary to remove this road-block, by putting united political pressure on Britain.

"Within the interstices of the above political structure, like small mammals in the undergrowth of the primeval jungles where all eyes were on the battles of the giant reptiles, lurk the political groupings of the Left. In the evolutionary process, the future lay with the mammals, because in their early stages they stuck to the undergrowth (avoiding the mistake of thinking that they had to do like the giant reptiles), and developed improved means of looking after their young. With this analogy I pass on to the statement of the problem, to which the foregoing is the background....

"I include in this (political Left) category the forces that made up the 'Left Alternative' grouping, which was by many regarded as a hopeful trend towards unity when it filled the Mansion House in 1976 and produced some preliminary ideas for concessions to be forced upon the Government in the matter of provision of jobs.

"The three groups concerned, the Communist Party of Ireland, the Liaison Committee of the Labour Left and Sinn Fein the Workers Party, came together for private talks in the previous period, initially at the suggestion of the Dublin Wolfe Tone Society. This coming together was possible because a tradition of mutual non-denunciation had established itself over a period of years, all three groupings being to some extent agreed on the common ground of British responsibility for the Northern crisis, and on the responsibility of the policy of permitting domination of the multinationals for the employment crisis.

"It was round the latter issue that they tried to build their fragile agreement. This fragility was rendered more pronounced by the existence of a school of thought in the SFWP that appeared positively to welcome the multinationals as a 'proletarianising' force. The former area proved more disputatious, particularly from the Labour quarter and no attempt was made to develop it....

"Another grouping subsequently emerged (known as the 'National Alternative') which attempted to develop a common standpoint on the Northern question. This included the CPI, the Irish Republican Socialist Party, the Irish Sovereignty Movement, Provisional Sinn Fein, Peoples Democracy and others.

"It was convened by a group of concerned individuals, the writer among them, who had long-standing Republican connections. SFWP were invited to participate, but declined because it would have meant sitting down with the Provisionals, to whose bombing campaign they attribute (with some justice) the decline in political development in the North (which showed some promise in the period 1968-70).

"This group produced a 'nearly agreed' document, which however foundered on the Provisionals' insistence of a particular wording describing the attitude to the use of force. Many of the participants had hoped that the politics of a ceasefire might have been explored positively, but these hopes proved illusory. On the negative side, the participation of the CPI in these talks gave rise to some strain in their relationship with the other parties in the original 'Left Alternative' group.

"The political left draws its forces from the working-class, self-employed and entrepreneurial bourgeoisie. The various groupings which make up the elements of the political left are composed of this mixture in varying degrees. They share a common attitude to their own development as organisations which can be described as bourgeois-competitive - in other words they see themselves as organisations or 'firms' competing for the same market (votes) and raw material supply (recruits). They each have a product (a political programme) which they develop in such a way as to be distinctive from competitors, while attempting to appeal to the same market.

"The market, however, is suspicious of this kind of political competition; it prefers on the whole to support the firm which has the largest 'market share' and a record of delivery of the goods.

"In the EEC Referendum, the anti-EEC forces presented themselves competitively, with the result that a credible alternative was in general not presented; in a few places where the political left submerged its competitive identities under the common banner of the Common Market Defence Campaign a reputable 'no' score was obtained (notably 50% in Nenagh town).

"The distinctive political wares of the competitive groups are worked out behind closed doors by leadership groups with varying degrees of informed expert input, and are steered through congresses by a more or less democratic process, rank-and-file members following the voting patterns of leading members who are influential and are good at rhetoric.

"Once the 'line' is adopted, it becomes incumbent on members to accept this as the entrenched position, and to support it against members of other groupings, irrespective of arguments. The strength of the discipline varies between the groupings.

"The fundamental weakness of this situation is that there is no effective means of allowing a freely interactive period of policy development covering common areas of agreement, such as to permit strengthening of inter-group co-operation, ultimately leading to the much sought after 'unity of the democratic forces'.

"...I (now) try to summarise the political objectives and develop a structural concept for a movement to achieve them.

"The key political objectives are:

"(a) the achievement of a negotiated settlement with the British on a secular democratic federal basis, with Britain transferring all financial support towards the promotion of all-Ireland institutions, and with all the Irish people involved in developing the new constitution without interference from the British.

"(b) the isolation of the landed-speculative parasitic element of the bourgeoisie, and the achievement of a democratic independent economic development policy with a leading role played by the State sector rather than the multinationals, based on alliance of the organised working-class, the self-employed and the productive entrepreneurial bourgeoisie.

"The organisation of a movement for achieving this democratic-revolutionary objective on the basis of a multi-class alliance is fraught with many problems, not the least of which is the fear on the part of the small property owners that those who shout for Socialist objectives will take their property from them. Similarly, those who have no property fear that in a democratic-revolutionary class alliance the lead would be taken by propertied elements, this, on the whole, being the historical experience.

"In Ireland at this time we are faced with a historic challenge: can we develop a movement in which there is enough mutual trust between the democratic anti-imperialist forces to permit a credible political alternative to develop? Can the Socialists be persuaded to lower the red flag and to promote a transition to socialism that is acceptable to self-employed and small entrepreneurs? Can the latter be got to believe in a process whereby a small private enterprise expands with the aid of public money to become a socialist enterprise, rather than a capitalist enterprise with the aid of the Stock Exchange, or a subsidiary of a multinational?

"These are the practical issues that must be teased out theoretically, if the 'Co-operative Democratic Federation' is to develop....

"...In the period of development of this movement, it will be necessary for the various groupings forming the federation to delete from the top of their agendas the question of electoral appeal. This will return later, when the spade-work has been done. Recognising that they are a rather small herd of political animals, the groupings composing the movement should consider retiring into the undergrowth and working out in concert how they can influence the battles of the political dinosaurs in the interests of the mammals (returning to the earlier evolutionary analogy).

"This is the period of 'guerrilla politics'; development of influential specialist lobbies with a low political profile on key issues such as civil liberty, neutrality, local democratic reform, land tenure reform, reform of the educational system, industrial democracy, the right to a job, taxation reform etc....

"The role of the leadership of the movement, and of various specialist groups of rank and file, is to co-ordinate and plan the development of policies appropriate to the various specialist lobbies in the light of the real needs (not some ideological imagined needs originating possibly in the Scriptures), with the knowledge that the grass-roots activists will assimilate them, adopt them and promote them in the appropriate broad organisations where their interests lead them to specialise.

"The principal strategic problem is how to isolate the parasitic sector of the bourgeoisie; how to drive a wedge between the parasitic sector of Fianna Fail support and the rest, and how to drive it along with Fine Gael into political isolation on the Right; parallel with this is the problem of how to develop a workable understanding between the Labour Party and the entrepreneurial wing of Fianna Fail.

"It is, perhaps, possible to achieve this by encouraging the development of demands from various democratic lobbies such as to render electorally attractive certain areas of common policy which already exist between Labour and Fianna Fail, such as:

"(a) In the area of management and control of the educational system, where both parties appear to favour a lay-managed system in contrast to the clerical denominational system inherited from the British and favoured by Fine Gael.

"(b) In the area of State enterprise, where all the principal State sponsored bodies owe their existence to Fianna Fail, and where Labour is ideologically committed to support of the principle.

"(c) In the area of foreign affairs, where Fine Gael is pro-NATO and Labour and (most of) Fianna Fail are neutralist....

"There are many obstacles to the 'left alternative', perhaps with or without one or more of the 'national alternative' groups, coming together in a Co-operative Democratic Federation. The principal obstacles are subjective: a type of quasi-religious megalomania, a 'holier than thou' tradition that echoes the sectaries of the 17th century. There are also histories of mutual recrimination, often on the basis of actual wrongs done.

"There are also 'objective' obstacles. The existence of vestigial or shadowy 'armed wings', links with organisations abroad of which the precise nature is not clear (association with an international movement or affiliation to a foreign State power?), the possession of embryonic parliamentary representation (on the part of the Labour Left, now become the Socialist Labour Party).

"The reality and extent of these obstacles is open to question, but there is no doubt that they exist as obstacles for as long as there are doubts in the minds of each group as to the nature of the credentials of the people they deal with in others: who is boss? whose writ runs? Army Council or Ard Comhairle? Administrative Council or Parliamentary Group? Political Committee or Moscow?...

"These obstacles can only be overcome by a process whereby the leaderships of the groupings agree to encourage their members to engage in common theoretical policy development work, along the lines suggested in this paper. There is a precedent for this, in that the Wolfe Tone Society has already hosted inter-group seminars on typical 'guerrilla-political' topics such as unemployment, civil liberties etc, and these seminars have lead to joint actions.

"To cement up this theoretical development, there is needed a reputable theoretical publication which would circulate in all associated groupings, containing printed versions of discussion papers and agreed common educational material.

"Is it too much to hope that some periodical such as *The Ripening of Time* might make a bid for this market, by associating itself with a consultative editorial committee having standing such as to ensure its general acceptability, but without any dead-hand or veto rights such as to stifle free discussion during common policy development?"

Appendix 10: National and Left-Wing Politics

Labour in the 1980s

Most of my time in the 1980s was spent in socio-technical consultancy work, but I did attempt to contribute to the Labour Party's understanding of the Northern scene, mostly via the International Affairs Committee. It was appropriate, in the aftermath of the disastrous Thatcher-Fitzgerald 'summit' of November 18-19 1984, to review Labour policies on the North, and to suggest ways in which they might be developed creatively in the new situation.

In this context I wrote a paper(19) which covered the historical background, the development of the Civil Rights movement and its sterilisation by violence, the evolution of Labour policy and its subversion by Conor Cruise O'Brien's two-nationism, the emergence of potential new Labour thinking via meetings of trade union activists, the New Ireland Forum, and so on. I identified the missing ingredient in the latter as the drawing of a proper distinction between Protestantism as a component of Irish culture, and Unionism as an externally-imposed political ideology, an imperial contrivance, with its origins in blood and Tory armed conspiracy. The Forum document, with its talk of 'accommodating the Unionist tradition', fudged this.

Contact during this period with the Labour Party was minimal and led to little in the way of visible achievements. I submitted a memorandum on the national question(20) to a Commission set up to study, in which I outlined the opportunities under the Anglo-Irish Agreement and in the European context. I gave some prominence to the question of sectarian education, and the problem of local government reform.

The Labour Party had planned its annual conference for December 1986 in Cork, in the City Hall. As a consequence of the Sovereignty Movement Campaign, led by Anthony Coughlan, there was a significant amount of informed opposition to the Single European Act (SEA), especially from the Trade Unions, and from residual elements of the Labour Left. The possibility existed of a conference decision against.

Coincidentally there happened to be an industrial dispute in Cork with the municipal workers, who manned the City Hall. This enabled Dick Spring to call off the Conference, in a pseudo-left act of 'solidarity'. He went on to make a personal television appearance, urging support for the SEA. This piece of political manoeuvring I found absolutely sickening. If they had wanted to defend party democracy and run the conference in the City Hall despite the strike, it should have been possible to do a deal with the municipal workers to come in for the necessary few days, to oblige the party, or some suitable agreement could have been made, such as to use the conference as a lever in support of the workers' claims. So in effect the Labour Party went into the ensuing referendum without any agreed policy, and with Dick Spring's TV appearance used as the means of establishing one, by default.

Shortly afterwards I met with Roger Garland and a few others, and became convinced that the banner of non-violent social-reform politics was passing to the Greens, with the addition of long-term sustainability and environmental concern. This was a step in the direction of the type of integration of science with social concern which I had been seeking over the years, and which the traditional European

Left, in all its forms, had ignored. So in the end I got around to joining the Green party, attending the local meetings in Rathmines.

The Green Party

In this context I initially became active in developing the use of the Internet as a tool for Green international networking. The opportunity also arose for producing some 'Theses for a Greened Euro-Left' which were accepted for publication by Rosemary Ross, editor of *Links Europa,* subject to some editing down, in the first issue of 1990. The context was a combination of the bicentenary of the French Revolution, and the aftermath of the referendum on the Single European Act. It represents a good summary of my end-decade political thinking at the Euro-level, and reflects accurately the thinking behind my transition to the Green Party(21).

In the Green context I retained an interest in Church and State issues, and in the Northern Ireland question, contributing articles, papers and reviews as the occasion arose(22).

Notes and References

1. I have scanned the CHS record (fortunately before the disastrous December 2000 fire) and they suggest a consistent liberal radical Irish-oriented political position. I have summarised them in the 1900s political module of the hypertext.

2. The Oxford debates show this political position developing further, to include support for women's suffrage. I have summarised what I found in the hypertext version of my introduction to *Civil War in Ulster*; this material is not in the printed version. The Gaelic League membership card is in the JJ papers archive, folder 71.

3. JJ's work for the Convention gets a mention of JA Gaughan's edited version of James Douglas's *Memoirs.* He probably acted as a *Manchester Guardian* correspondent during the Convention, and corresponded with Erskine Childers, then the Convention Secretary. This is treated in the 1910s module in the political stream of the hypertext. His work for the co-operative movement I have outlined in Appendix 4; he interacted with Horace Plunkett, George Russell, and probably with Standish O'Grady when the latter was promoting co-operative communes in Jim Larkin's *Irish Worker* in 1912-13. See his *To the Leaders of Our Working People,* ed EA Hagan, UCD Press 2002.

4. JJ's *Civil War in Ulster,* originally published in October 1913 in time for the November Ballymoney rally of the Ulster Liberal Protestant Home Rule supporters, was re-issued by UCD Press in 1999, with an introduction by the present writer. It is available in full in the hypertext. Also, for a scholarly analysis of *Partition in Ireland, India and Palestine* see a book of that title, by TG Fraser, published by Macmillan, London, 1984. The author adds to the title the phrase *Theory and Practice,* giving it the status of a 'Partitionists Handbook'. It was sponsored by the University of Ulster and the British Academy. It is a challenge to democratic political scholarship to review this book critically and develop alternative approaches to the colonial to post-colonial transition, avoiding the fuelling of religious fundamentalism, as British partitionist policies have done, in all three situations.

5. See the 1920s module of the political thread of the hypertext, which touches on his Boundary Commission work, and abstracts his 1923 *Manchester Guardian* articles. See also the 1920s Plunkett thread, where most of his effort seems to have gone, and the 1920s Seanad thread.

6. See the 1930s module of the hypertext political thread; see also *The Nemesis of Economic Nationalism.*

7. We first get interaction of political ideas across the generation gap in the 1940s and I go into this in some depth in the 1940s module of the hypertext political thread.

8. The 'signed menus and seating plans' are in folder 70 of the JJ papers archive. I have done some analysis of their content and the result is available in the hypertext.

9. Desmond Greaves (CDG) left a journal, which I have had the chance to scan, thanks to Anthony Coughlan of TCD. I have abstracted and overviewed most of his key references to Irish political developments, insofar as they relate to his interactions with the emergent Irish left. The detail is accessible from the overview, in separate modules, initially one per decade, but then more as the situation becomes more acute. The contact begins during our student period in the 1940s.

10. In the 1950s the Greaves journals give insights into how the more perceptive elements of the Western Marxist intellectuals reacted to the disastrous development in Eastern Europe. The need for the Left to understand the national question in the Irish context became more acute. The 1960s political module overviews and abstracts from all accessible relevant sources.

11. I have reproduced some of this correspondence, along with some notes on Owen Sheehy-Skeffington's widow's biography *Skeff* (Lilliput, Dublin 1991).

12. I have abstracted the Sinn Fein Ard Comhairle minutes from about 1960 onwards, indicating an increasing level of politicising activity. See also the Greaves journals for the early 1960s, and the Wolfe Tone Society's archive, which I have abstracted in the hypertext, a key document being the Open Letter to Lack Lynch, August 9 1971. Also I am indebted to Mick Ryan for drawing my attention to a special 1998 bicentenary publication *United Irishman* to which he contributed a memoir of his period as organiser of the movement and managing editor of the 1960s *United Irishman*. This commemorative publication was produced by Harry Donaghy, 24 Polard St, Belfast, BT12 7EX, and I understand is accessible in the Linen Hall Library. It is evident from Mick Ryan's memoir that the effective politicisation process, centred around the *United Irishman* under the editorship of Seamus Ó Tuathail, did not effectively begin until 1968. See also the Greaves journals, for the periods beginning 1966 and 1968.

13. The role of Fianna Fail in helping to create almost a Civil War situation in the North, in order to marginalise the role of the left-republicans in developing the political road via Civil Rights, has been treated in *The Arms Trial* by Justin O'Brien (Gill & Macmillan 2000), in a manner which gives some credit to the roles of Cathal Goulding and the present writer, though not without some significant misunderstandings, on which I have commented in the hypertext. See also my commentary on the memoirs of Mac Stiofain.

14. The Sinn Fein Ard Comhairle and Coisde Seasda minutes books are much richer for this period, as well as the files of *Nuacht Naisiunta* the internal newsletter which began in September 1969. See also the Greaves journal for 1969.

15. Derry Kelleher's books cover his experience of attempted politicisation of the republicanism from the 1940s onwards, and his attempts to swim against the tide of emigration, somewhat similarly to the present writer. His *Buried Alive in Ireland: a Story of a 20th Century Inquisition* and his *Irish Republicanism: the Authentic Perspective* are essential reading for the understanding of this process.

16. I give some details about the agenda of, and participation in, the 1973 Moscow peace conference in the 1970s political module of the hypertext.

17. Some documentation relating to some work I began on all-Ireland economics, but did not finish for lack of good sources, and to the CPI's role in the 'Left alternative' grouping, is also given in the 1970s political module.

18. My sister's paper is in the Wolfe Tone Society newsletter *Tuairisc* #2 (new series) May 1974, and my paper 'On the Problem of Democratic Unity' is accessible in full in *Ripening of Time* Issue #9, March 1978. Both are referenced from the 1970s political module of the hypertext.

19. I have reproduced this paper in full in the 1980s political module of the hypertext; it may have been published in *Links Europa*, the British Labour Left newsletter which networks with the European Left. The paper is dated November 28, 1984.

20. This memorandum, dated January 1986, is available in full in the hypertext. Although it had little or no impact at the time, I am making it available here as an indication of my then current thinking on the North.

21. I go into this further in the 1980s political module, where I describe how I managed to get the *1989 Green Manifesto* published on the GreenNet. The Links Europa Green-Left paper is also available in the hypertext.

22. I had a correspondence with Brendan Clifford in August 1990 which summarised well my then concerns; it arose out of my review of his book on 1798 and Belfast. I had earlier on 13/2/88 contributed a paper to the AGM of the Ulster Quaker Peace Committee: 'Violence and the Nation-Building Process - Some Reflections on Irish National Identity'.

Appendix 11: Science and Society

JJ in the 1920s as a result of his economic studies had early identified the role of intelligent enterprise, or 'know-how', among the 'factors of production'(1). Later, JJ in the Seanad in the 1940s was promoting investment into scientific research on peat as a raw material for a chemical industry. He also contributed to the debate on the Dublin Institute of Advanced Studies, on the occasion when TCD sold Dunsink Observatory to them, and used the occasion to regale the Seanad with the history of TCD contributions to world science(2).

JJ had encouraged me to study science, but had little actual scientific knowledge himself. I gave a paper to the Dublin University Experimental Science Association (DUESA) in or about 1947 or 48 on the historical interaction between discovery and political development. It was broadly based on the Hessen paper at the London 1932 *Science in History* conference, on the *Social and Economic Roots of Newton's Principia*. The conference was attended by a strong Marxist group from the USSR, which included Bukharin, Hessen and others. I recollect that much of the Hessen paper was devoted to the problem of finding position at sea, and its influence on trying to understand the movements of the moon and the planets, in the context of the longitude problem(3). PS O'Hegarty, a noted cultural activist and publisher, by then retired from the Civil Service, spoke to my paper. I remember him saying that 'any tool larger than a hand tool becomes a menace'.

This for me was an early introduction to the 'science and culture' problem in the national context.

During the 1950s in my Dublin Institute for Advanced Studies(4) epoch I was acutely aware of the mismatch between the DIAS as de Valera's implant, the Irish universities, and the Irish development process generally, such as it was in that black era.

The British Association met in Ireland in 1957; the Irish science community rallied round and welcomed it, though it had ceased to have the importance it had had in its 'belle epoque' in the previous century, of which I later analysed the Irish impact in 1983 in the *Crane Bag*(5). The BA meeting is basically a refresher course for schoolteachers on vacation, and as such it is important and useful. It is occasionally used for policy announcements by scientific 'heavies'. In the Irish context it may have had some influence in helping to initiate the 1964 OECD Report(6) by Patrick Lynch and Dusty Miller.

In the 1960s there was an encounter with the issue in the lead-up to the setting up of the National Science Council (NSC), and an unsuccessful attempt to influence the politics via several learned societies, whose representations were ignored in favour of a top-down nominated body(7).

Then in the 1970s I had the chance to shadow the work of the NSC via the *Irish Times* column(8), which ran from 1970 to 1976, thanks to Douglas Gageby, who bought the idea; it had not been done before in a national daily in Ireland; it had I believe been done in Britain by JG Crowther in the *Manchester Guardian*. As an example I give here some extracts from my April 18 1973 column, to indicate its prescient flavour:

"...I think that the following point is relevant to the animal wastes problem. Chemical fertiliser depends for its production on fossil fuels, which are liable to exhaustion. A far-sighted, conservationist economy would organise to recover, by biological means, all organic wastes, whether animal or human. Such wastes, already rich in phosphorus and nitrogen, can be concentrated still further by digestion, producing methane as by-product. The basic problem is one of mechanical handling; any economic solution will depend on the intelligent use of a gravity feed of slurries into a continuous digestion system...."

"...Theoretical solutions to the problem of dumps of old motor vehicles need also to be examined. There is more fossil fuel squandered in the manufacture of the vehicle than is burnt during its lifetime. This could be changed by introducing a system whereby vehicles were hired from the manufacturer, and were built for durability. There is no reason why a car should not last for 50 years or more, with good maintenance...."

In the 1970s there was some not very productive interaction with the then student Left, in an attempt to address the 'science and society' issue in Ireland within what I understood to be the Marxist canon. It was frustrated by the worsening corruption and dogmatism of the latter(9). More productive was the Kane-Bernal Society, which Derry Kelleher and I got going in TCD. It evolved into a sort of environmentalist lobby, fortified by my work with the *Irish Times* column(10).

The 'Science in Irish Culture' struggle

This could be said to have begun with my paper in the *Crane Bag* which looked at science in the Irish environment in the 19th century using the Irish meetings of the British Association as sort of snapshots. Then there was the Academy bicentenary in 1985, when a seminar was organised. The *Crane Bag* folded up but was replaced by the *Irish Review*, and I attempted to keep up the continuity, with rather minor and ephemeral success. To this day there is no journal which includes in its scope the scholarly study of 'science and society; issues in Ireland.

The *Crane Bag* Episode

In 1983 I persuaded Richard Kearney, who was then editing the *Crane Bag*, a cultural review published biennially, that the 'culture' concept in Ireland should include the culture of science in the national context. He accepted my 'history of science' paper, based on the records of the British Association meetings in Ireland(11). This however aroused some interest, and it was agreed with the Editor that I should organise a follow-up with a group of papers on related themes. I collected some, including one by James O'Hara in Hamburg on 19th century Irish mathematics, and one by Kieran Byrne in Mary Immaculate College, Limerick, on the RDS outreach lectures in the mid-19th century, which attempted to bring science to the Irish outside Dublin, and which interfaced with the Mechanics Institute movement for popular enlightenment. These however never saw the light of day, since after 1984 the *Crane Bag* folded, and I had to write apologetically to the frustrated authors. I had high hopes that the *Crane Bag* might have become a beacon for the scholarly integration of the culture of science into the general Irish cultural mainstream, but alas it was not to be.

Bernal Remembered

In the early 1980s I had made contact with the Bernal biographical project (which bore fruit finally in 1999, after much delay)(12). In this context I organised a Bernal Memorial Seminar in Dublin on Sept 20 1985. With this quite modest event I attempted to contribute to the Bernal rehabilitation process. It took the form of commemoration of the publication of Bernal's *World Without War*. It attracted some international participation, including Professor Roger Dittman from California, and a scientist from the German Democratic Republic who was in touch with Prof Brian Leonard in UCG. Dr Jane Bernal came from London, and Kevin Bernal, Desmond's brother, came up from Nenagh. Prof Dittman was (and remains) an activist on the network of the World Federation of Scientific Workers, founded by Bernal and Joliot-Curie after the war.

Irish support came from the ASTMS trade union, into which Bernal's old 'Association of Scientific Workers' had been subsumed; Michael Sharpe the IIRS patent specialist and ASTMS scientific staffs branch officer represented them. Martin Mansergh, political adviser to the Taoiseach, came. I contributed a paper 'Irish Neutrality, Disarmament and the 3rd World: the Bernal Message'(13) which took the basic ideas of the thinking of Bernal as outlined in his 1958 book *World Without War* and related them to contemporary Ireland, both as regards the development co-operation process itself and the global political problem of disarmament.

The Academy Bicentenary

This event attracted some scholarship from abroad, including O'Hara who came from Hamburg, and others. It was evident that Irish scholarship on the history of science in Ireland was largely lacking. There have always been a few amateur historians working in marginal time at the historical fringe of their scientific and professional specialties. Some papers, published obscurely, had been collected by Gordon Herries Davies, and made accessible in 1983 as a duplicated bibliography. I had hoped that the Academy event would publish a *Proceedings*, which might act as a focus for bringing into existence a centre of research into the cultural and political history of science in Ireland, but no such initiative was taken. I took it up with them, and the excuse was that all the papers were published separately in various scattered learned journals abroad. This of course is an absolute abdication of intellectual leadership, and highly reprehensible on the part of a body which claims to be a focus for Irish scholarship. The abstracts are I believe available in file somewhere in the Academy bureaucracy.

This hiatus was noticed by some activists in the field, and the result was a further conference, which took place the following year 1986 in TCD(14). But there still is no focus of continuity for the systematic study of science in Ireland in the colonial to post-colonial transition. This field is of course of crucial importance in the third world development economics domain, and the Irish as the pioneer nation in this process have a duty to provide the world with a relevant map of the various minefields with which the domain is littered.

The Irish Review
The gap left by the end of the *Crane Bag* was partially filled by the emergence of the *Irish Review* in 1986. This was less scholarly and more popularising, and the editorial team at its inception included Richard Kearney and Edna Longley. It was published by Cork UP. The first issue in 1986 included an offering by Hubert Butler on 'Ireland and the Nuclear Age', and one by Dorinda Outram, a historian of science who had been recruited to Joe Lee's Modern History Department in UCC, on 'Why Historians Deny Irish Science'. This was an opening and a challenge, to which I eventually managed to rise with my 'Science in a Post-Colonial Culture'(15). This however was subjected to editorial cuts, there being severe space constraints, and in effect it got emasculated. I gained the impression that the *Irish Review* was not seriously addressing the issue of science in Irish culture, and that the challenge indicated by Dorinda Outram remained extant.

Science and Culture in the 1990s
This proved to be a mainstream issue for me in the 1990s, and I made repeated efforts with various agencies. I continued the contact with Wrixon as best I could. I wrote reviews and used them as campaign material. I interacted with President Mary Robinson, giving her some material for an event in Lismore to celebrate Robert Boyle. I submitted a proposal to the Academy in 1993, when Aidan Clarke, the historian and son of Austin Clarke, was President, which however went down some black hole. I wrote an article 'The Practical Arts in Irish Culture' for of the then new Belfast publication *Causeway* on May 11 1993, I think as a result of an encounter with the editor. It was published in the first issue, which appeared shortly after. I contributed a paper entitled 'Science and Government', dated 3/10/93, in support of the Carlow 'Tyndall School', in the form of an article for the *Irish Times* using the School as leverage to get support for the academic study of the role of science in culture. There were numerous Green party science memoranda. The battle at the end of the century is still continuing(16).

Notes and References
1. See JJ's *Groundwork of Economics* (Educational Co of Ireland, 1925) where he identifies 'know-how' among the factors of production.
2. See Seanad reports for April 11 1946 on peat and February 26 1947 on Dunsink Observatory.
3. I put on record in more detail this and other related incidents in the 1940s Science and Society module. The Hessen paper influenced JD Bernal towards writing his *Social Function of Science* (Routledge Kegan Paul 1939).
4. I have touched on the Dublin Institute of Advanced Studies in the 1950s Science and Society module; this however undoubtedly needs and deserves critical treatment in depth, more than I am in a position to give now. JJ in the Seanad continued to promote the need for peat research, with ideas picked up from contact with Desmond Greaves and the present writer.
5. 'Science and Technology in Irish National Culture', RHW Johnston, *The Crane Bag* Forum Issue, Vol 7 no 2, 1983, p58.

6. I got to review the 1964 OECD Report in the December 1966 issue of *Development*, edited by Jim Gilbert. I have made this available in the 1960s Science and Society module of the hypertext.

7. There emerged a loose federation called the Council for Science and Technology in Ireland, under the stimulus of the Lynch-Miller OECD Report *Science and Irish Economic Development*, which attempted to co-ordinate the influence of the various science and engineering communities. I have put this into context in the 1960s Science and Society module of the hypertext. The experience fuelled a series of articles in the *Irish Times* in January 1967 by the present writer, *Science in Ireland*, which may perhaps have influenced the setting up of the National Science Council in 1969.

8. This column for most of the time was weekly; it started as a 'feature' and ended up on the financial page, with a change in emphasis. During the 1980s I collected it and edited it down into a book *In Search of Techne* for which I thought I had a publisher, Tycooley, who had specialised in the UN development agency market, for which the experience recorded in the column would have been relevant. Unfortunately Tycooley collapsed, but I have retained the edited *Irish Times* material, and it is available in the hypertext.

9. See the 1970s Science and Society module of the hypertext.

10. See also the 1970s Science and Society module of the hypertext.

11. This appeared in the *Crane Bag* Volume 7, #2, 1983, the 'Forum Issue', and I have reproduced it in the hypertext.

12. *JD Bernal: a Life in Science and Politics,* Verso, London, 1999. I have been able to use this as a source for the 2002 'who was who' publication by the Royal Irish Academy, *Irish Innovators*, edited by Charles Mollan et al, and also for *Physicists of Ireland* published in 2002 by the Institute of Physics, edited by Andrew Whitaker and Mark McCartney. The Bernal outline given here is based on the latter. The 1980s and 1990s in this stream were increasingly dominated by a perceived need, on the part of the present writer, to get the history of science, technology and the innovation process taken seriously in the Irish academic context, as an important background study in the business and humanities schools.

13. I make this paper available in full in the 1980s science and society module of the hypertext.

14. The proceedings were published by the TCD Physics Department; I got to review them.

15. My 1990 *Irish Review* (Spring 1990) paper *Science in a Post-Colonial Culture* is available in full here, and on the whole the printed version I consider unworthy and repudiate it. I went on to specify how a history of science centre might be developed, and I give in the 1980s science and society module of the hypertext some correspondence with Joe Lee in UCC and Gerry Wrixon in Eolas the science finding agency on this topic.

16. I have given documentation for all these still current 1990s issues in the 1990s science and society module of the hypertext.

Appendix 12: Socio-Technical Issues

Some comments on JJ's approach to innovation in the Irish agricultural context can be made in the same critical spirit as were developed by the writer during the 1990s. The obstacles were in the social dimension.

The key innovation which JJ tried to promote, over most of his working life, was not an innovation in the global context, nor was it technically an innovation in the Irish context. It was to combine livestock, tillage and market gardening in a single synergetic locally-based productive system, run as a managed business(1). Something like this had been standard estate practice for centuries in England, and was reflected in the management practices of some of the Irish estates. It required a fairly large-scale operational unit, if the synergy was to be demonstrated effectively.

In such a system it would be feasible to stall-feed the livestock in the winter, keeping up a steady flow of milk and meat production throughout the year, thus enabling industry to develop, supplying added-value products, effectively on the Danish model. This model however became more and more remote and unrealisable as the 'land for the people' slogan was interpreted in terms of division of estates into small individual subsistence farms(2). In the latter situation the 'easy way' was to allow the production to follow the growth of the grass, generating seasonal gluts of meat and milk, and making the marketing into a commodity disposal operation, rather than a profitable added-value employment-generating operation.

JJ attempted to modify aspects of his visionary system to adapt to the political fait-accompli of the existential smallholding community. In 1916 he was promoting local co-operative ownership of advanced American agricultural machinery(3). In the 1923 Report he supported the resurrection of the policies of the Horace Plunkett Department of Agriculture(4); also he put in a plea for the training of co-op managers(5). In his addendum to the 1926 Prices Commission Report he promoted co-operative marketing on the French model, coupled with value-added components in the distribution system(6).

In 1931 he was promoting winter milk production(7), but then under the influence of the economic war he went into polemical mode, aiming for the political arena, into which he arrived via the Seanad in 1938. Here he had a platform to promote aspects of his vision, taking up the support of the Mount St Club model(8), as a means of re-deploying some of the Dublin unemployed into productive agriculture, on the basis of his ideal synergetic large-farm system.

In the 1940s JJ's main attention was on the Post-Emergency Agricultural Commission and he succeeded in highlighting some key innovative issues having a socio-technical dimension. The third section on Production of Store and Fat Cattle is quite short, and states the problem of British policy on fat-cattle subsidy, with its 3-month residence requirement, generating an artificially high demand for 'forward stores', but takes it as a necessary constraint. JJ's arguments about the need to negotiate this politically, to get parity with Northern Ireland, and build up stall-feeding with consequential tillage-enhancement, was not at this stage taken on board. It was simply recommended that stores be de-horned for ease of transport. The idea of developing a trade in veal, on the continental pattern, was entertained.

In other words, JJ got them to recognise a key 'negative (economic) innovation' brought in by the British, but failed to get the socio-technical implications for the Irish economy put on the political agenda.

The fourth and final section on Feeding of Cattle homes in sharply on the key issue: winter feed supplies. No breeding programme will be any use unless the animals are fed adequately; and estimated extra 150 gallons of milk annually per cow was feasible with proper feeding alone. A radical change in grassland management was called for, with production of silage, supplemented by hay, roots, straw and green forage crops. This section contained what JJ had been campaigning for during the previous decade(9).

In his last attempt to bring together some shreds of his 'managed synergy' vision of Irish agriculture, JJ attempted to demonstrate (on his Grattan Lodge smallholding, near Vicarstown, Co Laois) that a market gardening enterprise could benefit by being associated with a few cows, adding value to their manure(10).

This completes the listing of episodes where JJ encountered obstacles to his technically innovative ideas, which were rooted in negative social forces. It is possible to conclude, in retrospect, that the key missing factor, preventing his vision from being realised, had been identified and called for by him in 1923: the provision of training for co-operative managers in the principles underlying the 'co-operative transformation of the estates' vision. Such people, had they existed, would have provided local leadership alternative to the village gombeens and the parish priests, and enabled 'project teams of motivated end-users' (to trespass into 90s socio-technical jargon) to have been built out of the working farmers and farm labourer populations of the rural communities. Isolated progressive priests like Fr McDyer of Glencolumcille were too little, too late.

Had this politics developed in the 1920s, as an alternative to the Fianna Fail land division and protected gombeen-capitalism policy which emerged in the 1930s, Irish rural and urban civilisation would have been able to follow a path closer to the Danish, with a strong labour movement.

***

During the 1940s in TCD I was very much aware of the obstacles in the way of doing good science in Ireland, and of the high emigration rate of science graduates. I was in process of absorbing the ideas of JD Bernal on the social function of science, and on how science interacted with the State, and with economic and technological progress. I read a paper to the Dublin University Experimental Science Association on these topics, perhaps around 1949(11).

During the 1950s in the Paris Ecole Polytechnique I became very aware of the importance of teamwork among people of complementary skills. I recognised the nature of the Bernal vision of the productive unit of the future Socialist society, organised as team of enthusiasts who understood the needs of their 'market', while not simply being motivated by greed(12). Subsequently in the Dublin Institute of Advanced Studies I was very much aware of the cultural gap between what we were doing in experimental science, and the needs of Irish industry, but was unable to address the issue in any organised way. There were, I think, articles in left-wing periodicals, like the *Plough* and the *Irish Democrat*. [If I find these I will reference them.]

Appendix 12: Socio-Technical Issues

I found time in the 1960s to address, at an abstracted level, various socio-technical issues; there was an organisation set up in 1965 called the Council for Science and Technology in Ireland, the objective of which was to lobby the Government in the context of the Lynch-Miller OECD Report *Science and Irish Economic Development*(13). This work was however at the level of 'science and society' politics; I was not concerned with the problem of how to adapt the productive team to the innovation in any specific context. I was of course concerned in Aer Lingus with techno-economic analysis of some specific innovations, and in investment decision support(14).

I repeatedly referenced the social dimension of the innovation process in the *Irish Times* series in the 1970s. There was also a social dimension implicit in some of the applied-research consultancy work implemented in the 1970s at the TCD-industry interface. The former projected critical views of various human structures and institutions relevant to the science scene, of the innovation process as it existed in Ireland, and on the problem of access to scientific and technical information. The latter covered areas like use of genetic resources by plant-breeders, and organisation of information relating to marine resources(15).

As an example of my contribution to the socio-technical debates which centred round the projected Dublin oil refinery in the mid-1970s, I reproduce the following:

January 30 1974

I have hesitated coming into the controversial area of the proposed Dublin oil refinery before this; basically I am 'environmentalist', while at the same time being in favour of upgrading the technological diversity of the Irish industrial base. These two objectives are not incompatible, provided the environmental legislation is adequate....

I have now had a chance to see the IIRS report on the pollution levels which are considered in the planning application for a refinery on reclaimed land in the Pigeon House area, and on the effluent control practice which is envisaged. The IIRS report states that '...the measures proposed by the applicants in regard to air and water pollution control represent the very best practice at this time....present pollution levels are not expected to show noticeable increase due to the proposed refinery; indeed SO2 levels may fall'.

The total daily emission of SO2 from the 100m stack is not to exceed 20 tonnes per day, compared to an overall Dublin emission variously estimated at 250 to 500 tonnes.

The mechanism for the conjectured fall in overall SO2 levels implied in the IIRS statement is that the total SO2 in the city includes that generated by refined oils consumed. The proposed refinery apparently plans to work on 'light Arabian and West African crude with sulphur content below 2%'. This must be compared with the oil which the ESB is currently burning at Ringsend. I am not currently in a position to make this comparison, but I can see that by operating an appropriate buying policy, by controlling the sulphur extraction during refinement subject to stringent effluent regulations, and by doing a deal with the ESB to take up the residual oil to fire its Ringsend generator, the net situation could be improved, and this is what is in the plan.

Most of the opposition to the Dublin refinery appears to be based on a figure of 100 tonnes per day of SO2 suggested by Dr Donal Flood, who in his retirement from the IIRS is acting as scientific adviser to the environmentalists. I do not doubt that this figure is a correct measure of refinery practice under conditions where effluent control is weak or non-existent. What Dr Flood is suggesting is that the proposed levels of control would be flouted consistently, due to inadequacy of effluent control legislation. So may I suggest that the debate be brought around to the issue of urban effluent control, and that the refinery debate be examined again by the environmentalists with a critical eye?

Firstly......do we need a refinery for the Irish home market? To answer this we need to go into the history of refining proposals in Ireland. The story goes back to 1939 when in the Fianna Fail 'self-sufficiency' epoch an effort was made by Seán Lemass to establish refinery capacity in Dublin, with the aid of London and Thames Oil Wharves ltd. This company (I don't know if it still exists) was an independent operator, outside the major multinational ring, which was prepared to do business with dangerous revolutionary countries like Mexico (which had just nationalised its oil) and Ireland (which had until recently been engaged in an 'economic war' with Britain, arising from the attempt by the de Valera Government to achieve some of the objectives of the 1921 Republicans which had not been conceded in the Treaty setting up the Irish Free State).

A refinery proposal was produced and discussed in the Press, but ultimately was blocked, apparently as a result of pressure by the major oil companies.

Then in the 1950s, under political pressure, the Government was instrumental in setting up the Whitegate refinery near Cork, under the joint ownership of three of the major oil companies. The effect of this joint ownership was to block all internally-generated development proposals, as any such had to be approved not just by one but by three boards abroad. Chemical engineering staff was allowed to run down, those remaining becoming disgruntled; it is now, I understand, a routine operation run by technicians. Whitegate supplies 50% of the market of the Republic.

Why was a refinery not built at Dublin at that time? Contemporaneously one was built a Belfast: a natural place, near its main market, minimising short-haul transport-costs. On this argument the only possible site for a refinery is Dublin.. The Belfast refinery raised no environmental storm; nor, for that matter, did Whitegate.

To answer that question, consider the recent fuel crisis..... Anyone who travelled to Britain by car-ferry over Christmas, as I did, will have noted that in Britain there is no visible shortage of petrol. I covered 600 miles and never saw a queue or a closed garage. Clearly the Irish market, as far as the oil majors is concerned, is an appendage of the British distribution system, and they want to keep it that way. It is, apparently, policy to concentrate refining capacity in Britain and to block the development of independent refining capacity in Ireland. Dublin is supplied from Pembroke.

The current Dublin refinery proposal has major implications for the oil multinationals. As far as I can gather, it is a joint venture between Irish and French interests, the latter being the French State oil company.

A refinery in Dublin, on the currently economic scale of operations, would be too big to be content with the 50% of the home market left by Whitegate. It would have to seek markets in Britain, supplying them with refined fuel by small coastal tanker. This is the reason for the French interest.....

A refinery in Dublin, independent of the major multinationals, would enable the Government to do an independent deal directly with an oil-producing country.

Consider now the problem of siting the refinery anywhere else. During the building phase you would have to import labour on a temporary basis, up to 2500, which would then run down on completion leaving a staff of possibly 300 for operations, maintenance and development. To build in an isolated place away from major centres, as well as being inherently a costly operation, is to condemn the completed unit to the status of a routine operation with minimal further technological development potential. For this to occur, an imaginative technological staff of high calibre has to be close to and interacting with other technological and scientific services, such as are only to be found near a major urban centre.

...The only possible site for a refinery is a major port, and in the interests of minimising short-haul costs it should be near its main market.

The task of the environmental lobby is, therefore, to press that the effluent, noise-levels and appearance are consistent with nationally-imposed standards. From what I have seen of the IIRS report, this should not be unduly difficult. Blanket opposition to a refinery on a declared and accepted industrial area at a major port is, I feel, overdoing the environmental watchdog role. So can the debate be re-started, with less heat and more light....?

On the question of oil spillage: to site the refinery in Dublin would involve a change in the method of handling of the oil volume consumed on the home market from a short-haul, small-vessel system to a long-haul, large vessel system. This would substantially reduce the number of fuel transfer operations, reducing spillage probability. Adding in some short-haul operations to supply the surplus to the British market would bring the total number of handlings to something like the present level. This would of course need to be evaluated and watched... We are already facing this risk at Whiddy Island, without any significant economic benefit or compensation. We have the means at Whiddy of measuring the spillage risk, so that the Dublin debate can be quantified in this regard.....

February 20 1974

Pollution by oil refineries was the subject of a lecture last week to the Institution of Chemical Engineers (Irish Section) by Mr P A Winchester, who is manager of the Whitegate Refinery.

Among the points he emphasised was the fact that there was no effective State-controlled pollution monitoring unit, with which a potential polluter could deal. This function, insofar is it exists, now lies with the IIRS, which will do an ad-hoc job when asked. This is not a substitute for a continuous independent monitoring body.

Mr Winchester pointed out that it is relatively inexpensive to build in pollution control at the design stage (e.g. segregated effluents which can be processed in the ways appropriate to the known contaminants, instead of a mess in a common sewer).

He then went into the economics and technology of water-treatment of crude oil: the sulphur tends to occur in the form of mercaptans, giving an offensive smell. These hydrolyse to H2S, which is then reacted with oxygen giving water and free sulphur. There is a market for this with the acid manufacturers. The process is tricky to control and consumes energy, but it can be done, and some of the cost is recovered with the sale of the sulphur.

Kuwait crude, which contains 4.3% sulphur, can be reduced to the 1% level, but to do so requires expenditure of 11% of the energy contained in the oil. For half the energy expenditure you can get the sulphur down to 2%. If you try to wash out the SO2 from the exhaust gases, you cool them, so that the plume does not rise well from the stack. The overall solution must be a compromise between good stack design and partial extraction of sulphur from the crude.

Noise, due mainly to furnaces and air cooling systems, can be designed out by totally enclosing the noise source and adding appropriate brick walls. (Again, there are no national noise standards, and no independent national or local noise monitoring service).

Mr Winchester called for a new breed, the 'environmental engineer', trained in a broad-based discipline familiar with all aspects of water and air pollution, whether by chemical, biological or physical (eg noise) processes.... The major industrial firms would have to employ such people, if they had to cope with a State monitoring service with teeth.

Plant managers, such as Mr Winchester, clearly want to employ such people.

Their Boards, however, are unlikely to sanction the spending of money in this direction unless their competitors are in the same position. So it is clearly up to the Government to legislate to introduce a statutory authority, and to the Universities to develop some sort of a masters-degree programme for converting our surplus of physicists, chemists and biologists into environmental engineers.

Most of the opposition to the Dublin Bay refinery proposal (which I am informed is based on a long-term contract option on Algerian oil at 2% sulphur) is based on the lack of such an authority, and on the presumed inability of Dubliners to press the Government politically to legislate for one.

According to the IIRS evaluation of the Dublin Bay project, all the design points mentioned by Mr Winchester are provided for at the start. With 600,000 Dubliners watching, I suggest that we are more likely to get legislation for a pollution monitor service than if the problem is banished to a green-field site, under the control of one of the 'big seven' oil-multinationals.

Mr Winchester analysed the history of the spillage of oil at Whitegate. Some 1500-1700 ships per annum are handled. In the four years 1970-1973 spills occurred on 7,5,4 and 1 occasions. This improving record is a result of a conscious effort to improve the management procedure governing the interaction between two crews, usually having a language barrier between them.

A State monitoring service could facilitate this learning process by being visibly present, and possibly even supplying interpreters, if necessary.

***

Appendix 12: Socio-Technical Issues

In the 1980s, as Techne Associates consultancy, the present writer produced several reports with a socio-technical dimension, initially in the context of the Institute of Physics Technology Group, and then later for Shannon Development and various State agencies, addressing issues like how to interface innovative enterprise development with technical colleges, and how to develop inter-regional linkages between innovative firms and sources of know-how(16).

But it was not until the 1990s that I had a chance to participate in an EU project in which a knowledge-base about the uptake of innovative IT was developed as a marketable product. This was not a success, but it is useful to analyse the socio-technical reasons why, using the knowledge embedded in the unsuccessful system. It led on to work in 'case-based reasoning' applications which enabled a systematic approach to be developed for indexing hypertext knowledge-bases(17).

The 'innovation uptake' paradigm also turns out to be helpful in understanding why JJ's technically innovative approach to agriculture failed to influence the politics.

I had been very much aware of the techno-economics of renewable energy sources, and had lobbied about the need for renewable energy in the 1970s and 1980s. The socio-economic aspect of the question has been incisively developed by Richard Douthwaite(18) though with a somewhat bleak future outlook.

Notes and References
1. The Orpen 'economic farm unit' concept is outlined in some detail in Chapter 19 of JJ's 1951 book *Irish Agriculture in Transition*.
2. JJ made his position on this issue quite clear in his contribution to the January 1939 debate in the Seanad on the Land Bill (1938). Farm labourers paid according to their worth on a well-managed estate would earn more than a subsistence 30-acre farmer.
3. JJ first recorded his support for co-operative mechanisation as early as his *1916 Albert Kahn Report* on food production in France during the war.
4. The 1923 *Agricultural Commission Report* was unfairly dismissed by the populist 'land for the people' lobby as a 'ranchers' charter', with the result that its progressive aspects did not have the impact they deserved.
5. JJ's contribution to the work of the Commission included a call for the education of co-op managers, who would have been crucial to the achievement of JJ's vision.
6. JJ's objective in his work on the 1926 Prices Commission was to draw attention to the role of friction in the distribution system, which gave rise to a big gap between farmers' and consumers' prices. He had studied this in the course of his Rockefeller Fellowship, from which he abstracted the French experience for his addendum to the *Prices Report*. He also called for a National Economic Council with a co-ordinating role.
7. In his *Plea for Winter Dairying* (JSSISI XV, 33, 1930-31) which was read on March 19 1931, JJ tried to develop arguments in favour of de-seasonalising milk production around the need for effective marketing of butter.
8. This proposal in the Seanad, which was debated on December 13 1939, was greeted with active hostility; it was suggested that the people concerned were ex-servicemen from the British Army who were being used to being told what to do.
9. This Post-Emergency Agriculture Report is accessed primarily from the Seanad and public service thread of the hypertext; it makes sense however to access it here in the socio-technical context.
10. In 1959 JJ regaled the SSISI, anecdotally, with this experience, in the context of a symposium on the Whitaker economic plan.

11. I expand on this in the <u>1940s science and society</u> module, this theme being overviewed in <u>Appendix 11</u>.

12. I have expanded on the work of the Ecole Polytechnique team in the <u>1950s academic</u> module, where I have located it, since its output was scientific papers, though the scale of the operation was industrial.

13. I outlined the work of the CSTI in the context of a series of <u>articles</u> I did for the *Irish Times*, which contributed to the *OECD Report* discussions, and the formation of public opinion in favour the Government organising to fund science, setting up the National Science Council.

14. This work is best followed in the techno-economic thread, overviewed below in <u>Appendix 13</u>.

15. The <u>1970s socio-technical</u> module gives an overview entry-point to the *Irish Times* series; the key socio-technical chapters are <u>1.2</u> Structures and Institutions, <u>3.3</u> Innovations and <u>5.2</u> Scientific and Technical Information. It goes on to outline the TCD genetic and marine work.

16. I have overviewed these projects in the <u>1980s socio-technical</u> module. In chronological order they were titled: 1981-1983: *The IPIB Technology Group* (this was marginal-time voluntary work); April and November 1985: *Local Enterprise and the RTCs* (Youth Employment Agency); October 1986: *RTD Linkages between LFRs* (National Board for Science and Technology); March 1988: *The Mentec Customer Analysis System.* They gave rise to various 'grey area' reports, some of which may be accessibly archived.

17. The experience gained here is at the root of the technology of the present hypertext publication. I outline it in a <u>case-based reasoning</u> essay associated with this theme. Related publications include Bergmann et al, *Developing Industrial Case-based Reasoning Applications* (Springer 1999). See also the <u>IT-USE project</u> funded by the EU Commission.

18. I have reproduced, with permission, in the supportive hypertext Richard Douthwaite's <u>essay</u> *When Should We Have Stopped?* published in the weekend supplement of the *Irish Times* of December 29 2001, and added some comments suggesting feasible policy changes. This builds on earlier work I had done, as noted in the <u>1970s techno-economic</u> module, which continued in the <u>1980s</u> with the Nairobi UN renewable energy conference, the momentum of which declined but revived again in the <u>1990s.</u>

Appendix 13: Techno-Economic Analysis

JJ's work on winter milk, as published in 1932, was a techno-economic critique of the whole underlying basis of Irish agriculture, which by insisting on allowing milk production to 'follow the grass' has condemned Irish farmers to bulk commodity production and acted as a barrier to value-added(1).

There is also a techno-economic aspect in JJ's concept of combining market gardening with cattle production. The modern 'organic farmers and growers' movement, of which JJ should be regarded as a pioneer, is beginning to take this up(2).

I can identify some pilot techno-economic analysis with which I was associated in the 1950s, when I was in my 'basic science research' phase in the DIAS, and when JJ had retired from the TCD political front-line to develop his market-gardening enterprise at Vicarstown in Laois. For JJ the key concept was the linking of small-scale livestock production with market gardening. JJ brought in the present writer via the analysis of the anaerobic digestion process for farm-yard manure, generating methane, and making the manure more easily handled in a market gardening context. I looked into this, with the aid of Padraig Ó Hailpin, a consulting engineer. I published a couple of articles in the *Irish Times*, in or around 1958, and there was some correspondence, but we concluded that on the scale JJ had in mind it was not feasible. The process has however been widely used in China and is beginning to be useful in Africa(3).

In the 1960s there was a sequence of episodes which illustrated the present writer's transition from being a 'pure scientist', through being an 'industrial applied-scientist', towards techno-economic analysis, in which mode he tended to operate during the 1970s.

Some of the most innovative techno-economic work was done with Aer Lingus in the 60s, where we predicted the performance of the IBM real-time reservations system, in the necessarily stochastic commercial environment, and explained why with American Airlines it had saturated at about a third of its planned capacity. This was, to the best of my knowledge, the first time a queue-theoretic approach was used for analysing the performance of a real-time system in a stochastic environment. This has since become the norm(4).

When with Professor FG Foster's Statistics and Operations Research MSc programme in TCD in the early 1970s I did an updated re-run of my father's 1932 winter milk analysis, in the form of a computer-based model for Bord Bainne. There were a number of other agricultural-oriented computer-modelling exercises done in the 1970s, on milk collection logistics, flax production etc(5).

The present writer's pioneering interest in techno-economic analysis declined in the 1980s and 1990s, as with the development of easy access to computing it became routine. The emphasis moved over to the socio-technical and political domains, and to issues related to science and society. Some of the socio-technical issues had a strong techno-economic dimension, especially those arising as a result of the energy crisis. I participated in the 1982 UN conference on renewable energy in Nairobi, and had a hand in trying to develop some follow-through. I had occasion to look into the Crumlin lignite deposits and how they might be utilised. I campaigned for the setting up of a focused national renewable energy centre, though unsuccessfully; the effort remains sporadic and scattered(6).

In the 1990s I found myself again interested in techno-economic analysis, though in marginal time, and on campaigning issues like public transport in Dublin. I submitted a paper to the Irish Planning Institute in which I made the case for a mesh route-map as an alternative preferable to the current centralist system, given the way Dublin has developed, with the emergence of a distributed set of distinct 'urban villages'(7).

Notes and References

1. See '<u>A Plea for Winter Dairying</u>' (JSSISI XV, 33, 1930-31)

2. See JJ's 1942 'Capitalisation of Irish Agriculture' (JSSISI xvi, 44, 1941-2) and his 1947 'An Economic Basis for Irish Rural Civilisation' (JSSISI xviii, 1, 1947-8), as outlined in the <u>1940s SSISI</u> module. The foregoing papers were later developed into an <u>important chapter</u> in JJ's subsequent book <u>*Irish Agriculture in Transition*</u>, published in 1951 (Blackwell, Oxford, and Hodges Figgis, Dublin). In this developed form it represents the most coherent version of JJ's vision for how he felt Irish agriculture should develop.

3. See the <u>1950s techno-economic</u> module in the hypertext. JJ reported on it anecdotally in the 1959 <u>SSISI</u> symposium on the Whitaker White Paper.

4. See the <u>1960s techno-economic</u> module of the hypertext, where these are outlined in some detail. The micro-economic analysis philosophy which emerged from this period forms the basis of a <u>short paper</u> published in the Aug-Sept 1970 issue of *Léargas*, the journal of the Institute of Public Administration.

5. See the <u>1970s techno-economic</u> module. The agricultural-oriented computer-modelling exercises are mostly on record in Julian Mac Airt's book on <u>*OR in Ireland*</u> (Mercier Press, Cork, 1988). See also my *Technology Ireland* January 1978 paper '<u>Technology and the Economy as Interacting Systems</u>' which constitutes an outline of the essentials of the techno-economic modelling philosophy which had evolved over the previous 15 years or so, interfacing with the socio-political domains.

6. I have expanded on these topics in the <u>1980s techno-economic</u> module of the hypertext.

7. See the <u>1990s techno-economic</u> module of the hypertext; also the 1991 Irish Planning Institute paper '<u>A Future for Dublin?</u>', which was submitted as an 'essay' and won a prize, but was never published.

Source Listing and Bibliography for JJ

I am indebted to my sister Dr Maureen Carmody for some marginal comments, most of which I have added in italics. RJ August 2001.

It is possible to classify JJ sources into
- (a) JJ's published works: books, papers, articles, pamphlets
- (b) Books possessed by JJ which relate to his publications and political evolution
- (c) Public records of his work eg government reports in which he participated, and his Seanad speeches
- (d) Minutes and other records of various bodies in which he participated
- (e) Public record office, national library and other such sources
- (f) Those papers left by him which have come into my possession and which I have attempted to catalogue.
- (g) Miscellaneous other institutional sources
- (h) Books relating to the background of JJ's work.

I hope to be able to deposit some or all of this material accessibly, perhaps in the Linenhall Library.

(a) Joe Johnston's Published Works
*Here I hope to list by title all his publications chronologically; they are stored in **Box 3**, unless otherwise stated. There is also a **Box X** which has unsorted background papers relating to his academic work, as well as some legal files relating to sales and purchases of houses.*

In this context the * is used as a marker for a title, where many are one-liners which would overflow if indented.

Books
* JJ's 1913 polemical book *Civil War in Ulster* (originally Sealy, Bryant and Walker, Dublin 1913; it has been re-published by UCD Press in 1999 with introduction by the present writer, and preface by Tom Garvin).
* *Report to the Trustees of the Albert Kahn Travelling Fellowships*, November 1914 - September 1916; August - October 1916. *(I count this as a 'published book' because some hundreds of copies were printed and circulated to university libraries. RJ Oct 2000)*
* *A Groundwork of Economics*, Educational Co of Ireland, Dublin, 1925. (Copy annotated by JJ, with dates suggesting when points in it were referenced.)
* *The Nemesis of Economic Nationalism*, PS King & Son, London, 1934.
* *Irish Agriculture in Transition*, Hodges Figgis, Dublin and Blackwell, London, 1951.
* *Why Ireland Needs the Common Market*, Mercier, Cork, 1962.
* *Bishop Berkeley's Querist in Historical Perspective*, Dundealgan Press, Dundalk, 1970.

Pamphlets etc
* *Food Supply in France* (1916; Albert Kahn Fellowship supplementary report).
* *The Trinity Co-op 1913-1921 and after*; foreword by AE; reprint of *Better Business* article, based on a paper read at the co-op AGM on March 1, 1921.
* *The Importance of Economy in the Distribution of Goods*, Irish Co-operative Conference Association, August 1933.
* 'Agriculture in our National Economy', introducing an *Irish Independent* series published as a pamphlet, undated, but probably circa 1946, under the general heading 'Post-war

Planning in Irish Agriculture. Other authors were Bro Jarlath Edwards, JN Greene, William J Hans, James Hughes TD, Dr Henry Kennedy, CJ Kerin, Mrs JP Nagle, PF Quinlan and Thomas Wade. There was also a critical analysis by Capt ER Orpen which includes the phrase '...judging from the recent Hot Springs Food Conference ...' which can help to date it.

* *The Sickness of the Irish Economy*, Irish Association, Parkside Press, 1957.
* *Irish Economic Headaches - A Diagnosis*, Aisti Eireannacha, Dublin. 1966.

Papers in Refereed Journals etc

* *Some Causes and Consequences of Distributive Waste*, (**JSSISI** vol XIV p353, 1926-7; this was read on 10 March 1927. It was a spin-off from his work on the Prices Tribunal.
* *National Transport Problems*, **JSSISI** XIV, 53, 1929-30.
* *A Plea for Winter Dairying*, *JSSISI* XV, 33, 1930-31.
* *Chronological Note on the Expedition of Leotychidas to Thessaly*, **Hermathena** XXI, 1931. This was with the momentum of his earlier classical scholarship; later classical papers show a trend into economics.
*An International Managed Currency in the 5th Century BC, **Hermathena** XXII, 1932; I have included the 11/04/33 Keynes letter with this, as it is related.
* *The World Crisis - Its Non-Monetary Background*, lecture delivered to the *Institute of Bankers*, Dublin, November 17 1932.
* *The Purchasing Power of Irish Free State Farmers in 1933*, in **The Economic Journal**, ed JM Keynes, September 1934.
* *Solon's Reform of Weights and Measures*, **Journal of Hellenic Studies**, Vol LIV, p180, 1934.
* *Aspects of the Agricultural Crisis at Home and Abroad*, **JSSISI** XV, 79, 1934-5.
* *Agriculture and the Sickness of the Free Economy*, **Studies** XXIV, no 94, June 1935.
* *Price Ratios in Recent Irish Agricultural Experience*, **The Economic Journal,** ed Keynes & Robinson, December 1934.
* I reference his unpublished 1937 wheat paper here in the academic stream.
* *The Monetary Theories of Berkeley*, **Economic History** (a supplement to the **Economic Journal**, ed JM Keynes and EAG Robinson), February 1938. (I have included the Keynes letter of 05/04/37 with this. RJ)
* *Irish Currency in the 18th Century*, **Hermathena** LII, November 1938.
* *Commercial Restrictions and Monetary Deflation in 18th Century Ireland*, **Hermathena** LIII, May 1939.
* *An Outlook on Irish Agriculture*, **Studies** XXVIII no 111, June 1939.
Reviews: *Irish Life in the 17the Century, by E McLysaght, and Economic History of Cork City, by W O'Sullivan*, **Economic History,** February 1940.
Berkeley and the Abortive Bank Project of 1720-21, **Hermathena** LIV, November 1939.
* *A Synopsis of Berkeley's Monetary Philosophy*, **Hermasthena** LV, May 1940.
Irish Agriculture Then and Now, **Manchester School** of Economic and Social Studies, October 1940.
* *Locke, Berkeley and Hume as Monetary Theorists*, **Hermathena** LVI, November 1940.
* *The Capitalisation of Irish Agriculture*, **JSSISI** XVI, 44, 1941-2. (cf TCD Library)
* *Bishop Berkeley and Kindred monetary Thinkers*, **Hermathena** LIX, May 1942.
* *An Economic Basis for Irish Rural Civilisation*, **JSSISI** xviii, 1, 1947-8
* Review: *Ireland - Its Physical, Historical, Social and Economic Geography*, by TW Freeman; **Hermathena** LXXVI, 1950, p99.
* *Raw Materials for Irish Animal Husbandry*, **JSSISI** XVIII, 392, 1950-51.
* *Economic Leviathans* **JSSISI** XIX pt 1, 42, 1952-3.

* *Berkeley's Influence as an Economist*, in **Hermathena,** *Homage to George Berkeley*, a commemorative issue, LXXXII, November 1953.

* Comments on *Agricultural Developments in Ireland, North and South*, by EA Attwood; **JSSISI** XXI, part V, 1966-67; JJ had supervised Attwood's PhD. He used the occasion to bid farewell to the SSISI, of which he had earlier been President. His comments are on record, p30.

* *Consumer Demand as the Basis of Credit*, 1969; JJ produced this as a 46-page stapled duplicated pre-print, for promotional circulation, with a view to getting it published; he never succeeded. It was rejected by the **JSSISI** under the influence of Roy Geary, as being philosophical and non-quantitative. I have reproduced it in full here.

* *Monetary Manipulation, Berkeleian and Otherwise*, **Hermathena** CX, 1970.

Articles

*From here on we use indentation and the * on occasion implies a categorisation.*

There is an article in the *London Times* ('from a correspondent') on September 8 1916, headed *Ireland Today / Spread of Sinn Fein / Political Cross-Currents*. I have reason to believe that this was by JJ, based on some travelling he did during the TCD summer vacation. *My sister Dr Maureen Carmody questions this, on the basis that he would have had to abandon her as a 3-month baby with our mother. I respond that he would have been quite capable of doing this, as indeed he did a couple of months later when he went to France on his final Albert Kahn Fellowship project, studying wartime agriculture. There must have been a support system, and it almost certainly involved our aunt Florrie, then working in Dublin as a 'typewriter'. RJ August 2001.*

If France Ruled Ireland / A Dream of Change*, by 'Viator'; September (?circa 18+) 1916, *Irish Times*(?); this was a series of three articles, two of which are preserved in a scrap-book which JJ lodged in the TCD Library in 1971.

Manchester Guardian articles, 1917, photocopies; probably by JJ, working in journalistic mode in the aftermath of 1916; they relate to travels which could have been done during the Easter vacation. Box 2.

War Agriculture in France / The Benefits of United Action / A Lesson to British Farmers, from a Correspondent in France, September 29 1916, *The Times*, London.

The *Anglo-Irish Economic Conflict*, in *Nineteenth Century and After,* Vol CXIX, #708, February 1936.

The Plight of Irish Agriculture, in *The Fortnightly* no 854, new series, London, February 1938.

The Prospects of Anglo-Irish Trade; I have this as galley-proof, and it is for the *Banker*; circa 1938 or 39; it refers to the recent trade agreement and the economic war as history.

Economic Development under Public Enterprise, Irish Times, April 16 1947; he referenced this in the Seanad on the same day. This was a report of a paper he had given in Athlone, possibly as Barrington Lecture.

Unfinished Programme, in *Sir Horace Plunkett Centenary Handbook*, National Co-operative Council, 1954.

'The Relevance of a Berkeleyan Theory of Credit to the Problems of Today', *Irish Press,* April 20 1965.

Fun

The Compleat Anglers: A Brazen Monument Immortalising the Tutorial System, by 'Jack Point', Dublin University Press, 1935.

Kottabistae, **Hermathena** LXVII, 1946; this is a set of translations into Latin verse of various poetic excerpts. JJ on p115 renders the Ogden Nash quatrain 'You dress yourself in floppy pants...' etc as follows:

Tegmine braccarum cumulasti membra saluto / Deliciae nostrae, sed tua membra tegis; / Adveniens simulas venerem sed versa retrorsun / Quantula tunc praestas, heu, simulacra deae.

(b) Some Residuals from the Books in JJ's Possession

*This is selective, on the basis that for a book to be included it must relate to one of the threads of this work. It is also incomplete, in that when JJ vacated his College rooms in 1971, much of his collection was scattered. It makes sense to classify it into History, Politics and Economics. It represents perhaps a selection from the books he possessed made by him in 1971 when he vacated finally his TCD rooms. I have retained these mostly in **Box 1**, unless otherwise stated.*

History, Philosophy

The History of Ireland During the Period of Parliamentary Independence, JW Barlow FTCD, Hodges Figgis, Dublin, 1873.

Seághan an Díomais / Shane the Proud, Conán Maol; Irish Book Co, Dublin, 1901; no 6 in the Léighean Éirean series, historical pamphlet published for didactic purposes in Irish and English on facing pages.

The Facts and Principles of Irish Nationality, Browne and Nolan, 1907, by 'Éireannaigh Éigin'; 83 pages, price 6d; this is a scholarly attempt to defend Irish history from Catholic-nationalist revisionism.

The Making of Ireland and her Undoing, by Alice Stopford Green, Macmillan, 1909; also by the same author *The Old Irish World*, Gill & Macmillan, 1912. I have treated ASG and her books at some length because I feel they were probably an important formative influence on JJ during his undergraduate and early postgraduate years.

Labour in Irish History, James Connolly, Maunsel 1910, copy autographed by JJ; Box JJ5.

For Ireland's Sake, or Under the Green Flag; a Romantic Irish Drama, J and JM Muldoon, Ponsonby (Dublin, 1910) Simkin, Marshall, Hamilton & Kent, (London 1910); this is a 'romantic-nationalist' drama, dedicated by the authors to the memory of Emmet, Fitzgerald and Tone. It seems JJ bought this in September 1915, wrote his name, address 30 TCD, and the date in it, there is an annotation in JJ's writing which suggests that he regarded the national aspirations as being 'fulfilled in John Redmond (under?) Asquith'. It has a strong local Dungannon flavour. Somehow it turned up via the Dungannon Royal School archivist Norman Cardell during my contact with him in 2000. It stimulated me to look into the Ulster dimension of the national theatre movement.

Sinn Fein Rebellion Handbook, 1917 issue, compiled by the Weekly *Irish Times*.

History of Trade Unionism 1666-1920, Sidney and Beatrice Webb, Workers Educational Association edition 1919; JJ acquired this on 22/02/46. There are annotations, some of which are in JJ's writing.

Scandinavian Relations with Ireland during the Viking Period, A Walsh, Talbot Press, 1922.

Glimpses of an Irish Felon's Life, Tom Clarke, Maunsel and Roberts, 1922.

Reprints of sermons in pamphlet form by Rev E Savell Hicks, preached at the Unitarian Church, Stephens Green, Dublin; there are seven, four of which are undated; the others are dated 1918, 1923 and 1925. The 1918 one commemorates the restoration of the Wilson Memorial Window, in memory of Thomas Wilson who fought in the American War of Independence, was aide-de-camp to George Washington and who became the first US Consul in Dublin. Other titles are 'Live and Let Live' (1923) and 'the Spirit of Innovations' (1925).

The New Departure in Irish Politics 1878-9 by TW Moody, reprint from *Essays in British and Irish History* ed HA Cronne, London 1949; inscribed by TWM to JJ.

Michael Davitt and the British Labour Movement 1882-1906, TW Moody; reprint from Transactions of the Royal Historical Society, 5th series, Vol 3, 1953; inscribed by TWM, and underlined by JJ, particularly Davitt's statement '...no one can say absolutely what is and what is not the duty of the State...it is for every successive generation... to say.. etc'.

The Seeker, poems by Maurice Wilkins, Dolmen Press, 1960, inscribed 'to JJ from his old friend the author, with every good wish...18th Oct 1960'. *My sister remembers him well as a frequent visitor during her childhood.*

Mrs George Berkeley and her Washing Machine, IC Tipton and EJ Furlong, **Hermathena** CI, Autumn 1965; this insight into the life of Berkeley through some notes left by his wife, at the end of their days in Oxford, contains the first literary reference to the term 'washing machine'.

The Case Against the Common Market; no named author, but probably Anthony Coughlan; Assessment pamphlet 2, the first one being *Labour and the Republican Movement*, by George Gilmore; this was published by the Dublin Wolfe Tone Society in May 1967, as from the then address of the present writer RJ. JJ had read this pamphlet and marked selected paragraphs. *My sister chaired the Nenagh anti-EEC campaign; it was her introduction to politics. She subsequently became a Labour Party activist and served on the Administrative Council, and on the Midwestern Health Board.*

The Irishness of the Irish, Estyn Evans; reprint of paper to the Irish Association, Armagh, September 22 1967.

Politics, pamphleteering

Diary of a Cabinet Minister, Olley and Co, Belfast, 1892 and 1893. This was a Unionist production which made fun of the idea of an Irish Cabinet under Home Rule.

How Ireland is Treated by her "Friends", William Pentland, Dublin 1898; this is a pamphlet highly critical of the Land League, by an author associated with the Tenants Right Movement in Westmeath.

'Lest We Forget', or questions and comments touching the evolution of the Home Rule or Fenian Conspiracy, by 'a Philosophic Radical'; Hodges Figgis, Dublin, no date given, but perhaps related to the 1906 election. There is an undated review of the booklet from a Belfast paper which on the reverse side has a reference to Wednesday September 9(?) and Friday August 28. There is a news item about a 'hunger march' at Lydd in Kent.

Religious Intolerance Under Home Rule ed Jeremiah MacVeagh MP; Irish Press Agency, 1911; this consisted of letters from over 100 prominent Protestants in favour of Home Rule, and discounting the 'Rome Rule' bogey as promoted by the Orangemen. This was a source-book for 'Civil War in Ulster'

Dublin Castle and the Irish People, R Barry O'Brien, Kegan Paul, Trench, Trubner & co, London 1912; this is inscribed AE Johnston, the Cottage, Stillorgan, which dates it acquisition to the early 1920s; my Aunt Annie probably got it to give her some background understanding of the Civil Service which she by then had joined. *My sister agrees with this.*

A Protestant Protest Ballymoney, October 24 1913, price one penny; this reprint of the proceedings of the famous Liberal Home Rule rally contains the records of speeches in the Ballymoney Town Hall. The Foreword is signed 'W'. The printed contributions are from Captain JR White DSO, Mrs JR Green, Sir Roger Casement, Mr Alex Wilson JP, Mr John Dinsmore (jr) and Mr William MacAfee BL. I have written about this in my Introduction to the 1999 re-edition of JJ's *Civil War in Ulster*

The Great Fraud of Ulster, TM Healy MP, Gill, Dublin, 1917.

* *Thoughts for a Convention: Memorandum on the State of Ireland*, by AE, Maunsel, 1917.

How to Settle the Irish Question, Bernard Shaw, Talbot Press, Dublin and Constable, London, December 1917.

Ourselves Alone in Ulster, Alice Stopford Green, Maunsel, Dublin, 1918.

Thomas Davis: The Thinker and the Teacher, collection with preface by Arthur Griffith, and essays by Gavan Duffy, John Blake Dillon, John Mitchel and others. Gill, Dublin 1918.

A Plea for Justice, AE, being a demand for a public enquiry into the attaches on co-operative societies in Ireland; Irish Homestead pamphlet, 1921.

The Inner and the Outer Ireland, by AE, Talbot Press, Dublin, 1921.

Ireland and the Empire at the Court of Conscience, AE, Talbot Press, Dublin, 1921.

Ulster in 1921, by 'the author of 'Tales of the RIC', Blackwood, Edinburgh and London; reprinted from Blackwood's Magazine, October 1922.

* *The Case for the Treaty*, Alfred O'Rahilly, Professor of the NUI, no date and no publisher's imprint.

The Truth about the Treaty, Robert Barton, National Series no 2, reprint from *The Republic of Ireland*, no date given, but probably 1922.

Free State Promises: Are They True?, unsigned, National Series no 4; this and the previous pamphlet presumably are examples of Erskine Childers' output at the time of the Treaty debates.

Arguments for the Treaty, Arthur Griffith, Martin Hester, Dublin, 1922(?); there is a similar one by Michael Collins.

Bulletin de la Societé Autour du Monde 1924, 1925, 1926, 1927, 1928, 1929; also Juin 1931 which includes the 1930 issue. JJ had a short outline of the current Irish situation in the 1926 issue. The delay in publication of the 1930 issue would have been due to financial constraints brought on by the 1929 financial crash. There were no subsequent issues in JJ's possession.

A Tour in Ireland, Arthur Young (1780), ed Constantia Maxwell, Cambridge UP 1925; acquired by JJ 1/06/28.

Towards a Better Ireland; report of a Conference on Applied Christianity held in Dublin, January 1926; speakers included RM Henry and Lionel Smith-Gordon. *(This seems to have been an attempt by the Home Rule-supporting Liberal Protestant community to develop a constructive critical voice in 'civil society' mode. RM Henry helped to lobby Asquith after the Ballymoney rally, and Smith-Gordon we have met as a Socialist in Oxford, and later at the 1924 Commonwealth Co-operative conference organised by the Plunkett Foundation. RJ Oct 2000.)*

The Political Future of India, James Johnston, PS King, London, 1933. This book by JJ's eldest brother gives useful insights into the British imperial system.

Can the Hindus Rule India?, James Johnston, PS King, London, 1935. James wrote this in his retirement; he compared the current proposals to pre-Reform England.

Hindu Domination in India, James Johnston, PS King, London, 1936; this is a sequel to the 1935 book. This sequel carries an advertisement by the publisher for JJ's 1934 'Nemesis of Economic Nationalism'.

The analysis of James Johnston's experience in the Indian Civil Service is outside the scope of this work, but it is evident that he was very critical of the Hindu culture, particularly regarding the treatment of the 'untouchables'. My sister regards his work as important and under-appreciated.

The Price of Irish Neutrality, by Henry Harrison OBE MC, Commonwealth Association, London, 1943; 'an invocation of historical truth in reply to Henry Steele Commager, Professor of History at Columbia University, New York'.

Czechoslovak Policy for Victory and Peace, Dr Edvard Benes, Czechoslovak Ministry of Foreign Affairs, London 1944.

Ireland's Economy; Radio Eireann talks on Ireland's part in the Marshall Plan; March and April 1949, three talks by Seán MacBride, with responses by JE Carrigan and WH Taft on behalf of the ECA Mission to Ireland.

PR in Ireland, Proinsias Mac Aonghusa; a reprint of six articles published in the *Irish Times*; undated; must have been 1959, when de Valera became President and the people rejected the constitutional amendment abolishing PR which was linked to his election.

I Accuse: A Monstrous Fraud which Deceived Two Continents, Herbert Ó Mackey; no date, no publisher's imprint, printed by Cahill; a copy signed by the author; it is a polemic exposing the Casement forgeries.

The Royal School Dungannon 1614 - 1964; commemorative booklet, with letter from James Kincade the Headmaster, thanking JJ for his donation to the building fund.

Burntollet; Bowes Egan and Vincent McCormack; LRS Publishers 1969; an illustrated blow-by-blow account of the ambush of the January 1969 Civil Rights march from Belfast to Derry.

New Ulster Movement - Interim Report to members, NUM, Belfast, April 1972

Economics, Co-operative Movement

* Publications marked thus were in a package with covering letter, dated 3 November 1971, from Malachi Prunty of the IAOS education section: '...we have most of them here and those we haven't got are not considered of great historical significance.'

Lombard Street, Walter Bagehot, ed E Johnston, 1904; no indication when purchased, but extensively marked; this would have been JJ's introduction to the understanding of the nature of money.

* *Plain Talks to Irish Farmers*, Sir Horace Plunkett, Eason, Dublin, 1910.

* *The Building Up of a Rural Civilisation*, George W Russell, Sealy Bryers and Walker, Dublin, 1910. (This is a reprint of AE's address to the IAOS on 10 December 1909.)

* *The Organisation of Co-operation for Credit...on Raiffeisen Principles*, German Co-operative Union, produced for the American Commission of Agricultural Inquiry, 1913.

* *The Rural Community: an Address to the American Commission of Agricultural Inquiry*, by George W Russell, at Plunkett House, Dublin, July 15 1913.

* *Inaugural Address by the President of the Co-operative Union*, Robert Fleming, at the Dublin Conference, 1 June 1914; Co-operative Union, Manchester, 1914.

Wealth of Nations, Adam Smith, 1905 edition, with introduction by Dugald Stuart; JJ put his name and address in it, 25 Fitzwilliam Square, and 38 TCD; this dates the purchase to sometime around 1915-16. It is extensively marked and annotated.

* *Templecrone: a Record of Co-operative Effort*, by AE, IAOS Leaflets no 22, new series, 1 December 1916.

Principles of Economic Geography, RN Rudmose Brown, Pitman, London, 1920. JJ wrote his name on this on 16/10/21, he then had rooms in 9 TCD; it is much marked.

* *Education Department programme of the Belfast Co-operative Society*, session 1920-21.

Rural Reconstruction, Henry W Wolff, Selwyn & Blount, New York, 1921; copy signed by JJ and dated 10/01/22, at 9 TCD; much underlined.

The Shannon Scheme, Thomas A MacLaughlin, Sackville Press, undated, probably 1924.

The Electrification of the Irish Free State; report of the experts appointed by the Government, Borgquist et al, 1925. The name of EH Alton was on this; he was the TCD representative in the Dáil at the time, and he must have passed it to JJ for comment.

The Dilemma of Thrift, WT Foster & W Catchings, Pollak Foundation, Newton, Massachusetts, 1926.

The Golden <u>Crucifixion</u> of John Bull, WH Wakinshaw & HJD Thompson, Economic Freedom League, Newcastle on Tyne, no date given, but there is in it a letter from the author dated 5/07/27, to which JJ replied.

Report of the Committee on Finance and Industry, HMSO 1931; this is the MacMillan Commission set up by the Treasury in November 1929. It is extensively marked and annotated by JJ.

The Querist, ed JM Hone, Talbot Press, Dublin, undated, but circa 1930 from internal evidence. Heavily annotated by JJ.

The Collapse of the Monetary System, Johan Jacobsen, published by the author, Copenhagen, March 1932.

Monetary Policy and the Depression, George O'Brien, **JSSISI** 5 October 1933, reprint.

To Tell you the Truth, WT Foster, Pollak Foundation, Newton, Massachusetts, 1933. This is a polemic aimed at the consumer alerting him to the high cost of hire-purchase credit.

Bishop Berkeley: the Querist, Ellen Douglass Leyburn, Proc RIAS, XLIV, Section C, No 3; read June 28 1937, published December 15 1937; this was in the context of a Yale PhD.

The State and Economic Life, Anwar Iqbal Qureshi, New Book Co, Bombay, 1938. The author had been a lecturer and research assistant in economics in TCD, and had become Head of the Economics Department, Osmania University, Hyderabad Deccan. "Being a Study of the Methods of State intervention in Economic Life in the Leading Countries of the world, with special reference to the Problems facing India". JJ had marked many passages. *My sister remembers him as a frequent visitor during her childhood.*

The Economics of War, GA Duncan, **Hermathena** XXVIII, 1939; compliments of author, much underlined. *Duncan, though junior to JJ, leapfrogged JJ to get the Chair of Economics in TCD, JJ being relatively less qualified, due to his classical background. They remained on good terms. JJ eventually had an Applied Economics Chair created for him.*

Food, Health and Income, John Boyd Orr, Macmillan, London, 1936 Papers by Henry Kennedy: *The Future of Agriculture in Ireland*, reprint from the *Irish Monthly*, October 1938; this was a Social Order Summer School contribution, and was marked in detail by JJ, and referenced directly or by implication in his <u>Seanad speeches</u>; the key message as to 'use the plough to grow better grass' and in support of systematic winter feeding of livestock. There is a compliments slip from the Secretary of the IAOS. Another one, *Agriculture and the Banking Commission* is a reprint from *Studies* December 1938, and is also heavily marked; the key message is the deterioration of agricultural practice in the context of the Economic War'. This was also Seanad material for JJ.

Can Britain Feed Herself on Home-produced Foods?, HH Jones; Vegetarian Society, Manchester, undated, but probably 1941. Unmarked, but contains typescript notes by JJ folded in, perhaps towards a review, the thrust of which it the mobilisation of the consumer co-operative movement in support of the Boyd Orr thesis.

A Select Bibliography of Economic Writings by Members of Trinity College, Dublin, RD Collison Black, **Hermathena** LXVI, 1945; with author's compliments.

National Investment, Louden Ryan, reprint from **Studies**, Winter 1945.

Report on Rural Electrification, Stationary Office, P6530, undated, but must have been 1945; this Report was produced for Seán Lemass (Industry and Commerce) and JJ welcomed it in the Seanad on March 7 1945.

The Irish Meat and Livestock Industry, Thomas Shaw; reprint from **Studies** September 1946. There are comments by JJ, TA Smiddy, J Hughes and EJ Sheehy in the same issue. JJ also used this in his Seanad arguments.

Farming in Irish Life, TW Freeman, reprint from the **Geographical Journal**, July-Sept 1947; this was a complimentary copy given to JJ by the author, and is marked.

Economic Studies at Trinity College Dublin, pt 1, RD Collison Black, **Hermathena** LXX, 1947; author's compliments. *Centenary 1847-1947 Proceedings*, SSISI, October 6-9 1947.

The Sterling Area, Paul Bareau, **British Commonwealth Affairs** no 3, Longmans, London, 1948. Heavily underlined by JJ.

Industrial Development in Ireland: a Statistical Review, RC Geary, **Manchester Statistical Society**, March 9 1949; extensively marked by JJ.

Ireland's External Assets, TK Whittaker, **JSSISI** 29 April 1949, reprint.

Britain's New Monetary Policy, WTC King, reprinted from **The Banker**, December 1951 and January 1952. Underlined by JJ.

Agricultural Co-operation in Ireland CC Ridall, JT Drought & Co, Dublin 1950; this booklet is an outline of the history of the IAOS, in the form of a reprint of articles in Agricultural Ireland by the Assistant Secretary of the IAOS, published in the period 1945-47. Although 'Charlie Riddell' receives honourable mention in Patrick Bolger's 1971 history, the latter does not reference this book. JJ however seems to have used it, as it is marked.

* *Co-operative Year Book 1956*, National Co-operative Council.

Planning for Economic Development, Patrick Lynch & CF Carter, Tuairim pamphlet 5, September 1959.

An Appraisement of Agricultural Co-operation in Ireland, P7467, Stationary Office (the Knapp Report) 1963.

Lauredale, Malthus and Keynes, Paul Lambert, reprint from *Annals of Public and Co-operative Economy*, 1966, no 1.

Irish Agricultural Production - Its Volume and Structure, Raymond Crotty, Cork University Press 1966; JJ got to review this in the *Irish Times*.

Free Trade with Britain, Garrett Fitzgerald, Business and Finance, undated, probably circa 1969, price one shilling.

Irish Journal of Agricultural Economics Vol 3 no 1, 1970; this has a paper by BC Hickey on *Economies of Size in Irish Farming* which contains a graph on p55 showing the rapidly declining cost per unit of output as a function of size. JJ must have kept this as a vindication of what he had been saying all along, though he was not referenced.

Lincoln College Record, 1970-71; this newsletter for Oxford alumni contains a review of JJ's Berkeley *Querist*.

(There were also selected for retention by JJ in 1971 several Government reports dating from the period of British rule: the 1836 Fisheries report, the 1894 Matheson Report on Surnames in Ireland, the Ordnance Survey Index (undated), the Vice regal Committees of Enquiry into Primary Education 1913 and 1918, the Educational Endowments (Ireland) Act 1885, the 1910 Railways Commission Report, the 1906 Poor Law Reform Commission,

Office of Public Works Reports 1879-80, 1906-07, 1907-09, 1914, 1916; Criminal Statistics 1900, Census 1901 (Antrim); also the Government of Ireland Act 1920. There is also a GSWR timetable of 1850 for the Dublin to Cork service; the express mail left Dublin at 10 am and arrived in Cork at 5 pm. He had also kept a copy of the 1925 Gaeltacht Commission, with associated maps. I have retained these in Box 4)

Records of JJ's Public Service

Box 2, unless otherwise indicated.

Handbook of the Ulster Question, ed Kevin O'Shiel, Stationary Office, 1923; this was the Report of the Boundary Commission, to which JJ contributed. *My sister remembers KO'S as a frequent visitor during her childhood.*
Reports of the <u>Commission on Agriculture</u>, Stationary Office, 1923-24. (TCD Library)
Report of the <u>Tribunal on Prices</u>, Stationery Office, 1926. (TCD Library)
Report of the Commission of Inquiry into the <u>Civil Service, 1932-1935</u>, Stationary Office, 1935. (TCD Library)
Reports of Committee of Inquiry on <u>Post-Emergency Agricultural Policy</u>, Stationary Office, Dublin, 1943-45.
Records of JJ's <u>Seanad speeches</u> I have photocopied and filed by year between 1938 and 1954.

(d) NGO Records

This includes notes abstracted from minutes and records of organisations with which JJ was connected, primarily the SSISI and Barrington material.
It also includes the Oldham / Collison Black / Salim Rachid material. It is in Box 2 along with the public service record.
I have also included in **Box 2** *some material which overflowed from the Albert Kahn folders: there is an album of photos, and some notes taken by JJ, mostly in India, background Brahmin material etc.*

(e) Public Record Office, National Library etc

In search of additional JJ sources I visited the National Library MS room on April 8 1999 and have made the following preliminary identification of items perhaps worth a look. This remains an aspirational agenda RJ April 2003

1912: 7448-9 cuttings relating to home rule activities.
1913: 9469 cuttings photos and letters relating to the Ulster Volunteers (Childers?); 10,453 Alice Stopford Green papers.
1916: 13,158-175 Bulmer Hobson papers; (p844) Redmond papers incl Irish Convention 1917.
1917: (p845) 8786 Barton papers.
1920-29: (p851)AS Green 160 letters to her 10,457.
1920: (p855) Capt George Berkeley and the Peace with Ireland Council MSS 7879-81; Irish Dominion League 10,920-1, 10,924-8; (p856) 11,426 recollection of Miss Stopford sec of PwIC; Monteagle papers 13,415 Irish Peace Conference 1920, 13.417 Dominion League.
TCD Library MS box under G Dermod O'Brien Irish Conference Committee and Irish Dominion League.

(p857)Sinn Fein minute book 1918-22 (Thomas Davis Society reference?)

1931: (p868) 13,478-526 TP Gill Sec Dept of Ag 1900-23 incl 500 letters from Horace Plunkett.

1940-49 (p870) Henry Harrison papers; anti-partition activities.

(f) JJ's papers

I have roughly classified and indexed these as follows, and sometimes referenced them to the hypertext narrative modules where there seems to be a good contact-point. The numbering referred to pockets in a current hanging file system in a steel cabinet; this for archiving has been transferred to numbered boxes, keeping the same numbering system as below for the files within boxes. **Boxes JJ4.x** *(decimalised)*

Relating to JJ's Academic Career

1. Albert Kahn background: includes deed of foundation, and stuff from the UCL archive relating to the early Fellowships; also the lists of the 1913 members of the Autour du Monde club, and the earlier reports of Takebe (1914), Dickenson (1913) and Back (1911-12).

2. AK travel notes, photos, including postcards collected in India and China; includes also some 1926 Rockefeller material. Also note dated August 15 1914 from the Foreign Office, arising from JJ's aborted start on his world tour via France.

3. AK Report by JJ.

4. AK correspondence (JJ), primarily Garnier, also Marquis MacSweeney *(known to my sister as a childhood visitor).* The August 1921 Lichtenberger comment on the Treaty talks, in the newspaper *La Victoire.* Review by Moody of Garnier's 1939 book.

5. AK contemporary material (RJ): includes current background AK material, extracts of mentions of JJ in the Bulletin, UCL material and current correspondence. Thee is also a file labelled 'AK 2002' which contains some material salvaged from the recovered 'Moscow' archive (as looted by the Nazis and recovered in 2001 from Moscow) and related correspondence.

6. AK report supplement: Food Production in France, with AE review.

8. Groundwork of Economics: reviews and photocopy,

9. Early TCD administrative stuff; dealings with pupils in the 20s.

10. Land Bank exam papers, 1924, 1925; Institute of Bankers 1932.

11. TCD oddments, circa 1910 and earlier.

12. Some files containing correspondence relating to the pre-history of the JJ biographical project.

(spare space)

18. Misc TCD notes and correspondence, 30s and 40s; includes his salary memorandum in draft; also extracts from McDowell's History of TCD relating to JJ's background.

19. Misc TCD correspondence, mostly 50s, containing some quite acrimonious material relating to the McConnell 'coup'. We may get around to analysing this in the context of what appears on the Board minutes.

20. Misc TCD correspondence, mostly 60s.

(spare space)

26. Misc correspondence re 'Consumer Demand as the Basis of Credit', mostly hostile or critical.

27. Early attempts to find a publisher for the *Querist* (1960s).

28. Later dealings with publishers, in the continuing attempt to find one for the *Querist* Receipt from National Library for copy of 1737 National Bank Queries.

29. Correspondence and feedback relating to the final publication of the *Querist* by Dundalgan; efforts to get it reviewed and sold were made, but without much success. In the end it was remaindered. Duncan took a dim view of the 'consumer demand and credit' aspect.

30. Misc CV-type material; obituaries; Academy citation 1943.

Relating to outreach, pamphleteering etc

31. Primarily relating to *Civil War in Ulster*, 1913 edition and 1999 edition, with RJ's background notes. I have added in a May 1914 issue of the Irish Volunteer, and an undated cutting relating to the 'Listowel emeute (terrorist tactics that failed)'. I have included here also the galley of his January 1916 published appeal to the Nationalists to support a fair national service conscription system, with a view to restoring the all-Ireland basis of Home Rule.

32. Irish Convention letters: <u>Childers</u>, Mahaffey; 1916 issue of *TCD*. Monteagle, Plunkett and the Dominion League.

33. 1920s material: correspondence with Blythe and Edgeworth; 1926 <u>Seanad election</u> material; letter from Cosgrave acknowledging subscription to the Party.

34. 1920s correspondence relating to Barrington Lectures, Busteed in Cork, Duncan in North Carolina, the Rockefeller Fellowship, the Fishermen's Association and the Dublin Labour movement, farmer to consumer.

35. <u>Political letters</u> relating to the War of Independence and Civil War period; Boundary Commission, Childers, Collins, Kevin O'Higgins, Dermot MacManus (to whom I think the Pierrepoint file can be attributed). *My sister remembers particularly Kevin O'Higgins and Erskine Childers.*

(space)

37. Feedback relating to the *Nemesis of Economic Nationalism*.

38. Lemass letter of 1932; the Fine Gael leadership meeting of 1934; a Spring Rice poem from PC Duggan; a letter from one J Warren, a Unionist, undated, but probably reacting to his Seanad maiden speech in 1938.

39. Paper written in 1937 and never published: *The Place of Wheat in Irish Agriculture*; JJ used the arguments of this repeatedly in the Seanad. It was clearly intended as an academic paper, so I reference it in that thread, and make it available in full.

40. Miscellaneous press cuttings relating to the economic war environment, 1933-37; raw material for JJ's then writings. There are also US-originating cuttings, relating to Roosevelt and the New Deal, and editorial comment on JJ's ideas.

41. JJ and Judge Wylie in 1941 on national emergency political economy; there is also an *Irish Times* poster for December 6 (1944?) which perhaps relates to an altercation between JJ and Aiken. A further cutting relates to the flag-burning incident in 1945. I have treated these in the <u>1940s political</u> module. I also include here a <u>letter</u> to the *Irish Times* dated June 1 1950, in response to one from the US Ambassador, relating to Irish neutrality during the war, and the question of US bases.

42. Correspondence with <u>Dermot MacManus</u> in 1965, relating to his Irish Literary Revival paper delivered at Harrogate, and his Killeaden paper on the Raftery background; also TR Henn.

43. JJ's <u>press campaign</u> during the Economic War. Includes US-originating stuff reviewing his book. I have also filed here JJ's 1939 passes for the Lords and the Commons, during his London visit in April of that year.

44. St John Ervine correspondence 1942 re Seanad; feedback re stove to heat glasshouses; George O'Brien re draft of ..*Transition;* Knocklong co-op 1948. There is also a letter dated 27 May 1941 from 'Meta' (signed also Margaret O'Flaherty) to JJ as Senator, relating to the deportation of Stella Jackson, who has been living (in 'sin') with Ewart Milne in Meta's house, Kilmacavea, Leap, Co Cork. The police raided at 4.30 a.m. Meta gave some Stella Jackson background; she was the author of a pamphlet of the Fabian Society on partition, and 'a person of some account'. Meta suspected that the deportation was on foot of her non-marital status, if so 'a contemptible reason'. She concludes 'tell Annie to come down and see me'. *According to my sister Meta was a friend of our aunt Ann.*

(I can add some background to this letter: Stella Jackson was the daughter of Thomas A Jackson, author of 'Ireland Her Own', the first attempt since Connolly to publish a Marxist history of Ireland. TAJ was a British Communist Party stalwart. The deportation took place before Hitler attacked the USSR, and the Russo-German Pact still nominally held; in this situation the CBGB was anti-war. There may therefore be more to this episode than met the eye at the time. There is a note on the envelope by my sister, as follows: 'Meta (née Barrington) married Professor Carter, left him for Liam O'Flaherty'. JJ had written on the envelope 're Meta O'F'

I had some contact with Stella Jackson in the early 60s when in London via the Connolly Association; it is a pity I was unaware of this episode at the time; I would certainly have explored it further had I known. RJ December 2000.)

45. Irish Association material, 40s and 50s. Includes 40s Bulletins (printed) and some 50s essays, including the printed prize essay by William Ward, and another one relating to the *Isles-Cuthbert Report.* Also the local press reports of the Kilkenny Debates, and the Mary McNeill History of the IA. I have included here also the 1948 Protestant school speech-day stuff (Drogheda and Dungannon), the signed 1951 Irish Association dinner menu, and the <u>Charter of TCD</u> verses by 'Rabach' which seem to relate to the 1948 'declaration of the republic' situation and the TCD response.

46. Irish Association 1960s material, including the Estyn Evans paper, and JJ's <u>1963 proposal</u> for a 'common market of these islands', and correspondence relating to it. There is correspondence with Irene Calvert, and a positive assessment of the incoming President Martin Wallace by Sir Graham Larmour, with an attached article by him attacking the Orange Order.

47. Plunkett House Library stuff, including Irish Statesman material.

48. Seanad Election addresses; correspondence with James Douglas in 1950 relating to JJ's standing down as TCD Senator; his 1939 'speech book'. Also Dev's 1951 nomination telegram, and a letter from Dev thanking him for his book *Irish Agriculture in Transition.* Also a short press report of the 1959 Seanad election, when JJ stood but lost to Fearon.

49. Some 50s correspondence; includes Bob Barton letter re hobby farming in Wicklow; also Tolstoy and Couris letters (the Collon Russian emigre group). There is also a letter from one F O'Hanlon, who it seems occupied a flat in Fitzwilliam Square near to JJ in 1918; he had read a report in Peace News of an address to the Church of Ireland Peace Fellowship. He enclosed an article of his in the paper *Labour's West Sussex Voice,* in which he had been critical of Labour policy on rearmament etc, and expressed empathy with JJ. I have also included here an account book which JJ kept, in a 'desk diary for 1933', accounts for a period in the 40s and 50s. This may throw light on the economics of his Grattan Lodge market gardening experiment. Also the Thekla Beere letter about the Naas rail-link, noted in the 50s Barrington or 'outreach' thread.

50. Material relating to the Dublin Universities merger debate in the 60s; also the closure of the Albert College. I have reproduced and abstracted this in the <u>1960s political</u> module.

51. *Irish Press* article series '<u>Freedom from Hunger</u>', commencing April 19 1963. There is also a 'reply to professor Yudkin's paper at UCC on Sunday April 28, 1963' which covers similar ground; it was given by one C Murphy who may have been a JJ acolyte.

52. Contains misc correspondence to JJ in the 60s, including Seán T Kelly of the Multifarnham Agricultural College, Julian Mac Airt of the TCD Statistics Dept, and also re a primary school near Vicarstown. There is also a notebook covering some travelling JJ did in Mayo in the mid-60s, in which he recorded meeting some contacts given him by RJ.

53. Correspondence in the mid 60s relating to, and reviews of, *Irish Economic Headaches,* including a letter from MJ Costello, and T O'Leary of the Irish House-owners Association, who had read a review. He sent a memorandum for consideration.

54. Early 60s papers and comments related to *Why Ireland Needs the Common Market.* Includes an acknowledgement from BR Sen the DG of the UNFAO. There is also a <u>paper</u> *The Common Market and the Communist Menace* which appeared in the *Sunday Press* on 23/12/1962. The 'communist menace' is in fact a label he uses for centralist bureaucratic price-fixing. In a separate folder is correspondence with Mercier Press the publisher, and in a further separate folder some records relating to the Nenagh anti-common market campaign; JJ was living in Nenagh with my sister at the time.

55. Late 60s and early 70s papers relating to the anti-EEC campaign; some of these are worth reproducing as JJ's '<u>last political fling</u>'. There is also an 'inland waterways' file; he had taken out supportive membership, and there are early memoranda on the campaign to get the Shannon-Erne Canal re-opened. He used this in his abortive attempt to develop a paper on transport.

56. Peace movement letters, relating to Northern Ireland and to Vietnam, from Peadar O'Donnell, Moira Woods and Conor Farrington; the latter is a copy of a joint letter submitted to the press signed by notables; it is undated but relates to the situation post August 1969. One of the CF letters notes the appreciation on the part of Catholic victims of the concern by Southern Protestants. There is a JJ membership card of the Irish Anti-Apartheid Movement dated 1971, and an Irish Democrat book-list.

57. Letters and drafts from the mid-60s showing his continuing attempts to publish for a lay 'opinion-leading' readership; they include an attempt to get his 1937 '<u>wheat</u>' paper published through the Agricultural Institute, and a development of his comments on Attwood's related SSISI paper published in the *Economist*.

58. Late 60s letters and drafts relating to the Northern Ireland question, including a typescript embodying some of his Boundary Commission experience, to the effect that the Border, if drawn to minimise the number of unwilling citizens, should run from the northern tip of Monaghan to a point just east of the entrance to Lough Foyle. There is also a letter from Professor W McC Stewart of Bristol, with an enclosed copy of an article by him, supportive of the status of Magee College in Derry, critical of the Lockwood Report, and the situation in the Coleraine campus of the New University of Ulster, staffed mainly with English academics. He had hoped to meet JJ at the 1969 scholar's dinner in TCD, but there is a copy of a letter from his sister Anne indicating JJ's imminent hospitalisation for a hip replacement.

59. A further letter from Attwood, dated 16/04/68, declining a submission by JJ to a planned conference in the Montrose Hotel. This occurs with, and may be related to, a copy of a paper by Alfred Latham-Koenig on *Intermediate Technologies for Developing Countries*, read at the Milan International Development Conference on June 7-10 1967.

60. Letter from the Taoiseach Seán Lemass dated 23/03/65 thanking JJ for his paper on the *Berkeley Theory of Credit*. He sent the same paper to de Valera, apparently after a meeting with him, and received an acknowledgement from him dated 03/10/66, in which Dev expressed the hope that it would revive interest in Berkeley's economic work, and that there would be a demand for the projected *Querist* book.

This was JJ's unpublished 'Consumer Demand as the Basis of Credit' monograph, which the then SSISI influentials *(Geary, Whitaker et al) had declined as being too philosophical and not econometric enough. RJ December 2000.*

61. Miscellaneous draft letters from his last few years, some unpublished, mostly published, in which case they were kept by my mother in her scrap-book (see 75 below), and where they exist loose I have transferred them to this folder. There is also a response, dated 20/06/66, from John Carroll, then Chief Industrial Officer of the Irish Transport and General Workers' Union, later President of the union, with some critical comments on a paper JJ had sent him. I have been unable to identify which paper it was; by then JJ was having trouble in getting things published, and he tended to work in 'samizdat' mode, with duplicated copies. Carroll took exception to JJ's assertion that CIE workers were 'regular recipients of taxpayers' bounty'. He was however supportive of JJ's attempts to get the issues discussed.

62. 1. RJ-Oxford correspondence, see below. Also 2. RJ-Tuam correspondence re Bobby Burke; see also below.

Primarily Relating to the family

63. Recent correspondence between RJ and various people in Dungannon (see below under 'various institutional sources').

64. Letters from James; papers dealing with Alan's final years, cremation and scattering of the ashes at Killygarvan.

65. Extracts from the Dungannon Royal School records, re JJ and brothers. I include also in this folder a photo, some correspondence and a lock of hair relating to some lady with a Scottish connection who is not my mother. I seem to remember my mother remarking about some such connection which was prior to her own.

66. Miscellaneous letters, family-related, but some with a political flavour, from the 1910s and 1920s period, sources mostly unidentified; includes a letter from Uncle Henry (Geddes) in Vancouver dated 1913, seeking a job back home, also my uncle Harry's (JJ's elder brother, the medical) commission in the RAMC; there is also an acknowledgement from the Provisional Government of JJ's letter of condolence on the death of Michael Collins, and a 1926 driving licence. There is also a begging letter to JJ from one James Stern, Balnagor, 1929, who had been schooled by John Johnston in Tullyarran, confirming the latter link.

67. JJ's 1945 notebook 'History of the Johnstons'; this contains a partial family tree going back to 1748, and pointers to how it might be further researched. There is some insight into the MacLean connection, and a letter from a John Philip Johnston in Alabama. I have included in this folder some pedigree material found in a separate box-file, labelled 'family'. I have also included in this folder also my own correspondence with Gordon and Kaye Johnston, of Goff's Harbour, NSW, Australia; this includes a draft family tree going back to a Joseph Johnston circa 1720. In this it is suggested that a brother of my grandfather went to Australia, and that his family would be as close to ours as are the Achesons. There are however discrepancies, and I have not pursued it. The Johnstons are a somewhat numerous tribe in Tyrone; this must in my time remain unfinished business.

68. Folder 1 Contains a notebook of my mother's dating from circa 1908, and also her 1916 'Ladies Yearbook 1915' with her diary of her Australian trip; it also contains her brother

Harry's 1915 recruiting paper, her 1911 teaching diploma, a lesson plan relating to Christchurch Cathedral, presumably a graduation test, and marriage certificates of her mother's parents and her maternal grandmother's parents (1825). Folder 2 contains my father's letters to her when separated on the world tour. There are also photos of my mother at her school circa 1913-4.

69. Folder relating to a 'Rutherford Mayne' portrait presentation, containing also photo of old John Johnston, several photos of JJ in unidentified situations, including one in the company of Harold Laski, probably at a TCD event, circa 1946 or 47 (when I remember Laski addressing the College Historical Society). There is also a set of family photos taken in or about 1926 in the Albert Kahn Foundation, using their pioneering colour process.

Here is serendipity at work. I had no idea who Rutherford Mayne was, but it turns out he was one of the leading lights in the Belfast manifestation of the Irish theatre movement in the 1900s. So I have given some pointers to this, in a short essay in the <u>political</u> channel.

70. Envelope containing various dinner menus and seating plans. I have analysed these for <u>insights</u> into where JJ stood in the 'pecking order' inside and outside College, over the period 1920 to 1960. I have also filed here some press reports of speeches made by notables, including Dukes the 1917 Chief Secretary, and by Sir Horace Plunkett in 1920.

71. Envelope containing a selection of mostly family letters which JJ kept for one reason or another, mostly peripheral to this work. Among them is his last letter from Limerick hospital, before they operated (he succumbed to the effects of the anaesthetic); it is dated 19 August 1972; also letters re James's death in 1937; Cynthia from Africa in 1944 on war service, mentioning RJ at school (she must have been in touch). Germane to the present study are: (a) JJ's 22/07/1914 Masonic parchment, accrediting his membership (he had joined the Longford lodge to please my mother's father; he resigned after he had got married); (b) Oxford membership cards, including Craobh Ollscoile Oxford of Connradh na Gaedhilge, and the Lincoln College Fleming Society; (c) listing of items found on the bodies of 1916 casualties: JC Larkin, J Larkin, J Kelly, it is not clear how he got this, but he has pencilled a note 'found on casualties of Easter' on the paper, which is signed by one J Reynolds; (d) part of a letter seeking to find jobs for RIC men who had resigned; dated September 1920, the lower part is chopped off.

72. Three sets of letters illustrating the scattering of TCD graduates globally; they were JJ's contemporaries, with whom he kept in touch. There was one Sandy in Hereford, Frank Apperley in Virginia USA, and one Austin, who is seems was my sister's godfather, from the front in the first world war; he was killed. Also Jack Poynton who ended up in the University of South Carolina in 1925. *Bessy(?) Apperley, Frank's wife, was my sister's godmother. The Poyntons were friends via my mother's mother 'Granny Wilson'; they were her neighbours in Ballymahon Co Longford; there was a brother Noel and a sister Kathleen.*

73. Folder containing papers relating to the present writer RJ, including early school reports from 1935, letters from school to home during the 1940s, correspondence from France in the 1950s; there is also a copy of a critical letter I wrote to the *Irish Times* in 1966 relating to science and technology policy, in my then capacity as Secretary of the <u>CSTI</u> (Council for Science and Technology in Ireland). He had additionally included in this folder Adare's 1841 document proposing to the Primate a plan for an '<u>Irish Collegiate School</u>', the foundation document of St Columba's College, the philosophy of which JJ clearly approved; it enshrined the ideas of the Gaelicising and aspirant Protestant nation-building landed gentry, of whom Claude Chevasse was a vestigial representative. *My sister remembers Claude Chevasse as a visitor during her childhood.*

74. Miscellaneous letters and cuttings, mostly non-political, curiosities, including some cuttings from Indian newspapers. Some could be letters from ex-students at the front in 1914-18. I have also filed here some stuff which turned up later: JJ's birth certificate, and his marriage certificate to my mother Timahoe Church, Queens County, July 21 1914. Also a vaccination certificate for my grandmother (Mary Geddes), Sept 17 1877, and a military pass for my other grandmother, Mrs CJ Wilson, to go to Broadstone in May 1916.

75. Scrap-book kept by my mother, mostly in the 1960s; this has some of JJ's and my letters to the paper, including one from me about the TCD-UCD merger, as from the Wolfe Tone Society. She added miscellaneous earlier material.

76. Extensive set of letters from William in India, over a long period of time; primarily to do with the 'family fund', and issues relating to Geddes, Tommy and Alec.

77. Letters of condolence etc re the death in 1929 of William's daughter Shiela, in Glengara Park School, where she was boarding with my sister Maureen, her parents William and Ruby being in India.

78. Letter re Eddie: Priorland 1931, from Bob Nesbitt 1931, and in mental hospital (1934), and letter from Tim (1967) re mother's 80th birthday. Letters from CJJ to JJ over period 1909 to 1914; photos of my mother when teaching at a national school at Ballivor, or perhaps Timahoe.

79. Letters from Annie in Budapest, where she was attending a World Student Christian Federation convention.

80. Letter from Sam when in Newcastle Sanatorium, dated 2 May 1919. Letters from Alec, including one in 1939 from military service, and one in 1969 detailing transitional retirement lodging arrangements for JJ. Notebook belonging to Sam's widow Elizabeth, with letters showing how she took up nursing, and some family photos.

81. Letters from JJ's brother Harry when on active service; he was torpedoed off Italy in May 1917, but survived.

82. Material relating to JJ's brother John, including Dungannon Royal School records, and letters to JJ, relating to the 'family fund' and Geddes. *The 'family fund' existed, with contributions according to ability, to help take care of Sam's children, Tommy, Alec and Geddes, after Sam died.*

83. Harpur letters (Ernest, Ballinclea)

84. Letters from 'Auntie Moodie' in Australia.

85. Contains Alamein Memorial records, including photo of Geddes's name on the memorial stone; also correspondence from his O/C relating to the episode on January 22-23 1943 in which Geddes lost his life.

86. Letters from the Traill ranch, and other Argentine sources, relating to Geddes.

87. Voluminous correspondence from various members of the family relating to Geddes, who clearly was in process of becoming the 'black sheep' of the family. There is the makings of a thesis, book, play or saga in some appropriate medium, which however I must leave on one side.

My sister was very familiar with this period; from 1923 up to 1929 when she was 7 to 13 the 3 lads became part of the family; she was very fond of Geddes.

88. Geddes's letters and earlier works, including his poems in praise of Stillorgan and Tyrone. There is also a letter from JJ to him, echoing the 'prodigal son' epic in the Bible.

89. Correspondence re the purchase of the Glen near Drogheda, in May 1940, from Col Jury (of Jury's Hotel). There are indications from this correspondence that JJ mobilised extended family funding for the purpose, and conceived the project in terms of a strategic investment in the interest of the extended family, in the then wartime context.

90. Documents relating to the purchase in 1953 and sale in 1959 of Grattan Lodge, Vicarstown, Co Laois. This property was built in 1882 by the Grattan-Bellew family and they were there until 1947.

91. Account-books relating to farming and market-gardening operations at the Glen, 1940-41.

92. Account-books and inventories covering period 1920s to 1960s sporadically.

93. Miscellaneous financial papers relating to JJ's last couple of years. living in the extension to my sister's house at Stoneyhigh near Nenagh.

94. Correspondence with the Bank and the Revenue relating to JJ's final years. It includes correspondence with the Bank of Ireland in Cookstown, where he moved his business during the bank strike.

95. Letters re JJ's and my mother's deaths and funerals, and JJ's memorial service in the TCD Chapel. There is also correspondence relating to the ownership of the plot in Mount Jerome. File of correspondence re sale of JJ's books to various libraries etc.

***

I have set up a box X which contains supportive material for JJ's lectures and publications: I have not been able to sort it in detail; also legal documents to do with the sale of various houses JJ lived in, from McCracken's solicitors office.

(g) Miscellaneous other institutional sources

Folder containing correspondence with the Horace Plunkett Foundation in Oxford, which has supplied material relating to JJ's piloting of the consumer co-op concept in TCD, and the College archives in Oxford, which contains records of student debates. I have also included material from the Plunkett House library.

Folder containing notes and extracts from the SSISI and Barrington archives.

Photocopies of the 1917 Manchester Guardian articles which can credibly be attributed to JJ, and which I have abstracted in the political module.

The foregoing material is also in folders in Box 2.

Folder containing sources in Dungannon relating to JJ's background, including correspondence between RJ and the Dungannon Heritage Centre, which came up with John Johnston's marriage certificate, and the Castle Caulfield parish records courtesy of Adrian McLernon. Also Dungannon Royal School correspondence, and the Donaghmore schools record. I have filed this in folder 63, as under 'family' above.

Folder containing correspondence between RJ and Oxford sources relating to JJ (Bodleian Library etc) see 62.1 above.

Folder containing correspondence with Maurice Laheen in Tuam re RM Burke and his co-operative farm; also the JJ encounter in 1947 on the Barrington circuit; see 62.2 above.

(h) Books relating to the background of JJ's work

I have collected some of these in Box(es) JJ5(+). The natural place for most of them is in a special location on my own bookshelves, where they have ended up, though it may be appropriate to transfer some of them to the Linen Hall Library. Those which I have had to access from the TCD Library I have marked as such, and where relevant abstracted. RJ December 2002.

Home Rule: Imperial and National and *Real Representation for Great Britain and Ireland*, AE Dobbs, Ponsonby Dublin 1908 and 1910; these arguments for Home Rule and for Proportional Representation came in via the Carmody collection, and are representative of the contemporary thinking of the Ulster Liberal Home Rule community.

The Strange Death of Liberal England, George Dangerfield, Smith & Haas, New York, 1934; Stanford UP & Serif 1997.

With Plunkett in Ireland: the Co-op Organiser's Story, RA Anderson, Macmillan, London, 1935; reprinted Irish Academic Press 1983.

The *Centenary Volume* of the Proceedings of the Statistical and Social Inquiry Society of Ireland was published in 1947, edited by R D Collison Black. TCD Library.

The Ulster Crisis, ATQ Stewart, Faber & Faber 1967, Blackstaff 1997.

Alice Stopford Green, a Passionate Historian, RB McDowell, (Allen Figgis, Dublin, 1967). TCD Library.

Ireland, Yesterday and Tomorrow, Bulmer Hobson, Anvil, Dublin, 1968; Carmody collection; I include this as an example of a parallel political evolution. JJ did not have much contact with the author, although distantly related. See Note 6 Chapter 2 for a minor contact-point.

The Irish Convention 1917-18, RB McDowell, Routledge and Kegan Paul, London, 1970. TCD Library.

Whitehall Diaries: Vol III, Ireland 1918-25, Thomas Jones, ed Keith Middlemas, Oxford University Press, 1971.

The Blueshirts, Maurice manning, Gill & Macmillan (1971, 1987); this mentions Dermot Macmanus. TCD Library.

The Years Flew By, Sydney Gifford Czira, Gifford and Craven, Dublin 1974.

The Riddle of Erskine Childers, Andrew Boyle, Hutchinson, London, 1977.

The Irish Co-operative Movement, its History and Development, Patrick Bolger, Institute of Public Administration, 1977. TCD Library.

Partition in Ireland, India and Pakistan - Theory and Practice, TG Fraser, Macmillan, London, 1984. (TCD Library)

Escape from the Anthill, Hubert Butler, Lilliput 1985; see this for Butler's assessment of Standish O'Grady, considered as a JJ influence. TCD Library.

Sam Thompson and Modern Drama in Ulster, Hagal Mengel, Peter Lang 1986; Bremer Beitrage zur Literatur und Ideologiegeschichte #3. TCD Library.

Arthur J Balfour and Ireland 1974-1922, Catherine B Shannon, CUA Press 1988.

The Dissenting Voice, Flann Campbell, Blackstaff, Belfast, 1991.

The Impact of Land Re-distribution in Ireland 1923-1974, Patrick Commins, Rural Economy Research Unit, Teagasc, Michael Dillon Memorial Lecture, RDS, Dublin 3 December 1993.

Fruits of a Century ed Maurice Henry, with Trevor West and Pat Bolger, ICOS 1994. TCD Library.

Ancestral Voices, Conor Cruise O'Brien, Poolbeg, Dublin 1994.

1922 - The Birth of Irish Democracy, Tom Garvin, Gill & Macmillan, Dublin, 1996.

Modern Irish Lives, ed Louis McRedmond, Gill & Macmillan, Dublin 1996.

The Spirit of Earnest Inquiry, Mary E Daly, SSISI 1997; this is a 150th anniversary history..

Dermot MacManus is also mentioned in *Blueshirts and Irish Politics*, Mike Cronin, Four Courts Press (1997); this documents the Yeats episode. TCD Library.

Who's Who in the Irish War of Independence and in Civil War 1916-23, Padraic O'Farrell, Lilliput, Dublin, 1997.

Memoirs of Senator James G Douglas, Concerned Citizen, J Anthony Gaughan, UCD Press, Dublin 1998.

The Long Gestation: Irish Nationalist Life, Patrick Maume, Gill & Macmillan, 1999. TCD Library.

UCD, a National Idea, Donal McCartney, Gill & MacMillan 1999.

New Liberalism, JL Hammond and the Irish Problem, 1897-1949, GK Peatling, **Historical Research**, Vol 73, no 180, February 2000.

Standish O'Grady's association with Jim Larkin and *The Irish Worker* has been researched by Edward A Hagan (U Conn) who edited O'Grady's *To the Leaders of Our Working People*, UCD Press, 2002. I had occasion to review this for the December 2002 *Irish Democrat*. Thus O'Grady in the 1912-14 period, as a JJ influence, should be seen as co-operative, democratic, left-wing, rather than feudal-romantic.

Source Listing and Bibliography for RJ

It is possible to classify RJ sources into

- (a) My published works: books, papers, articles, pamphlets;
- (b) Books possessed by me which relate to my publications and political evolution;
- (c) Public records of my work eg government reports in which I participated;
- (d) Minutes and other records of various bodies in which I participated;
- (e) Public record office, national library and other such sources;
- (f) Those papers in my possession and which I have attempted to catalogue;
- (g) Miscellaneous other institutional sources;
- (h) Books relating to the background of my work.
-

I hope to be able to deposit some or all of this material accessibly, perhaps in the Linen Hall Library, or other relevant library. An approximate key to the current provisional box numbering is given below. This classification is not absolute, because stuff sometimes turns up unexpectedly, and gets put in the current box when dealt with. Much of the material remains currently on my bookshelves. RJ Oct 2005.

Box RJ1 is mostly 1970s and 80s socio-technical.
Box RJ2 is mostly techno-economic and socio-technical.
Box RJ3 has books and publications of direct political interest to the narrative.
Box RJ4 is mostly published work with a science flavour.
Box RJ5 is mostly unpublished files of papers related to political developments, covering the 1950s, 60s and 70s.
Box RJ6 is mostly the 1980s, and Box RJ7+ the 90s.

(a) Published Works

Books
Up to the present I can't claim a complete book under my own authorship; I can however claim to have contributed chapters and editing services to published books, and I list these; they are accessibly currently in m,y library:
Unstable Heavy Particles 1947-55, ed H Yukawa, for Physical Society of Japan. *This contains several papers with which I was associated, one of which has my name on it.*
Renewable Energy Ireland, a Report summarising the Irish contribution to the UN Conference on New and Renewable Sources of Energy, Nairobi, August 1981, edited by RJ and published by the Irish United Nations Association.
Operations Research in Ireland, ed Julian Mac Airt, Mercier Press 1988; I contributed chapter 6, on techno-economic modelling of mostly biological systems, based on the 1970s experience of the TCD MSc in OR and Statistics.
JD Bernal - a Life in Science and Politics, ed Brenda Swann and Francis Aprahamian, Verso 1999; the writer contributed Chapter 2, on the early Irish influences. I summarise this in the 'Science and Society' thread, Bernal having been a significant early influence on my own political development in the 1940s and subsequently. .
Developing Industrial 'Case-based Reasoning', R Bergmann et al, Springer verlag 1999, this is the INRECA project report, which was published as a case-based reasoning manual; the writer is among the 10 named authors on page xix. His main contribution was in the use of n-dimensional 'fuzzy' parametric indexing in technical catalogue search.

Irish Innovators in Science and Technology, ed Mollan, Davis & Finucane, Royal Irish Academy, 2002: I contributed the chapter on Bernal. There is also a book on Irish physicists, edited by Andrew Whitaker of QUB and published in 2002 by the Institute of Physics, to which I contributed a chapter on Bernal in somewhat greater depth. Both are largely based on the Verso 1999 book.

Scientific papers, mostly during the DIAS epoch, but some later:

Proc. Congres Internationale sur le Rayonnement Cosmique, University de Toulouse, avec l'appui de l'UNESCO, Bagners re Bigorre, Juillet 1953; this includes contributions under the following titles, with RJ as a named member of the group:

Production of a V01 by a 1BeV negative primary; WB Fretter, BP Gregory, RHW Johnston, A Lagarrigue, H Mayer, F Muller and C Peyrou; p26.

Quelques Resultats sur les V-chargés; with group as above; P101.

Mesures de Masse de Particules S par Moment-Parcours, with group as above; p113.

The foregoing is in Box RJ4, as are the following scientific papers. From 1954 the sequence continues with reports of work done in DIAS; I have outlined something of the scientific thinking behind this in the 1950s academic module:

Evidence for the Nuclear Interaction of a Charged Hyperon Arrested in Photographic Emulsion; RHW Johnston and C Ó Ceallaigh; **Phil Mag**, ser 7, vol 45, p424, April 1954.

Further Evidence (etc as above); **Il Nuovo Cimento**; *1 Marzo 1955, 1, 468-472.*

Observations on Negative K-mesons; MW Friedlander, D Keefe and MGK Menon (Bristol), RHW Johnston and C Ó Ceallaigh (DIAS), and A Kernan (UCD); **Phil Mag** ser 7, vol 45 p144, February 1955.

Further Evidence for the Electron-Decay of K-Mesons; RHW Johnston and C Ó Ceallaigh, **Phil Mag** ser 7, vol 46, p393, April 1955.

Conferenza Internationale sulle Particelle Elementari, Pisa June 1955; this contains many papers from the Ecole Polytechnique group, and several from the Dublin Institute for Advanced Studies, including 2 by the present writer, and several in which he participated. Most of this material appeared as separate publications subsequently. Box RJ4.

The G-stack collaboration, in its first publication: *On the Masses and Modes of Decay of Heavy Mesons Produced by Cosmic Radiation;* JH Davies et al, **Il Nuovo Cimento**, serie X, Vol 2, pp1063-1103, Novembre 1955; this paper had all of 36 named authors, 10 from Bristol, 6 from Copenhagen, 3 from DIAS (including the present writer), 3 from UCD, 9 from 4 locations, three in Italy and one in Brussels, and 5 from 2 other Italian locations.

A Scattering Calibration Experiment; RHW Johnston, n2 del Supplemento al Vol 4 Serie X del **Nuovo Cimento**, pp456-459, 1956.

On the Relation between Blob-density and Velocity of a Singly Charged Particle in G-5 Emulsion; G Alexander and RHW Johnston, **Il Nuovo Cimento**, Serie X, Vol 5, pp363-379, Febbraio 1957.

The Relative Frequencies of the Decay Modes of Positive K-Mesons and the Decay Spectra of Modes K-mu-3 and K-beta; G Alexander, RHW Johnston and C Ó Ceallaigh, **Il Nuovo Cimento,** Serie X, Vol 6, pp 478-5000, Settembre 1957.

The G-stack collaboration, with variable composition, produced 3 more papers on negative K-mesons: *The Interaction and Decay of K- mesons in Photographic Emulsion;* Part 1, General Characteristics of K- Interactions: B Bhowmik et al, **Il Nuovo Cimento,** Serie X, Vol 13, pp690-729, Agosto 1959; Part 2, The Emission of Hyperons from Kinteractions at rest: B Bhowmik et al, Il Nuovo Cimento, Serie X, Vol 14, pp315-364, Ottobre 1959; Part 3 has no additional sub-title, but is in effect an addendum to part 2: D Evans et al, Il Nuovo Cimento, Serie X, Vol 15, pp873-898, Marzo 1960;

On the Ionisation-Velocity Relation in Photographic Emulsion for Singly Charged Particles, 1961, unpublished, with MA Shaukat (DIAS) and D Prowse (UCLA). *This was my last scientific paper; it is filed with some Ó Ceallaigh correspondence; he was in the end not happy to publish it because it was inconclusive. We had reached the fringe of applicability of the experimental technology, and were attempting to quantify the 'relativistic rise' on the high-energy side of the minimum. Prowse had supplied the raw material. We had in fact gone up a cul-de-sac, and Ó Ceallaigh recognised it.* Box RJ4.

A Special-Purpose Computer for the Analysis of Measurements of Multiple Scattering in Photographic Emulsion, paper by RJ in **Electronic Engineering**, June 1963; Box RJ4.

The Development of a Method for Measuring the Concentration of Suspended Solids, paper by RJ in **Research and Development for Industry**, no 31, March 1964; this is in a folder along with internal Guinness reports on the continuous fermentation process; also 3 Guinness Patents: 976,663 Examining Solutions Photo-electrically, 986,343 Controlling Yeast Fermentation, 1,004,693 Continuous Production of Alcoholic Beverages; Box RJ4.

An Analytical Approach to the Simulation of a Real-time System, paper by RJ at the 5th Annual Symposium of AGIFORS, Chicago, 1965; also at the same conference, with Oisin Ó Siochrú, *Long-term Fleet Planning as a Step Towards an Integral Company Model.* Both these are in a folder in box RJ4.

Organisational Structure, presentation to the Aer Lingus General Manager, from Innovation Group 18, July 1967. This group effort as well as the present writer involved Maurice Foley, Ken Holden and 4 others. It was a bottom-up response to a call for innovative management ideas. One can perhaps see the influence of Stafford Beer. I abstracted this experience into a presentation which I made in the Irish Management Institute in 1968, and I have reproduced this in the 1960s socio-technical module. Box RJ4.

Simulation and Validation, response to Prof TH Naylor, **Proceedings of the 1972 IFORS Conference**, p219, North Holland / American Elsevier 1973; also in same Proceedings, *Report on the Discussion Forum*, p703. Both are accessible in full.

An Approach to National Manpower Planning in Science and Technology, Proceedings of the **Statistical and Social Inquiry Society**, Vol XXIII Part II, p21); this was delivered on January 9 1975 by RJ, co-authored with Genevieve Franklin.

Folder in Box RJ2 contains many of the above papers.

Articles, Reviews and Letters in quality journals:
There is a letter headed *Uneven Development in Technology* in the US-published *International Science and Technology* (March 1963), and a review in *Development* (December 1966) of the OECD Report *Science and Irish Economic Development*. Box RJ2.

Irish Times **Features:** there was a series of five articles on January 9-13 1967 under the generic title *Science in Ireland* which was my contribution to the public discussions arising out of the 1964 OECD Report and the subsequent lobbying of the Council for Science and Technology in Ireland (CSTI) regarding the structuring of the then projected National Science Council. Box RJ2.

There were several in-depth reviews written during the 1960s, and these are collected in a folder, along with related correspondence. There is a letter from Maurice Harmon, editor of the *University Review*, seeking to publish the 1967 *Irish Times* series as a single integrated long paper. I sent him the material, but have no record whether it appeared or not. They might possibly be in the June 1967 issue. There is a copy of the Ray Keary *Geology* article in the *Irish Times* of May 26 1966, and my supportive letter as from the CSTI of June 7 1966. There is an article in Hibernia, May 1967, reviewing a book by Brian Murphy *The Computer in Society* which raises most of the key socio-technical issues which remained endemic up to the 1990s and even today. There is a critical review of Michael Woods *Research in Ireland* published in the August 1970 issue of the **Irish Journal of Agricultural Research and Rural Sociology**. There is a copy of a paper published in *Léargas,* August-September 1970, published by the Institute of Public Administration, entitled *The Computer as an Analytical Mathematical Tool.* Box RJ2.

The foregoing paved the way for the *Irish Times Science and Technology Column* which ran from January 1970 to December 1976, and is in principle available in full in ASCII, but I made a selection in the mid-1980s with a view to publication of a book by Tycooley, entitled *In Search of Techne*, and this is the basis of what is available here, being what I then considered to be perhaps of lasting interest, in the context of possible future studies of science and society, or science and government. Tycooley however collapsed, and I was left with an unpublished book on my hands, which at the time I had to leave on one side. It may however be of interest here in the context of studies of science and politics in the third world, ie the process of transition from colonial to post-colonial government, and the recognition of that science is not necessarily always simply and imperial tool. Bound printouts of two edited versions of *In Search of Techne* are in Box RJ2.

Government by Duplicity, a review by RJ of Tom Jones *Whitehall Diaries* Volume III (on Ireland); this appeared in *Atlantis* 4, September 1972; box RJ3.

The New Ireland - Utopian or Scientific? paper by RJ in *Atlantis* 5, April 1973. I reproduce this in full in the hypertext; it encapsulates the essentials of my vision at the beginning of my post-SF epoch. *This vintage issue of a publication edited by Seamus Deane contained papers by Desmond Greaves, Desmond Fennell, Jack Bennett, JW Foster, WJ McCormack, Lelia Doolan, Ed Walsh and many others; Atlantis was beginning to assume a mantle not unlike that of* the Bell *and the* Irish Statesman*; it is a pity if did not survive.*

Reviews in Books Ireland and the *Irish Times*; these are in a folder in Box RJ2:
* *Hamilton Academicals* a review of TL Hankins' biography of WR Hamilton, Books Ireland December 1981;
* 'Why the Sky is Blue' a review of the Brock et al collected essays on *John Tyndall* Books Ireland, May 1982;
* *The 1986 Science in Ireland 1800-1930 Conference Report* with the sub-title *Tradition and Reform* edited by JR Nudds et al, TCD and published by the TCD Physics Dept. I was asked by John Banville to review it for the *Irish Times*.

Science and Technology in Irish National Culture, in *The Crane Bag*, Forum Issue, Vol 7 no 2, 1983, p58. This was very badly proofed and has appalling misprints, but I have reproduced a corrected version which is related to the 'science and society' thread. Box RJ4.

JD Bernal - Some Irish Influences, paper by RJ in **Notes and Records of the Royal Society**, London, Vol 47(1), 93-101 (1991). *Ann Synge (who contributed Chapter 1 on the early Bernal, complementing my Chapter 2, to the book finally published by Verso in 1999) and I between us contributed two papers to NRRS in successive issues, based in the work we had done towards our respective chapters in the then projected Bernal biography; we were in despair at its ever coming out! Ann alas did not live to see her chapter in print.* Box RJ4.

Physics on the Fringe, **Physics World**, July 1992; this career overview in its published form was edited down from the original version available here. Box RJ4.

Science, Technology and Nationality - *an Irish Example*, paper by RJ in **Planet** the Welsh bi-monthly review, no 110, April-May 1995. Box RJ4.

Sustainable Development, report on the 1996 INES conference in Amsterdam, *MSF Journal (Ireland)* no 2, 1996. Along with other conference material, in Box RJ8.

Science in India, review in **Science and Public Policy** Vol 24 #1, February 1997, of *The Science of Empire*, Z Baber, SUNY 1996.

Tableau 2 - Futures + Directions, ed June O'Reilly, Cork RTC, 1997; this contains my 'Green Science' paper.

New Perspectives on Ireland, ed Daltun Ó Ceallaigh, Leirmheas 1998; this is mainly based on Greaves School papers, but includes an edited version of my *Science and National Culture* material.

Biotechnology and Sustainability: a Local and Global Political Perspective, in *Farm and Food*, Spring 2001 (Teagasc, ed Con O'Rourke). Box RJ4, with Planet.

Occasional **Newspaper** Articles:

*Publications in journals of the **Irish left** (*Review, Irish Democrat, the Plough, United Irishman): alas I do not have these; to resurrect them would be a major work; perhaps later during subsequent development of the hypertext knowledge-base.*

(b) Selected Books and Papers in my possession, relating to Scientific and Political Development

Folder containing SF Ard Fheis records (incomplete) from 1964 to 1969; also the Roy Garland (UUP) version of the 1969 *Garland Commission Report* I have included a 1962 report on the state of the IRA from the Minister for Justice to the Cabinet with these. Box RJ3.

Where We Stand, Tomás Mac Giolla; Carrickmore Republican Clubs Conference, 1972; reprinted by Workers Party 2000; Box RJ3.

The Years Flew By, Sidney Gifford Czira, Gifford and Craven, Dublin 1974; I have used her Ferguson aircraft reference on several occasions..

Economic and Social Implications of the Political Alternatives that may be open to Northern Ireland, ed Norman Gibson, NUU Social Sciences, 1975.

The Ripening of Time - this pocket-sized left-wing theoretical quarterly ran from December 1975 at least up to October 1980 and perhaps later; I have a complete series Nos 1 to 13 (January 1980). It was produced by a group which preferred to remain obscure; it had an anarcho-Trotskyist flavour, and was critical of the USSR. I read a paper to the Wolfe Tone Society on January 24 1978, and I sent them a copy, which they published in No 9, March 1978. Derry Kelleher had a paper in No 11, February 1979. The RoT people lumped these together, and did a critical reply to mine in No 13, October 1980, and promised one on Kelleher, but I don't have it. This is raw material for the 1970s political thread. Box RJ3.

Co-operation and Community Development in the West of Ireland, Patrick Commins, 5th international seminar on marginal regions, TCD, July-August 1979; Box RJ3.

De Valera Centenary Publication Dublin Institute of Advanced Studies, 1982; this was a stimulus for the present writer to try to reopen relations with it, as a follow-on from the TCD Applied Research Consultancy contract. There is correspondence with Ken Whitaker, Stan Nielsen and others. It was a false trail.

On to the Republic, Derry Kelleher, Ripening of Time, 1982;

Coalition?, Derry Kelleher, Justice Books 1, 1984;

Garret's Bloodied Scenario, Derry Kelleher, Justice Books 2, 1986;

An Alien Ideology, Derry Kelleher, Justice Books 3, 1986;

Operations Research in Ireland, Julian Mac Airt, Mercier Press, Cork, 1988.

An Open Letter to Ian Paisley, Derry Kelleher, Justice Books 6, 1990;

1916 as History, C Desmond Greaves, Fulcrum Press 1991;

Skeff, Andrée Sheehy-Skeffington, Lilliput 1991; there is inserted also the original of my September 1978 MS notes for Andrée S-S, which she used as the basis for her references to the 1940s student left in the book, without acknowledgement, and MS letters from OSS to RJ dated 23-25/04/56, on issues relating to the exposure of Stalin;

Patterns of Betrayal, Seán Garland et al; Workers Party, 1992; this is their response to the Democratic Left breakaway; Box RJ3.

Caorthann 1994-95, a fringe Green theoretical publication edited by Laurence Cox, this includes material published by me, in particular a paper on A Green Paradigm for Nationality. Box RJ7.

Independent Spirit, essays by Hubert Butler, Farrar, Strauss and Giroux, New York, 1996;

Bodenstown 1998, Seán Garland, Workers Party 1998; Box RJ3.

Folder containing Cathal Goulding funeral record, 1999 Ard Fheis agenda, Goulding oration at Jim Sullivan's funeral 1991. Box RJ3

Buried Alive in Ireland, Derry Kelleher, Justice Books, 2001;

Irish Republicanism - the Authentic Perspective, Derry Kelleher, Justice Books, 2001; *NB The Kelleher material is in print and accessible via Athol on Belfast. RJ April 2002.*

'Republican Sinn Fein' stuff received from Ruairi Ó Brádaigh, 2001; Box RJ3.

(c) Reports for Government Agencies, Project Reports etc

This group sub-divides into broadly-defined techno-economic and socio-technical areas. The former addresses the question 'how will this technological innovation affect the economics of the operation?' The latter addresses the question 'how will this innovation affect the people concerned, and how can they be best motivated to implement it?'

There were various reports published in the 70s and 80s, mostly in consultancy mode; these are 'grey' publications, in some cases accessible in the libraries of the client organisations, but never actually 'published'.

There were also some EU project reports in the 1990s, mostly in the domain of knowledge-base and learning-resource architecture.

Techno-economic

Folder containing technical papers and correspondence relating to the production of methane gas from farmyard manure, circa 1958. This led to an article in the *Irish Times* Methane from Manure; there is a typescript copy. The correspondence is with F Mignotte in France and engineer Padraig Ó Hailpin in Dublin. Box RJ2.

A folder containing some notes on techno-economic analysis of business processes, produced in 1970 as raw material for postgraduate supervision work, Box RJ5.

An Empirical Model of a Commercial Tomato Production Unit in Ireland, RJ with JS Hickey, IA Kinsella and PC O'Kane; this was an account of a techno-economic modelling MSc project implemented by the group. Circa 1972. Box RJ2.

Report and source-programme relating to an analysis of fishing-port performance, sponsored by Gaeltarra Eireann, 1974. Box RJ2

A folder containing a selection of TCD-related OR-type project material from the period 1971 to 1975 is retained in Box RJ5.

Legislation, Energy Conservation and the Balance of Payments; (Conserve 1975); this memorandum was circulated to TDs from an ad-hoc group of engineers and concerned citizens convened by RJ, the objective being to oppose the then proposed investment in a nuclear power plant at Carnsore Point Co Wexford. Along with supportive documentation it resides in a folder in Box RJ2.

Folder containing <u>anaerobic digestion</u> correspondence, notes, papers, articles associated with the period 1973-75 resides in Box RJ5.

Technology and the Economy as Interacting Systems, paper by RJ in *Technology Ireland*, vol 9 no 10, January 1978; Box RJ4.

Biomass System Analysis; report by RJ for the National Board for Science and Technology, 1980; Box RJ2.

Folder with *New Hibernia* correspondence (Breasal Ó Caollai) and unpublished article re the IIRS management crisis; also Kelleher material re techno-economics of Whitegate Refinery. December 1984. Box RJ1.

Socio-technical

On the Variability of Concert Audiences: <u>Memo</u> prepared for the Committee of the Culwick Choral Society, circa 1958, containing an analysis of concerts from 1939 to 1957, with ticket sales analysed by outlet, and concerts analysed by genre. *This I count as a pioneering episode in what later emerged in operations research as the 'philosophy of the unplanned experiment'.* Box RJ2.

Folder containing papers relating to the Council for Science and Technology in Ireland (CSTI) (mid-1960s), followed by those of the Kane-Bernal Association which followed in (early 1970s), in association with Derry Kelleher. Box RJ2.

A Paper folder in Box RJ2 contains, along with the above *Books Ireland* reviews, 3 documents relating to socio-technical work in the 1970s:

* An article in Business and Finance 19 December 1974 discussing the need for a National Board for Science and Technology.

* A conference contribution to a meeting of the Society of College Lecturers, being a <u>reply</u> to a paper by Páid McMenamin of the Industrial Development Authority, on *Industrial Expansion and the Composition of the Labour Force*; I made the case for a procedure for converting science graduates to engineers in a postgraduate process.

* An article entitled <u>ARC</u> in the May 1980 issue of *Trade and Industry* outlining the experience of the TCD Applied Research Consultancy Group in its 4 years of prior existence.

On the Feasibility of a European Regional <u>Genetic Resources</u> Information Network; Robert Friel and RHW Johnston; TCD Applied Research and Consultancy Group, January 1979. Box RJ1

A National <u>Marine</u> Data-Bank; Robert Friel, RHW Johnston and Daphne Levinge; TCD ARC Group, May 1979. Box RJ1

Folder containing notes towards a briefing for the Ballymun Community Co-op identifying potential enterprise opportunities; this leaned on the experience of Mike Cooley's 'Greater London Enterprise Board'. There was some Youth Employment Agency support, and a projected link with the National Institute of Higher Education (NIHE Dublin) in Glasnevin. Circa 1984. Box RJ1

Community Enterprise and the RTCs, Reports to the Youth Employment Agency and the National Enterprise Agency, April and November 1985; the <u>first</u> covered Dundalk, Athlone and Tralee, and the <u>second</u> covered the other six, NIHE Limerick, the Dublin Institute of Technology and University College Dublin. Box RJ1.

Community Enterprise and the 3rd-level Colleges; <u>Practical Manual</u> for the use of Community Enterprise Activists, December 1986; this was based on the earlier Reports to the YEA and NEA, April and November 1985. Box RJ1

Folder containing material relating to the Shannon Development project on identifying regional linkages with Brittany; 1986; Box RJ1.

Research and Technological Development <u>Linkages</u> between Less Favoured Regions of the European Community; National Board for Science and Technology, 1986; cf Dr Stan Nielsen. Box RJ1

The NIHE as an Accessible <u>Technology Business</u> Resource...; Shannon Development, July 1987. There is also an associated file of correspondence with the NIHE people and with Shannon Development. Box RJ1

The <u>Mentec</u> *Customer Analysis System*; March 1988; cf Dr Mike Peirce. *This failed because it ran into socio-technical barriers of a type subsequently identified.* Box RJ1

Folder containing profiles of various small Irish high-tech firms, translated into French, which were used in an exploratory mission seeking to identify potential partnerships via the BC-NET process, circa 1989. Box RJ1

(d) Minutes and other records of relevant organisations

Folders (grouped by year) containing internal Irish Workers League material from the period 1949 to 1954, including conference resolutions, and a leaflet on the Ballyfermot Co-op. The 1949 folder contains a memo from Muriel McSwiney dated 1944, which however is outside the scope of this study. I have abstracted as much of this material as seems relevant, starting with the <u>1940s political</u> module and continuing into the <u>1950s module</u>. Box RJ5.

The <u>Sinn Fein</u> minutes from the 1960s and early 70s, and the Ard Fheis reports, which were made accessible courtesy of the Workers' Party, which has organisational continuity with the 1960s Sinn Fein. These contain in 1964 a reference to, and outline of, the present writer's *Economic Resistance* article in the *United Irishman*, and later in 1970 a reference to the *Freedom Manifesto* published after the Ard Fheis; this is hot-linked to a copy of the complete document, of which the present writer was the author. The latter 2 documents are in Box RJ3.

I have cross-referenced my analysis of the Garland January 1966 '<u>captured documents</u>' from the Sinn Fein record; they help fill a gap in the Ard Fheis sequence, and relate to how the Army Council saw Sinn Fein during 1965-66. These are available via the National Archive (ref 98/6/495) and I am indebted to Matt Treacy a TCD postgraduate student for picking them up, in the context of his researches into the period. This and my SF Minutes notes are in Box RJ3, in a blue IPA folder. This also contains the *Commission Report* of 1969 (which I have scanned in; this version arrived via a Quaker Unionist NI source) and the 1998 special *United Irishman* commemorative issue which contains the memoir by <u>Mick Ryan</u>. Also in RJ3 is a folder containing some backup documentation relating to the Commission meetings, which I have not attempted to analyse; the work of the Commission during 1969 was overtaken by events, and I judged the latter to be more relevant to the narrative.

A file of the weekly internal Sinn Fein newsletter *Nuacht Naisiunta*, running from its initiation in September 1969 up to June 1976 was kept by Derry Kelleher, and I have used it extensively, especially for the period <u>1969-70</u>. This has been donated to the Workers Party archive, on the understanding that it will be set up accessibly for historical scholarship. This archive contains much useful pre-split republican material.

The Dublin Wolfe Tone Society <u>minutes</u> are in the custody of Anthony Coughlan; he has enabled me to abstract them, and my abstract is available, subject to his copyright. The WTS archive includes a copy of a TCD student publication entitled 1916-1966 published in 1966 as a commemoration; it has papers from 17 authors, including an outline political manifesto by RJ entitled <u>Ahead</u>. Some of my own <u>WTS papers</u> relating to the WTS I have also abstracted, and these are available in Box RJ5; these include some <u>notes from 1965</u> relating to republican politicisation at the basic grassroots level, and an abstract of the <u>1967 Coughlan plan</u> for WTS development. The WTS held a conference in Carrickmacross in November 1972, and C Desmond Greaves read a paper *England's Responsibility for the Crisis in Ireland*. This was subsequently published in Atlantis, No 5, April 1973, and is <u>here reproduced</u> in full, along with my own <u>*Irish Utopias*</u> paper which appeared in the same issue.

Minutes of the <u>Technology Group</u> of the Institute of Physics (Irish Branch) exist in a folder in box RJ1. Some relevant points in these have been abstracted in the 1980s socio-technical stream.

Green Party records are incomplete, but I have grouped such material as is available in folders by year, and sometimes by topic within year. This should not be seen as a history of the Green party, but simply an indication of the present writer's contribution to it.

'Green Party' folder 1990-1991 includes notes on the use of the <u>Internet</u>, and material on <u>regional policy</u> development. Box RJ7.

Folder 1992 has some Green policy development papers, and included letters to Roger Garland and then to Trevor Sargent, after the latter's election, attempting to make the case for taking seriously the potential of the <u>Internet</u>. Box RJ7.

'Green' folder 1993 has some record of an attempt to introduce the '<u>social wage</u>' concept into the political currency, both via the Green Party and also via Ruairi Quinn and the Labour Party. Box RJ7.

There is a 1994 Green folder containing miscellaneous policy material relating to the European election, including records of an <u>expedition to the West</u> in support of Richard Douthwaite's candidacy. Box RJ7.

There is more to come for the 1990s in this sequence, and I hope to add to it in the hypertext support system.

(e) Public Record Office Sources

New Ireland Forum, Report of proceedings, public session, October 11 1983; contains submission by the present writer, Micheál Ó Loingsigh and others; box RJ3.

The *Garland January 1966* '<u>*captured documents*</u>'*;* these help fill a gap in the Ard Fheis sequence, and relate to how the Army Council saw Sinn Fein during 1965-66. These are available via the National Archive (ref 98/6/495) and I am indebted to Matt Treacy for picking them up, in the context of his researches into the period. I have put them in an 'Institute of Public Administration' folder along with some Ard Fheis material, and a 1962 Government assessment of the risk of a general release, in Box RJ2.

I have attempted to track down a record of the Lynch-Heath talks which took place in 1971-72, without much success; these related to the EEC and to the North. At the time we suspected the gestation of a 'Federal deal' in the context of the EEC accession, with Ireland going in as a British satellite, in return for concessions leading towards 'national unity'. I regard the analysis of this aspect as unfinished business; I have attempted to outline what I thought at the time in the <u>1970s political</u> module of the hypertext.

(f) Personal Papers, letters etc.

Personal papers relating to various political and scientific processes; correspondence relating to possible employments, project proposals etc.

Folder with 1950s correspondence: Owen Dudley Edwards and the 1913 Club, Brian Farrington on Stalin, *Plough* material in draft, notes on the Wolfe Tone diaries; raw material for the development of politics in the black 1950s. Box RJ5.

Folder with Connolly Association correspondence, mostly with Desmond Greaves, from the period 1963-68. *(I have copied the Greaves letters for the Coughlan archive.)* Box RJ5.

Folder with material relating to the 1964 Sinn Fein draft social and economic programme, including some critical notes by RJ. Box RJ5.

Folder containing Wolfe Tone material 1964-66, including correspondence with George Gilmore in 1966, and 'economic resistance' papers. Also the Minister Des O'Malley correspondence re Griffith Barracks and the housing crisis. Box RJ5.

Folder containing the earlier *Irish Times* series January 9-13 1967 on 'Science in Ireland', and the original more extended paper from which the series was condensed. Box RJ2.

Folder with material relating to the Pierre Tielhard de Chardin Society of Ireland; circa 1967; Derry Kelleher and the writer took an interest in this, in the then fashionable spirit of enquiry into issues relating to Marxism and Christianity. This episode has been placed on record by Risteard Ó Glaisne in Irish published by Coscéim in 1994. Box RJ2.

Entropy papers: two folders dating from the period 1965-1969 containing my attempts to formulate an information-theoretical theory of management costs, extending the Shannon definition of entropy, and introducing a temperature-analogue identified as a measure of management skill. There are some TCD seminar papers, courtesy of Frank Drechsler in the Business School. I published some summary notes in the basic concepts via the Institute of Physics, in Physics Today, July 1992, and this is accessible. Box RJ6.

Folder containing a limited amount of 1967-68 Sinn Fein-related material, including correspondence with Derek Peters and Betty Sinclair about the NICRA and how to improve its relationship with the Republican Clubs, primarily regarding arrest without trial etc. It also includes letters from Anthony Coughlan on the abstention question, 'Definition of Socialism' material, draft recruiting leaflet material for the 26 and 6 counties, and miscellaneous correspondence relating to educational conferences etc. Box RJ5.

Folder containing Wolfe Tone Society material mostly from 1968, supplementary to the Society's records as salvaged and retained by Anthony Coughlan. It includes a copy of the 'Text-books in Irish' report compiled by Micheál Ó Loingsigh et al in May 1968, and a report of the Maire Mac an tSaoi lecture of July 1967. It includes the August 1968 circular which enshrined the present writer's still-persisting broad-spectrum agenda, at a time when the focus was already narrowing to Civil Rights in the North. There is also a copy of the abortive August 1968 Dungannon Declaration which Anthony Coughlan had attempted to convey as the public message from the Coalisland-Dungannon march, but for which the transmission procedure failed through an unfortunate misunderstanding, between the Dublin WTS people and the NICRA. Box RJ5.

Folder with some 'dirty tricks department' material attempting to undermine the politicisation process 1964-73; some from 'ultra-left' sources, others Special Branch forgeries. Box RJ5.

Folder containing a few papers related to the NICRA, including the original Constitution, the January 1969 constitutional revision memorandum, a slanted press cutting suggesting 'IRA infiltration', the June 1969 'Ultimatum to Stormont' leaflet, and a September 1969 draft of a document supportive of the 'Civil and Political Rights Covenant' campaign. Box RJ5.

Folder containing miscellaneous correspondence relating to local SF work in 1969; this includes the record of the meeting of the Pearse Cumann with George Gilmore and the

Rev Ned Watson, the correspondence with Mercy Simms. and also the draft notes for organisers for November 1969, prior to the Ard Fheis on January 1970. Box RJ5.

Folder with some cuttings and correspondence arising out of the August 1969 crisis, including letters to Bernadette Devlin, Noel Browne and Justin Keating; this material has mostly been abstracted in the 1960s political thread, in its context. Box RJ5.

Folder with some Sinn Fein material circa 1970; includes the Crowe episode, where an aging bachelor farmer was seeking a successor. Box RJ6.

'Boat Project' folder: we market-researched demand in 1971 for a boat service between the Aran Islands, Ros a Mhichil and Doolin, as a possible community co-operative project. Box RJ6.

Miscellaneous cuttings and correspondence etc connected with my resignation from SF in January 1972. Box RJ6.

Bofin: some correspondence relating to a community co-operative project on Inis Bofin; we attempted this in 1972-3. Box RJ6.

Resources Study Group material dating circa 1972. Box RJ6.

Miscellaneous Common Market (Study Group and Defence Campaign) notes from the period 1966 to 1972. Box RJ6.

A folder with some 1973 Moscow Peace Conference material contains support for some initiatives relating to technology transfer to the third world, treated in the techno-economic stream. It also contains material relating to the political stream, as regards the composition of the group attending the conference, in the context of the republican politicisation process, and the convergence with the Left. Box RJ5.

Folder containing some CPI material relating to the period 1974-1978, selected papers from which I have reproduced in the 1970s module of the political stream; these relate to partition economics, the 'left alternative' and the 'science and society' question. Box RJ6.

Folder with material relating to the 'Irish Alternative' meetings which took place in 1977 around Sunningdale-time; this was an attempt to reach out to the IRSP and the Provisionals from the Left, which proved abortive. Box RJ6.

Folder with Operations Research Society of Ireland material for the period 1977-1980, including conference abstracts and attendances, and some lecture demonstration notes (in a separate folder). Box RJ6.

Renewable Energy conference folder (1981) containing the Nairobi conference report, and some records of attempts to follow it up with some energy consultancy based on contacts made; these did not bear fruit. Box RJ5.

Paddy Farrington in Vietnam 1981-82; correspondence. Box RJ1.

Folder with material relating to the Peace Technology Group, Futures Society etc, circa 1982, done via TCD Industrial Liaison Office. Box RJ1

Folder with ORSI Bulletin file covering 1979 to 1987, giving some insights into the thinking of the 'management science' community in Ireland, as they increasingly led the way towards the micro-computing revolution. Some issues contain an 'RJ Column', one of which, in January 1983, outlines a response to some questions raised in the international Operations Research community (IFORS) context, indicating collective self-doubt. Box RJ6.

Folder with report of Toulouse meeting on 'European Strategy in Research and Technology', February 1984, and associated correspondence, mainly Brendan Halligan. I attended this in behalf of the Labour Party. Box RJ1.

'Techne Papers' folder outlining RJ's approach to building on the TCD Applied Research Consultancy experience, via a network to support a dynamic flow of innovative companies from the university research system towards commercial viability. This at the time was stillborn, but it represents a model which was valid but perhaps premature in the context. I have reproduced a summary 'Innovation' paper dated 19/10/1984 in the 'socio-technical' stream as an example. Box RJ6.

Associated with the foregoing is a file of correspondence with HMS 'Dusty' Miller covering the period 1982-84, relating to an abortive attempt to develop a venture-seeding business on a commercial basis. There is also a file of correspondence with the IDA, the CII, the IIRS, the NBST and the YEA, relating to the Techne project. I attempted, unsuccessfully, a 'rearguard action' with the College, in the form of a letter to the Provost at the end of 1983. This I have included in the 1980s module of the 'Academic' stream, along with some related interactions with Kader Asmal. Box RJ6.

Crane Bag folder containing follow-up material on my 1983 *British Association meetings in Ireland* paper which I collected for an aborted issue of the biennial, projected for 1985, but it folded, Its niche was partially filled by the *Irish Review* from 1986, to which I contributed a paper *Science in a Post-Colonial Culture*. This was subjected to editorial cuts, but the full version is available. Box RJ3.

There is a folder labelled 'Foster / UNU 1986' which contains records of an attempt I made to re-establish my earlier 'research associate' status with the Statistics and Operations Research Laboratory in TCD. It also contains correspondence relating to the termination of the TCD contract. A further folder labelled 'dealing with the College 1984-88' is associated. Box RJ6.

Folder containing correspondence in 1983-94 with the Minister Ruairi Quinn, Niall Greene who headed the Youth Employment Agency, and others, which indicates that there was some hope for the Techne concept, with some State support, via the Youth Employment Agency. There is here an implicit political dimension. This also contains correspondence with Joe Watson the Limerick Industrial Liaison Officer, and Ron Cox in TCD Engineering, in February 1984, relating to the RJ resurrection project 'Techne'. I have made this available in the 1980s module of the socio-technical stream.

Folder with material relating to the Brittany trip in 1985 in search of linkages between college research groups and small high-tech firms, on an inter-regional basis. Included is a paper on the 'quad-linkage' concept. Box RJ6.

Folder entitled 'Aran Islands / Agriculture Biologique' which contains some correspondence with the Inis Mean co-operative (Tarlach de Blacam) and with various agencies about the organic food market. I had identified the latter in Brittany where I had encountered the 'agriculture biologique' movement. This related to some Aran development concepts. Box RJ5.

Folder contain the Strasbourg divorce documentation, application #9697/82, with the Report of the Commission as adopted on March 5 1985. There is an article by Alan Shatter as published in the *Irish Times* of December 19 1986, entitled *What the Johnston Decision Means for Irish Law*. Box RJ6.

Folder with *Links Europa* file, incomplete, from 1986 to 1993, with some correspondence with the Editor Rosemary Ross. Box RJ6.

Associated folder containing material which arose out of the 1789 French Revolution bicentenary; this led to a paper published in Links Europa in 1990, in which a new approach to the nation-State structure of Europe was urged in the context of a Left-Green convergence. Box RJ6.

Folder with EU proposal for 'distributed intellectual resources database' project, in association with Foster in TCD; 1985. Box RJ1

Folder with papers relating to the Crumlin (Lough Neagh) lignite deposits, as taken up on behalf of the Irish United Nations Association, at the instigation of Seán MacBride, circa Feb 1986. Box RJ1

Two folders relating to the Constitution Club, which existed in the period 1986-1988, and involved the present writer along with Desmond Fennell, Tom Barrington, Ray Crotty, John Robb and a few others in an attempt to influence public opinion in the direction of Regional Government. One folder collects most if not all of the papers presented, including one by the present writer on the *Regional Technopole* concept, while the other contains minutes and correspondence. Box RJ6.

Folder entitled 'Cork-Rennes' which contains some material relating to attempts in the period 1986 to 1988 to build on the 'inter-regional linkage' concept, as piloted in earlier work. This did not bear fruit; it deserves a brief mention in the 1980s socio-technical stream. Box RJ6.

Folder containing political feelers to Haughey, Spring, Quinn re Science & Technology policy, 1984-88. Box RJ1

Folder containing miscellaneous material relating to the Dublin transport network issue; this helped generate my 1984 and 1991 papers on this topic, the latter winning an Irish Planning Institute prize. Box RJ7.

Folder entitled 'Techsear' containing documentation about a relational database, developed with Mike Peirce for Mentec in 1988, aimed at servicing the need in industry for innovation expertise, in a marketing context. Box RJ6.

The TII file contains correspondence relating to the attempt I made with Michael Byrne of Byrne Lowe Associates to set up a technology transfer and innovation brokerage, with the aid of a European network. This never came to anything; the supportive information-technology was flawed. There is a brief note on this in the 1980s module of the socio-technical stream. Box RJ6.

Folder with political correspondence late 1980s, including a Brendan Clifford review and subsequent correspondence; includes also a 1989 memo on the Gorbachev situation in the USSR. Box RJ5.

Towards the end of the 1980s I attempted unsuccessfully to re-establish a relationship with the *Irish Times*, and there is some correspondence about this in a folder saved in Box RJ5.

Folder containing miscellaneous papers and letters to do with the Desmond Greaves Summer School, extended over the 1990s. I have abstracted some of this in a dedicated posthumous 1990s Greaves module of the hypertext. Box RJ7.

Folder dated 1991 with material relating to my tenure of the Presidency of the Operations Research Society of Ireland, during which I attempted to negotiate mergers, the Society being sub-viable. Box RJ8.

Folder dated 1991 relating to the Irish Planning Institute prize essay scheme, which led to my prize-winning *A Future for Dublin?* paper. Box RJ8.

Folder containing correspondence in 1991-92 relating to the Institution of Engineers of Ireland and their attempt to develop the electrical and electronic division towards computer applications. This was not successful, but it has surfaced again a decade later and looks like it might run this time. Box RJ8.

Folder with Campaign for Democracy material 1991-1993, and Robert Lynd School material 1992; also correspondence with Senator Gordon Wilson. It contains also the original of my *Irish Times* letter dated 11/12/1992 relating John Taylor and the Donegal-Derry question to the opportunities presented by Maastricht. Box RJ8.

Folder containing 1994 correspondence with the US Embassy relating to the projected Clinton visit, the Wilson heritage near Strabane and the neglected Protestant aspect of the Irish influence on the US Presidency. Box RJ7.

Folder containing material relating to the 1994 Gralton School and related correspondence with Declan Bree TD. Box RJ8.

Associated with the above is a folder with NW regional material, including an Arigna Mines position paper, and a record of a regional conference in June 1990 in Manorhamilton. I had picked up on this network thanks to attendance at a 1990 Gralton event. Box RJ8.

Folder containing some Green party material for 1995, including correspondence with Patricia McKenna and Anthony Coughlan about the divorce referendum. Box RJ7.

Folder containing Green party 1996 material, mostly to do with the party constitutional reform process. There are 2 further folders for 1997 continuing this process; one also contains some science policy material. Box RJ7.

Folder with correspondence re the Spanish Civil War memorial (O Riordain, Jan 1996); this includes a list of those who contributed. The memorial consists of the names of the volunteers who fought in the Connolly Column, inscribed on the base of the Connolly Memorial opposite Liberty Hall in Dublin. Contributions ranged from £5 to £150, and included ones from Trades Councils and Trade Union branches. RJ contributed £25. Box RJ8.

Copy of the 1992 *Towards a Lasting Peace in Ireland* manifesto published by Sinn Fein, containing 1994 *Irish Times* letter and related correspondence with Gerry Adams, and a 1996 fax to John Hume. Box RJ8.

Folder with material relating to INES the international network of engineers and scientists, focused in the August 1996 Amsterdam Sustainable Development conference, which I attended with MSF sponsorship, and reported on subsequently. It includes an account *Some Sustainable Development Challenges* published in the October 1996 Engineers Journal. Box RJ8.

The 1998 Green Party folder contains more science policy material, substantially as published in the Cork *Tableau*, which I have reproduced in the 1990s 'science and society' module of the hypertext.. Box RJ7.

Folder with correspondence between the present writer and leading members of the Orange Order, covering the period 1996-1999. The contacts where Henry Reid and Cecil Kilpatrick. I have reproduced some of the outgoing correspondence, but the incoming is handwritten. I later got to review Kilpatrick's popularising biography of William of Orange for Books Ireland, providing an opportunity to link it with Kelleher's 1798 bicentenary offering. Box RJ7.

Folder with misc correspondence re the 'science and Irish culture' question, 1994-98, mostly with Peter Bowler and the Queens science history people, but also including correspondence with Feargal Quinn in the RDS context, and with President Mary McAleese on her election. Box RJ7.

Folder with material relating to the NI Peace Process, mainly to and from Derry Kelleher and Nodhlag Ó Gaire. Box RJ8.

(g) Miscellaneous other archival sources

The Desmond Greaves Journals, which I have scanned courtesy of Anthony Coughlan his executor, have proved to be a useful source of insights into the development of the political left from the mid 1940s onwards. I have abstracted them in decade modules, as feeders for the political thread. I have overviewed them in a sequence of 2 modules which are associated with the political Appendix. The decade detail modules are also available; the 1940s module contains Volumes 7, 8 and 9; the earlier volumes I pass over, though they will of course be of great interest to any biographer; we first encountered Greaves in 1946 when we were active as the student left in the Promethean Society. The 1950s module contains Volumes 10 to 13, and the 1960s modules contain Volumes 14 to 21. There are 3 successive chained modules of Greaves material in the 1960s. *(The 60s are much richer needless to say.)* There are two chained modules in the 1970s, and one in the 1980s.

Miscellaneous documentation related to the development of the Irish Green party.

(h) Other Relevant Books, mostly but not always in my possession

Those marked * have indexed references to me in their texts. I hope to go through these systematically, and to deliver 'hot-linked' critical responses via the hypertext support for this 'Century' book, where I have not done so already. I want to place on record here that none of the authors mentioned ever checked things out with me, though I was always available at the time the book was written. Any other books I find which reference me I will add to this list, and add responses if I consider it necessary. My experience of most of these references is that they are often erroneous and dependent totally on mentions in the contemporary press.

The Social Function of Science, JD Bernal FRS, Routledge Kegan Paul 1939; this book was influential during the early TCD Promethean Society epoch; see also his subsequent *The Freedom of Necessity,* RKP 1949. (TCD Library).

The Life and Times of James Connolly and *Liam Mellows and the Irish Revolution,* C Desmond Greaves, Lawrence and Wishart, 1960 and 1971 respectively. Box RJlib1. Greaves had set himself the task of encouraging the development of independent Marxist thought within Ireland, and ensuring that the Irish when they emigrated to Britain learned to act politically in the Irish interest, the vehicle for this being the Connolly Association, with its paper the Irish Democrat. I have partially abstracted his journal, which he kept from the 1930s to his death in 1988, where it bears on this narrative, in the hypertext. An overview is accessible from Appendix 10.

The WTS History sub-committee was helpful in the production of *The First Dáil* by Maire Comerford, published by Joe Clarke, 1969. She was a regular attender at the WTS meetings. RJlib1.

The Irish Crisis, C Desmond Greaves, Lawrence and Wishart, 1972. (TCD Library)

* *Ireland Since the Famine,* FSL Lyons, Collins/Fontana 1973. Box RJlib2.

* *Memoirs of a Revolutionary,* Seán Mac Stiofain, Gordon Cremonesi, 1975; this has references to the present writer, and provides several anchor-points for comment (TCD Library).

* *The IRA, the Secret Army,* J Bowyer Bell, Academy Press, 1979; this also deserves critical comment and remains on the agenda. Box RJlib2.

* *Communism in Modern Ireland,* Mike Milotte, Gill & Macmillan 1984; also needs critical comment. Box RJlib2.

* *Disillusioned Decades,* Tim Pat Coogan, Gill & Macmillan 1987. Box RJlib2.

* *The Provisional IRA,* P Bishop & E Mallie, Heinemann, London, 1987. Box RJlib2.

* Andrée Sheehy-Skeffington, Owen Sheehy-Skeffington's widow, wrote a biography *Skeff* which was published by Lilliput in 1991. I contributed material to her, which she acknowledged. Box RJ3.

* *Heresy: the Battle of Ideas in Modern Ireland,* Desmond Fennell, Blackstaff 1993. Box RJlib2.

* *20th Century Ireland, Nation and State,* Dermot Keogh, Gill & Macmillan, 1994. Box RJlib2.

Maurice Laheen, the Tuam local historian, put me in touch with John Cunningham who wrote a chapter on RM Burke's life and times for John A Claffey's *Glimpses of Tuam since the Famine* (Tuam 1997; ISBN_0_9530250_0_4).

Home Rule as Rome Rule, Derry Kelleher, Justice Books, 1997, based on his November 1996 address to the UCC Philosophical Society. Box RJlib1.

* *Memoir: My Life and Themes,* Conor Cruise O'Brien, Poolbeg, 1998. Box RJlib2.

* Science and Colonialism in Ireland, Nicholas Whyte, Cork UP 1999. Box RJlib2.

Elephants Against Rome, C Desmond Greaves, Learmheas 1999; preface by Anthony Cronin and introduction by Anthony Coughlan; an epic poem dealing with the writer's early experience in left-wing anti-fascist politics in the 1930s and 40s. Box RJlib1.

* Ireland and Empire, Stephen Howe, Oxford UP, 2000. RJlib2.

The Arms Trial, Justin O'Brien, Gill & Macmillan 2000; this has references to the present writer on which I have hung some commentary. It also confirms contemporary 'official' republican analyses, as outlined in *Nuacht Naisiunta* during the Easter 1970 period (TCD Library).

For Protestant Self-Determination, CM Hussey, Dunesk Press, 2001; this thoughtful historical analysis of the Ulster situation deserves in-depth review, and I hope to do this in the current context, with further additions to the hypertext. Box RJlib2.

* Sinn Fein: 100 Turbulent Years, Brian Feeney, O'Brien Press, 2002. Box RJlib2.

Ireland and Postcolonial Theory, ed Clare Carroll and Patricia King, Cork University Press, 2003. This important offering based on mostly US scholarship breaks new ground in Irish cultural studies; I review it for the October 2003 *Irish Democrat*. Attic, case 1, shelf 5R.

JD Bernal: the Sage of Science, Andrew Brown, Oxford UP 2005. This definitive biography is based on extensive researches in the Bernal archive, acknowledging the Brenda Swann work; it complements effectively the 1999 Verso publication listed above, #4 in the RJ authorship section. Attic, case 1, shelf 3R.

Indexes

I am providing here four indexes, on differing principles:

1. Names of people who were participants in the events, or influences in the background
2. Organisations and Institutions, including some relevant periodical publications
3. Abstract concepts or topics
4. Significant events within the decade chapters, in historical sequence

1. People

2. Organisations, Institutions, Periodicals

3. Concepts, Topics

4. Significant Events